PITMAN'S SHORTHAND DICTIONARY

PITMAN'S SHORTHAND DICTIONARY

BASED ON THE ORIGINAL WORK OF
SIR ISAAC PITMAN

ELEVENTH EDITION (NEW ERA)
REPRINTED WITH APPENDIX OF ADDITIONAL WORDS

Isaac Pitman

LONDON
SIR ISAAC PITMAN & SONS LTD.

SIR ISAAC PITMAN AND SONS LTD.
Pitman House, Parker Street, Kingsway, London, W.C.2
Pitman House, Bouverie Street, Carlton, Victoria 3053, Australia
P.O. Box 7721, Johannesburg, Transvaal, S. Africa
P.O. Box 6038, Portal Street, Nairobi, Kenya

PITMAN PUBLISHING CORPORATION
20 East 46th Street, New York, N.Y. 10017

SIR ISAAC PITMAN (CANADA) LTD.
Pitman House, 381-383 Church Street, Toronto

SBN: 273 40956 5

MADE IN GREAT BRITAIN AT THE PITMAN PRESS, BATH
F8—(S.170)

PREFACE

THE first Dictionary of stenographic outlines ever published in connection with Pitman's Shorthand was produced from lithographic transfers written by the Inventor of Phonography in the year 1846, and had the following title: *A Phonographic Dictionary of the English Language; containing the most usual words to the number of Twelve Thousand.* By Isaac Pitman. In succeeding years improved editions of the work written by the same hand were produced by the lithographic process; but in 1878, with the title of *A Phonetic Shorthand and Pronouncing Dictionary of the English Language*, the Inventor of Phonography produced a Dictionary of larger size, and for the first time the shorthand characters were engraved on metal blocks. Besides the shorthand outline, this edition gave the pronunciation of each word in phonetic printing, and also its definition. The work contained twenty-six thousand shorthand forms. In subsequent editions the phonotypic pronunciations and the definitions were discarded, and the Dictionary was issued with merely the common longhand spelling of the words after the shorthand outlines; while, from time to time, considerable additions were made to the vocabulary. The Dictionary containing shorthand outlines and meanings was subsequently revived, and is now known as *Pitman's English and Shorthand Dictionary.* The New Era edition contains outlines and definitions for over 60,000 words.

In the present Edition of the Shorthand Dictionary is a valuable "Introduction" which explains at length the treatment of particular classes of words, and this feature will, no doubt, prove of great service to students, teachers, and practitioners.

The Publishers tender their hearty thanks to the large number of correspondents who have contributed suggestions with a view to ensuring the greater accuracy and completeness of the Dictionary.

CONTENTS

INTRODUCTION

IN the present work standard forms are furnished for the words of the English language, written in accordance with the rules of Pitman's Shorthand (New Era Edition). Every writer of the system is aware that the use of the many regularized abbreviating devices which results in brief and facile outlines being obtained for the great majority of words without the help of any arbitrary abbreviation, also involves, in many instances, a choice between two or more possible forms, and the SHORTHAND DICTIONARY provides those outlines which experience has shown can be recommended for general adoption. Hence the importance and utility of the work as a book of reference for teachers, students, and practitioners.

In this edition of the Dictionary some further words have been incorporated in the Appendix.

Every effort has been made to render the Dictionary reliable and consistent in regard to pronunciation and the selection of the shorthand forms. There will, no doubt, be differences of opinion with regard to the outlines for certain words, since a form which is the most convenient to one writer is not invariably so to another writer. It is strongly recommended, however, that the closest possible adherence to Dictionary outlines be observed, since they have been decided upon as the result of experience and the most careful thought. No Dictionary outline, therefore, should be rejected in favour of another until an attempt has been made to ascertain whether there is not some special reason for its adoption. It is obvious that uniformity of outline is especially helpful in the case of writers who have to read or transcribe one another's notes.

PRONUNCIATION—REPRESENTATION OF VOWELS, ETC.

With respect to pronunciation, this has been carefully checked throughout, the *New English Dictionary* (edited by the late Sir James A H. Murray, LL.D., and others) being taken as the authority in practically all cases, so far as that work is available.

The following observations with regard to the vowel sounds, etc., in certain classes of words may be found helpful—

(*a*) The sound of the vowel "*a*" in such words as b*a*r, h*a*rm, emb*a*rk, is *ah*.

There are, on the other hand, many words in which the vowel "*a*" before *r* has a short or indistinct sound; *e.g.*, *tariff*, *globular*, *pillar*, Compare *tarry* (adjective) with *tarry* (verb).

(*b*) *aw* and not *ah* is used in such words as *taunt, launch, saunter.*

(*c*) " *o* " when occurring medially and sounded indistinctly is represented by *ŭ*, as in *custom, mason, London, monopoly, gallop.*

A long vowel tends to become short when it is unaccented, and in some words, such as *proclaim, biograph,* the vowels *ō* and *ŭ* are practically indistinguishable as ordinarily pronounced. In others, however, *e.g.*, *flotation, hotel, rotate, nobility,* the vowel is unmistakably *ō* although unaccented.

(*d*) The unaccented " *a* " in such words as *accurate, breakage, palace,* including most adjectives ending in *-ate*, is represented by *ĕ*.

Here, again, the long vowel tends to become short when it is unaccented. Compare *lace* with *palace.* In some cases, however, including all *verbs* ending in *-ate*, the vowel "*a*" is long, although it may be unaccented. Compare *moderate* (adjective) with *moderate* (verb).

(*e*) *ĭ* is used in  *marriage,* *carriage,* etc.

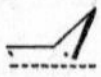

(*f*) The diphthong *ī* is used in words ending in *-ization, e.g., realization, capitalization.*

(*g*) The vowel sound after *j* or *r* in such words as J*ew*, j*uice*, per*use*, is *ōō* and not *ū*. After *l*, also, *ū* is generally represented as *ōō* unless it begins **a** syllable; *e.g.,* *include,* *flute,* *solution,* but *soluble,* *valuer.*

(*h*) In French words such as *patois, boudoir, soirée,* etc., *oi* is pronounced *wah.*

(*i*) *French eu.* When the usual sign representing the vowel sound of *eu* in French words cannot be conveniently employed, it may be treated as *ŭ*; thus, 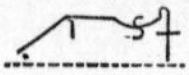 *raconteur,* *restaurateur.*

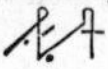

(*j*) In such words as *ranch, French, inch, punch,* with regard to which authorities differ, *ch,* which is believed to represent the more usual pronunciation, is employed.

NOTES AS TO THE PLACING OF VOWEL-SIGNS, ETC.

(1) Diphthong *ū* between two Strokes.—The diphthong *ū* when occurring between two strokes is treated in the same way as a third-place vowel; *i.e.*, it is always written before the second of the two strokes; thus,  *Hercules,* *culinary,* *accurate,* *valueless.*

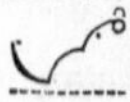

(2) Diphthongs *ī* and *ow*. The diphthong *ī* is written out of its

ordinary position for the purpose of joining finally to *n*, as in *deny*; and also in a few instances when following a third-place vowel; *e.g.*, *radii*, *nuclei*, *genii*. The diphthong *ow* is written out of its ordinary position for the purpose of joining initially to *l*, as in *owl*.

(3) Diphthong *oi*.—It is permissible to write the first tick of the diphthong *oi* upward (i.e. as in the diphone *awi*), instead of horizontally, when it is more convenient to do so. This is the case especially when it is joined initially to *l*, thus, *oil*.

(4) The small circle used to represent a vowel occurring between the two consonants expressed by a stroke hooked for *r* or *l* is written *after* the stroke unless the presence of a hook or a stroke or of another vowel-sign renders the other side more convenient; thus, *garnish*, but *regard*; *side-car*, but *motor-car*; *shilling*, but *virulent*; *parlour*, but *parallel*.

(5) Third-place Vowel occurring on same side of Stroke as *shun* Hook.—Any vowel- (or diphthongal-) sign other than a *dot* vowel is placed *outside final shun* hook; thus *delusion*, *fusion*, *alleviation* (but *vision*). All third place signs are written inside medial *shun* hook; thus, *educational*.

(6) Vocalization in Derivative Words.—A vowel in a derivative word, whether occurring in a (grammatical) prefix or suffix, such as *re-*, *pre-*, *-able*, *-ance*, or in the portion representing the root word, follows the ordinary rules as regards the stroke to which it is to be placed, and if it is immediately followed by another vowel, a diphone is used; thus, *prefigure*, *measurable*, *severance*, *singer*, *unopened*, *unaccented*, *re-examine*.

This does not apply to Compound Words, in which case the vowel-signs are generally placed as in the original words unless there is some special reason to the contrary; thus, *headache*, *steam-engine*, *crab-apple*; but *seaman*, *black-eyed*, to avoid placing a vowel-sign in an angle.

SUPPLEMENTARY RULES FOR THE CHOICE OF OUTLINES

The following rules and explanations are given in order to show the practice which has been followed in the selection of the outlines for various classes of words—

DIPHTHONG Ū AND CONSONANT Y

Stroke is used whenever convenient in words beginning with the sound of *ū;* thus, *Europe,* *utilize,* *eulogy,* *unique.* Note, however, *usury* and *Euphrates.*

ABBREVIATED W USED MEDIALLY

The abbreviated form of the consonant *w* is not joined medially to a preceding stroke except in a few COMPOUNDS of "woman," in which it joins easily, such as *needlewoman,* *charwoman,* and in *sidewalk;* hence *woodwork,* *saleswoman,* *work-woman,* *silkworm.*

W (SEMICIRCLE AND STROKE)

Initial *w* followed by a DIPHONE or a TRIPHONE is represented by the stroke ; thus, *weigher,* *wooer,* *Wyoming.*

S (DIRECTION OF CIRCLE)

In writing *n s m* the circle *s* is placed *inside* the *m* in the following cases—

(*a*) In DERIVATIVES and COMPOUNDS from words in which the circle is written inside the *m; e.g.,* *unseemly,* *unsummoned,* *tinsmith* (compare *newsmonger*); also in the word *insomnia.*

(*b*) In words containing the syllable *-some, e.g.* *noisome,* *handsome.*

NOTE.—It will be found that, with only two or three exceptions, *e.g.,* *mincemeat,* *Norseman,* and *nursemaid,* the form is used for *n s m* and the form for *n z m,* most of the examples of the latter being words ending in *-ism, e.g.,* *communism,* *galvanism.*

S, Z (CIRCLE AND STROKE)

(1) Words ending in *-nese* and *-nize,* most of which are DERIVATIVES, are written with stroke *n* and circle *s* (*z*) whenever convenient;

thus, *Japanese*, *Americanize*, *humanize*, *modernize*. Note, however, *revolutionize*.

(2) Words ending in *-nism* are written with unless a better outline is obtained by writing hook *n* and . The latter is found to be the more convenient form after [but not or] or Examples: *Puritanism*, *religionism*, *anachronism*; but *mechanism*, *paganism*. *modernism*, *Wesleyanism*.

(3) Words ending in *-ess*. All words (feminines) ending in *-ess* cannot conveniently be treated uniformly, but the following shows the practice which has been followed—

(*a*) In words ending with the *syllable -ess*, stroke *s* is used if necessary for the purpose of distinguishing the feminine singular from the masculine plural when no other means of distinction is available; thus, *poetess*, (*poets*), *heiress* (*heirs*), *Jewess*, (*Jews*).

(*b*) With regard to those words ending in *-eress*, *-oress*, *-dess*, *-n(t)ess* or *-fess* in which alternative methods of distinction are available, stroke *s* is used after or ; thus, *archeress*, *manageress*, *tutoress*, *murderess*, *vicaress*, *deaconess*, *countess*, *championess*, *chiefess*: but in other cases the circle is written, *e.g.*, *viscountess*, *giantess*, *lioness*, *baroness*, *mayoress*, *authoress*.

(*c*) In words ending in *-ress* immediately preceded by a consonant, the final *s* sound is always represented by the circle; thus, *actress*, *waitress*, *tigress*.

(4) Words ending in *-zoon* are written with stroke *z*; thus, *epizoon*, *polyzoon* (plural *polyzoa*); but adjectives ending in *-zoic* have the circle; thus, *paleozoic*, *protozoic*.

(5) DERIVATIVES from words with outlines containing stroke *s* (see also paragraph 48 of the *Instructor* and No. (3) below).

Derivatives formed by adding a suffix beginning with a vowel to a *primitive* word ending with *s* or *z* and a vowel retain stroke *s* or *z*; thus, *cosier*, *lazier*, *pursuance*, *Sadducean*, *Puseyism*, *laziest*, *busiest.*

Compare—(*a*) *Secondary derivatives*, such as *spiciest*, *sauciest*, *glossier*, the primitives of which are written with circle *s*; and (*b*) Derivatives in which the suffix does not commence with a vowel; *e.g.*, *drowsiness*, *merciless*, *ensued*, *busily.*

S (STROKE AND CIRCLE); ST (AND LOOP)

(1) Initial *s* or *st* followed by a DIPHONE is written as follows—

(*a*) With stroke *s* or in DERIVATIVES such as *sower*, *seer*, *stayer*, *stowage.*

(*b*) With the circle or loop in other words, such as *sahib*, *séance*, *sienna*, *stoic*, *Styrian.*

Initial *s* or *st* followed by a TRIPHONE is written with stroke *s* or ; thus, *Siam*, *suet*, *Stuart*, *steward*, *Stowell.*

(2) Contrary to the general rule for words beginning with *s* vowel *s*, several words beginning with *sĭst* or (*con*)*sĭst* are more conveniently written with circle *s* first; *e.g.*, *system*, *cistern*, *consist*, *consistent*, *sisterly.*

(3) While words ending in *-ous* preceded by a diphthong are written with stroke *s* in accordance with paragraph 48 (*c*) of the *Instructor*, their DERIVATIVES ending in *-īously*, *-uously*, *-uousness* and *-uosity* are generally written with the circle; thus, *piously*, *strenuously*, *ambiguously*, *impetuosity.*

The following, however, are cases in which the stroke is retained for the purpose of distinction— *joyously*, *joyousness*, *ingenuously,* *ingenuousness,* *tenuously,* *tenuousness,* *sinuosity.*

(3*a*) In other words containing *s, z* or *st* preceded by a TRIPHONE or by a DIPHONE, the circle or loop is used; *e.g., bias,* *biased.* *quiesce,* *acquiesce,* *Genoese,* *essayist,* *truest,* *deist,* *Judaism,* *statuesque.* The following are exceptions to this— *prowess,* (*principles*), *dais,* *chaos,* *newest,* (*next*), *highest.*

(4) Words ending in *-astic* or *-istic* are written as follows—

(*a*) With *st* loop after *t, d, j* or *l;* thus, *artistic,* *deistic,* *logistic,* *elastic.*

(*b*) With in other cases; thus, *plastic.* *theistic,* *sophistic.*

(5) is retained in DERIVATIVES from words with outlines containing, except the monosyllabic past tenses *stayed,* *stewed,* etc.; thus, *stowage,* *dustiness,* *majestic,* *lustier.*

ST (LOOP AND) ST)

Words ending in *-nest, -nist; -fest, -vest, -vist; -test, -tist, -dest,* etc., are written with the *st* loop unless a distinctly better outline is obtained by means of the stroke; thus, *keenest,* *greenest,* *organist,* *briefest,* *bravest,* *faintest,* *fondest,* *artist,* but *plainest,* *earnest,* *toughest,* *positivist,* *kindest,* *hardest.*

SST (, AND)

Words ending in *-cest, -cist* and *-sest* are generally written with ; thus, *fiercest,* *publicist,* *closest;* but is more convenient after *n* or *r*, as in *nicest,* *empiricist;* *densest.* is used in verbs ending in *-sist, e.g., subsist,* *desist.*

SZD (AND)

COMPOUND WORDS ending in *-sized* are written with except when gives a better joining (as after *f*, *v*, or *n*); thus, *fair-sized*, *full-sized*, *large-sized*; but *oversized*, *undersized*.

SS, SZ (LARGE CIRCLE, AND)

(1) Words ending in *-sis* and *-sus* are written with the large circle; thus, *basis*, (plural *bases*), *narcissus*. Note also *Francis*.

(2) Words ending with the sound of *sĕs* or *zĕs*, or with *s* – $\frac{s}{z}$ separated by a diphthong or a diphone (including words ending in *-cess*, *-cize* and *-size*), are generally written with or ; thus, *access*, *possess*, *capsize*, *gaseous*; but after *th*, *n* or upward *r*, affords a better joining, *e.g.*, *Gothicize*, *princess*, *Frances*, *recess*, *exorcize*. The form is used also in *diocese* and *decease* for distinction; and the common words *success*, *exercise* and *emphasize*, are written with the large circle for convenience.

(3) Words ending in *-cism* are generally written with the large circle; thus, *fanaticism*, *Gallicism*; but after *th*, *n* or *r*, the form gives more convenient and distinctive outlines; thus, *Gothicism*, *cynicism*, *laconicism*, *exorcism*, *Doricism*.

HOOKED STROKE AND STROKE R OR L

(1) Words ending in *-metry* and *-metric* are written with stroke *r* whenever practicable; thus, *geometry*, *barometric*, but *planimetry*.

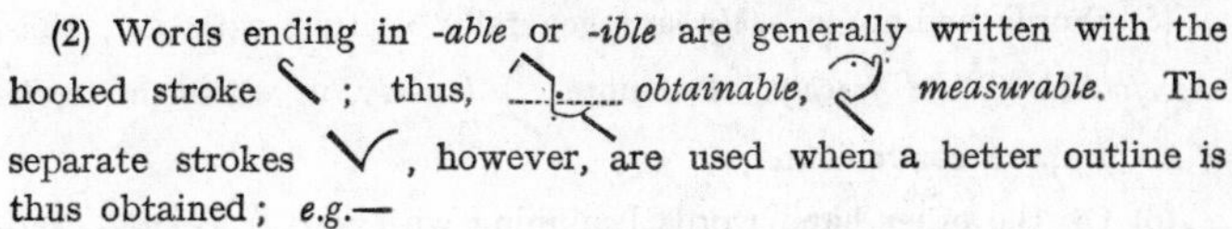

(2) Words ending in *-able* or *-ible* are generally written with the hooked stroke ; thus, *obtainable*, *measurable.* The separate strokes , however, are used when a better outline is thus obtained; *e.g.*—

(*a*) After , , , or after a circle following a "right" curve (but not after or); thus, *excusable*, *accessible*, *invincible*, *reversible*, *forcible* (but *feasible*, *serviceable*).

(*b*) After or ; thus, *contestable*, *digestible.*

(*c*) After , or a downstroke hooked for *v*; thus, *explainable*, *discernible*, *provable.*

(*d*) After a half-length stroke hooked for *n*; thus, *accountable*, *lamentable.* (But note *insurmountable.*)

(*e*) After a *shun* hook; thus, *actionable*, but in *mentionable* disjoined is more convenient.

(3) Words ending in *-tal* or *-dal* preceded by *r* are written with stroke *l*; thus, *parietal*, *spheroidal.* Compare the words *rattle*, *riddle.* A number of words ending in *-tal* preceded by *n* are also written with stroke *l*; *e.g.*, *mental*, *horizontal.* Compare the word *mantle.*

(4) Words ending in *-ful* and *-fully* are written with stroke *l* in cases where a distinction between the adjective and the adverb can easily be shown by means of the downward and the upward *l* respectively; *e.g.*, after , , , , or a straight upstroke; thus, *wakeful*, *wakefully*, *manful*, *wrongful*, *sorrowful.* In other words, including verbs, ***fl*** and ***vl*** occurring after the strokes mentioned above are represented by the hooked forms ; thus, *scuffle*, *interval*, *upheaval.*

(5) Words ending in *-shly* are generally written with , thus, *foolishly*, *freshly*. But note *harshly*, in which the stroke *l* is more convenient.

(6) On the other hand words beginning with *unr-*, *enr-*, *unl-*, *enl-*, formed by a prefix from words beginning with *r* or *l* generally retain the separate *r* or *l*; thus, *unrest*, *unreasoning*, *unleavened*, *enlist*. But note *enlighten* and *enliven*.

(7) Words ending in *-ary*, *-ery*, *-ory*, etc., are treated as follows—

(*a*) The hooked strokes are used when they give a more easily written outline than the separate *r*; thus, *drapery*, *rookery*, *treasury*, *luminary*.

(*b*) The hooked strokes are retained in adjectives derived from words written with a final hooked stroke, such as *tottery*, *silvery*, *savoury*.

(*c*) In other cases the separate *r* or *l* is written; thus, *statutory*, *notary*, *factory*, *fishery*.

(8) DERIVATIVES ending in *-ally* and *-alize* from words written with a final hooked stroke retain the hooked form; thus, *brutally*, *brutalize*, *locally*, *localize*. But note *totally* which is considered a more convenient form.

(9) Words ending in *-erate* or *-orate* are often written with separate *rt* if the latter gives an easily written outline and one which enables that of the past tense to be easily formed from it; thus, *exaggerate*, *exaggerated*; *adulterate*, *adulterated*; *enumerate*, *enumerated*. Compare *deliberate*, *deliberated*, *decorate*, *decorated*. The outline *elaborate* is necessary for distinction.

(10) DERIVATIVES from words written with hooked forms of the *pr*, *pl* series are generally also written with the hooked forms if practicable, even if the *r* or *l* is no longer in the same syllable as the preceding consonant; thus, *tippler*, *trampling*, *saddling*,

tackling, *doubly*. Compare such words as *seedling*, *duckling*, which are not so derived.

(11) In COMPOUND WORDS, when the second part of the compound begins with *r* or *l*, that *r* or *l* is, as a rule, not combined with the last letter of the first part; hence, *typewritten*, *bricklayer*, *necklace*. But note *typewriter* and *typewriting*.

(12) In the case of *verbs* the hooked forms are generally preferred so as to enable past tenses to be written on the same principle; thus, *bridle*, *bridled* (compare *bridal*), *model*, *modelled*.

DUPLICATE FORMS FOR FR, VR, ETC.

(1) In DERIVATIVES and COMPOUNDS from words written with , etc., the form of *fr*, or *vr*, used in the primitive should, when convenient, also be used in the derivative or compound, without regard to the practice adopted in other words; thus, *freeness*, (compare *furnace*), *offerer* (compare *friar*).

Subject to the above—

(2) The "left" curves are used if more convenient for joining than the "right" curves. This is the case—

(*a*) When *fr* or *vr* occurs either before or after *t*, *d*, *ch*, *j*, *f*, *v*, *th*, *s* or *z*, as in *tougher*, *leverage*, *effervesce*, *survivor*, *froth*, *zephyr*.

(*b*) Generally before a character beginning with the same motion, viz. the "left" motion, as in *friable*, *freckle*, *frank*, *France*.

(3) In other cases the "right" curves are generally used, as *verbose*, *Africa*, *fresh*, *frame*.

(4) As regards *thr* and *THr*, are used initally when preceded by a vowel (*i.e.*, as when standing alone); thus, *Atherton*, *Atherley*, *otherwise*; and

(5) In other cases the "right" curves are used, as *thread*, *thrive*, *thrash*, *throttle*, *tether*, *zither*, *Arthur*.

DOUBLE CONSONANTS (VOCALIZED) AND SEPARATE R OR L

(1) Medial *r* or *l* preceded by a strongly-sounded vowel is generally represented by separate *r* or *l* unless a hooked form is necessary in order to avoid an awkward or a too lengthy outline; thus *ulterior*, *internal*, *fraternal*, *repel*, but *repulsive*.

(2) Words ending in *-torial* are generally written with separate *r*, but the hooked form is used in a few cases to avoid an awkward or a very lengthy outline; thus, *tutorial*, *equatorial*, *piscatorial*, but *reportorial*, *spectatorial*, *dictatorial*.

(3) Words ending in *-tarium*, *-torium*, etc., are generally written with the hooked *tr*; thus, *cometarium*, *moratorium*.

(4) Words ending in *-chord* are written with half-length *kr*; thus, *tetrachord*, *monochord*.

(5) Words ending in *-form* are written with the hooked form, or , after ; thus, *stalactiform*, *spongiform*, *aciform*, *curviform*, *vermiform*. In other cases separate *r* is used; thus, *napiform*, *cuneiform*, *metalliform*, *variform*.

(6) Words ending in *-culate*, *-gulate*, *-cular*, *-gular*, and *-culum* are generally written with the hooked strokes *kl* or *gl*; thus, *calculate*, *speculate*, *gesticulate*, *reticulate*, *articulate*, *circulate*, *matriculate*, *coagulate*, *regulate*, *binocular*, *angular*, *singular*, *curriculum*.

(7) The prefix *for-* is represented by or, when this is inconvenient, by ; thus, *forsake*, *forbear*, but *forget*. This does not apply to the prefix *fore-*, which should be written with separate *r* (downward in preference) when convenient; thus, *forecast*, *forenoon*, *foresight* (compare *ferocity*); otherwise the hooked form is used: thus, *foretell*, *foreshorten*, *forewarn*.

(8) COMPOUND WORDS ending in *-bird* and *-board* are written with the half-length *br* whenever convenient; thus, *jailbird*, *mocking-bird*, *blackboard*, *switchboard*. But note *pasteboard*; also *keyboard*, for distinction.

FINAL N (STROKE AND HOOK)

(1) Words ending in *-nian* are generally written with the hook for the final *n*, even in the case of DERIVATIVES from words with outlines ending with hook *n*; thus, *Etonian*, *Hamiltonian*, but note *Gladstonian*, *Augustinian*, *Athenian*.

(2) Words ending in *-n nt* are generally written with hook *n* finally; thus, *anent*, *assonant*, *dissonant*. Final *-n nt* preceded by *p*, stroke *t* or *v*, or *m* is, however, written with stroke *nt* finally; thus, *pennant*, *tenant*, *convenient*, *dominant*, as are also the words *consonant* and *sonant*.

(3) Words ending in *-t n* or *-d n* are generally written with the hook for the final *n*; thus, *fatten*, *wheaten*, *abandon*.

(4) The final *n* is, however, represented by the stroke in the following cases—

(*a*) Words ending in *-rt n* or *-j st n*, such as *Spartan*, *martin*, *congestion*. Compare *puritan*, *baritone*, *Samaritan*, in which a vowel occurs between the *r* and the *t*.

(*b*) Most words ending in *-ntine, e.g.* *turpentine*.

(*c*) The words *fountain*, *mountain*, *plantain*, *pontoon*, *bounden*, and *garden*.

N PRECEDED BY TWO VOWEL-SOUNDS

Stroke *n* is used—(*a*) After a TRIPHONE consisting of *ū* and a vowel; thus, *genuine*, *constituent*, *pursuant*. Compare *lion*, *client*, *compliance*, *buoyancy*, in which the *n* is preceded by other triphones.

(*b*) After two separate vowel-signs; thus, *triune*.

(*c*) In the words *pioneer*, *giant*, *buoyant*, *heroine*, *ruin*, and several words ending in *-fluent*, *e.g.*, *fluent*, *mellifluent*. Compare other words in which *n* occurs after a diphone, *e.g.*, *crayon*, *cayenne*, *hygiene*.

Note also words like *recurrence*, *concurrent*, in which stroke *n* is used although the two vowel sounds do not occur together.

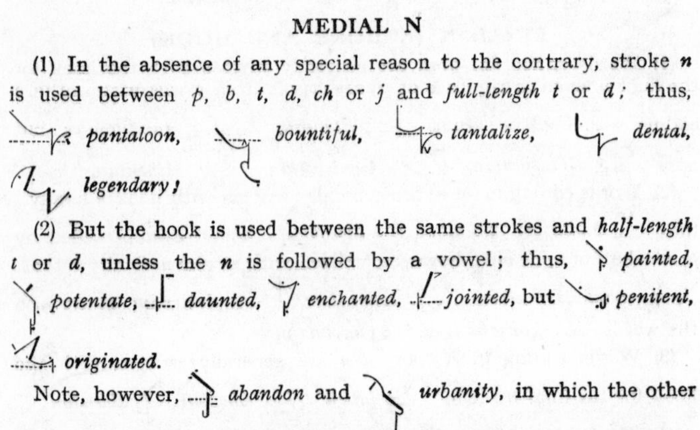

MEDIAL N

(1) In the absence of any special reason to the contrary, stroke *n* is used between *p*, *b*, *t*, *d*, *ch* or *j* and *full-length t* or *d*; thus, *pantaloon*, *bountiful*, *tantalize*, *dental*, *legendary*;

(2) But the hook is used between the same strokes and *half-length t* or *d*, unless the *n* is followed by a vowel; thus, *painted*, *potentate*, *daunted*, *enchanted*, *jointed*, but *penitent*, *originated*.

Note, however, *abandon* and *urbanity*, in which the other circular movement in the outlines renders the hook more convenient.

Stroke *n* is used after only one downstroke having an initial attachment on the opposite side; thus, *stranded*, *reprinted*, *branded*. Compare *disappointed*, *suspended*.

(3) Hook *n* is used between *r* and *n* in such words as *barrenness*, *modernness*, but stroke *n* is preferred between *sr* or *w* and *n*; thus, *sereneness*, *oneness*. Similarly *roundness*, but *windiness*.

(4) Stroke *n* is generally retained in DERIVATIVES from words written with the stroke, other than those ending in *-ic* or *-cy;* thus, *funnier*, *puniness*; but *euphonic*, *subserviency*.

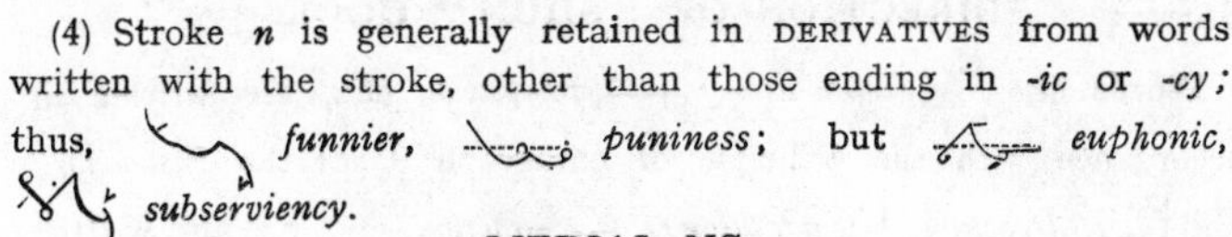

MEDIAL NS

(5) Stroke *n* is used medially before *s* or *z*, unless the hook is clearly more convenient; thus, *Wednesday*, *wainscot*, *caravansary*, but *ransom*, *lonesome*, *Ironside*.

(6) Two hooks together are generally avoided; hence *plunger*, *ranger*. They are, however, allowed in *kindred*, *hundred*, *manger*, *philanthropist*, and one or two uncommon words, as well as certain compound words (see next paragraph).

(7) In COMPOUND WORDS hook *n* is often retained medially, even where it would be avoided in other words; *e.g.*, *open-mouthed*, *penman*, *mainmast*, *rainproof*, *earthenware*.

F, V (HOOK AND STROKE)

(1) Words ending in *-tive* (other than those which are contracted) are generally written with ; thus, *receptive*, *inventive*. Exceptions to the above are *captive*, *plaintive*, *comparative*, and such words as *attentive*, *retentive*, *digestive*, *suggestive*.

(2) The stroke is used for *f* or *v* occurring between *p* or *b* (without an initial attachment) and *t* or *d;* thus, *pivot*, *buffet*. After or , however, the hook is more convenient; thus, *private*, *brevity*.

(3) Hook *f* or *v* is used between *t*, *d* or *ch* and *t* or *d* in DERIVATIVES as well as other words; thus *sanctified*, *Cheviot*. Note, however, *defied*, *edified* and *deified*, for distinction.

DIRECTION OF "SHUN" HOOK

Words like *probation*, *correction*, etc., are written in accordance with the principle of paragraph 95 of the *Instructor;* and *decoction*, *adoption*, *inaction*, etc., are also written in accordance with the spirit, though not the letter, of paragraph 96.

THE ASPIRATE

(1) Initial *h* followed by a TRIPHONE is represented by the upward or the downward stroke, and not by the tick; thus, *Higham*, *Howard*, *hierarchy*, *hyaline*, *Howell*.

(2) Downward *h* is used in a few cases to create a clear distinction of outline, as *heritor* (*inheritor*), *heritable* (*inheritable*), or to provide a more easily written form, as *heritage*.

(3) Words beginning with *hetero-* are written with except before — ⌒ or (, when is more convenient; thus, *heterogeneous*, *heterodox;* but *heterogamous*, *heteromorphous*, *heterology*.

(4) COMPOUND WORDS ending in *-house* are written as under—

(*a*) With if convenient for joining, *i.e.* after *p, b, t, d, f* or a straight upstroke; thus, *chop-house*, *club-house*, *gate-house*, *coffee-house*, *warehouse*, *hothouse*.

(*b*) With after *k, g, m* or *l;* thus, *workhouse*, *log-house*, *summer-house*, *ale-house*.

(*c*) When stroke *s* gives a better joining than either or , *i.e.* after *ch, s, sh, n, ng*, a circle or a hook; thus, *coach-house*, *ice-house*, *wash-house*, *pigeon-house*, *alms-house*, *greenhouse*.

(5) Downward *h* is retained in DERIVATIVES and COMPOUNDS of words in which *h* is the only consonant, if a *syllable* is added to the primitive word; thus, *highness*, *highest*, *hoer*, *high-bred*.

hay-loft. Compare *hoed,* *hewn,* etc., in which there is no added syllable.

(6) Medial *h.* With regard to words ending in *-hold, -holed,* etc.—

(*a*) The form is used after *p, b, f, v,* TH, or *h*; thus, *uphold,* *copyhold,* *behold,* *foothold,* *overhauled,* *withhold,* *high-heeled.*

(*b*) In other cases dot *h* and either or, if more convenient, are written; thus, *pigeon-holed,* *stronghold,* *strangle-hold,* *leasehold.*

UPWARD AND DOWNWARD R AND L

(1) Words beginning with *st* (*vowel*) *r* followed by stroke *n* have upward *r*; thus, *consternation,* *sternutation,* *Stornoway.*

(2) Final *r* is written upward (among other cases) after *kr, gr* or *lk*; thus, *crier,* *grower,* *luckier*; but downward after *sk,* or *fk*; thus, *obscure,* *fakir.*

(3) Final *r* in COMPOUNDS, as in other words is written upward after two downstrokes; thus, *tax-gatherer,* *shooting-star.*

(4) In words ending in *-rest, -rist, -lest* or *-list* the *r* or *l* is written upward or downward as when followed by a final vowel; thus, *barest,* *fairest,* *imperialist,* *fullest,* *annalist.*

(5) Medial *r* is nearly always written downward before *m*; thus, *barium,* *emporium,* *forum.* After *th,* however, it is written upward; thus, *theorem.*

(6) Medial *r* is also written downward in most DERIVATIVES from words written with downward *r*; thus, *declarable,* *powerful,* *barely,* *furrier,* *maturely*; but in words ending in *-rial, -ral* or *-rhal* upward *r* is used; thus, *armorial,* *mayoral,* *catarrhal.*

(7) Final *l* after or is written as after ; thus, *egotistical*, *methodistical*, *logistical*, *fantastically*.

(8) *L* occurring finally, or with only a circle or loop following, is written downward after a half-length or double-length stroke if a more convenient outline is so obtained; thus, *completely*, *shiftless*, *vividly*, *pectoral*, *structural*. Note *actual* and *actually* for distinction.

(9) Final *l* is written upward after downward *l* in *genteelly*, *foully*, etc., but downward after *ld* or *lr* in *mildly*, *scholarly*, etc.

(10) Final *l* is written downward in COMPOUNDS of words written with upward *l* if the upward form would be quite inconvenient for joining, as in *sand-eel*, *train-oil*, but the upward form is retained if at all practicable, as in *port-hole*, *stock-list*.

(11) Medial *l* is written upward in *biliousness* and *superciliousness*, but downward in words ending in *-lescence* or *-lescent*; *e.g.*, *opalescence*, *coalescent*. It is also written upward before whenever practicable; thus, *realism*, *imperialism*, but *sensationalism*, *naturalism*.

UPWARD AND DOWNWARD SH

(1) Final *sh* is written downward after *t* (or *st*); but upward after *d*; thus, *latish*, *coquettish*, *crustacea*, *moustache*, but *radish*, *Swedish*. Exception— *brutish*.

(2) Final *-shŭs* is written upward after *t*, *d* or *sd*, but downward after *st*; thus, *fictitious*, *seditious*, but *superstitious*.

(3) The words *mopish* and *mobbish* are written with upward *sh* on the same principle as *brush* (see *Instructor*, par. 120).

(4) Final *sh* or *sh s* after upward *l* is written downward; thus, *lash, slash, polish, malicious;* but in the past tenses *lashed, polished,* etc., upward *sh* is more convenient.

COMPOUND CONSONANTS

(1) *Wl* and *wh l*. The compound consonants and are used in all words beginning with *w l d* and *wh l d* respectively; thus, *wailed, weld, wild, wilder, wheeled.*

(2) *Rr*. The use of is strictly confined to derivatives from words written with final downward *r*; hence, *sorcerer, fruiterer, usurer.*

The compound consonant is not used after *l*; hence, *cellarer.*

(3) The word *queer* is so written in order to keep it quite distinct from *clear.*

(4) *Kw* and *mp, mb* in COMPOUND WORDS. A consonant at the end of the first part of a compound word is not combined with a consonant beginning the second part; hence *silk-worm, dumb-bell, tomboy.* An exception to this is the word *lukewarm.*

HALVING PRINCIPLE

(1) A stroke is not halved when a better outline is obtained by means of the full *t* or *d*; thus, *hotel, flotsam, graduation, indulge, integer, interior, tautology, litigious, lemonade.*

(2) Words ending in *-tatory, -datory, -ditary,* etc., are treated as follows—

(*a*) In the case of the termination *-tatory* the last *t* is generally written in full; thus, *rotatory, excitatory, saltatory;* but

(*b*) When the termination is *-datory, -ditary,* the halving principle is generally applied; thus, *consolidatory, hereditary.*

(3) Words ending in *-tively* following stroke *t* or *tr* are written with full *t*; thus, *authoritatively*, *illustratively*.

(4) Words ending in *-ctary*, *-ctory*, *-catory*, *-gatory*, *-ctarian*, etc., are generally written with full *t*; thus, *directory*, *purgatory*, *Tractarian*. A better outline, however, is obtained by halving in such words as *secretary*, *migratory*.

(5) Words ending in *-taceous* and *-dacious* are written with full *t* or *d*; thus, *cretaceous*, *mendacious*.

(6) Although the halving principle is generally applied for the addition of either *t* or *d* in words of more than one syllable, in primitive words a thin stroke (other than or which can be thickened as well as halved) is not halved standing alone to add *d*, or a thick stroke standing alone to add *t*, unless there is a final hook or a joined diphthong; thus, *acrid*, *applaud*, *adroit*, *sedate*, *seclude*. Exceptions to this are— *convert*, *concord* and *conclude*.

In past tenses of more than one syllable, however, a thin stroke may generally be halved; thus, *seated*, *stated*, *uttered*, *offered*, *supplied*, *construed*, *committed*, *commuted*; but note *echoed* and *essayed*.

(7) The more common words ending in *-pid* are written with half-length *p*; thus, *tepid*, *insipid*; but

(8) Words ending in *-pade*, *-ped*, *-pede* or *-pod* are generally written with full *d*; thus, *escapade*, *uniped*, *centipede*, *tripod*. But note *quadruped*, to avoid a lengthy outline.

(9) Words ending in *k* (vowel) *d* are generally written with full *d*; thus, *arcade*, *naked*, *decoyed*; but half-length *k* is used in a few words of more than two syllables, *e.g.*, *barricade*, *cavalcade*, and in the word *rescued*.

(10) Words ending in *g* (vowel) *t*, however, are generally written with half-length *g*; thus, *frigate*, *target*. *nugget*.

(11) As a rule the halving principle is not applied if the resulting outline would not be capable of full vocalization. It is, however, applied in the case of a number of words ending in *-tism* or *-dism* in which a more facile outline is obtained by disregarding the "*i*," viz., *despotism*, *Jacobitism*, *patriotism*, *blackguardism*, *favouritism*, *scepticism*, and several words ending in *-matism* such as, *rheumatism*. Compare such words as *absolutism*, *conservatism*, etc., in which the full outline is quite convenient.

(12) The halving principle is, as a rule, applied when *t* or *d* is preceded by a DIPHONE; thus, *create*, *druid*, *radiate*; but the *t* is written in full in *poet*, *silhouette*, and a few uncommon words and proper names.

(13) Stroke *t* or *d* is retained when convenient in the following classes of DERIVATIVES, viz.—

(*a*) Words derived, either directly or indirectly, from *primitive* words with outlines containing stroke *t* or *d* and not more than one other stroke consonant; *e.g.*, *pitiful*, *cottony*, *gluttonous*, *bedeck*, *undivided*, *becloud*, *overrate*, *outspread*, *overcrowd*. The following are exceptional— *beautify*, *beautiful*, *written*, *writing*, *undefined*, *indebted*, *subdivide*.

(*b*) Certain secondary derivatives from *primary derivatives* written with stroke *t* or *d*, in which the stroke is retained for the purpose of distinction; *e.g.*, *weightiness*, *greediness*, *heartily*, *flightiness*.

(*c*) In words ending in *-tieth*, in order to prevent the possibility of confusion between *seventieth* and *seventh*; *fiftieth*, and *fifth*, etc.

(14) In COMPOUNDS of words with outlines ending in stroke *t* or *d* that *t* or *d* is generally expressed by halving; thus, *copyright, backbite, ice-boat, cow-hide, go-ahead, brush-wood.* Stroke *t* or *d* is, however, retained after one half-length stroke, as in *tit-bit, catboat,* and also in a few cases in which the full *t* or *d* gives a more distinct outline, *e.g., rosewood, jolly-boat, row-boat.*

(15) In COMPOUNDS of words commencing with *t* or *d*, that *t* or *d* is not expressed by halving; thus, *time-table, grave-digger, quarter-deck.* Exceptions— *sometimes* and *beforetime.*

(16) *Lt* is generally written upward as in *fault, quilt, exult;* but it is written downward—

(*a*) When preceded by an initial vowel and followed by *m*, as in *ultimo,* and

(*b*) After *n, ng, vs* or *ns* as in *knelt, ringlet, vacillate, insult;* also in the word *dwelt.*

(17) *Rd.* With regard to final *rd*, the forms *veered, persevered,* etc., are adopted because, although not strictly in accordance with the rule, they are quite distinct and more convenient than the possible alternatives , , etc. On the other hand, in such words as *geared,* is a better form than , which latter would become indistinct in practice.

(18) In addition to cases in which would be actually inconvenient, is used for final *rd* in such past tenses as *rendered, surrendered, wintered.* (Compare *windward.*)

(19) *Ld.* When would be inconvenient *ld* is represented by the full form ; thus, *quarrelled, belittled, scheduled, leasehold.* Note: is sufficiently convenient in *retailed, mild, lulled,* etc.

DOUBLING PRINCIPLE

(1) The doubling principle is not applied in words ending in *-lateral* and *-literal*, double-length *l* being used only in words in which it occurs *finally* and in words derived from these; hence, *lateral* (compare *latterly*), *pluriliteral*, *poulterer* (compare *slaughterer*), *liturgy* (compare *lighterage*).

(2) The doubling principle, which is applied in the case of most common words ending in *-ture*, is not applied in the following instances— *literature*, *capture* (the outline being required for *captor*), *furniture*, and words like *departure* and *candidature*.

(3) When the vowel in the termination *tor* is sounded distinctly, as in the legal terms *grantor*, *vendor*, *guarantor*, the doubling principle is not applied.

(4) The doubling principle is applied in a few cases although there is an accented vowel between *t* and *r*; *e.g.*, *interpret*, *enteric*, *dysenteric*, *tartaric*, *material*.

(5) The doubling principle is also applied in the following cases, notwithstanding that there is no vowel between the *t* or *d* and the *r*—

(*a*) Several words containing *central*, *centri-* or *-centric*, *e.g.*, *central*, *concentric*, *eccentric*, *centrifugal*.

(*b*) *theatrical*, *cylindric*.

(6) Words ending in *-erate* or *-orate*, although derived from words written with a double-length stroke, are written by means of the halving principle (*i.e.*, in the same way as past tenses such as *centred*); thus, *directorate*, *stadtholderate*.

(7) The doubling principle is not applied when *tr* is preceded by a triphone representing a diphthong and a long vowel; thus, *extenuator*, *punctuator*. Compare *proprietor*, *radiator*.

(8) Joining of Strokes of Unequal Length. Paragraph 142 (*a*) of the *Instructor* applies to double-length as well as half-length strokes. Double-length *n*, however, is sufficiently distinct after *t* or downward *l*; thus, *detonator*, *alienator*.

(9) Double-length *l* is written upward, except after *n*, *ng*, *ns* or *sk*; thus, *filter*, *beholder*, *gilder*, but *penholder*, *ringleader*, *insulter*, *scolder*, *helter-skelter*.

(10) Double-length strokes may be used in such COMPOUND WORDS as the following—*backbiter*, *chaff-cutter*, *muzzle-loader*.

PREFIXES

Trans- is contracted by the omission of the *n* when it is followed by *p*, *m*, upward *l*, or the hooked letters *pl*, *kr*, *gr*, *fr*, and *fl*; thus, *transparent*, *transmit*, *translation*, *transplant*, *transcribe*, *transgress*, *transfer*, *transfluent*.

SUFFIXES

(1) With reference to *-ing* the stroke is used after , although it does not give a very convenient joining, as the dot might be mistaken for a vowel-sign; thus, *utilizing*, *releasing*.

(2) When adding *-ing*, the outline of the original word is almost invariably left unaltered; thus, *fancying*, *freezing*, *shelling*, *cleansing*, *hoeing*, *allowing*, *failing*, *piercing*, *pushing*, *rating*. Exceptions to this are *losing*, *lacing*, etc., *ailing*, *coalescing*, *convalescing*, and *writing*.

(3) When the outline of the present tense ends with a joined diphthong, the latter is not retained if stroke can be joined; thus, *renewing*, *pursuing*, *bowing*.

(4) Outlines containing stroke *ng*, when used in the representation of the suffix *-ing* are vocalized in the ordinary way, whether the vowel is a third-place vowel or otherwise; thus, *laying*, *gnawing*.

(5) *-ality*, *-ility*, *-arity*, etc., are expressed by means of a disjoined stroke in the great majority of cases, including practically all of the large number of words ending in *-bility*. The words which are written in full include—

(*a*) Words ending in *-alty*, *-iality*, *erty*, or *-iority*, if the full outline is quite convenient; thus, 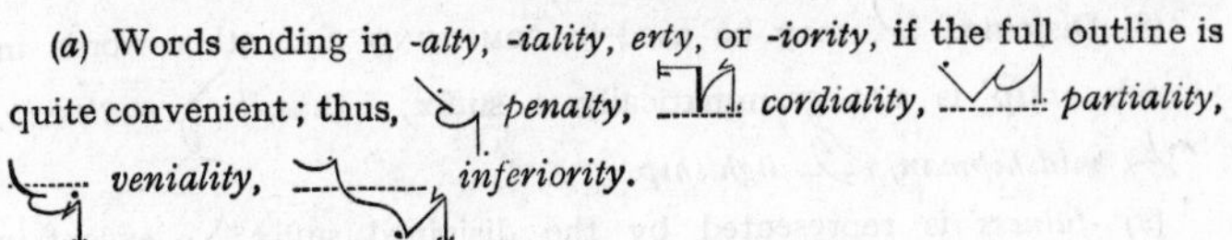 *penalty*, *cordiality*, *partiality*, *veniality*, *inferiority*.

(*b*) Words in which the full outline is particularly facile, especially after a half-length stroke; *e.g.*, *fertility*, *austerity*, *maturity*, *verticality*, *personality*.

(*c*) Words in which the *-ality*, etc., is preceded by only one stroke or by *s* or *shun*; thus, *hilarity*, *facility*, *nationality*.

(*d*) In a few cases for the purpose of distinction; *e.g.*, *juniority* (*geniality*), *locality* (*legality*), *disparity* (*disability*).

(*e*) *compatibility*, *accessibility*, *asperity*, and a few other miscellaneous words.

A vowel preceding the disjoined consonant indicating the suffix *-ality*, etc., may, if necessary, be disregarded; thus, *visibility*.

(6) *-ment* is represented by after or , or a hook to which the full form cannot conveniently be joined; thus, *consignment*, *preferment*, *effacement*, *commencement*, *enchantment*, *pavement*; also in *enlistment*. When can be made convenient, it is often written in preference to the contracted form; thus, *discernment*, *rescindment*, *amendment*, *assortment*.

(7) The suffix may be joined when occurring after full-length *r*, *n* or *ng*, also, when convenient, after a hook (the preceding part of the outline remaining unaltered); thus, *censorship*, *companionship*, *kingship*, *friendship*, *relationship*. *-Ship* is written in full after *l*, as in *fellowship*; also in *airship*.

(8) Disjoined may be used in COMPOUND and other words in which *-ship* is not grammatically a suffix; thus, *battleship, midshipman, lightship.*

(9) *-fulness* is represented by the disjoined suffix except in *delightfulness, doubtfulness* and *beautifulness.*

GRAMMALOGUES

DERIVATIVES and COMPOUNDS from grammalogues are written by retaining the logogram (unvocalized) in the outline whenever a convenient and legible form is so obtained; thus, *golden, thankless, deliverer, advantageous, would-be, twofold.*

CONTRACTIONS

(1) With reference to the omission of medial *t* after *s*—see *Instructor*, par. 183 (*c*), when a vowel occurs immediately after the *t*, the latter is not omitted except in the following instances; viz. *postal, postage, post-office, testament, testimony, procrastinate, investigate, mistake, domestic, pessimistic, optimistic, euphemistic, mediumistic, bombastic, futuristic, substitute, substitution, destitute, destitution, institute, institution, celestial,* and derivatives from these words (*mistook* excepted). Compare *pistol, vestige, sophisticate, mystic, plastic, rustic*, etc., in which the *t* is expressed.

(2) In addition to the contractions appearing in the lists in the textbooks, contracted forms are also given in the Dictionary, as alternatives to the full outlines, for some other words, which are not considered to be of such frequent occurrence in general matter as to warrant their inclusion in the lists.

DERIVATIVE WORDS

The derivation of words must be regarded as one of a number of considerations affecting the choice of outlines, but while in the outlines of many derivatives the outline of the primitive word, or some particular feature of it, is retained, there are, on the other hand, many cases in which derivatives are written in accordance with the ordinary rules and principles of the system, without regard to derivation ; *e.g.*, *remove*, *remover* ; *bitter*, *embitter* ; *hawk*, *hawker* ; *ail*, *ailment* ; *royal*, *royalist*.

Words described as "derivatives" are taken to include any words that are *apparently* derived from other English words.

In the above notes, attention is drawn by means of capitals to the treatment of certain classes of derivative and compound words.

DERIVATIVES ANTICIPATED

In certain cases, including some verbs previously mentioned, words are written in a particular way so that their outlines may agree with those of derivatives formed from them, *e.g.*, *meddle*, *meddled* ; *wanton*, *wantonly* ; *clandestine*, *clandestinely* ; *captive*, *captivate* ; *inadvertent*, *inadvertently* ; *exist*, *existence*, *sister*, *sisterly* ; *scientific*, *scientifically* ; *shelter*, *sheltered*.

COMPOUND WORDS

A number of classes of compound words have already been dealt with in connection with the various principles involved. With regard to cases in which the outlines of the primary words will not join conveniently, they are written disjoined if a better outline is not obtainable by altering one or both of them so as to admit of joining. (See also next par.)

DISJOINING

(1) Disjoining is not resorted to if a better outline can otherwise be obtained ; thus, *tactics*, *locate*. *densely*, *rearrange*, but *misfeasance*, *steadfast*, *mentionable*, *deaf-mute*, *spendthrift*.

(2) Three straight strokes that would not make an angle are not joined together ; hence *picture-gallery*, *turkey-cock*.

(3) Outlines in which one at least of three strokes is a curve are generally allowable although there is no angle; thus, *papacy*, *clockwork*; but the combination is avoided; hence, *luckier*.

(4) Sometimes an angle is shown in order to make a joining allowable; thus, *escheat*, *Hebraized*.

(5) More than two successive downstrokes including *p b*, *d t*, etc., are generally avoided by disjoining in such words as *top-boots*, *red-tapism*, *quarter-deck*. Compare *copy-book*, *seed-time*, *tea-dealer*, in which there are only two downstrokes.

OUTLINES AND VOWELS

Outlines, as a rule, are not varied in order to permit of a vowel-sign being placed exactly in its proper place; thus, *legislation*, *ceaseless*, *ingeniously*, *appropriately*, *meanwhile*. In a few cases, however, in which an outline that can be more accurately vocalized is a better one from a practical point of view, it is adopted, *e.g.*, *doubtless* *unsoiled*.

In certain cases in which it would be difficult to insert an intersected vowel-sign it is disregarded; *e.g.*, *figurative*, *calculated*, *partiality*.

SPECIAL OUTLINES

It will be recognized that there are many pairs or groups of words which, from their meaning, are liable to clash, and every precaution is necessary in such cases to avoid the risk of confusion. In a great majority of cases the application of the ordinary rules of the system affords adequate means of distinction, but in a comparatively few of these pairs of words, such as *favoured*, *favourite*; *Australian*, *Australasian*, *birth*, *burial*; which otherwise would be written with the same or a very similar form, a special outline is adopted for one of them in order to provide a clear distinction. Again, in a few instances, such as *solicitor*, *affidavit*, *oxyhydrogen*, *tartaric*, *sincerely*, *necessarily*, it has been found advisable, in order to secure the most convenient outline, to adopt a form which is not capable of being fully vocalized, or which is not written in accordance with the usual practice. A list of these special outlines, in addition to those already mentioned in this Introduction, is given below. It should be borne in mind that such outlines, except in the case of some derivatives from the words in question, must not necessarily be regarded as models for the formation of other outlines.

The following outlines are written out of their proper position for the purpose of distinction— *human*, *woman*.

The Index to the Introduction will be found most useful where it is desired to refer to any word or class of word.

LIST OF SPECIAL OUTLINES

afresh
agent
alcohol
alkali
alliance
allowance
antithesis
assuredly
avert
avoidance
bachelor
bankrupt
beerhouse
bold
candlestick
capital
caused

*child*less
conciliatory
considerate
constitute
*dear*est
delightful
descriptions
desert
destiny
diffract
discern
downright
edification
editor
editorial
erudite
eventually

explode
eyesight
eyesore
fallen
farmer
fiscal
flannelette
foundation
further
futile
futurism
garnet
Gentile
girth
gradually
guidance
hardiest

heartily
hearty
hospital
hyoid
ignominy
illness
impercepti-ble
indigent
indolent
inert
inevitable
intromission
junior
marital
merchandise
moodily
moral
mortal
Mrs.
narrate
needful
needless
notable
officiated
omniscient
orator

ordinal
ornament
ornamental
outburst
oval
partake
*particular*ly
pattern
pennon
persecute
poorest
preciseness
pre-eminent
proprietary
Protestant
protestation
pure
qualify
quality
queerly
railroad
rebate
rebut
regret
revere
reverie

secretariat
separate
shortened
shrinker
sightseer
solitary
standardize
start
statute
subvert
swerved
synod
temperate
transept
trivial
undoubted
unlikely
unluckily
upright
ursiform
verbal
veritable
vesture
virile
vitiated
vitiation

PROPER NAMES

In connection with these the pronunciation has been checked from the *Century Cyclopedia of Proper Names*, the *Standard Dictionary*, and other sources. It should be remembered that proper names have frequently more than one accepted pronunciation. In some instances, such as *Grantham, Evesham*, etc., there is a local and also an "outside" pronunciation, and in the case of foreign names some have an anglicized pronunciation while others are given a native pronunciation only. From the shorthand point of view some proper names require special consideration, and the following observations will serve to indicate the practice which has been adopted in various groups of words—

(1) When the ***nses*** circle is used, the vowel is understood to be ***ĕ***: it is therefore necessary to write stroke ***n*** and the *ses* circle when another vowel occurs, as in  *Albigenses*, *Waldenses.*

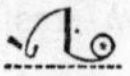

(2) Proper names ending in *-ley* preceded by the sound of *k* are generally written with the hooked letter; thus, *Brockley*, *Hinckley.*

(3) Words ending in *-shire* are generally written with the hooked letter *shr*; thus, *Ayrshire*, *Aberdeenshire.*

(4) Words ending in *-ford* are generally written with the half-length hooked letter (or); thus, *Woodford*, *Catford*, *Oxford.* The separate however is used after etc., as in  *Swinford*, *Cinderford*, *Chingford.*

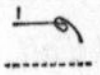

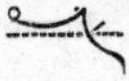

(5) The hooked letter is used for the terminations *-borough, -burgh, -bury*, when it is more convenient than the separate *b-r*, including cases in which it occurs after *t, d, m, ms, l, ls*; thus, 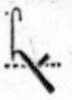 *Attleborough*, *Flamborough*, *Aldeburgh*, *Bloomsbury*, *Tilbury*, *Halsbury.*

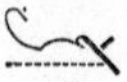

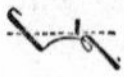

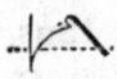

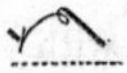

(6) Proper names ending in *-ton* or *-don* are treated in the same way as other words having those terminations (see page xxi); thus, 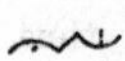 *Merton*, *Pemberton*, *Cheriton*, *Clifton*, *Bandon.*

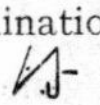

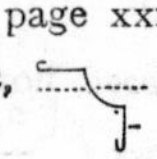

(7) Words ending in *-field* are generally written with , but after / or / hook *f* is used; thus, *Duffield,* but *Lichfield,* *Sedgfield.*

(8) In the majority of words ending in *-ham* the *h* is silent, *e.g.,* *Clapham,* *Seaham,* *Ashburnham,* *Tottenham,* *Rotherham,* but in a few names of more than two syllables ending in *-ingham,* such as *Birmingham, Nottingham,* the aspirate is pronounced by some persons. There are also a number of names ending in *-sham* or *-tham* in which custom has sanctioned the sound of *sh* and *th* respectively, *e.g.,* *Horsham,* *Waltham,* *Bentham,* though in others the *s* or *t* sound is retained, *e.g.,* *Topsham,* *Cheetham,* *Greatham.*

(9) The *h* in the termination *-hurst* is generally represented by the dot; thus, *Lyndhurst,* *Billingshurst.* In a few instances, however, it is disregarded in order to obtain a more convenient outline, *e.g.,* *Pankhurst,* *Parkhurst.*

(10) After *k* (among other cases) the terminations *-wall, -well,* are most conveniently written with ; thus, *Kirkwall,* *Bakewell.* After upward *l,* however, is sufficiently convenient; as *Holywell.*

(11) When the vowel in the termination *-ville* is sounded distinctly, the separate *l* is written if convenient; thus, *Sackville,* *Granville,* but *Nashville.*

(12) The termination *-gate* is written with full *t;* thus, *Bishopsgate,* *Deansgate,* *Cripplegate.*

(13) *-wood,* however, is generally written with half-length *w;* thus, *Attwood,* *Kingswood.* Exception, *Heywood,* to distinguish from *Hayward.*

(14) Words having the termination *-worth* are written with ; thus, *Saddleworth*, *Nailsworth;* or when necessary to avoid an awkward or too lengthy outline, with vocalized with *wŭ;* thus, *Wandsworth*, *Wordsworth*.

(15) In words ending in *-ing*, the dot is used after or or after following another stroke; thus, *Epping*, *Wapping*, *Hastings*, *Twining*, *Spalding*. In other cases stroke is written; thus, *Tooting*, *Kettering*, *Hutchings*, *Harding*, *Jennings*, *Behring*.

(16) In proper names *p* is not omitted when it occurs between *m* and *t* or *m* and *sh; e.g.*, *Hampstead* (*Hamstead*), *Ampthill*, *Compton*, *Assumption*, *Hampshire*. In *Campden* the *p* is silent.

(17) In proper names having their origin in uncontracted logograms the logograms are retained, but may be vocalized; thus, *Child*, *Gold*, *Short*. Proper names having their origin in contracted grammalogues are written in full; thus, *Lord*, *Liberty*, *Wordsworth*, *Yardley*, *Goodyear*, *Young*.

(18) In several place names such as *Kingston-on-Thames*, *Stratford-on-Avon*, *Burton-on-Trent*, *Clacton-on-Sea*, *Southend-on-Sea* the preposition may be omitted.

(19) The following are so written in order to obtain an easy or distinct outline— *Surat*, *Shetland*, *Thetford*, *Dudley*. *Jedburgh*, *Ushant*, *London*, *Carruthers*, *Sutherland*, *Weymouth*.

DISTINGUISHING OUTLINES

The following distinguishing outlines should be noted— *Frances*, *Francis*; *Persia*, *Prussia*; *Tenby*, *Denbigh*; *Dunbar*, *Edinburgh*; *Didsbury*, *Dewsbury*; *Bute*, *Bude*; *Symonds*, *Simmons*; *Wyndham*, *Wenham*; *Cobbett*, *Cobb*; *Hindley*, *Huntley*; *Wales*, *Wells*; *Mather*, *Modder*; *Barmen*, *Bremen*.

NEW ERA CHANGES

The following is a summary of the changes introduced in the "New Era" edition of the system by practically all of which some simplification of a rule is effected—

New Era Outline. | Centenary Outline.

"Right" semicircle used to express initial *w* before *k, g, m,* and *r* (upward or downward).

were *worse*

worry *world*

Triphones used to represent a diphthong and *any* vowel (either short or long).

hyaena

St loop used in words like *steady, steadied,* etc.

steady *steadied*

study *studio*

Shr always written downward.

Devonshire

fissure

Shl always written upward.

freshly *judicial*

Singer, wringer, etc., now vocalized regularly.

singer *wringer*

"Right" curves *fl* and *vl* discontinued except after *k, g, n, ng,* or a straight upstroke.

afflict *flock*

level *impulsively*

"Right" forms of *thl* and *THl* discontinued.

lethal *Bethel*

Words ending in *-cular* and *-gular* are now as a rule written with the hooked strokes.

(*Note.*—The contractions *regular* and *irregular* are retained.)

binocular

angular

singular

In the case of *spr, str,* etc., following another stroke, the *r* hook is now shown whether the two strokes make an angle or not.

prosper *destroy*

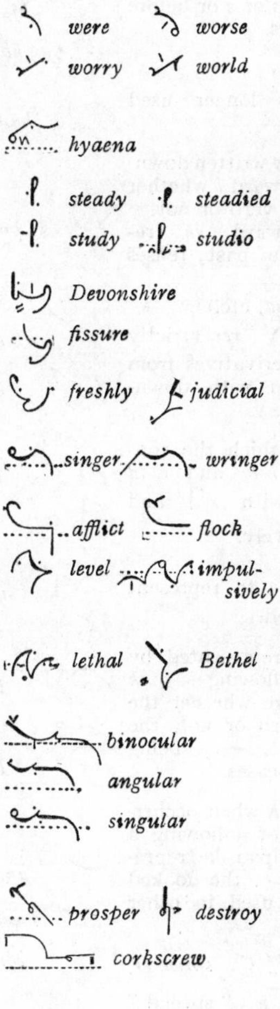

corkscrew

	New Era Outline.	*Centenary Outline.*
-uation. The outlines etc., now vocalized with triphone.	*accentuation*	
Tick *h* no longer used before stroke *s* or *z* or before hooked strokes.	*Hesse* *hazy* *history* *Hastings* *hatred* *Huddersfield*	
Dot *h* no longer used initially.	*handed* *hundred*	
Final *sh* now written downward after upward *l* whether the word is a verb or not. (*Note.*—Upward *sh* retained in the past tenses *polished*, etc.)	*polish* *relish*	
Use of *rer* strictly confined to derivatives from words written with downward *r* finally.	*sorcerer* *fruiterer*	
Words in which the consonants are *h-ld* and *w-ld* now written with and respectively.	*held* *wild*	
Use of to represent *ld* discontinued.	*quarrelled* *mildly*	
Mpr, mbr represented by when following — *k* or an upstroke whether the word is a verb or not, the double-length being used in other cases.	*lumber* *Cumberland* *Humber*	
Ng-kr, ng-gr when occurring initially or following a circle or an upstroke represented by , the hooked stroke being used in other cases. (*Note.* *shrinker*, retained as a "special" outline.)	*anchor* *anchorage* *hanker* *linger* *conger*	

	New Era Outline.	Centenary Outline.
Doubling principle no longer applied to or	conqueror, slumberer	
Y diphthongs discontinued (with exception of diphthong *u*), and diphone used for *ia*, *ie*, etc., even when monosyllabic. (=*ya*, *ye*, etc.)	lawyer, vineyard, Spaniard, million	
W diphthongs restricted to medial use, and initial, joined semicircle used to represent consonant *w* only.	water, washer, withstand, railway, walk	
Use of for *Wil*- discontinued.	Wilson, William	
Com in *-coming* is now indicated by disjoining.	becoming, becomingly, welcoming	
Inter- and *enter*- are now written in accordance with the rule for doubling and is given as a prefix representing *intro*-.	enterprise, intermingle, introduce	
The hook prefix *in*- is no longer used before *spr*.	inspiration	
Words which are uncontracted and are written in their regular position are excluded from the list of Grammalogues and a few other Grammalogues are discontinued.	happy, happen, children, suggest, suggested, suggestive, suggestion, journal, half, Heaven, initial, holy, whither, will, met, ye, youth, youths	
Logogram for *for* altered.	for	

A few other contracted logograms and a number of contractions are excluded from the lists and are now given in the Dictionary only as alternatives to the full outlines.

New Era Outline			Centenary Outline.
	or	religious	
	or	religion	
	or	generation	
	or	Christian	
	or	Christianity	
	or	constitutional-ly	
	or	Phonography	
	or	saviour	
	or	scripture	

Logogram *he* now used only when joined to a preceding character.

In addition to the alterations referred to above, the outlines of a number of words have been regularized, *e.g.*, *travel*, *forefather*, *vastly*, *income*. On the other hand, a few further words are given "special" outlines either for the purpose of distinction, *e.g.*, *burial*, *further*, *secretariat*, or for convenience, *e.g.*, *typewriter*.

Certain contractions which it has not been thought necessary to retain in the lists in the textbooks are now given in the Dictionary as alternatives to the full outlines; and alternative contracted forms are also given for some further words for which safe contractions may at times be desired.

INDEX TO INTRODUCTION

A. Subjects

B. Illustrative Words

T

U

NOTES

(*a*) All grammalogues and contractions, other than those which are fully vocalized (such as .... *cramped*), are printed in italic; also any portions of derivative or compound words for which logograms or contractions are retained.

(*b*) Only logograms and contractions (and their derivatives when the primitive forms are retained) occupying a first or a third position have their positions shown by a dotted line.

(*c*) Capitals are employed initially only where such is the ordinary usage, as in the case of proper names and terms. In botanical, zoological, and similar scientific terms, the names of genera are capitalized; with species bearing the same name a capital would not, of course, be used. For example, *Ranunculus*, the genus; but *ranunculus*, a plant of this genus.

Pitman's Shorthand Dictionary

A

A
Aaron'ic
Aaron'ical
aback'
ab'acus
Abad'don
abaft'
aban'don
aban'doned
abandonee'
aban'doner
aban'doning
aban'donment
abarticula'tion
abase'
abased'
abase'ment
abash'
abashed'
abash'ment
abash'ing
aba'sing
abat'able
abate'
aba'ted
abate'ment
aba'ter
aba'ting
ab'atis
ab'atised
aba'tor
abattoir'
abb
Ab'ba
ab'bacy
abba'tial
abbat'ical
ab'bé
ab'bess
ab'bey
ab'bot
ab'botship
abbre'viate
abbre'viated
abbre'viating
abbrevia'tion
abbre'viator
abbre'viatory
abbre'viature
ab'dicant
ab'dicate
ab'dicated

ab'dicating
abdica'tion
ab'dicative
ab'ditory
abdo'men
abdom'inal
abdominos'copy
abdom'inous
abduce'
abduced'
abdu'cent
abdu'cing
abduct'
abduct'ed
abduct'ing
abduc'tion
abduct'or
Abeceda'rian
abed'
abele'
Abel'ian
A'belite
aber'rance
aber'rancy
aber'rant
aberra'tion
abet'
abet'tal
abet'ted
abet'ting
{ abet'ter
{ abet'tor
abey'ance
abey'ant
abhor'
abhorred'
abhor'rence
abhor'rency
abhor'rent
abhor'rer
abhor'ring
A'bib
abi'dance
abide'
abi'der
abi'ding
abi'dingly
Ab'igail
abil'ity
abintest'ate
ab'ject, *a.* & *n.*
abject', *v.*

ab'jectly
ab'jectness
abjec'tion
abjudica'tion
abjura'tion
abju'ratory
abjure'
abjured'
abju'ring
abju'rer
ablacta'tion
abla'tion
ab'lative
ablaze'
a'ble
a'ble-bodied
a'bleness
ab'lepsy
ab'luent
ablu'tion
ablu'tionary
a'bly
ab'negate
ab'negated
ab'negating
abnega'tion
ab'negative
ab'negator
abnor'mal
abnor'mity
abnor'mous
aboard'
abode'
abol'ish
abol'ishable
abol'ished
abol'isher
abol'ishing
abol'ishment
aboli'tion
aboli'tionism
aboli'tionist
abom'inable
abom'inableness
abom'inate
abom'inated
abomina'tion
aborig'inal
aborig'ines
abor'tion
abor'tive
abor'tively

abor'tiveness
abound'
abound'ed
abound'ing
about'
above'
abracadab'ra
abrade'
abra'ded
abra'ding
Abraham'ic
abra'sion
abreast'
abridge'
abridged'
abridg'er
abridg'ing
abridg'ment
abroach'
abroach'ment
abroad'
ab'rogate
ab'rogated
ab'rogating
abroga'tion
abrupt'
abrup'tion
abrupt'ly
abrupt'ness
ab'scess
abscind'
ab'sciss
abscis'sion
abscond'
abscond'ed
abscond'er
abscond'ing
ab'sence
ab'sent, *a.*
absent', *v.*
absent'ed
absentee'
absentee'ism
absent'er
absent'ing
ab'sinth
absin'thian
absin'thiated
absin'thin
ab'solute
ab'solutely
ab'soluteness
absolu'tion
ab'solutism
ab'solutist
absol'utory
absol'vatory
absolve'
absolved'
absolv'er
absolv'ing
ab'sonant
absorb'
absorbabil'ity
absorb'able
absorbed'
absorb'ent
absorb'ing
absorp'tion
absorp'tive

abstain'
abstain'er
abstain'ing
abste'mious
abste'miously
abste'miousness
absten'tion
absterge'
absterged'
abster'gent
abster'ging
absterse'
abster'sion
abster'sive
ab'stinence
ab'stinent
ab'stinently
abstract', *v.*
ab'stract, *a.* & *n.*
abstract'ed
abstract'edly
abstract'edness
abstract'er
abstract'ing
abstrac'tion
abstrac'tive
ab'stractly
ab'stractness
abstruse'
abstruse'ly
abstruse'ness
absurd'
absurd'ity
absurd'ly
absurd'ness
abun'dance
abun'dant
abun'dantly
abuse', *v.*
abuse', *n.*
abused'
abu'ser
abus'ing
abu'sive
abu'sively
abu'siveness
abut'
abut'ment
abut'tal
abut'ted
abut'ter
abut'ting
abysm'
abys'mal
abyss'
Abyssin'ian
aca'cia
Aca'cian
acade'mial
acade'mian
academ'ic
academ'ical
academi'cian
acad'emist
acad'emy
Aca'dian
Acca'dian
Acale'phae
acan'tha
acantha'ceous

acan'thine
acan'thus
acar'diac
ac'arus
acatalec'tic
acat'alepsy
acatalep'tic
acau'lous
accede'
acce'ded
acce'ding
accel'erate
accel'erated
accel'erating
accelera'tion
accel'erative
accel'eratory
accend'ible
accen'sion
ac'cent, *n.*
accent', *v.*
accent'ed
accent'ing
accent'or
accent'ual
accent'uate
accent'uated
accentua'tion
accept'
acceptabil'ity
accept'able
accept'ableness
accept'ance
accepta'tion
accept'ed
accept'er
accept'ing
accep'tion
accep'tive
accept'or
ac'cess, access'
ac'cessarily
ac'cessary
accessibil'ity
acces'sible
acces'sibly
acces'sion
acces'sional
acces'sive
accesso'rial
ac'cessorily
ac'cessory
ac'cidence
ac'cident
acciden'tal
accip'ient
accip'iter
accip'itrine
acclaim'
acclama'tion
acclam'atory
accli'mate
accli'mated
accli'mating
acclima'tion
acclimatiza'tion
accli'matize
accli'matized
accli'matizing
accli'mature

accliv'ity
accli'vous
accolade'
accom'modable
accom'modate
accom'modated
accom'modating
accommoda'tion
accom'modative
accom'modator
accom'panied
accom'panier
accom'paniment
accom'panist
accom'pany
accom'panying
accom'plice
accom'plish
accom'plishable
accom'plished
accom'plisher
accom'plishing
accom'plishment
accord'
accord'ance
accord'ancy
accord'ant
accord'antly
accord'ed
accord'er
accord'ing
accord'ingly
accord'ion
accost'
accost'able
accost'ed
accost'ing
accou'chement
accoucheur'
accoucheuse'
account'
accountabil'ity
account'able
account'ableness
account'ant
account'antship
account'-book
account'ed
account'ing
accoup'le
accoup'led
accoup'lement
accoup'ling
{ accou'tre
{ accou'ter
accou'tred
accou'trements
accou'tring
accred'it
accred'ited
accres'cence
accres'cent
accre'tion
accre'tive
accroach'
accrue'
accrued'
accru'ing
accuba'tion
accum'bency
accum'bent
accu'mulate
accu'mulated
accu'mulating
accumula'tion
accu'mulative
accu'mulatively
accu'mulator
ac'curacy
ac'curate
ac'curately
ac'curateness
accurse'
accursed'
accurs'ed
accurs'ing
accu'sable
accu'sant
accusa'tion
accu'sative
accu'satively
accu'satory
accuse'
accused'
accus'er
accus'ing
accus'tom
accus'tomarily
accus'tomary
accus'tomed
accus'toming
ace
Acel'dama
acen'tric
Aceph'ala
aceph'alous
ace'-point
a'cer
ac'erate
acerb'
ac'erbate
acerb'ity
ac'erose
ac'erous
aces'cence
aces'cency
aces'cent
aceta'rious
acet'ary
ac'etate
ac'etated
acet'ic
acet'ified
acet'ify
acet'ifying
acetom'eter
ac'etone
ac'etose
acetos'ity
ac'etous
ace'tum
acet'ylene
Achai'an
Ache'an
ache
ached
achiev'able
achieve'
achieved'
achieve'ment
achiev'er
achiev'ing
ach'ing
a'chor
achromat'ic
achro'matism
achro'matize
acic'ular
acic'ulate
acic'uliform
ac'id
acidif'erous
acidifi'able
acidifica'tion
acid'ified
acid'ifier
acid'ify
acid'ifying
acidim'eter
acid'ity
ac'idness
acid'ulae
acid'ulate
acid'ulated
acid'ulating
acidula'tion
acid'ulous
a'ciform
acknowl'edge
acknowl'edged
acknowl'edger
acknowl'edging
acknowl'edgment
ac'me
ac'ne
acol'ogy
acol'othist
ac'olyte
ac'onite
acon'itine
a'corn
a'corned
acotyle'don
acotyle'donous
acou'chy
acous'tic
acoust'ical
acquaint'
acquaint'ance
acquaint'ance-ship
acquaint'ed
acquaint'ing
acquest'
acquiesce'
acquiesced'
acquies'cence
acquies'cent
acquies'cing
acquirabil'ity
acquir'able
acquire'
acquired'
acquire'ment
acquir'er
acquir'ing
acquisi'tion
acquis'itive
acquis'itively
acquis'itiveness

acquit'
acquit'ment
acquit'tal
acquit'tance
acquit'ted
acquit'ting
Ac'rasy
a'cre
a'creage
a'cred
ac'rid
acrid'ity
ac'ridness
acrimo'nious
acrimo'niously
acrimo'niousness
ac'rimony
acrit'ical
ac'ritude
acroat'ic
ac'robat
Acrocerau'nian
ac'rogen
acrog'enous
acrog'raphy
ac'rolith
acron'ych
Acrop'olis
ac'rospire
ac'rospired
across'
acros'tic
acros'tical
acros'tically
ac'roter
acrote'ria
act
act'ed
Ac'tian
act'ing
actin'ic
actin'iform
ac'tinism
actin'ograph
actin'olite
actinol'ogy
actinom'eter
ac'tion
ac'tionable
ac'tionary
ac'tionist
ac'tionless
ac'tive
ac'tively
activ'ity
act'or
act'ress
act'ual
actual'ity
act'ualize
act'ually
actua'rial
actua'rially
act'uary
act'uate
act'uated
act'uating
actua'tion
actuos'ity
acu'leate

acu'leated
acu'leous
acu'men
acu'minate
acu'minated
acu'minating
acumina'tion
acu'minous
acupress'ure
acupunctura'tion
acupunct'ure
acute'
acute'ly
acute'ness
adac'tyl
ad'age
ada'gio
ad'amant
adamante'an
adaman'tine
Adam'ic
Ad'amite
Adamit'ic
Ad'am's-ap'ple
adapt'
adaptabil'ity
adapt'able
adapt'ableness
adapta'tion
adapt'ed
adapt'edness
adapt'er
adapt'ing
adapt'ive
add
adden'da
adden'dum
ad'der
addibil'ity
ad'dible
addict'
addic'ted
addict'edness
addict'ing
addic'tion
addic'tive
ad'ding
addit'ament
addi'tion
addi'tional
ad'dle
ad'dled
ad'dle-head'ed
ad'dle-pa'ted
ad'dling
address'
addressed'
addressee'
address'er
address'ing
adduce'
adduced'
addu'cent
addu'cer
addu'cible
addu'cing
adduct'
adduc'tion
adduc'tive
adduc'tor

ad'eling
adel'opode
adel'phia
ademp'tion
adenog'raphy
ad'enoid
adenolog'ical
adenol'ogy
adeno'ma
ad'enose
adenot'omy
ad'enous
ad'eps
adept'
ad'equacy
ad'equate
ad'equately
ad'equateness
adhere'
adhered'
adhe'rence
adhe'rency
adhe'rent
adhe'rently
adhe'rer
adhe'ring
adhe'sion
adhe'sive
adhe'sively
adhe'siveness
adhib'it
adhib'ited
adhibi'tion
adhor'tatory
adiaph'orous
adieu'
adipoc'erate
ad'ipocere
ad'ipose
adipo'sis
ad'ipous
ad'ipsy
ad'it
adja'cence
adja'cency
adja'cent
adja'cently
adject'
adject'ed
adject'ing
adjec'tion
adjecti'val
ad'jective
ad'jectively
adjoin'
adjoined'
adjoin'ing
adjourn'
adjourned'
adjourn'ing
adjourn'ment
adjudge'
adjudged'
adjudg'ing
adju'dicate
adju'dicated
adju'dicating
adjudica'tion
adju'dicator
adju'dicature

ad'junct
adjunc'tion
adjunc'tive
adjunc'tively
adjunct'ly
adjura'tion
adju'ratory
adjure'
adjured'
adjur'er
adjur'ing
adjust'
adjust'able
adjust'ed
adjust'er
adjust'ing
adjust'ive
adjust'ment
ad'jutancy
ad'jutant
ad'jutant-*general*
adju'tor
adju'trix
ad'juvant
admeas'ure
admeas'urement
admensura'tion
admin'ister
admin'istered
administe'rial
admin'istering
admin'istrable
admin'istrate
administra'tion
admin'istrative
admin'istrator
admin'istrator-
ship
admin'istratrix
admirabil'ity
ad'mirable
ad'miral
ad'miralship
Ad'miralty
admira'tion
admire'
admired'
admir'er
admir'ing
admir'ingly
admissibil'ity
admis'sible
admis'sion
admis'sory
admit'
admit'table
admit'tance
admit'ted
admit'ter
admit'ting
admix'
admixed'
admix'tion
admix'ture
admon'ish
admon'ished
admon'isher
admon'ishing

admoni'tion
admon'itive
admon'itor
admon'itory
admortiza'tion
adnas'cence
ad'nate
adnom'inal
ado'
ado'be
adoles'cence
adoles'cency
adoles'cent
Adone'an
Adon'ic
adopt'
adopt'ed
adopt'er
adopt'ing
adop'tion
adop'tionist
adop'tive
ador'able
ador'ableness
adora'tion
adore'
adored'
ador'er
ador'ing
ador'ingly
adorn'
adorned'
adorn'er
adorn'ing
adorn'ment
adoscula'tion
adown'
adrift'
adroga'tion
adroit'
adroit'ly
adroit'ness
adry'
adsciti'tious
adsciti'tiously
ad'script
adstric'tion
adula'tion
ad'ulator
ad'ulatory
adult'
adul'terant
adul'terate
adul'terated
adul'terating
adultera'tion
adul'terator
adul'terer
adul'teress
adul'terous
adul'terously
adul'tery
adult'ness
adum'bra
adum'brant
ad'umbrate
ad'umbrated
ad'umbrating
adumbra'tion
adust'

advance'
advanced'
advance'-guard
advance'ment
advan'cer
advan'cing
advan'cive
advan'tage
advan'taged
advanta'geous
advanta'geously
advanta'geous-
ness
advant'aging
advene'
adve'nient
ad'vent
adventi'tious
adventi'tiously
adventi'tious-ness
advent'ual
adven'ture
adven'tured
adven'turer
adven'turesome
adven'turess
adven'turing
adven'turous
adven'turously
adven'turous-ness
ad'verb
adverb'ial
adverb'ially
adversa'ria
ad'versary
adver'sative
ad'verse
ad'versely
ad'verseness
adver'sity
advert'
advert'ed
advert'ence
advert'ency
advert'ent
advert'ently
advert'ing
ad'vertise
ad'vertised
adver'tisement
ad'vertiser
ad'vertising
advice'
advisabil'ity
advis'able
advis'ableness
advis'ably
advise'
advised'
advis'edly
advis'er
advise'ment
advis'ing
advis'ory
ad'vocacy

ad′vocate *n. v.*
ad′vocated
ad′vocateship
ad′vocating
advoca′tion
advow′ee
advow′son
adynam′ic
ad′ytum
adze
ae′dile, etc., (*see* e′dile)
ae′gis
aegro′tat
Aene′id
Aeo′lian
ae′on
a′erate
a′erated
a′erating
aera′tion
ae′rial
a′erie
aerifica′tion
a′erified
a′eriform
a′erify
a′erodrome
aerodynam′ics
aerog′raphy
a′erolite
a′erolith
aerolit′ic
aerolog′ical
aerol′ogist
aerol′ogy
a′eromancy
aerom′eter
aeromet′ric
aerom′etry
a′eronaut
aeronau′tic
a′erophyte
a′eroplane
a′eroplanist
aeros′copy
a′erostat
aerostat′ics
aerosta′tion
aesthet′ic (*see* esthetic)
aesthet′ical
afar
afeard′
affabil′ity
af′fable
af′fableness
af′fably
affair′
affect′
affecta′tion
affect′ed
affect′edly
affect′edness
affect′er
affectibil′ity
affect′ible
affect′ing
affect′ingly
affec′tion

affec′tional
affec′tionate
affec′tionately
affec′tionateness
affec′tioned
affec′tive
affec′tively
affi′ance
affi′anced
affi′ancer
affi′ancing
affiche′
affida′vit
affied′
affil′iate
affil′iated
affil′iating
affilia′tion
af′finage
affin′ity
affirm′
affirm′able
affirm′ably
affirm′ance
affirm′ant
affirma′tion
affirm′ative
affirm′atively
affirmed′
affirm′er
affirm′ing
affix′, *v.*, af′fix, *n.*
affixed′
affix′ing
affix′ture
affla′ted
affla′tion
affla′tus
afflict′
afflict′ed
afflict′er
afflict′ing
afflic′tion
afflict′ive
af′fluence
af′fluency
af′fluent
af′fluently
af′flux
afflux′ion
afford′
afford′ed
afford′ing
affor′est
afforesta′tion
affran′chise
affran′chisement
affray′
affreight′
affright′
affright′ed
affright′er
affright′ing
affront′
affront′ed
affront′ing
affront′ive
affuse′
affused′

affu′sing
affu′sion
Af′ghan
afield′
afire′
afloat′
afoot′
afore′
afore′*going*
afore′*hand*
afore′mentioned
afore′named
afore′said
afore′thought
afore′time
a fortio′ri
afoul′
afraid′
afresh′
Af′ric
Af′rican
Af′ricander
af′rit
afront′
aft
aft′er
aft′er-ages
aft′er-birth
aft′er-clap
aft′er-cost
aft′er-crop
aft′er-damp
aft′er-*guard*
aft′er-hours
aft′er-math
aft′er-*most*
afternoon′
aft′er-pains
aft′er-piece
aft′er-thought
aft′erward
aft′erwards
aft′er-wit
a′ga
again′
against′
agal′ma
ag′amist
ag′amous
ag′apae
ag′ape
agape′
Agapem′one
ag′aric
ag′ate
aga′ve
agaze′
agazed′
age
a′ged
a′gedly
a′geing
a′gency
agen′da
a′gent
aggera′tion
agglom′erate
agglom′erated
agglom′erating

agglomera'tion
agglu'tinant
agglu'tinate
agglu'tinated
agglu'tinating
agglutina'tion
agglu'tinative
ag'grandize
ag'grandized
aggrand'izement
ag'grandizer
ag'grandizing
ag'gravate
ag'gravated
ag'gravating
aggrava'tion
ag'gregate, *a. v.*
ag'gregated
ag'gregately
ag'gregating
aggrega'tion
ag'gregative
ag'gregator
aggress'
aggressed'
aggress'ing
aggres'sion
aggress'ive
aggress'iveness
aggress'or
aggriev'ance
aggrieve'
aggrieved'
aggriev'ing
aggroup'
aggrouped'
aggroup'ing
aghast'
ag'ile
ag'ileness
agil'ity
ag'io
ag'iotage
agist'
agist'ment
agist'or
ag'itable
ag'itate
ag'itated
ag'itating
agita'tion
ag'itative
ag'itator
a'glet
aglow'
agmatol'ogy
ag'nail
ag'nate
agnat'ic
agna'tion
agni'tion
agno'men
agnos'tic
agnos'ticism
ago'
agog'
ago'ing
agone'
agon'ic

ag'onism
ag'onist
agonis'tes
agonis'tic
agonis'tical
ag'onize
ag'onized
ag'onizing
ag'onizingly
ag'ony
ag'ora
agou'ti
agraph'ia
agra'rian
agra'rianism
agra'rianize
agree'
agreeabil'ity
agree'able
agree'ableness
agreed'
agree'ing
agree'ment
agres'tic
ag'ricultor
agricul'tural
ag'riculture
agricul'turist
ag'rimony
agriol'ogy
agrostog'raphy
agrostol'ogy
aground'
a'gue
a'gued
a'guish
ah
aha'
ahead'
aheap'
ahem'
ahoy'
ahull'
aid
aid'ance
aide'-de-camp
aid'ed
aid'er
aid'ful
aid'ing
aid'less
ai'glet
ai'grette
ai'guille
ail
ailed
ail'ing
ail'ment
aim
aimed
aim'er
aim'ing
aim'less
aim'lessly
ain't
air
air'-bed

air'-brake
air'-cells
aired
air'er
air'-gun
air'-hole
air'ily
air'iness
air'ing
air'less
air'-pump
air'-shaft
air'-ship
air'-tight
air'y
aisle
ait
ajar'
aj'utage
akim'bo
akin'
al'abaster
alack'
alack'-a-day
alac'rity
à la mode
à la mort'
alarm'
alarmed'
alarm'ing
alarm'ingly
alarm'ist
alar'um
a'lary
alas'
a'late
alb
Alba'nian
alba'ta
al'batross
albe'it
albes'cent
Al'bin
albi'ness
al'binism
albi'no
albi'noism
albugin'eous
albu'go
al'bum
albu'men
albu'minize
albu'minized
albu'min
albu'minoid
albuminu'ric
albu'minous
albur'num
al'ca
alcade'
alcahest'
Alca'ic
al'cazar
alchem'ic
alchem'ical
al'chemist
alchemis'tic

al′chemy
al′cohol
al′coholate
alcohol′ic
alcoholiza′tion
al′coholize
alcoholom′eter
Al′coran
Alcoran′ic
Alcoran′ist
al′cove
Aldeb′aran
al′dehyde
al′der
al′derman
alderman′ic
Al′dine
ale
aleak′
a′leatory
alec′tryomancy
alee′
a′legar
ale′hoof
ale′house
alem′bic
alem′broth
alert′
alert′ness
alette′
aleu′romancy
aleurom′eter
Aleu′tian
aleu′tic
ale′wife
Alexan′drian
Alexan′drine
alexiphar′mic
alexiter′ic
alexiter′ical
alfres′co
Al′gae
al′gebra
algebra′ic
algebra′ical
al′gebraist
Algerine′
Al′gol
al′gor
al′gorithm
al′gum
Alham′bra
a′lias
al′ibi
a′lien
alienabil′ity
a′lienable
a′lienage
a′lienate
a′lienated
a′lienating
aliena′tion
a′lienator
a′liene
alienee′
a′lienism
alif′erous
al′iform
alight′
alight′ed
alight′ing
align′, aline′
align′ment
alike′
al′iment
aliment′al
aliment′ary
alimenta′tion
aliment′iveness
alimo′nious
al′imony
al′iped
al′iquant
al′iquot
a′lish
alive′
aliz′arine
al′kahest
alkahest′ic
alkales′cency
alkales′cent
al′kali
al′kalifiable
al′kalified
al′kalify
al′kalifying
alkalig′enous
alkalim′eter
alkalimet′ric
alkalimet′rical
alkalim′etry
al′kaline
alkalin′ity
alkaliza′tion
al′kalize
al′kaloid
al′kanet
Al′koran
all
Al′lah
al′lanite
allanto′ic
allan′toid
allan′tois
allay′
allayed′
allay′er
allay′ing
allega′tion
allege′
allege′able
alleged′
alleg′er
alle′giance
alleg′ing
allegor′ic
allegor′ical
al′legorist
al′legorize
al′legorized
al′legorizer
al′legorizing
al′legory
allegret′to
allegris′simo
alle′gro
allelu′ia
allemande′
alle′viate
alle′viated
alle′viating
allevia′tion
alle′viative
alle′viator
al′ley
All Fools′ Day
all-fours′
all-hail′
All-Hal′lows
allia′ceous
alli′ance
allied′
allies′
alliga′tion
al′ligator
alli′sion
allit′erate, *a.* & *v.*
allitera′tion
allit′erative
al′lium
al′locate
al′located
al′locating
alloca′tion
alloca′tur
al′lochroite
allocu′tion
allo′dial
allo′dium
al′lograph
allonge′
allopath′ic
allopath′ically
allop′athist
allop′athy
al′lophane
allot′
allot′ment
allot′ted
allot′ter
allot′ting
allot′ropy
allow′
allow′able
allow′ableness
allow′ably
allow′ance
allow′anced
allow′ancing
allowed′
allow′er
allow′ing
alloy′
alloy′age
alloyed′
alloy′ing
All Saints′ Day
all-see′ing
All Souls′ Day
all′spice
allude′
allud′ed
allud′ing
allure′
allured′
allure′ment
allur′er

allur'ing
allur'ingly
allu'sion
allu'sive
allu'sively
allu'sory
allu'vial
allu'vion
allu'vium
all-wise'
ally'
ally'ing
Al'magest
al'ma ma'ter
al'manac
al'mandine
*al*might'iness
*al*might'y
a'lmond
al'moner
al'monry
al'most
alms
alms'-house
al'mug
al'oe
aloet'ic
aloet'ical
aloft'
alogot'rophy
al'omancy
alone'
along'
along'side
aloof'
aloof'ness
alope'cia
aloud'
alp
alpac'a
alp'enstock
al'pha
al'phabet
alphabeta'rian
alphabet'ic
alphabet'ical
alphon'sin
al'phus
Al'pine
*al*read'y
al'so
Alta'ic
al'tar
al'tarage
al'tar-cloth
al'tar-piece
al'ter
alterabil'ity
al'terable
al'terableness
al'terably
al'terant
altera'tion
al'terative
al'tercate
al'tercating
alterca'tion
al'tered
al'terer
al'tering

al'tern
altern'ate, *a.*
al'ternate, *v.*
al'ternated
altern'ately
al'ternating
alterna'tion
alter'native
alter'natively
Althae'a
although'
altim'eter
altim'etry
altis'onant
al'titude
al'to
altogeth'er
alto-relie'vo
al'truism
altruis'tic
alu'del
al'um
alu'mina
alu'minate
al'umine
aluminif'erous
alu'minite
alumin'ium
alu'minous
al'umish
alum'nus
al'veary
al'veolar
al'veolary
al'veolate
al'veolite
al'veolus
al'vine
*al'*way
*al'*ways
am
am'adou
a'mah
amain'
amal'gam
amal'gamate
*amal'gama*ted
*amal'gama*ting
amalgama'tion
amanuen'sis
am'aranth
amaranth'ine
amaranth'us
Amaryl'lis
amass'
amassed'
amass'ing
amass'ment
am'ateur
am'ative
am'ativeness
amato'rial
am'atory
amauro'sis
amaze'
amazed'
amaze'ment
amaz'ing
amaz'ingly

Am'azon
Amazo'nian
am'bage
ambas'sador
ambas'sadress
am'ber
am'bergris
ambidex'ter
ambidexter'ity
ambidex'trous
ambidex'trously
am'bient
ambig'enal
ambigu'ity
ambig'uous
ambig'uously
ambig'uousness
am'bit
ambi'tion
ambi'tious
ambi'tiously
am'ble
am'bled
am'bler
am'bling
amblyo'pia
am'bo
ambro'sia
ambro'sial
Ambro'sian
am'brotype
am'bry
ambs'-ace
am'bulance
am'bulant
ambula'tion
am'bulator
am'bulatory
am'bury
ambuscade'
ambusca'ded
ambusca'ding
am'bush
am'bushment
ameer', amir'
ame'liorate
ame'liorated
ame'liorating
ameliora'tion
ame'liorative
ame'liorator
amen'
amenabil'ity
ame'nable
ame'nably
amend'
amend'able
amend'atory
amend'ed
amend'er
amend'ing
amend'ment
amends'
amen'ity
ament'
amenta'ceous
amen'tia
ament'um
amerce'
amerce'able

amerced'
amerce'ment
amerc'er
amerc'ing
Amer'ican
Amer'icanism
Amer'icanize
am'ethyst
amethyst'ine
Amhar'ic
amiabil'ity
a'miable
a'miableness
a'miably
amian'thus
amicabil'ity
am'icable
am'icableness
am'ice
amid'
am'idine
amid'ships
amidst'
amiss'
am'ity
am'meter
ammo'nia
ammo'niac
am'monite
ammo'nium
ammuni'tion
amne'sia
amne'sic
am'nesty
am'nion
am'nios
amniot'ic
amoe'ba
Amo'mum
among'
amongst'
Amontilla'do
am'orist
amoro'so
am'orous
am'orously
am'orousness
amor'phism
amor'phous
amort'
amortiza'tion
amor'tize
amor'tizement
amount'
amount'ed
amount'ing
amour'
ampère'
am'persand
am'phi
Amphib'ia
amphib'ian
amphib'ious
amphib'iously
amphib'iousness
amphibol'ogy
amphib'olous
am'phibrach

Amphictyon'ic
Amphic'tyons
amphisbae'na
amphithe'atre / amphithe'ater
amphitheat'ric
amphitheat'rical
Am'phitrite
am'phora
am'phoral
am'ple
am'pleness
amplifica'tion
am'plified
am'plifier
am'plify
am'plifying
am'plitude
am'ply
ampul'la
am'putate
am'putated
am'putating
amputa'tion
amuck'
am'ulet
amus'able
amuse'
amused'
amuse'ment
amus'er
amus'ing
amus'ingly
amu'sive
amyg'dalate
amyg'daline
amyg'daloid
am'yl
amyla'ceous
am'ylin
an
an'a
Anabap'tism
Anabap'tist
Anabaptist'ic
anab'olism
anacamp'tics
anacar'dic
anacathar'tic
anach'ronism
anachronis'tic
anaclas'tic
anacolu'thon
anacon'da
Anacreon'tic
an'adem
anae'mia
anaem'ic
anaesthe'sia
anaesthet'ic
an'aglyph
anaglyph'ic
anaglyp'tic
anagno'sis
an'agogy

an'agram
anagrammat'ic
anagrammat'ical
anagram'matist
anagram'matize
an'agraph
a'nal
an'alects
analec'ta
analec'tic
analem'ma
an'alepsy
analep'tic
analog'ical
anal'ogism
anal'ogist
anal'ogize
anal'ogized
anal'ogizing
anal'ogous
anal'ogously
an'alogue
anal'ogy
anal'ysis
an'alyst
analyt'ic
analyt'ical
an'alysable
analysa'tion
an'alyse
an'alysed
an'alyser
an'alysing
anamor'phosis
ana'nas
anan'drous
an'apest
anapes'tic
anaph'ora
anarch'ic
anarch'ical
an'archism
an'archist
an'archy
anar'throus
anasar'ca
anasar'cous
anas'tasis
anastat'ic
anas'tomose
anas'trophe
anath'ema
anathemat'ical
anath'ematism
anathematiza'-tion
anath'ematize
anath'ematized
anath'ematizer
anath'ematizing
anatif'erous
anatom'ic
anatom'ical
anat'omizing
anat'omist
anatomiza'tion

anat'omize
anat'omized
anat'omy
anatrep'tic
an'ceps
an'cestor
ancesto'rial
ances'tral
an'cestress
an'cestry
anch'or
anch'orable
anch'orage
anch'ored
anch'oress
anch'oret
anchoret'ic
anchoret'ical
anch'oring
anch'orite
ancho'vy
an'chylose
an'cient
an'ciently
an'cientry
an'cillary
ancip'ital
ancip'itous
an'come
an'con
an'cones
and
andan'te
andanti'no
Ande'an
and'iron
andranat'omy
androg'ynal
androg'ynism
androg'ynous
an'droid
android'al
android'es
an'dron
an'drous
an'ecdotal
an'ecdote
anecdot'ic
anecdot'ical
an'ecdotist
ane'mia
anemog'raphy
anemol'ogy
anemom'eter
anemom'etry
anem'one
anem'oscope
anent'
an'eroid
anesthe'sia
an'eurism
anew'
anfract'uous
an'gel
angel'ic
angel'ica
angel'ical
angelol'ogy

an'gelot
an'gelus
an'ger
an'gered
an'gering
an'gina
angiocarp'ous
angiog'raphy
angiol'ogy
angiot'omy
an'gle
an'gled
an'gler
An'glican
An'glicanism
An'glice
An'glicism
an'glicize
an'glicized
an'glicizing
an'gling
An'glomania
An'glo-Sax'on
ango'la
an'gor
ango'ra
an'grily
an'gry
anguil'liform
anguin'eal
an'guish
an'guished
an'guishing
an'gular
angular'ity
an'gularly
an'gulated
anhela'tion
anhy'drous
an'il
an'ile
an'iline
anil'ity
an'ima
animadver'sion
animadvert'
animadvert'ed
animadvert'er
animadvert'ing
an'imal
animal'cula
animal'cular
animal'cule
animal'culine
animal'culist
animal'culum
an'imalism
animal'ity
animaliza'tion
an'imalize

an'imalized
animal'izing
an'imate
an'imated
an'imating
an'imatingly
anima'tion
an'imative
an'imator
an'imism
an'imist
animos'ity
an'imus
an'ion
an'ise
an'iseed
an'isette
an'ker
an'kle
an'kle-bone
an'kled
an'klet
an'na
an'nalist
an'nalize
an'nals
an'nats
anneal'
annealed'
anneal'ing
annel'idan
annex'
annex'able
annexa'tion
annexa'tionist
annexed'
annex'ing
anni'hilable
anni'hilate
anni'hilated
anni'hilating
annihila'tion
anni'hilator
anniver'sary
an'no Dom'ini
an'no mun'di
an'notate
an'notated
an'notating
annota'tion
an'notator
an'notatory
annot'to
announce'
announced'
announc'ement
announc'er
announc'ing
annoy'
annoy'ance
annoyed'
annoy'er
annoy'ing
an'nual
an'nually
annu'itant
annu'ity
annul'
an'nular

an'nulate
an'nulated
annula'tion
an'nulet
annulled'
annul'ler
annul'ling
annul'ment
Annulo'sa
an'nulose
an'nulus
annu'merate
annu'merated
annu'merating
annumera'tion
annun'ciate
annun'ciated
annun'ciating
annuncia'tion
annun'ciator
annun'ciatory
an'ode
an'odyne
anoint'
anoint'ed
anoint'er
anoint'ing
anoint'ment
anom'alism
anom'alist
anomalist'ic
anomalist'ical
anom'alous
anom'alously
anom'aly
anon'
anonym'ity
anon'ymous
anon'ymously
anon'ymousness
anorex'ia
anorm'al
anos'mia
anoth'er
anot'ta
an'serated
an'serine
an'swer
an'swerable
an'swered
an'swerer
an'swering
ant
an'ta
antac'id
antag'onism
antag'onist
antagonist'ic
antag'onize
antag'onized
antag'onizing
antal'gic
antal'kali
Antarc'tic
antarthrit'ic
antasthmat'ic
ant'-eater
antecede'
antece'ded
antece'dence
antece'dent
antece'dently
antece'ding
anteces'sor
an'techamber
an'techapel
an'tedate
an'tedated
an'tedating
antedilu'vial
antedilu'vian
an'telope
antemerid'ian
antemun'dane
antemu'ral
anteni'cene
anten'na
anten'nae
antenup'tial
antepas'chal
an'tepast
antepenult'
antepenult'imate
antepilep'tic
ante'rior
anterior'ity
ante'riorly
an'te-room
an'them
an'ther
an'theroid
ant'-hill
anthol'ogy
an'thracite
anthracit'ic
an'thrax
anthropog'raphy
an'thropoid
anthropol'ogist
anthropol'ogy
anthropomor'-phism
anthropomor'-phist
anthropomor'-phize
anthropomor'-phous
anthropop'athy
anthropoph'agi
anthropoph'-agous
anthropoph'agy
an'ti
antibil'ious
an'tic
An'tichrist
antichrist'ian
antic'ipant
antic'ipate
antic'ipated
antic'ipating
anticipa'tion
antic'ipative
antic'ipator
antic'ipatory
anticli'max
anticli'nal
anticy'clone
an'tidotal
an'tidote
antidot'ical
antifeb'rile
antifed'eral
antifed'eralism
an'tigraph
antilog'arithm
antil'ogy
antim'eter
antimonarch'ical
antimo'nial
antimo'niate
antimo'nious
an'timony
Antino'mian
Antino'mianism
antin'omy
Antio'chian
antipa'pal
antipathet'ic
antipath'ic
antip'athy
antiphlogis'tic
an'tiphon
antiph'onal
antiph'ony
antiph'rasis
antip'odal
an'tipode
antipode'an
antip'odes
antipyret'ic
antipy'rin
antiqua'rian
antiqua'rianism
an'tiquary
an'tiquate
an'tiquated
antiqua'tion
antique'
antique'ly
antique'ness
antiq'uities
antiq'uity
antirheumat'ic
antiscorbu'tic
antiscript'ural
antisep'tic
antislav'ery
antiso'cial
antispasmod'ic
antis'tasis
antis'trophe
antistroph'ic
antith'eses
antith'esis
antithet'ic

antithet'ical
antitrinita'rian
antitox'in
an'titype
antityp'ical
ant'ler
ant'lered
ant'like
antonoma'sia
ant'onym
Anu'bis
a'nus
an'vil
anxi'ety
anx'ious
anx'iously
anx'iousness
an'y
*an'y*body
*an'y*how
*an'y*one
an'ything
*an'y*where
*an'y*wise
Ao'nian
a'orist
aoris'tic
aor'ta
aorti'tis
apace'
apago'ge
ap'anage
apart'
apart'ment
apathet'ic
apathet'ical
ap'athist
ap'athy
ap'atite
ape
apeak'
aped
apel'lous
Ap'ennine
apep'sia
ape'rient
aper'itive
ap'erture
apet'alous
a'pex
apha'sia
aphe'lion
aphe'resis
aph'ides
aphilan'thropy
a'phis
aphlogis'tic
apho'nia
aph'orism
aph'orist
aphorist'ic
aphorist'ical
aph'orize
aph'rite
aph'thae
aph'thong
apia'rian

a'piarist
a'piary
ap'ices
apic'ulated
a'piculture
apiece'
a'ping
A'pis
a'pish
a'pishly
a'pishness
aplas'tic
aplomb'
apoc'alypse
apocalyp'tic
apocalyp'tical
apocar'pous
apoc'opate
apoc'ope
apocrus'tic
Apoc'rypha
apoc'ryphal
a'podal
a'pode
apod'osis
ap'ogee
ap'ograph
Apol'lo
apollon'icon
Apoll'yon
apologet'ic
apologet'ical
apol'ogist
apol'ogize
apol'ogized
apol'ogizer
apol'ogizing
ap'ologue
apol'ogy
ap'ophthegm
apoph'yge
apoplec'tic
apoplec'tical
ap'oplexy
apos'tasy
apos'tate
apostat'ical
apos'tatize
apos'tatized
apos'tatizing
a posterio'ri
apos'til
apos'tle
apos'tleship
apos'tolate
apostol'ic
apostol'ical
apostolic'ity
apos'trophe
apostroph'ic
apos'trophize
apos'trophized
apos'trophizing
apos'tume
apoth'ecary
ap'othegm
apothegmat'ic
apotheo'sis

apothe'osize
apot'omy
appal'
Appalach'ian
appalled'
appall'ing
appall'ingly
ap'panage
appara'tus
appar'el
appar'elled
appar'elling
appa'rent
appa'rently
appari'tion
appar'itor
appeal'
appeal'able
appealed'
appeal'er
appeal'ing
appear'
appear'ance
appeared'
appear'er
appear'ing
appeas'able
appeas'ableness
appease'
appeased'
appease'ment
appeas'er
appeas'ing
appel'lant
appel'late
appella'tion
appel'lative
appel'latively
appel'latory
appellee'
appel'lor
ap'penage
append'
append'age
append'ant
append'ed
appen'dices
appendici'tis
append'ing
appen'dix
appen'dixes
appercep'tion
appertain'
appertained'
appertain'ing
appertain'ment
ap'petence
ap'petency
ap'petent
ap'petite
ap'petitive
ap'petize
ap'petizer
ap'petizing
Ap'pian
applaud'
applaud'ed
applaud'er
applaud'ing
applause'

applau'sive
ap'ple
ap'ple-tree
appli'ance
appli'ancy
applicabil'ity
ap'plicable
ap'plicableness
ap'plicancy
ap'plicant
ap'plicate
applica'tion
ap'plicative
ap'plicatory
applied'
appli'er
appliqué'
apply'
apply'ing
appoggiatu'ra
appoint'
appoint'able
appoint'ed
appointee'
appoint'er
appoint'ing
appoint'ment
Apollina'rian
appor'tion
appor'tioned
appor'tioner
appor'tioning
appor'tionment
appos'er
ap'posite
ap'positely
ap'positeness
apposi'tion
appos'itive
apprais'al
appraise'
appraised'
appraise'ment
apprais'er
apprais'ing
appre'ciable
appre'ciably
appre'ciate
appre'ciated
appre'ciating
apprecia'tion
appre'ciative
appre'ciatory
apprehend'
apprehend'ed
apprehend'er
apprehend'ing
apprehen'sible
apprehen'sion
apprehen'sive
apprehen'sively
apprehen'sive- [ness
appren'tice
appren'ticed
appren'ticeship
appren'ticing

apprise', apprize'
apprised'
appris'er
appris'ing
approach'
approach'able
approached'
approach'er
approach'ing
approach'ment
ap'probate
ap'probated
ap'probating
approba'tion
ap'probative
ap'probatively
ap'probativeness
ap'probatory
appro'priable
appro'priate
appro'priated
appro'priately
appro'priateness
appro'priating
appropria'tion
appro'priative
appro'priator
approv'able
approv'al
approve'
approved'
approve'ment
approv'er
approv'ing
approv'ingly
approx'imate, *n.a*
approx'imate, *v.*
approx'imated
approx'imately
approx'imating
approxima'tion
approx'imative
appui'
appulse'
appul'sion
appul'sive
appur'tenance
appur'tenant
a'pricot
A'pril
A'pril-fool
a prio'ri
a'pron
a'proned
apropos'
apse
ap'sidal
ap'sides
ap'sis
apt
ap'tera
ap'teral
ap'terous
ap'teryx
apt'itude
apt'ly
apt'ness
ap'tote
a'qua

aquafor'tis
aquarelle'
aqua'rial
aqua'rian
aqua'rium
Aqua'rius
aquat'ic
aq'uatint
a'qua vi'tae
aq'ueduct
a'queous
a'queousness
aq'uiline
aq'uilon
Ar'ab
arabesque'
arabesqued'
Ara'bian
Ar'abic
Arab'ical
ar'abine
ar'abist
ar'able
Arach'nida
arach'noid
arachnol'ogy
ar'agonite
Arame'an
Arama'ic
ara'tion
ar'balist
ar'balister
ar'biter
ar'bitrable
arbit'rament
***ar'bitrar**ily*
***ar'bitrar**iness*
ar'bitrary
ar'bitrate
***ar'bitrat**ed*
***ar'bitrat**ing*
arbitra'tion
ar'bitrator
***ar'bitrat**rix*
ar'bitress
ar'bour, ar'bor
ar'boured
arbo'reous
arbores'cence
arbores'cent
ar'boret
arbore'tum
arboricult'ural
ar'boriculture
arboricult'urist
ar'boriform
ar'borist
arboriza'tion
ar'borous
ar'buscle
arbus'cular
arbut'ean
ar'butus
arc
arcade

arca'ded
Arca'dian
arca'na
arca'num
arch
archaeolog'ic
archaeolog'ical
archaeol'ogist
archaeol'ogy
archa'ic
ar'chaism
archan'gel
archangel'ic
archapos'tle
archbish'op
archbish'opric
archem'ic
archdea'con
archdea'conry
archdea'conship
archdi'ocese
archdru'id
archdu'cal
archduch'ess
archduch'y
archduke'
archduke'dom
arched
arch'er
arch'eress
arch'ery
ar'chetypal
ar'chetype
archfiend'
arch'ical
archidiac'onal
archiepis'copacy
archiepis'copal
ar'chil
Archilo'chian
archiman'drite
Archime'dean
arch'ing
archipel'ago
ar'chitect
ar'chitective
architecton'ic
{ *architect ural*
{ *ar'chitecture*
ar'chitrave
archi'val
ar'chives
ar'chivist
ar'chivolt
arch'ly
arch'ness
ar'chon
archpres'byter
archpres'bytery
archpriest'
archpri'mate

arch'stone
arch'way
arch'wise
ar'cograph
arcta'tion
Arc'tic
Arctu'rus
ar'cuate
arcua'tion
ar'cubalist
ar'dency
ar'dent
ar'dently
ar'dour, ar'dor
ar'duous
ar'duously
ar'duousness
are
a'rea
Ar'eca
arefac'tion
ar'efy
are'na
arena'ceous
arena'tion
arenose'
are'ola
are'olar
are'olate
areola'tion
areom'eter
areomet'ric
areomet'rical
areom'etry
Areop'agist
Areop'agite
Areop'agus
ar'gal
ar'gand
ar'gent
argent'al
argent'ic
argentif'erous
ar'gentine
ar'gil
argilla'ceous
argillif'erous
argil'lous
Ar'give
ar'gol
ar'gon
Ar'gonaut
Argonaut'ic
ar'gosy
ar'got
ar'guable
ar'gue
ar'gued
ar'guer
ar'guing
ar'gument
argumenta'tion
argumen'tative
argumen'tatively
argumen'tative-[ness
ar'gus
a'ria
A'rian

A'rianism
ar'id
arid'ity
ar'idness
A'ries
ariet'ta
aright'
ar'il
arise'
aris'en
aris'ing
ar'istarch
aristarch'ian
aristoc'racy
ar'istocrat
aristocrat'ic
aristocrat'ical
Aristote'lian
Aristotel'ic
ar'ithmancy
arith'metic
arithmet'ical
arithmeti'cian
ark
arm
arma'da
armadil'lo
ar'mament
ar'mature
arm'-*chair*
armed
Arme'nian
arm'ful
arm'hole
ar'miger
armig'erous
armil'la
armil'lary
arm'ing
Armin'ian
Armin'ianism
armip'otence
armip'otent
arm'istice
arm'less
arm'let
ar'mor, ar'mour
{ ar'morer
{ ar'mourer
armo'rial
Armor'ic
Armor'ican
ar'mourist
ar'mour-pla'ted
{ ar'moury
{ ar'mory
arm'pit
arms
arm's'-length
ar'my
ar'nica
arnot'to
aro'ma
aromat'ic
aromat'ical

aro'matize
aro'matizer
aro'matous
arose'
around'
arouse'
aroused'
arous'ing
arpeg'gio
ar'pent
arquebusade'
ar'quebuse / ar'quebus
arquebusier'
ar'rack
ar'ragonite
arraign'
arraigned'
arraign'er
arraign'ing
arraign'ment
arrange'
arranged'
arrang'ement
arrang'er
arrang'ing
ar'rant
ar'rantly
ar'ras
array'
arrayed'
array'er
array'ing
arrear'
arrear'age
arrears'
arrest'
arrest'ed
arrest'er / arrest'or
arrest'ing
arrest'ment
arrière
ar'ris
arri'val
arrive'
arrived'
arriv'ing
ar'rogance
ar'rogancy
ar'rogant
ar'rogantly
ar'rogate
ar'rogated
ar'rogating
arroga'tion
arrondisse'ment
arro'sion
ar'row
ar'row-head
ar'rowroot
ar'row-shaped
ar'rowy
ar'senal
arse'niate
ar'senic, *n.* / arsen'ic, *adj.*
arsen'ical
arsen'icate
arsen'icated
arsen'icating
arse'nious
ar'senite
ar'sis
ar'son
art
arte'rial
arterializa'tion
arte'rialize
arte'rialized
arte'rializing
arteriol'ogy
arteriot'omy
ar'tery
arte'sian
art'ful
art'fully
art'fulness
arthrit'ic
arthri'tis
arthrod'ic
ar'tichoke
ar'ticle
ar'ticled
ar'ticling
articu'lar
artic'ularly
articula'ta
artic'ulate, *n.& a.*
artic'ulate, *v.*
artic'ulated
artic'ulately
artic'ulating
articula'tion
art'ifice
artif'icer
artifi'cial
artificial'ity
artifi'cialness
artil'lerist
artil'lery
artil'leryman
ar'tisan
art'ist
artiste'
artist'ic
artist'ical
artist'ically
art'less
art'lessly
art'lessness
Arunde'lian
arundif'erous
arus'pice
arus'picy
Ar'yan
as (a coin)
as
asafoet'ida
asbes'tine
asbes'tos
as'caris
ascend'
ascend'able
ascend'ant
ascend'ent
ascend'ed
ascend'ency
ascend'er
ascend'ing
ascen'sion
Ascen'sion Day
ascen'sional
ascent'
ascertain'
ascertain'able
ascertained'
ascertain'er
ascertain'ing
ascertain'ment
ascet'ic
ascet'icism
ascit'ic
asciti'tious
ascrib'able
ascribe'
ascribed'
ascrib'ing
ascrip'tion
asep'sis
asep'tic
asex'ual
ash
ashamed'
ash'en
ash'ery
ash'es
ash'-hole
ash'lar
ash'laring
ashore'
ash'-pan
ash'-pit
Ash Wed'nesday
ash'y
A'sian
Asiat'ic
Asiat'icism
aside'
as'inine
asit'ia
ask
askance'
askant'
asked
ask'er
askew'
ask'ing
aslant'
asleep'
aslope'
Asmone'an
aso'matous
asp
aspar'agine
aspar'agus
as'pect
as'pen
as'perate
as'perated
as'perating
aspera'tion
asper'ges
aspergil'lus
asper'ity
asperm'ous
asperse'
aspersed'
aspers'er

aspers'ing
arper'sion
asper'sive
asperso'rium
aspers'ory
as'phalt
asphal'tic
asphal'tum
as'phodel
asphyx'ia
asphyx'iate
asphyx'iated
asphyx'y
aspi'rant
as'pirate, *n.*
as'pirate, *v.*
as'pirated
as'pirating
aspira'tion
as'pirator
aspi'ratory
aspire'
aspired'
aspir'er
aspir'ing
aspir'ingly
asquint'
ass
as'sagai
assa'i
assail'
assail'able
assail'ant
assailed'
assail'er
assail'ing
assas'sin
assas'sinate
assas'sinated
assas'sinating
assassina'tion
assas'sinator
assault'
assault'ed
assault'er
assault'ing
assay'
assayed'
assay'er
assay'ing
assem'blage
assem'ble
assem'bled
assem'bler
assem'bling
assem'bly
assent'
assent'ed
assen'ter
assen'tient
assent'ing
assert'
assert'ed
assert'ing
asser'tion
assert'ive
assert'ively
assert'or
assert'ory

assess'
assess'able
assessed'
assess'ing
assess'ment
assess'or
as'sets
assev'erate
assev'erated
assev'erating
assevera'tion
as'sident
assidu'ity
assid'uous
assid'uously
assid'uousness
assign'
assign'able
as'signat
assigna'tion
assigned'
assignee'
assign'er
assign'ing
assign'ment
assignor'
assigns'
assim'ilable
assim'ilate
assim'ilated
assim'ilating
assimila'tion
assim'ilative
assim'ilatory
assist'
assist'ance
assist'ant
assist'ed
assist'ing
assize'
assized'
assize'ment
assiz'er
assiz'es
assiz'or
associabil'ity
asso'ciable
asso'ciate
asso'ciated
asso'ciating
associa'tion
associa'tional
asso'ciative
assoil'zie
as'sonance
as'sonant
assort'
assort'ed
assort'er
assort'ing
assort'ment
assuage'
assuaged'
assuag'ement
assuag'er
assuag'ing
assua'sive
assuefac'tion
assume'
assumed'

assum'er
assum'ing
assum'ingly
assump'sit
assump'tion
assump'tive
assump'tively
assur'ance
assure'
assured'
assur'edly
assur'edness
assur'er
assur'ing
assur'ingly
assur'or
Assyr'ian
astat'ic
as'teism
as'ter
aste'ria
aste'riated
as'terisk
as'terism
as'terite
astern'
as'teroid
asteroid'al
asthen'ic
asthenol'ogy
asth'ma
asthmat'ic
asthmat'ical
astigmat'ic
astig'matism
astir'
aston'ied
aston'ish
aston'ished
aston'ishing
aston'ishingly
aston'ishment
astound'
astound'ed
astound'ing
astrad'dle
as'tragal
as'tral
astray'
astrict'
astric'tion
astric'tive
astride'
astringe'
astrin'gency
astrin'gent
astrog'raphy
as'troid
as'troite
as'trolabe
astrol'oger
astrolog'ic
astrolog'ical
astrol'ogize
astrol'ogy
astron'omer

astronom'ic
astronom'ical
astron'omy
as'troscope
astrotheol'ogy
astrut'
astute'
astute'ly
astute'ness
asun'der
asy'lum
asymmet'ric
asymmet'rical
asym'metry
as'ymptote
at
at'abal
at'avism
at'axy
ate
atelier'
athal'amous
Athana'sian
a'theism
a'theist
atheist'ic
atheist'ical
ath'eling
athenae'um
Athe'nian
athirst'
ath'lete
athlet'ic
at-home
athwart'
atilt'
Atlante'an
atlan'tes
Atlan'tic
At'las, at'las
atmol'ogy
atmom'eter
at'mosphere
atmospher'ic
atmospher'ical
atoll'
at'om
atom'ic
atom'ical
at'omism
at'omist
at'omize
atomol'ogy
aton'able
atone'
atoned'
atone'ment
aton'er
aton'ic
aton'ing
at'ony
atop'
atrabila'rian
atrabila'rious
atrabil'iary
atrabil'ious
atramenta'ceous
atrament'al
atramenta'rious
atrament'ous

atrip'
a'trium
atro'cious
atro'ciously
atro'ciousness
atroc'ity
at'rophied
at'rophy
attach'
attach'able
atta'ché
attached'
attach'ing
attach'ment
attack'
attack'able
attacked'
attack'er
attack'ing
attain'
attainabil'ity
attain'able
attain'ableness
attaind'er
attained'
attain'ing
attain'ment
attaint'
attaint'ed
attaint'ing
attaint'ment
attaint'ure
at'tar
attem'per
attem'pered
attem'pering
attem'perment
attempt'
attempt'able
attempt'ed
attempt'er
attempt'ing
attend'
attend'ance
attend'ant
attend'ed
attend'er
attend'ing
attent'
atten'tion
atten'tive
atten'tively
atten'tiveness
atten'uant
atten'uate
atten'uated
atten'uating
attenua'tion
attest'
attesta'tion
attest'ed
{ attest'er
{ attest'or
attest'ing
At'tic, at'tic
At'ticism
At'ticize
At'ticized
At'ticizing
attire'

attired'
attir'er
attir'ing
at'titude
attitu'dinal
attitu'dinize
attol'lent
attor'ney
Attor'ney-*Gen'-eral*
attor'neyship
attract'
attractabil'ity
attract'able
attract'ed
attract'ile
attract'ing
attract'ingly
attrac'tion
attract'ive
attract'ively
attract'iveness
attract'or
at'trahent
attrib'utable
{ at'tribute, *n.*
{ attrib'ute, *v.*
attrib'uted
attrib'uting
attribu'tion
attrib'utive
attrite'
attri'tion
attune'
attuned'
attun'ing
atyp'ic
aubin'
au'burn
auc'tion
auctioneer'
auctioneer'ing
auda'cious
auda'ciously
auda'ciousness
audac'ity
audibil'ity
au'dible
au'dibleness
au'dibly
au'dience
audiom'eter
au'diphone
au'dit
au'dited
au'diting
au'ditor
audito'rium
au'ditory
Auge'an
au'ger
au'get
aught
au'gite
{ aug'ment, *n.*
{ augment', *v.*
augment'able
augmenta'tion
augment'ative
augment'ed

augment'er
augment'ing
au'gur
au'gural
au'gured
au'guring
au'gurship
au'gury
Au'gust, *n.*
august', *a.*
Augus'tan
Augus'tin
Augustin'ians
august'ness
auk
aula'rian
au'lic
au'lin
aunt
aunt'ie
au'ra
au'ral
au'rate
au'rated
au'reate
aure'lia
aure'lian
aure'ola
au'reole
au'ric
au'ricle
au'ricled
auric'ula
auric'ular
auric'ularly
auric'ulate
auric'ulated
aurif'erous
au'riform
aurig'raphy
au'rist
au'rochs
auro'ra
auro'ra borea'lis
auro'ral
au'rum
ausculta'tion
aus'cultator
auscul'tatory
au'spicate
au'spice
au'spices
auspi'cious
auspi'ciously
auspi'ciousness
au'ster
austere'
austere'ly
auster'ity
aus'tral
Australa'sian
Austra'lian
Aus'trian
aus'tromancy
authen'tic
authen'tical
authen'ticate

authen'ticated
authen'ticating
authentica'tion
authentic'ity
au'thor
au'thoress
author'itative
author'itatively
author'itative-ness
author'ity
au'thorizable
authoriza'tion
au'thorize
au'thorized
au'thorizing
au'thorship
autobiog'rapher
autobiograph'ic
autobiograph'-ical
autobiog'raphy
autoch'thon
autoch'thonous
autoc'racy
au'tocrat
autocrat'ic
autocrat'ical
au'to-da-fé
autog'enous
au'tograph
autograph'ic
autograph'ical
autog'raphy
autom'ata
au'tomath
automat'ic
automat'ical
autom'atism
autom'aton
autom'atous
automobile'
automor'phic
au'tomotor
autonom'ic
auton'omize
auton'omous
auton'omy
au'tonym
autop'sia
autop'sy
au'totype
au'tumn
autum'nal
auxil'iar
auxil'iaries
auxil'iary
avail'
availabil'ity
avail'able
avail'ableness
availed'
avail'ing
av'alanche
av'arice
avari'cious
avari'ciously
avari'ciousness
avast'

avatar'
avaunt'
a've
A've Mari'a
avenge'
avenged'
aveng'er
aveng'ing
av'ens
av'entail
av'enue
aver'
av'erage
av'eraged
av'eraging
aver'ment
averred'
aver'ring
averrun'cate
averse'
averse'ly
aver'sion
avert'
avert'ed
avert'er
avert'ible
avert'ing
a'viary
avia'tion
a'viator
avid'ious
avid'ity
avoca'tion
avoc'ative
av'ocet
avoid'
avoid'able
avoid'ance
avoid'ed
avoid'er
avoid'ing
avoirdupois'
av'oset
avoset'ta
avouch'
avouched'
avouch'er
avouch'ing
avouch'ment
avow'
avow'able
avow'al
avowed'
avow'edly
avowee'
avow'er
avow'ing
avow'ry
avulse'
avul'sion
avun'cular
await'
await'ed
await'ing
awake'
awaked'
awa'ken
awa'kened
awa'kening

award'
award'ed
award'er
award'ing
aware'
away'
awe
a-weath'er
awed
a-weigh'
awe'less
awes
awe'-struck
aw'ful
aw'fully
aw'fulness
awhile'
aw'ing
awk'ward
awk'wardly
awk'wardness
awl

awn
awn'ing
awoke'
awry'
ax'al
axe
axe'head
ax'ial
axif'erous
ax'iform
ax'il
ax'ile
axil'la
ax'illar
ax'illary
ax'inite
ax'iom
axiomat'ic
axiomat'ical
ax'is
ax'le

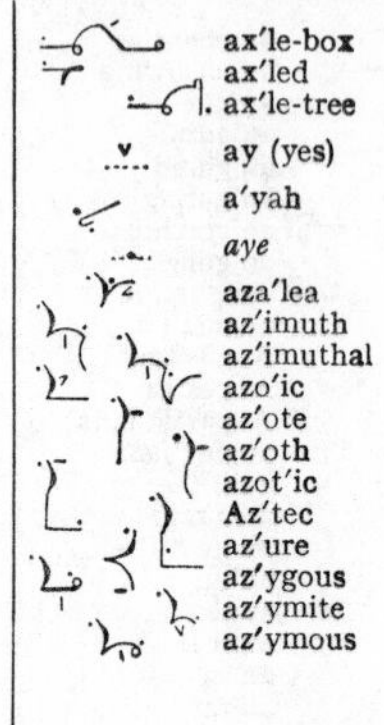

ax'le-box
ax'led
ax'le-tree
ay (yes)
a'yah
aye
aza'lea
az'imuth
az'imuthal
azo'ic
az'ote
az'oth
azot'ic
Az'tec
az'ure
az'ygous
az'ymite
az'ymous

B

baa
Ba'al
bab'ble
bab'bled
bab'blement
bab'bler
bab'bling
babe
Ba'bel
ba'bery
ba'boo, ba'bu
baboon'
ba'by
ba'byhood
ba'byish
Babylo'nian
Babylo'nish
baccalau'reate
baccara', bacca-[rat'
bac'cate
bac'chanal
bacchana'lian
bac'chant
bacchan'te
bac'chic
baccif'erous
bacciv'orous
bach'elor
bach'elorship
bacil'li
baci'lus
back
back'bar
back'bite
back'biter
back'biting
back'board
back'bone
back'door
backed
back'er
backgam'mon
back'ground
back'handed
back'house
back'ing
back'side
back'sight
back'slide
back'slider
back'sliding
back'stairs
back'stay
back'sword
back'ward
back'wardly
back'wardness

back'wards
back'water
back'woods
back'woodsman
back'yard
ba'con
Baco'nian
bacte'ria
bacteriol'ogy
bacte'rium
bad
bade
badge
badg'er
badg'ered
badg'ering
badi'geon
bad'inage
bad'ly
bad'minton
bad'ness
baf'fle
baf'fled
baf'fler
baf'fling
bag
bagatelle'
bag'gage
bagged
bag'ging
bag'gy
bag'man
bagn'io
bag'pipe
bag'piper
bail
bail'able
bailed
bailee'
bail'er
bai'lie
bai'liff
bail'ing
bai'liwick
bail'ment
bailor'
bairn
bait
bait'ed
bait'ing
baize
bake
baked
bake'house
bake'meat
bak'er
bak'ery
bak'ing

bak'sheesh
bal'ance
bal'anced
bal'ancer
bal'ance-sheet
*bal'anc*ing
bal'conied
bal'cony
bald
bal'dachin
bal'derdash
bald'est
bald'head
bald'ly
bald'ness
bal'dric
bale
Balear'ic
baled
bale'-fire
bale'ful
bale'fully
bale'fulness
bal'ing
balize'
balk
balked
balk'er
balk'ing
ball
bal'lad
bal'lad-mon'ger
bal'last
bal'lasted
bal'lasting
ball'-cock
balled
bal'let
bal'let (a little [ball)
ball'ing
ballis'ta
ballis'ter
ballis'tic
balloon'
balloon'ing
balloon'ist
bal'lot
bal'lot-box
bal'loted
bal'loting
ball'-room
balm
balm'ily
balm'iness
balm'y
bal'neal
bal'sam
balsam'ic

balsam'ical
balsamif'erous
Bal'tic
bal'uster
bal'ustered
balustrade'
bamboo'
bamboo'zle
bamboo'zled
bamboo'zling
ban
ban'al
banal'ity
bana'na
ban'co
band
band'age
band'aged
band'aging
bandan'na
band'box
band'ed
band'elet
ban'der
ban'derole
ban'dicoot
band'ied
band'ing
ban'dit
bandit'ti
ban'dog
bandoleer'
bandolier'
bandore'
band'roll
band-stand
ban'dy
ban'dying
ban'dy-leg
bane
bane'ful
bane'fulness
bang
banged
bang'ing
ban'gle
bangue
ban'ish
ban'ished
ban'isher
ban'ishing
ban'ishment
ban'ister
ban'jo
bank
bank'able
bank'bill
bank'-book
banked
bank'er
bank'ing
bank'-note
bank'rupt
bank'ruptcy
bank'rupted
bank'rupting
bank'-stock
ban'ner
ban'nered
ban'neret

ban'nerol
ban'ning
ban'nock
banns
ban'quet
ban'queted
ban'queter
ban'queting
banquette'
bans
ban'shee
ban'stickle
ban'tam
ban'ter
ban'tered
ban'terer
ban'tering
bant'ling
ban'yan
ba'obab
bap'tism
baptis'mal
Bap'tist
bap'tistery
baptis'tic
baptis'tical
bapti'zable
baptize'
baptized'
bapti'zer
bapti'zing
bar
barb
bar'bacan
Barba'dian
barba'rian
barbar'ic
bar'barism
barbar'ity
bar'barize
bar'barized
bar'barizing
bar'barous
bar'barously
bar'barousness
bar'bate
bar'becue
bar'becued
bar'becuing
barbed
bar'bel
bar'bellate
bar'ber
bar'berry
bar'bet
barbette'
bar'bican
bar'bule
bar'carole
bard
bard'ic
bard'ism
bare
bare'bone
bared
bare'faced
bare'facedness
bare'foot
bare'footed
barège'

bare'headed
bare'ly
bare'ness
bar'est
bar'gain
bar'gained
bargainee'
bar'gainer
bar'gaining
barge
barge'man
baril'la
bar'ing
bar'-iron
bar'itone
ba'rium
bark
barked
bar'keeper
bark'er
bark'ery
bark'ing
bark'y
bar'ley
bar'ley-broth
bar'ley-corn
bar'ley-meal
barm
bar'maid
Bar'mecide
barm'y
barn
bar'nacle
bar'olite
barom'eter
baromet'ric
baromet'rical
barom'etry
bar'on
bar'onage
bar'oness
bar'onet
bar'onetage
bar'onetcy
baro'nial
bar'ony
bar'oscope
baroscop'ic
baroscop'ical
barouche'
barque
bar'quentine
bar'racan
bar'rack
barracoon'
bar'ras
bar'rator
bar'ratrous
bar'ratry
barred
bar'rel
bar'relage
bar'relled
bar'rel-organ
bar'ren
bar'renness
barricade'
barrica'ded
barrica'ding
bar'rier

bar'ring
bar'rister
bar'row
bar'-shot
bar'ter
bar'tered
bar'terer
bar'tering
bartizan'
bar'ton
bary'ta
bary'tes
baryt'ic
bar'ytone
bary'tum
ba'sal
basalt'
basalt'ic
basalt'iform
basalt'ine
bas'anite
base
base'ball
base'born
based
base'less
base'ly
base'ment
base'-minded
base'ness
bashaw'
bash'ful
bash'fully
bash'fulness
bash'i-bazouk'
ba'sic
bas'ify
bas'ifying
bas'ified
bas'ifier
bas'il
bas'ilar
bas'ilary
basil'ic
basil'ica
basil'ical
basil'icon
bas'ilisk
ba'sin
ba'sing
ba'sis
bask
basked
bas'ket
bask'ing
Basque
bas-relief'
bass (a hassock)
bass (in music)
bas'set
bas'seted
bas'seting
bassinet' *or* -ette
bassoon'
bassoon'ist
bass'-viol
bass'wood
bas'tard
bas'tardize
bas'tardized

bas'tardizing
bas'tardly
bas'tardy
baste
bast'ed
bastile', bastille'
bastina'do
bastina'doed
bast'ing
bast'ion
bast'ioned
bas'yle
bat
ba'table
Bata'vian
batch
bate
bateau'
ba'ted
bath
bathe
bathed
bath'er
bath'ing
bath'os
bath'-room
bat'ing
batiste'
bat'let
bat'man
bat'on
Batra'chia
batra'chian
bat'rachite
bat'rachoid
Batrachomy-om'achy
bats'man
bat'ta
battal'ia
battal'ion
battal'ioned
bat'ted
bat'tel
bat'teler, bat'tler
bat'ten
bat'tened
bat'tening
bat'ter
bat'tered
bat'terer
bat'tering
bat'tering-ram
bat'tery
bat'ting
bat'tish
bat'tle
bat'tle-array
bat'tle-axe
bat'tled
bat'tledore
bat'tle-field
bat'tlement
bat'tlemented
bat'tler
bat'tleship
bat'tling
battol'ogy
battue'
baubee'

bau'ble
baulk
Bava'rian
ba'vin
bawbee'
baw'ble
bawd
bawd'ily
bawd'y
bawl
bawled
bawl'er
bawl'ing
bawn
bay
bayadère'
bay'ard
bay'berry
bayed
bay'ing
bay'onet
bay'oneted
bay'oneting
bay'ou
bay'-salt
bay'-tree
bay'-window
bazaar', bazar'
bdell'ium
be
beach
beached
beach'ing
beach'y
bea'con
bea'conage
bea'coned
bea'coning
bead
bead'ing
bead'le
bead'-roll
beads'-man
bea'gle
beak
beaked
beak'er
beam
beamed
beam'-ends
beam'ing
beam'less
beam'y
bean
bean-feast
bear
bear'able
bear'-baiting
beard
beard'ed
beard'ing
beard'less
beard'lessness
bear'er
bear'-garden
bear'ing
bear'ish
bear'like
bear's'-foot
bear's'-grease

bear'skin
beast
beast'liness
beast'ly
beat
beat'en
beat'er
beatif'ic
beatif'ical
beatifica'tion
beat'ify
beat'ing
beat'itude
beau
beau-ide'al
beau'ish
beau-monde'
beau'teous
beau'teously
beau'teousness
beau'tified
beau'tifier
beau'tiful
beau'tifulness
beau'tify
beau'tifying
beau'ty
beau'ty-spot
beaux
bea'ver
bea'vered
bea'verteen
bebee'rine
becalm'
becalmed'
becalm'ing
became'
because'
beccafi'co
bechance'
becharm'
bêche'-de-mer
beck
becked
beck'et
beck'ing
beck'on
beck'oned
beck'oning
becloud'
becloud'ed
becloud'ing
become'
*be*com'ing
*be*com'ingly
*be*com'ingness
bed
bedab'ble
bedab'bled
bedab'bling
bedag'gle
bedark'en
bedash'
bedaub'
bedaubed'
bedaub'ing
bedaz'zle
bed'*-chair*
bed'chamber
bed'-clothes

bed'ded
bed'ding
bedeck'
bedecked'
bedeck'ing
bed'eguar
be'del, be'dell
bedev'il
bedew'
bedewed'
bedew'ing
bed'fellow
bed'-hangings
bedight'
bedim'
bedi'zen
bed'lam
bed'lamite
bed'maker
bed'mate
Bed'ouin
bed'-plate
bed'-post
bed'-quilt
bedrag'gle
bed'rid
bed'ridden
bed'room
bed'side
bed'stead
bed'straw
bed'tick
bed'time
bee
bee'bee
bee'bread
beech
beech'en
beech'-nut
beef
beef'eater
beef'steak
bee'-hive
bee'house
beele
bee'-line
Beel'zebub
bee'-master
been
beer
beer'-barrel
beer'house
beer'shop
beest'ings
bees'wax
beet
beet'le
beet'le-brow
beet'ling
beet'-root
beeves
befall'
befal'len
befal'ling
befell'
befit'
befit'ted
befit'ting
befog'
befool'

befooled'
befool'ing
before'
before'*hand*
before'time
befoul'
befriend'
befriend'ed
befriend'ing
befringe'
beg
began'
beget'
beget'ter
beget'ting
beg'gar
beg'gared
beg'garing
beg'garliness
beg'garly
beg'gary
begged
beg'ging
begin'
begin'ner
begin'ning
begird'
begird'ed
begird'ing
begirt'
beg'lerbeg
begone'
bego'nia
begot'
begot'ten
begrime'
begrimed'
begrim'ing
begrudge'
begrudged'
begrudg'ing
beguile'
beguiled'
beguile'ment
beguil'er
beguil'ing
be'gum
begun'
behalf'
behave'
behaved'
beha'ving
behav'iour / behav'ior
behead'
behead'ed
behead'ing
beheld'
be'hemoth
behest'
behind'
behind'*hand*
behold'
behold'en
behold'er
behold'ing
behoof'
behoove' / behove'
behooved'

behoved'
*be'*ing
{ bela'bour
{ bela'bor
bela'boured
bela'bouring
belate'
belat'ed
belay'
belayed'
belay'ing
belch
belched'
belch'ing
bel'dam, bel'-
belea'guer [dame
belea'guered
belea'guering
belem'nite
bel'fry
Bel'gian
Bel'gic
Be'lial
belie'
belied'
belief'
*believ'*able
{ *believe'*
{ *believed'*
believ'er
*believ'*ing
believ'ingly
belit'tle
belit'tled
belit'tling
bell
belladon'na
bell'-bird
belle
belles-let'tres
bell'-founder
bell'-foundry
bell'-hanger
bel'licose
bel'lied
bellig'erency
bellig'erent
bell'man
bell'-metal
bel'low
bel'lowed
bel'lower
bel'lowing
bel'lows
bell'pull
bell'ringer
bell'-wether
bel'ly
bel'ly-band
bel'lyful
bel'lying
bel'omancy
belong'
belonged'
belong'ing
belove'
beloved'
belov'ed
below'
belt

Bel'tane
bel'ted
belt'ing
bely'ing
bel'vedere
bemire'
bemired'
bemoan'
bemoaned'
bemoan'er
bemoan'ing
bemuse'
ben
bench
bench'er
bend
bend'able
bend'ed
bend'er
bend'ing
bend'let
bend'y
beneath'
Ben'edict
Benedic'tine
benedic'tion
benedic'tive
benedic'tory
Benedic'tus
benefac'tion
benefac'tor
benefac'tress
ben'efice
ben'eficed
benef'icence
benef'icent
benef'icently
benefi'cial
benefi'cially
benefi'ciary
ben'efit
ben'efiting
ben'efited
benev'olence
benev'olent
benev'olently
Bengalese'
Bengal'i
benight'
benight'ed
benight'ing
benign'
benig'nant
benig'nantly
benig'nity
benign'ly
ben'ison
ben'net
bent
benth'al
benumb'
benumbed'
ben'zene
ben'zine
benzo'ic
benzo'in
ben'zol
ben'zoline
bequeath'
bequeathed'

bequeath'er
bequeath'ing
bequest'
berate'
berat'ed
berat'ing
ber'berine
Bere'an
bereave'
bereaved'
bereave'ment
bereav'er
bereav'ing
bereft'
ber'gamot
ber'gander
berg'mote
ber'iberi
Ber'nardine
Bernese'
Ber'oe
ber'ried
ber'ry
ber'serker
berth
ber'yl
ber'ylline
beseech'
beseech'er
beseech'ing
beseech'ingly
beseem'
beseem'ing
beseem'ly
beset'
beset'ting
beshrew'
beside'
besides'
besiege'
besieged'
besieg'er
besieg'ing
besmear'
besmeared'
besmear'ing
be'som
besot'
besot'ted
besot'ting
besought'
bespang'le
bespat'ter
bespat'tered
bespat'tering
bespeak'
bespeak'er
bespeak'ing
bespoke'
bespok'en
bespread'
besprin'kle
Bes'semer
best
bes'tial
bestial'ity
best'ialize
bestir'
bestirred'
bestir'ring

bestow'
bestow'al
bestowed'
bestow'er
bestow'ment
bestrad'dle
bestrew'
bestrewed'
bestrew'ing
bestrid'
bestrid'den
bestride'
bestrid'ing
bestud'
bet
betake'
betak'en
be'tel
beth'el
bethink'
bethink'ing
bethought'
betide'
betimes'
beto'ken
beto'kened
beto'kening
bet'ony
betook'
betray'
betray'al
betrayed'
betray'er
betray'ment
betroth'
betroth'al
betrothed'
betroth'ing
betroth'ment
bet'ted
bet'ter
bet'tered
bet'tering
bet'terment
bet'ters
bet'ting
bet'ty
between'
betwixt'
bev'el
bev'elled
bev'eled
bev'elling
bev'eling
bev'el-wheels
bev'erage
bev'y
bewail'
bewail'able
bewailed'
bewail'er
bewail'ing
beware'
bewil'der
bewil'dered
bewil'dering
bewil'derment
bewitch'
bewitched'
bewitch'er
bewitch'ery
bewitch'ing
bewitch'ment
bewray'
bey
beyond'
bez'el
bezique'
be'zoar
bezoar'dic
bhang
bian'gular
bian'nual
bi'as
bi'ased
bi'asing
biax'ial
bib
biba'cious
bib'ber
bib'itory
Bi'ble
Bi'bler
Bib'lical
Bib'licist
bibliog'rapher
bibliograph'ic
bibliograph'ical
bibliog'raphy
bibliol'atry
bibliolog'ical
bibliol'ogy
bib'liomancy
biblioma'nia
biblioma'niac
bibliomani'acal
bibliom'anist
bib'liophile
bibliopho'bia
bib'liopole
bibliop'olism
bibliop'olist
bibliothe'ca
Bib'list
bib'ulous
bical'carate
bicap'sular
bicar'bonate
bice
bicen'tenary
biceph'alous
bi'ceps
bichro'mate
bicip'ital
bicip'itous
bick'er
bick'ered
bick'erer
bick'ering
bick'ern
bicon'jugate
bi'corn
bicorn'ous
bicor'poral
bicru'ral
bicus'pid
bi'cycle
bi'cyclist
bid
bid'den
bid'der
bid'ding
bide
bidet'
bid'ing
bien'nial
bien'nially
bier
bifa'rious
bif'erous
bif'fin
bi'fid
bif'idate
bif'idated
biflo'rous
bi'fold
bifo'liate
bi'forate
bif'orine
bi'form
bi'formed
bi'furcate *a.*
bi'furcate *v.*
bi'furcated
bifurca'tion
bifur'cous
big
big'amist
big'amy
big'arreau
bigen'tial
big'gin
bight
big'ness
Bigno'nia
big'ot
big'oted
big'otry
big'wig
bijou'
bijou'try
bi'jugate
bi'jugous
bila'biate
bilam'ellate
bilam'ellated
bil'ander
bilat'eral
bil'berry
bil'bo
bil'boes
bild'stein
bile
bile'-duct
bilge
bilged
bilge'water
bil'iary
bilin'gual
bilin'guist
bilin'guous
bil'ious
bil'iousness
bilit'eral
bilk
bilked
bilk'ing
bill
bill'book
billed

bil'let
billet-doux'
bil'leted
bil'leting
bill'hook
bill'iards
bil'ling
bil'lingsgate
bil'lion
bil'lot
bil'low
bil'lowy
bill'-sticker
bilo'bate
bi'lobed
biloc'ular
bil'tong
bimac'ulate
bim'ana
bi'mane
bim'anous
bimar'ginate
bime'dial
bimen'sal
bimes'trial
bimet'allism
bimet'alism
bimonth'ly
bin
bi'nary
bi'nate
bind
bind'er
bind'ery
bind'ing
bind'weed
binerv'ate
bin'nacle
bin'ocle
binoc'ular
binoc'ulate
bino'mial
binom'inal
binom'inous
binot'onous
bi'nous
bioc'ellate
biodynam'ics
biogen'esis
bi'ograph
biog'rapher
biograph'ic
biograph'ical
biog'raphize
biog'raphy
biolog'ical
biol'ogy
biolyt'ic
biom'etry
bi'oplasm
bi'otaxy
bip'arous
bipart'ible
bipart'ile
bipart'ient
bipart'ite
biparti'tion
bipec'tinate
bi'ped
bi'pedal
bipel'tate
bipen'nate
bipen'nated
bipet'alous
bipin'nate
bi'plane
bipo'lar
bipolar'ity
bi'pont
bipont'ine
bipunct'ual
biquad'rate
biquadrat'ic
biquint'ile
bira'diate
bira'diated
bira'mous
birch
birch'en
bird
bird'-cage
bird'catcher
bird'-like
bird'-lime
bird's'-eye
bi'reme
biret'ta
biros'trate
biros'trated
birth
birth'day
birth'-mark
birth'place
birth'right
Biscay'an
bis'cotin
bis'cuit
bisect'
bisect'ed
bisect'ing
bisec'tion
biseg'ment
bise'rial
biser'rate
bise'tose
bise'tous
bisex'ous
bisex'ual
bish'op
bish'opric
bisk
bis'muth
bis'muthal
bi'son
bisque
bissex'tile
bistip'uled
bis'tort
bis'toury
bis'tre, bis'ter
bisul'cate
bisul'phate
bisul'phuret
bit
bitch
bite
bit'er
bitern'ate
bit'ing
bitt
bit'ted
bit'ten
bit'ter
bit'terish
bit'terly
bit'tern
bit'terness
bit'ters
bit'tersweet
bit'terweed
bit'ting
bitu'men
bitu'minate
bitu'minize
bitu'minous
bi'valve
bivalv'ous
bivalv'ular
bivault'ed
biven'tral
biv'ious
biv'ouac
biweek'ly
bizarre'
blab
blabbed
blab'ber
blab'bing
black
black'amoor
black'art
black'ball
black'balled
black'-balling
black'beetle
black'berry
black'bird
black'board
black'-book
black'-cap
black'-cattle
black'-death
blacked
black'en
black'ened
black'ener
black'ening
black'-eyed
black'fish
black'*guard*
black'*guard*ism
black'ing
black'ish
black'-lead
black'leg
black'letter
black'ly
black'mail
black'ness
Black'Rod
black'smith
black'thorn
blad'der
blade
blade'-bone
blad'ed
blain
blame
blame'able
blamed

blame'ful
blame'less
blame'lessness
blam'er
blame'worthy
blanch
blanched
blanchim'eter
blanch'ing
blancmange'
bland
blandil'oquence
bland'ish
bland'ished
bland'isher
bland'ishing
bland'ishment
bland'ness
blank
blank'et
blank'eted
blank'eting
blank'ness
blare
blar'ney
blasé
blaspheme'
blasphemed'
blasphe'mer
blasphe'ming
blas'phemous
blas'phemously
blas'phemy
blast
blast'ed
blaste'ma
blast'er
blast'-furnace
blast'ing
blastocar'pous
blas'toderm
blast'pipe
bla'tant
blat'ter
blay
blaze
blazed
blaz'ing
bla'zon
bla'zoned
bla'zoner
bla'zoning
bla'zonry
bleach
bleached
bleach'er
bleach'ery
bleach'ing
bleak
bleak'ish
bleak'ly
bleak'ness
blear
bleared
blear'-eyed
bleat
bleat'ed
bleat'er
bleat'ing
bleb

bled
bleed
bleed'ing
blem'ish
blem'ished
blem'ishing
blench
blenched
blend, blende
blend'ed
blend'er
blend'ing
blen'ny
blent
bles'-bok
bless
blessed
bless'ed
bless'edly
bless'edness
bless'er
bless'ing
blest
blet
blet'onism
blet'onist
blew
blight
blight'ed
blight'ing
blight'ingly
blind
blind'ed
blind'er
blind'fold
blind'folded
blind'folding
blind'ing
blind'ly
blind'man's-buff
blind'ness
blind'-side
blink
blink'ard
blinked
blink'er
blink'ing
bliss
bliss'ful
bliss'fulness
blis'ter
blis'tered
blis'tering
blis'tery
blithe
blithe'ful
blithe'ly
blithe'some
blithe'someness
bliz'zard
bloat
bloat'ed
bloat'edness
bloat'er
bloat'ing
blob'ber
blob'ber-lipped
block
blockade'
blockad'ed

blockad'ing
block'-book
blocked
block'head
block'house
block'ing
block'ish
block'-tin
blond, blonde
blood
blood'ed
blood'-guiltiness
blood'-heat
blood'hound
blood'ily
blood'iness
blood'ing
blood'less
blood'-red
blood'-relation
blood'root
blood'shed
blood'shot
blood'stained
blood'sucker
blood'thirsty
blood'-vessel
blood'wort
blood'y
bloom
bloom'ary
bloomed
bloom'er
bloom'ery
bloom'ing
bloom'ingly
bloom'y
blos'som
blos'somed
blos'soming
blot
blotch
blote
blot'ted
blot'ter
blot'ting
blouse
blow
blow'er
blow'ing
blown
blow'-pipe
blow'-valve
blowze
blowzed
blowz'y
blub'ber
blub'bered
blub'bering
bluch'er or
blud'geon
blue
blue'-bell
blue'berry
blue'-bird
blue'book
blue'bottle
blue'-light
blue'ness
blues

blue'-stocking
blue'-stone
blu'ey
bluff
bluff'ness
bluf'fy
blu'ish
blu'ishly
blun'der
blun'derbuss
blun'dered
blun'derer
blun'derhead
blun'dering
blunt
blunt'ed
blunt'ing
blunt'ish
blunt'ly
blunt'ness
blur
blurred
blur'ring
blurt
blurt'ed
blurt'ing
blush
blushed
blush'ing
blush'ingly
blus'ter
blus'tered
blus'terer
blus'tering
{ blus'terous
{ blus'trous
bo
bo'a
bo'a-constric'tor
Boaner'ges
boar, board
board'able
board'ed
board'er
board'ing
board'ing-house
board'ing-*school*
board'-wages
boar'ish
boast
boast'ed
boast'er
boast'ful
boast'fulness
boast'ing
boast'ingly
boat
boat'able
boat'bill
boat'builder
boat'hook
boat'ing
boat'man
boat'swain
bob
bobbed
bob'bin
bob'binet
bob'bing
bob'olink

bob'stay
bob'tail
bob'tailed
boc'asin
bock'ing
bock'land
bode
bod'ed
bode'ga
bod'ice
bod'ied
bod'iless
bod'ily
bod'ing
bod'kin
Bodlei'an
bod'y
bod'y-clothes
bod'y-*guard*
bod'ying
bod'y-pol'itic
Boeo'tian
Boer
bog
bog'gle
bog'gled
bog'gler
bog'gling
bog'gy
bo'gie
bog'-land
bo'gus
bo'gy
boh'
bohea'
Bohe'mian
boil
boiled
boil'er
boil'er-plate
boil'ery
boil'ing
boil'ing-point
bois'terous
bois'terously
bo'lar
bold
bold'er
bold'est
bold'ly
bold'ness
bole
bole'ro
boll
bol'lard
Bolognese'
Bolo'gnian
bol'ster
bol'stered
bol'stering
bolt
bolt'ed
bolt'er
bolt'ing
bolting-cloth
bolus
bomb
bom'bard, *n*
bombard', *v.*
bombard'ed

bombardier'
bombard'ing
bombard'ment
bombasine'
bom'bast
bombast'ic
bombazette'
bombazine'
bomb'-proof
bomb'-shell
bom'byx
bon-accord'
bonan'za
Bonapart'ean
Bo'napartism
Bo'napartist
bona'sus
bonas'sus
bon'-bon
bond
bond'age
bond'ed
bond'holder
bond'ing
bond'maid
bond'man
bond'servant
bonds'man
bond'woman
bone
boned
bone'lace
bone'set
bone'setter
bone'setting
bone'shaker
bon'fire
bonhomie'
Bon'iface
bon'ing
bon mot
bonne' bouche
bon'net
bon'neted
bon'nily
bon'ny
bo'nus
bon'y
bonze
boo'by
boo'dle
book
book'-account
book'binder
book'bindery
book'binding
book'case
book'-debt
book'ing
book'ish
book'ishness
book'-keeper
book'-keeping
book'-*knowledge*
book'land
book'let
book'-maker
book'mark
book' post
book'rack

book'seller
book'selling
book'shelf
book'stall
book'store
book'worm
boom
boomed
boom'erang
boom'ing
boon
boop'ic
boor
boor'ish
boor'ishly
boose
boos'er
boos'y
boot
boot'ed
bootee'
booth
boot'ikin
boot'jack
boot'less
boot'lessly
boot'-tree
boot'y
booze
booz'y
bopeep'
borac'ic
bor'age
bo'rate
bo'rax
bor'der
bor'dered
bor'derer
bor'dering
bor'der-land
bor'dure
bore
bo'real
Bo'reas
bore'cole
bored
bore'dom
bor'er
bo'ric
bo'ring
born
borne
bo'ron
bor'ough
bor'row
bor'rowed
bor'rower
bor'rowing
bos
bos'cage
bosh
bosk'et
bosk'y
bos'om
bos'omed
boss
bos'sage
bossed
bos'sy
bot
botan'ic
botan'ical
bot'anist
bot'anize
bot'anizing
botanol'ogy
bot'any
botar'go
botch
botched
botch'er
botch'ery
botch'ing
botch'y
bote
bot'-fly
both
both'er
both'ered
both'ering
both'ie, both'y
Both'nian
Both'nic
bot'ryoid
botryoid'al
bot'ryolite
bots, botts
bot'tine
bot'tle
bot'tled
bot'tling
bot'tom
bot'tomed
bot'toming
bot'tomless
bot'tomry
bouche
boudoir'
bough
bought
bou'gie
bouil'li
bouil'lon
boul'der
boul'evard
bounce
bounced
bounc'er
bounc'ing
bounc'ingly
bound
bound'ary
bound'ed
bound'en
bound'er
bound'ing
bound'less
bound'lessly
bound'lessness
boun'teous
boun'teously
boun'teousness
boun'tiful
boun'tifulness
boun'ty
bouquet'
Bour'bonism
Bour'bonist
bourgeois'
bour'geois
bourgeois'ie
bour'geon
bourn, bourne
bourse
bouse
boustrophe'don
bous'y
bout
bouts-rimés'
bo'vine
bov'ril
bow (part of violin; a weapon)
bow (part of a ship; to bend the body)
Bowd'lerize
bowed
bow'elled
bow'els
bow'er
bow'ery
bow'ie-knife
bow'ing
bow'knot
bowl
bowl'der
bowled
bow'-leg
bow'-legged
bowl'er
bow'line
bowl'ing
bowl'ing-green
bow'man
bowse
bow'sprit
bow'-string
bow'-window
bow'-wow
box
boxed
box'en
box'er
box'ing
box'-tree
box'-wood
boy
boy'au
boy'cott
boy'hood
boy'ish
boy'ishly
boy'ishness
boy's'-play
brac'cate
brace
braced
brace'let
bra'cer
brach'ial
brach'iate
brach'iopod
brachyg'rapher
brachyg'raphy
brachyl'ogy
bra'cing
brack'en
brack'et
brack'eted

brack'eting
brack'ish
brack'ishness
bract
brac'tea
bract'eate
brad
brad'awl
brad'ypod
brag
braggado'cio
brag'gart
bragged
brag'ger
brag'ging
Brah'ma
Brah'man
Brah'min
Brahmin'ical
braid
braid'ed
braid'ing
{ brail
{ Braille
brain
brained
brain'less
brain'pan
brait
brake
brake'man
brakes'man
brak'y
bram'ble
bram'bling
bram'bly
bran
branch
branched
bran'chial
branch'ing
branch'iopod
branch'less
branch'let
branch'y
brand
brand'ed
brand'er
bran'died
brand'ing
bran'dish
bran'dished
bran'dishing
brand'ling
brand'-new
bran'dy
bran'gle
bran'gler
bran'gling
bran'lin
bran'ny
brant
brash
{ brass
{ brasse
bras'sard
bras'sart
brass'-band
bras'sica
brass'iness

brass'y
brat
brava'do
brave
braved
brave'ly
brave'ness
brav'er
brav'ery
brav'est
brav'ing
bra'vo
bravu'ra
brawl
brawled
brawl'er
brawl'ing
brawn
brawn'y
brax'y
bray
brayed
bray'er
bray'ing
braze
brazed
bra'zen
bra'zen-faced
bra'zenness
bra'zier
brazil'
Brazil'ian
brazil'wood
braz'ing
breach
bread
bread'-corn
bread'-fruit
bread'stuff
breadth
bread'winner
break
break'able
break'age
break'-down
break'er
break'fast
break'fasted
break'fasting
break'ing
break'man
break'water
bream
bream'ing
breast
breast'ed
breast'fast
breast'ing
breast'knot
breast'pin
breast'plate
breast'wheel
breast'work
breath
breath'able
breathe
breathed
breath'er
breath'ing
breath'less

brec'cia
bred
breech
breeched
breech'es
breech'ing
breech'loader
breed
breed'er
breed'ing
breeze
breez'y
Bre'hon
brent
bret
breth'ren
bret'tice
breve
brev'et
brev'eted
brev'eting
bre'viary
brevier'
brev'iped
brevipen'nate
brev'ity
brew
brew'age
brewed
brew'er
brew'ery
brew'house
brew'ing
brew'is
brew'ster
bri'ar
Bria'rean
bribe
bribed
brib'er
brib'ery
brib'ing
bric'-à-brac
brick
brick'bat
brick'-kiln
brick'layer
brick'maker
brick'work
brick'yard
bri'dal
bride
bride'cake
bride'chamber
bride'groom
bride'less
bride'maid
bride'man
brides'maid
brides'man
bride'well
bridge
bridged
bridg'ing
bri'dle
bri'dled
bri'dler
bri'dling
bridoon'
brief

brief'er
brief'est
brief'less
brief'ly
brief'ness
bri'er
bri'ered
bri'ery
brig
brigade'
brigadier'
brig'and
brig'andage
brig'andine
brig'antine
bright
bright'en
bright'ened
bright'ening
bright'-eyed
bright'ly
bright'ness
Bright's disease'
brigue
brill
bril'liance
bril'liancy
bril'liant
bril'liantly
brim
brim'ful
brim'less
brimmed
brim'mer
brim'ming
brim'stone
brind'ed
brind'led
brine
brine'pan
bring
bring'er
bring'ing
brin'ish
brink
brin'y
brisk
brisk'et
brisk'ly
brisk'ness
bris'tle
bris'tled
bris'tling
bris'tly
brit
Britan'nic
Brit'ish
Brit'on
brit'tle
brit'tleness
britz'ka
broach
broached
broach'er
broach'ing
broad
broad'-arrow
broad'-awake
broad'-axe
broad'cast

broad'cloth
broad'en
broad'er
broad'ish
broad'ly
broad'ness
broad'side
broad'sword
brocade'
brocad'ed
bro'cage
broc'coli
brochure'
brock
brock'et
brog
bro'gan
brogue
broid'er
broil
broiled
broil'er
broil'ing
broke
bro'ken
bro'kenly
bro'kenness
bro'ker
bro'kerage
bro'ma
bro'mal
bro'mate
bromatol'ogy
bro'mide
bro'mine
bron'chia
bron'chial
bronchi'tis
bron'chus
bronze
bronzed
bronz'ing
brooch
brood
brood'ed
brood'ing
brood'y
brook
brook'let
broom
broom'stick
broom'y
brose
broth
broth'el
broth'er
broth'erhood
broth'er-in-law
broth'erly
brough'am
brought
brow
brow'beat
brow'beaten
brow'beating
brown
browned
brown'er
brown'est

brown'ie
brown'ing
brown'ish
brown' stud'y
browse, browze
browsed
brows'er
brows'ing
bru'in
bruise
bruised
bruis'er
bruis'ing
bruit
bru'mal
brunette'
brunt
brush
brushed
brush'er
brush'ing
brush'wood
brush'y
brusque
brusque'ness
brus'querie
Brus'sels sprouts
bru'tal
brutal'ity
bru'talize
bru'talized
bru'talizing
bru'tally
brute
bru'tified
bru'tify
bru'tifying
bru'tish
bru'tishly
bru'tishness
bryol'ogy
bry'ony
bub'ble
bub'bled
bub'bler
bub'bling
bub'bly
bu'bo
bubon'ic
buc'cal
buccaneer' / buccanier'
buccaneer'ing
buc'cinal
Bucel'las
bucen'taur
bu'ceros
buck
buck'et
buck'etful
buck'ing
buck'ish
buc'kle
buc'kled
buck'ler
buck'ling
buck'ram
buck'skin
buck'thorn
buck'wheat

bucol'ic
bucol'ical
bud
bud'ded
Bud'dhism
Bud'dhist
Buddhis'tic
bud'ding
bud'dle
Bude'-light
budge
budged
budg'er
budg'et
budg'ing
bud'let
buff
buf'falo
buf'fel
buf'fer
buf'fet
buf'feted
buf'feter
buf'feting
buf'fo
buffoon'
buffoon'ery
buffoon'ing
buf'fy
bug
bug'bear
bug'gy
bu'gle
bu'gler
bu'gloss
buhl
buhl'-work
buhr'-stone
build
build'ed
build'er
build'ing
built
bulb
bulbed
bulbif'erous
bulb'let
bulb'ous
bul'bul
bulb'ule
bulge
bulged
bulg'ing
bulim'ia
bulk
bulk'head
bulk'iness
bulk'y
bull
bul'la
bull'dog
bul'let
bul'letin
bul'let-proof
bull'-fight
bull'finch
bull'frog
bul'lied
bul'lion
bul'lionist

bul'list
bul'lock
bull''s-eye
bul'ly
bul'lying
bul'rush
bulse
bul'wark
bum
bumbail'iff
bum'ble-bee
bum'boat
bum'kin
bump
bumped
bump'er
bump'ing
bump'kin
bump'tious
bump'tiousness
bun
bunch
bunch'iness
bunch'y
bun'co
bun'combe
bun'dle
bun'dled
bun'dling
bung
bun'galow
bung'-hole
bun'gle
bun'gled
bun'gler
bun'gling
bun'glingly
bun'ion
bunk
bunk'er
bunk'o
bun'kum
bunt
bunt'ine
bunt'ing
buoy
buoy'ancy
buoy'ant
buoy'antly
buoyed
bur
bur'bot
bur'den
bur'dened
bur'dening
bur'densome
bur'densomeness
bur'dock
bureau'
bureau'cracy
bureaucrat'ic
bureaucrat'ical
bureau'cratist
burette'
burg
burg'age
bur'gess
burgh
burgh'er

burg'lar
burgla'rious
burgla'riously
burg'lary
burg'mote
burg'omaster
burgoo'
bur'grave
Bur'gundy
bur'ial
bur'ial-place
bur'ied
bur'ier
bu'rin
burke
burked
burk'er
burk'ing
burk'ism
burl
burled
burl'er
burlesque'
burlesqued'
burlesqu'ing
burlet'ta
bur'liness
bur'ly
Burmese'
burn
burn'able
burned
burn'er
burn'ing
bur'nish
bur'nished
bur'nisher
bur'nishing
burnous'
burnt
burnt'-offering
bur, burr
bur'ral
bur'rel
bur'rock
bur'row
bur'rowed
bur'rowing
bur'ry
bur'sar
bur'sary
burst
burst'er
burst'ing
bur'then
bur'ton
bur'y
bur'ying
bur'ying-ground
bus, 'bus
bus'by
bush
bush'el
bush'iness
bush'ing
bush'man
bush'y
bus'ier
bus'iest
bus'ily

bus'iness
bus'iness-like
busk
bus'ket
bus'kin
bus'kined
busk'y
buss
bust
bus'tard
bus'tle
bus'tled
bus'tler
bus'tling
bus'y
bus'ybody
bus'ying
but
butch'er
butch'ered
butch'ering
butch'erly
butch'ery
but'ler
but'lerage
but'lership
but'lery
but'ment
butt
butt'ed

butt'-end
but'ter
but'tercup
but'tered
but'terfly
but'terine
but'tering
but'termilk
but'ter-tooth
but'tery
butt'-hinge
but'ting
but'tock
but'ton
but'toned
but'tonhole
but'toning
but'tress
but'tressed
but'tressing
butts
but'ty
butyra'ceous
butyr'ic
bu'tyrin
bux'eous
buxi'na
bux'ine
bux'om
bux'omly

bux'omness
buy
buy'er
buy'ing
buzz
buz'zard
buzzed
buz'zer
buz'zing
buz'zingly
by
by ***and*** by
bye
by-elec'tion
by'-end
by'gone
by'-lane
by'-law
by'-name
by'-path
by'-play
by'-prod'uct
bys'sine
by'stander
by'-street
by the by
by'-way
by'*word*
Byzan'tian
Byzan'tine

C

Ca'aba
cab
cabal'
cab'ala
cab'alism
cab'alist
cabalis'tic
cabalis'tical
cabal'ler
cab'alline
cab'aret
cab'bage
cab'bala
ca'ber
cab'in
cab'in-boy
cab'ined
cab'inet
ca'ble
ca'bled
ca'blegram
ca'bling
cab'man
cabob'
caboose'
cabriolet'
caca'o
cach'alot
cache
ca'chet
cachex'ia
cachex'y
cachinna'tion
cach'olong
cachou'
cacique'
cack'le
cack'led
cack'ler
cack'ling
cacochym'ic
cac'ochymy
cac'odoxy
cacoe'thes
cacog'raphy
cacol'ogy
cacophon'ic
cacoph'onous
cacoph'ony
cacta'ceous
cac'tus
cad
cadaver'ic
cadav'erous
cadav'erously
cadav'erousness
cad'dis
cad'dy
cade
ca'dence
caden'za
cadet'
cadg'er
ca'di
cadil'lac
Cadme'an
cad'mia
cad'mium
ca'dre
cadu'cean
cadu'ceus
cadu'cous
cae'cum
caesu'ra
ca'fé
caffe'ic
caf'feine
Caf'fre
caf'tan
cage
caged
cag'ing
ca'hier
caïque'
cairn
cairngorm'
cais'son
cai'tiff
cajole'
cajoled'
cajole'ment
cajo'ler
cajo'lery
cajo'ling
caj'uput
cake
caked
cak'ing
cal'abash
calaboose'
Cala'brian
calaman'co
cal'amar
cal'amary
calamif'erous
cal'amine
cal'amite
calam'itous
calam'itously
calam'itousness
calam'ity
cal'amus
calash'
cal'car
cal'carate
calca'reous
calca'reousness
cal'ceated
cal'cedon
calceola'ria
cal'cify
calcin'able
calcina'tion
calcin'atory
cal'cine
cal'cined
cal'cium
calcog'raphy
cal'culable
cal'culary
cal'culate
cal'culated
cal'culating
calcula'tion
cal'culative
cal'culator
cal'culatory
cal'culous
cal'culus
cal'dron
Caledo'nian
calefa'cient
calefac'tion
calefac'tory
cal'endar
cal'ender
cal'endered
cal'enderer
cal'endering
cal'ends
cal'enture
cales'cence
calf
calf's'-foot
calves'-foot
cal'ibre, cal'iber
calibra'tion
cal'ice
cal'ico
cal'id
cal'if
cal'ifate
caligraph'ic
calig'raphy
cal'ipash
calipee'
cal'iper
cal'iph
cal'iphate

calisay'a
{ calisthen'ics
{ callisthen'ics
cal'iver
cal'ix
calk, caulk
calked
calk'er
calk'ing
call
called
call'er
callig'raphy
call'ing
calli'ope
callos'ity
cal'lous
cal'lously
cal'lousness
cal'low
cal'lus
calm
calmed
calm'er
calm'est
calm'ing
calm'ly
calm'ness
cal'omel
calores'cence
calor'ic
calorif'ic
calorifica'tion
calorim'eter
calorimo'tor
calotte'
cal'otype
calum'ba
cal'umet
calum'niate
calum'niated
calum'niating
calumnia'tion
calum'niator
calum'niatory
calum'nious
calum'niously
calum'niousness
cal'umny
Cal'vary
calve
calved
calves
calv'ing
Cal'vinism
Cal'vinist
Calvinis'tic
Calvinis'tical
calx
cal'ycine
cal'ycle
cal'yx
cam
cam'ber
cam'bered
cam'bering
cam'bial
cam'bist
cam'bistry
cam'bium
camboose'
Cam'brian
cam'bric
came
cam'el
camel'lia
camel'opard
cam'eo
cam'era
cam'era lu'cida
cam'era obscu'ra
cameralis'tic
cam'erate
cam'erated
camera'tion
Camero'nian
Cam'isard
cam'isole
cam'let
cam'omile
Camor'ra
camp
campaign'
campaign'er
campani'le
campanol'ogy
campan'ula
camped
cam'phene
cam'phine
cam'phogen
cam'phor
cam'phorate
cam'phorated
camp'ing
cam'pion
can
Ca'naanite
Ca'naanitish
Cana'dian
canaille'
canal'
canalic'ulate
canaliza'tion
ca'nalize
canard'
cana'ry
can'cel
can'cellate
can'cellated
cancella'tion
can'celled
can'celling
can'cer
can'cerate
cancera'tion
can'cerous
can'cerously
can'cerousness
can'criform
can'crine
can'crinite
candela'bra
candela'brum
can'dent
can'did
can'didate
can'didature
can'didly
can'didness
can'died
can'dle
Can'dlemas
can'dlestick
can'dor, can'dour
can'dy
can'dying
can'dytuft
cane
cane'-brake
caned
cangue, cang
canic'ular
can'ine
ca'ning
can'ister
can'ker
can'kered
can'kering
can'kerous
can'ker-worm
can'kery
can'nel-coal
can'nibal
can'nibalism
can'nikin
can'non
cannonade'
cannona'ded
cannona'ding
{ cannoneer'
{ cannonier'
can'non-proof
can'non-shot
can'not
can'nula
can'nular
can'ny
canoe'
can'on
cañ'on
can'oness
canon'ic
canon'ical
canon'icals
can'onist
canoniza'tion
can'onize
can'onized
can'onizing
can'onry
can'opied
can'opy
cano'rous
canst
cant
can't
Can'tab
canta'bile
Canta'brian
Cantabrig'ian
can'taliver
can'taloup
cantan'kerous
canta'ta
canta'tion

cantatri'ce
cant'ed
canteen'
can'tel
can'ter
can'tered
can'tering
canthar'ides
canthar'idin
can'ticle
can'tilate
cantila'tion
can'tilever
cant'ing
can'tle
can'to
can'ton
can'tonal
can'toned
Cantonese'
can'toning
can'tonize
canton'ment
can'vas, can'vass
can'vassed
can'vasser
can'vassing
ca'ny
can'yon
canzo'ne
canzonet'
caout'chouc
caout'choucin
cap
capabil'ity
ca'pable
ca'pableness
ca'pably
capa'cious
capa'ciously
capa'ciousness
capac'itate
capac'itated
capac'ity
cap-à-pie'
capar'ison
capar'isoned
capar'isoning
cape
cap'elet, cap'ellet
ca'per
capercail'zie
ca'pering
cap'ias
capilla'ceous
capillaire'
capillar'ity
cap'illary
capil'liform
cap'ital
cap'italist
capitaliza'tion
cap'italize
cap'itate
capita'tion
Cap'itol
Cap'itoline
capit'ular
capit'ularly

capit'ulary
capit'ulate
capit'ulated
capit'ulating
capitula'tion
capit'ulator
capit'ulum
capi'vi
cap'lin
cap'nomancy
cap'nomor
ca'pon
capot'
capote'
capped
cap'per
cap'ping
caprice'
capri'cious
capri'ciously
capri'ciousness
Cap'ricorn
Cap'ricornus
cap'rid
caprifica'tion
cap'riform
caprig'enous
cap'rine
cap'riole
cap'sicum
capsize'
capsized'
capsi'zing
cap'stan
cap'sular
cap'sulary
cap'sule
cap'tain
cap'taincy
cap'tainship
cap'tion
cap'tious
cap'tiously
cap'tiousness
cap'tivate
cap'tivated
cap'tivating
captiva'tion
cap'tive
captiv'ity
cap'tor
cap'ture
cap'tured
cap'turing
Cap'uchin
cap'ulet
car
carabinier'
car'acal
car'ack
car'acole
car'acoly
carafe'
car'amel
car'at
car'avan
caravaneer'

caravan'serai
car'avel
car'away
car'bine
carbineer'
carbol'ic
car'bolize
car'bon
carbona'ceous
Carbona'ri
car'bonate, *n.*
car'bonate, *v.*
car'bonated
carbon'ic
carbonif'erous
carboniza'tion
car'bonize
car'bonized
car'bonizing
car'boy
car'buncle
car'buncled
carbun'cular
carbuncula'tion
car'buret
car'buretted-ted
car'burettor-ter
car'cajou
car'canet
car'cass, car'case
carcinol'ogy
carcino'ma
carcino'matous
card
car'damine
car'damom
card'board
card'-case
card'ed
card'er
car'diac
cardi'acal
cardiag'raphy
cardial'gia
cardial'gy
car'dinal
car'dinalate
card'ing
car'dioid
cardiog'raphy
cardiol'ogy
cardi'tis
cardoon'
care
cared
careen'
careen'age
careened'
careen'ing
career'
*care'*ful
*care'*fully
*care'*fulness
*care'*less
*care'*lessly
*care'*lessness
caress'

caressed'
caress'ing
caress'ingly
car'et
*care'*worn
car'go
car'goose
car'ib
Caribbe'an
Car'ibee
caribou'
car'icature
car'icatured
car'icaturing
car'icaturist
car'icous
ca'ries
car'illon
cari'na
car'inate, *adj.*
car'inate, *v.*
car'inated
*car'*ing
car'iole
carios'ity
ca'rious
cark
cark'ing
car'line
Carlovin'gian
car'man
Car'melite
car'minated
car'minative
car'mine
car'nage
car'nal
carnal'ity
car'nalize
car'nalizing
car'nally
car'nal-mind'ed
carna'tion
carna'tioned
carne'lian
car'neous
car'ney
carnifica'tion
car'nified
car'nify
car'nifying
car'nival
carniv'ora
carniv'orous
car'nous
carnos'ity
car'ol
car'oled-lled
car'oling-lling
carot'id
carou'sal
carouse'
caroused'
carous'er
carous'ing
carp
car'pal
Carpa'thian
carped

car'pel
car'pellary
carpel'lum
car'penter
car'pentry
carp'er
car'pet
car'peted
car'peting
carp'ing
car'polite
carpol'ogist
carpol'ogy
car'pus
car'raway
car'rel
car'riage
car'ried
car'rier
car'rion
carronade'
car'rot
car'roty
car'ry
car'ry-all
car'rying
cart
cart'age
carte
carte blanche'
carte-de-visite'
cart'ed
car'tel
cart'er
Carte'sian
Carthagin'ian
car'thamin
cart'-horse
Carthu'sian
car'tilage
cartilag'inous
cart'ing
cart'-load
cartog'rapher
cartograph'ic
cartog'raphy
cartoon'
cartoon'ist
cartouche'
car'tridge
car'tulary
cart'-way
cart'-wheel
cart'wright
carun'cle
carun'cular
carun'culate
carun'culated
carve
carved
car'vel
carv'er, carv'ing
car'yate
caryat'ic
caryat'id
caryat'ides
cas'cabel
cascade'
cascal'ho
cas'cara sagra'da

cascaril'la
case
cased
case'harden
case'hardening
ca'seic
ca'sein
case'-knife
case'mate
case'mated
case'ment
case'mented
ca'seous
casern'
case'-shot
cash
cash'-account
cash'-book
cash'-boy
cash'-girl
cashed
cashew'
cashier'
cashiered'
cashier'ing
cash'ing
cash'keeper
cash'mere
cashoo'
ca'sing
casi'no
cask
cas'ket
casque
cassa'da
cas'sareep
cassa'tion
cassa'va
cas'sia
cas'simere
cas'sius
cas'sock
cas'socked
cas'sowary
cast
Casta'lian
cas'tanet
cast'away
caste
cas'tellan
cas'tellany
cas'tellated
cas'ter, cast'or
cas'tigate
cas'tigated
castiga'tion
cas'tigating
cas'tigator
cas'tigatory
Cas'tile soap
Castil'ian
cast'ing
cast'ing net
cast'ing-vote
cast'-iron
cas'tle
cas'tled
cast'ling
cas'tor
cas'tor-oil

castrameta'tion
cas'trate
cas'trated
cas'trating
castra'tion
cas'trel
cas'ual
cas'ualty
cas'uist
casuis'tic
casuis'tical
cas'uistry
cat
catab'olism
catacaus'tic
catachre'sis
catachres'tic
cat'aclysm
cataclys'mist
cat'acomb
catacous'tics
catadiop'tric
cat'afalque
catagmat'ic
Cat'alan
catalec'tic
cat'alepsis
cat'alepsy
catalep'tic
catallac'tics
cat'alogue
cat'alogued
cat'aloguing
Catalo'nian
catal'ysis
catalyt'ic
catamaran'
catame'nia
catame'nial
cat'amount
cat'apan
catapet'alous
cataphon'ics
cat'aphract
cat'aplasm
cat'apult
catapult'ic
cat'aract
catarac'tous
catarrh'
catarrh'al
catas'tasis
catas'trophe
catastroph'ic
cat'bird
cat'boat
cat'*call*
catch
catch'er
catch'fly
catch'ing
catch'penny
catch'pole
catch'up
catch'*word*
catechet'ic
catechet'ical
cat'echism
cat'echist
catechist'ic
catechiza'tion
cat'echize
cat'echized
cat'echizer
cat'echizing
cat'echu
catechu'men
catechumen'ic
catechumen'ical
categoremat'ic
categor'ical
cat'egorize
cat'egory
cate'na
catena'rian
cate'nary
cat'enate
cat'enated
catena'tion
ca'ter
cat'eran
ca'tered
ca'terer
ca'teress
ca'tering
cat'erpillar
cat'erwaul
cates
cat'fish
cat'gut
Cath'ari
cathar'sis
cathar'tic
cathar'tical
cat'-head
cathe'dra
cathe'dral
catheret'ic
cath'eter
cath'ode
cathod'ic
cath'olic
Cathol'icism
catholic'ity
Cathol'icize
cathol'icon
Catilina'rian
cat'ion
cat'kin
cat'-like
cat'ling
cat'mint
cat'-nip
Cato'nian
cat-o'-nine'-tails
catop'tric
catop'tromancy
cat's'-paw
cat'sup
cat'tle
cat'tle-show
caubeen'
Cauca'sian
cau'cus
cau'dal
cau'date
cau'dated
cau'dle
cauf
caught
caul
caul'dron
caules'cent
caulic'olous
cau'licule
caulif'erous
cau'liflower
cau'liform
cau'line
caulk
caus'al
causal'ity
causa'tion
caus'ative
caus'atively
cause
caused
cause'less
cause'lessly
cause'lessness
caus'er
cause'rie
causeuse'
cau'sey
cause'way
cau'seyed
causid'ical
caus'ing
caus'tic
caustic'ity
cau'ter
cau'terant
cauteriza'tion
cau'terize
cau'terized
cau'terizing
cau'tery
cau'tion
cau'tionary
cau'tioned
cau'tioner
cau'tioning
cau'tious
cau'tiously
cau'tiousness
cavalcade'
cavalier'
cavalier'ly
cav'alry
cavass'
cavati'na
cave
ca'veat
ca'veator
caved
cav'ern
cav'erned
cav'ernous
cav'esson
cavet'to
caviar', caviare'
cav'icorn
cav'il
cav'illed-led
cav'iller-ler
cav'illing-ling
cav'illingly-lingly
cav'in

cav'ing
cav'ity
ca'vy
caw
cawed
caw'ing
cawk
cax'on
cayenne'
cay'man
cazique'
cease
ceased
cease'less
cease'lessly
ceas'ing
ce'city
ce'dar
ce'dared
ce'darn
cede
ce'ded
ce'der
cedil'la
ce'ding
ce'drat, ce'drate
ce'drin, ce'drine
ceil
ceiled
ceil'ing
cel'adon
cel'andine
cel'ature
cel'ebrant
cel'ebrate
cel'ebrated
cel'ebrating
celebra'tion
cel'ebrator
celeb'rity
celer'iac
celer'ity
cel'ery
celes'tial
celes'tialize
Cel'estine
cel'estine
ce'liac
cel'ibacy
cel'ibate
celidog'raphy
cell
cel'lar
cel'larage
cel'larer
cel'laret
celled
'cell'ist
'cell'o
cel'lular
cel'lulated
cel'lule
cellulif'erous
cel'luloid
cel'lulose
Cel'sius
Celt
Celtibe'rian
Celt'ic
Celt'icism

Celt'ish
cement'
cementa'tion
cement'atory
cement'ed
cement'er
cement'ing
cementi'tious
cem'etery
cen'obite
cenobit'ical
cenog'amy
cen'otaph
cense
censed
cen'ser
cens'ing
cen'sor
censo'rial
censo'rious
censo'riously
censo'riousness
cen'sorship
cen'sual
cen'surable
cen'surableness
cen'sure
cen'sured
cen'surer
cen'suring
cen'sus
cent
cent'age
cen'tal
cen'taur
cen'taury
centena'rian
cen'tenary
centen'nial
cen'ter
cen'tering
centes'imal
centesima'tion
centifo'lious
cen'tigrade
cen'tigramme
cen'tiliter-tre
centime'
cen'timeter-tre
cen'tipede
cen'to
cen'tral
central'ity
centraliza'tion
cen'tralize
cen'tralized
cen'tralizing
cen'tre
cen'tre-bit
cen'tred
cen'tric
cen'trical
centric'ity
centrif'ugal
cen'tring
centrip'etal
centum'vir
centum'virate
cen'tuple
centu'rial

centu'rion
cen'tury
cephalal'gic
ceph'alalgy
cephal'ic
ceph'alopod
ceph'alous
cera'ceous
ceram'ic
cer'asin
cer'asite
ce'rate
ce'rated
cer'atin
Cerbe'rean
cere
ce'real
cerebel'lum
cer'ebral
cerebra'tion
cerebrospi'nal
cer'ebrum
cere'cloth
cere'ment
ceremo'nial
ceremo'nialism
ceremo'nious
ceremo'niously
cer'emony
ce'reous
cer'evis
ce'ric
ce'rin
cer'iph
cerise'
ce'rite
ce'rium
cern
cerne
cer'niture
cerog'raphy
ce'romancy
ceroon'
ceroplas'tic
cer'tain
cer'tainly
cer'tainty
cer'tes
certif'icate
certifica'tion
cer'tified
cer'tifier
cer'tify
cer'tifying
certiora'ri
cer'titude
ceru'lean
ceru'men
ce'ruse
ce'rused
cer'vical
cer'vine
Cesa'rean
ces'pitous
cess
cessa'tion
ces'ser
ces'sion
ces'sionary
ces'sor

cess'pool
cest
ces'tui
ces'tus
cesu'ra
cesu'ral
Ceta'cea
ceta'cean
ceta'ceous
ce'tic
ce'tin
ce'tine
cetol'ogy
Chab'lis
chad
chafe
chafed
cha'fer
cha'fery
chaff
chaff'-cutter
chaffed
chaf'fer
chaf'fered
chaf'ferer
chaf'fering
chaf'finch
chaf'fy
cha'fing
cha'fing-dish
chagreen'
chagrin'
chagrined'
chain
chained
chain'ing
chain'-pump
chain'-shot
chain'-stitch
chair
chaired
*chair'*ing
*chair'*man
*chair'*manship
chaise
chalcedon'ic
chalced'ony
chalcog'rapher
chalcog'raphy
Chalda'ic
Chal'daism
Chalde'an
Chaldee'
chal'dron
cha'let
chal'ice
chal'iced
chalk
chalked
chalk'iness
chalk'ing
chalk'-pit
chalk'-stone
chalk'y
chal'lenge
chal'lengeable
chal'lenged
chal'lenger
chal'lenging
chalyb'eate

cham
chamade'
cham'ber
cham'bered
cham'berer
cham'ber-fellow
cham'berlain
cham'bermaid
chame'leon
cham'fer
cham'fered
cham'ois
cham'omile
champ
champagne'
cham'paign
cham'perty
cham'pion
cham'pioned
cham'pioness
cham'pionship
chance
chanced
chan'cel
chan'cellery
chan'cellory
chan'cellor
chan'cellorship
chan'cery
chanc'ing
chan'cre
chan'crous
chandelier'
chand'ler
chand'lery
chan'frin
change
changeabil'ity
change'able
change'ableness
change'ably
changed
change'ful
change'less
change'ling
chan'ger
chan'ging
chan'nel
chan'nelled
chan'nelling
chan'son
chansonette'
chant
chant'ed
chant'er
chant'ey
chan'ticleer
chant'ing
chant'ress
chant'ry
cha'os
chaot'ic
chap
chape
chapeau'
chap'el
chap'elry
chap'eron
chap'eronage
chap'fallen

chap'iter
chap'lain
chap'laincy
chap'lainship
chap'let
chap'man
chapped
chap'py
chaps
chap'ter
chap'trel
char (a fish)
char (to work by the day)
char'-à-banc
char'acter
characterist'ic
*characteris'tic*ally
*characteriza'*tion
char'acterize
char'acterized
char'acterizing
*char'acter*less
charade'
char'coal
chard
chare
charge
chargeabil'ity
charge'able
charge'ably
charged
chargé d'affaires'
char'ger
charg'ing
cha'rily
cha'riness
char'iot
charioteer'
char'ism
char'itable
char'itableness
char'ity
chariva'ri
char'latan
charlatan'ic
char'latanism
char'latanry
char'lock
charm
charmed
charm'er
charm'ing
charm'ingly
char'nel
char'nel-house
char'pie
char'poy
charred
char'ring
char'ry
chart
char'ta
charta'ceous
char'ter
char'tered
char'terer
char'ter-party
chart'ism
chart'ist

chartog'rapher
chartog'raphy
chartom'eter
Char'treuse
Char'treux
char'woman
cha'ry
chas'able, chase'-
chase [able
chased
chas'er
chas'ing
chasm
chasse'pot
chasseur'
chas'sis
chaste
chaste'ly
chast'en
chast'ened
chast'ener
chast'ening
chastise'
chastised'
chas'tisement
chastis'er
chastis'ing
chas'tity
chas'uble
chat
château'
chat'elaine
chat'ellany
chat'ted
chat'tel
chat'ter
chat'terbox
chat'tered
chat'terer
chat'tering
chat'ty
chat'wood
chauf'feur
chauvin
chau'vinism
chau'vinist
cheap
cheap'en
cheap'ened
cheap'ener
cheap'ly
cheap'ness
cheat
cheat'able
cheat'ed
cheat'er
cheat'ing
check
check'-book
checked
check'er
check'er-board
check'ered
check'ers
check'er-work
check'ing
check'mate
check'mated
check'mating
check'string

cheek
cheek'-tooth
cheep'er
cheer
cheered
cheer'er
cheer'ful
cheer'fulness
cheer'ily
cheer'iness
cheer'ing
cheer'ingly
cheer'less
cheer'y
cheese
cheese'-cake
cheese'-cutter
cheese'monger
cheese'-press
chee'sy
chee'tah
chef
chef-d'œuvre'
Cheirop'tera
cheirop'terous
chem'ic
chem'ical
chemise'
chemisette'
chem'ist
chem'istry
chenille'
cheque
cheq'uer
cher'ish
cher'ished
cher'isher
cher'ishing
cheroot'
cher'ry
cher'sonese
chert
chert'y
cher'ub
cheru'bic
cher'ubim
cher'vil
ches'nut
chess
chess'board
chess'man
chest
chest'ed
chest'nut
che'tah
cheval'
chevaux' de frise'
chevalier'
chev'ron
chev'ronel
chew
chewed
chew'ing
Chiant'i
chiaroscu'ro
chib'bal
chibouk', chi'-
chic [bouque
chicane'

chica'ner
chica'nery
chich
chich'ling
chick
chick'abiddy
chick'en
chick'en-pox
chick'ling
chick'pea
chick'weed
chic'ory
chid
chide
chid'ed
chid'er
chid'ing
chief
chief'ess
chief'ly
chief'tain
chief'tainship
chiel
chield
chiffon
chiffonier'
chi'gnon
chig'oe
chil'blain
child
child'-bed
child'birth
childe
child'hood
child'ing
child'ish
child'ishly
child'ishness
child'less
child'like
chil'dren
chil'iad
chil'iagon
chil'iarch
chil'iasm
chill
chilled
chil'li
chil'liness
chil'ling
chil'ly
chi'lopod
Chil'tern
Hun'dreds
chime
chimed
chim'er
chime'ra
chimer'ical
chim'ing
chim'ney
chim'ney-board
chim'ney-piece
chim'ney-pot
chim'ney-sweep
chimpan'zee
chin
chi'na
chi'na-aster
chi'na-clay

chin'capin
chinchil'la
chin'-cough
chine
chined
Chinese'
chink
chinked
chink'ing
chink'y
chinned
chinse
chintz
chip
chipped
Chip'pendale
chip'per
chip'ping
chip'py
chirag'ra
chi'rograph
chirog'rapher
chirograph'ic
chirog'raphist
chirog'raphy
chirolog'ical
chirol'ogy
chi'romancy
chiroman'tic
chiron'omy
chi'roplast
chirop'odist
chiros'ophy
chirp-ed
chirp'er
chirp'ing
chir'rup
chir'ruped
chir'ruping
chis'el
chis'eled-lled
chis'eler-ller
chis'eling-lling
chiselly
Chis'leu
chit
chit'-chat
chi'ton
chit'terlings
chit'ty
chival'ric
chiv'alrous
chiv'alry
chive
chlo'ral
chlo'rate
chlo'ric
chlo'rid, chlo'ride
chlo'ridate
chlo'rine
chlo'rite
chlorit'ic
chlo'rodyne
chlo'roform
chlorom'eter
chlorom'etry
{ chlo'rophyl
{ chlo'rophyll
chloro'sis
chlo'rous

chock
chock'-full
choc'olate
choice
choi'cer
choi'cest
choir
choke
choked
choke'-damp
choke'-full
chok'er
chok'ing
chok'y
chol'er
chol'era
cholera'ic
chol'era mor'bus
chol'eric
chondri'tis
chondrom'eter
choose
choos'er
choos'ing
chop
cho'pin
chop'-house
chopped
chop'per
chop'ping
chops
chop'sticks
chorag'ic
cho'ral
cho'ralist
chord
chord'ed
chord'ing
chore
chore'a
choree'
chore'us
choriam'bic
choriam'bus
cho'rion
chor'ist
chor'ister
chorog'rapher
chorograph'ic
chorog'raphy
cho'roid
cho'rus
chose
chos'en
chough
chouse
choused
chow'-chow
chow'der
chrematis'tics
chrestom'athy
chrism
chris'mal
chris'matory
chris'om
Christ
Christ'-cross
chris'ten

Chris'tendom
chris'tened
chris'tening
Chris'tian
Christian'ity
Christ'ianize
Christ'ianized
Christ'ianizing
Christ'ianly
Christ'mas
Christ'mas-box
Christ'mas-day'
Christol'ogy
chro'mate
chromat'ic
chromat'ics
chromatog'raphy
chromatol'ogy
chromatom'eter
chrome
chro'mic
chro'mium
chro'mograph
chromolithog'-raphy
chro'mosphere
chron'ic
chron'ical-cle
chron'icled
chron'icler
chron'icles
chron'icling
chron'ogram
chron'ograph
chronogram-mat'ic
chronog'rapher
chronog'raphy
chronol'oger
chronolog'ic
chronolog'ical-ly
chronol'ogist
chronol'ogy
chronom'eter
chronomet'ric
chronom'etry
chron'opher
chron'oscope
chrys'alid
chrys'alis
chrysan'themum
chrysog'raphy
chrys'olite
chrysol'ogy
chrysop'rasus
chrys'otype
chub
chubbed
chub'by
chuck
chucked
chuck'ing
chuck'le
chuck'led
chuck'ling
chud'dar
chuff
chuf'fily
chuf'finess

chuf'fy
chum
chump
chu'nam
chunk
chunk'y
church
churched
church'ing
church'ism
church'man
church'-rate
churchward'en
church'*yard*
churl
churl'ish
churl'ishly
churl'ishness
churn
churned
churn'ing
chute
chut'ney
chyla'ceous
chyle
chylifac'tive
chylif'erous
chylifica'tion
chy'lous
chyme
chymifica'tion
chym'ify
ciba'rious
cib'ol
cibo'rium
cica'da
cic'atrice
cicatri'sive
cica'trix
cicatriza'tion
cic'atrize
cic'atrized
cic'atrizing
cic'ely
cicero'ne
Cicero'nian
cichora'ceous
Cid
ci'der
ci'derist
ci'derkin
ci-devant'
cierge
cigar'
cigarette'
cil'ia
cil'iary
cil'iate
cil'iated
Cili'cian
cili'cious
cil'iform
cil'iograde
cil'ium
ci'ma
cim'bal
Cim'bric
Cimme'rian
cim'olite
cinch
Cincho'na
cincho'nic
cin'chonine
cinct'ure
cinct'ured
cin'der
cin'derous
cin'dery
cinemat'ograph
cinefac'tion
cinera'ceous
cinera'ria
cin'erary
cinera'tion
cinera'tious
Cingalese'
cin'nabar
cin'nabarine
cin'namon
cinnamon'ic
cinq, cinque
cinque'-foil
Cinque' ports
ci'pher
ci'phered
ci'phering
cip'olin
Circas'sian
Circe'an
cir'cinal
cir'cinate
cir'cle
cir'cled
cir'cler
cir'clet
cir'cling
cir'cuit
cir'cuited
circu'itous
circu'itously
circu'ity
cir'culable
cir'cular
cir'cularism
circular'ity
cir'cularize
cir'cularly
cir'culate
cir'culated
cir'culating
circula'tion
cir'culative
cir'culatory
circumam'bient
cir'cumcise
cir'cumcised
cir'cumciser
cir'cumcising
circumci'sion
cir'cumduct
circum'ference
circumferen'tial
circumferen'tor
cir'cumflect
cir'cumflex
circumflex'ion
circum'fluence
circum'fluent
circum'fluous
circumfuse'
circumfused'
circumfu'sile
circumfu'sion
circumgy'rate
circumgyra'tion
circumja'cence
circumja'cent
circumlocu'tion
circumloc'utory
circum'mure
circummured'
circumnav'igable
circumnav'igate
circumnav'igated
circumnaviga'tion
circumnav'igator
circumplica'tion
circumpo'lar
circumrota'tion
circumro'tary
circumro'tatory
circumscrib'able
circumscribe'
circumscribed'
circumscrib'er
circumscrib'ing
circumscrip'tion
circumscrip'tive
cir'cumspect
circumspec'tion
circumspec'tive
cir'cumspectly
cir'cumspectness
cir'cumstance
cir'cumstanced
circumstan'tial
circumstantial'ity
circumstan'tiate
circumstan'tiated
circumstan'tiating
circumval'late
circumvalla'tion
circumvent'
circumvent'ed
circumven'tion
circumven'tive
circumvola'tion
circum'volute
circumvolu'tion
circumvolve'
cir'cus
cirrho'sis
cirrif'erous
cir'riform
cirrig'erous
cir'riped
cirro-cu'mulus
cir'rose
cirro-stra'tus
cir'rus, cir'socele
cisal'pine
cisatlan'tic
cismon'tane
cis'soid
cist
cist'ed
Cister'cian
cis'tern
cis'tic
cit

ci'table
cit'adel
cita'tion
ci'tatory
cite
cited
cit'er
cith'ara
cit'igrade
ci'ting
cit'izen
cit'izenship
cit'rate
cit'rene
cit'ric
cit'ril
cit'rine
cit'ron
cit'y
civ'et
civ'et-cat
civ'ic
civ'il
civ'il engineer'
civil'ian
civil'ity
civ'ilizable
civiliza'tion
civ'ilize
civ'ilized
civ'ilizer
civ'ilizing
civ'illy
civ'ism
clab'ber
clack
clacked
clack'er
clack'ing
clad
claim
claim'able
claim'ant
claimed
claim'er
claim'ing
clair-obscure'
clairvoy'ance
clairvoy'ant
clam
cla'mant
clam'ber
clam'bered
clam'bering
clammed
clam'ming
clam'miness
clam'my
clam'or, clam'our
clam'ored
clam'orer
clam'oring
clam'orous
clamp
clamped
clamp'ing
clan
clandes'tine
clandes'tinely

clang
clanged
clang'ing
clan'gor, clan'gour
clan'gorous
clank
clanked
clank'ing
clan'nish
clan'nishly
clan'ship
clans'man
clap
clap'board
clapped
clap'per
clap'per-claw
clap'ping
clap'trap
claq'uer
claqueur'
clarabel'la
Clar'enceux, Clar'encieux
clar'et
clarifica'tion
clar'ified
clar'ifier
clar'ify
clar'ifying
clar'inet
clar'ion
clarionet'
clash
clashed
clash'ing
clasp
clasped
clasp'er
clasp'ing
clasp'-knife
class
classed
class'able
clas'sic
clas'sical
classical'ity
clas'sicist
classif'ic
classifica'tion
clas'sified
clas'sifier
clas'sify
clas'sifying
class'ing
clas'sis
class'man
class'mate
clat
clat'ter
clat'tered
clat'terer
clat'tering
clause
claus'tral
clau'sular
cla'vate
cla'vated
clave
clav'iary
clav'ichord

clav'icle
clavic'ular
clavier'
clavig'erous
cla'vis
claw
clawed
claw'ing
clay
clayed
clay'ey
clay'ing
clay'ish
clay'more
clean
cleaned
clean'er
clean'est
clean'ing
clean'lily
clean'liness
clean'ly, *adj.*
clean'ly, *adv.*
clean'ness
cleanse
cleansed
cleans'er
cleans'ible
cleans'ing
clear
clear'age
clear'ance
cleared
clear'er
clear'est
clear'ing
clear'ing-house
clear'ly
clear'ness
clear'-sighted
cleat
cleav'age
cleave
cleaved
cleav'er
cleav'ing
cledge
cledg'y
clef
cleft
cleg
clem'atis
clem'ency
clem'ent
Clem'entine
clench
clench'er
clench'ing
clep'sydra
clere'story
cler'gy
cler'gyman
cler'ic
cler'ical
clerk
clerk'ship
cle'romancy
clev'er
clev'erly

clev'erness
clev'is
clev'y
clew
cliché'
click
clicked
click'er
click'et
click'ing
cli'ent
cli'entage
clientele'
cliff
clift
climac'teric
cli'mate
climat'ic
climat'ical
cli'matize
cli'matized
climatog'raphy
climatol'ogist
climatol'ogy
cli'max
climb
climb'able
climbed
climb'er
climb'ing
clime
clinch
clinched
clinch'er
clinch'ing
cling
cling'er
cling'ing
cling'stone
cling'y
clin'ic
clin'ical
clink
clinked
clink'er
clink'ered
clink'ing
clinoceph'aly
cli'nograph
cli'noid
clinom'eter
clinomet'ric
clinomet'rical
clin'quant
clip
clipped
clip'per
clip'ping
clique
cli'quish
cli'quism
clish-ma-cla'ver
cliv'ers
cloak
cloaked
cloak'ing
clob'ber
cloche
clo'cher

clock
clock'-maker
clock'-work
clod
clod'dy
clod'-hopper
clod'-hopping
clod'pate
clod'pated
clod'poll
cloff
clog
clogged
clog'giness
clog'ging
clog'gy
clois'ter
cloisonné'
clois'teral
clois'tered
clois'terer
clois'tering
clon'ic
close, *v.*
close, *adj.*
close'-bodied
closed
close'ly
close'ness
clo'ser
clos'est
clos'et
clos'eted
clos'eting
clos'ing
clo'sure
clot
clot'-bur
cloth
clothe
clothed
clothes
clothes'-basket
clothes'-horse
clothes'-line
cloth'ier
cloth'ing
clot'ted
clot'ting
clot'ty
cloud
cloud'-capt
cloud'-capped
cloud'ed
cloud'ily
cloud'iness
cloud'ing
cloud'less
cloud'lessly
cloud'y
clough
clout
clout'ed
clout'ing
clout'-nail
clove
clo'ven
clo'ven-footed
clo'ver
clo'vered

clown
clown'ish
clown'ishly
clown'ishness
cloy
cloyed
cloy'ing
club
club'bable
clubbed
club'bist
club'-footed
club'-house
club'-law
club'-room
cluck
clucked
cluck'ing
clue
clump
clum'sily
clum'siness
clum'sy
clunch
clung
Clu'niac
clus'ter
clus'tered
clus'tering
clus'tery
clutch
clutched
clutch'ing
clut'ter
clut'tered
clut'tering
clys'mic
clys'ter
coach
coach'-horse
coach'-house
coach'man
co-ac'tion
coac'tive
coadjust'
coad'jutant
coadju'tor
coadju'trix
coadven'ture
coag'ulable
coag'ulant
coag'ulate
coag'ulated
coag'ulating
coagula'tion
coag'ulative
coag'ulator
coag'ulatory
coag'ulum
co'-aid
coal
coal'-field
coaled
coalesce'
coalesced'
coales'cence
coales'cent
coalesc'ing
coal'ing

coali'tion
coali'tionist
co-ally'
coal'-mine
coal'-pit
coal'y
coam'ing
coapta'tion
coarc'tate
coarcta'tion
coarse
coarse'ly
coarse'ness
coars'er
coars'est
coast
coast'ed
coast'er
coast'-*guard*
coast'ing
coast'-line
coast'wise
coat
coat'ed
coatee'
coat'ing
coax
coaxed
coax'er
coax'ing
coax'ingly
cob
co'balt
cobalt'ic
co'baltine
cob'bing
cob'ble
cob'bled
cob'bler
cob'ble-stone
cob'bling
cob'by
Cob'denism
cob'nut
co'bra
cob'web
co'ca
Cocagne'
co'caine
coc'culus
coc'cyx
coch'ineal
coch'lea
coch'lear
cochlear'iform
coch'leate
cock
cockade'
cocka'ded
Cockaigne'
cockatoo'
cock'atrice
cock'bill
cock'boat
cock'chafer
cock'-crow
cock'-crowing

cocked
cock'er
cock'erel
cock'et
cock'-eyed
cock'-fight
cock'-horse
cock'ing
cock'le
cock'led
cock'ling (*part.*)
cock'ling (cock-[erel]
cock'-loft
cock'ney
cock'neyfy
cock'neyism
cock'pit
cock'roach
cocks'comb
cock'-sparrow
cock'spur
cock'swain
cock'-tail
co'co, co'coa
co'coa-nib
co'co-nut
cocoon'
cocoon'ery
coc'tion
cod
co'da
cod'dle
cod'dled
cod'dling
code
code'ine
co'dex
cod'fish
codg'er
cod'icil
codicil'lary
codifica'tion
cod'ified
cod'ifier
cod'ify
codil'la
codille'
cod'ling
co'don
co-effi'ciency
coeffi'cient
coe'liac
coemp'tion
coenog'amy
coe'qual
coequal'ity
coerce'
coerced'
coer'cible
coer'cibleness
coerc'ing
coer'cion
coer'cive
coessen'tial
coessential'ity
coeta'neous
coeter'nal
coeter'nity

coe'val
coexist'
coexist'ed
coexist'ence
coexist'ent
coexist'ing
coextend'
coexten'sion
coexten'sive
cof'fee
cof'fee-house
cof'fee-pot
cof'fer
cof'fer-dam
cof'fered
cof'ferer
cof'fin
cof'fined
cog
co'gency
co'gent
co'gently
cogged
cog'ger
cog'ging
cog'itable
cog'itate
cog'itated
cog'itating
cogita'tion
cog'itative
co'gnac
cog'nate
cog'nateness
cogna'tion
cogni'tion
cog'nitive
cog'nizable
cog'nizance
cog'nizant
cog'nize
cognizee'
cog'nizor
cogno'men
cognom'inal
cog'-wheel
cohab'it
cohab'itant
cohabita'tion
cohab'ited
cohab'iter
cohab'iting
coheir'
coheir'ess
cohere'
cohered'
coher'ence
coher'ency
coher'ent
coher'ently
coher'ing
cohesibil'ity
cohe'sible
cohe'sion
cohe'sive
cohe'siveness
cohib'it
cohibi'tion

co'hobate
co'hort
coif
coifed
coiffeur'
coiffure'
coign, coigne
coil
coiled
coil'ing
coin
coin'age
coincide'
coin'cidence
coin'cident
coin'cidently
coindica'tion
coined
coin'er
co-inhab'itant
coin'ing
coir
coit
coi'tion
coju'ror
coke
coked
cok'ing
co'ker-nut
col'ander
col'chicum
col'cothar
cold
cold'er
cold'est
cold'hearted
cold'ish
cold'ly
cold'ness
cole
coleop'tera
coleop'terist
coleop'terous
cole'seed
cole'wort
col'ic
col'icky
col'in
Colise'um
collab'orate
collabora'tion
collab'orator
collapse'
collapsed'
collaps'ible
collaps'ing
col'lar
col'lared
{ col'laret
{ collarette'
col'laring
colla'table
collate'
colla'ted
collat'eral
collat'eralness
collat'ing
colla'tion
colla'tive

colla'tor
col'league
col'leagueship
col'lect, *n.*
collect', *v.*
collect'able
collecta'nea
collecta'neous
collect'ed
collect'edly
collect'edness
collect'ible
collec'tion
collect'ive
collect'ively
collect'iveness
collect'ivism
collect'or
collect'orship
col'leen
col'lege
colle'gial
colle'gian
colle'giate
col'let
collide'
colli'ded
colli'ding
col'lie
col'lier
col'liery
col'ligate
colliga'tion
col'limate
collima'tion
col'limator
collinea'tion
colliq'uative
colli'sion
col'locate
col'located
col'locating
colloca'tion
collocu'tion
collo'dion
collo'dionize
col'loid
col'lop
collo'quial
collo'quialism
col'loquist
col'loquy
col'lotype
collude'
collu'ded
collu'der
collu'ding
collu'sion
collu'sive
collu'sively
col'ly
col'ocynth
colocyn'thin
col'ombin
co'lon
col'onel
col'onelcy
colo'nial

col'onist
coloniza'tion
coloniza'tionist
col'onize
col'onized
col'onizing
colonnade'
col'ony
col'ophon
col'ophony
col'or, col'our
{ col'orable
{ col'ourable
col'orableness
col'orably
colora'tion
col'orature
{ col'ored
{ col'oured
colorif'ic
{ col'oring
{ col'ouring
{ col'orist
{ col'ourist
{ col'orless
{ col'ourless
colos'sal
colosse'an
Colosse'um
Colos'sian
Colos'sus
col'portage
col'porteur
col'staff
colt
colt'ish
colt'er
colts'foot
col'uber
col'ubrine
colum'ba
columba'rium
col'umbary
Colum'bian
colum'bic
columbif'erous
col'umbin
col'umbine
colum'bite
colum'bium
columel'la
col'umn
colum'nar
columna'tion
col'umned
columnia'tion
colure'
col'za
co'ma
co'-mate
co'matose
comb
com'bat
com'batable
com'batant
com'bated

com'bater
com'bating
com'bative
com'bativeness
combed
comb'er
combin'able
combina'tion
combine'
combined'
combi'ner
comb'ing
combin'ing
comb'less
combust'
combustibil'ity
combus'tible
combus'tibleness
combus'tion
combus'tive
come
come-at'-able
come'dian
comédienne'
comediet'ta
come'-down
com'edy
come'lier
come'liest
come'lily
come'liness
come'ly
come-out'er
com'er
comes'tible
com'et
cometa'rium
com'etary
comet'ic
cometog'raphy
com'fit
com'fiture
com'fort
com'fortable
com'fortableness
com'forted
com'forter
com'forting
com'fortless
com'frey
com'ic
com'ical
comical'ity
com'ically
com'icalness
*com'*ing
comi'tia
com'ity
com'ma
command'
commandant'
command'atory
command'ed
commandeer'
command'er
command'ery
command'ing
command'ingly
command'ment
comman'do
commat'ic
com'matism
commeas'urable
commem'orable
commem'orate
commem'orated
commem'orating
commemora'tion
commem'orative
commem'orator
commem'oratory
commence'
commenced'
commence'ment
commenc'ing
commend'
commend'able
commend'ably
commen'dam
commenda'tion
com'mendator
commend'atory
commend'ed
commend'ing
commen'sal
commensurabil'ity
commen'surable
commen'surate
commensura'tion
com'ment
com'mentary
com'mentate
commenta'tion
com'mentator
com'mented
com'menter
com'menting
commenti'tious
com'merce
commer'cial
*commer'cia*lism
commer'cialize
commer'cially
commina'tion
commin'atory
commin'gle
commin'gled
commin'gling
com'minute
comminu'tion
commis'erable
commis'erate
commis'erated
commis'erating
commisera'tion
commis'erative
commis'erator
commissa'rial
commissa'riat
com'missary
com'missary-*gen'eral*
commis'sion
commissionaire'
commis'sioned
commis'sioner
commis'sionership
commis'sioning
com'missure
commit'
commit'ment
commit'tal
commit'ted
commit'tee
committee'
commit'ter
commit'ting
commit'tor
commix'
commixed'
commix'ing
commix'tion
commix'ture
com'modate
commode'
commo'dious
commo'diously
commo'diousness
commod'ity
com'modore
com'mon
com'monable
com'monage
com'monalty
com'mon coun'cil
com'moner
com'monest
com'mon law
com'monly
com'monness
com'monplace
com'monplace-book
Com'mon Pleas
com'mons
com'mon sense
com'monweal
com'monwealth
com'morancy
commo'tion
com'munal
com'munalize
com'mune / commune'
communed'
communicabil'ity
commun'icable
commun'icant
commun'icate
commun'icated
commun'icating
communica'tion
commun'icative
commun'icator
commun'icatory
commun'ing
commun'ion
commun'ionist
com'munism
com'munist
communis'tic
commu'nity
com'munize
commutabil'ity
commu'table
commuta'tion
commu'tative

commute'
commu'ted
commu'ter
commu'ting
commu'tual
compact
compact'ed
compact'edly
compact'ing
compac'tion
compact'ly
compact'ness
compa'ges
compag'inate
compag'ination
compan'ion
compan'ionable
compan'ionless
compan'ionship
com'pany
com'parable
compar'ative
compar'atively
compare'
compared'
compar'er
compar'ing
compar'ison
compart'
compart'ed
compart'ing
compart'ment
com'pass
com'passable
com'pass-box
com'passed
com'passes
com'passing
compas'sion
compas'sionate, *a*
compas'sionate, *v*
compas'sionated
compas'sionately
compas'sionate-
ness
compas'sionating
compatibil'ity
compat'ible
compat'ibleness
compat'ibly
compa'triot
compa'triotism
compear', com-
compel' [peer'
compel'lable
compella'tion
compelled'
compel'ler
compel'ling
com'pend
compen'dious
compen'diously
compen'dious-
ness
compen'dium
com'pensate
com'pensated
com'pensating
compensa'tion
compen'sative

compen'satory
compete'
compet'ed
com'petence
com'petency
com'petent
com'petently
compet'ing
competi'tion
compet'itive
compet'itor
compila'tion
compile', com-
compi'ler [piled'
compi'ling
compla'cence
compla'cency
compla'cent
compla'cently
complain'
complain'able
complain'ant
complained'
complain'er
complain'ing
complaint'
complais'ance
complais'ant
complais'antly
com'plement
complemen'tal
complemen'tary
complete'
comple'ted
complete'ly
complete'ness
complet'ing
comple'tion
comple'tive
comple'tory
com'plex
complex'ion
complex'ional
complex'ionary
complex'ioned
complex'ity
com'plexness
complex'us
compli'able
compli'ance
compli'ant
compli'antly
com'plicacy
com'plicate
com'plicated
com'plicating
complica'tion
complic'ity
complied'
compli'er
com'pliment
compliment'al
compliment'ary
com'plimenter
{ com'plin
{ com'pline
com'plot, comp-
complot'ted [lot'
complot'ter
complot'ting

complot'tingly
Compluten'sian
comply'
comply'ing
com'po
compone'
compo'nent
comport'
comport'ed
comport'ing
compose'
composed'
compo'sedly
compo'sedness
compo'ser
compo'sing
com'posite
composi'tion
compos'itive
compos'itor
com'post
compo'sure
com'pote
compota'tion
compound
compound'able
compound'ed
compound'er
compound'ing
compreca'tion
comprehend'
comprehend'ed
comprehend'er
comprehend'ing
comprehensibil'ity
comprehen'sible
comprehen'sibly
comprehen'sion
comprehen'sive
comprehen'sively
comprehen'sive-
ness
compress
compressed'
compressibil'ity
compress'ible
compress'ible-
ness
compress'ing
compres'sion
compress'ive
compress'or
compress'ure
compris'al
comprise'
comprised'
compris'ing
com'promise
com'promised
com'promiser
com'promising
compromit'
compromit'ted
compromit'ting
compt'ograph
comptoir'
comptom'eter
comptrol'ler
compul'satory
compul'sion

compul'sive
compul'sively
compul'siveness
compul'sorily
compul'sory
compunc'tion
compunc'tious
compurga'tion
com'purgator
compu'table
computa'tion
compute'
compu'ted
compu'ter
compu'ting
compu'tist
com'rade
Com'tist
con
cona'tus
conax'ial
concam'erate
concat'enate
concat'enated
concat'enating
concatena'tion
con'cave
con'caved
con'cavely
con'caveness
concav'ity
conceal'
conceal'able
concealed'
conceal'er
conceal'ing
conceal'ment
concede'
conce'ded
conce'ding
conceit'
conceit'ed
conceit'edly
conceit'edness
conceiv'able
conceiv'ableness
conceive'
conceived'
conceiv'er
conceiv'ing
concent'
concen'ter
concen'tre
con'centrate
con'centrated
con'centrating
concentra'tion
concen'trative
concen'trative-ness
con'centrator
concen'tric
concen'trical
concentric'ity
concen'tual
con'cept
concep'tacle
concep'tion
concep'tive
concern'

concerned'
concern'edly
concern'ing
concern'ment
concert
concertan'te
concert'ed
concerti'na
concert'ing
concer'to
con'cert-pitch
conces'sion
conces'sionary
conces'sionist
conces'sive
conces'sory
conch
con'cha
Conchif'era
conchif'erous
con'chite
con'choid
conchoi'dal
concholog'ical
conchol'ogist
conchol'ogy
conchom'eter
concierge'
concil'iate
concil'iated
concil'iating
concilia'tion
concil'iator
concil'iatory
concin'nity
concise'
concise'ly
concise'ness
conci'sion
con'clave
conclude'
conclu'ded
conclud'er
conclu'ding
conclu'sion
conclu'sive
conclu'sively
conclu'siveness
conclu'sory
concoct'
concoct'ed
concoct'er
concoct'ing
concoc'tion
concoc'tive
concom'itance
concom'itant
con'cord
concord'ance
concord'ant
concord'antly
concord'at
concord'ist
con'course
concres'cence
concres'cible
concrete
concre'ted
con'cretely

con'creteness
concre'ter
concre'ting
concre'tion
concre'tional
concre'tionary
concre'tive
concre'tor
concu'binage
concu'binary
con'cubine
concu'piscence
concu'piscent
concur'
concurred'
concur'rence
concur'rent
concur'rently
concur'ring
concus'sion
concus'sive
condemn'
condemn'able
condemna'tion
condem'natory
condemned'
condemn'er
condemn'ing
condensabil'ity
condens'able
condens'ate
conden'sated
conden'sating
condensa'tion
condens'ative
condense'
condensed'
condens'er
condens'ing
condescend'
condescend'ed
condescend'ing
condescend'ingly
condescen'sion
condign'
condign'ly
condign'ness
con'diment
condi'tion
condi'tional
condi'tionally
condi'tioned
condo'latory
condole'
condoled'
condole'ment
condo'lence
condo'ler
condo'ling
condona'tion
condone'
condoned'
condon'ing
con'dor
condottie're
conduce'
conduced'
conducibil'ity
condu'cible
condu'cing

condu'cive
conduct
conduct'ed
conductibil'ity
conduct'ible
conduct'ing
conduc'tion
conduct'ive
conductiv'ity
conduct'or
conduct'ress
con'duit
condu'plicate
con'dyle
con'dyloid
cone
cones
co'ney
confab'ulate
confab'ulated
confab'ulating
confabula'tion
confect
confect'ed
confec'tion
confec'tionary
confec'tioner
confec'tionery
confec'tory
confed'eracy
confed'erate, *v.*
confed'erate, *n.a.*
confed'erated
confed'erater
confed'erating
confedera'tion
confed'erative
confer'
con'ference
confer'rable
conferred'
confer'rer
confer'ring
confess'
confess'ant
confessed'
confes'sedly
confess'ing
confes'sion
confes'sional
confes'sionary
confess'or
confet'ti
confet'to
confidant' / confidante'
confide'
confi'ded
con'fidence
con'fident
confiden'tial
con'fidently
confi'der
confi'ding
config'urate
config'urating
configura'tion
config'ure
config'ured
confi'nable

confine'
confined'
confine'ment
confi'ner
confi'ning
confirm'
confirm'able
confirma'tion
confirm'ative
confirm'atively
confirm'atory
confirmed'
confirm'edly
confirmee'
confirm'er
confirm'ing
confis'cable
con'fiscate
con'fiscated
con'fiscating
confisca'tion
con'fiscator
confis'catory
con'fitent
conflagra'tion
conflict
conflict'ed
conflict'ing
conflict'ive
con'fluence
con'fluent
con'flux
conform'
conformabil'ity
conform'able
conform'ably
conforma'tion
conformed'
conform'ing
conform'ist
conform'ity
confound'
confound'ed
confound'edness
confound'er
confound'ing
confrater'nity
confrère'
confront'
confront'ed
confront'er
confront'ing
Confu'cian
confus'able
confuse'
confused'
confu'sedly
confu'sedness
confu'sing
confu'sion
confu'sional
confu'table
confuta'tion
confu'tative
confute'
confu'ted
confu'ter
confu'ting
congé
congeal'

congeal'able
congealed'
congeal'ing
congeal'ment
con'gee
congela'tion
con'gener
congener'ic
conge'nial
congenial'ity
conge'nialness
congen'ital
con'ger
con'ger-eel'
conge'ries
congest'
congest'ed
congest'ible
conges'tion
congest'ive
con'globate
congloba'tion
conglob'ulate
conglom'erate, *n.a*
conglom'erate, *v.*
conglom'erated
conglom'erating
conglomera'tion
conglu'tinant
conglu'tinate
conglu'tinated
conglu'tinating
conglutina'tion
conglu'tinative
Con'go
con'gou
congrat'ulant
congrat'ulate
congrat'ulated
congrat'ulating
congratula'tion
congrat'ulator
congrat'ulatory
con'gregate
con'gregated
con'gregating
congrega'tion
congrega'tional
Congrega'tionalism
Congrega'tionalist
con'gress
congres'sional
congres'sionist
con'greve
con'gruence
con'gruent
congru'ity
con'gruous
con'gruously
con'gruousness
con'ic
con'ical
con'ically
con'ic sec'tion
co'nifer
Conif'erae
conif'erous
co'niform

co'nite
conjec'turable
conjec'tural
conjec'ture
conjec'tured
conjec'turer
conjec'turing
conjoin'
conjoined'
conjoin'ing
conjoint'
conjoint'ly
conjoint'ness
con'jugal
conjugal'ity
con'jugate
con'jugated
con'jugating
conjuga'tion
conjuga'tional
conju'gial
conjunct'
conjunc'tion
conjunc'tional
conjuncti'va
conjunc'tive
conjunc'tively
conjunc'ture
conjura'tion
conjure'
con'jure
conjured'
con'jured
conjur'er
con'jurer
conjur'ing
con'juring
conjur'or
connas'cent
con'nate
connat'ural
connat'uralize
connect'
connect'ed
connect'edly
connect'ing
connec'tion
connect'ive
connect'ively
connect'or
conned
con'ner
connex'ion
con'ning
con'ning-tower
conni'vance
connive'
connived'
conni'ver
conni'ving
connoisseur'
connota'tion
connote'
connu'bial
connubial'ity
connumera'tion
co'noid
conoi'dal
conoi'dic
co'noscope
con'quer
con'querable
con'quered
con'quering
con'queror
con'quest
consanguin'eal
consanguin'eous
consanguin'ity
con'science
conscien'tious
conscien'tiously
conscien'tiousness
con'scionable
con'scious
con'sciously
con'sciousness
conscript
conscrip'tion
con'secrate
con'secrated
con'secrating
consecra'tion
con'secrator
con'secratory
consec'tary
consecu'tion
consec'utive
consec'utively
consec'utiveness
consen'sual
consen'sus
consent'
consenta'neous
consent'ed
consent'er
consen'tient
consent'ing
con'sequence
con'sequent
consequen'tial
consequen'tially
con'sequently
conserv'able
conserv'ancy
conserva'tion
conserv'atism
conserv'ative
conserv'atively
conserv'atoire
con'servator
conserv'atory
conserve'
conserved'
conserv'er
conserv'ing
consid'er
consid'erable
consid'erably
consid'erate
consid'erately
consid'erateness
considera'tion
consid'ered
consid'erer
consid'ering
consign'
consigned'
consignee'
consign'er
consign'ing
consign'ment
consignor'
consist'
consist'ed
consist'ence
consist'ency
consist'ent
consist'ently
consist'ing
consisto'rial
consis'tory
conso'ciate
conso'ciated
conso'ciating
consocia'tion
consol'
consol'able
consola'tion
consol'atory
console'
consoled'
conso'ler
consol'idate
consol'idated
consol'idating
consolida'tion
consol'idator
consol'idatory
consol'ing
consols'
consommé'
con'sonance
con'sonancy
con'sonant
consonan'tal
con'sonous
con'sort
consort'
consort'ed
consort'ing
conspec'tus
conspic'uous
conspic'uously
conspic'uousness
conspir'acy
conspira'tion
conspir'ator
conspire'
conspired'
conspir'er
conspir'ing
con'stable
constab'ulary
con'stancy
con'stant
con'stantly
con'stat
con'stellate
constella'tion
consterna'tion
con'stipate
con'stipated
con'stipating
constipa'tion
constit'uency
constit'uent
con'stitute
con'stituted
con'stituter

con'stituting
constitu'tion
constitu'tional
constitu'tionalist
constitutional'-ity
constitu'tionally
constitu'tioned
constitu'tionist
con'stitutive
con'stitutively
con'stitutor
constrain'
constrain'able
constrained'
constrain'er
constrain'ing
constraint'
constrict'
constrict'ed
constrict'ing
constric'tion
constrict'ive
constrict'or
constringe'
constringed'
constrin'gent
constrin'ging
construct'
construct'ed
construct'er
construc'tion
construc'tional
construc'tionist
construct'ive
construct'ively
construct'iveness
construct'or
con'strue
con'strued
con'struer
con'struing
consubstan'tial
consubstan'tial-ist
consubstantial'ity
consubstan'tiate
consubstantia'-tion
con'suetude
consuetu'dinal
consuetu'dinary
con'sul
con'sulage
con'sular
con'sulate
con'sulship
consult'
consult'ant
consulta'tion
consul'tative
consul'tatory
consult'ed
consult'er
consult'ing
consu'mable
consume'
consumed'
consu'mer
consu'ming

consum'mate
con'summate
con'summated
consum'mately
con'summating
consumma'tion
consum'mative
con'summator
consump'tion
consump'tive
consump'tively
consump'tive-ness
con'tact
conta'gion
conta'gionist
conta'gious
conta'giously
conta'giousness
contain'
contain'able
contain'ant
contained'
contain'er
contain'ing
contam'inable
contam'inate
contam'inated
contam'inating
contamina'tion
contam'inative
contan'go
contemn'
contemned'
contem'ner
contemn'ing
con'template
con'templated
con'templating
contempla'tion
contem'plative
contem'platively
contem'plative-ness
con'templator
contempora'-neous
contempora'-neousness
contem'porary
contempt'
contempt'ible
contempt'ibly
contemp'tuous
contemp'tuously
contemp'tuous-ness
contend'
contend'ed
contend'er
contend'ing
content
content'ed
content'edly
content'edness
content'ing
conten'tion
conten'tious
conten'tiously
conten'tiousness

content'ment
contents'
conter'minable
conter'minous
contest
contest'able
contest'ant
contesta'tion
contest'ed
contest'ing
con'text
context'ural
contex'ture
contigu'ity
contig'uous
contig'uously
con'tinence
con'tinency
con'tinent
continen'tal
con'tinently
contin'gence
contin'gency
contin'gent
contin'gently
contin'uable
contin'ual
contin'ually
contin'uance
contin'uant
continua'tion
contin'uative
contin'uator
contin'ue
contin'ued
contin'uer
contin'uing
continu'ity
contin'uous
contin'uously
contort'
contort'ed
contort'ing
contor'tion
con'tour
con'tra
con'traband
contract
contract'able
contract'ed
contract'edly
contract'edness
contractibil'ity
contract'ible
contract'ile
contractil'ity
contract'ing
contrac'tion
contract'or
contract'ual
contrac'ture
con'tra-dance
contradict'
contradict'ed
contradict'ing
contradic'tion
contradic'tious
contradict'ive
contradict'or
contradict'ory

contradistinct'
contradistinc'-tion
contradistin'-guish
contradistin'-guished
contradistin'-guishing
contral'to
con'traries
contrari'ety
con'trarily
con'trariness
contra'rious
con'trariwise
con'trary
contrast
contrast'ed
contrast'ing
contravalla'tion
contravene'
contravened'
contrave'ner
contrave'ning
contraven'tion
contraver'sion
con'tretemps
contrib'utable
contrib'ute
contrib'uted
contrib'uting
contribu'tion
contrib'utive
contrib'utor
contrib'utory
con'trite
con'tritely
contri'tion
contri'vable
contri'vance
contrive'
contrived'
contri'ver
contri'ving
control'
control'lable
controlled'
control'ler
control'lership
control'ling
control'ment
controver'sial
controver'sialist
con'troversy
controvert'
controvert'ed
controvert'ible
controvert'ing
controvert'ist
contuma'cious
contuma'ciously
contuma'cious-ness
con'tumacy
contume'lious
con'tumely
contuse'
contused'

contu'sing
contu'sion
conun'drum
convalesce'
convalesced'
convales'cence
convales'cency
convales'cent
convales'cing
convec'tion
convec'tive
conven'able
convene'
convened'
conve'ner
conve'nience
conve'niency
conve'nient
conve'niently
con'vent
conven'ticle
conven'ticler
conven'tion
conven'tional
conven'tionalism
conven'tionalist
conventional'ity
conven'tionary
conven'tionist
conven'tual
converge'
converged'
conver'gence
conver'gency
conver'gent
conver'ging
convers'able
convers'ableness
con'versance
con'versant
conversa'tion
conversa'tional
conversa'tionist
convers'ative
conversazio'ne
converse
conversed'
con'versely
convers'er
convers'ible
convers'ing
conver'sion
convers'ive
convert
convert'ed
convert'er
convertibil'ity
convert'ible
con'vex
con'vexed
convex'ity
con'vexly
convey'
convey'able
convey'ance
convey'ancer
convey'ancing
conveyed'
convey'er-or
convey'ing

convict
convict'ed
convict'ing
convic'tion
convict'ive
convince'
convinced'
convince'ment
convin'cer
convin'cible
convin'cing
convin'cingly
conviv'ial
conviv'ialist
convivial'ity
con'vocate
con'vocated
con'vocating
convoca'tion
convoca'tional
convoke'
convoked'
convo'king
con'volute
con'voluted
convolu'tion
convolve'
convolved'
convolv'ing
convol'vulus
convoy
convoyed'
convoy'ing
convulse'
convulsed'
convuls'ing
convul'sion
convul'sionary
convuls'ive
convuls'ively
co'ny
coo, cooed
coo'ing
cook
cooked
cook'ery
cook'ing
cook'y
cool
cooled
cool'er
cool'est
cool'-headed
coo'lie
cool'ing
cool'ish
cool'ly
cool'ness
cool'y
coom
coon
coop
cooped
coop'er
coop'erage
co-op'erant
co-op'erate
co-op'erated
co-op'erating
co-opera'tion

co-op'erative
co-op'erator
coop'ering
coop'ery
co-opt'
co-op'tate
co-op'tion
co-or'dinance
co-or'dinate, *v.*
co-or'dinate, *n.a.*
co-or'dinately
co-or'dinateness
co-ordina'tion
coot
cop
copai'ba
copai'vic
co'pal
copar'cenary
copart'ner
copart'nership
copart'nery
copas'torate
co-pa'triot
cope
co'peck
coped
Coper'nican
cope'-stone
cop'iable
cop'ied
cop'ier
co'ping
co'pious
co'piously
co'piousness
copi'vi
cop'per
cop'peras
cop'pered
cop'per-faced
cop'perhead
cop'pering
cop'perish
cop'perize
cop'perplate
cop'persmith
cop'per-works
cop'pery
cop'pice
copres'ence
cop'rolite
cop'rolith
coprolit'ic
coproph'agous
copse
cops'y
Copt
Cop'tic
cop'ula
cop'ulate
cop'ulated
cop'ulating
copula'tion
cop'ulative
cop'ulatively
cop'y
cop'y-book
cop'ygraph
cop'yhold

cop'ying
cop'ying-press
cop'yist
cop'yright
coquet'
co'quetry
coquette'
coquet'ted
coquet'ting
coquet'tish
coquet'tishly
cor'acle
cor'acoid
cor'al
coralla'ceous
corallif'erous
coral'liform
cor'alline
cor'allite
coralloid'al
cor'ban
cor'beil *or* cor'bel
cord
cord'age
cor'date
cord'ed
cordelier'
cordelle'
cor'dial
cordial'ity
cor'dially
cor'diform
cordille'ra
cord'ing
cor'dite
cor'don
cor'doned
cor'dovan
cor'duroy
cord'wainer
core
cored
co-re'gent
co-relig'ionist
coreop'sis
co-respond'ent
corf
coria'ceous
corian'der
Corin'thian
cork
cork'age
corked
cork'ing
cork'screw
cork'-tree
cork'y
cor'morant
corn
corn'bread
corn'-chandler
corn'-cockle
corn'-crake
cor'nea

corned
cor'nel
corne'lian
cor'neous
cor'ner
cor'nered
cor'nering
cor'ner-stone
cor'net
cor'net-à-pis'ton
cor'netcy
corn'field
cor'nice
cor'nicle
cornic'ulate
cor'niform
corn'ing
Cor'nish
cor'nist
corn'-land
corn'-laws
cor'no
corno'pean
corn'-plaster
cornuco'pia
cornute'
cornu'ted
corn'y
cor'ody
corol'la
corolla'ceous
corol'lary
cor'ollate
cor'ollated
coro'na
cor'onach
coro'nal
cor'onary
cor'onated
corona'tion
cor'oner
cor'onet
cor'oneted
coro'niform
cor'onoid
coro'nule
cor'poral
corporal'ity
cor'porally
cor'poralship
cor'porate
cor'porateness
corpora'tion
cor'porative
cor'porator
corpo'real
corporeal'ity
corpo'really
corpo'realness
corpore'ity
cor'posant
corps
corpse
cor'pulence
cor'pulency
cor'pulent
cor'pus
cor'puscle
corpus'cular
corpuscula'rian

corral′
corral′ling
correct′
correct′ed
correct′ible
correct′ing
correc′tion
correc′tional
correct′ive
correct′ly
correct′ness
correct′or
cor′relate
cor′related
correla′tion
correl′ative
correl′atively
correl′ativeness
correspond′
correspond′ed
correspond′ence
correspond′ent
correspond′ing
cor′ridor
corrigen′da
corrigen′dum
corrigibil′ity
cor′rigible
cor′rigibleness
corrob′orant
corrob′orate
corrob′orated
corrob′orating
corrobora′tion
corrob′orative
corrob′oratory
corroboree′
corrode′
corro′ded
corro′dent
corro′dible
corro′ding
cor′rody
corro′sible
corro′sibleness
corro′sion
corro′sive
corro′sively
corro′siveness
cor′rugant
cor′rugate
cor′rugated
cor′rugating
corruga′tion
cor′rugator
corrupt′
corrupt′ed
corrupt′er
corruptibil′ity
corrupt′ible
corrupt′ibleness
corrupt′ibly
corrupt′ing
corrup′tion
corrupt′ive
corrupt′ly
corrupt′ness
cor′sage
cor′sair
corse

corse′let
cor′set
Cor′sican
cors′ned
cortège′
Cor′tes
cor′tex
cor′tical
cor′ticate
cor′ticated
corticif′erous
corun′dum
corus′cant
cor′uscate
cor′uscated
cor′uscating
corusca′tion
corvée′
corvette′
cor′vine
cor′vus
cor′ybant
coryban′tic
coryphae′us
coryphée′
cor′yphene
coryphe′us
cory′za
cose′cant
cosh′er
co′sily
co′sine
cosmet′ic
cos′mic
cos′mical
cos′mically
cosmog′onal
cosmog′onist
cosmog′ony
cosmog′rapher
cosmograph′ic
cosmog′raphy
cos′molabe
cosmol′atry
cosmolog′ical
cosmol′ogist
cosmol′ogy
cosmoplas′tic
cosmopol′itan
cosmopol′itan-ism
cosmop′olite
cosmora′ma
cosmoram′ic
cos′mos
Cos′sack
cos′set
cost
cost′al
cos′tard
cos′tate
cos′tated
cost′-book
cos′termonger

cos′tive
cos′tively
cos′tiveness
cost′liness
cost′ly
cost′mary
cos′tume
costu′mer
costu′mier
co′sy
cot
cotan′gent
cote
cotempora′neous
cotem′porary
co′terie
co-ter′minous
cothurn′ate
cothur′nus
cotil′lion
co-trustee′
Cots′wold
cot′ta
cot′tage
cot′tager
cot′ter
cot′tier
cot′ton
cot′ton-gin
cot′tony
cotyle′don
cotyle′donous
cotyl′iform
cot′yloid
couch
couch′ant
couché′
couched
couch′er
couch′-grass
couch′ing
cou′gar
cough
coughed
cough′er
cough′ing
could
coulisse′
coul′ter
coun′cil
coun′cil-board
coun′cillor / coun′cilor
coun′sel
coun′selled / coun′seled
coun′selling / coun′seling
coun′sellor / coun′selor
coun′sellorship / coun′selorship
count
count′able
count′ed
coun′tenance
coun′tenanced
coun′tenancer
coun′tenancing
count′er

counteract'
counteract'ed
counteract'ing
counterac'tion
counteract'ive
counteract'ively
counter-attrac'tion
counter*bal'ance*
counter*bal'ance*d
counter*bal'anc*ing
count'erbrace
count'ercharge
count'ercharm
count'ercheck
count'erclaim
count'erfeit
count'erfeited
count'erfeiter
count'erfeiting
count'erfoil
count'er*guard*
count'er-ir'ritant
count'er-jumper
countermand'
countermand'ed
countermand'ing
count'ermarch
count'ermark
count'ermine
count'er-motion
count'ermure
count'erpane
count'erpart
count'er-plea
count'erplot
count'erplot'ted
count'erplot'ting
count'erpoint
count'erpoise
count'erpoised'
count'erpois'ing
count'erscarp
count'ersign
count'ersigned
count'ersigning
count'ersink
count'er-stroke
count'er-tenor
countervail'
countervailed'
countervail'ing
countervalla'tion
count'erview
count'erweigh
count'erweighed
count'er-weighing
count'erweight
count'erwork
count'ess
count'ing
count'ing-house
count'less
count'rified
count'ry

count'ry-dance
count'ryman
count'ry-seat
count'y
count'y-court
coup
coup de main'
coup d'état'
coupé'
coupee'
coup'er
coup'le
coup'led
coup'ler
coup'let
coup'ling
cou'pon
cour'age
coura'geous
coura'geously
coura'geousness
cour'ant
cour'bash
cou'rier
course
coursed
cours'er
cours'ing
court
court'-chaplain
court'ed
court'eous
court'eously
court'eousness
court'er
court'esan
court'esy (civility)
courte'sy (a bending)
courte'sying
court'-*hand*
court'-house
court'ier
court'-lands
court'-leet
court'like
court'liness
court'ling
court'ly
court-mar'tial
court'-plaster
court'ship
court'-yard
cous'in
cous'in ger'man
couteau'
couvade'
cove
cov'enant
cov'enanted
covenantee'
cov'enanter
cov'enantor
cov'enanting
cov'er
cov'ered
cov'erer
cov'ering
cov'erlet

cov'ert
cov'ertly
cov'erture
cov'et
cov'etable
cov'eted
cov'eter
cov'eting
cov'etous
cov'etously
cov'etousness
cov'ey
cov'in, co'ving
cov'inous
cow
cow'an
cow'ard
cow'ardice
cow'ardliness
cow'ardly
cow'boy
cow'catcher
cowed
cow'er
cow'ered
cow'ering
cow'hage
cow'herd
cow'-hide
cowl
cowled
co-work'er
cow'-pox
cow'rie *or* cow'ry
cow'slip
cox'comb
coxcomb'ical
coxcom'ical
cox'combry
coxcomical'ity
cox'swain
coy
coy'ish
coy'ly
coy'ness
coyo'te
coz'en
coz'enage
coz'ened
coz'ener
coz'ening
co'zily
co'zy
crab
crab'-apple
crab'bed
crab'bedly
crab'bedness
crab'bing
crab'by
crab'-tree
crab'-yaws
crack
crack'-brained
cracked
crack'er
crack'ing
crack'le
crack'led

crack'ling
crack'nel
cracks'man
cra'dle
cra'dled
cra'dling
craft
craft'ily
craft'iness
crafts'man
craft'y
crag
crag'ged
crag'giness
crag'gy
crake
cram
cram'bo
crammed
cram'mer
cram'ming
cramp
cramped
cramp'-fish
cramp'ing
cramp'-iron
cram'pon
crampoon'
cra'nage
cran'berry
crane
cranes'bill
cra'nial
craniog'nomy
craniolog'ical
craniol'ogist
craniol'ogy
craniom'eter
craniomet'rical
craniom'etry
cranios'copy
cra'nium
crank
crank'le
crank'led
crank'ling
crank'y
cran'nied
cran'ny
crape
crap'ulence
crap'ulent
crap'ulous
crash
crashed
crash'ing
crass
crass'itude
cratch
cratch'-cradle
cratch'es
crate
cra'ter
crater'iform
craunch
craunched
cravat'
crave
craved

cra'ven
cra'ver
cra'ving
cra'vingly
cra'vingness
craw
craw'fish
crawl
crawled
crawl'er
crawl'ing
cray'fish
cray'on
craze
crazed
cra'zily
cra'ziness
cra'zing
cra'zy
creak
creaked
creak'ing
cream
cream'-cheese'
creamed
cream'ery
cream'ing
cream'y
crease
creased
creas'er
creas'ing
crea'table
create'
crea'ted
crea'ting
crea'tion
crea'tive
crea'tiveness
crea'tor
crea'tural
crea'ture
crea'turely
crèche
cre'dence
creden'da
creden'dum
cre'dent
creden'tial
credibil'ity
cred'ible
cred'ibleness
cred'ibly
cred'it
cred'itable
cred'itably
cred'ited
cred'iting
cred'itor
credu'lity
cred'ulous
cred'ulously
cred'ulousness
creed
creek
creek'y
creel
creep
creep'er
creep'ing

creep'ingly
cremate'
crema'tion
cremato'rium
Cremo'na
cre'nate
cre'nated
cren'ature
{ cren'ellate
{ cren'elate
{ cren'ellated
{ cren'elated
{ crenella'tion
{ crenela'tion
crenelle'
{ cren'elled
{ cren'eled
cren'ulate
cre'ole
creo'lian
cre'osote
cre'pance
crep'itant
crep'itate
crep'itated
crep'itating
crepita'tion
crep'on
crept
crepus'cular
crepus'cule
crepus'culous
crescen'do
cres'cent
cress
cres'set
crest
crest'ed
crest'fallen
creta'ceous
Cre'tan
cre'tin
cre'tinism
cretonne'
crevasse'
crev'ice
crew
crew'el
crib
crib'bage
cribbed
crib'bing
crib'ble
crib'bled
crib'riform
crick
crick'et
crick'eter
cri'coid
cried
crier
crime
crim'inal
criminal'ity
crim'inally
crim'inate
crim'inated
crim'inating
crimina'tion

crim'inative
crim'inatory
criminol'ogy
crimp
crimped
crimp'ing
crimp'ing-iron
crim'ple
crim'pled
crim'pling
crim'son
crim'soned
crim'soning
cri'nal
cri'nate
cri'natory
cringe
cringed
cringe'ling
crin'ger
crin'ging
crin'gingly
crin'gle
crinicul'tural
crinig'erous
cri'nite
crin'kle
crin'kled
crin'oid
crinoi'dal
crinoi'dean
crin'oline
crip'ple
crip'pled
crip'pling
cri'sis
crisp
cris'pated
crisped
crisp'er
Cris'pin
crisp'ly
crisp'ness
crisp'y
criss'-cross
cris'tate
cris'tated
crite'ria
crite'rion
crit'ic
crit'ical
crit'ically
crit'icalness
crit'icism
crit'icize
crit'icized
crit'icizer
crit'icizing
critique'
criz'zle
croak
croaked
croak'er
croak'ing
Cro'at
Croa'tian
croche
cro'chet

cro'cheted
cro'cheting
crock
crock'ery
crock'et
croc'odile
crocodil'ian
crocodil'ity
cro'cus
croft
croft'er
croft'ing
crois'ant
crome
crom'lech
cromor'ne
crone
cro'ny
crook
crooked
crook'ed
crook'edly
crook'edness
crook'ing
crop
cropped
crop'per
crop'ping
cro'quet
crore
cro'sier (*or* -zier)
cro'siered
cros'let
cross
cross'-action
cross'-armed
cross'-bar
cross'-barred
cross'-bearer
cross'bill
cross'bow
cross'-breed
cross'-cut
crossed
cross-examina'-tion
cross-exam'ine
*cross-exam'in*ing
cross'-eyed
cross'-grained
cross'-head
cross'ing
cross'-legged
cross'let
cross'ly
cross'ness
cross'-purpose
cross'-question
cross'-road
cross'tree
cross'ways
cross'wise
crotch
crotched
crotch'et
crotch'eted
crotch'ety
cro'ton

croton'ic
cro'ton-oil
crouch
crouched
crouch'ing
croup
croupade'
crou'pier
crout
crow
crow'bar
crowd
crowd'ed
crowd'er
crowd'ing
crowd'y
crowed
crow'foot
crow'ing
crown
crowned
crown'er
crown'-glass
crown'ing
crown'-law
crown'-lawyer
crown'less
crown'-post
crown'prince
crown'-wheel
crow's'-foot
crow's'-nest
cro'zier (*or* -sier)
cro'ziered
cru'cial
cru'ciate
cru'cible
crucif'erous
cru'cified
cru'cifier
cru'cifix
crucifix'ion
cru'ciform
cru'cify
cru'cifying
crude
crude'ly
crude'ness
cru'dity
cru'el
cru'elly
cru'elty
cru'et
cruise
cruised
cruis'er
cruis'ing
crumb
crumb'-cloth
crumb'ing
crum'ble
crum'bled
crum'bling
crum'my
crump
crum'pet
crum'ple
crum'pled
crum'pling
crunch

crup'per
cru'ral
crusade'
crusa'der
crusa'ding
cruse
crush
crushed
crush'er
crush'ing
crust
Crusta'cea
crusta'cean
crustaceol'ogy
crusta'ceous
crusta'ceousness
crustal'ogy
crusta'ted
crusta'tion
crust'ed
crust'ily
crust'iness
crust'ing
crust'y
crutch
crutched
crutch'ing
crux
cry
cry'ing
cryoph'orus
crypt
crypt'ic
crypt'ical
cryp'togam
Cryptoga'mia
cryptogam'ic
cryptog'amist
cryptog'amous
cryptog'amy
cryp'togram
cryp'tograph
cryptog'rapher
cryptograph'ic
cryptograph'ical
cryptog'raphy
crys'tal
crys'talline
crys'tallite
crys'tallizable
crystalliza'tion
crys'tallize
crys'tallized
crys'tallizing
crystallog'rapher
crystallograph'ic
crystallog'raphy
crys'talloid
crystal'ology
crys'tallotype
cte'noid
cub
Cu'ban
cuba'tion
cu'bature
cubbed
cub'bing
cube
cu'beb

cu'bic
cu'bicle
cu'biform
cu'bit
cu'bital
cu'bited
cu'boid
cuboi'dal
cuck'ing-stool
cuck'old
cuck'oo
cu'cullate
cu'cullated
cu'cumber
cucur'bit
cud
cud'bear
cud'dle
cud'dled
cud'dling
cud'dy
cudg'el
{ cudg'eled
{ cudg'elled
cudg'eller
cudg'elling
cud'weed
cue
cuff
cuffed
cuff'ing
cuirass'
cuirassier'
cuish
cuisine'
cuisse
Cul'dee
cul-de-sac'
culic'iform
cu'linary
cull
culled
cul'lender
cull'er
cull'ing
cul'lion
cul'lis
cul'ly
culm
culmif'erous
cul'minate
cul'minated
cul'minating
culmina'tion
culpabil'ity
cul'pable
cul'pableness
cul'pably
cul'prit
cul'tivable
cul'tivatable
cul'tivate
cul'tivated
cul'tivating
cultiva'tion
cul'tivator
cul'trate
cul'trated
cul'triform
cul'tural

cul'ture
cul'tured
cul'tus
cul'ver
cul'verin
cul'vert
cum'bent
cum'ber
cum'bered
cum'berer
cum'bering
cum'bersome
cum'bersomely
cum'bersome-
ness
Cum'brian
cum'brous
cum'brously
cum'brousness
cum'in, cum'min
cum'merbund
cu'mulate
cu'mulated
cu'mulating
cumula'tion
cu'mulative
cu'mulose
cumulo-cirro-
stra'tus
cumulo-stra'tus
cu'mulus
cu'neal
cu'neate
cu'neated
cu'neiform
cun'ning
cun'ningly
cun'ningness
cup
cup'bearer
cup'board
cu'pel
cupella'tion
cup'ful
Cu'pid
cupid'ity
cu'pola
cupped
cup'per
cup'ping
cup'ping-glass
cu'preous
cuprif'erous
cu'pule
cupulif'erous
cur
curabil'ity
cur'able
cur'ableness
{ curaçao'
{ curaçoa'
cu'racy
cura're
cu'rarize
curas'sow
cu'rate
cur'ative
cura'tor
curb
curbed

curb'ing
curb'-roof
curb'stone
curcu'lio
curd
curd'ed
curd'iness
cur'dle
cur'dled
cur'dling
curd'y
cure
curé
cured
cure'less
cur'er
curette'
cur'few
cu'ria
cu'rial
cur'ing
cu'rio
curios'ity
curio'so
cu'rious
cu'riously
cu'riousness
curl
curled
curl'er
cur'lew
curl'icue
curl'iness
curl'ing
curl'y
curmudg'eon
cur'rant
cur'rency
cur'rent
cur'rently
cur'ricle
curric'ula
curric'ulum
cur'ried
cur'rier
cur'rish
cur'ry
cur'ry-comb
cur'rying
curse
cursed
curs'ed
curs'edness
curs'ing
cur'sitor
cur'sive
cur'sorily
cur'soriness
cur'sory
curt
curtail
curtailed'
curtail'er
curtail'ing
curtail'ment

cur'tain
cur'tained
cur'tate
curta'tion
cur'tilage
curt'ly
curt'ness
curt'sy
cu'rule
curv'ate
curv'ated
curva'tion
curv'ature
curve
curved
cur'vet
cur'veted
cur'veting
cur'viform
curvilin'eal
curvilin'ear
curv'ing
curv'ity
cush'at
cush'ion
cush'ioned
cusp
cusped
cus'pid
cus'pidal
cus'pidated
cus'tard
custo'dial
custo'dian
cus'tody
cus'tom
cus'tomable
cus'tomarily
cus'tomary
cus'tomed
cus'tomer
cus'tom-house
cus'toms
cus'tos
cut
cuta'neous
cute
cute'ness
cu'ticle
cutic'ular
cu'tis
cut'lass
cut'ler
cut'lery
cut'let
cut'-out
cut'purse
cut'ter
cut'throat
cut'ting
cut'tle-fish
cut'ty
cut'-water
cy'anate

cyan'ic
cy'anid
cy'anide
cyan'ogen
cyanom'eter
cyan'uret
cyanu'ric
cyc'lamen
cy'cle
cyc'lic
cyc'lical
cy'cling
cy'clist
cy'clograph
cy'cloid
cycloi'dal
cyclom'eter
cyclom'etry
cy'clone
cyclope'an
cyclope'dia
cyclope'dic
cyclope'dical
cyclop'ic
Cy'clops
cyg'net
cyl'inder
cylin'dric
cylin'drical
cylin'driform
cyl'indroid
cylindromet'ric
cy'ma
cym'bal
cym'biform
cyme
cy'mose
Cym'ric
cynan'che
cynan'thropy
cyn'ic
cyn'ical
cyn'icism
cyn'osure
cy'phonism
cy'press
Cyp'rian
cyp'rine
Cyp'riote
Cyrena'ic
Cyre'nian
cyriolog'ic
cyst
cyst'ic
cysti'tis
cys'tocele
cystot'omy
Cythere'an
czar
czar'evitch
czarev'na
czari'na
czar'owitz
Czech

D

dab
dabbed
dab'bing
dab'ble
dab'bled
dab'bler
dab'bling
dab'chick
dab'ster
dace
dachs'hund
Da'cian
dacoit'
dac'tyl
dac'tylar
dactyl'ic
dac'tylist
dactyl'oglyph
dactylog'raphy
dactylol'ogy
dad
dad'dy
da'do
dae'dal
daed'alus
daff
daf'fodil
daft
dag'ger
dag'gle
Da'gon
daguer'rean
daguerre'otype
dahabee'yah
dah'lia
dai'ly
dain'tily
dain'tiness
dain'ty
dai'ry
dai'rymaid
da'is
dai'sied
dai'sy
dak
dale
dall
dal'liance
dal'lied
dal'lier
dal'ly
dalmat'ic
Dal'tonian
dalt'onism
dam
dam'age
dam'ageable
dam'aged
dam'aging
Dam'ascene
dam'ask
dam'asked
damaskeen'
damaskeened'
dam'assin
dame
dammed
damn
damnabil'ity
dam'nable
dam'nableness
dam'nably
damna'tion
dam'natory
damned
dam'ned
dam'nify
dam'ning
damp
damped
damp'en
damp'ened
damp'ening
damp'er
damp'est
damp'ing
damp'ish
damp'ness
dam'sel
dam'son
dan
dance
danced
dan'cer
dan'cing
dan'delion
dan'der
dan'dify
dan'dle
dan'dled
dan'dler
dan'dling
dan'druff
dan'dy
dan'dyish
dan'dyism
Dane
Dane'geld
Dane'gelt
dane'wort
dan'ger
dan'gerous
dan'gerously
dan'gerousness
dan'gle
dan'gled
dan'gler
dan'gling
Da'nish
dank
danseuse'
Danu'bian
dap
Daph'ne
dap'per
dap'perling
dap'ple
dap'pled
dap'pling
dar
dare
dared
dar'er
dar'ic
dar'ing
dar'ingly
dar'ingness
dark
dark'en
dark'ened
dark'ener
dark'ening
dark'er
dark'est
dark'-eyed
dark'ish
dark'ling
dark'ly
dark'ness
dark'some
dar'ling
darn
darned
dar'nel
darn'er
darn'ing
dart
dart'ed
dart'er
dart'ing
dart'ingly
Dar'winism
dash
dash'-board
dashed
dash'er
dash'ing
das'tard
das'tardliness
das'tardly
das'tardy
da'ta
da'table, date'-able
data'ria

da'tary
date
da'ted
date'less
da'ter
da'ting
da'tive
da'tum
datu'ria
{ datu'rin
{ datu'rine
daub
daubed
daub'er
daub'ing
daub'y
daugh'ter
daugh'terly
daunt
daunt'ed
daunt'er
daunt'ing
daunt'less
daunt'lessly
daunt'lessness
dau'phin
dau'phiness
dav'enport
dav'it
da'vy
daw
daw'dle
daw'dled
daw'dler
daw'dling
dawk
dawn
dawned
dawn'ing
day
day'book
day'break
day'-dream
day'-labourer
day'light
day'spring
day'-star
day'time
day'-work
daze
daz'zle
daz'zled
daz'zling
dea'con
dea'coness
dea'conry
dea'conship
dead
dead'en
dead'ened
dead'ening
dead'eye
dead'head
dead'heat
dead'-letter
dead'lier
dead'lift
dead'light
dead'liness
dead'lock

dead'ly
dead'-march
dead'ness
dead'-weight
deaf
deaf'en
deaf'ened
deaf'ening
deaf'-mute
deaf'ness
deal
deal'er
deal'ing
dealt
dean
dean'ery
dear
dear' er
dear' est
dear' ly
dear' ness
dearth
dear'y
dea'sil
death
death'-bed
death'less
death'like
death'ly
death'-rate
death's'-head
death'-warrant
débâc'le
debar'
debark'
debarka'tion
debarked'
debark'ing
debarred'
debar'ring
debase'
debased'
debase'ment
deba'ser
deba'sing
deba'table
debate'
deba'ted
deba'ter
deba'ting
debauch'
debauched'
debauchee'
debauch'er
debauch'ery
debauch'ing
debauch'ment
deben'ture
deben'tured
debil'itate
debil'itated
debil'itating
debilita'tion
debil'ity
deb'it
deb'ited
deb'iting
debonair'
debouch'
débris'

debt
debtee'
debt'less
debt'or
début'
débutant
débutante
dec'achord
dec'adal
dec'ade
dec'adence
dec'adency
dec'agon
dec'agram
Decagyn'ia
decahe'dral
decahe'dron
{ dec'aliter
{ dec'alitre
decal'ogist
Dec'alogue
Decam'eron
{ dec'ameter
{ dec'ametre
decamp'
decamped'
decamp'ing
decamp'ment
deca'nal
Decan'dria
decan'drian
decan'drous
decan'gular
decant'
decanta'tion
decant'ed
decant'er
decant'ing
decaphyl'lous
decap'itate
decap'itated
decap'itating
decapita'tion
dec'apod
decap'odous
decar'bonate
decarboniza'tion
decar'bonize
decar'bonized
decar'bonizing
dec'astich
dec'astyle
decasyllab'ic
decay'
decayed'
decay'er
decay'ing
decease'
deceased'
deceas'ing
deceit'
deceit'ful
deceit'fulness
deceit'less
deceiv'able
deceive'
deceived'
deceiv'er
deceiv'ing
Decem'ber

decem′fid
decem′vir
decem′viral
decem′virate
de′cency
decen′nary
decen′nial
decen′nium
de′cent
de′cently
decen′tralize
decep′tion
decep′tious
decep′tive
decep′tively
decep′tiveness
decern′
decerp′tion
deci′dable
decide′
deci′ded
deci′dedly
deci′der
deci′ding
decid′uous
decid′uousness
dec′igram
{ dec′ilitre
{ dec′iliter
decil′lion
decil′lionth
dec′imal
dec′imalize
dec′imate
dec′imated
dec′imating
decima′tion
{ dec′imeter
{ dec′imetre
deci′pher
deci′pherable
deci′phered
deci′pherer
deci′phering
deci′sion
deci′sive
deci′sively
deci′siveness
deck
decked
deck′er
deck′ing
declaim′
declaim′er
declaim′ing
declama′tion
declam′atory
declar′able
declara′tion
declar′ative
declar′atively
declar′atory
declare′
declared′
declar′er
declar′ing
declen′sion
decli′nable
declina′tion
dec′linator

decli′natory
decline′
declined′
decli′ner
decli′ning
declinom′eter
decli′nous
decliv′itous
decliv′ity
decli′vous
decoct′
decoct′ed
decoct′ible
decoct′ing
decoc′tion
decoct′ive
decohere′
decol′late
decol′lated
decol′lating
decolla′tion
décolleté′
{ decol′or
{ decol′our
decol′orant
decolora′tion
decol′o(u)red
decol′o(u)ring
decol′orize
decol′orized
decol′orizing
decompo′sable
decompose′
decomposed′
decompo′sing
decom′posite
decomposi′tion
decompound′
decompound′ed
decompound′ing
decon′secrate
dec′orate
dec′orated
dec′orating
decora′tion
dec′orative
dec′orativeness
dec′orator
deco′rous
deco′rously
deco′rousness
decor′ticate
decor′ticated
decor′ticating
decortica′tion
deco′rum
decoy′
decoy′-duck
decoyed′
decoy′ing
decrease′
decreased′
decreas′ing
decreas′ingly
decree′
decreed′
decre′er
decree′ing
dec′rement
decrep′it

decrep′itate
decrep′itated
decrep′itating
decrepita′tion
decrep′itness
decrep′itude
decres′cent
decre′tal
decre′tist
decre′tive
decre′tory
decri′al
decried′
decrusta′tion
decry′
decry′ing
decum′bence
decum′bency
decum′bent
dec′uple
dec′upled
dec′upling
decu′rion
decur′rent
decur′sive
decurve′
decus′sate
decus′sated
decus′sating
decussa′tion
decus′satively
de′dal
deda′lian
ded′alous
ded′icate
ded′icated
ded′icating
dedica′tion
ded′icator
ded′icatory
deduce′
deduced′
deduce′ment
dedu′cing
deducibil′ity
dedu′cible
deduct′
deduct′ed
deduct′ing
deduc′tion
deduct′ive
deed
deed′less
deem
deemed
deem′ing
deem′ster
deep
deep′en
deep′ened
deep′ening
deep′er
deep′est
deep′ly
deep′ness
deep′-seated
deer
deer′-stalker
deface′
defaced′

deface'ment
defa'cer
defa'cing
de fac'to
defal'cate
defal'cated
defal'cating
defalca'tion
de'falcator
defama'tion
defam'atory
defame'
defamed'
defa'mer
defa'ming
default'
default'ed
default'er
default'ing
defea'sance
defea'sible
defea'sibleness
defeat'
defeat'ed
defeat'ing
def'ecate
def'ecated
def'ecating
defeca'tion
def'ecator
defect'
defect'ible
defec'tion
defect'ive
defect'ively
defect'iveness
defence'
defenced'
defence'less-ness
defend'
defend'able
defend'ant
defend'ed
defend'er
defend'ing
defensibil'ity
defen'sible
defen'sive
defen'sively
defen'sory
defer'
def'erence
def'erent
deferen'tial
deferred'
defer'rer
defer'ring
defeu'dalize
defi'ance
defi'ant
defi'ciency
defi'cient
defi'ciently
def'icit
defied'
defi'er
defile'
defiled'
defile'ment
defi'ler
defi'ling
defi'nable
define'
defined'
defi'ner
defi'ning
def'inite
def'initely
def'initeness
defini'tion
defin'itive
defin'itively
deflagrabil'ity
def'lagrable
def'lagrate
def'lagrated
def'lagrating
deflagra'tion
def'lagrator
deflate'
deflect'
deflect'ed
deflect'ing
deflec'tion
deflex'ion
deflect'or
deflo'rate
deflora'tion
deflow'er
deflow'ered
deflower'er
deflux'ion
defo'liated
defolia'tion
deforce'
defor'est
deforesta'tion
deform'
deformed'
deform'er
deform'ing
deform'ity
defraud'
defraud'ed
defraud'er
defraud'ing
defray'
defrayed'
defray'er
defray'ing
deft
deft'ly
deft'ness
defunct'
defy'
defy'ing
degen'eracy
degen'erate. *adj.*
degen'erate, *v.*
degen'erated
degen'erately
degen'erateness
degen'erating
degenera'tion
degen'erative
deglu'tinate
deglu'tinated
degluti'tion
degrada'tion
degrade'
degra'ded
degra'ding
degra'dingly
degree'
dehisce'
dehis'cence
dehort'
dehorta'tion
dehort'ative
dehort'atory
de'icide
deif'ic
deifica'tion
de'ified
de'ifier
de'iform
de'ify
de'ifying
deign
deigned
deign'ing
deil
Deipnos'ophist
de'ism
de'ist
deis'tic
deis'tical
de'ity
deject'
deject'ed
deject'edly
deject'edness
deject'er
deject'ing
dejec'tion
deject'ory
dé'jeuner
de ju're
delaine'
delay'
delayed'
delay'er
delay'ing
de'le
del'eble
delec'table
delecta'tion
del'egate, *n.,a.,v.*
del'egated
del'egating
delega'tion
delete'
delete'rious
dele'tion
delf
de'liac
delib'erate, *adj.*
delib'erate, *v.*
delib'erated
delib'erately
delib'erateness
delib'erating
delibera'tion
delib'erative
delib'erator
del'ible
del'icacy
del'icate
del'icately
del'icateness

delicatesse'
deli'cious
deli'ciously
deli'ciousness
deliga'tion
delight'
delight'ed
delight'ful
delight'fulness
delight'ing
delight'some
delim'it
delimita'tion
delin'eament
delin'eate
delin'eated
delin'eating
delinea'tion
delin'eator
delin'eatory
delin'quency
delin'quent
del'iquate
deliqua'tion
deliquesce'
deliquesced'
deliques'cence
deliques'cent
deliques'cing
delir'ious
delir'iously
delir'ium
delir'ium tre'-[mens
deliv'er
*deliv'er*able
deliv'erance
deliv'ered
*deliv'er*er
*deliv'er*ing
deliv'ery
dell
Della-Crus'can
Del'phian
del'phic
Delsar'tian
del'ta
del'toid
delu'dable
delude'
delu'ded
delu'der
delu'ding
del'uge
del'uged
del'uging
delu'sion
delu'sive
delu'sively
delu'sory
delve
delved
delv'er
delv'ing
demag'netize
demagog'ic
dem'agogism
dem'agogue
demain'
demand'
demand'able
demand'ant
demand'ed
demand'er
demand'ing
de'marcate
demarca'tion
demean'
demeaned'
demean'ing
{ demean'our
{ demean'or
dement'ate
dement'ed
demen'tia
demer'it
demersed'
demer'sion
demesne'
dem'i
dem'igod
dem'ijohn
dem'ilune
dem'i-monde
dem'iquaver
dem'irep
demisabil'ity
demi'sable
demise'
demised'
dem'isemiqua'-[ver
demi'sing
demis'sion
demit'
dem'itone
demo'bilize
democ'racy
dem'ocrat
democrat'ic
democrat'ical
demoiselle'
demol'ish
demol'ished
demol'isher
demol'ishing
demoli'tion
de'mon
demonetiza'tion
demon'etize
demo'niac
demoni'acal
demo'nian
demon'ic
de'monism
de'monist
de'monize
de'monized
de'monizing
demonol'atry
demonol'ogy
demonstrabil'ity
demon'strable
dem'onstrate
*dem'onstrat*ed
*dem'onstrat*ing
demonstra'tion
demon'strative
demon'stratively
dem'onstrator
demon'stratory
demoraliza'tion
demor'alize
demor'alized
demor'alizing
de'mos
Demosthen'ic
demote'
demot'ic
demp'ster
demul'cent
demul'sion
demur'
demure'
demure'ly
demure'ness
demur'rage
demurred'
demur'rer
demur'ring
demy'
den
denar'cotize
dena'rius
den'ary
dena'tionalize
dena'tionalized
dena'tionalizing
den'driform
den'drite
dendrit'ic
dendrit'ical
den'droid
dendrol'ogist
dendrol'ogy
den'gue
deni'able
deni'al
denied'
deni'er
den'igrate
deniza'tion
den'izen
denom'inable
denom'inate
denom'inated
denom'inating
{ *denomina'tion*
{ *denomina'tional*
denom'inative
denom'inator
deno'table
denota'tion
denote'
deno'ted
deno'ting
dénoue'ment
denounce'
denounced'
denounce'ment
denounc'er
denounc'ing
dense
dense'ly
dense'ness
den'ser
den'sest
den'sity
dent
den'tal
den'talize
den'tate

den'tated
denta'tion
dent'ed
dentelle'
den'ticle
dentic'ulate
dentic'ulated
denticula'tion
den'tiform
den'tifrice
den'til
dent'ing
den'tist
dentis'tic
den'tistry
denti'tion
den'toid
den'ture
den'udate
denuda'tion
denude'
denu'ded
denu'ding
denun'ciate
denun'ciated
denun'ciating
denuncia'tion
denun'ciator
denun'ciatory
deny'
deny'ing
deobstruct'
deob'struent
deoc'ulate
de'odand
de'odar
deodoriza'tion
deo'dorize
deo'dorized
deo'dorizer
deo'dorizing
deontol'ogy
deox'idate
deox'idated
deox'idating
deoxida'tion
deox'idize
deox'idized
deox'idizing
deox'ygenate
deox'ygenize
depart'
depart'ed
depart'er
depart'ing
depart'ment
department'al
department'ally
depar'ture
depas'ture
depau'perate
depau'perize
depend'
depend'able
depend'ant
depend'ed
depend'ence
depend'ency
depend'ent
depend'ently

depend'er
depend'ing
dephos'phorize
depict'
depict'ed
depict'er
depict'ing
depic'tion
depic'ture
depic'tured
depic'turing
dep'ilate
dep'ilated
dep'ilating
depila'tion
depil'atory
deplete'
deple'ted
deple'ting
deple'tion
deple'tory
deplor'able
deplor'ableness
deplor'ably
deplora'tion
deplore'
deplored'
deplor'er
deplor'ing
deplor'ingly
deploy'
deployed'
deploy'ing
deploy'ment
deplume'
depo'larize
depo'nent
depop'ularize
depop'ulate
depop'ulated
depop'ulating
depopula'tion
depop'ulator
deport'
deporta'tion
deport'ed
deport'ing
deport'ment
depo'sable
depo'sal
depose'
deposed'
depo'ser
depo'sing
depos'it
depos'itary
depos'ited
depos'iting
deposi'tion
depos'itor
depos'itory
dep'ot
deprava'tion
deprave'
depraved'
depra'ver
depra'ving
deprav'ity
dep'recable
dep'recate

dep'recated
dep'recating
dep'recatingly
depreca'tion
dep'recative
dep'recator
dep'recatory
depre'ciate
depre'ciated
depre'ciating
deprecia'tion
depre'ciative
depre'ciator
depre'ciatory
dep'redate
dep'redated
dep'redating
depreda'tion
dep'redator
depred'atory
depress'
depressed'
depress'ing
depress'ingly
depres'sion
depress'ive
depress'or
depri'vable
depriva'tion
deprive'
deprived'
depri'ver
depri'ving
depth
depth'less
depul'sion
dep'urate
dep'urated
dep'urating
depura'tion
dep'urator
depu'ratory
deputa'tion
depute'
depu'ted
depu'ting
dep'uty
derail'
derail'ment
derange'
derange'able
deranged'
derange'ment
derang'ing
der'elict
derelic'tion
deride'
deri'ded
deri'der
deri'ding
deri'dingly
deris'ible
deri'sion
deri'sive
deri'sively
deri'siveness
deri'sory
deriv'able
deriva'tion
deriva'tional

deriv'ative
deriv'atively
derive'
derived'
deri'ving
derm
der'mal
dermat'ic
der'matoid
dermatol'ogy
der'mic
dermog'raphy
der'moid
dermot'omy
der'nier
der'ogate
der'ogated
der'ogating
deroga'tion
derog'atory
der'rick
der'ringer
der'vish
descant
descant'ed
descant'er
descant'ing
descend'
descend'ant
descend'ed
descend'ent
descend'er
descendibil'ity
descend'ible
descend'ing
descen'sion
descen'sional
descen'sive
descent'
descri'bable
describe'
described'
descri'ber
descri'bing
descried'
descri'er
descrip'tion
descrip'tions
descrip'tive
descrip'tively
descry'
descry'ing
des'ecrate
des'ecrated
des'ecrating
desecra'tion
desert
desert'ed
desert'er
desert'ing
deser'tion
desert'less
deserve'
deserved'
deserv'edly
deserv'er
deserv'ing
deserv'ingly
deshabille'

des'iccate
des'iccated
des'iccating
desicca'tion
des'iccative
des'iccator
desid'erate
desid'erated
desid'erating
desid'erative
desidera'tum
design'-able
des'ignate
des'ignated
des'ignating
designa'tion
des'ignator
designed'
design'edly
design'er
design'ing
design'less
desirabil'ity
desir'able
desir'ableness
desire'
desired'
desir'er
desir'ing
desir'ous
desist'
desist'ance
desist'ed
desist'ing
desi'tion
desk
desmol'ogy
des'olate, *adj.*
des'olate, *v.*
des'olated
des'olateness
des'olating
desola'tion
des'olator
despair'
despaired'
despair'ing
despair'ingly
despatch'
despatched'
despatch'ing
despera'do
des'perate
des'perately
despera'tion
des'picable
des'picableness
des'picably
despi'sable
despise'
despised'
despi'ser
despi'sing
despite'
despite'ful
despoil'
despoiled'
despoil'er
despoil'ing
despoil'ment

despolia'tion
despond'
despond'ed
despond'ence
despond'ency
despond'ent
despond'ing
des'pot
despot'ic
despot'ical
des'potism
des'potize
des'pumate
des'pumated
des'pumating
despuma'tion
des'quamate
desquama'tion
dessert'
dessert'spoonful
destina'tion
des'tine
des'tined
des'tining
des'tiny
des'titute
destitu'tion
destroy'
destroyed'
destroy'er
destroy'ing
destructibil'ity
destruc'tible
destruc'tion
destruc'tive
destruc'tively
*destruc'tive*ness
destruc'tor
desuda'tion
des'uetude
des'ultorily
des'ultoriness
des'ultory
detach'
detached'
detach'ing
detach'ment
de'tail, *n.*
detail', *v.*
detailed'
detail'er
detail'ing
detain'
detained'
detain'er
detain'ing
detect'
detect'able
detect'ed
detect'er-or
detect'ing
detec'tion
detec'tive
detent'
deten'tion
deter'
deterge'
deterged'
deter'gent
deter'ging

dete'riorate
dete'riorated
dete'riorating
deteriora'tion
deter'ment
deter'minable
deter'minant
deter'minate
deter'minately
determina'tion
deter'minative
deter'mine
deter'mined
deter'minedly
deter'miner
deter'mining
deter'minism
deterred'
deter'rent
deter'ring
deter'sion
deter'sive
detest'
detest'able
detesta'tion
detest'ed
detest'er
detest'ing
dethrone'
dethroned'
dethrone'ment
dethro'ner
dethro'ning
det'inue
det'onate
det'onated
det'onating
detona'tion
det'onator
detoniza'tion
det'onize
det'onized
det'onizing
detor'sion
detort'
detour'
detract'
detract'ed
detract'ing
detrac'tion
detract'ive
detract'or
detract'ory
det'riment
detrimen'tal
detri'tal
detri'tion
detri'tus
detrude'
detrud'ed
detrud'ing
detrun'cate
detrun'cated
detrunca'tion
detru'sion
deuce
deuterog'amist
deuterog'amy
Deuteron'omy
deuterop'athy
deutox'ide
devapora'tion
dev'astate
dev'astated
dev'astating
devasta'tion
devel'op
devel'oped
devel'oper
devel'oping
devel'opment
devest'
de'viate
de'viated
de'viating
devia'tion
device'
dev'il
{ dev'iling
{ dev'illing
dev'ilish
dev'ilishly
dev'ilry
de'vious
de'viously
de'viousness
devi'sable
devise'
devised'
devisee'
devi'ser
devi'sing
devi'sor
devi'talize
devitrifica'tion
devit'rify
devo'calize
devoid'
devoir'
devolu'tion
devolve'
devolved'
devolv'ing
Devo'nian
dev'onport
devote'
devo'ted
devo'tedness
devotee'
devo'ter
devo'ting
devo'tion
devo'tional
devour'
devoured'
devour'er
devour'ing
devout'
devout'ly
devout'ness
dew
dewan'
dew'drop
dew'iness
dew'lap
dew'-point
dew'y
dex'ter
dexter'ity
dex'terous
dex'trous
{ dex'terously
{ dex'trously
dex'tral
dextral'ity
dex'trin(e)
dextrors'al
dex'trose
Dey
dho'bi
dho'ti
dhow
dhur'rie
diabe'tes
diabe'tic
dia'blerie
diabol'ic
diabol'ical
diab'olism
diab'olo
diacaus'tic
diach'ylon
diac'onal
diac'onate
diacous'tic
diacrit'ic
diacrit'ical
di'adem
{ diaer'esis
{ dier'esis
diagno'sis
diagnos'tic
diagom'eter
diag'onal
diag'onally
di'agram
diagrammat'ic
di'agraph
diagraph'ic
di'al
di'alect
dialec'tic
dialec'tical
dialecti'cian
di'alist
di'allage
{ di'alling
{ di'aling
dial'ogism
dial'ogist
dialogis'tic
dial'ogize
di'alogue
di'al-plate
dial'ysis
diamagnet'ic
diam'eter
diam'etral
diamet'ric
diamet'rical
di'amond
Dian'dria
dian'drian
dian'drous
Dian'thus
diapa'son
di'aper
di'aphane
diaphane'ity
diaphan'ic

diaphanom'eter
diaph'anous
diaphon'ic
diaphore'sis
diaphoret'ic
di'aphragm
diaph'ysis
dia'rian
di'arist
{ diarrhoe'a
{ diarrhe'a
diarrhoet'ic
diarthro'sis
di'ary
di'astase
dias'tole
di'astyle
Diates'saron
diather'mal
diather'manous
diath'esis
Diatoma'ceae
diaton'ic
di'atribe
dib
dib'ble
dib'bled
dib'bler
dib'bling
dib'stone
dice
dice'-box
diceph'alous
di'cer
dichot'omize
dichot'omous
dichot'omy
dichromat'ic
di'cing
dick'ens
dick'er
dick'ey, dick'y
dicotyle'don
dicotyle'donous
dictate
dicta'ted
dicta'ting
dicta'tion
dicta'tor
dictato'rial
dicta'torship
dic'tion
dic'tionary
dic'tum
did
didac'tic
didac'tical
didac'tyl
didac'tylous
did'dle
did'dled
did'dling
didecahe'dral
didst
did'ymous
didyna'mian
didyn'amous
die
died
die'-hard

die'-sinker
di'esis
di'et
di'etary
di'eted
di'eter
dietet'ic
dietet'ical
di'etine
di'eting
dif'fer
dif'fered
dif'ference
dif'ferenced
dif'ferencing
dif'ferent
differen'tia
differen'tial
differen'tiate
differentia'tion
dif'ferently
dif'ficult
dif'ficulty
dif'fidence
dif'fident
dif'form
diffract'
diffract'ed
diffract'ing
diffrac'tion
{ diffuse', *adj.*
{ diffuse', *v.*
diffused'
diffuse'ly
diffu'ser
diffusibil'ity
diffu'sible
diffu'sing
diffu'sion
diffu'sive
diffu'sively
diffu'siveness
dig
digam'ma
digas'tric
di'gest, *n.*
digest', *v.*
digest'ed
digest'er
digestibil'ity
digest'ible
digest'ing
diges'tion
digest'ive
digged
dig'ger
dig'ging
dig'it
dig'ital
digita'lis
dig'itate, *adj.*
dig'itate, *v.*
dig'itated
digita'tion
dig'itigrade
di'glyph
dig'nified
dig'nify
dig'nifying
dig'nitary

dig'nity
di'graph
digress'
digressed'
digress'ing
digres'sion
digres'sional
digres'sive
digyn'ian
dig'ynous
dihe'dral
dihe'dron
diju'dicate
dijudica'tion
dike
diked
di'king
dilac'erate
dilap'idate
dilap'idated
dilap'idating
dilapida'tion
dilap'idator
dilatabil'ity
dila'table
dilata'tion
dilate'
dila'ted
dila'ting
dila'tion
dila'tor
dil'atorily
dil'atoriness
dil'atory
dilem'ma
dilettan'te
dilettan'tism
dil'igence
dil'igent
dil'igently
dill
dil'uent
dilute'
dilu'ted
dilu'ter
dilu'ting
dilu'tion
dilu'vial
dilu'vian
dilu'vium
dim
dime
dimen'sion
dim'eter
dimid'iate
dimin'ish
dimin'ished
dimin'ishing
diminuen'do
diminu'tion
dimin'utive
dim'issory
dim'ity
dim'ly
dimmed
dim'ming
dim'mish
dim'ness
dimor'phism
dimor'phous

dim'ple
dim'pled
dim'pling
dim'ply
din
dine
dined
di'ner
ding
ding'-dong
dinged
din'gey, din'ghy
din'giness
ding'ing
din'gle
din'go
din'gy
di'ning
di'ning-room
din'ner
din'ning
din'nerless
dinothe'rium
dint
dint'ed
dioc'esan
di'ocese
Dioe'cia
dioe'cian
diop'ter
diop'tric
diop'trical
diora'ma
diora'mic
diortho'sis
diox'ide
dip
dipet'alous
di'phone
diphon'ic
diphthe'ria
diph'thong
diphthon'gal
dip'loe
diplo'ma
diplo'macy
dip'lomat
dip'lomated
diplomat'ic
diplomat'ically
diplo'matist
dipped
dip'per
dip'ping
dips
dipsoma'nia
Dip'tera
dip'teral
dip'tote
dip'tych
diradia'tion
dire
direct'
direct'ed
direct'ing
direc'tion
direct'ive
direct'ly
direct'ness
direct'or
direct'orate
directo'rial
direct'ory
direct'ress
direct'rix
dire'ful
dire'fulness
dir'er
dir'est
dirge
dir'igent
dir'igible
dirk
dirt
dirt'ied
dirt'ier
dirt'iest
dirt'ily
dirt'iness
dirt'y
dirt'ying
Dis
disabil'ity
disa'ble
disa'bled
disa'bling
disabuse'
disabused'
disabus'ing
dis*advan'tage*
dis*advanta'ge*ous
dis*advanta'ge*ously
disaffect'
disaffect'ed
disaffect'ing
disaffec'tion
disaffirm'
disaffirm'ance
disaffirmed'
disaffirm'ing
disaffor'est
disagree'
disagree'able
disagree'ableness
disagree'ably
disagreed'
disagree'ing
disagree'ment
disallow'
disallow'able
disallow'ance
disallowed'
disallow'ing
disan'imate
disannul'
disannulled'
disannul'ling
disappear'
disappear'ance
disappeared'
disappear'ing
disappoint'
disappoint'ed
disappoint'ing
dis*appoint'ment*
disapproba'tion
disap'probatory
disappro'priate
disapprov'al
disapprove'
disapproved'
disapprov'ingly
disarm'
disarm'ament
disarmed'
disarm'ing
disarrange'
disarranged'
disarrange'ment
disarrang'ing
disarray'
disarrayed'
disarray'ing
disasso'ciate
disassocia'tion
disas'ter
disas'trous
disas'trously
disavow'
disavow'al
disavowed'
disavow'ing
disband'
disband'ed
disband'ing
disband'ment
disbelief'
disbelieve'
disbelieved'
disbeliev'er
disbeliev'ing
disbur'den
disbur'dened
disbur'dening
disburse'
disbursed'
disburse'ment
disburs'er
disburs'ing
disc
discard'
discard'ed
discard'ing
discern
discerned'
discern'er
discern'ible
discern'ing
discern'ingly
discern'ment
{ *discharge'*
{ *discharged'*
dischar'ger
*discharg'*ing
dis'ciform
disci'ple
disci'pleship
dis'ciplinable
disciplina'rian
dis'ciplinary
dis'cipline
dis'ciplined
dis'ciplining
disclaim'
disclaimed'
disclaim'er
disclaim'ing
disclose'
disclosed'
disclo'ser

disclo'sing
disclo'sure
dis'coid
discoi'dal
{ discol'or
{ discol'our
discolora'tion
discol'ored
discol'oring
discom'fit
discom'fited
discom'fiter
discom'fiting
discom'fiture
discom'fort
discom'forted
discom'forting
discommend'
discommode'
discommo'ded
discommo'ding
discommo'dious
discompose'
discomposed'
discompo'sing
discompo'sure
disconcert'
disconcert'ed
disconcert'ing
disconnect'
disconnect'ed
disconnect'ing
disconnec'tion
discon'solate
discontent'
discontent'ed
discontent'edly
discontent'ing
discontent'ment
discontin'uance
discontinua'tion
discontin'ue
discontin'ued
discontin'uing
discontinu'ity
discontin'uous
discord
discord'ance
discord'ancy
discord'ant
discos'tate
discount
discount'able
discount'ed
discoun'tenance
discoun'tenanced
discoun'tenanc- [ing
dis'counter
discount'ing
discour'age
discour'aged
discour'agement
discour'ager
discour'aging
discourse'
discoursed'
discours'er
discours'ing
discours'ive
discour'teous

discour'teously
discour'tesy
dis'cous
discov'er
discov'erable
discov'ered
discov'erer
discov'ering
discov'erture
discov'ery
discred'it
discred'itable
discred'ited
discred'iting
discreet'
discreet'ly
discreet'ness
discrep'ance
discrep'ancy
discrep'ant
discrete'
discre'tion
discre'tional
discre'tionary
discre'tive
discrim'inate, *a.*
discrim'inate, *v.*
discrim'inated
discrim'inately
discrim'inating
discrimina'tion
discrim'inative
discrim'inator
discrim'inatory
discrown'
discrowned'
discrown'ing
discur'sion
discur'sive
discur'sively
discur'sory
dis'cus
discuss'
discussed'
discuss'er
discuss'ing
discus'sion
discuss'ive
discu'tient
disdain'
disdained'
disdain'ful
disdain'fully
disdain'ing
disease'
diseased'
diseas'ing
disembark'
disembarka'tion
disembar'rass
disembar'rassed
disembar'rassing
disembar'rassment
disembod'ied
disembod'iment
disembod'y
disembod'ying
disembogue'
disembow'el
disembow'elled

disembow'elling
disembroil'
disembroiled'
disembroil'ing
disena'ble
disena'bled
disena'bling
disenam'oured
disenchant'
disenchant'ed
disenchant'er
disenchant'ing
disenchant'ment
disencum'ber
disencum'bered
disencum'bering
disencum'brance
disendow'ment
disenfran'chise
disengage'
disengaged'
disengage'ment
disengag'ing
disenno'ble
disenno'bled
disenno'bling
disenrol'
disenslave'
disenslaved'
disenslav'ing
disentan'gle
disentan'gled
disentan'gling
disenthrall'
disenthrone'
disentrance'
{ dis*estab'lish*
{ dis*estab'lished*
{ dis*estab'lish-* [*ment*
disesteem'
disesteemed'
disesteem'ing
disestima'tion
{ disfa'vor
{ disfa'vour
disfa'voured
disfa'vouring
disfigura'tion
disfig'ure
disfig'ured
disfig'urement
disfig'urer
disfig'uring
disfran'chise
disfran'chised
disfran'chise- [ment
disgorge'
disgorged'
disgorge'ment
disgorg'ing
disgrace'
disgraced'
disgrace'ful
disgrace'fully
disgrac'ing
disguise'
disguised'
disgui'ser
disgui'sing
disgust'

disgust'ed
disgust'ful
disgust'ing
dish
dishabille'
dish'-cloth
disheart'en
disheart'ened
disheart'ening
dished
dishev'el
{dishev'elled
{dishev'eled
dishev'elling
dish'ing
dishon'est
dishon'estly
dishon'esty
{dishon'or
{dishon'our
dishon'ourable
dishon'orary
dishon'oured
dishon'ourer
dishon'ouring
disillu'sion
disinclina'tion
disincline'
disinclined'
disincli'ning
disincor'porate
disincor'porated
disincor'porating
disincorpora'tion
disinfect'
disinfect'ant
disinfect'ed
disinfec'tion
disingenu'ity
disingen'uous
disingen'uously
disingen'uous-[ness
disinher'it
disinher'itance
disinher'ited
disinher'iting
disin'tegrable
disin'tegrate
disin'tegrated
disin'tegrating
disintegra'tion
disinter'
dis*in'terested*
dis*in'terested*ly
dis*in'terested*ness
disinter'ment
disinterred'
disinthrall'
disjoin'
disjoined'
disjoin'ing
disjoint'
disjoint'ed
disjoint'ing
disjunct'
disjunc'tion
disjunct'ive
disjunct'ively
disk
dislike'

disliked'
disli'ker
disli'king
dis'locate
dis'located
dis'locating
disloca'tion
dislodge'
dislodged'
dislodg'ing
dislodg'ment
disloy'al
disloy'ally
disloy'alty
dis'mal
dis'mally
disman'tle
disman'tled
disman'tling
dismask'
dismast'
dismast'ed
dismast'ing
dismay'
dismayed'
dismay'ing
disme
dismem'ber
dismem'bered
dismem'bering
dismem'berment
dismiss'
dismiss'al
dismissed'
dismiss'ing
dismis'sion
dismiss'ive
dismiss'ory
dismount'
dismount'ed
dismount'ing
disobe'dience
disobe'dient
disobe'diently
disobey'
disobeyed'
disobey'er
disobey'ing
disoblige'
disobliged'
disobli'ging
disor'der
disor'dered
disor'dering
disor'derliness
disor'derly
dis*organiza'tion*
{dis*or'ganize*
{dis*or'ganized*
dis*or'ganizer*
disown'
disowned'
dispar'age
dispar'aged
dispar'agement
dispar'ager
dispar'aging
dispar'agingly
dis'parate
dispar'ity

dispart'
dispart'ed
dispart'ing
dispas'sion
dispas'sionate
dispatch'
dispel'
dispelled'
dispel'ling
dispen'sable
dispen'sary
dispensa'tion
dis'pensator
dispen'satory
dispense'
dispensed'
dispen'ser
dispen'sing
dispeo'ple
dispeo'pled
disper'mous
disperse'
dispersed'
dispers'er
dispers'ing
disper'sion
dispers'ive
dispir'it
dispir'ited
dispir'iting
displace'
displaced'
displace'ment
displac'ing
displant'
displant'ed
displant'ing
display'
displayed'
display'er
display'ing
displease'
displeased'
displeas'er
displeas'ing
dis*pleas'ure*
displode'
displo'sion
displo'sive
displume'
displumed'
displum'ing
dispone'
dispo'ner
disport'
disport'ed
disport'ing
dispo'sable
dispo'sal
dispose'
disposed'
dispo'ser
dispo'sing
disposi'tion
dispossess'
dispossessed'
dispossess'ing
disposses'sion
dispossess'or
dispraise'

disproof'
dis*propor'tion*
dispropor'tionable
dispropor'tional
dis*propor'tionate*
dis*propor'tioned*
disprov'able
disprov'al
disprove'
disproved'
disprov'er
disprov'ing
dis'putable
dis'putant
disputa'tion
disputa'tious
dispu'tative
dispute'
dispu'ted
dispu'ter
dispu'ting
disqualifica'tion
disqual'ified
disqual'ify
disqual'ifying
disqui'et
disqui'eted
disqui'eting
disqui'etude
disquisi'tion
disquisi'tional
disregard'
disregard'ed
disregard'ful
disregard'ing
disrel'ish
disrel'ished
disrel'ishing
disrepair'
disrep'utable
disrepute'
dis*respect'*
dis*respect'*ful
dis*respect'*fully
disrobe'
disrobed'
disro'ber
disro'bing
disrup'tion
disrup'tive
disrup'ture
dis*satisfac'tion*
dis*satisfac'tory*
dissat'isfied
dissat'isfy
dissat'isfying
dissect'
dissect'ed
dissect'ible
dissect'ing
dissec'tion
dissect'or
{ disseise'
{ disseize'
disseized'
disseizee'
disseiz'in
disseiz'ing
disseiz'or
dissem'blance

dissem'ble
dissem'bled
dissem'bler
dissem'bling
dissem'inate
dissem'inated
dissem'inating
dissemina'tion
dissem'inator
dissen'sion
dissent'
dissent'ed
dissent'er
dissen'tient
dissent'ing
disserta'tion
disserve'
disserved'
disserv'ice
disserv'iceable
disserv'ing
dissev'er
dissev'erance
dissevera'tion
dissev'ered
dissev'ering
dis'sidence
dis'sident
dissil'ient
dissim'ilar
dissimilar'ity
dissimila'tion
dissimil'itude
dissim'ulate
dissimula'tion
dis'sipate
dis'sipated
dis'sipating
dissipa'tion
disso'ciable
disso'cial
disso'ciate
disso'ciated
disso'ciating
dissocia'tion
dissolubil'ity
dis'soluble
dis'solute
dis'solutely
dis'soluteness
dissolu'tion
dissolvabil'ity
dissolv'able
dissolve'
dissolved'
dissolv'ent
dissolv'er
dissolv'ing
dis'sonance
dis'sonancy
dis'sonant
dissuade'
dissua'ded
dissua'der
dissua'ding
dissua'sion
dissua'sive
dis'taff
distain'
distained'

distain'ing
dis'tance
dis'tanced
dis'tancing
dis'tant
dis'tantly
distaste'
distast'ed
distaste'ful
distem'per
distem'perance
distem'pered
distem'pering
distend'
distend'ed
distend'ing
distensibil'ity
disten'sible
disten'sion
disten'sive
dis'tich
distil', distill'
distil'lable
distil'late
distilla'tion
distil'latory
distilled'
distil'ler
distil'lery
distil'ling
distinct'
distinc'tion
distinct'ive
distinct'ively
distinct'iveness
distinct'ly
distinct'ness
distin'guish
*distin'guish*able
distin'guished
distin'guisher
*distin'guish*ing
distort'
distort'ed
distort'ing
distor'tion
distort'ive
distract'
distract'ed
distract'ing
distrac'tion
distract'ive
distrain'
distrain'able
distrained'
distrain'er
distrait'
distraught'
distress'
distressed'
distress'ful
distress'ing
distrib'utary
distrib'ute
distrib'uted
distrib'uter
distrib'uting
distribu'tion
distrib'utive
distrib'utor

dis'trict
distrin'gas
dis'trix
distrust'
distrust'ed
distrust'er
distrust'ful
distrust'ing
distrust'less
disturb'
disturb'ance
disturbed'
disturb'er
disturb'ing
disul'phate
disul'phuret
disulphu'ric
disun'ion
disun'ionist
disunite'
disunit'ed
disuni'ter
disunit'ing
disu'nity
disu'sage
disuse', *n.*
disuse', *v.*
disused'
disus'ing
disval'ue
disyllab'ic
disyl'lable
ditch
ditched'
ditch'er
ditch'ing
ditch'-water
di'theism
di'theist
ditheis'tic
dith'yramb
dithyram'bic
di'tone
dit'tany
dit'to
dit'ty
diure'sis
diuret'ic
diur'nal
divaga'tion
divan'
divar'icate
divar'icated
divar'icating
divarica'tion
dive
dived
di'ver
diverge'
diverged'
diver'gence
diver'gency
diver'gent
diver'ging
di'vers
diverse'
diverse'ly
diversifica'tion
diver'sified
diver'siform
diver'sify
diver'sifying
diver'sion
diver'sity
divert'
divert'ed
divert'er
divert'ing
diver'tisement
divert'ive
divest'
divest'ed
divest'ible
divest'ing
dives'ture
divi'dable
divide'
divi'ded
div'idend
divi'der
divi'ding
divina'tion
div'inator
divine'
divined'
divine'ly
divi'ner
di'ving
di'ving-bell
divi'ning
divin'ity
divisibil'ity
divis'ible
divis'ibleness
divi'sion
divi'sional
divi'sive
divi'sively
divi'sor
divorce'
divorced'
divor'cer
divor'cible
divor'cing
divorce'ment
divulge'
divulged'
divul'ger
divul'ging
divul'sion
di'zen
diz'ziness
diz'zy
do
dob'bin
do'cent
do'cile
docil'ity
doc'imasy
docimas'tic
docimol'ogy
dock
dock'age
dock'et
dock'eted
dock'eting
dock'ing
dock'yard
doc'tor
doc'toral
doc'torate
doc'tored
*doc'tor*ing
doc'tress
doctrinaire'
doc'trinal
doc'trine
doc'ument
documen'tal
documen'tary
dod
dod'der
dod'dered
dodec'agon
dodecagyn'ian
dodecahe'dron
dodecan'drian
dodecan'drous
dodecasyl'lable
dodge
dodged
dodg'er
dodg'ing
do'do
doe
do'er
does, *v.*
doe'skin
doff
doffed
doff'er
doff'ing
dog
dog'berry
dog'-cart
dog'-days
doge
dog'-eared
dog-fish
dogged
dog'ged
dog'gedly
dog'gedness
dog'ger
dog'gerel
dog'gish
dog'ma
dogmat'ic
dogmat'ical
dogmat'icalness
dogmat'ics
dog'matism
dog'matist
dog'matize
dog'matized
dog'matizer
dog'matizing
dog'-rose
dog's'-ear
dog's'-eared
dog's'-meat
dog'-star
dog'tooth
dog'-trot
dog'-watch
dog'wood
dohl
doi'ly
do'ing
do'ings

doit
dol'ce
dol'drums
dole
doled
dole'ful
dole'fulness
dole'some
dole'somely
dole'someness
do'ling
do'-little
doll
dol'lar
dolly
dol'man
dol'omite
dolomit'ic
do'lor / do'lour
dolorif'erous
dolorif'ic
dol'orous
dol'orously
dol'phin
dolt
dolt'ish
dolt'ishness
domain'
dome
domed
Domes'day
domes'tic
domes'ticate
domes'ticated
domes'ticating
domestica'tion
domestic'ity
dom'icile, *n.*
dom'icile, *v.*
dom'iciled
domicil'iary
domicil'iate
domicil'iated
domicil'iating
domicilia'tion
dom'iciling
dom'inant
dom'inate
dom'inated
dom'inating
domina'tion
dom'inative
dom'inator
domineer'
domineered'
domineer'ing
Domin'ical
Domin'ican
dom'inie
domin'ion
dom'ino
dom'inoes
dom'inus
don
do'na
donate'
dona'ted
dona'ting
dona'tion

Don'atism
Don'atist
don'ative
done
donee'
don'jon
don'key
don'key-engine
don'na
donned
don'ning
do'nor
doo'lie, doo'ly
doom
doomed
doom'ing
dooms'day
door
door'-keeper
door'-nail
door'-step
door'way
dop'per
dor, dorr
Dor'cas
do'ree
Do'rian
Dor'ic
Dor'icism
dor'mancy
dor'mant
dor'mer
dor'mitive
dor'mitory
dor'mouse
dor'sal
dor'sel
dor'sum
do'ry
do'sage
dose
dosed
do'sing
dos'sal
dos'ser
dossier'
dos'sil
dost
dot
do'tage
do'tard
dota'tion
dote
do'ted
do'tel
do'ter
doth
do'ting
do'tingly
dot'tard
dot'ted
dot'terel
dot'ting
douane'
doub'le
doub'le-bar'relled
doub'led
doub'le-deal'ing
doub'le-face
doub'le-faced

doub'leness
doub'let
doub'ling
doubloon'
doub'ly
doubt
doubt'able
doubt'ed
doubt'er
doubt'ers
doubt'ful
doubt'fully
doubt'fulness
doubt'ing
doubt'ingly
doubt'less
doubts
douceur'
douche
dough
dough'nut
dough'tily
dough'tiness
dough'ty
dough'y
douse
doused
dous'ing
dove
dove'-cot
dove'like
dove'tail
dove'tailed
dove'tailing
dow'able
dow'ager
dow'dy
dow'dyish
dow'el
dow'elled / dow'eled
dow'elling-eling
dow'er
dow'ered
dow'erless
dow'las
down
down'cast
down'fall
down'haul
down'hearted
down'-hill
down'iness
down'pour
down'right
down'sitting
down'stairs
down'stroke
down'ward
down'y
dow'ry
dowse
doxol'ogy
dox'y
doyen'
doze
dozed
doz'en
do'zer
do'ziness

do'zing
do'zy
drab
drab'ble
drab'bled
drab'bling
drachm
drach'ma
Dracon'ic
draff
draff'y
draft
draft'ed
draft'ing
drafts'man
drag
dragged
drag'ging
drag'gle
drag'gled
drag'gling
drag'-net
drag'oman
drag'on
drag'onet
drag'on-fly
drag'onish
dragonnade'
dragoon'
dragooned'
dragoon'ing
drain
drain'able
drain'age
drained
drain'er
drain'ing
drain'-trap
drake
dram
dra'ma
dramat'ic
dramat'ical
dramat'ically
dram'atist
dram'atize
dram'atized
dram'atizing
dram'-drinker
dram'-shop
drank
drape
draped
dra'per
dra'pery
dra'ping
dras'tic
draught
draught'-board
draught'-engine
draught'-horse
draught'iness
draughts
draughts'man
draught'y
Dravid'ian
draw
draw'back
draw'bridge
drawee'
draw'er
draw'ers
draw'ing
draw'ing-master
draw'ing-pen
draw'ing-room
drawl
drawled
drawl'er
drawl'ing
drawn
draw'-net
dray
dray'-cart
dray'-horse
dray'man
dread
dread'ed
dread'ful
dread'fully
dread'fulness
dread'ing
dread'less
dread'lessness
dread'nought
dream
dreamed
dream'er
dream'iness
dream'ing
dream'ingly
dream'less
dreamt
dream'y
drear
drear'ily
drear'iness
drear'y
dredge
dredged
dredg'er
dredg'ing
dredg'ing-box
dreg'giness
dreg'gy
dregs
drench
drenched
drench'ing
Dres'den
dress
dress'coat
dressed
dress'er
dress'ing
dres'sing-case
dres'sing-gown
dres'sing-room
dres'sing-table
dress'maker
dress'y
drib'ble
drib'bled
drib'bling
drib'let
dried
dri'er
dri'est
drift
drift'ed
drift'ing
drift'wood
drill
drilled
drill'ing
drill'-plough
drill'-sergeant
dri'ly
drink
drink'able
drink'er
drink'ing
drink'-offering
drip
dripped
drip'ping
drip'ping-pan
drip'pings
drive
driv'el
driv'eled
driv'elled
driv'eller
driv'elling
driv'en
dri'ver
dri'ving
dri'ving-shaft
driz'zle
driz'zled
driz'zling
driz'zly
droll
droll'ery
drom'edary
drone
droned
dro'ning
dro'nish
droop
drooped
droop'ing
droop'ingly
drop
drop'let
dropped
drop'ping
drop'-scene
drop'sical
drop'sy
drosh'ky
dros'ky
dross
dross'iness
dross'y
drought
drought'y
drouth
drove
dro'ver
drown
drowned
drown'ing
drowse
drow'sily
drow'siness
drows'ing
drow'sy
drub
drubbed

drub'bing
drudge
drudged
drudg'er
drudg'ery
drudg'ing
drudg'ingly
drug
drugged
drug'get
drug'ging
drug'gist
dru'id
dru'idess
druid'ic
druid'ical
dru'idism
drum
drum'head
drum'-major
drummed
drum'mer
drum'ming
drum'stick
drunk
drunk'ard
drunk'en
drunk'enness
Druse, druse
dry
dry'ad
dry'asdust
dry'-dock
dry'er
dry'-goods
dry'ing
dry'ly
dry'ness
dry'-nurse
dry'-rot
dry'salter
dry'-shod
du'al
du'alism
du'alist
dual'ity
du'archy
dub
du'bash
dubbed
dub'ber
dub'bing
dubi'ety
du'bious
du'biously
du'biousness
du'bitable
dubita'tion
du'cal
duc'at
ducatoon
duch'ess
duch'y
duck
ducked
duck'er
duck'ing
duck'ling
duck'weed
duct
duc'tile
ductil'ity
dud'der
dude
dudg'eon
due
du'el
du'eller, du'eler
du'elling, du'eling
du'ellist, du'elist
duel'lo
duen'na
duet'
duet'to
duff
duf'fel
duf'fer
dug
dug'out
duke
duke'dom
dul'cet
dul'cified
dul'cify
dul'cifying
dul'cimer
duli'a
dull
dull'ard
dulled
dull'er
dull'est
dul'ly
dull'ness
dulse
du'ly
dumb
dumb'-bell
dumbfound'
dumbfound'ed
dumbfound'ing
dumb'ly
dumb'ness
dumb'show
dum'my
dump
dump'ish
dump'ling
dumps
dump'y
dun
dunce
dun'der
dune
dun'fish
dung
dungaree
dunged
dun'geon
dung'hill
dung'ing
dung'y
dung'-yard
duniwas'sal
Dunlop'
dun'nage
dunned
dun'ner
dun'ning
dun'nish
du'o
duodecen'nial
duodec'imal
duodec'imo
duodec'uple
duoden'ary
duode'num
duolit'eral
du'ologue
du'pable
dupe
duped
du'pery
du'ping
du'ple
du'plex
du'plicate, *n.* & *a.*
du'plicate, *v.*
du'plicated
du'plicating
duplica'tion
du'plicative
du'plicator
du'plicature
duplic'ity
durabil'ity
du'rable
du'rableness
du'ra ma'ter
du'rance
dura'tion
dur'bar
du'ress
dur'ing
durst
dusk
dusk'ily
dusk'iness
dusk'ish
dusk'ishness
dusk'y
dust
dust'-cart
dust'ed
dust'er
dust'-hole
dust'iness
dust'ing
dust'man
dust'-pan
dust'y
Dutch
Dutch'man
du'teous
du'teously
du'teousness
du'tiable
du'tiful
du'tifully
du'tifulness
du'ty
duum'vir
duum'viral
duum'virate
dux
dwale
dwarf
dwarfed
dwarf'ing
dwarf'ish

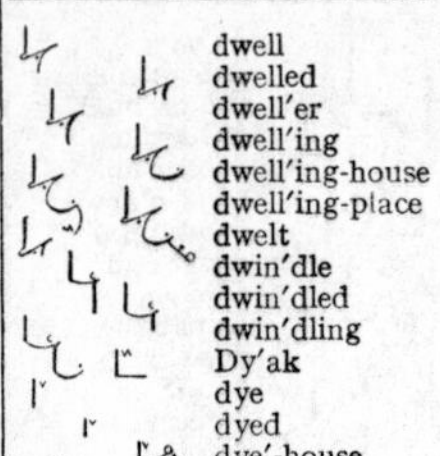

dwell
dwelled
dwell'er
dwell'ing
dwell'ing-house
dwell'ing-place
dwelt
dwin'dle
dwin'dled
dwin'dling
Dy'ak
dye
dyed
dye'-house

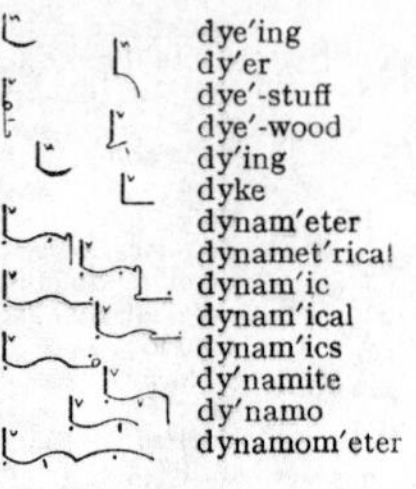

dye'ing
dy'er
dye'-stuff
dye'-wood
dy'ing
dyke
dynam'eter
dynamet'rical
dynam'ic
dynam'ical
dynam'ics
dy'namite
dy'namo
dynamom'eter

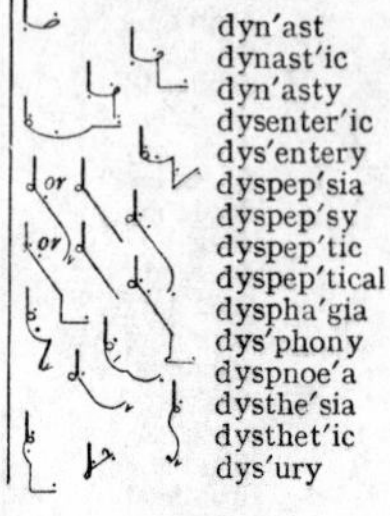

dyn'ast
dynast'ic
dyn'asty
dysenter'ic
dys'entery
dyspep'sia
dyspep'sy
dyspep'tic
dyspep'tical
dyspha'gia
dys'phony
dyspnoe'a
dysthe'sia
dysthet'ic
dys'ury

E

each
ea'ger
ea'gerly
ea'gerness
ea'gle
ea'gle-eyed
ea'glet
ea'gre
ear
ear'-ache
ear'drum
eared
ear'ing
earl
earl'dom
ear'less
ear'lier
ear'liness
ear'ly
ear'mark
earn
earned
earn'er
ear'nest
ear'nestly
ear'nest-money
ear'nestness
earn'ing
earn'ings
ear'-ring
ear'shot
earth
earth'-born
earthed
earth'en
earth'enware
earth'liness
earth'ling
earth'ly
earth'quake
earth'worm
earth'y
ear'-trumpet
ear'-wax
ear'wig
ear'-witness
ease
eased
ease'ful
ea'sel
ease'less
ease'ment
eas'ier
eas'iest
eas'ily
eas'iness
eas'ing
east
East'er
east'erly
east'ern
east'ward
eas'y
eas'y-*chair*
eas'y-going
eat
eat'able
eat'en
eat'er
eat'ing
eat'ing-house
eau-de-Cologne'
eau-de-vie'
eaves
eaves'dropper
ebb
ebbed
ebb'ing
ebb'tide
eb'on
eb'onize
eb'ony
ebri'ety
ebul'liency
ebul'lient
ebulli'tion
écar'té
ec'basis
ecbat'ic
ec'bole
eccen'tric
eccen'trical
eccentric'ity
eccle'sia
eccle'siarch
Ecclesias'tes
ecclesias'tic
ecclesias'tical
ecclesias'ticism
Ecclesias'ticus
ecclesiolog'ical
ecclesiol'ogist
ecclesiol'ogy
eccrit'ic
ech'elon
ech'inate
echi'nus
ech'o
ech'oed
ech'oing
echom'eter
echom'etry
éclat'
eclec'tic
eclec'tical
eclec'ticism
eclipse'
eclipsed'
eclips'ing
eclip'tic
ec'logue
econom'ic
econom'ical
econ'omist
econ'omize
econ'omized
econ'omizing
econ'omy
écraseur'
ecru'
ec'stasy
ecstat'ic
ecstat'ical
ec'stasis
ectro'sis
ec'typal
e'cu
ecumen'ical
ec'zema
eczem'atous
eda'cious
edac'ity
Ed'da
ed'der
ed'died
ed'dy
ed'dying
e'delweiss
edem'atous
E'den
eden'tate
eden'tated
edge
edged
edge'less
edge'-rail
edge'-tool
edge'ways
edge'wise
edg'ing
ed'ible
ed'ibleness
e'dict
edifica'tion
ed'ifice
ed'ified
ed'ify
ed'ifying
e'dile
ed'it
ed'ited
ed'iting
edi'tion

ed'itor
edito'rial
ed'itorship
ed'itress
ed'ucable
ed'ucate
ed'ucated
ed'ucating
educa'tion
educa'tional
educa'tionist
ed'ucator
educe'
educed'
edu'cible
edu'cing
educ'tion
educ'tor
edul'corant
edul'corate
edul'corator
eel
e'en
ee'rie
ef'fable
efface'
efface'able
effaced'
efface'ment
effa'cing
effect'
effect'ed
effect'ible
effect'ing
effec'tion
effect'ive
effect'ively
effect'iveness
effect'or
effects'
effec'tual
effec'tually
effec'tuate
effec'tuated
effec'tuating
effectua'tion
effem'inacy
effem'inate, *adj.*
effem'inate, *v.*
effem'inated
effem'inately
effem'inateness
effem'inating
Effen'di
ef'ferent
effervesce'
effervesced'
efferves'cence
efferves'cent
effete'
effica'cious
effica'ciously
effica'ciousness
ef'ficacy
effi'ciency
effi'cient
effi'ciently

effig'ies
ef'figy
effloresce'
effloresced'
efflores'cence
efflores'cency
efflores'cent
efflores'cing
ef'fluence
ef'fluent
efflu'vium
ef'flux
efflux'ion
ef'fort
ef'fortless
effront'ery
effulge'
efful'gence
efful'gent
effuse'
effused'
effu'sing
effu'sion
effu'sive
effu'sively
effu'siveness
eft
eges'tion
egg
egged
egg'ing
egg'-shell
e'gis
eg'lantine
eg'oism
eg'oist
eg'otism
eg'otist
egotis'tic
egotis'tical
eg'otize
egre'gious
egre'giously
e'gress, *n.*
egress', *v.*
egres'sion
eg'ret
Egyp'tian
Egyptol'ogy
eh
ei'der
ei'der-down
ei'der-duck
ei'dograph
eight
eighteen
eighteenth
eight'fold
eighth
eighth'ly
eight'ieth
eight'score
eight'y
eigne
eire'nicon
Eistedd'fod
ei'ther
ejac'ulate
ejac'ulated
ejac'ulating

ejacula'tion
ejac'ulatory
eject'
eject'ed
eject'ing
ejec'tion
eject'ment
eject'or
eke
eked
e'king
elab'orate, *adj.*
elab'orate, *v.*
elab'orated
elab'orately
elab'orating
elabora'tion
elab'orative
elab'orator
ela'in
élan
elapse'
elapsed'
elaps'ing
elas'tic
elas'tically
elastic'ity
elate'
ela'ted
ela'ting
ela'tion
el'bow
el'bow-*chair*
el'bowed
el'bowing
el'bow-room
el'der
el'derberry
eld'erly
eld'est
El Dora'do
elecampane'
elect'
elect'ed
elect'ing
elec'tion
electioneer'
electioneered'
electioneer'ing
elec'tive
elect'or
elect'oral
elect'orate
elec'tress
elec'tric
elec'trical
elec'trically
electri'cian
electric'ity
elec'trifiable
electrifica'tion
elec'trified
elec'trify
elec'trifying
elec'tro
elec'trocute
elec'trode
electrolier'
electrol'ogy

electrol'ysis
elec'trolyte
elec'trolyzable
elec'trolyze
electro-mag'net
electro-mag'-netism
electrom'eter
electromo'tor
electrop'athy
electroph'orus
elec'troplate
elec'troscope
elec'trotype
elec'trotyped
elec'trotyping
elec'trum
elec'tuary
eleemos'ynary
el'egance
el'egancy
el'egant
el'egantly
elegi'ac
elegi'acal
el'egist
el'egy
el'eme
el'ement
elemen'tal
elemen'tary
el'emi
elen'chus
el'ephant
elephan'ta
elephanti'asis
elephan'tine
elephan'toid
Eleusin'ian
eleuthe'rian
el'evate
el'evated
el'evating
eleva'tion
el'evator
elev'en
elev'enth
elf
elf'in
elf'ish
elf'ishness
elic'it
elic'ited
elic'iting
elide'
eli'ded
eli'ding
eligibil'ity
el'igible
elim'inate
elim'inated
elim'inating
elimina'tion
eliqua'tion
eli'sion
élite'
elix'ir

Elizabe'than
elk
ell
ellipse'
ellip'sis
ellip'soid
ellipsoi'dal
ellip'tic
ellip'tical
elliptic'ity
ellip'toid
elm
elm'en
elm'y
elocu'tion
elocu'tionary
elocu'tionist
eloge'
el'ogy
El'ohim
e'longate
e'longated
e'longating
elonga'tion
elope'
eloped'
elo'ping
elope'ment
el'oquence
el'oquent
el'oquently
else
else'where
elu'cidate
elu'cidated
elu'cidating
elucida'tion
elu'cidative
elu'cidator
elu'cidatory
elude'
elu'ded
elu'dible
elu'ding
elu'sion
elu'sive, elu'sive-[ly
elu'soriness
elu'sory
elves
Elys'ian
Elys'ium
El'zevir
em
ema'ciate
ema'ciated
ema'ciating
emacia'tion
em'anant
em'anate
em'anated
em'anating
emana'tion
em'anative
eman'cipate
eman'cipated
eman'cipating
emancipa'tion
emancipa'tionist
eman'cipator
emas'culate

emas'culated
emas'culating
emascula'tion
embale'
embaled'
embalm'
embalmed'
embalm'er
embalm'ing
embank'
embanked'
embank'ing
embank'ment
embar'go
embar'goed
embark'
embarka'tion
embarked'
embark'ing
embar'rass
embar'rassed
embar'rassing
embar'rassment
embas'sador
em'bassy
embat'tle
embat'tled
embat'tling
embay'
embayed'
embed'
embed'ded
embed'ding
embel'lish
embel'lished
embel'lisher
embel'lishing
embel'lishment
em'ber
em'ber-week
embez'zle
embez'zled
embez'zlement
embez'zler
embez'zling
embit'ter
emblaze'
emblazed'
embla'zing
embla'zon
embla'zoned
embla'zoner
embla'zoning
embla'zonry
em'blem
emblemat'ic
emblemat'ical
emblem'atize
em'blement
embod'ied
embod'ier
embod'iment
embod'y
embod'ying
embold'en
embold'ened
embold'ening
em'bolism
embolis'mal

embolis'mic
em'bolus
embonpoint'
embor'der
embos'om
emboss'
embossed'
emboss'ing
emboss'ment
embow'el
{ embow'elled / embow'eled }
{ embow'eller / embow'eler }
{ embow'elling / embow'eling }
{ embow'ellment / embow'elment }
embow'er
embrace'
embraced'
embra'cer
embra'cery
embra'cing
embra'sure
em'brocate
em'brocated
em'brocating
embroca'tion
embro'glio
embroid'er
embroid'ered
embroid'erer
embroid'ering
embroid'ery
embroil'
embroiled'
embroil'ing
embroil'ment
em'bryo
embryog'raphy
embryol'ogy
em'bryonate
em'bryonated
embryon'ic
embryot'ic
embryot'omy
Emeer'
emend'
emend'able
emen'dals
emenda'tion
em'endator
emend'atory
emend'ed
emend'ing
em'erald
emerge'
emerged'
emer'gence
emer'gency
emer'gent
emer'ging
emer'ited
emer'iti
emer'itus
em'erods
em'eroid
emersed'
emer'sion

em'ery
em'esis
emet'ic
emet'ical
e'meu, emu
émeute'
em'icant
em'igrant
em'igrate
em'igrated
em'igrating
emigra'tion
em'inence
em'inency
em'inent
em'inently
Emir'
em'issary
emis'sion
emis'sive
em'issory
emit'
emit'ted
emit'ting
em'met
emolles'cence
emol'liate
emol'liated
emol'liating
emol'lient
emol'ument
emo'tion
emo'tional
emo'tive
empale'
empaled'
empale'ment
empa'ling
empan'el
{ empan'elled / empan'eled }
{ empan'elling / empan'eling }
empark'
em'peror
em'phasis
em'phasize
em'phasized
em'phasizing
emphat'ic
emphat'ical
emphat'ically
em'pire
empir'ic
empir'ical
empir'icism
empir'icist
emplas'tic
employ'
employed'
{ employ'é / employ'ée }
employee'
employees'
employ'er
employ'ing
employ'ment
empoi'son
empo'rium
empow'er

empow'ered
empow'ering
em'press
emp'tied
emp'tier
emp'tiest
emp'tiness
emp'ty
emp'tying
emp'tyings
empur'ple
empur'pled
empur'pling
empye'ma
empyr'eal
empyre'an
empyreu'ma
empyreumat'ic
empyreumat'ical
empyr'ical
e'mu
em'ulate
em'ulated
em'ulating
emula'tion
em'ulative
em'ulator
emul'gent
em'ulous
em'ulousness
emul'sion
emul'sive
emunc'tory
ena'ble
ena'bled
ena'bling
enact'
enact'ed
enact'ing
enact'ive
enact'ment
enact'or
enam'el
{ enam'elled / enam'eled }
{ enam'elling / enam'eling }
{ enam'eller / enam'eler }
{ enam'or / enam'our }
enam'oured
enam'ouring
enarmed'
enarthro'sis
e'nate
encage'
encaged'
encag'ing
encamp'
encamped'
encamp'ing
encamp'ment
encan'this
encar'pus
encase'
encaus'tic
encave'
enceinte'

{ encae'nia
{ ence'nia
encephal'ic
enceph'alon
enceph'alos
enchafe'
enchain'
enchained'
enchain'ing
enchant'
enchant'ed
enchant'er
enchant'ing
enchant'ingly
enchant'ment
enchant'ress
enchase'
enchased'
encha'sing
enchirid'ion
encho'rial
encir'cle
encir'cled
encir'cling
enclasp'
enclave'
enclit'ic
enclit'ical
enclose'
enclosed'
enclo'sing
enclo'sure
enco'miast
encomias'tic
encomias'tical
enco'mium
encom'pass
encom'passed
encom'passing
encore'
encored'
encor'ing
encoun'ter
encoun'tered
encoun'tering
encour'age
encour'aged
encour'agement
encour'ager
encour'aging
encour'agingly
encroach'
encroached'
encroach'er
encroach'ing
encroach'ment
encrust'
encum'ber
encum'bered
encum'bering
encum'brance
encyc'lical
{ encyclopae'dia
{ encyclope'dia
encyclope'dian
encyclope'dic
encyclope'dist
encyst'
encyst'ed
end

en*dan'ger*
en*dan'gered*
en*dan'gering*
endear'
endeared'
endear'ing
endear'ment
{ endeav'or
{ endeav'our
endeav'ored
endeav'oring
endec'agon
end'ed
endem'ic
endem'ical
ender'mic
end'ing
en'dive
end'less
end'lessly
end'lessness
en'dogen
endog'enous
endorse'
endorsed'
endorse'ment
endors'er
endors'ing
endos'mose
en'dosperm
en'dostome
endow'
endowed'
endow'er
endow'ing
endow'ment
Endozo'a
endue'
endued'
endu'ing
endur'able
endur'ance
endure'
endured'
endur'ing
end'ways
end'wise
Ene'id
en'ema
en'emy
energet'ic
energet'ical
en'ergize
en'ergized
en'ergizer
en'ergizing
en'ergy
en'ervate
en'ervated
en'ervating
enerva'tion
enfee'ble
enfee'bled
enfee'blement
enfee'bling
enfeoff'
enfeoffed'
enfeoff'ing
enfeoff'ment

enfilade'
enfila'ded
enfila'ding
enfold'
enfold'ed
enfold'ing
enforce'
enforce'able
enforced'
enforc'edly
enforce'ment
enforc'er
enforc'ing
enfran'chise
enfran'chised
enfran'chisement
enfran'chising
engage'
engaged'
engage'ment
enga'ging
enga'gingly
engen'der
engen'dered
engen'dering
en'gine
engineer'
engineered'
engineer'ing
en'ginery
engird'
engird'ed
engird'ing
engir'dle
Eng'lish
Eng'lishman
engorge'
engorged'
engorge'ment
engraft'
engraft'ed
engrail'
engrailed'
engrail'ing
engrail'ment
engrain'
engrained'
engrain'ing
engrave'
engraved'
engra'ver
engra'ving
engross'
engrossed'
engross'er
engross'ing
engross'ment
engulf'
enhance'
enhanced'
enhance'ment
enhan'cing
enharmon'ic
enharmon'ical
enheart'en
enig'ma
enigmat'ic
enigmat'ical
enig'matist

enig'matize
enjoin'
enjoined'
enjoin'ing
enjoy'
enjoy'able
enjoyed'
enjoy'ing
enjoy'ment
enkin'dle
enkin'dled
enkin'dling
enlard'
enlard'ed
enlarge'
enlarged'
*enlarge'*ment
enlar'ger
*enlar'*ging
enlight'en
enlight'ened
enlight'ener
enlight'ening
enlight'enment
enlist'
enlist'ed
enlist'ing
enlist'ment
enli'ven
enli'vened
enli'vener
enli'vening
en'mity
en'neagon
Ennean'dria
enno'ble
enno'bled
enno'blement
enno'bling
ennui'
enor'mity
enor'mous
enor'mously
enor'mousness
enough'
enounce'
enounced'
enoun'cing
enquire'
enrage'
enraged'
enra'ging
enrap'ture
enrap'tured
enrap'turing
enrav'ish
enrav'ished
enrav'ishing
enrav'ishment
enrich'
enriched'
enrich'er
enrich'ing
enrich'ment
enrobe'
enrobed'
enrob'ing
enrol', enroll'
enrolled'

enroll'er
enroll'ing
enrol'ment
enroot'
enroot'ed
enroot'ing
ens
ensam'ple
ensam'pled
ensam'pling
ensan'guine
ensconce'
ensconced'
ensconc'ing
enseal'
ensealed'
enseam'
ensem'ble
enshield'
enshrine'
enshrined'
enshrin'ing
enshroud'
enshroud'ed
enshroud'ing
en'siform
en'sign
en'signcy
en'silage
enslave'
enslaved'
ensla'ver
enslave'ment
enslav'ing
ensnare'
ensnared'
ensnar'er
ensnar'ing
ensphere'
ensphered'
enspher'ing
enstamp'
enstamped'
enstamp'ing
ensue'
ensued'
ensu'ing
ensure'
entab'lature
entail'
entailed'
entail'ing
entail'ment
entan'gle
entan'gled
entan'glement
entan'gling
en'tasis
entente'
en'ter
en'tered
en'terer
enter'ic
enteri'tis
en'tering
enterol'ogy
en'terprise
en'terprised
en'terpriser
en'terprising

en'terprisingly
entertain'
entertained'
entertain'er
entertain'ing
entertain'ment
entheoma'nia
enthrall'
enthralled'
enthrone'
enthroned'
enthrone'ment
enthro'ning
enthroniza'tion
enthu'siasm
enthu'siast
enthusias'tic
enthusias'tical
*enthusias'tic*ally
entice'
enticed'
entice'ment
enti'cer
enti'cing
enti'cingly
entire'
entire'ly
entire'ness
entire'ty
enti'tle
enti'tled
enti'tling
en'tity
entomb'
entombed'
entomb'ing
entomb'ment
entom'ic
entom'ical
en'tomoid
entomolog'ical
entomol'ogist
entomol'ogy
entomoph'agous
enton'ic
entourage'
Entozo'a
entozo'on
en'tr'acte
en'trails
entrain'
entram'mel
entram'melled
entram'meled
entram'melling
entram'meling
entrance
entranced'
entranc'ing
en'trant
entrap'
entrapped'
entrap'ping
entreat'
entreat'ed
entreat'er
entreat'ing

entreat'ingly
entreat'y
entrée'
entremets'
entrench'
entrench'ment
en'trepôt
entrepreneur'
en'tresol
entrust'
en'try
entwine'
entwined'
entwin'ing
entwist'
enu'cleate
enu'cleated
enu'cleating
enuclea'tion
enu'merate
enu'merated
enu'merating
enumera'tion
enu'merative
enu'merator
enun'ciate
enun'ciated
enun'ciating
enuncia'tion
enun'ciative
enun'ciatory
envel'op
en'velope
envel'oped
envel'oping
envel'opment
enven'om
enven'omed
enven'oming
en'viable
en'viably
en'vied
en'vier
en'vious
en'viously
envi'ron
envi'roned
envi'roning
envi'ronment
envi'rons
en'voy
en'voyship
en'vy
en'vying
enwrap'
enwreathe'
E'ocene
Eo'lian
Eol'ic
eol'ipile
e'on
Eozo'ic
Eozo'on
ep'act
ep'arch
ep'archy
epaule'ment
ep'aulet
epen'thesis

épergne'
e'phah
ephem'era
ephem'eral
ephem'eris
ephem'eron
Ephe'sian
eph'od
eph'or
ep'ic
epican'thus
ep'icarp
ep'icene
epicra'nium
Epicte'tian
ep'icure
Epicure'an
Epicure'anism
ep'icurism
ep'icycle
epicy'cloid
epidem'ic
epidem'ical
epider'mal
epider'mis
epigas'tric
epiglot'tic
epiglot'tis
ep'igram
epigrammat'ic
epigrammat'ical
epigram'matist
ep'igraph
ep'ilepsy
epilep'tic
ep'ilogue
Epiph'any
epiph'ysis
ep'iphyte
epis'copacy
epis'copal
Episcopa'lian
episcopa'lianism
epis'copate
ep'isode
ep'isodial
ep'isperm
epis'tle
epis'tolary
epis'tolize
ep'istyle
ep'itaph
epithala'mium
ep'ithet
epithet'ic
epit'ome
epit'omist
epit'omize
epit'omized
epit'omizer
epit'omizing
ep'itrite
Epizo'a
epizo'an
epizo'ic
epizoot'ic
ep'och
ep'ode

epod'ic
ep'onym
epopee'
eprouvette'
epura'tion
equabil'ity
e'quable
e'quably
e'qual
equal'ity
equaliza'tion
e'qualize
e'qualized
e'qualizing
{ *e'qualled*
{ *e'qualed*
e'qualling
e'qually
equan'gular
equanim'ity
equa'tion
equa'tor
equato'rial
eq'uerry
eques'trian
eques'trianism
equian'gular
equidis'tant
equilat'eral
equili'brate
equili'brated
equili'brating
equilibra'tion
equilib'rious
equil'ibrist
equilib'rity
equilib'rium
e'quine
equinoc'tial
e'quinox
equip'
eq'uipage
equip'ment
e'quipoise
equipol'lence
equipol'lency
equipol'lent
equipon'derance
equipon'derant
equipped'
equip'ping
equiso'nance
equiso'nant
eq'uitable
eq'uitably
eq'uitant
equita'tion
eq'uites
eq'uity
equiv'alence
equiv'alency
equiv'alent
equiv'ocal
equiv'ocally
equiv'ocate
equiv'ocated
equiv'ocating
equivoca'tion
equiv'ocator

e'quivoque
equiv'orous
e'ra
era'diate
eradia'tion
erad'icable
erad'icate
erad'icated
erad'icating
eradica'tion
eradi'cative
era'sable
erase'
erased'
erase'ment
era'ser
era'sing
era'sion
Eras'tian
Eras'tianism
era'sure
ere
Er'ebus
erect'
erect'able
erect'ed
erect'ile
erectil'ity
erect'ing
erec'tion
erect'ly
erect'ness
erect'or
ere'long
er'emite
eremit'ic
eremit'ical
er'ethism
erg
er'go
er'got
er'gotism
Eri'ca
eriom'eter
er'mine
er'mined
erode'
ero'ded
ero'dent
ero'ding
ero'sion
ero'sive
erot'ic
erpetol'ogy
err
er'rand
er'rant
er'rantry
erra'ta
errat'ic
errat'ical
errat'ically
erra'tum
er'rhine
erred
er'ring
erro'neous
erro'neously
erro'neousness
er'ror

Erse
erst
erst'while
erubes'cence
erubes'cent
eruct'ate
eructa'tion
er'udite
er'uditely
er'uditeness
erudi'tion
eru'ginous
erupt'
erupt'ed
erup'tion
erup'tive
erysip'elas
erysipel'atous
erythe'ma
escalade'
escala'ded
escala'ding
escal'lop
escapade'
escape'
escaped'
escape'ment
escap'ing
escarp'
escarped'
escarp'ing
escarp'ment
eschalot'
es'char
escharot'ic
eschatol'ogy
escheat'
escheat'able
escheat'ed
escheat'ing
escheat'or
eschew'
eschewed'
eschew'ing
Fsco'rial
{ es'cort, *n.*
{ escort', *v.*
escort'ed
escort'ing
escritoire'
escrito'rial
Escula'pian
es'culent
escutch'eon
escutch'eoned
esoph'agus
esoter'ic
espal'ier
espar'to
{ *espe'cial*
{ *espe'cially*
Esperan'to
espi'al
espied'
es'pionage
esplanade'
espou'sal
espouse'
espoused'
espous'er

espous'ing
espy'
espy'ing
Es'quimau
esquire'
es'say
essayed'
essay'er
essay'ing
es'sayist
es'sence
es'senced
es'sencing
Essene'
essen'tial
essential'ity
essen'tially
{ *estab'lish*
{ *estab'lished*
estab'lisher
estab'lishing
estab'lishment
estafette'
estate'
esteem'
esteem'able
esteemed'
esteem'ing
esthet'ic
es'timable
es'timate, *n.*
es'timate, *v.*
es'timated
es'timating
estima'tion
es'timator
est'ival
estiva'tion
estop'
estopped'
estop'pel
esto'vers
estrade'
estrange'
estranged'
estrange'ment
estran'ging
estrapade'
estray'
estreat'
estreat'ed
estreat'ing
estrepe'ment
es'tuary
es'tuate
estua'tion
et cet'era
etch
etched
etch'er
etch'ing
eter'nal
eter'nally
eter'nity
eter'nize
eter'nized
eter'nizing
ete'sian
eth'al
e'ther

ethe'real
ethe'realize
ethe'realized
ethe'realizing
e'theriform
e'therism
etheriza'tion
e'therize
e'therized
e'therizing
eth'ic
eth'ical
eth'ically
eth'ics
E'thiop
Ethio'pian
Ethiop'ic
eth'moid
ethmoi'dal
eth'narch
eth'nic
eth'nical
ethnog'rapher
ethnograph'ic
ethnograph'ical
ethnog'raphy
ethnolog'ic
ethnol'ogist
ethnol'ogy
etholog'ic
etholog'ical
ethol'ogist
ethol'ogy
eth'yl
e'tiolate
etiol'ogy
et'iquette
Etne'an
Eto'nian
Etrus'can
etui'
etymolog'ic
{ etymolog'ical
{ etymolog'ically
etymol'ogist
etymol'ogy
et'ymon
Eucalyp'tus
eucalyp'tol
Eu'charist
eucharis'tic
eucharis'tical
eu'crasy
eudiom'eter
eudiomet'ric
eudiom'etry
eugen'ic
eu'logist
eulogis'tic
eulo'gium
eu'logize
eu'logized
eu'logizing
eu'logy
eu'nomy
eu'nuch
eupep'sy
eupep'tic
eu'phemism

eu'phemist
euphemist'ic
eu'phemize
euphon'ic
eupho'nious
eu'phonism
eu'phony
eu'phrasy
eu'phuism
eu'phuist
euphuis'tic
Eura'sian
eure'ka
eurhyth'my
euri'pus
Euroc'lydon
Europe'an
Eusta'chian
eu'style
eutec'tic
Euter'pean
euthana'sia
euthan'asy
evac'uant
evac'uate
evac'uated
evac'uating
evacua'tion
evac'uative
evac'uator
evade'
eva'ded
eva'der
eva'ding
evanes'cence
evanes'cent
evan'gel
evangel'ic
evangel'ical
evan'gelism
evan'gelist
evangeliza'tion
evan'gelize
evan'gelized
evan'gelizing
evan'ish
evap'orable
evap'orate
evap'orated
evap'orating
evapora'tion
evap'orative
eva'sible
eva'sion
eva'sive
eva'sively
eva'siveness
eve
evec'tion
e'ven
e'vened
eve'ning
e'venly
e'venness
e'vensong
event'
event'ful
event'fulness
e'ventide

even'tual
even'tually
eventual'ity
even'tuate
ev'er
ever'circulator
ev'ergreen
everlast'ing
everlast'ingly
ever-liv'ing
ever*more'*
ev'ery
ev'erybody
ev'ery-day
ev'erything
ev'erywhere
evict'
evict'ed
evict'ing
evic'tion
ev'idence
ev'idenced
ev'idencing
ev'ident
eviden'tial
ev'idently
e'vil
e'vil-doer
e'vil-eyed
evince'
evinced'
evin'cible
evin'cing
evin'cive
evis'cerate
evis'cerated
evis'cerating
eviscera'tion
ev'itable
evoke'
evoked'
ev'olute
evolu'tion
evolu'tionary
evolu'tionist
evolve'
evolved'
evolve'ment
evolv'ing
evul'sion
ewe
ew'er
ew'ery, ew'ry
exac'erbate
exac'erbated
exac'erbating
exacerba'tion
exact'
exact'ed
exact'er
exact'ing
exac'tion
exact'itude
exact'ly
exact'ness
exact'or
exag'gerate
exag'gerated
exag'gerating

exaggera'tion
exalt'
exalta'tion
exalt'ed
exalt'edness
exalt'ing
exam'inable
exam'inant
examina'tion
exam'ine
exam'ined
exam'iner
exam'ining
exam'ple
exanthe'ma
exanthem'atous
exanthe'sis
ex'arch
ex'archate
exas'perate
exas'perated
exas'perating
exaspera'tion
excandes'cent
ex'cavate
ex'cavated
ex'cavating
excava'tion
ex'cavator
exceed'
exceed'ed
exceed'ing
exceed'ingly
excel'
excelled'
ex'cellence
ex'cellency
ex'cellent
ex'cellently
excel'ling
excel'sior
except'
except'ed
except'ing
excep'tion
excep'tionable
excep'tional
except'ive
except'or
ex'cerpt, *v.*, *n.*
excerp'ta
excerp'tion
excess'
excess'ive
excess'ively
excess'iveness
exchange'
*exchange*abil'ity
*exchange'*able
exchanged'
exchan'ger
*exchan'*ging
excheq'uer
exci'sable
excise'
excised'
excise'man
exci'sing
exci'sion
excitabil'ity

exci'table
exci'tant
excita'tion
exci'tative
exci'tatory
excite'
exci'ted
excite'ment
exci'ter
exci'ting
exci'tingly
exclaim'
exclaimed'
exclaim'er
exclaim'ing
exclama'tion
exclam'ative
exclam'atory
exclude'
exclu'ded
exclu'ding
exclu'sion
exclu'sionist
exclu'sive
exclu'sively
exclu'siveness
excog'itate
excog'itated
excog'itating
excogita'tion
excommu'nicable
excommu'nicate
excommu'nicated
excommu'nicating
excommunica'tion
excommu'nication
excommu'nicator
exco'riate
exco'riated
exco'riating
excoria'tion
excor'ticate
excortica'tion
ex'crement
excremen'tal
excrementi'tious
excres'cence
excres'cent
excre'ta
excrete'
excre'ted
excre'ting
excre'tion
excre'tive
excre'tory
excru'ciate
excru'ciated
excru'ciating
excrucia'tion
excul'pable
ex'culpate
ex'culpated
ex'culpating
exculpa'tion
excul'patory
excur'sion
excur'sionist

excur'sive
excur'sus
excu'sable
excu'sably
excu'satory
excuse'
excused'
excuse'less
excu'ser
excu'sing
ex'ecrable
ex'ecrably
ex'ecrate
ex'ecrated
ex'ecrating
execra'tion
ex'ecratory
exec'utant
ex'ecute
ex'ecuted
ex'ecuting
execu'tion
execu'tioner
exec'utive
exec'utor
executo'rial
*exec'utor*ship
exec'utory
exec'utrix
exege'sis
exeget'ic
exeget'ical
exem'plar
exem'plarily
exem'plary
exemplifica'tion
exem'plified
exem'plifier
exem'plify
exem'plifying
exempt'
exempt'ed
exempt'ing
exemp'tion
exequa'tur
ex'equies
ex'ercisable
ex'ercise
ex'ercised
ex'erciser
ex'ercising
exercita'tion
exergue'
exert'
exert'ed
exert'ing
exer'tion
exfo'liate
exfo'liated
exfo'liating
exfolia'tion
exfo'liative
exha'lable
exha'lant
exhala'tion
exhale'
exhaled'
exha'ling
exhale'ment

exhaust'
exhaust'ed
exhaust'ible
exhaust'ing
exhaus'tion
exhaust'ive
exhaust'less
exhib'it
exhib'ited
exhib'iting
exhibi'tion
exhibi'tioner
exhib'itive
exhib'itor
exhib'itory
exhil'arant
exhil'arate
exhil'arated
exhil'arating
exhilara'tion
exhort'
exhorta'tion
exhort'ative
exhort'atory
exhort'ed
exhort'er
exhort'ing
exhuma'tion
exhume'
exhumed'
exhu'ming
exigeant
ex'igency
ex'igent
exig'uous
ex'ile
ex'iled
ex'iling
exinani'tion
exist'
exist'ed
exist'ence
exist'ent
exist'ible
existibil'ity
exist'ing
ex'it
ex-may'or
ex'ode
exo'dium
Ex'odus
ex'ogen
exog'enous
exon'erate
exon'erated
exon'erating
exonera'tion
exon'erative
exon'erator
ex'orable
exor'bitance
exor'bitancy
exor'bitant
exor'bitantly
ex'orcise
ex'orcised
ex'orciser
ex'orcising
ex'orcism
ex'orcist

exor'dial
exor'dium
exosto'sis
exoter'ic
exoter'ical
exot'ic
exot'icism
expand'
expand'ed
expand'er
expand'ing
expanse'
expansibil'ity
expan'sible
expan'sion
expan'sive
expa'tiate
expa'tiated
expa'tiating
expatia'tion
expa'tiator
expa'tiatory
expa'triate
expa'triated
expa'triating
expatria'tion
expect'
expect'ance
expect'ancy
expect'ant
expect'antly
expecta'tion
expect'ed
expect'er
expect'ing
expect'ingly
expec'torant
expec'torate
expec'torated
expec'torating
expectora'tion
expe'dience
expe'diency
expe'dient
expe'diently
ex'pedite
ex'pedited
ex'peditely
ex'pediting
expedi'tion
expedi'tionary
expedi'tious
expedi'tiously
expel'
expelled'
expel'ler
expel'ling
expend'
expend'ed
expend'ing
expend'iture
expense'
expen'sive
expen'sively
expen'siveness
expe'rience
expe'rienced
expe'riencing
exper'iment

experimen'tal
experimen'talist
experimen'talize
experimen'tally
exper'imented
exper'imenter
exper'imenting
exper'imentist
ex'pert
expert'ly
expert'ness
ex'piable
ex'piate
ex'piated
ex'piating
expia'tion
ex'piator
ex'piatory
expir'able
expira'tion
expir'atory
expire'
expired'
expir'ing
expi'ry
explain'
explain'able
explained'
explain'er
explain'ing
explana'tion
explan'atory
ex'pletive
ex'pletory
ex'plicable
ex'plicate
ex'plicated
ex'plicating
explica'tion
ex'plicative
ex'plicatory
explic'it
explic'itly
explic'itness
explode'
explo'ded
explo'der
explo'ding
exploit'
exploita'tion
explora'tion
explor'atory
explore'
explored'
explor'er
explor'ing
explo'sion
explo'sive
explo'sively
expo'nent
exponen'tial
export
export'able
exporta'tion
export'ed
export'er
export'ing
expose'
exposé

exposed'
expo'ser
expo'sing
exposi'tion
expos'itive
expos'itor
expos'itory
expos'tulate
expos'tulated
expos'tulating
expostula'tion
expos'tulator
expos'tulatory
expo'sure
expound'
expound'ed
expound'er
expound'ing
ex-pres'ident
express'
express'age
expressed'
express'ible
express'ing
expres'sion
expres'sionless
express'ive
express'ively
express'iveness
express'ly
exprobra'tion
expro'priate
expro'priated
expro'priating
expropria'tion
expul'sion
expul'sive
expunc'tion
expunge'
expunged'
expun'ging
ex'purgate
ex'purgated
ex'purgating
expurga'tion
ex'purgator
expur'gatory
ex'quisite
ex'quisitely
ex'quisiteness
exsan'guious
exscind'
exscind'ed
exscind'ing
exsic'cant
ex'siccate
exsicca'tion
exsuc'tion
ex'tant
extempora'neous
extem'porary
extem'pore
extem'porize
extem'porized
extem'porizer
extem'porizing
extend'
extend'ed
extend'er

extend'ible
extend'ing
extensibil'ity
exten'sible
exten'sile
exten'sion
exten'sive
exten'sively
exten'siveness
exten'sor
extent'
exten'uate
exten'uated
exten'uating
extenua'tion
exten'uator
exte'rior
exte'riorly
exter'minate
exter'minated
exter'minating
extermina'tion
exter'minator
exter'minatory
extern'
exter'nal
exter'nalism
external'ity
exter'nalize
exter'nally
exter'sion
extinct'
extinc'teur
extinc'tion
extin'guish
*extin'guish*able
extin'guished
extin'guisher
*extin'guish*ing
extin'guishment
ex'tirpate
ex'tirpated
ex'tirpating
extirpa'tion
ex'tirpator
extol'
extolled'
extol'ler
extol'ling
extor'sive
extort'
extort'ed
extort'er
extort'ing
extor'tion
extor'tionary
extor'tionate
extor'tioner
ext'ra
extract
extract'able
extract'ed
extract'ing
extrac'tion
extrac'tive
ex'tradite
ex'tradited

extradi'tion
extra'dos
extrajudi'cial
extramun'dane
extramu'ral
extra'neous
extra'neously
extraor'dinarily
extraor'dinary
extrav'agance
extrav'agant
extrav'agantly
extravagan'za
extrav'asate
extrav'asated
extrav'asating
extravasa'tion
extreme'
extreme'ly
extre'mist
extrem'ity
ex'tricable
ex'tricate
ex'tricated
extrica'tion
extrin'sic
extrin'sical
extrin'sically
extrude'
extru'ded
extru'ding
extru'sion
exu'berance
exu'berant
exu'berantly
exuda'tion
exude'
exu'ded
exu'ding
exul'cerate
exul'cerated
exul'cerating
exulcera'tion
exult'
exult'ant
exulta'tion
exult'ed
exult'ing
exult'ingly
exu'viae
eye
eye'ball
eye'brow
eyed
eye'-glass
eye'ing, ey'ing
eye'lash
eye'less
eye'let
eye'let-hole
eye'lid
eye'mark
eye'piece
eye'-pit
ey'er
eye'-salve
eye'-servant
eye'-serve
eye'-server

eye′-service
eye′shot
eye′sight
eye′sore
eye′spot

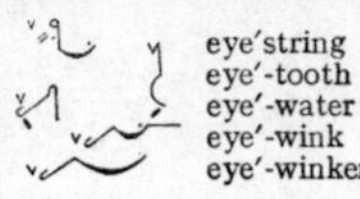

eye′string
eye′-tooth
eye′-water
eye′-wink
eye′-winker

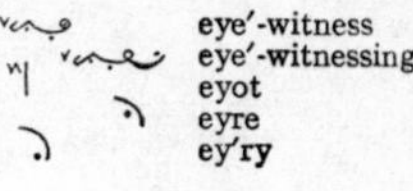

eye′-witness
eye′-witnessing
eyot
eyre
ey′ry

F

Fa'bian
fa'ble
fa'bled
fa'bler
fa'bling
fab'ric
fab'ricant
fab'ricate
fab'ricated
fab'ricating
fabrica'tion
fab'ricator
fab'ulist
fab'ulous
façade'
face
faced
fac'et
fac'eted
face'tiae
face'tious
face'tiously
face'tiousness
fa'cia
fa'cial
fac'ile
facil'itate
facil'itated
facil'itating
facilita'tion
facil'ity
fa'cing
facsim'ile
fact
fac'tion
fac'tionist
fac'tious
fac'tiously
fac'tiousness
facti'tious
facti'tiously
fac'titive
fac'tor
fac'torage
facto'rial
fac'tory
facto'tum
fac'ula
fac'ultative
fac'ulty
fad
fad'dist
fad'dle
fade
fa'ded
fade'less
fadge

fa'ding
fae'ces
faec'ula
fag
fag'-end
fagged
fag'ging
fag'ot
Fah'renheit
faience'
fail
failed
fail'ing
faille
fail'ure
fain
fainéant'
faint
faint'ed
faint'er
faint'est
faint-heart'ed
faint'ing
faint'ish
faint'ly
faint'ness
fair
fair'er
fair'est
fair'ly
fair'ness
fair'y
fair'y-land
faith
faith'ful
faith'fully
faith'fulness
faith'less
faith'lessness
fake
fakir'
falcade'
fal'cate
fal'cated
falca'tion
fal'chion
fal'con
fal'coner
fal'conet
fal'conry
fald'stool
Faler'nian
fall

falla'cious
falla'ciously
falla'ciousness
fal'lacy
fall'en
fallibil'ity
fal'lible
fall'ing
Fallo'pian
fal'low
fal'low deer
fal'lowed
fal'lowing
false
false'-hearted
false'hood
false'ly
false'ness
fal'ser
fal'sest
falset'to
fal'sifiable
falsifica'tion
fal'sified
fal'sifier
fal'sify
fal'sity
fal'ter
fal'tered
fal'tering
fal'teringly
fame
famed
famil'iar
familiar'ity
familiariza'tion
famil'iarize
famil'iarized
famil'iarizing
famil'iarly
fam'ily
fam'ine
fam'ish
fam'ished
fam'ishing
fa'mous
fa'mously
fan
fanat'ic
fanat'ical
fanat'icism
fan'cied
fan'cier
fan'ciful
fan'cifulness
fan'cy
fan'cying
fandan'go

fane
fanfare'
fanfaron'
fanfaronade'
fang
fanged
fan'gled
fang'less
fan'light
fanned
fan'ner
fan'ning
fan'tail
fanta'sia
fan'tasies
fan'tasm
fantas'tic
fantas'tical
fantas'tically
fan'tasy
fan'tom
far
far'ad
faradiza'tion
farce
farceur'
far'cical
far'cin
far'cy
far'del
fare
fared
farewell'
far'-fetched
fari'na
farina'ceous
far'ing
far'inose
farm
farm'able
farmed
farm'er
farm'ery
farm'house
farm'ing
farm'-labourer
farm'*yard*
fa'ro
farra'ginous
farra'go
far'rier
far'riery
far'row
far'sighted
far'ther
far'ther*most*
far'thest
far'thing
far'thingale
fas'ces
fas'cia
fas'cicle
fas'cicled
fascic'ular
fascic'ulate
fascic'ulated
fascic'ulus
fas'cinate
fas'cinated
fas'cinating
fascina'tion
Fa'scist
fash
fash'ion
fash'ionable
fash'ionably
fash'ioned
fash'ioner
fash'ioning
fash'ionist
fast
fast'-day
fast'en
fast'ened
fast'ening
fast'er
fast'est
fastid'ious
fastid'iously
fastid'iousness
fast'ing
fast'ness
fat
fa'tal
fa'talism
fa'talist
fatalis'tic
fatal'ity
fa'tally
fate
fa'ted
fate'ful
fates
fa'ther
fa'thered
fa'therhood
fa'thering
fa'ther-in-law
fa'ther'and
fa'therless
fa'therliness
fa'therly
fath'om
fath'omable
fath'omed
fath'oming
fath'omless
fatigue'
fatigued'
fatigu'ing
fat'ling
fat'ly
fat'ness
fat'ted
fat'ten
fat'tened
fat'tener
fat'tening
fat'ter
fat'test
fat'tiness
fat'ting
fat'tish
fat'ty
fatu'itous
fatu'ity
fat'uous
faubourg
fau'ces
fau'cet
faugh
fault
fault'ily
fault'iness
fault'less
fault'lessly
fault'lessness
fault'y
faun
fau'na
fau'nist
or fauteuil'
faux pas
fa'vor, fa'vour
fa'vourable
fa'vourably
fa'voured
fa'vourer
fa'vouring
fa'vourite
fa'vouritism
fawn
fawned
fawn'er
fawn'ing
fawn'ingly
fay
fay'ing
feal
fe'alty
fear
feared
fear'ful
fear'fulness
fear'ing
fear'less
fear'lessly
fear'lessness
fear'some
feasibil'ity
fea'sible
fea'sibleness
feast
feast'-day
feast'ed
feast'er
feast'ing
feat
feath'er
feath'er-bed
feath'ered
feath'er-edge
feath'ering
feath'ery
fea'ture
fea'tured
febrifa'cient
feb'rifuge
feb'rile
febril'ity
Feb'ruary
fe'cal
fe'ces
fec'ula
fec'ulence
fec'ulent
fec'und
fec'undate
fecunda'tion

fecun'dity
fed
fed'eral
fed'eralism
fed'eralist
fed'eralize
fed'eralized
fed'eralizing
fed'erate
federa'tion
fed'erative
fee
fee'ble
fee'bleness
fee'bier
fee'blest
fee'bly
feed
feed'er
feed'ing
fee'-farm
fee'ing
feel
feel'er
feel'ing
feel'ingly
fee sim'ple
feet
fee' tail
feign
feigned
feign'edly
feign'ing
feign'ingly
feint
feld'spar
felic'itate
felic'itated
felic'itating
felicita'tion
felic'itous
felic'itously
felic'ity
fe'line
fell
fel'lah
fellaheen'
felled
fell'er
fell'ing
fell'monger
fel'loe, fel'low
fel'low-creature
fel'low-heir
fel'lowship
fel'ly
fe'lo-de-se
fel'on
felo'nious
felo'niously
fel'ony
fel'spar
felspath'ic
felt
felt'ed
felt'er
felt'ing
feluc'ca
fe'male
feminal'ity
fem'inine
feminin'ity
fem'inize
fem'oral, fe'mur
fen
fence
fenced
fence'less
fen'cer
fen'cible
fen'cing
fend
fend'ed
fend'er
fend'ing
fenes'tral
fenes'trate, *adj.*
fenes'trate, *v.*
fenestra'tion
Fe'nian
Fe'nianism
fen'nel
fen'ny
feoff
feoffee'
feoff'er
feoff'ment
fera'cious
ferac'ity
fe'rae
fe'rial
fe'rine
ferment
fermentabil'ity
ferment'able
fermenta'tion
ferment'ative
ferment'ed
ferment'ing
fern
fern'ery
fern'y
fero'cious
fero'ciously
fero'ciousness
feroc'ity
fer'rous
fer'ret
fer'reted
fer'reting
fer'riage
fer'ric
fer'ried
ferrif'erous
ferru'ginated
ferru'ginous
fer'rule
fer'ry
fer'ry-boat
fer'ry-man
fer'tile
fertil'ity
fertiliza'tion
fer'tilize
fer'tilized
fer'tilizer
fer'tilizing
fer'ula
ferula'ceous
fer'ule
fer'vency
fer'vent
fer'vently
fer'vid
fer'vidly
fer'vor, fer'vour
fes'cue
fesse
fes'tal
fes'ter
fes'tered
fes'tering
fes'tival
fes'tive
fes'tively
festiv'ity
festoon'
festooned'
fe'tal
fetch
fetched
fetch'ing
fête
fet'id
fetif'erous
fe'tish, fe'tich
fet'lock
fe'tor
fet'ter
fet'tered
fet'tering
fe'tus
feu
feud
feu'dal
feu'dalism
feudaliza'tion
feu'dalize
feu'dalized
feu'dalizing
feu'dary
feu'datory
feud'ist
feuilleton'
fe'ver
fe'vered
fe'verfew
fe'verish
fe'verishly
fe'verishness
few
few'er
few'ness
fez
fiacre
fiancé, fiancée
fias'co
fi'at
fib
fibbed
fib'ber
fib'bing
fi'bre
fi'bril
fibril'la
fi'brillous
fi'brin
fi'brinous
fi'broid
fi'brous

fib'ula
fichu'
fick'le
fick'leness
fick'ly
fi'co
fic'tile
fictil'ia
fic'tion
fic'tionist
ficti'tious
ficti'tiously
ficti'tiousness
fic'tor
fi'cus
fid
fid'dle
fid'dled
fid'dler
fid'dle-stick
fid'dling
fidel'ity
fidg'et
fidg'eted
fidg'etily
fidg'etiness
fidg'eting
fidg'ety
fidu'cial
fidu'ciary
fie
fief
field
field'-bed
field'-book
field'er
field'fare
field'-glass
field'-hos'pital
field'-officer
field'-piece
fiend
fiend'ish
fiend'like
fierce
fierce'ly
fierce'ness
fierc'er
fierc'est
fi'eri-fa'cias
fi'eriness
fi'ery
fife
fifed
fi'fer
fi'fing
fifteen
fifteenth
fifth
fifth'ly
fif'tieth
fif'ty
fig
fight
fight'er
fight'ing
fig-leaf
fig'ment
fig-tree
figurabil'ity
fig'urable
fig'ural
fig'urate
fig'urated
figura'tion
fig'urative
fig'uratively
fig'ure
fig'ured
fig'ure-head
fig'uring
fila'ceous
fil'acer
fil'ament
filamen'tous
filan'der
fil'atory
fil'ature
fil'bert
filch
filched
filch'er
filch'ing
file
filed
fil'emot
fi'ler
fil'ial
filia'tion
fil'ibuster
fil'ibustering
fil'ibusterism
fil'icoid
fil'igree
fil'igreed
fi'ling
Filio'que
fill
filled
fill'er
fil'let
fil'leted
fil'leting
fil'libeg
fill'ing
fil'lip
fil'liped
fil'ly
film
film'iness
film'y
fi'lose
fil'ter
fil'tered
fil'tering
filth
filth'ily
filth'iness
filth'y
fil'trate
fil'trated
fil'trating
filtra'tion
fim'briate
fin
fi'nable
fi'nal
fina'le
final'ity
fi'nally
finance'
financed'
finan'cing
finan'cial
finan'cially
finan'cier
finch
find
find'er
find'ing
fine
fined
fine'draw
fine'drawer
fine'drawing
fine'drawn
fine'ly
fine'ness
fi'ner
fi'nery
fine'spun
finesse'
finess'ing
fi'nest
fine'-still
fin'ger
fin'gered
fin'gering
fin'ger-ring
fin'ial
fin'ical
finical'ity
fin'icalness
fin'icking
fin'ikin
fi'ning
fi'nis
fin'ish
fin'ished
fin'isher
fin'ishing
fi'nite
fi'nitely
fi'niteness
fin'itude
fin'less
Finn
finned
fin'ny
fin'-toed
fiord, fjord
fir
fire
fire'arm
fire'brand
fire'-brick
fire'-brigade
fire'-clay
fire'-damp
fired
fire'-engine
fire'fly
fire'lock
fire'man
fire'-place

fire'-plug
fire'proof
fir'er
fire'ship
fire'side
fire'stone
fire'-wood
fire'work
fir'ing
fir'kin
firm
fir'mament
firmamen'tal
fir'man
firm'er
firm'ly
firm'ness
first
first'-born
first'-class
first'-fruits
first'-hand
first'ling
first'ly
first'-rate
firth
fir'tree
fisc
fis'cal
fish
fished
fish'er
fish'erman
fish'ery
fish'gig
fish'-hook
fish'ing
fish'ing-line
fish'-market
fish'monger
fish'-pond
fish'-tackle
fish'-shop
fish'wife
fish'y
fis'sile
fissil'ity
fis'sion
fissip'arous
fis'siped
fis'sure
fis'sured
fist
fist'ic
fist'icuffs
fis'tula
fis'tular
fis'tulary
fis'tulous
fit
fitch
fitch'et
fit'ful
fit'ly
fit'ness
fit'ted
fit'ter
fit'test

fit'ting
fit'tingly
fit'tings
fitz
five
five'fold
fives'-court
fix
fix'able
fixa'tion
fix'ative
fixed
fix'edly
fix'edness
fix'ing
fix'ity
fix'ture
fiz'gig
fizz
fiz'zle
fiz'zled
fiz'zling
fjeld
flab'bergast
flab'biness
flab'by
flabel'late
flabella'tion
flac'cid
flaccid'ity
flac'cidness
flag
flagell'ant
flag'ellate
flag'ellated
flag'ellating
flagella'tion
flageolet'
flagged
flag'giness
flag'ging
flag'gy
flagi'tious
flag'-officer
flag'on
fla'grance
fla'grancy
fla'grant
fla'grantly
flag'-ship
flag'staff
flag'-stone
flail
flair
flake
flaked
flake'-white
fla'kiness
fla'ky
flam
flam'beau
flamboy'ant
flame
flamed
fla'men
fla'ming
flamin'go
Flamin'ian
flammabil'ity
flam'mable

flam'meous
fla'my
flanch
flange
flank
flanked
flank'er
flank'ing
flan'nel
flan'nelette
flan'nelled, flan'neled
flap
flap'dragon
flapped
flap'per
flare
flared
flar'ing
flash
flashed
flash'er
flash'-house
flash'ily
flash'ing
flash'y
flask
flas'ket
flat
flat'-boat
flat'fish
flat'-iron
flat'ly
flat'head
flat'ness
flat'ted
flat'ten
flat'tened
flat'tening
flat'ter
flat'tered
flat'terer
flat'tering
flat'tery
flat'test
flat'ting
flat'tish
flat'ulence
flat'ulency
flat'ulent
fla'tus
flaunt
flaunt'ed
flaunt'er
flaunt'ing
flaut'ist
fla'vor, fla'vour
fla'vorous
fla'voured
fla'vouring
fla'vourless
flaw
flawed
flaw'less
flaw'y
flax
flax'en
flax'seed
flax'y
flay

flayed
flay'er
flay'ing
flea
flea'bane
flea'-bite
fleam
flea'wort
fleck
flecked
fleck'er
fleck'less
flec'tion
flec'tor
fled
fledge
fledged
fledge'ling
fledg'ing
flee
fleece
fleeced
flee'cer
flee'cy
fle'er
fleer, *v.*
fleered
fleer'er
fleer'ing
fleet
fleet'ed
fleet'est
fleet'ing
fleet'ness
Flem'ing
Flem'ish
flense
flensed
flens'ing
flesh
flesh'-brush
flesh'-colour
fleshed
flesh'er
flesh'iness
flesh'ings
flesh'liness
flesh'ly
flesh'y
fletch
fleur-de-lis'
flew
flexibil'ity
flex'ible
flex'ibly
flex'ile
flex'ion
flex'or
flex'uous
flex'ure
flib'bertigib'bet
flick
flick'er
flick'ered
flick'ering
fli'er
flies
flight
flight'iness
flight'y
flim'siest
flim'sily
flim'siness
flim'sy
flinch
flinched
flinch'ing
fling
fling'er
fling'ing
flint
flint'iness
flint'y
flip
flip'-flap
flip'pancy
flip'pant
flip'pantly
flip'pantness
flip'per
flirt
flirta'tion
flirt'ed
flirt'ing
flit
flitch
flit'ted
flit'ter
flit'ting
float
float'age
float'ed
float'er
float'ing
float'y
floccilla'tion
floc'culence
floc'culent
floc'cus
flock
flock'-bed
flocked
flock'ing
flock'y
floe
flog
flogged
flog'ger
flog'ging
flong
flood
flood'ed
flood'-gate
flood'ing
floo'kan
flook'ing
floor
floored
floor'ing
flop
flopped
flop'ping
flo'ra
flo'ral
Flor'entine
flores'cence
flores'cent
flo'ret
floricul'tural
flo'riculture
flor'id
flor'idness
florif'erous
flo'riform
flor'in
flor'ist
flos'cular
flos'cule
flos'culus
floss
flo'ta
flota'tion
flotil'la
flot'sam
flounce
flounced
floun'cing
floun'der
floun'dered
floun'dering
flour
floured
flour'ing
flour'ish
flour'ished
flour'isher
flour'ishing
flour'y
flout
flout'ed
flout'er
flout'ing
flow
flow'age
flowed
flow'er
flower-de-luce'
flow'ered
flow'eret
flow'eriness
flow'ering
flow'erless
flow'ery
flow'ing
flow'ingly
flow'ingness
flown
flu'ate
flu'can, fluc'can
fluctif'erous
fluc'tuate
fluc'tuated
fluc'tuating
fluctua'tion
flue
flu'ency
flu'ent
flu'ently
fluff'y
flu'gelman
flu'id
fluid'ity
flu'idize
flu'idness
fluke
flume

flu'minous
flum'mery
flum'mox
flung
flunk'ey
flunk'eyism
flu'or
fluor'ic
flu'oride
flu'orine
flu'or-spar
flur'ried
flur'ry
flur'rying
flush
flushed
flush'er
flush'ing
flus'ter
flus'tered
flus'tering
flute
flu'ted
flu'ter
flu'ting
flu'tist
flut'ter
flut'tered
flut'tering
flu'ty
flu'vial
flu'vialist
flu'viatile
flux
fluxa'tion
fluxed
flux'ibility
flux'ible
flux'ion
flux'ional
flux'ionary
flux'ionist
fly
fly'blow
fly'-catcher
fly'er
fly'ing
fly'ing-fish
fly'ing-machine'
fly'-leaf
fly'-trap
fly'-wheel
foal
foaled
foal'ing
foam
foamed
foam'ing
foam'y
fob
fobbed
fob'bing
fo'cal
focim'eter
fo''c'sle
fo'cus
fo'cus(s)ed
fo'cus(s)ing
fod'der

fod'dered
fod'dering
foe
foe'man
foe'tal
foet'icide
foe'tor
foe'tus
fog
fog'-bank
fogged
fog'giness
fog'gy
fog'-horn
fo'gy
Foh, foh
foi'ble
foil
foiled
foil'er
foil'ing
foist
foist'ed
foist'er
foist'ing
fold
fold'age
fold'ed
fold'er
fold'ing
folia'ceous
fo'liage
fo'liate
fo'liated
folia'tion
fo'liature
fo'lier
foliif'erous
fo'lio
fo'liomort
fo'lious
folk
folk'land
folk'-lore
folk'moot
folk'mote
fol'licle
follic'ular
follic'ulated
follic'ulous
fol'low
fol'lowed
fol'lower
fol'lowing
fol'ly
foment'
fomenta'tion
foment'ed
foment'er
foment'ing
fond
fon'dant
fond'est
fon'dle
fon'dled
fon'dler
fon'dling
fond'ly
fond'ness
font

font'al
fontanelle'
food
food'less
fool
fooled
fool'ery
fool'hardiness
fool'hardy
fool'ing
fool'ish
fool'ishly
fool'ishness
fools'cap
foot
foot'ball
foot'-board
foot'boy
foot'-bridge
foot'ed
foot'er
foot'fall
foot'-*guards*
foot'hold
foot'ing
foot'lights
foot'man
foot'mark
foot'-muff
foot'-pace
foot'pad
foot'-path
foot'print
foot'-soldier
foot'sore
foot'stalk
foot'step
foot'stool
foot'-warmer
foot'way
fop
fop'ling
fop'pery
fop'pish
fop'pishly
fop'pishness
for
for'age
for'aged
for'ager
for'aging
fora'men
for'aminated
Foraminif'era
foraminif'erous
forasmuch'
for'ay
forbad', forbade'
forbear', for'bear
forbear'ance
forbear'ing
forbid'
forbid'den

forbid'der
forbid'ding
forbid'dingly
forbore'
forborne'
force
forced
force'ful
force'fulness
force'less
force'-meat
for'ceps
force'-pump
for'cer
for'cible
for'cibly
for'cing
for'cipated
forcipa'tion
for'cite
ford
ford'able
ford'ed
ford'ing
fore
fore'arm
forebode'
forebo'ded
forebo'der
forebo'ding
fore'brace
forecast
forecast'ing
fore'castle
fore'chains
foreclose'
foreclosed'
foreclo'sing
foreclo'sure
foredate'
foredat'ed
foredat'ing
fore'-deck
foredoom'
fore'father
forefend'
fore'finger
fore'foot
fore'front
foregath'er
forego'
forego'ing
foregone'
fore'ground
fore'handed
fore'head
for'eign
for'eigner
for'eignness
forejudge'
foreknew'
foreknow'
foreknow'er
foreknow'ing
fore*knowl'edge*
foreknown'
fore'land

fore'lock
fore'man
fore'mast
fore'*most*
fore'name
fore'named
forenoon'
foren'sic
foreordain'
foreordained'
foreordain'ing
foreordina'tion
fore'part
fore'rank
fore-run'
forerun'ner
forerun'ning
fore'said
fore'sail
foresee'
foresee'ing
foreseen'
forese'er
foreshad'ow
foreshad'owed
foreshad'owing
fore'-sheet
fore'shore
foreshort'en
foreshort'ened
foreshort'ening
foreshow'
foreshowed'
foreshow'ing
fore'side
fore'sight
fore'skin
for'est
forestall'
forestall'er
for'ester
for'estry
foret'
fore'taste
fore*tell'*
fore*tell'*er
fore*tell'*ing
fore'thought
foreto'ken
foreto'kened
foretold'
fore'top
forev'er
forewarn'
forewarned'
forewarn'ing
fore'woman
for'feit
for'feitable
for'feited
for'feiter
for'feiture
forfend'
for'fex
forgath'er
forgave'
forge

forge'able
forged
forge'man
for'ger
for'gery
forget'
forget'ful
forget'fulness
for'getive
forget'-me-not
forget'table
forget'ter
for'ging
for*giv'*able
for*give'*
for*give'*ness
forgiv'er
for*giv'*ing
forgo'
forgot'
forgot'ten
forjudge'
fork
forked
fork'edness
fork'y
forlorn'
forlorn'ness
form
form'al
formal'dehyde
form'alism
form'alist
formal'ity
form'alize
form'alized
form'alizing
form'ally
for'mat
forma'tion
form'ative
forme
formed
for'mer
for'merly
for'mic
for'micate
formica'tion
formidabil'ity
for'midable
for'midably
form'ing
form'less
for'mula
for'mularize
for'mulary
for'mulate
formula'tion
for'nicate
for'nicated
for'nicating
fornica'tion
for'nicator

for'nicatress
for'nix
forsake'
forsa'ken
forsa'ker
forsa'king
forsook'
forsooth'
forswear'
forswear'er
forswore'
forsworn'
fort
fort'alice
forte
for'te
forth
forth'coming
forthwith'
for'tieth
for'tifiable
fortifica'tion
for'tified
for'tifier
for'tify
for'tifying
fortis'simo
for'titude
fort'night
fort'nightly
for'tress
fortu'itous
fortu'itously
fortu'itousness
fortu'ity
for'tunate
for'tunately
for'tune
for'tune-hunter
for'tune-*tell*er
for'ty
fo'rum
for'ward
for'warded
for'warder
for'warding
for'wardness
for'wards
forzan'do
fosse
fosse'way
fos'sick
fos'sicker
fos'sil
fossilif'erous
fossilifica'tion
fos'silist
fossiliza'tion
fos'silize
fos'silized
fos'silizing
fossil'ogy
fosso'rial
foss'way
fos'ter
fos'terage
fos'ter-brother
fos'ter-*child*

fos'tered
fos'terer
fos'ter-father
fos'tering
fos'terling
fos'ter-sister
fos'ter-son
foth'er
foth'ered
fought
foul
foulard'
fouled
foul'est
foul'ing
foul'ly
foul'ness
fou'mart
found
founda'tion
founda'tioner
founda'tion-
found'ed [stone
foun'der
foun'dered
foun'derous
foun'dery
found'ing
found'ling
found'ress
foun'dry
fount
foun'tain
foun'tain-head
four
fourchette'
four'fold
four'-footed
Fou'rierism
four'-*in-hand*
four'-poster
four'score
four'-square
fourteen'
fourteenth'
fourth
fourth'ly
four'-wheeler
fou'ty
fo'vea
fo'veate
fo'veolate
fovil'la
fowl
fowl'er
fowl'ing
fowl'ing-piece
fox
fox-case
fox-chase
foxed
fox'glove
fox'hound
fox'iness
fox'like
fox'tail

fox'y
foyer'
fracas
frac'tion
frac'tional
frac'tious
frac'tiously
frac'tiousness
frac'ture
frac'tured
frac'turing
frag'ile
frag'ilely
fragil'ity
frag'ment
frag'mentary
fra'grance
fra'grancy
fra'grant
fra'grantly
frail
frail'est
frail'ness
frail'ty
fra'mable
frame
framed
fra'mer
frame'work
fra'ming
franc
fran'chise
fran'chisement
fran'chising
Francis'can
franc-tireur'
frangibil'ity
fran'gible
fran'gipane
frangipa'ni
frank
franked
frank'incense
frank'ing
frank'lin
frank'ly
frank'ness
fran'tic
fran'tically
fran'ticness
frap
frater'nal
frater'nity
fraterniza'tion
frat'ernize
frat'ernized
frat'ernizer
frat'ernizing
frat'ricidal
frat'ricide
fraud
fraud'ful
fraud'ulence
fraud'ulency
fraud'ulent
fraud'ulently

fraught
fray
frayed
fray'ing
freak
freak'ish
freck'le
freck'led
freck'ling
freck'ly
free
free'-bench
free'booter
free'-born
freed
freed'man
free'dom
free'hold
free'holder
free'ing
free'-liver
free'ly
free'man
free'mason
free'masonry
free'-minded
free'ness
free'port
fre'er
free'-spoken
fre'est
free'stone
free'thinker
freethink'ing
free-*trade*
free-tra'der
free-wheel
free-will'
freeze
freez'ing
freez'ing-point
freight
freight'age
freight'ed
freight'er
freight'ing
French
French' horn
French'ified
French'ify
French'man
frenet'ic
fren'ulum
fren'zied
fren'ziedly
fren'zy
fre'quency
fre'quent
frequent'
frequent'ed
frequent'er
frequent'ing
fre'quently
fres'co
fres'coed
fresh
fresh'en
fresh'ened
fresh'ening
fresh'er
fresh'est
fresh'et
fresh'ly
fresh'man
fresh'ness
fret
fret'ful
fret'fully
fret'fulness
fret'ted
fret'ter
fret'ting
fret'ty
fret'work
friabil'ity
fri'able
fri'ar
fri'ary
fria'tion
frib'ble
frib'bler
frib'bling
fricandeau'
fricassee'
fricasseed'
fric'ative
fric'tion
fric'tionless
Fri'day
fried
friend
friend'less
friend'liest
friend'liness
friend'ly
friend'ship
fri'er
frieze
frig'ate
fright
fright'en
fright'ened
fright'ening
fright'ful
fright'fully
fright'fulness
frig'id
frigida'rium
frigid'ity
frig'idly
frig'idness
frigorif'ic
frill
frilled
frill'ing
fringe
fringed
fring'ing
fring'y
frip'per
frip'perer
frip'pery
frisette'
friseur'
frisk
frisked
frisk'er
frisk'et
frisk'ily
frisk'iness
frisk'ing
frisk'y
frit
frith
frit'ter
frit'tered
frit'tering
frivol'ity
friv'olous
friv'olously
friv'olousness
friz
frizzed
friz'zle
friz'zled
friz'zler
friz'zling
fro
frock
frock'coat
frocked
Froebel'ian
frog
frog'hopper
frol'ic
frol'icked
frol'icking
frol'icsome
frol'icsomeness
from
frond
frondesce'
frondes'cence
frondose'
fron'dous
front
front'age
front'ager
fron'tal
front'ed
fron'tier
front'ing
fron'tispiece
front'less
front'let
frost
frost'-bite
frost'-bitten
frost'ed
frost'ily
frost'iness
frost'ing
frost'work
frost'y
froth
froth'ily
froth'iness
froth'ing
froth'y
frou'-frou
frounce
frounced
froun'cing
frou'zy
fro'ward
fro'wardly
fro'wardness
frown

frowned
frown'ing
frown'ingly
frow'zy
froze
fro'zen
fructes'cence
fructif'erous
fructifica'tion
fruc'tified
fruc'tify
fruc'tifying
fru'gal
frugal'ity
fru'gally
frugif'erous
frugiv'orous
fruit
fruit'age
fruit'erer
fruit'eress
fruit'ery
fruit'ful
fruit'fulness
fruit'ing
frui'tion
fruit'less
fruit'lessly
fruit'lessness
fruit'y
frumenta'ceous
fru'menty
frump
frush
frus'trate
frus'trated
frus'trating
frustra'tion
frus'tum
frutes'cence
frutes'cent
fruticose'
fru'ticous
frutic'ulose
fry
fry'er
fry'ing
fry'ing-pan
fu'ar
fu'cate
fu'cated
fuch'sia
fuciv'orous
fu'coid
fucoi'dal
fu'cus
fud'dle
fud'dled
fud'dler
fud'dling
fudge
Fue'gian
fu'el
fuga'cious
fugac'ity
fu'gal
fu'gitive
fu'gitively
fu'gleman

fugue
fu'guist
ful'crate
ful'crum
fulfil'
fulfilled'
fulfil'ler
fulfil'ling
fulfil'ment
ful'gency
ful'gent
fulig'inous
ful'gor, ful'gour
ful'gural
full
full'-aged
full'-blown
fulled
full'er
full'ers' earth
full'ery
full'est
full'ing
full'ing-mill
full'-length
full'ness
full-swing
full'y
ful'mar
ful'minant
ful'minate
ful'minated
ful'minating
fulmina'tion
ful'minatory
ful'mine
ful'ness
ful'some
ful'someness
ful'vid
ful'vous
fum'atory
fum'ble
fum'bled
fum'bler
fum'bling
fume
fumed
fumif'erous
fu'migate
fu'migated
fu'migating
fumiga'tion
fu'migator
fu'ming
fu'mitory
fu'my
fun
funam'bulate
funambula'tion
funam'bulatory
funam'bulist
func'tion
func'tional
func'tionary

fund
fun'dament
fundamen'tal-ly
fund'ed
fund'-holder
fund'ing
fun'dus
fu'neral
fune'real
fun'gi
Fun'gia
fun'gic
fun'giform
fun'goid
fun'gous
fun'gus
fu'nicle
funic'ular
funk
fun'nel
fun'nier
fun'niest
fun'ny
fun'ny-bone
fur
fur'below
fur'bish
fur'bished
fur'bisher
fur'bishing
fur'cate
fur'cated
furca'tion
fur'fur
furio'so
fu'rious
fu'riously
fu'riousness
furl
furled
furl'ing
fur'long
fur'lough
fur'menty
fur'nace
fur'nish
fur'nished
fur'nisher
fur'nishing
fur'niture
fu'ror
furo're
furred
fur'rier
fur'riery
fur'ring
fur'row
fur'rowed
fur'ry
fur'ther
fur'therance
fur'thered
fur'therer
fur'thering
fur'ther*more*
fur'ther*most*
fur'thest
fur'tive

fur'tively
fu'ry
furze
furz'y
fusca'tion
fus'cous
fuse
fused
fusee'
fusibil'ity
fu'sible
fu'siform
fu'sil
fusilier'
fusillade'
fu'sing
fu'sion
fuss
fussed
fuss'ily
fuss'ing
fuss'y
fust
fus'tian
fus'tic
fustiga'tion
fust'iness
fust'y
fu'tile
fu'tilely
futil'ity
fut'tock
fu'ture
fu'turist
futu'rity
fuze
fuzz
fuzz'ily
fuzz'iness
fuzz'y
fy
fyrd

G

gab
gab'ble
gab'bled
gab'bler
gab'bling
ga'bel
gab'erdine
ga'bion
gabionade'
ga'ble
ga'bled
ga'blet
ga'by
gad
gad'ded
gad'der
gad'ding
gad'fly
Gael
Gael'ic
gaff
gaf'fer
gaf'fle
gag
gage
gaged
ga'ger
gagged
gag'ger
gag'ging
gag'gle
gag'gled
gag'gling
ga'ging
gai'ety, gay'ety
gai'ly, gay'ly
gain
gained
gain'er
gain'ful
gain'fulness
gain'less
gain'ly
gain'said
gain'say
gain'sayer
gain'saying
gair'ish
gair'ishly
gair'ishness
gait
gait'er
ga'la
galac'tic
galactom'eter

galan'gal
gal'antine
Gala'tian
gal'axy
gal'banum
gale
ga'lea
ga'leate
ga'leated
gale'na
Galen'ic
Ga'lenism
Ga'lenist
Gali'cian
Galile'an
gal'iot
gal'ipot
gall
gallant
gallant'ing
{ gal'lantly
{ gallant'ly
gallant'ness
gal'lantry
galled
gal'leon
gal'lery
gal'ley
gal'ley-slave
gal'liard
Gal'lic
Gal'lican
Gal'licism
Gal'licize
galligas'kins
gallimau'fry
gallina'ceous
gall'ing
gal'linipper
gal'linule
gal'lipot
gallivant'
gallivant'ing
gall'nut
gal'lon
galloon'
gallooned'
gal'lop
gallopade'

gal'loped
gal'loper
gal'loping
gal'loway
gal'lows
gall'stone
gal'op
galore'
galosh'
galvan'ic
gal'vanism
gal'vanist
gal'vanize
gal'vanized
gal'vanizer
gal'vanizing
galvanol'ogist
galvanol'ogy
galvanom'eter
galvan'oscope
Galwe'gian
gam
gam'ba
gambade'
gamba'do
gam'bit
gam'ble
gam'bled
gam'bler
gam'bling
gamboge'
gambo'gian
gam'bol
gam'boled-lled
gam'boling-lling
gam'brel
game
game'-cock
gamed
game'ful
game'keeper
game'some
game'ster
gam'in
ga'ming
gam'ma
gam'mel
gam'mon
gam'moned
gam'moning
gamopet'alous
gamosep'alous
gamp

gam'ut
ga'my
ganch
ganched
ganch'ing
gan'der
gang
gang'er
gan'gliac
gan'gliform
gan'glion
gan'glionary
ganglion'ic
gan'grenate
gan'grene
gan'grened
gan'grening
gan'grenous
gangue
gang'way
gan'net
gan'oid
gant'let
gan'try
gaol
gaol'er
gap
gape
gaped
ga'per
ga'ping
ga'pingly
gar
garage
garb
gar'bage
gar'ble
gar'bled
gar'bler
gar'bles
gar'bling
garçon'
gar'dant
gar'den
gar'dened
gar'dener
gar'dening
gare
gar'fish
gar'garize
gar'garism
gar'get
gar'gil
gar'gle
gar'gled
gar'gling
gar'goyle
gar'ish
gar'ishly
gar'ishness
gar'land
gar'lic
gar'ment
gar'ner
gar'nered
gar'nering
gar'net
gar'nish
gar'nished
garnishee'
garnisheed'
gar'nisher
gar'nishing
gar'nishment
gar'niture
garotte'
garrotte'
gar'-pike
ga'rous
gar'ret
garreteer'
gar'rison
gar'risoned
gar'rot
garrotte'
garrot'ted
garrot'ter
garrot'ting
garru'lity
gar'rulous
gar'rulously
gar'rulousness
gar'ter
gar'tered
gar'tering
ga'rum
gas
Gas'con
gasconade'
gascona'ded
gascona'der
gascona'ding
gas'conism
gaselier'
gas'eous
gas'fitter
gas'-fitting
gash
gashed
gash'ing
gas'-holder
gasifica'tion
gas'ified
gas'iform
gas'ify
gas'ifying
gas'-jet
gas'ket
gas'kin
gas'light
gas'-meter
gas'ogen
gas'ogene
gas'olene
gasom'eter
gasom'etry
gasp
gasped
gasp'ing
gasp'ingly
gas'sing
gas'sy
gastral'gia
gas'tric
gastril'oquist
gastril'oquy
gastri'tis
gas'trocele
gastrol'ogy
gas'tromancy
gas'tronome
gastron'omer
gastronom'ic
gastron'omist
gastron'omy
gas'tropod
gastrop'odous
gas'-works
gat
gate
gate'house
gate'man
gate'way
gath'er
gath'ered
gath'erer
gath'ering
gauche
gaucherie'
Gau'cho
gaud
gaud'iest
gaud'ily
gaud'iness
gaud'y
gauf'fering
gauge
gauge'able
gauged
gau'ger
gau'ging
Gaul
Gaul'ish
gault
gaunt
gaunt'let
gaunt'leted
gaunt'ly
gaun'try
gauze
gauz'iness
gauz'y
gave
gav'el
gav'elkind
gavotte'
gawk
gawk'y
gay
gay'est
gay'ety
gay'ly
gaze
gazed
gazelle'
ga'zer
gazette'
gazet'ted
gazetteer'
ga'zing
ga'zing-stock
gaz'ogene
gear

geared
gear'ing
gec'ko
gee
gee'-gee
geese
Gehen'na
gei'sha
gel'able
gelat'inate
gelat'inated
gelat'inating
gelatina'tion
gel'atine
gelat'inous
gela'tion
geld
geld'ed
geld'er
geld'ing
gel'id
gem
Gema'ra
gemar'ic
gem'el
gemina'tion
Gem'ini
gem'inous
gem'ma
gem'mary
gem'mate
gem'mated
gemma'tion
gemmed
gem'meous
gemmif'erous
gem'ming
gemmip'arous
gem'mule
gem'my
gems'bok
gendarme'
gendarm'erie
gendarm'ery
gen'der
genealog'ical-ly
geneal'ogist
geneal'ogy
gen'era
gen'eral
generalis'simo
general'ity
generaliza'tion
gen'eralize
gen'eralized
gen'eralizing
gen'erally
*gen'eral*ship
gen'erant
gen'erate
gen'erated
gen'erating
genera'tion
gen'erative
gen'erator
genera'trix
gener'ic

gener'ical
generos'ity
gen'erous
gen'erously
Gen'esis
gen'et
geneth'liac
genet'ic
genette'
Gene'van
Gene'vanism
Genevese'
ge'nial
genial'ity
ge'nially
genic'ulate
genic'ulated
genicula'tion
ge'nii
genis'ta
gen'ital
gen'itive
gen'itor
gen'iture
gen'ius
Genoese'
genre
gens
genteel'
genteel'ly
gen'tian
gen'til
Gen'tile
Gen'tilism
gentil'ity
gen'tle
gen'tlefolk
gen'tleman
*gen'tleman*like
*gen'tleman*ly
gen'tlemen
gen'tleness
gen'tlest
gen'tlewoman
gen'tly
gentoo'
gen'try
ge'nu
gen'uflect
genuflex'ion
gen'uine
gen'uinely
gen'uineness
ge'nus
geocen'tric
geocen'trical
ge'ode
geodes'ic
geodes'ical
geod'esy
geodet'ic
geodet'ical
geodif'erous
geog'eny
geognos'tic
geognos'tical
geog'nosy

geogon'ic
geog'rapher
geograph'ic
geograph'ical
geog'raphy
geolog'ical
geol'ogize
geol'ogist
geol'ogy
ge'omancer
ge'omancy
geoman'tic
geom'eter
geomet'ric
geomet'rical
geomet'rically
geometri'cian
geom'etry
geon'omy
George
Geor'gian
geor'gic
Geor'gium Si'dus
geos'copy
ge'rah
gera'nium
ger'falcon
germ
Ger'man
german'der
germane'
German'ic
Ger'manism
Ger'manize
ger'micide
ger'minal
ger'minant
ger'minate
ger'minated
ger'minating
germina'tion
geroco'mia
geroc'omy
gerryman'der
ger'und
gerun'dial
gesta'tion
ges'tatory
ges'tic
gestic'ulate
gestic'ulated
gestic'ulating
gesticula'tion
gestic'ulator
gestic'ulatory
ges'ture
ges'tured
ges'turing
get
get'ter
get'ting
gew'gaw
gey'ser
ghar'ry
ghast'lier
ghast'liness
ghast'ly

gha'zi
ghee
gher'kin
Ghet'to
Ghib'elline
ghost
ghost'like
ghost'ly
ghoul
ghoul'ish
ghur'ry
gialloli'no
gi'ant
gi'antess
giaour
gib
gib'berish
gib'bet
gib'beted
gib'beting
gib'bon
gib'bose
gibbos'ity
gib'bous
gib'-cat
gibe
gibed
gi'ber
gi'bing
gib'let
gib'-staff
gid'dier
gid'diest
gid'dily
gid'diness
gid'dy
gier'-eagle
gift
gift'ed
gig
gigante'an
gigan'tic
gig'gle
gig'gled
gig'gler
gig'gling
gig'ot
Gilber'tian
gild
gild'ed
gild'er
glid'ing
gill (of a fish)
gill (a measure)
gil'lie
gil'lyflower
gil'py
gilt
gim'bal
gim'crack
gim'let
gimp
gin
gin'gal
gin'gall
gin'ger
gin'gerbread
gin'gerly
gin'gery
ging'ham
gin'ging
gingi'val
gin'gle
gin'gled
gin'gling
ginned
gin'ning
gin'seng
gip
gip'sy, gyp'sy
gip'syism
giraffe'
gir'andole
gir'asol
gird
gird'ed
gird'er
gird'ing
gir'dle
gir'dled
gir'dler
gir'dling
girl
girl'hood
girl'ish
girl'ishness
Giron'dist
girt
girth
gist
git'tern
gius'to
give
giv'en
giv'er
gives
*giv'*ing
giz'zard
gla'brous
glacé
gla'cial
glac'ier
gla'cis
glad
glad'den
glad'dened
glad'dening
glade
gla'diate
glad'iator
gladiato'rial
glad'iole
gladi'olus
glad'ly
glad'ness
glad'some
glad'someness
Gladsto'nian
glair
glaired
glair'ing
glair'y
glaive
glam'orous
glam'or-our
glance
glanced
glan'cing
gland
glan'dered
glan'ders
glandif'erous
gland'iform
glan'dular
glandula'tion
glan'dule
glandulos'ity
glan'dulous
glare
glared
glar'eous
glar'iness
glar'ing
glar'y
glass
glass'-cutter
glass'ful
glass'house
glas'siness
glass'-works
glass'wort
glass'y
Glaswe'gian
glau'cine
glauco'ma
glauco'matous
glauco'sis
glau'cous
glaze
glazed
gla'zer
gla'zier
gla'zing
gleam
gleamed
gleam'ing
gleam'y
glean
gleaned
glean'er
glean'ing
glebe
gle'by
glee
glee'ful
glee'some
gleet
glen
gle'ne
glengar'ry
glenliv'et
gle'noid
glib
glib'ly
glib'ness
glide
gli'ded
gli'der
gli'ding
gli'dingly
glim'mer
glim'mered
glim'mering
glimpse
glissade'
glis'ten

glis'tened
glis'tening
glis'ter
glis'tered
glis'tering
glit'ter
glit'tered
glit'tering
gloam'ing
gloat
gloat'ed
gloat'ing
glo'bate
glo'bated
globe
glo'bose
globos'ity
glo'bous
glob'ular
glob'ule
glob'ulin
glob'ulous
glome
glom'erate
glom'erated
glom'erating
glomera'tion
gloom
gloom'ier
gloom'iest
gloom'ily
gloom'iness
gloom'ing
gloom'y
glo'ried
glorifica'tion
glo'rified
glo'rify
glo'rifying
glo'rious
glo'riously
glo'ry
glo'rying
gloss
glossa'rial
glos'sarist
glos'sary
glossed
gloss'er
gloss'ier
gloss'iest
gloss'ily
gloss'iness
gloss'ing
glossog'rapher
glossograph'ical
glossog'raphy
glossolog'ical
glossol'ogist
glossol'ogy
gloss'y
glot'tal
glot'tis
glottol'ogy
glove
gloved
glov'er
glow
glowed

glow'er
glow'ing
glow'-worm
gloxin'ia
gloze
glozed
glo'zer
glo'zing
glu'cic
gluci'na
glu'cine
gluci'num
glu'cose
glue
glued
glu'er
glu'ey
glu'ing
glum
gluma'ceous
glume
glu'mous
glut
glute'al
glu'ten
glu'tinate
glu'tinated
glu'tinating
glu'tinous
glut'ted
glut'ting
glut'ton
glut'tonize
glut'tonous
glut'tony
glyc'erine
glyco'nian
glycon'ic
glyph
glyph'ic
glyph'ograph
glyphog'rapher
glyphograph'ic
glyp'tic
glyptog'raphy
glyptothe'ca
gnarl
gnarled
gnarl'ing
gnarl'y
gnash
gnashed
gnash'ing
gnat
gnaw
gnawed
gnaw'er
gnaw'ing
gneiss
gneiss'ose
gnome
gno'mic
gno'mon
gnomon'ic
gnomon'ical
gnomon'ics
gnomonol'ogy
gno'sis
gnos'tic
gnos'ticism

gnu
go
goad
goad'ed
goad'ing
go'-ahead
goal
goat
goatee'
goat'herd
goat'ish
goat'sucker
gob
gobang'
gob'bet
gob'bing
gob'ble
gob'bled
gob'bler
gob'bling
gob'elin
gob'let
gob'lin
go'by
go'-by
go'-cart
God
god'child
god'daughter
god'dess
Gode'tia
god'father
God'head
god'less
god'like
god'liness
god'ly
god'mother
god'parent
god'send
god'son
God'-speed
god'ward
go'er
gof'fer
gog'gle
gog'gled
gog'gle-eyed
gog'let
*go'*ing
goi'tre
goi'trous
gold
gold'-beater
*gold'*en
gold'-field
*gold'*finch
*gold'*fish
gold'-foil
*gold'*hammer
gold'ilocks
*gold'*lace
gold' plate
gold'-size
*gold'*smith
gold'-stick
*gold'*thread
gold'-wire
golf
Goli'ath

golosh'
gomphi'asis
gompho'sis
gomu'tis
gon'dola
gondolier'
gone
gon'falon
gong
goniom'eter
goniomet'ric
goniomet'rical
goniom'etry
good
good-bye'
good-day'
good-hu'moured
good'ish
good'iness
good'lier
good'liest
good'liness
good'ly
good-na'ture
good-na'tured
good-na'turedly
good'ness
good-night'
goods
goods'-train
good'wife
goodwill'
good'y
Goor'kha, Ghoor'ka
goosan'der
goose
goose'berry
goose'neck
goos'ery
go'pher
Gor'dian
Gor'dian knot
gore
gored
gorge
gorged
gor'geous
gor'geously
gor'geousness
gor'get
gor'ging
gor'gon
gorgo'nian
gorgonzo'la
goril'la
gor'ing
gor'mand
gor'mandism
gor'mandize
gor'mandized
gor'mandizer
gor'mandizing
gorse
gor'y
gos'hawk
gos'ling
gos'pel
gos'peled
gos'peller
gos'samer
gos'samery
gos'sip
gos'siped
gos'siping
got
Goth
Go'thamite
Goth'ic
Goth'icism
Goth'icize
got'ten
gouge
gouged
gou'ging
gourd
gourd'y
gour'mand
gourmet'
gout
gout (taste)
gout'ily
gout'iness
gout'y
gov'ern
*gov'ern*able
gov'ernance
gov'ernante
gov'erned
gov'erness
gov'erning
gov'ernment
governmen'tal
gov'ernor
gov'ernor-*general*
gov'ernorship
gow'an
gown
gowned
gown'man
gowns'man
grab
grabbed
grab'bing
grab'ble
grace
graced
grace'ful
grace'fully
grace'fulness
grace'less
grace'lessness
gra'ces
gra'cing
gra'cious
gra'ciously
gra'ciousness
gradate'
grada'ted
grada'ting
grada'tion
grada'tional
gra'datory
grade
gra'ded
gra'dient
gra'ding
grad'ual
grad'ually
grad'uate
grad'uated
grad'uating
gradua'tion
grad'uator
gra'dus
graf, graff
graffi'ti
graffi'to
graft
graft'ed
graft'er
graft'ing
grail
grain
grained
grain'er
grain'ing
grains
grain'y
gral'lic
gral'loch
gram
gramin'eal
gramin'eous
graminif'erous
graminiv'orous
gram'malogue
gram'mar
gramma'rian
grammat'ic
grammat'ical
grammat'ically
gram'matist
gramme
gram'ophone
gram'pus
gran'ary
grand
gran'dam
gran'dame
grand'-daughter
grandee'
grand'er
grand'est
gran'deur
grand'father
grandil'oquence
grandil'oquent
gran'diose
grand-ju'ror
grand ju'ry
grand'ly
grand'mother
grand'parent
grand'sire
grand'son
grange
gran'ger
gran'gerism
gran'gerize
granif'erous
gran'iform
gran'ite
granit'ic
gran'itoid
graniv'orous
grant
grant'able
grant'ed

grantee'
grant'er
grant'ing
grant'or
gran'ular
gran'ulary
gran'ulate
gran'ulated
gran'ulating
granula'tion
gran'ule
gran'ulose
gran'ulous
grape
gra'pery
grape'-shot
grape'-sugar
grape'-vine
graph'ic
graph'ical
graph'ically
graph'ite
graph'olite
grapholog'ic
grapholog'ical
graphol'ogy
graphom'eter
graphomet'ric
graphomet'rical
graph'otype
grap'nel
grap'ple
grap'pled
grap'pling
grap'pling-iron
grasp
grasp'able
grasped
grasp'er
grasp'ing
grass
grassed
grass'hopper
grass'iness
grass'ing
grass'-plot
grass'y
grate
gra'ted
grate'ful
grate'fully
grate'fulness
gra'ter
gratic'ulate
graticula'tion
gratifica'tion
grat'ified
grat'ifier
grat'ify
grat'ifying
gra'ting
gra'tingly
gra'tis
grat'itude
gratu'itous
gratu'itously
gratu'ity
grat'ulant
grat'ulate
grat'ulated
grat'ulating
gratula'tion
grat'ulatory
grava'men
grave
grave'-clothes
graved
grave'-digger
grav'el
grave'less
grav'elled-led
grav'elling-ling
grav'elly
grave'ly
gra'ven
grave'ness
gra'ver
graves
gra'vest
grave'stone
grave'yard
gravim'eter
gra'ving
gra'ving-dock
grav'itate
grav'itated
grav'itating
gravita'tion
grav'itative
grav'ity
gra'vy
gray, grey
gray'beard
gray'ish
gray'ling
gray'wacke
graze
grazed
gra'zer
gra'zier
gra'zing
grease
greased
greas'ier
greas'iest
greas'ily
greas'iness
greas'ing
greas'y
great
great'coat
*great'*er
great'est
*great'*ly
great' ness
greaves
grebe
Gre'cian
Gre'cism
greed
greed'ily
greed'iness
greed'y
Greek
Greek'-fire
green
green'back
green'cloth
green'er
green'ery
green'est
green'-eyed
green'finch
green'gage
green'grocer
green'horn
green'house
green'ing
green'ish
green'ness
green'-room
greens
green'sand
green'stone
green'sward
green'wood
greet
greet'ed
greet'er
greet'ing
greffier
grega'rious
grega'riously
Grego'rian
greg'ory-pow'der
grenade'
grenadier'
gren'adine
gresso'rial
grew
grey
grey'beard
grey-haired
grey'hound
grey'ness
grid'dle
gride
gri'ded
grid'elin
gri'ding
grid'iron
grief
griev'ance
grieve
grieved
griev'er
griev'ing
griev'ous
griev'ously
griev'ousness
grif'fin
grig
grill
grillade'
gril'lage
grille, grill
grilled
grill'ing
grim
grimace'
grimaced'
grima'cing
grimal'kin
grime
grimed
gri'mier
gri'miest
gri'mily
gri'miness
gri'ming

grim'ly
grim'mer
grim'mest
grim'ness
gri'my
grin
grind
grind'er
grind'ing
grind'stone
grinned
grin'ner
grin'ning
grip
gripe
griped
gri'per
grippe
grip'per
grip'ping
grisaille'
grisette'
gris'kin
gris'liness
gris'ly
gris'on
Grisons'
grist
gris'tle
gris'tly
grit
grit'-stone
grit'tiness
grit'ty
griz'zle
griz'zled
griz'zly
groan
groaned
groan'ing
groat
groats
gro'cer
gro'cery
grog
grog'gery
grog'giness
grog'gy
grog'ram
grog'shop
groin
groined
Gro'lier
grom'met
groom
groomed
groom'ing
grooms'man
groove
grooved
groov'er
groov'ing
grope
groped
gro'per
gro'ping
gros'beak
gross
gross'est
gross'ly
gross'ness
gros'sular
grot
grotesque'
grotesque'ly
grotesque'ness
grot'to
ground
ground'age
ground'-ash
ground'ed
ground'ing
ground'less
ground'lessness
ground'-line
ground'ling
ground'-nut
ground'-plot
ground'-rent
ground'sel
ground'sill
ground'work
group
grouped
group'ing
grouse
grout
grout'ed
grout'ing
grove
grov'el
grov'elled
grov'eled
grov'eller
grov'eler
grov'elling
grov'eling
grow
grow'er
grow'ing
growl
growled
growl'er
growl'ing
growl'ingly
grown
growth
groyne
grub
grubbed
grub'ber
grub'bing
grudge
grudged
grudg'er
grudg'ing
grudg'ingly
gru'el
grue'some
gruff
gruff'est
gruff'ly
gruff'ness
grum
grum'ble
grum'bled
grum'bler
grum'bling
grum'blingly
grume
grum'ly
grum'met
gru'mous
grump
grump'ily
grump'y
grun'dy
grunt
grun'ted
grunt'er
grunt'ing
Gruyère'
guai'acum
guanif'erous
gua'no
guarantee'
guaranteed'
guarantee'ing
guarantor'
guar'anty
guard
guard'ed
guard'edly
guard'edness
guard'er
guard'ian
guard'ianship
*guard'*ing
gua'va
gubernato'rial
gudg'eon
guelder rose
Guelph
Guelph'ic
guer'don
guerril'la
guess
guessed
guess'er
guess'ing
guess'-work
guest
guffaw'
guid'able
guid'ance
guide
guide-book
guid'ed
guide'-post
guid'er
guid'ing
guild
guild'er
guild'hall
guile
guile'ful
guile'fulness
guile'less
guile'lessly
guile'lessness
guil'lemot
guilloche'
guillotine'
guillotined'
guillotin'ing
guilt
guilt'ier
guilt'iest
guilt'ily
guilt'iness

guilt'less
guilt'y
guim'bard
guin'ea
guin'ea-fowl
guin'ea-pig
guise
guitar'
gulch
gul'den
gules
gulf
gull
gulled
gul'let
gullibil'ity
gul'lible
gul'lied
gul'ling
gul'ly, gul'ley
gulp
gulped
gulp'ing
gum
gum-ar'abic
gum'boil
gum-elas'tic
gummed
gummif'erous
gum'miness
gum'mous
gum'my
gump'tion
gum-res'in
gum'-tree
gun
gun'-barrel
gun'boat
gun'-carriage
gun'-cotton
gun'-metal
gun'nel
gun'ner
gun'nery
gun'ning
gun'ny
gun'powder
gun'-room
gun'shot
gun'smith
gun'-stick
gun'-stock
gun'wale, gun'nel
gurge
gur'geons
gur'gle
gur'gled
gur'gling
Gur'kha
gur'nard
gur'net
gush
gushed
gush'ing
gush'ingly
gus'set
gust
gus'tatory
gus'to
gust'y
gut
gut'ta
gut'ta-per'cha
gut'tated
gut'ted
gut'ter
gut'tered
gut'tering
guttif'erous
gut'ting
gut'tural
gut'turally
gut'turalness
guy
guz'zle
guz'zled
guz'zler
guz'zling
gybe
gybed
gyb'ing
gym'khana
gymna'siarch
gymna'sium
gym'nast
gymnas'tic
gymnas'tical
gymnas'tics
gymnos'ophist
gym'nosperm
gymnosperm'ous
gym'note
gynaecol'ogy
gynan'der
gynan'drian
gynan'drous
gyn'archy
gyne'cian
gynecoc'racy
gynoc'racy
gyp'seous
gypsif'erous
gyp'sum
gyp'sy
gyp'syism
gy'ral
gy'rate
gy'rated
gy'rating
gyra'tion
gy'ratory
gyre
gyroid'al
gyr'omancy
gy'roscope
gy'rose
gyve
gyved
gyv'ing

H

ha
ha'beas cor'pus
hab'erdasher
hab'erdashery
hab'erdine
hab'ergeon
habil'iment
habil'itate
hab'it
habitabil'ity
hab'itable
hab'itancy
hab'itat
habita'tion
hab'ited
hab'iting
habit'ual
habit'ually
habit'uate
habit'uated
habit'uating
habitua'tion
hab'itude
habitué'
hacien'da
hack
hacked
hack'er
hack'ing
hack'le
hack'ler
hack'ling
hack'ly
hack'matack
hack'ney
hack'ney-coach
hack'neyed
hack'neying
had
had'dock
hade
Ha'des
hadj
hadj'i
hae'mal
haemat'ic
hae'matin
hae'matite
haematit'ic
haemato'sis
haem'orrhage
haemorrhoid'al
haem'orrhoids
haemostat'ic
haft
haft'ed
hag
hag'gard
hag'ged
hag'gis
hag'gish
hag'gle
hag'gled
hag'gler
hag'gling
ha'giarchy
hagioc'racy
ha'giograph
Hagiog'rapha
hagiog'rapher
hagiog'raphy
hagiol'ogist
hagiol'ogy
hah
ha'-ha
hail
hailed
hail'ing
hail'stone
hail'-storm
hail'y
hair
hair'breadth
hair'cloth
hair'dresser
haired
hair'iness
hair'less
hair'pin
hair'stroke
hair'y
hake
hal'berd
halberdier'
hal'cyon
hale
half
half'-blood
half'-caste
half'-pay
half'pence
half'penny
half'-way
half'-witted
half'-*year*
hal'ibut
hal'idom
hal'ing
haliog'rapher
haliog'raphy
hall
hall'age
hallelu'iah-jah
hal'liard
hall'-mark
halloo'
hallooed'
halloo'ing
hal'low
hal'lowed
Hallow-e'en'
hal'lowing
Hal'lowmas
hallucina'tion
hallu'cinatory
ha'lo
hal'ogen
halog'enous
hal'oid
ha'loscope
halt
halt'ed
hal'ter
halt'ing
halt'ingly
halve
halved
halves
halv'ing
hal'yard
ham
hamadry'ad
ha'mate
ha'mated
ham'ble
hame
Hamilto'nian
Hamit'ic
ham'let
ham'leted
ham'mer
ham'merable
ham'mer-cloth
ham'mered
ham'merer
ham'mering
ham'merman
ham'mock
ha'mous
ham'per
ham'pered
ham'pering
ham'shackle
ham'ster
ham'string
ham'stringed
ham'stringing
ham'strung
han'aper
hance

hand
hand'-bill
*hand'*book
*hand'*breadth
*hand'*cart
*hand'*cuff
*hand'*cuffed
hand'ed
*hand'*ful
hand'-gallop
*hand'*icap
*hand'*icapper
*hand'*icraft
*hand'*icraftsman
*hand'*ier
hand'iest
*hand'*ily
*hand'*iness
hand'iwork
hand'kerchief
*hand'*le
*hand'*led
*hand'*ler
*hand'*ling
hand'maid
hand'maiden
hand'-rail
hand'-saw
hand'screw
*hand'*sel
*hand'*selled-led
*hand'*some
*hand'*somely
*hand'*someness
*hand'*somest
*hand'*spike
hand'-work
*hand'*writing
hand'y
hang
hang'bird
hang'dog
hanged
hang'er
hang'er-on
hang'ing
hang'man
hang'nail
hang'-nest
hank
hank'er
hank'ered
hank'ering
Hanove'rian
Han'sard
hanse
Hanseat'ic
han'som
hap
haphaz'ard
hap'less
hap'ly
hap'pen
hap'pened
hap'pening
hap'pier
hap'piest
hap'pily
hap'piness
hap'py
harangue'
harangued'
harangu'er
harangu'ing
har'ass
har'assed
har'asser
har'assing
har'binger
har'bour, har'bor
har'boured
har'bourer
har'bouring
har'bourless
hard
hard'-earned
hard'en
hard'ened
hard'ener
hard'ening
hard'er
hard'est
hard'-fought
hard'head
hard'-hearted
hard'ier
hard'iest
hard'ihood
hard'ily
hard'iness
hard'ly
hard'ness
hards
hard'ship
hard'ware
har'dy
hare
hare'bell
hare'brained
hare'foot
hare'lip
ha'rem
har'icot
hark
harl
Harle'ian
har'lequin
harlequinade'
har'lot
har'lotry
harm
harmat'tan
harmed
harm'ful
harm'fully
harm'fulness
harm'ing
harm'less
harm'lessly
harm'lessness
harmon'ic
harmon'ica
harmon'ical
harmon'icon
harmo'nious
harmo'niously
harmon'iphon
har'monist
harmo'nium
har'monize
har'monized
har'monizer
har'monizing
harmonom'eter
har'mony
har'most
har'motome
har'ness
har'nessed
har'nesser
har'nessing
harp
harped
harp'er
harp'ing
harp'ings
harp'ist
harpoon'
harpooned'
harpooneer'
harpoon'er
harpoon'ing
harp'sichord
har'py
har'quebus
har'ried
har'rier
har'row
har'rowed
har'rower
har'rowing
har'ry
har'rying
harsh
harsh'er
harsh'est
harsh'ly
harsh'ness
hars'let
hart
harts'horn
har'um-scar'um
harus'pex
harus'pice
harus'picy
har'vest
har'vested
har'vester
har'vesting
has
hash
hashed
hash'ish
has'let
hasp
hasped
has'sock
hast
hast'ate
hast'ated
haste
ha'sted
ha'sten
ha'stened
ha'stener

ha'stening
ha'stier
ha'stiest
ha'stily
ha'stiness
ha'sting
ha'sty
ha'sty-pud'ding
hat
hat'band
hat'box
hatch
hatched
hatch'el
hatch'elled-led
hatch'eller-ler
hatch'elling-ling
hatch'er
hatch'es
hatch'et
hatch'ing
hatch'ment
hatch'way
hate
hate'able
ha'ted
hate'ful
hate'fully
hate'fulness
ha'ter
hath
ha'ting
ha'tred
hat'ter
hatti-sherif'
hau'berk
haugh
haugh'tiest
haugh'tily
haugh'tiness
haugh'ty
haul
haul'age
hauled
haul'er
haul'ing
haulm
haunch
haunched
haunt
haunt'ed
haunt'er
haunt'ing
haut'boy
haut'eur
haut-goût'
Havan'a
have
ha'ven
hav'ersack
hav'ildar
hav'ing
hav'oc
haw
Hawai'ian
hawed
haw-haw'
haw'ing
hawk
hawked
hawk'er
hawk'ey
hawk'-eyed
hawk'ing
hawk'weed
hawse
haw'ser
haw'thorn
hay
hay'cock
hay'field
hay'ing
hay'loft
hay'maker
hay'mow
hay'rick
hay'stack
haz'ard
haz'arded
haz'arding
haz'ardous
haze
hazed
ha'zel
ha'ziness
ha'zing
ha'zy
or *he*
head
head'ache
head'band
head'-dress
head'ed
head'er
head'-gear
head'ily
head'iness
head'ing
head'land
head'less
head'line
head'long
head'man
head'master
or head'quarters
heads'man
head'stall
head'stone
head'strong
head'way
head'wind
head'work
head'y
heal
heal'able
{ heald
{ healed
heal'er
heal'ing
health
health'ful
health'fully
health'fulness
health'ier
health'iest
health'ily
health'iness
health'y
heap
heaped
heap'er
heap'ing
heap'y
hear
heard
hear'er
hear'ing
heark'en
heark'ened
heark'ener
heark'ening
hear'say
hearse
heart
heart'ache
heart'-broken
heart'burn
heart'felt
hearth
hearth'stone
heart'ier
heart'iest
heart'ily
heart'iness
heart'less
heart'lessness
heart'-rending
hearts'ease
heart'-sick
heart'y
heat
heat'ed
heat'er
heath
hea'then
hea'thendom
hea'thenish
hea'thenism
hea'thenize
hea'thenized
hea'thenizing
heath'er
heath'ery
heath'y
heat'ing
heave
heaved
heav'en
heav'enly
heav'enward
heav'er
heaves
heav'ier
heav'iest
heav'ily
heav'iness
heav'ing
heav'y
heav'y-la'den
hebdom'adal
heb'etate
hebeta'tion
heb'etude
Hebra'ic
He'braism
He'braist
Hebraist'ic

He'braize
He'braized
He'braizing
He'brew
He'brewess
Hebrid'ian
hec'atomb
heck'le
hec'tare
hec'tic
hec'tical
hec'togramme
hec'tograph
hec'tolitre-ter
hec'tometre-ter
hec'tor
hec'tored
hec'toring
hec'torism
hed'dle
hedera'ceous
hed'eral
hederif'erous
hedge
hedged
hedge'hog
hedg'er
hedge'row
hedg'ing
hedon'ic
heed
heed'ed
heed'ful
heed'ing
heed'less
heed'lessly
heed'lessness
heel
heeled
heel'er
heel'ing
heel'-tap
heft
hegemon'ic
he'gemony
Heg'ira, Hej'ira
heif'er
heigh'-ho
height
height'en
height'ened
height'ener
height'ening
hei'nous
hei'nously
hei'nousness
heir
heir-appa'rent
heir'dom
heir'ess
heir'less
heir'loom
heir'ship
held
he'liac
heli'acal
hel'ical
hel'icite
hel'icoid

Hel'icon
Helico'nian
heliocen'tric
he'liochrome
he'liograph
heliograph'ic
heliog'raphy
heliol'ater
heliol'atry
heliom'eter
he'lioscope
he'liostat
he'liotrope
he'liotype
helispher'ic
he'lium
hel'ix
hell
hel'lebore
Helle'nian
Helle'nic
Hel'lenism
Hel'lenist
Hellenist'ic
Hel'lenize
Hel'lenized
Hel'lenizing
Hellespon'tine
hell'-hound
hell'ish
hell'ward
helm
helmed
helm'et
helm'eted
helmin'thic
helminthol'ogy
helms'man
hel'ot
hel'otism
help
helped
help'er
help'ful
help'fully
help'fulness
help'less
help'lessly
help'lessness
help'mate
help'meet
hel'ter-skel'ter
helve
helved
Helve'tian
Helvet'ic
helv'in
helv'ing
hem
hem'achate
hemastat'ical
hem'atin
hem'atite
hematit'ic
hemicra'nia
hem'icycle
hemihe'dral
hemi'na

hem'iopsy
hemiple'gia
hem'iplegy
hemip'teral
hemip'terous
hem'isphere
hemispher'ic
hemispher'ical
hemispheroid'al
hem'istich
hem'itrope
hem'lock
hemmed
hem'ming
hem'orrhage
hemorrhoid'al
hem'orrhoids
hemostat'ic
hemp
hemp'en
hemp'seed
hem'-stitch
hen
hen'bane
hence
henceforth'
hencefor'ward
hench'man
hen'coop
hendec'agon
hendec'asyllable
hen'house
hen'na
hen'otheism
hen'peck
hepat'ic
hepat'ical
hep'atite
hepatiza'tion
hep'atize
hep'atized
hepatol'ogy
hepatos'copy
hep'tachord
hep'tagon
heptag'onal
heptagyn'ia
heptahe'dron
heptan'drian
heptan'gular
hep'tarch
hep'tarchy
her
her'ald
her'alded
heral'dic
her'aldry
herb
herba'ceous
herb'age
herb'al
herb'alism
herb'alist
herba'rium
her'bary

herbes'cent
herbif'erous
Herbiv'ora
herbiv'orous
herboriza'tion
her'borize
her'borized
her'borizing
herb'ous
herb'y
Hercu'lean
herd
herd'ed
herd'er
herd'ing
herds'man
here
here'about
hereaf'ter
hereat'
hereby'
hered'itable
heredit'ament
hered'itary
hered'ity
here*in'*
hereof'
hereon'
hereout'
her'esiarch
heresiog'rapher
her'esy
her'etic
heret'ical
heretofore'
hereunto'
hereupon'
herewith'
her'iot
her'iotable
her'isson
her'itable
her'itage
her'itor
her'itrix
hermaph'rodite
hermaphrodit'ic
hermeneu'tical
hermeneu'tics
hermet'ic
hermet'ical
hermet'ically
her'mit
her'mitage
her'mitary
hermit'ical
her'nia
her'nial
he'ro
Hero'dian
hero'ic
hero'ical
hero'ically
her'oine
her'oism
her'on
her'onry
he'ro-worship
her'pes
herpet'ic
herpetol'ogy
her'ring
hers
herse
herself'
her'sillon
hes'itancy
hes'itant
hes'itate
hes'itated
hes'itating
hes'itatingly
hesita'tion
hes'itative
Hes'per
Hespe'rian
Hes'perus
Hes'sian
hetae'ra
hetae'ria
heterocar'pous
heterochro'mous
het'eroclite
heteroclit'ic
heteroclit'ical
heterodac'tyl
het'erodont
het'erodox
het'erodoxy
heterog'amous
heteroge'neal
heterogene'ity
heteroge'neous
heterog'raphy
heterol'ogy
heteromor'phic
heteromor'phous
heteron'omy
het'eronym
heteropath'ic
heterop'athy
heteropha'sia
het'erophemy
het'eropod
het'man
heuris'tic
hew
hewed
hew'er
hew'ing
hewn
hews
hex'achord
hexadac'tylous
hex'ad
hexaë'meron
hex'agon
hexag'onal
hexagyn'ian
hexag'ynous
hexahe'dral
hexahe'dron
hexam'eter
hexamet'ric
hexamet'rical
hexan'dria
hexan'drous
hexan'gular
hexapet'alous
hexaphyl'lous
hex'apla
hex'aplar
hex'apod
hex'astich
hex'astyle
Hex'ateuch
hey
hey'-day
hia'tus
hiber'nacle
hiber'nal
hi'bernate
hi'bernated
hi'bernating
hiberna'tion
Hiber'nian
Hiber'nianism
Hiber'nicism
hi'bernize
{ hic'cup
{ hic'cough
hic'cuped
hic'cuping
hick'ory
hick'wall
hid
hi'dage
hidal'go
hid'den
hid'denly
hide
hide'bound
hid'eous
hid'eously
hi'der
hi'ding
hie
hied
hi'erarch
hierarch'al
hierarch'ical
hi'erarchy
hierat'ic
hieroc'racy
hi'eroglyph
hieroglyph'ic
hieroglyph'ical
hi'erogram
hierogrammat'ic
hierogram'matist
hierog'rapher

hierograph'ic
hierograph'ical
hierog'raphy
hierolog'ic
hierol'ogist
hierol'ogy
hi'eromancy
hi'erophant
hieros'copy
hig'gle
hig'gled
hig'gledy-pig'-[gledy
hig'gler
hig'gling
high
high'-born
high'-bred
high'-church
high'-class
high'er
high'est
high-falu'tin
high'-flown
high'-flyer
high-hand'ed
high'-heeled
high'land
high'lander
high'low
high'ly
high'-minded
high'ness
high'-pressure
high'-priest
high'road
high'-spirited
high'-toned
high'ty-tigh'ty
high'-water
high'way
high'wayman
high'-wrought
hila'rious
hilar'ity
Hil'ary
hill
hill'iness
hill'ock
hill'-side
hill'y
hilt
hilt'ed
hi'lum
him
Hima'layan
himself'
hin
hind
hind'berry
hind'er
hin'der
hin'dered
hin'derer
hin'dering
hind'er*most*
hind'*most*
hin'drance
Hin'du
Hin'duism
Hindusta'ni
hinge
hinged
hin'ging
hin'ny
hint
hint'ed
hin'terland
hint'ing
hint'ingly
hip
hipped
hippocam'pus
hip'pocras
Hippocrat'ic
hip'podrome
hip'pogriff
hippoph'agy
hippopot'amus
hippu'ric
hip'-roof
hip'-shot
hir'cine
hir'cus
hire
hired
hire'ling
hir'er
hir'ing
hir'sute
his
his'pid
hiss
hissed
hiss'ing
hiss'ingly
hist
histog'raphy
histolog'ical
histol'ogist
histol'ogy
histo'rian
histor'ic
histor'ical
historiog'rapher
historiog'raphy
his'tory
histrion'ic
his'trionism
hit
hitch
hitched
hitch'er
hitch'ing
hith'er
hith'er*most*
hither*to'*
hith'erward
hit'ter
hit'ting
hive
hived
hives
hi'ving
ho
hoar
hoard
hoard'ed
hoard'er
hoard'ing
hoar'frost
hoar'hound
hoar'iness
hoarse
hoarse'ly
hoarse'ness
hoar'y
hoax
hoaxed
hoax'ing
hob
hob'ble
hob'bled
hob'bledehoy
hob'bler
hob'bling
hob'by
hob'by-horse
hobgob'lin
hob'nail
hob'nailed
hob'-nob
hock
hocked
hock'ey
hock'ing
hock'le
ho'cus
ho'cus-po'cus
hod
hod'den-grey
hodge'-podge
hodier'nal
hod'man
hoe
hoed
hoe'ing
hoes
hog
hogged
hog'gery
hog'ging
hog'gish
hog'gishly
hogmanay'
hogs'head
hoi'den, hoy'den
hoist
hoist'ed
hoist'ing
hoi'ty-toi'ty
ho'key-po'key
hold
hold'-all
hold'en
hold'er
hold'fast
hold'ing
hole

holed
hol'iday
ho'lier
ho'liest
ho'lily
ho'liness
ho'ling
hol'la
hol'laed
hol'laing
Hol'lander
hol'lands
hol'loa
hol'loaed
hol'loaing
hol'low
hol'lowed
hol'low-eyed'
hol'lowing
hol'lowness
hol'ly
hol'lyhock
holm
hol'ocaust
hol'ograph
hol'ster
hol'stered
ho'ly
ho'ly-day
ho'ly-rood
ho'lystone
hom'age
home
home'-bred
home'-brewed
home'-felt
home'less
home'lessness
home'lier
home'liest
home'liness
home'ly
home'-made
Homer'ic
home'sick
home'spun
home'stead
home'ward
homici'dal
hom'icide
homilet'ic
hom'ilist
hom'ily
ho'ming
hom'iny
hom'mock
homocen'tric
homochro'mous
homoeopath'ic
homoeop'athist
homoeop'athy
homog'amous
homoge'neal
homogene'ity
homoge'neous
homog'eny
homolog'ical
homol'ogous
hom'ologue

homol'ogy
hom'onym
homonym'ic
homon'ymous
homon'ymy
ho'mophone
homoph'onous
homoph'ony
homot'ropal
ho'motype
hone
honed
hon'est
hon'estly
hon'esty
hone'wort
hon'ey
hon'ey-bag
hon'ey-bee
hon'eycomb
hon'ey-dew
hon'eyed
hon'eymoon
hon'eysuckle
hong
hon'ing
hon'or, hon'our
honora'rium
hon'orary
hon'ourable
hon'ourably
hon'oured
hon'ourer
hon'ouring
hon'oursman
hood
hood'ed
hood'wink
hoof
hoofed
hook
hoo'kah
hooked
hook'er
hook'-nosed
hook'y
hoo'ligan
hoop
hooped
hoop'ing
hoop'ing-cough
hoo'poe
hoot
hoot'ed
hoot'ing
hoove
hop
hop-bine
hope
hoped
hope'ful
hope'fully
hope'fulness
hope'less
hope'lessly
hope'lessness
ho'per
hop'-flea

ho'ping
hopped
hop'per
hop'-pick'er
hop'ping
hop'ple
hop'pled
hop'ples
hop'scotch
ho'ral
ho'rary
horde
hori'zon
horizon'tal
horizon'tally
horn
horn'beam
horn'bill
horn'blende
horn'-book
horned
horn'er
hor'net
horn'ing
horn'less
horn'pipe
horn'y
horog'raphy
hor'ologe
horolog'ical
horologiog'raphy
horol'ogist
horol'ogy
horom'eter
horom'etry
hor'oscope
horos'copy
hor'rent
hor'rible
hor'ribleness
hor'ribly
hor'rid
hor'ridly
horrif'ic
hor'rified
hor'rify
hor'rifying
hor'ror
horse
horse'back
horse'-breaker
horse'-chestnut
horse'-cloth
horse'-flesh
horse'-guards
horse'hair
horse'-jockey
horse'-leech

horse'-litter
horse'man
horse'manship
horse'-play
horse'-power
horse'shoe
horse'tail
horse'whip
horse'woman
hors'ing
hors'y
horta'tion
hor'tative
hor'tatory
hor'ticultor
horticul'tural
hor'ticulture
horticul'turist
hor'tulan
hor'tus sic'cus
hosan'na
hose
ho'sier
ho'siery
hos'pice
hos'pitable
hos'pitably
hos'pital
hospital'ity
hos'pitaller
hos'podar
host
hos'tage
hos'tel
hos'telry
host'ess
hos'tile
hos'tilely
hostil'ity
hos'tler
hot
hot'bed
hot'-blooded
hotch'potch
hot cock'les
hotel'
hot'-headed
hot'house
hot'ly
hot'-pressed
hot'-pressing
hot'spur
hot'spurred
Hot'tentot
hot'ter
hot'test
hough
houghed
hound
hound'ish
hour
hour'-glass
hour'-hand
hou'ri
*hour'*ly
house

house'-boat
house'breaker
house'breaking
housed
house'ful
house'hold
house'holder
house'keeper
house'less
house'maid
house'-sur'geon
house'wife
house'wifery
house'wright
hous'ing
hove
hov'el
hov'er
hov'ered
hov'ering
how
howbe'it
how'dah
howev'er
how'itzer
how'ker
howl
howled
howl'er
how'let
howl'ing
howsoev'er
hoy
hoy'den
hoy'denish
hub
hub'bub
huck
huck'aback
huck'le
huck'lebacked
huckle'berry
huck'ster
huck'stered
huck'stering
hud'dle
hud'dled
hud'dler
hud'dling
Hudibras'tic
hue
huff
huffed
huff'er
huff'iness
huff'ish
huff'y
hug
huge
huge'ly
hugged
hug'ger-mug'ger
hug'ging
Hu'guenot
hulk
hull
hullabaloo'

hulled
hull'er
hull'ing
hum
hu'man
humane'
humane'ly
hu'manism
hu'manist
humanita'rian
humanita'rian-[ism
human'ity
humaniza'tion
hu'manize
hu'manized
hu'manizer
hu'manizing
hu'mankind
hu'manly
hum'ble
hum'ble-bee
hum'bled
hum'bleness
hum'bler
hum'blest
hum'bling
hum'bly
hum'bug
hum'bugged
hum'bugging
hum'drum
hu'meral
hu'merus
hum'hum
hu'mic
hu'mid
humid'ify
humid'ity
hu'mify
humil'iate
humil'iated
humil'iating
humilia'tion
humil'ity
hummed
hum'mer
hum'ming
hum'ming-bird
hum'mock
hu'mor, hu'mour
hu'moral
hu'morous
hu'morously
hu'moured
hu'mouring
hu'morist
hu'mourless
hu'moursome
hu'moursomely
hump
hump'back
hump'backed
humped
hump'ty-dump'-[ty
hu'mulin
hu'mus

hun
hunch
hunch'back
hun'dred
hun'dredfold
hun'dredth
hun'dredweight
hung
Hunga'rian
hun'ger
hun'gered
hun'gering
hun'griest
hun'grily
hun'gry
hunks
hunt
hunt'ed
hunt'er
hunt'ing
hunt'ress
hunts'man
hur'dle
hur'dled
hur'dling
hur'dy-gur'dy
hurl
hurl'bat
hurl'bone
hurled
hur'ler
hurl'ing
hur'ly-bur'ly
hurrah'
hur'ricane
hur'ried
hur'riedly
hur'rier
hur'ry
hur'rying
hur'ry-skur'ry
hurt
hurt'er
hurt'ful
hurt'fulness
hur'tleberry
hus'band
hus'banded
hus'banding
hus'bandman
hus'bandry
hush
hushed
hush'ing
hush'-money
husk
husked
husk'ier
husk'iest
husk'ily
husk'iness
husk'ing
husk'y
hussar'
hus'sy
hust'ings
hus'tle
hus'tled
hus'tler
hus'tling
hut
hutch
hutched
hutch'ing
hut'ted
hut'ting
Hutto'nian
huzza'
huzzaed'
huzza'ing
hy'acinth
hyacin'thine
Hy'ades
Hy'ads
hyae'na
hy'aline
hy'aloid
hy'brid
hy'bridize
hybridiza'tion
hy'bridous
hy'datid
hy'datis
hy'datism
hy'dra
hydrac'id
hy'dragogue
Hydran'gea
hy'drant
hydrar'gyrum
hy'drate
hy'drated
hydrau'lic
hy'driad
hy'drid
hy'dride
hydrobro'mic
hydrocar'bon
hydrocar'bonate
hydrocar'buret
hy'drocele
hydroceph'alus
hydrochlo'rate
hydrochlo'ride
hydrocy'anate
hydro-elec'tric
hydro-galvan'ic
hy'drogen
hy'drogenize
hydrog'enous
hydrog'rapher
hydrograph'ic
hydrograph'ical
hydrog'raphy
hy'droid
hydrolog'ical
hydrol'ogist
hydrol'ogy
hydrol'ysis
hy'dromancy
hy'dromel
hydrom'eter
hydromet'ric
hydrom'etry
hydropath'ic
hydrop'athist
hydrop'athy
hy'drophane
hydroph'anous
hydropho'bia
hydropho'bic
hy'drophyte
hydrop'ic
hy'droplane
hy'drosalt
hy'droscope
hydrostat'ic
hydrostat'ics
hydrosul'phate
hydrosul'phuret
hydrot'ic
hy'drous
hydrox'ide
hydrox'y
hydrox'yl
hye'mal
hye'na
hygei'an
hy'giene
hygien'ic
hygrol'ogy
hygrom'eter
hygromet'ric
hygrom'etry
hy'groscope
hy'lobate
hy'loist
hy'lotheism
hylozo'ic
hylozo'ism
hy'men
hymene'al
hymene'an
Hymenop'tera
hymenop'teral
hymn
hym'nal
hymn'-book
hymned
hym'nic
hymn'ing
hym'nody
hymnog'rapher
hymnol'ogist
hymnol'ogy
hy'oid
Hyoscy'amus
hyperbat'ic
hyper'baton
hyper'bola
hyper'bole
hyperbol'ic
hyperbol'ical
hyperbol'ically
hyper'bolism
hyper'bolist

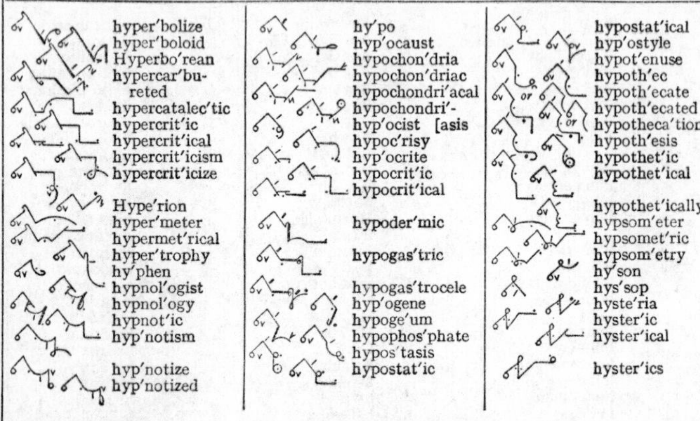

hyper'bolize
hyper'boloid
Hyperbo'rean
hypercar'bu-
reted
hypercatalec'tic
hypercrit'ic
hypercrit'ical
hypercrit'icism
hypercrit'icize
Hype'rion
hyper'meter
hypermet'rical
hyper'trophy
hy'phen
hypnol'ogist
hypnol'ogy
hypnot'ic
hyp'notism
hyp'notize
hyp'notized

hy'po
hyp'ocaust
hypochon'dria
hypochon'driac
hypochondri'acal
hypochondri'-
hyp'ocist [asis
hypoc'risy
hyp'ocrite
hypocrit'ic
hypocrit'ical
hypoder'mic
hypogas'tric
hypogas'trocele
hyp'ogene
hypoge'um
hypophos'phate
hypos'tasis
hypostat'ic

hypostat'ical
hyp'ostyle
hypot'enuse
hypoth'ec
hypoth'ecate
hypoth'ecated
hypotheca'tion
hypoth'esis
hypothet'ic
hypothet'ical
hypothet'ically
hypsom'eter
hypsomet'ric
hypsom'etry
hy'son
hys'sop
hyste'ria
hyster'ic
hyster'ical
hyster'ics

I

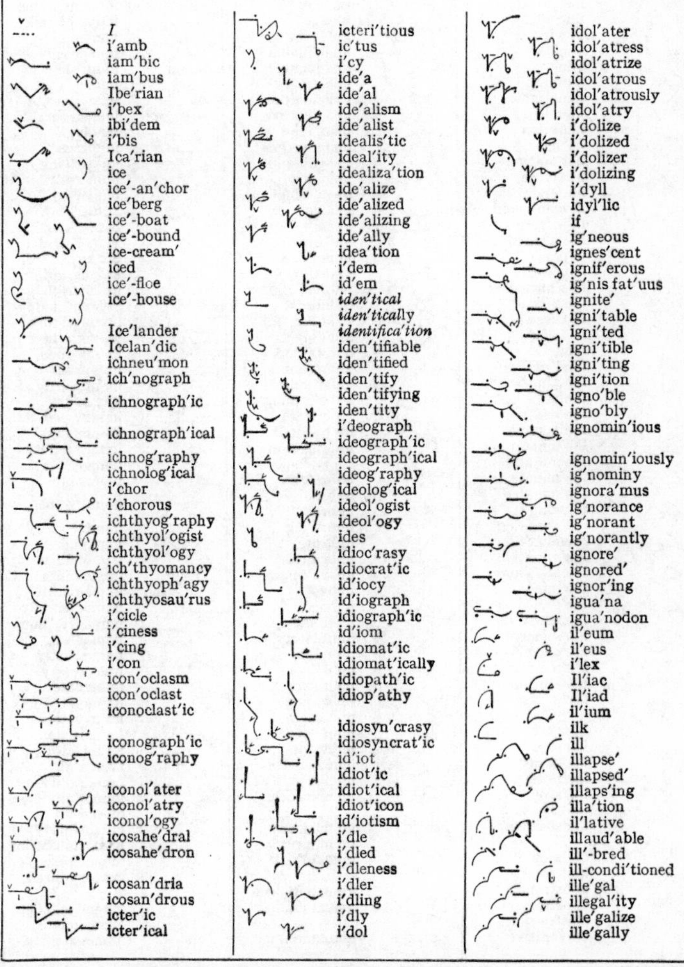

I
i'amb
iam'bic
iam'bus
Ibe'rian
i'bex
ibi'dem
i'bis
Ica'rian
ice
ice'-an'chor
ice'berg
ice'-boat
ice'-bound
ice-cream'
iced
ice'-floe
ice'-house
Ice'lander
Icelan'dic
ichneu'mon
ich'nograph
ichnograph'ic
ichnograph'ical
ichnog'raphy
ichnolog'ical
i'chor
i'chorous
ichthyog'raphy
ichthyol'ogist
ichthyol'ogy
ich'thyomancy
ichthyoph'agy
ichthyosau'rus
i'cicle
i'ciness
i'cing
i'con
icon'oclasm
icon'oclast
iconoclast'ic
iconograph'ic
iconog'raphy
iconol'ater
iconol'atry
iconol'ogy
icosahe'dral
icosahe'dron
icosan'dria
icosan'drous
icter'ic
icter'ical
icteri'tious
ic'tus
i'cy
ide'a
ide'al
ide'alism
ide'alist
idealis'tic
ideal'ity
idealiza'tion
ide'alize
ide'alized
ide'alizing
ide'ally
idea'tion
i'dem
id'em
iden'tical
*iden'tical*ly
identifica'tion
iden'tifiable
iden'tified
iden'tify
iden'tifying
iden'tity
i'deograph
ideograph'ic
ideograph'ical
ideog'raphy
ideolog'ical
ideol'ogist
ideol'ogy
ides
idioc'rasy
idiocrat'ic
id'iocy
id'iograph
idiograph'ic
id'iom
idiomat'ic
idiomat'ically
idiopath'ic
idiop'athy
idiosyn'crasy
idiosyncrat'ic
id'iot
idiot'ic
idiot'ical
idiot'icon
id'iotism
i'dle
i'dled
i'dleness
i'dler
i'dling
i'dly
i'dol
idol'ater
idol'atress
idol'atrize
idol'atrous
idol'atrously
idol'atry
i'dolize
i'dolized
i'dolizer
i'dolizing
i'dyll
idyl'lic
if
ig'neous
ignes'cent
ignif'erous
ig'nis fat'uus
ignite'
igni'table
igni'ted
igni'tible
igni'ting
igni'tion
igno'ble
igno'bly
ignomin'ious
ignomin'iously
ig'nominy
ignora'mus
ig'norance
ig'norant
ig'norantly
ignore'
ignored'
ignor'ing
igua'na
igua'nodon
il'eum
il'eus
i'lex
Il'iac
Il'iad
il'ium
ilk
ill
illapse'
illapsed'
illaps'ing
illa'tion
il'lative
illaud'able
ill'-bred
ill-condi'tioned
ille'gal
illegal'ity
ille'galize
ille'gally

illegibil'ity
illeg'ible
illeg'ibly
illegit'imacy
illegit'imate, *n.*, *a.*
illegit'imate, *v.*
illev'iable
ill-fa'voured
ill-hu'mour
illib'eral
illiberal'ity
illib'erally
illic'it
illic'itly
illic'itness
illimitabil'ity
illim'itable
illim'ited
illini'tion
illi'sion
illit'eracy
illit'erate
illit'erateness
ill-man'nered
ill-na'ture
ill-na'tured
ill'ness
illog'ical
ill-o'mened
ill-starred'
ill-timed'
ill-treat'
illude'
illud'ed
illud'ing
illume'
illumed'
illu'minable
illu'minant
illu'minary
illu'minate
illu'minated
illumina'ti
illu'minating
illumina'tion
illu'minative
illu'minator
illu'mine
illu'mined
illuminee'
illu'miner
illu'ming
illu'mining
illu'minism
illu'minize
ill'-used
illu'sion
illu'sionism
illu'sionist
illu'sive
illu'sively
illu'siveness
illu'sory
ill'ustrate
ill'ustrated
ill'ustrating
illustra'tion
illus'trative
illus'tratively
ill'ustrater
ill'ustrator
illus'tratory
illus'trious
illus'triously
illus'triousness
ill-will'
ill-wish'er
im'age
im'ageable
im'aged
im'agery
imag'inable
imag'inably
imag'inary
imagina'tion
imag'inative
imag'ine
imag'ined
imag'iner
im'aging
imag'ining
ima'go
imam'
im'becile
imbecil'ity
imbed'
imbibe'
imbibed'
imbi'ber
imbi'bing
imbibi'tion
imbo'som
imbo'somed
imbo'soming
im'bricate
im'bricated
imbrica'tion
imbro'glio
imbrue'
imbrued'
imbru'ing
imbrute'
imbru'ted
imbru'ting
imbue'
imbued'
imbu'ing
imitabil'ity
im'itable
im'itate
im'itated
im'itating
imita'tion
im'itative
im'itator
immac'ulate
immac'ulateness
im'manence
im'manency
im'manent
immate'rial
immate'rialism
immate'rialist
immaterial'ity
immate'rially
immature'
immatured'
immature'ly
immatur'ity
immeas'urable
immeas'urably
imme'diate
*imme'diate*ly
immed'icable
immem'orable
immemo'rial
immense'
immense'ly
immense'ness
immen'sity
immensurabil'ity
immen'surable
immerge'
immerged'
immer'ging
immerse'
immersed
immers'ing
immer'sion
immer'sionist
immethod'ical
im'migrant
im'migrate
im'migrated
im'migrating
immigra'tion
im'minence
im'minent
im'minently
immin'gle
immin'gled
immin'gling
immiscibil'ity
immis'cible
immis'sion
immit'igable
immix'
immo'bile
immobil'ity
immo'bilize
immod'erate
immod'erately
immodera'tion
immod'est
immod'estly
immod'esty
im'molate
im'molated
im'molating
immola'tion
im'molator
immor'al
immoral'ity
immor'ally
immor'tal
immortal'ity
immortaliza'tion
immor'talize
immor'talized
immor'talizing
immortelle'
immovabil'ity

immov'able
immov'ably
immune'
immu'nity
immuniza'tion
im'munize
immure'
immured'
immur'ing
immutabil'ity
immu'table
immu'tably
imp
impact
impact'ed
impact'ing
impair'
impaired'
impair'er
impair'ing
impale'
impaled'
impale'ment
impal'ing
impalpabil'ity
impal'pable
impana'tion
impan'el
impan'elled-led
impan'elling-ling
impar'adise
imparisyllab'ic
impar'ity
impark'
imparl'
imparl'ance
impart'
impart'ed
impart'er
impart'ing
impar'tial
impartial'ity
impar'tially
impar'tialness
impartibil'ity
impart'ible
impart'ment
impas'sable
impasse'
impassibil'ity
impas'sible
impas'sion
impas'sionate
impas'sioned
impas'sive
impas'sively
impas'siveness
impassiv'ity
impasta'tion
impaste'
impa'sted
impa'sting
impa'tience
impa'tient
impa'tiently
impawn'
impawned'
impawn'ing
impeach'
impeach'able
impeached'
impeach'er
impeach'ment
impearl'
impearled'
impearl'ing
impeccabil'ity
impec'cable
impec'cancy
impec'cant
impecunios'ity
impecu'nious
impede'
imped'ed
impe'dient
imped'iment
impedimen'ta
impedimen'tal
impe'ding
impel'
impelled'
impel'lent
impel'ler
impel'ling
impen'
impend'
impend'ed
impend'ence
impend'ency
impend'ent
impend'ing
impenetrabil'ity
impen'etrable
impen'itence
impen'itency
impen'itent
impen'itently
impen'nate
impen'nous
imperati'val
imper'ative
imper'atively
impera'tor
imperato'rial
imper'atory
imperceptibil'ity
impercep'tible
impercep'tibleness
impercep'tibly
imper'fect
imperfec'tion
imper'fectly
imper'fectness
imper'forable
imper'forate
imper'forated
imperfora'tion
impe'rial
impe'rialism
impe'rialist
impe'rialistic
impe'rially
imper'il
imper'illed
imper'illing
impe'rious
impe'riously
impe'riousness
imper'ishable
imper'ishable-ness
imper'manence
imper'manent
impermeabil'ity
imper'meable
imper'sonal
impersonal'ity
imper'sonally
imper'sonate
imper'sonated
imper'sonating
impersona'tion
impersua'sible
imper'tinence
imper'tinency
imper'tinent
imper'tinently
imperturb'ability
imperturb'able
imperturba'tion
imperviabil'ity
imper'viable
imper'vious
imper'viousness
impeti'go
im'petrate
impetra'tion
impetuos'ity
impet'uous
impet'uously
im'petus
im'pi
impierce'
impi'ety
impinge'
impinged'
impinge'ment
impin'ging
im'pious
im'piously
im'piousness
imp'ish
implacabil'ity
impla'cable
impla'cably
implant'
implanta'tion
implant'ed
implant'ing
implausibil'ity
implau'sible
implau'sibleness
implead'
implead'ed
implead'er
implead'ing
im'plement
imple'tion
im'plex
im'plicate
im'plicated
im'plicating

implica'tion
im'plicative
implic'it
implic'itly
implic'itness
implied'
implied'ly
implora'tion
implore'
implored'
implor'er
implor'ing
implor'ingly
implumed'
imply'
imply'ing
impol'icy
impolite'
impolite'ly
impolite'ness
impol'itic
impolit'ical
imponderabil'ity
impon'derable
impon'derous
imporos'ity
impo'rous
import
import'able
impor'tance
impor'tant
*impor'tant*ly
importa'tion
import'ed
import'er
import'ing
impor'tunate
impor'tunately
importune'
importuned'
importun'er
importun'ing
importu'nity
impo'sable
impose'
imposed'
impo'ser
impo'sing
impo'singly
impo'sing-stone
imposi'tion
impossibil'ity
impos'sible
im'post
imposthuma'tion
impos'thume
impos'tor
impos'ture
impos'tured
im'potence
im'potency
im'potent
im'potently
impound'
impound'ed
impound'er
impound'ing
impov'erish
impov'erished
impov'erisher
impov'erishing
impov'erishment
im*practicabil'*ity
im*prac'ticable*
im'precate
im'precated
im'precating
impreca'tion
im'precatory
impreci'sion
impregn'
impregnabil'ity
impreg'nable
impreg'nably
impreg'nate
impreg'nated
impreg'nating
impregna'tion
impresa'rio
imprescrip'tible
impress
impressed'
impressibil'ity
impress'ible
impress'ing
impres'sion
impres'sionable
impres'sionism
impres'sionist
impress'ive
impress'ively
impress'ment
impress'ure
imprima'tur
impri'mis
imprint
imprint'ed
impris'on
impris'oned
impris'oning
impris'onment
im*probabil'ity*
im*prob'able*
im*prob'ably*
improb'ity
impromp'tu
improp'er
improp'erly
impro'priate
impro'priated
impro'priating
impropria'tion
impro'priator
impropri'ety
*improv*abil'ity
improv'able
improv'ableness
improve'
improved'
improve'ment
improv'er
improv'idence
improv'ident
improv'idently
*improv'*ing
*improv'*ingly
improvisa'tion
improv'isator
improvisato're
improvise'
improvised'
improvi'ser
improvi'sing
impru'dence
impru'dent
impru'dently
im'pudence
im'pudent
im'pudently
impudic'ity
impugn'
impugned'
impugn'er
im'pulse
impul'sion
impul'sive
impul'sively
impul'siveness
impu'nity
impure'
impure'ly
impure'ness
impu'rity
impur'ple
impu'table
imputa'tion
impu'tative
impute'
impu'ted
impu'ter
impu'ting
imputres'cible
in
inabil'ity
inaccessibil'ity
inaccess'ible
inaccess'ibly
inac'curacy
inac'curate
inac'curately
inac'tion
inac'tive
inact'ively
inactiv'ity
inad'equacy
inad'equate
inad'equately
inad'equateness
inadmissibil'ity
inadmis'sible
inadvert'ence
inadvert'ent
inadvert'ently
ina'lienable
inamora'ta
inamora'to
inane'
inan'imate
inan'imated
inani'tion
inan'ity
inap'petence
inap'petency
inapplicabil'ity

inap'plicable
inapplica'tion
inap'posite
inappre'ciable
inappro'priate
inapt'
inapt'itude
inapt'ly
inapt'ness
inarch'
inartic'ulate
inartic'ulately
inarticula'tion
inartifi'cial
inartis'tic
inasmuch'
inatten'tion
inatten'tive
inatten'tively
inatten'tiveness
inaudibil'ity
inaud'ible
inau'gural
inau'gurate
inau'gurated
inau'gurating
inaugura'tion
inau'gurator
inauspi'cious
inauspi'ciously
in'born
inbreathe'
in'bred
in'ca
incage'
incal'culable
incales'cence
incales'cency
incales'cent
incandes'cence
incandes'cent
incanta'tion
incan'tatory
incapabil'ity
inca'pable
incapa'cious
incapac'itate
incapac'itated
incapac'ity
incar'cerate
incar'cerated
incar'cerating
incarcera'tion
incar'nate, *adj.*
incar'nate, *v.*
incar'nated
incar'nating
incarna'tion
incar'native
incase'
incased'
incas'ing
incatena'tion
incau'tion
incau'tious
incau'tiously
incau'tiousness

in'cavated
incava'tion
incen'diarism
incen'diary
in'cense
incen'sive
incen'sor
incen'tive
incep'tion
incep'tive
incep'tor
incera'tion
incer'titude
inces'sancy
inces'sant
inces'santly
in'cest
inces'tuous
inch
inch'meal
in'choate
in'choately
inchoa'tion
incho'ative
in'cidence
in'cident
inciden'tal
inciden'tally
incin'erate
incin'erated
incin'erating
incinera'tion
incip'ience
incip'iency
incip'ient
incip'iently
incise'
incised'
inci'sing
inci'sion
inci'sive
inci'sor
inci'sory
incis'ure
inci'tant
incita'tion
incite'
inci'ted
incite'ment
inci'ter
inci'ting
incivil'ity
inclasp'
inclasped'
inclasp'ing
inclave'
inclem'ency
inclem'ent
incli'nable
inclina'tion
incli'natory
incline'
inclined'
incli'ner
incli'ning
inclinom'eter
inclose'
inclosed'

inclo'sing
inclo'sure
include'
inclu'ded
inclu'ding
inclu'sion
inclu'sive
inclu'sively
incoer'cible
incog.
incog'nita
incog'nito
incog'nizable
incog'nizance
incog'nizant
incoher'ence
incoher'ency
incoher'ent
incoher'ently
incoin'cident
incombustibil'ity
incombus'tible
in'come
in'coming
incommensurability
incommen'surable
incommen'surate
incommode'
incommo'ded
incommo'ding
incommo'dious
incommunicabil'ity
incommu'nicable
incommu'nicative
incommu'table
incompact'
incom'parable
incom'parably
incompass'ionate
incompatibil'ity
incompat'ible
incom'petence
incom'petency
incom'petent
incom'petently
incomplete'
incomplete'ly
incomplete'ness
incompli'ant
incom'posite
incomprehensibil'ity
incomprehen'sible
incomprehen'sive
incompressibil'ity
incompress'ible
incompu'table
inconceiv'able
inconclu'sive
inconclu'sively
incondens'able

incon'gruent
incongru'ity
incon'gruous
incon'gruously
incon'sequence
incon'sequent
inconsequen'tial
inconsid'erable
inconsid'erate
*inconsid'erate*ly
inconsidera'tion
inconsist'ency
inconsist'ent
inconsist'ently
inconsol'able
incon'sonance
inconspic'uous
inconspic'uously
incon'stancy
incon'stant
incon'stantly
inconsum'able
incontest'able
incon'tinence
incon'tinent
incon'tinently
incontrol'lable
incontrovertibil'ity
incontrovert'ible
inconve'nience
inconve'nienced
inconve'nient-ly
inconvertibil'ity
inconvert'ible
inco-or'dinate
inco-ordina'tion
incor'porate, *adj.*
incor'porate, *v.*
incor'porated
incor'porating
incorpora'tion
incorpo'real
incorpore'ity
incorrect'
incorrect'ly
incorrect'ness
incorrigibil'ity
incor'rigible
incor'rigibleness
incor'rigibly
incorro'dible
incorrupt'
incorruptibil'ity
incorrupt'ible
incorrup'tion
incorrupt'ness
incras'sate, *adj.*
incras'sate, *v.*
incrassa'tion
incras'sative
increase
increased'
increas'er
increas'ing
increasingly'
incredibil'ity
incred'ible

incred'ibly
incredu'lity
incred'ulous
incred'ulousness
in'crement
incremen'tal
incrim'inate
incrim'inatory
incrust'
incrust'ate
incrusta'tion
incrust'ed
incrust'ing
in'cubate
in'cubated
in'cubating
in'cubation
in'cubator
in'cubus
in'culcate
in'culcated
in'culcating
inculca'tion
in'culcator
incul'pable
incul'pate
incul'pated
incul'pating
inculpa'tion
incul'patory
incum'bency
incum'bent
incur'
incurabil'ity
incur'able
incur'ably
incu'rious
incu'riously
incurred'
incur'rence
incur'ring
incur'sion
incur'sive
incurv'ate, *adj.*
incurv'ate, *v.*
incurv'ated
incurv'ating
incurva'tion
incurve'
incurved'
incurv'ing
indebt'ed
indebt'edness
inde'cency
inde'cent
inde'cently
indecid'uous
indeci'pherable
indeci'sion
indeci'sive
indeci'sively
indecli'nable

indeco'rous
indeco'rousness
indeco'rum
indeed'
indefatigabil'ity
indefat'igable
indefeasibil'ity
indefea'sible
indefensibil'ity
indefen'sible
indefen'sibly
indefin'able
indef'inite
indef'initely
indef'initeness
indelibil'ity
indel'ible
indel'ibly
indel'icacy
indel'icate
indel'icately
indemnifica'tion
indem'nified
indem'nify
indem'nifying
indem'nity
indent'
indenta'tion
indent'ed
indent'ing
inden'ture
independ'ence
independ'ent
independ'ently
indescri'bable
indestructibil'ity
indestruc'tible
indeter'minable
indeter'minate
indeter'minately
indetermina'tion
indevout'
in'dex
in'dexed
in'dexer
index'ical
in'dexing
indexter'ity
In'diaman
In'dian
in'dia-rub'ber
in'dicant
in'dicate
in'dicated
in'dicating
indica'tion
indic'ative
indic'atively
in'dicator
in'dicatory
ind'ices
indict'

indict'able
indict'ed
indict'er
indict'ing
indic'tion
indic'tive
indict'ment
{ *indif'ference*
{ *indif'ferent*
indif'ferentism
indif'ferently
in'digence
in'digene
indig'enous
in'digent
indigest'ed
indigestibil'ity
indigest'ible
indiges'tion
indig'nant
indig'nantly
indigna'tion
indig'nity
in'digo
indigom'eter
in'digotin
indirect'
indirec'tion
indirect'ly
indirect'ness
indiscern'ible
indiscern'ibly
indis'cipline
indiscreet'
indiscreet'ly
indiscrete'
indiscre'tion
indiscrim'inate
indiscrim'inately
indiscrimina'tion
{ *indispen'sable*
{ *indispen'sably*
indispose'
indisposed'
indisposi'tion
indis'putable
indis'putably
indissolubil'ity
indis'soluble
indis'solubly
indissol'vable
indistinct'
indistinct'ly
indistinct'ness
indistin'guish-able
indite'
indi'ted
indite'ment
indi'ter
indi'ting
individ'ual
individ'ualism
individual'ity

individualiza'tion
individ'ualize
individ'ualized
individ'ualizing
individ'ually
indivisibil'ity
indivis'ible
indoc'ile
indocil'ity
indoc'trinate
indoc'trinating
indoctrina'tion
in'dolence
in'dolent
in'dolently
indom'itable
in'door
indors'able
indorse'
indorsed'
indorsee'
indorse'ment
indors'er
indors'ing
in'draught
in'drawn
indu'bitable
indu'bitably
induce'
induced'
induce'ment
indu'cer
indu'cible
indu'cing
induct'
induct'ed
induct'ile
inductil'ity
induct'ing
induc'tion
induc'tive
induc'tively
inductom'eter
induct'or
indue'
indued'
indu'ing
indulge'
indulged'
indul'gence
indul'gent
indul'gently
indul'ger
indul'ging
in'durate
in'durated
in'durating
indura'tion
indus'trial
indus'trious
indus'triously
in'dustry
in'dwelling
ine'briant
ine'briate
ine'briated

ine'briating
inebria'tion
inebri'ety
ined'ited
inef'fable
inef'fableness
inef'fably
ineffice'able
ineffective'
ineffect'ual
ineffect'ually
ineffica'cious
inef'ficacy
{ *inefi'ciency*
{ *inefi'cient*
{ *inefi'ciently*
inelas'tic
inelastic'ity
inel'egance
inel'egant
inel'egantly
ineligibil'ity
inel'igible
inept'
inept'itude
inept'ly
inept'ness
in*equal'*ity
ineq'uitable
inerad'icable
inerrabil'ity
inerr'able
iner'rancy
iner'rant
inert'
iner'tia
inert'ly
inert'ness
inessen'tial
ines'timable
ines'timably
inev'itable
inev'itably
inexact'
inexact'ness
inexcus'able
inexcu'sableness
inexcu'sably
inexer'tion
inexhal'able
inexhaust'ed
inexhaust'ible
inexhaust'ibly
inexist'ence
inexist'ent
inex'orable
inex'orably
inexpe'diency
inexpe'dient
inexpen'sive
inexpe'rience
inexpe'rienced
inexpert'

inex'piable
inex'plicable
inex'plicably
inexplic'it
inexpress'ible
inexpress'ibly
inexpress'ive
inexpug'nable
inextinct'
in*extin'guish*able
inex'tricable
inex'tricably
infallibil'ity
infal'lible
infal'libly
in'famous
in'famously
in'famy
in'fancy
in'fant
infan'ta
infan'te
infan'ticide
in'fantile
in'fantine
in'fantry
infat'uate
infat'uated
infat'uating
infatua'tion
infea'sible
infect'
infect'ed
infect'ing
infec'tion
infec'tious
infec'tiously
infec'tiousness
infec'tive
infec'tor
infec'und
infecun'dity
infeft'ment
infelic'itous
infelic'ity
infer'
infer'able
in'ference
inferen'tial
infe'rior
inferior'ity
infer'nal
infer'nally
infer'no
infer'rable
inferred'
infer'ring
infer'tile
infertil'ity
infest'
infesta'tion
infest'ed
infest'er
infest'ing
infestiv'ity
in'fidel
infidel'ity
infil'trate
infil'trated
infil'trating
infiltra'tion
in'finite
in'finitely
in'finiteness
infinites'imal
infin'itive
infin'itude
infin'ity
infirm'
infir'mary
infir'mity
infirm'ly
infix'
inflame'
inflamed'
infla'mer
infla'ming
inflammabil'ity
inflam'mable
inflamma'tion
inflam'matory
infla'table
inflate'
infla'ted
infla'ter
infla'ting
infla'tion
infla'tionary
inflect'
inflect'ed
{ inflec'tion
{ inflex'ion
inflec'tional
inflec'tive
inflexed'
inflexibil'ity
inflex'ible
inflex'ibly
inflict'
inflict'ed
inflict'er
inflict'ing
inflic'tion
inflic'tive
inflores'cence
inflow
in'fluence
in'fluenced
*in'fluenc*ing
in'fluent
{ *influen'tial*
{ *influen'tially*
influen'za
in'flux
influx'ion
infold'
infold'ed
infold'ing
info'liate
inform'
inform'al
informal'ity
inform'ally
inform'ant
informa'tion
informed'
inform'er
*inform'*ing
infract'
infrac'tion
infract'or
infran'gible
infre'quence
infre'quency
infre'quent
infringe'
infringed'
infringe'ment
infrin'ger
infrin'ging
infruc'tuous
infrugif'erous
infundib'ular
infu'riate
infu'riated
infu'riating
infus'cate
infuse'
infused'
infu'ser
infusibil'ity
infu'sible
infu'sing
infu'sion
infu'sive
Infuso'ria
infuso'rial
infu'sory
in'gather
in'gathering
ingen'erate, *adj.*
ingen'erate, *v.*
ingenera'tion
inge'nious
inge'niously
inge'niousness
ingénue'
ingenu'ity
ingen'uous
ingen'uously
ingen'uousness
ingest'
inges'ta
inges'tion
in'gle
inglo'rious
inglo'riously
in'got
ingraft'
ingraft'ed
ingraft'ing

ingraft'ment
ingrain'
ingrained'
ingrain'ing
in'grate
ingra'tiate
ingra'tiated
ingra'tiating
ingrat'itude
ingre'dient
ingress
ingres'sion
in'growing
in'growth
in'guinal
ingulf'
ingulfed'
ingur'gitate
ingurgita'tion
inhab'it
inhab'itable
inhab'itancy
inhab'itant
inhabita'tion
inhab'itativeness
inhab'ited
inhab'iter
inhab'iting
inhab'itiveness
inhala'tion
inhale'
inhaled'
inha'ler
inha'ling
inharmon'ic
inharmo'nious
inharmo'niously
inharmo'nious-ness
inhere'
inhered'
inher'ence
inher'ency
inher'ent
inher'ently
inher'it
inher'itable
inher'itance
inher'ited
inher'iting
inher'itor
inher'itrix
inhib'it
inhib'ited
inhib'iting
inhibi'tion
inhib'itory
inhos'pitable
inhos'pitably
inhospital'ity
inhu'man
inhu'manly
inhuman'ity

inhuma'tion
inhume'
inhumed'
inhu'ming
inim'ical
inim'ically
inim'itable
inim'itably
iniq'uitous
iniq'uity
ini'tial
ini'tialled-led
ini'tially
ini'tiate
ini'tiated
ini'tiating
initia'tion
ini'tiative
ini'tiatory
inject'
inject'ed
inject'ing
injec'tion
injudi'cial
injudi'cious
injudi'ciously
injunc'tion
in'jure
in'jured
in'jurer
in'juring
inju'rious
inju'riously
in'jury
injus'tice
ink
ink'horn
ink'iness
in'kle
ink'ling
ink'stand
ink'y
inlace'
inlaced'
inla'cing
inlaid'
in'land
in'lander
inlay
in'layer
inlay'ing
inleague'
in'let
inlock'
in'ly
in'mate
in'most
inn
innate'
innate'ly
innate'ness
innav'igable
in'ner
in'ner*most*
innerv'ate
innerva'tion

innerve'
innerved'
innerv'ing
in'ning
inn'keeper
in'nocence
in'nocency
in'nocent
in'nocently
innoc'uous
innoc'uously
innom'inate
in'novate
in'novated
in'novating
innova'tion
in'novator
innox'ious
innox'iously
innuen'do
innu'merable
innu'merably
innu'merous
innutri'tion
innutri'tious
innu'tritive
inobtru'sive
inobtru'sively
inobtru'siveness
inoc'ulable
inoc'ular
inoc'ulate
inoc'ulated
inoc'ulating
inocula'tion
inoc'ulator
ino'dorous
inoffen'sive
inoffen'sively
inoffi'cial
inoffi'cious
inop'erative
inopportune'
inopportune'ly
inor'dinacy
inor'dinate
inor'dinately
inordina'tion
inorgan'ic
inos'culate
inos'culated
inoscula'tion
in'quest
inqui'etude
inquir'able
inquire'
inquired'
inquiren'do

inquir'er
inquir'ing
inquir'y
inquisi'tion
inquisi'tional
inquis'itive
inquis'itively
inquis'itiveness
inquis'itor
inquisito'rial
inquisito'rially
in'ro
in'road
in'rush
insaliva'tion
insalu'brious
insalu'brity
insal'utary
insane'
insane'ly
insan'ity
insatiabil'ity
insa'tiable
insa'tiableness
insa'tiably
insa'tiate
insa'tiately
insati'ety
inscri'bable
{ *inscribe'*
{ *inscribed'*
inscri'ber
inscri'bing
inscrip'tion
inscrip'tive
inscroll'
inscrolled'
inscrutabil'ity
inscru'table
inseam'
in'sect
insecta'rium
insec'ticide
in'sectile
insec'tion
insectiv'orous
insecure'
insecure'ly
insecu'rity
insem'inate
insemina'tion
insen'sate
{ *insensibil'ity*
{ *insen'sible*
{ *insen'sibly*
insen'tient
inseparabil'ity
insep'arable
insep'arableness
insep'arably
insert'
insert'ed
insert'ing
inser'tion
Insesso'res

insesso'rial
in'set
in'shore
insicca'tion
in'side
insi'der
insid'ious
insid'iously
in'sight
insig'nia
in*signif'icance*
in*signif'icancy*
in*signif'icant*
insincere'
insincere'ly
insincer'ity
insin'uate
insin'uated
insin'uating
insin'uatingly
insinua'tion
insin'uative
insin'uator
insip'id
insipid'ity
insip'idly
insip'ience
insip'ient
insist'
insist'ed
insist'ence
insist'ency
insist'ent
insist'ently
insist'ing
insi'tion
in si'tu
insnared'
insnar'er
insnar'ing
insobri'ety
inso'ciable
in'solate
in'solated
insola'tion
in'solence
in'solent
in'solently
insolid'ity
insolubil'ity
insol'uble
insolv'able
insolv'ency
insolv'ent
insom'nia
*in*somuch'
insouciance'
inspan'
{ *inspect'*
{ *inspect'ed*
*inspect'*ing
inspec'tion
inspec'tive
inspec'tor
or inspector-*gen'eral*
inspir'able

inspira'tion
inspir'atory
inspire'
inspired'
inspi'rer
inspi'ring
inspir'it
inspir'ited
inspir'iting
inspis'sate
inspis'sated
inspis'sating
inspissa'tion
instabil'ity
insta'ble
install'
installa'tion
installed'
install'ing
instal'ment
in'stance
in'stanced
in'stancing
in'stant
instanta'neous
instanta'neously
instan'ter
in'stantly
instate'
instead'
insteep'
in'step
in'stigate
in'stigated
in'stigating
instiga'tion
in'stigator
instil', instill'
instilla'tion
instilled'
instil'ler
instil'ling
instil'ment
in'stinct
instinc'tive
instinc'tively
in'stitute
in'stituted
in'stituting
institu'tion
institu'tional
institu'tionary
in'stitutist
in'stitutive
in'stitutor
instruct'
instruct'ed
instruct'ing
instruc'tion
instruc'tive
instruct'or
instruct'ress
in'strument
instrumen'tal
instrument'alist
{ instrumental'ity
{ instrument'ally
instrumenta'tion

in*subjec'tion*
insubor'dinate
insubordina'tion
in*substan'tial*
insubstantial'ity
in*substan'tially*
insuf'ferable
insuf'ferably
{ in*suffi'ciency*
in*suffi'cient*
in*suffi'ciently*
insuf'flate
insuffla'tion
in'sufflator
in'sular
in'sularism
insular'ity
in'sulate
in'sulated
insula'tion
in'sulator
in'sult, insult'
insult'ed
insult'er
insult'ing
insult'ingly
insuperabil'ity
insu'perable
insu'perably
insupport'able
insupport'ably
insuppres'sible
insur'able
insur'ance
insure'
insured'
insur'er
insur'ing
insur'gent
insurmount'able
insurmount'ably
insurrec'tion
insurrec'tionary
insurrec'tionist
insusceptibil'ity
insuscep'tible
insuscep'tive
intact'
inta'glio
in'take
intangibil'ity
intan'gible
in'teger
in'tegral
in'tegrant
in'tegrate
in'tegrated
in'tegrating
integra'tion
integ'rity
integ'ument
integumen'tary
in'tellect
intellec'tion
intellec'tive
intellec'tual
intellec'tualism
intellec'tualist
intellectual'ity
intellec'tually
intel'ligence
intel'ligencer
intel'ligent
intelligen'tial
intel'ligently
intelligibil'ity
{ *intel'ligible*
intel'ligibly
intem'perance
intem'perant
intem'perate
intem'perately
intem'perateness
intend'
intend'ancy
intend'ant
intend'ed
intend'ing
intend'ment
intense'
intense'ly
intense'ness
intensifica'tion
inten'sified
inten'sifier
inten'sify
inten'sifying
inten'sion
inten'sity
inten'sive
intent'
inten'tion
inten'tional
inten'tionally
inten'tioned
intent'ly
intent'ness
inter'
interact'
interbreed'
interbreed'ing
inter'calar
inter'calary
inter'calate
inter'calated
inter'calating
intercala'tion
intercede'
interce'ded
interce'dent
interce'der
interce'ding
intercept'
intercept'ed
intercept'er
intercept'ing
intercep'tion
intercep'tor
interces'sion
interces'sional
interces'sor
interces'sory
interchain'
interchange'
in'terchange
interchangeabil'ity
interchange'able
interchange'ableness
interchange'ably
interchanged'
interchang'ing
intercolo'nial
intercolum'nar
intercolumnia'tion
intercommu'nion
intercommu'nicate
intercommu'nity
intercos'tal
in'tercourse
intercur'rent
interdepend'ence
interdepend'ent
interdict'
in'terdict
interdict'ed
interdict'ing
interdic'tion
interdict'ive
interdict'ory
in'terest
in'terested
in'teresting
interfa'cial
interfere'
interfered'
interfer'ence
interfer'er
interfer'ing
interfer'ingly
interfuse'
in'terim
inte'rior
interja'cent
interject'
interject'ed
interject'ing
interjec'tion
interjec'tional
interlace'
interlaced'
interla'cing
interlard'
interlard'ed
interlard'ing
interleave'
interleaved'
interleav'ing
interline'
interlin'eal
interlin'ear
interlinea'tion
interlined'
interlin'ing
interlink'
interlock'

interlocked'
interlock'ing
interloc'utor
interloc'utory
in'terloper
interlu'cent
in'terlude
interlu'nar
interlu'nary
intermar'riage
intermar'ried
intermar'ry
intermar'rying
intermed'dle
intermed'dled
intermed'dler
intermed'dling
interme'dial
interme'diary
interme'diate
intermedia'tion
inter'ment
intermez'zo
inter'minable
inter'minable-ness
inter'minably
intermin'gle
intermin'gled
intermin'gling
intermis'sion
intermis'sive
intermit'
intermit'ted
intermit'tent
intermit'ting
intermix
intermixed'
intermix'ing
intermix'ture
intermu'ral
intern'
inter'nal
inter'nally
interna'tional
interna'tionalism
interna'tionalist
interna'tionally
interne'cine
intern'ment
internun'cial
internun'cio
interocean'ic
interpari'etal
interpel'late
interpel'lated
interpella'tion
interplan'etary
interplead'
interplead'er
interplead'ing
inter'polate
inter'polated
inter'polater
inter'polating
interpola'tion
interpose'
interposed'
interpo'ser
interpo'sing
interposi'tion
inter'pret
inter'pretable
interpreta'tion
inter'preted
inter'preter
inter'pretive
interred'
interreg'num
inter'ring
inter'rogate
inter'rogated
interroga'tion
interrog'ative
inter'rogator
interrog'atory
interrupt'
interrupt'ed
interrupt'er
interrupt'ing
interrup'tion
interscap'ular
interse'cant
intersect'
intersect'ed
intersect'ing
intersec'tion
intersec'tional
in'terspace
intersperse'
interspersed'
intersper'sing
intersper'sion
interstel'lar
interstel'lary
inter'stice
inter'stices
intersti'tial
intertex'ture
intertri'bal
intertrop'ical
intertwine'
intertwined'
intertwi'ning
intertwi'ningly
intertwist'
intertwist'ed
intertwist'ing
in'terval
intervene'
intervened'
interve'ner
interve'nient
interve'ning
interven'tion
in'terview
in'terviewed
in'terviewer
in'terviewing
interweave'
interweaved'
interweav'ing
interwov'en
intes'table
intes'tacy
intes'tate
intes'tinal
intes'tine
in'timacy
in'timate, *n., adj.*
in'timate, *v.*
in'timated
in'timately
in'timating
intima'tion
intim'idate
intim'idated
intim'idating
intimida'tion
intit'uled
in'to
intol'erable
intol'erably
intol'erance
intol'erant
intol'erantly
in'tonate
in'tonated
in'tonating
intona'tion
in'tonator
intone'
intoned'
intox'icant
intox'icate
intox'icated
intox'icating
intoxica'tion
intractabil'ity
intrac'table
intrac'tably
intra'dos
intramu'ral
intranquil'lity
intran'sigent
intran'sitive
intransmis'sible
intrench'
intrenched'
intrench'ing
intrench'ment
intrep'id
intrepid'ity
intrep'idly
in'tricacy
in'tricate
in'tricately
intrigue'
intrigued'
intrigu'er
intrigu'ing
intrin'sic
intrin'sically
introces'sion
introduce'
introduced'

introdu'cer
introdu'cing
introduc'tion
introduc'tive
introduc'tory
intro'it
intromis'sion
intromit'
intromit'ted
intromit'ting
introrse'
introspect
introspec'tion
introspec'tive
introver'sion
introvert
introvert'ed
intrude'
intru'ded
intru'der
intru'ding
intru'sion
intru'sive
intrust'
intrust'ed
intrust'ing
intuba'tion
intui'tion
intu'itive
intu'itively
intumesce'
intumesced'
intumes'cence
intumes'cing
intussuscep'tion
intwine'
intwined'
intwin'ing
intwist'
inum'brate
in'undate
in'undated
in'undating
inunda'tion
inure'
inured'
inure'ment
inur'ing
inurn'
inurned'
inurn'ing
inu'tile
inutil'ity
invade'
inva'ded
inva'der
inva'ding
in'valid
inval'id
inval'idate
inval'idated
inval'idating
invalid'ity
inval'uable
invariabil'ity
inva'riable

inva'riableness
inva'riably
inva'sion
inva'sive
invec'tive
inveigh'
inveighed'
inveigh'er
inveigh'ing
invei'gle
invei'gled
invei'gler
invei'gling
invent'
invent'ed
invent'ing
inven'tion
invent'ive
invent'or
in'ventory
inverse'
inverse'ly
inver'sion
invert'
invert'ant
inver'tebral
inver'tebrate
inver'tebrated
invert'ed
invert'edly
invert'ing
invest'
invest'ed
inves'tigable
inves'tigate
inves'tigated
inves'tigating
investiga'tion
inves'tigative
inves'tigator
invest'ing
inves'titure
invest'ment
invest'or
invet'eracy
invet'erate
invid'ious
invid'iously
invig'orate
invig'orated
invig'orating
invigora'tion
invincibil'ity
invin'cible
invin'cibly
inviolabil'ity
invi'olable
invi'olably
invi'olate
invisibil'ity
invis'ible
invis'ibly
invita'tion
invi'tatory
invite'
invi'ted
invi'ter

invi'ting
invi'tingly
invit'rifiable
in'vocate
invoca'tion
in'voice
in'voiced
in'voicing
invoke'
invoked'
invo'king
invol'ucel
involucel'late
involu'cral
involu'crate
in'volucre
in'volucred
involu'cret
involu'crum
invol'untarily
invol'untary
in'volute
in'voluted
involu'tion
involve'
involved'
involv'ing
invulnerabil'ity
invul'nerable
in'ward
in'wardly
in'wardness
in'wards
inweave'
in'working
inwrap'
inwrapped'
inwrap'ping
inwrought'
i'odate
iod'ic
i'odide
i'odine
i'odize
i'odized
i'odizing
io'doform
i'odous
iod'uret
i'olite
i'on
Io'nian
Ion'ic
io'ta
ipecacuan'ha
ip'so fac'to
Ira'nian
irascibil'ity
iras'cible
iras'cibleness
iras'cibly
irate'
ire
ire'ful
ire'fully
i'renarch

iren'ical
ire'nicon
i'rid
i'rides
irides'cence
irides'cent
irid'ium
i'ris
i'risated
i'riscope
I'rish
I'rishism
I'rishman
I'rishry
iri'tis
irk
irk'some
irk'someness
i'ron
i'ronclad
i'roned
i'roner
iron-grey
iron'ic
iron'ical
iron'ically
i'roning
i'ronmaster
i'ronmonger
i'ronmongery
i'ron-mould
i'ronside
i'ronwork
i'rony, *adj.*
i'rony, *n.*
irra'diance
irra'diancy
irra'diant
irra'diate
irra'diated
irra'diating
irradia'tion
irra'tional
irrational'ity
irra'tionally
irreclaim'able
irreclaim'ably
irreconci'lable
irreconci'lably
irrec'onciled
{ *irrecov'erable*
{ *irrecov'erably*
irredeem'able
irredeem'ably
Irreden'tist
irredu'cible
irrefragabil'ity
irref'ragable
irrefu'table
irreg'ular
irregular'ity
irreg'ularly
irrel'ative
irrel'evance
irrel'evancy
irrel'evant
irrelig'ion
irrelig'ious
irreme'diable
irremis'sible
irremis'sive
irremov'able
irremu'nerable
irreparabil'ity
irrep'arable
irrep'arably
irrepealabil'ity
irrepeal'able
irrepeal'ably
irreplace'able
irreprehen'sible
irrepres'sible
irreproach'able
irreproach'ably
irreprov'able
irresistibil'ity
irresist'ible
irresist'ibly
irres'oluble
irres'olute
irresolu'tion
irresolvabil'ity
irresolv'able
irrespec'tive
irrespec'tively
{ *irresponsibil'ity*
{ *irrespon'sible*
irretriev'able
irretriev'ably
irrev'erence
irrev'erent
irrev'erently
irrevers'ible
irrevocabil'ity
irrev'ocable
irrev'ocably
ir'rigate
ir'rigated
ir'rigating
irriga'tion
irrig'uous
irri'sion
irritabil'ity
ir'ritable
ir'ritant
ir'ritate
ir'ritated
ir'ritating
irrita'tion
ir'ritative
ir'ritatory
irrora'tion
irrup'ted
irrup'tion
irrup'tive
Ir'vingite
is
isagog'ics
ischaid'ic
is'chiagra
ischuret'ic
ischu'ria
is'chury
Ish'maelite
Ish'maelitish
isid'ia
isid'ium
i'singlass
Is'lam
Is'lamism
Is'lamite
Islamit'ic
is'land
is'lander
isle
is'let
ism
i'sobar
isobar'ic
isobaromet'ric
isochromat'ic
isoch'ronal
isoch'ronism
isoch'ronous
i'sogon
i'solate
i'solated
i'solating
isola'tion
isomer'ic
isom'erism
isomet'ric
isomet'rical
isomor'phism
isomor'phous
isonom'ic
ison'omy
i'sopod
isop'odous
isos'celes
isostem'onous
isoth'eral
i'sothere
i'sotherm
isother'mal
isoton'ic
Is'raelite
Is'raelitic
Is'raelitish
is'suable
is'sue
is'sued
is'suer
is'suing
Isth'mian
isth'mus
it
Ital'ian
Ital'ianize

Ital'ic
ital'icize
ital'icized
ital'icizing
itch
itched
itch'ing
itch'y
i'tem
it'erant
it'erate
it'erated
it'erating
itera'tion
it'erative
itin'erancy
itin'erant
itin'erary
itin'erate
itin'erated
itin'erating
its
itself'
i'vied
i'vory
i'vy
Ix'ia
Ix'ora

J

jab'ber
jab'bered
jab'berer
jab'bering
jac'amar
ja'cent
jac'inth
jack
jack-a-dan'dy
jack'al
Jack'-a-Lent
jack'anapes
jack'ass
jack'-block
jack'-boots
jack'daw
jack'et
jack'eted
jack'-knife
jack'-plane
jack'-pudding
jack'-screw
Jack-tar'
jack'-wood
Jacobe'an
Jac'obin
Jacobin'ic
Jacobin'ical
Jac'obinism
Jac'obite
Jacobit'ical
Jac'obitism
Ja'cob's-lad'der
jac'onet
Jacquard'
jacta'tion
jactita'tion
jacula'tion
jac'ulator
jac'ulatory
jade
ja'ded
ja'ding
ja'dish
jag
jagged
jag'ged
jag'gedness
jag'ger
jag'gy
jaghire'
jag'uar
Jah
jail
jail'bird
jail'er
Jain
Jain'ism

jal'ap
jalousie'
jam
jamb
jammed
jam'ming
Jane
jan'gle
jan'gled
jan'gler
jan'gling
jan'itor
janiza'rian
jan'izary
Jan'senism
Jan'senist
Jan'uary
Japan'
Japanese'
japanned'
japan'ner
japan'ning
jape
Japhet'ic
jar
jarara'ca
jarde
jar'gon
jargonelle'
jar'rah
jarred
jar'ring
jar'ringly
jar'vey
jas'hawk
jas'mine
jas'per
jas'perated
jas'pery
jaspid'ean
jaun'dice
jaun'diced
jaunt
jaun'ted
jaun'tily
jaunt'ing
jaun'ty
Javanese'
jave'lin
jaw
jaw'bone
jawed
jaw'y
jay
jeal'ous
jeal'ously
jeal'ousy
Jean, jean

jeer
jeered
jeer'er
jeer'ing
Jeho'vah
Joho'vist
jejune'
jejune'ness
jel'lied
jel'lify
jel'ly
jel'ly-fish
jem'adar
jem'my
jen'net
jen'neting
jen'ny
jeof'ail
jeop'ard
jeop'arded
jeop'arding
jeop'ardize
jeop'ardized
jeop'ardizing
jeop'ardous
jeop'ardy
jerbo'a
jeremi'ad
jer'falcon
jerk
jerked
jerked'-beef
jerk'er
jer'kin
jerk'ing
jer'ry
jer'ry-builder
jer'sey
jess
jes'samine
Jes'se
jest
jest'ed
jest'er
jest'ing
jest'ingly
Jes'uit
Jes'uitess
Jesuit'ic
Jesuit'ical
Jes'uitism
jet
jet d'eau'
jet'sam
jet'tee
jet'tison
jet'ty
jeu d'esprit'

Jew
jew'el
jew'elled-led
jew'eller-ler
jew'elling-ling
jew'ellery, -lry
jew'elly-ly
Jew'ess
Jew'ish
jew's'-ear
jew's'-harp
Jez'ebel
jib
jibbed
jib'ber
jib'bing
jib'-boom
jibe
jif'fy
jig
jig'ger
jig'ging
jill
jilt
jilt'ed
jilt'ing
jim'my
jimp
jin'gal
jin'gle
jin'gled
jin'gling
Jin'go
Jin'goism
jinn
jin'nee
jinrick'sha
jip'po
job
jobbed
job'ber
job'bery
job'bing
jock'ey
jock'eyed
jock'eying
jock'eyism
jock'eyship
jocose'
jocose'ly
jocose'ness
joc'ular
jocular'ity
joc'ularly
joc'und
jocund'ity
jog
jogged
jog'ger
jog'ging
jog'gle
jog'gled
jog'gling
johan'nes
join
join'der
joined
join'er
join'ery
join'-*hand*
join'ing
joint
joint'ed
joint'er
joint'ing
joint'ly
joint'ress
joint-ten'ant
join'ture
join'tured
join'turing
join'turess
joist
joist'ed
joist'ing
joke
joked
jo'ker
jo'king
jo'kingly
jole
jollifica'tion
jol'lily
jol'lity
jol'ly
jol'ly-boat
jolt
jolt'ed
jolt'er
jolt'ing
jolt'ingly
jon'quil
jo'rum
joss
joss'-house
jos'tle
jos'tled
jos'tling
jot
jot'ted
jot'ting
joule
jounce
jounced
jour'nal
jour'nalism
jour'nalist
journalis'tic
jour'nalize
jour'nalized
jour'nalizing
jour'ney
jour'neyed
jour'neyer
jour'neying
jour'neyman
jour'ney-work
joust
joust'ed
joust'er
joust'ing
jo'vial
jovial'ity
jo'vially
jowl
jowl'er
joy
joyed
joy'ful
joy'fully
joy'fulness
joy'ing
joy'less
joy'lessly
joy'lessness
joy'ous
joy'ously
joy'ousness
ju'bilant
ju'bilate
jubila'tion
ju'bilee
Juda'ic
Juda'ical
Ju'daism
Judaiza'tion
Ju'daize
Ju'daized
Ju'daizer
Ju'daizing
Ju'das
judge
judged
judg'er
judge'ship
judg'ing
judg'ment
ju'dicative
ju'dicatory
ju'dicature
judi'cial
judi'cially
judi'ciary
judi'cious
judi'ciously
jug
ju'gal
ju'gated
Jug'gernaut
jug'gle
jug'gled
jug'gler
jug'glery
jug'gling
ju'gular
jugula'tion
juice
juice'less
jui'ciness
jui'cy
ju'jube
ju'lep
Ju'lian
julienne'
July'
ju'mart
jum'ble
jum'bled
jum'bler
jum'bling
jumelle'
jump
jumped
jump'er
jump'ing
junc'tion
junc'ture
June
jun'gle
ju'nior

jun'iorate
junior'ity
ju'niper
junk
jun'ket
jun'keted
jun'keting
Ju'no
jun'ta
jun'to
jupe
Ju'piter
jupon
Juras'sic
ju'rat
jura'tion
ju'ratory
jurid'ical
jurid'ically
jurisconsult'
jurisdic'tion
*jurisdic'tion*al
jurisdic'tive
jurispru'dence
jurispru'dent
ju'rist
ju'ror
ju'ry
ju'ryman
ju'ry-mast
just
just'ed
jus'tice
justi'ciary
jus'tifiable
jus'tifiably
justifica'tion
justif'icative
justif'icatory
jus'tified
jus'tifier
jus'tify
jus'tifying
just'ing
jus'tle
jus'tled
just'ling
just'ly
just'ness
jut
jute
jut'ted
jut'ting
jut'ty
Juvena'lian
juvenes'cence
juvenes'cent
ju'venile
juvenil'ity
juxtaposi'tion

K

Ka'aba
kack'le
Kaf'ir, Kaf'fir
ka'go
kail, kale
Kai'ser
kale
kalei'doscope
kaleidoscop'ic
ka'li
Kal'muck
kamptu'licon
kamsin'
kangaroo'
Kant'ian
Kant'ism
Kant'ist
ka'olin
kar'ma
karoo'
katab'olism
kath'ode
ka'tydid
kau'ri
ka'va
kavass'
kaw
kayles
keb
keck'le
keck'led
keck'ling
keck'sy
keck'y
kedge
kedged
kedg'er
kedg'eree
kedg'ing
keel
keel'age
keeled
keel'er
keel'haul
keel'hauled
keel'hauling
keel'ing
keel'man
keel'son
keen
keen'er
keen'est
keen'ly
keen'ness
keep
keep'er
keep'ing
keep'sake

keeve
keg
ke'lis
kelp
kel'pie, kel'py
Kelt
Kelt'ic
kemp
ken
ken'nel
ken'nelled
ken'nelling
ke'no
kenogen'esis
Kent'ish
ken'tle
kent'ledge
kep'i
kept
ker'asine
kerb
kerb'-stone
ker'chief
ker'chiefed
kerf
ker'mes
kern
ker'nel
ker'nelled-led
ker'nelly-ly
ker'osene
ker'rie
ker'sey
ker'seymere
kes'trel
ketch
ketch'up
ket'tle
ket'tle-drum
kev'el
kex
key
key-board
keyed
key'hole
key'less
key'-note
key'stone
kha'ki
kham'sin
khan
khan'ate
Khedive'
kib'ble
kib'bled
kib'bler
kibe
kibed

kibit'ka
ki'by
kib'lah
kick
kicked
kick'er
kick'ing
kick'shaw
kid
kid'der
Kid'derminster
kid'dle
kid'dow
kid'ling
kid'nap
kid'napped
kid'napper
kid'napping
kid'ney
kil'derkin
kill
kill'dee
killed
kill'er
kill'ing
kiln
kiln'-dried
kiln'-dry
kiln'-drying
{ kil'ogram
{ kil'ogramme
{ kilogramme'ter
{ kilogramme'tre
{ kil'olitre
{ kil'oliter
{ kil'ometer
{ kil'ometre
kilt
kilt'ed
kilt'ing
kim'bo
kin
kind
kind'er
kin'dergarten
kind'est
kind'hearted
kin'dle
kind'lier
kind'liest
kin'dled
kin'dler
kind'liness
kin'dling
kind'ly
kind'ness
kin'dred
kine

kinemat'ic
kinemat'ical
kinemat'ics
kinemat'ograph
kinet'ic
kinet'ics
king
king'-bird
king'-crab
king'craft
king'cup
king'dom
king'fisher
king'let
king'like
king'liness
king'ling
king'ly
king'-post
king's e'vil
king'ship
kink
kin'kajou
ki'no
kins'folk
kin'ship
kins'man
kins'woman
kiosk'
kip
kip'per
kip'skin
kirk
kirsch'wasser
kir'tle
kir'tled
kis'met
kiss
kissed
kiss'er
kiss'ing
kit
kit'-cat
kitch'en
kitch'ener
kite
kith
kit'ling
kit'ten
kit'tenish
ki'wi
kleptoma'nia
klick
klicked
knab
knabbed
knab'bing
knack
knack'er
knag
knag'giness
knag'gy
knap'sack
knap'weed
knar
knarred
knarled
knave
kna'very
kna'vish
kna'vishly
kna'vishness
knead
knead'ed
knead'er
knead'ing
knee
knee'-cap
kneed
knee'-deep
knee'-joint
kneel
kneeled
kneel'er
kneel'ing
knee'pan
knell
knelt
knew
knick'er
knick'erbocker
knick'-knack
knife
knife'-board
knife'-cleaner
knife'-grinder
knight
knight'age
knight'ed
knight'-errant
knight'-errantry
knight'hood
knight'liness
knight'ly
knit
knit'table
knit'ter
knit'ting
knit'ting-needle
knit'tle
knives
knob
knobbed
knob'biness
knob'by
knock
knocked
knock'er
knock'ing
knock'-kneed
knoll
knolled
knoll'ing
knop
knop'pern
knot
knot'berry
knot'-grass
knot'ted
knot'tiness
knot'ting
knot'ty
knout
know
know'able
know'er
know'ing
know'ingly
knowl'edge
known
knuck'le
knuck'led
knuck'le-duster
knuck'ling
knurl
knurled
knurl'y
ko'ba
ko'dak
kohl
kohl'rabi
koo'doo
koo'lah
ko'pek
kop'je
Ko'ran
ko'sher
kotow'
kou'miss
kour'bash
kraal
kra'ken
krem'lin
kre'osote
kreut'zer
krieg'spiel
krish'na
krout
kru'ka
krul'ler
ku'dos
ku'fic
ku'miss
ku'ril
kur'saal
ky'anite
ky'anize
ky'anized
ky'anizing
Ky'rie
kyriolog'ical

L

la
laa'ger
laa'gered
laa'gering
Lab'adist
lab'arum
la'bel
la'belled
la'beled
la'belling
la'beling
label'lum
la'bent
la'bial
la'biate
labioden'tal
lab'oratory
labo'rious
labo'riously
la'bour, la'bor
la'boured
la'bourer
la'bouring
la'boursome
Lab'radorite
la'brose
labur'num
lab'yrinth
labyrin'thian
labyrin'thine
lac
lac'cic
lac'cin
lace
laced
lac'erable
lac'erate
lac'erated
lac'erating
lacera'tion
lac'erative
Lacer'ta
lacer'tian
lacer'tine
laches
lach'rymal
lach'rymary
lach'rymatory
lach'rymose
la'cing
lack
lackadai'sical
lack'adaisy
lack'-a-day
lacked
lack'ey, lac'quey
lack'eyed
lack'eying
lack'ing
lack'-lustre
lacon'ic
lacon'ical
lacon'ically
lacon'icism
la'conism
lac'quer, lack'er
lac'quered
lac'quering
lac'rimose, etc.
see lach-
lacrosse'
lac'tarene
lac'tarine
lac'tary
lac'tate
lacta'tion
lac'teal
lac'tean
lactes'cence
lactes'cent
lac'tic
lactif'erous
lactom'eter
lacu'na
lacu'nar
lacu'nose
lacus'tral
lacus'trine
lad
lad'anum
lad'der
lad'die
lade
la'ded
la'den
la'ding
la'dle
la'dleful
la'dy
la'dybird
La'dy Day
la'dylike
la'dy-love
la'dy's-fin'ger
la'dyship
la'dy's-maid
la'dy's-slipper
laffitte'
lag
la'ger beer
lag'gard
lagged
lag'ger
lag'ging
Lag'omys
lagoon'
la'ic
la'ical
laiciza'tion
la'icize
laid
lain
lair
laird
la'ity
lake
lake'let
lalla'tion
la'ma
La'maism
La'maist
La'maite
lamb
lam'bative
lam'bent
lamb'ing
lamb'kin
lamb'like
lamb'skin
lamb's'-wool
lame
lamed
lamel'la
lamel'lar
lam'ellate
lam'ellated
lamellif'erous
lamel'liform
lame'ly
lame'ness
lament'
lam'entable
lam'entably
lamenta'tion
lament'ed
lament'er
lament'ing
lam'ina
laminabil'ity
lam'inable
lam'inar
lam'inary
lam'inate
lam'inated
lam'inating
lamina'tion
la'ming
laminif'erous
la'mish
Lam'mas
lam'mergeyer
lamp
lam'pas
lamp'black

lam'per-eel
lamp'ic
lamp'light
lamp'lighter
lampoon'
lampooned'
lampoon'er
lampoon'ing
lampoon'ry
lamp'-post
lam'prey
la'nary
la'nate
la'nated
Lancaste'rian
Lancas'trian
lance
lanced
lan'ceolar
lan'ceolate
lan'ceolated
lan'cer
lan'ces
lan'cet
lance'wood
lan'ciform
lan'cinate
lancina'tion
lan'cing
land
lan'damman
lan'dau
landaulet'
land'ed
land'er
land'grave
landgra'viate
land'gravine
land'holder
land'ing
land'lady
land'less
land'lock
land'locked
land'locking
land'loper
land'*lord*
land'*lord*ism
land'lubber
land'man
land'mark
land'owner
land'owning
land'-rail
land'reeve
land'scape
land'slide
land'slip
lands'man
land'sturm
land'ward
land'wehr
lane
lan'grage
lan'grel
langsyne'
lan'guage
Languedoc
lan'guid
lan'guidly
lan'guish
lan'guished
lan'guisher
lan'guishing
lan'guishment
lan'guor
lan'guorous
lanif'erous
lanig'erous
lank
lank'ness
lank'y
lan'ner
lan'neret
lan'olin
lans'quenet
lan'tern
lan'ternist
lan'thanum
lanu'ginous
lan'yard
Laoc'oon
Laodice'an
lap
lap'-dog
lapel'
lap'ful
lapida'rian
lap'idary
lap'idate
lapida'tion
lapides'cence
lapides'cent
lapidif'ic
lapid'ified
lapid'ify
la'pis
lap'is laz'uli
Lap'lander
Lapp
lapped
lap'per
lap'pet
lap'ping
laps'able
lapse
lapsed
lap'sided
laps'ing
lap'-stone
lap'sus
lap'wing
lar
lar'board
lar'ceny
larch
lard
larda'ceous
lard'ed
lard'er
lard'ing
La'res
large
large'ly
large ness
larg'er
larg'ess
larg'est
larghet'to
larghis'simo
lar'go
lar'iat
lark
lark'spur
lar'mier
lar'rikin
lar'ry
lar'um
lar'va
lar'vae
lar'val
lar'vated
laryn'geal
laryn'gean
laryngi'tis
laryn'goscope
laryngoscop'ic
laryngot'omy
lar'ynx
lascar'
lasciv'ious
lasciv'iously
lasciv'iousness
lash
lashed
lash'er
lash'ing
lass
las'sie
las'situde
las'so
last
last'ed
last'ing
last'ingly
last'ly
latch
latched
latch'et
latch'ing
latch'-key
late
lateen'
late'ly
la'tency
late'ness
la'tent
la'tently
la'ter
lat'eral
lat'erally
Lat'eran
laterifo'lious
lateri'tious
lath
lathe
lathed
lath'er
lath'ered
lath'ering
lath'ing
lath'y
latib'ulize
lat'iclave
laticos'tate
latiden'tate
latifo'lious
Lat'in
Lat'inism
Lat'inist

Latin'ity
Lat'inize
Lat'inized
Lat'inizing
la'tish
lat'itat
lat'itude
latitu'dinal
latitudina'rian
latitudina'rianism
latitu'dinous
la'trant
latri'a
latrine'
lat'robite
lat'ten
lat'ter
lat'terly
lat'tice
lat'ticed
lat'ticing
laud
laud'able
laud'ableness
laud'ably
laud'anum
lauda'tion
laud'atory
laud'ed
laud'er
laud'ing
laugh
laugh'able
laugh'ably
laughed
laugh'er
laugh'ing
laugh'ingly
laugh'ter
launch
launched
launch'ing
laun'der
laun'derer
laun'dress
laun'dry
lau'reate
lau'reated
lau'reateship
laurea'tion
lau'rel
lau'relled-led
lau'rustine
lau'rustinus
la'va
lava'bo
lav'atory
lave
lav'ender
la'ver
la'ving
lav'ish
lav'ished
lav'isher
lav'ishing
lav'ishly
law
law'ful
law'fully
law'fulness

law'giver
law'less
law'lessly
law'lessness
law'-maker
lawn
lawn-ten'nis
law'suit
law'yer
lax
laxa'tion
lax'ative
lax'ity
lax'ly
lax'ness
lay
lay'er
lay'ering
layette'
lay'ing
lay'man
laz'ar
lazaret'
lazaret'to
Laz'arist
laze
la'zier
la'ziest
la'zily
la'ziness
laz'uli
la'zy
lazzaro'ne
lea
leach
leached
leach'ing
lead (a metal)
lead (to conduct)
lead'ed
lead'en
lead'er
leaderette'
lead'ership
lead'ing
lead-pen'cil
lead'ing-strings
leads'man
leaf
leaf'age
leafed
leaf'iness
leaf'ing
leaf'less
leaf'let
leaf'y
league
leagued
lea'guer
lea'guing
leak
leak'age
leaked
leak'iness
leak'ing
leak'y
leal
leam
lean
leaned

lean'er
lean'est
lean'faced
lean'ing
lean'ness
leant
lean'-to
leap
leaped
leap'er
leap'-frog
leap'ing
leap'-*year*
learn
learned
learn'ed
learn'edly
learn'er
learn'ing
learnt
leas'able
lease
leased
lease'hold
lease'holder
leash
leashed
leas'ing
least
leath'er
leatherette'
leath'ern
leath'ery
leave
leaved
leav'en
leav'ened
leav'ening
leaves
leav'ing
leav'ings
lech'er
lech'erous
lech'ery
lec'tern
lec'tion
lec'tionary
lec'tor
lec'ture
lec'tured
lec'turer
lec'tureship
lec'turing
led
ledge
ledg'er
led'-horse
lee
leech
leech'craft
leeched
leech'ing
leek
leer
leered
leer'ing
leer'ingly
lees
lee'shore
leet

lee'ward
lee'way
left
left'-handed
left'-off
leg
leg'acy
le'gal
le'galism
le'galist
legal'ity
legaliza'tion
le'galize
le'galized
le'galizing
le'gally
leg'ate
legate'
legatee'
lega'tion
lega'to
lega'tor
leg'end
leg'endary
leg'erdemain
leg'er-line
legged
leg'ging
leg'gy
leghorn'
legibil'ity
leg'ible
leg'ibly
le'gion
le'gionary
leg'islate
leg'islated
leg'islating
legisla'tion
leg'islative
leg'islator
leg'islature
legit'imacy
legit'imate, *adj.*
legit'imate, *v.*
legit'imated
legit'imately
legit'imating
legitima'tion
legit'imatize
legit'imist
leg'ume
legu'men
legu'min
legu'minous
lei'surable
lei'sure
lei'sured
lei'surely
lem'ma
lem'ming
lem'on
lemonade'
le'mur
lend
lend'able
lend'er
lend'ing
length
length'en
length'ened
length ening
length'ily
length'iness
length'wise
length'y
le'nience
le'niency
le'nient
le'niently
le'nified
le'nify
len'itive
len'ity
le'no
lens
Lent, lent
lent'en
lentic'ular
len'tiform
lentig'inous
lenti'go
len'til
len'to
Le'o
le'onine
leop'ard
lep'er
lep'idolite
Lepidop'tera
lepidop'terous
lepido'sis
lep'idote
lep'orine
lep'rosy
lep'rous
leptodac'tyl
le'pus
Les'bian
lese-maj'esty
le'sion
less
lessee'
les'sen
les'sened
les'sening
les'ser
les'son
lessor'
lest
let
le'thal
lethar'gic
leth'argy
Le'the
Lethe'an
lethif'erous
Lett
let'ter
let'tered
let'tering
let'ter-paper
let'terpress
let'ters
let'ter-*writer*
let'ting
let'tuce
Levant'
levant'er
Levant'ine
leva'tor
lev'ee
lev'el
lev'elled / lev'eled
lev'eller / lev'eler
lev'elling / lev'eling
le'ver
le'verage
lev'eret
lev'iable
levi'athan
lev'ied
lev'igate
lev'igated
lev'igating
leviga'tion
lev'itate
levita'tion
Le'vite
Levit'ical
Levit'icus
lev'ity
lev'y
lev'ying
lewd
lewd'ly
lewd'ness
lew'is
lex
lex'ical
lexicog'rapher
lexicograph'ic
lexicograph'ical
lexico'graphy
lexicol'ogy
lex'icon
lexigraph'ic
lexig'raphy
ley
Ley'den
li
liabil'ity
li'able
li'ableness
liaison'
li'ar
li'as
liba'tion
li'bel
li'bellant / li'belant
li'belled / li'beled
li'beller / li'beler
li'belling / li'beling
li'bellous / li'belous
lib'er
lib'eral
lib'eralism
lib'eralist
liberal'ity
lib'eralize
lib'eralized
lib'eralizing

lib'erally
lib'erate
lib'erated
lib'erating
libera'tion
lib'erator
liberta'rian
liber'ticide
lib'ertine
lib'ertinism
lib'erty
libid'inous
Li'bra
libra'rian
libra'rianship
li'brary
li'brate
li'brated
li'brating
libra'tion
li'bratory
libret'tist
libret'to
Lib'yan
lice
li'cence
li'cense
li'censed
licensee'
li'censer
li'censing
licen'tiate
licen'tious
licen'tiously
licen'tiousness
lich
li'chen
lichenog'raphy
lic'it
lic'itly
lick
licked
lick'er
lick'erish
lick'ing
lick'spittle
lic'orice
lic'tor
lid
lid'less
lie
Lie'big
lief
liege
li'en
li'entery
li'er
lieu
lieuten'ancy
lieuten'ant
lieuten'ant (*Amer. pron.*)
lieuten'ant-col'onel
life
life'-belt
life'-blood
life'-boat
life'-*giving*
life'*guard*
life' *insurance*
life'less
life'lessness
life'like
life'long
life'-preserver
life'time
lift
lift'ed
lift'er
lift'ing
lig'ament
ligamen'tal
ligamen'tous
li'gan
liga'tion
lig'ature
light
light'ed
light'en
light'ened
light'ening
light'er
light'erage
light'erman
light'-fingered
light'-footed
light'-headed
light'-hearted
light'-horse
light'house
light'-in'fantry
light'ing
light'ly
light'-minded
light'ness
light'ning
lights
light'ship
light'some
light'-spir'ited
lign-al'oes
lig'neous
lignifica'tion
lig'niform
lig'nify
lig'nifying
lig'nin
lig'nite
lignit'ic
lig'num-vi'tae
lig'ula
lig'ulate
lig'ulated
lig'ure
like
like'able
liked
like'lihood
like'liness
like'ly
li'ken
li'kened
like'ness
like'minded
li'kening
like'wise
li'king
li'lac
lilia'ceous
lil'ied
lillibulle'ro
Lillipu'tian
lilt
lil'y
lima'ceous
li'mature
limb
lim'bate
limbed
lim'ber
lim'bered
lim'berness
limb'ing
lim'bo
lim'bus
lime
limed
li'ming
lime'kiln
lime'light
lime'stone
lime'-wash
lime'-water
lim'it
lim'itable
lim'itary
limita'tion
lim'ited
lim'iting
lim'itless
limn
lim'ner
lim'ning
limp
limped
limp'er
lim'pet
lim'pid
limpid'ity
lim'pidness
limp'ing
limp'ingly
li'my
lin
linch
linch'pin
lin'den
line
lin'eage
lin'eal
lineal'ity
lin'eally
lin'eament
lin'ear
linear'ity
linea'tion
lined
lin'en
lin'en-draper
li'ner
ling
lin'ger
lin'gered
lin'gering
lin'gerie
lin'go
lin'gual
lin'guiform
lin'guist

linguis'tic
linguis'tical
linguoden'tal
lin'iment
li'ning
link
link'boy
linked
link'ing
Linne'an
lin'net
lino'leum
li'notype
lin'seed
lin'sey-wool'sey
lin'stock
lint
lin'tel
li'on
li'oness
li'on-hearted
li'onize
li'onized
li'onizing
li'on-like
lip
lip'ogram
lipogrammat'ic
lipogram'matist
lipoth'ymy
lipped
lip'pitude
lip'-salve
liq'uable
liqua'tion
liquefac'tion
liquefi'able
liq'uefied
liq'uefier
liq'uefy
liq'uefying
liques'cency
liques'cent
liqueur' (or)
liq'uid
liq'uidate
liq'uidated
liq'uidating
liquida'tion
liq'uidator
liquid'ity
liq'uidize
liq'uidized
liq'uidizing
liq'uor
liq'uorice
Lis'bon
lisp
lisped
lisp'er
lisp'ing
lis'som
list
list'ed
lis'tel
lis'ten
lis'tened
lis'tener
lis'tening
Lis'terism
list'ing
list'less
list'lessly
list'lessness
lit
lit'any
lit'eral
lit'eralism
lit'eralist
literal'ity
lit'erally
lit'erary
lit'erate
litera'ti
litera'tim
lit'erature
lith'arge
lithe
lithe'ness
lithe'some
lith'ia
lith'ic
lith'ium
lith'oglyph
lithoglyph'ic
lith'ograph
lith'ographed
lithog'rapher
lithograph'ic
lithograph'ically
lith'ographing
lithog'raphy
lith'oid
lithoi'dal
litholog'ic
{ litholog'ical
{ litholog'ically
lithol'ogy
lith'omancy
lithontrip'tic
lithoph'agous
lith'ophane
lith'otint
lith'otome
lithot'omist
lithot'omy
lithot'rity
lit'igant
lit'igate
lit'igated
lit'igating
litiga'tion
lit'igator
litig'ious
lit'mus
litram'eter
li'tre, li'ter
lit'ter
litte'rateur
lit'tered
lit'tering
lit'tle
lit'tleness
lit'toral
litur'gic
litur'gical
lit'urgy
live
live
live'-bait
lived, *v.*
lived, *adj.*
live'lier
live'liest
live'lihood
live'liness
live'long
live'ly
liv'er
liv'eried
liv'erwort
liv'ery
liv'eryman
lives
lives, *pl.*
live'stock
liv'id
livid'ity
liv'idness
liv'ing
Livo'nian
li'vre
lixiv'ial
lixiv'iate
lixiv'iated
lixiv'iating
lixivia'tion
lixiv'ium
liz'ard
lla'ma
lo
loach
load
load'ed
load'ing
load'star
load'stone
loaf
loaf'er
loaf'ing
loam
loam'y
loan
loan'able
loaned
loan'ing
loan'-office
loath, loth
loathe
loathed
loath'ing
loath'some
loath'someness
loaves
lob
lo'bate
lo'bated
lob'by
lob'byist
lob'by-*member*
lobe
lobe'lia
lob'lolly
lob'scouse
lob'ster
lob'ular
lob'ule
local', locale'
lo'cal
lo'calism

local'ity
localiza'tion
lo'calize
lo'calized
lo'calizing
lo'cally
locate'
loca'ted
loca'ting
loca'tion
loc'ative
loch
lock
lock'age
locked
lock'er
lock'et
lock'ing
Lock'ist
lock'-jaw
lock'-out
lock'smith
lock'-up
Loco-fo'co
locomo'tion
lo'comotive
lo'comotor at'axy
loc'ulament
loc'ular
loc'ulus
lo'cum-te'nens
lo'cus
lo'cust
locu'tion
lode
lode'star
lode'stone
lodge
lodged
lodg'er
lodg'ing
lodg'ing-house
lodg'ment
loft
loft'ier
loft'iest
loft'ily
loft'iness
loft'y
log
log'arithm
logarith'mic
log'-book
logged
log'gerhead
log'gia
log'ging
log'house
log'hut
log'ic
log'ical
log'ically
logi'cian
logis'tic
logis'tical
log'-line
log'ogram
logograph'ic
logog'raphy

logom'achist
logom'achy
logom'eter
logomet'ric
Log'os
log'otype
log'wood
loin
loi'ter
loi'tered
loi'terer
loi'tering
loll
Lol'lard
Lol'lardism
lolled
loll'ing
lol'lipop
Lom'bard
Lombar'dic
lo'ment
Lon'doner
lone
lone'lier
lone'liest
lone'liness
lone'ly
lone'some
lone'someness
long
long'-boat
long'-bow
long'-cloth
long'-clothes
longed
long'er, *n.*
lon'ger, *adj.*
lon'gest
longe'val
longev'ity
longe'vous
long'*hand*
long'-headed
longim'anous
long'ing
long'ish
lon'gitude
longitu'dinal
long'-lived
long'-run
long'-sight
long'-sighted
long-sight'edness
long'-stop
long'-suffering
long'-winded
long'wise
loo
loo'by
loof
look
looked
look'er
look'ing
look'ing-glass
look'out
loom
loomed
loom'ing
loon

loop
looped
loop'er
loop'hole
loop'holed
loop'ing
loose
loosed
loose'ly
loos'er
loos'est
loos'en
loos'ened
loose'ness
loot
loo'-table
lop
Lophi'odon
lopped
lop'per
lop'ping
lop'-sided
loqua'cious
loqua'ciously
loquac'ity
lor'cha
lord
lord'ed
lord'ing
*lord'*like
*lord'*liness
*lord'*ling
*lord'*ly
*lord'*ship
Lord's Sup'per
lore
lorgnette'
lor'icate
lor'icated
lorica'tion
lorn
lor'ry
lo'ry
lose
los'er
los'ing
loss
lost
lot
lo'ta, lo'tah
lote'-tree
loth
lo'tion
lot'tery
lot'to
lo'tus
loud
loud'er
loud'ly
loud'ness
lough
lou'is
lou'is d'or
lounge
lounged
loung'er
loung'ing
louse
lous'y
lout

lout'ish
lout'ishly
lou'ver
lov'able
lov'age
love
love'-apple
love'-bird
loved
love'-feast
love'-knot
love'less
love'-letter
love'lier
love'liest
love'liness
love'-lorn
love'ly
lov'er
love'-sick
lov'ing
loving-kind'ness
lov'ingly
low
low'-born
low'-bred
Low'-church
lowed
low'er
low'er
low'ered
low'ered
low'ering
low'ering
lower'*most*
low'ery
low'est
low'ing
low'land
Low'lander
low'lier
low'liest
low'lily
low'liness
low'ly
low'-minded
low'-mindedness
low'ness
low'-spirited
low'-wines
loxodrom'ic
loy'al
loy'alist
loy'ally
loy'alty
loz'enge
lub'ber
lub'berly
lu'bric
lu'brical
lu'bricant
lu'bricate
lu'bricated
lu'bricating
lubrica'tion
lu'bricator
lubric'ity
lu'bricous
luce
lu'cent

lucer'nal
lucerne'
lu'cid
lucid'ity
lu'cidly
lu'cidness
lu'cifer
lucif'erous
lucif'ic
lu'ciform
lucim'eter
luck
luck'ier
luck'iest
luck'ily
luck'less
luck'y
lu'crative
lu'cre
lu'cubrate
lucubra'tion
lu'culent
Lud'dite
lu'dicrous
lu'dicrously
luff
luffed
luff'er
luff'ing
lug
lug'gage
lugged
lug'ger
lug'ging
lugu'brious
luke'warm
luke'warmness
lull
lull'aby
lulled
lull'ing
lumachel'la
lu'machelle
lumba'ginous
lumba'go
lum'bar
lum'ber
lum'bered
lum'berer
lum'bering
lum'ber-room
lumbri'cal
lu'minary
luminif'erous
luminos'ity
lu'minous
lump
lumped
lump'er
lump'ing
lump'ish
lump'ishly
lump'y
Lu'na
lu'nacy
lu'nar
luna'rian
lu'nary
lu'nate
lu'nated

lu'natic
luna'tion
lunch
lunched
lunch'eon
lunch'ing
lune
lunette'
lung
lunge
lunged
lun'ging
lung'wort
lu'niform
luniso'lar
lunt
lu'nular
lu'nulate
lu'nulated
Lu'percal
lu'pine, *adj.*
lu'pine, lu'pin
lu'pulin
lu'pus
lurch
lurched
lurch'er
lurch'ing
lure
lured
lu'rid
lu'ring
lurk
lurked
lurk'er
lurk'ing
lurk'ing-place
lus'cious
lus'ciously
lus'ciousness
lush
Lu'siad
lu'sory
lust
lust'ed
lust'ful
lust'ier
lust'iest
lust'ily
lust'iness
lust'ing
lus'tral
lus'trate
lustra'tion
lus'tre
lus'tring
lus'trous
lus'trously
lus'trum
lust'y
lu'tanist
luta'rious
luta'tion
lute
lut'ed
lu'teous
lute'string
Lu'theran
Lu'theranism
lu'thern

lut'ing
lu'tose
lu'tulent
lux'ate
lux'ating
luxa'tion
luxu'riance
luxu'riancy
luxu'riant
luxu'riate
luxu'riated
luxu'riating
luxu'rious

luxu'riously
lux'ury
lycan'thropy
lyce'um
lyd'dite
Lyd'ian
lye
ly'ing
ly'ing-in'
lymph
lymphat'ic
lynch
lynched

lynch'er
lynch'ing
lynx
lynx'-eyed
ly'ra
ly'rate
ly'rated
lyre
lyr'ic
lyr'ical
lyr'icism
lyr'ist
lyte'rian

M

Mab
macadamiza'-
tion
macad'amize
macad'amized
macad'amizing
{ macaro'ni
{ maccaro'ni
macaron'ic
macaroon'
macaw'
Maccabe'an
ma'ccoboy
mace
mace'-bearer
Macedo'nian
mac'erate
mac'erated
mac'erating
macera'tion
Machiavel'lian
Machiavel'lian-
ism
Machiavel'lism
machic'olate
machic'olated
machicola'tion
mach'inate
mach'inated
mach'inating
machina'tion
machine'
machined'
machin'ery
machin'ing
machin'ist
mack'erel
mack'intosh
mack'le
macro'bian
macrocephal'ic
mac'rocosm
macrom'eter
mac'ula
mac'ulate
mac'ulated
mac'ulating
macula'tion
mad
{ mad'am
{ mad'ame
mad'cap
mad'ded
mad'den
mad'dened
mad'dening
mad'der
mad'dest
mad'ding
made
Madei'ra
mademoiselle'
mad'house
mad'ly
mad'man
mad'ness
madon'na
mad'repore
mad'rigal
mael'strom
mae'nad
maesto'so
Mafi'a
magazine'
mag'dalen
magen'ta
mag'got
mag'goty
Ma'gi
Ma'gian
mag'ic
mag'ical
mag'ically
magi'cian
mag'ic lant'ern
magilp'
magiste'rial
magiste'rially
mag'istracy
mag'istrate
mag'ma
Mag'na Char'ta
magnanim'ity
magnan'imous
magnan'imously
mag'nate
magne'sia
magne'sian
magne'sium
mag'net
{ *magnet'ic*
{ *mag'netism*
mag'netize
mag'netized
mag'netizer
mag'netizing
magne'to-elec-
tric
magne'to-elec-
tricity
magnetom'eter
magnetomet'ric
magne'to-mo'tor
magnif'ic
Magnif'icat
magnif'icence
magnif'icent
magnif'icently
mag'nified
mag'nifier
mag'nify
mag'nifying
magnil'oquence
magnil'oquent
mag'nitude
magno'lia
mag'num
mag'pie
Mag'yar
{ Mahara'ja
{ Mahara'jah
mahat'ma
Mah'di
mahl'stick
mahog'any
Mahom'etan
Mahom'etanism
mahout'
maid
maid'en
maid'enhair
maid'enhood
maid'enish
maid'en-like
maid'enly
Maid-Ma'rian
maid'servant
mail
mail'-cart
mailed
mail'ing
maim
maimed
maim'ing
main
main'land
main'ly
main'mast
main'prize
main'sail
main'spring
main'stay
maintain'
maintain'able
maintained'
maintain'er
maintain'ing
main'tenance

main'top
maisonette'
maize
majes'tic
majes'tical
majes'tically
maj'esty
majol'ica
ma'jor
ma'jor-do'mo
ma'jor-*gen'eral*
major'ity
majus'cule
make
make'bate
make'-believe
ma'ker
make'shift
make'-up
make'weight
ma'king
mal'achite
malacol'ogy
maladministra'tion
maladroit'
mal'ady
Mal'aga
mal'anders
mal'apert
malapropos'
ma'lar
mala'ria
mala'rial
mala'rious
malassimila'tion
ma'late
Malay'
Malay'an
mal'content
male
maledic'tion
mal'efactor
mal'efactress
malef'ic
malev'olence
malev'olent
malfea'sance
malforma'tion
ma'lic
mal'ice
mali'cious
mali'ciously
mali'ciousness
malign'
malig'nancy
malig'nant
maligned'
malign'er
malign'ing
malig'nity
malign'ly
malin'ger
malin'gered
malin'gerer
malin'gering
mal'ison
mal'kin
mall
mall (a walk)
mal'lard
malleabil'ity
mal'leable
mal'leate
mal'leated
mallea'tion
malle'olar
mal'let
mal'low
mal'lows
malm
malm'sey
malprac'tice
malt
malt'ed
Maltese'
mal'tha
Malthu'sian
malt'ing
maltreat'
maltreat'ed
maltreat'ing
maltreat'ment
malt'ster
malt'y
malva'ceous
malversa'tion
mam
mama'
mam'elon
mam'eluke
mam'illary
mam'illated
mamma'
mam'mal
mamma'lia
mamma'lian
mammal'ogist
mammal'ogy
mam'mary
mam'mifer
mammif'erous
mam'miform
mam'millary
mam'millated
mam'mon
mam'monist
mam'moth
man
man'acle
man'acled
man'acling
man'age
man'ageable
man'aged
man'agement
man'ager
man'ageress
manage'rial
man'aging
man'akin
manatee'
manchineel'
Manchu'
Manchoo'
man'ciple
manda'mus
man'darin
man'date, *n.*
mandate', *v.*
man'datory
man'dible
mandib'ular
mandib'ulate
Mandin'go
man'dolin
man'drake
man'drel
man'dril
man'ducate
manduca'tion
mane
man'-eater
manège'
ma'nes
man'ful
man'fully
man'fulness
man'gabey
man'ganese
mangane'sian
mangan'ic
mange
man'gel-wur'zel
man'ger
man'giness
man'gle
man'gled
man'gler
man'gling
man'go
man'grove
man'gy
man-ha'ter
man'hood
ma'nia
ma'niac
mani'acal
Manichae'an
Man'ichaeism
Manichee'
man'ichord
man'icure
man'icurist
man'ifest
man'ifestable
manifesta'tion
man'ifested
man'ifesting
man'ifestly
manifes'to
man'ifold
man'ikin
manil'la
man'ioc

man'iple
manip'ular
manip'ulate
manip'ulated
manip'ulating
manipula'tion
manip'ulative
manip'ulator
ma'nis
man'itou
mankind'
man'lier
man'liest
man'like
man'liness
man'ly
man'na
manned
man'ner
man'nered
man'nerism
man'nerist
man'nerliness
man'nerly
man'ning
man'nish
manoeu'vre
manoeu'vred
manoeu'vrer
manoeu'vring
man'-of-war'
manom'eter
manomet'rical
man'or
man'or-house
mano'rial
man'sard
manse
man'servant
man'sion
man'slaughter
man'suetude
man'tel
man'tel-board
man'telet
man'telpiece
mantil'la
mantis'sa
man'tle
man'tled
man'tling
man'-trap
man'tua
man'tua-maker
man'ual
manuduc'tion
manuduc'tor
manufac'tory
manufac'ture
manufac'tured
manufac'turer
manufac'turing
manumis'sion
manumit'
manumit'ted
manumit'ting
manumo'tor
manure'
manured'
manur'er
manu'rial
manur'ing
man'uscript
Manx
man'y
Mao'ri
map
ma'ple
mapped
map'pery
map'ping
mar
mar'abou
Mar'about
marana'tha
maraschi'no
maras'mus
maraud'
maraud'ed
maraud'er
maraud'ing
marave'di
mar'ble
mar'bled
mar'bler
mar'bling
marc
mar'casite
marces'cent
march
marched
march'er
march'ing
mar'chioness
mar'cid
marcid'ity
mare
mare's'-nest
mare's'-tail
margar'ic
mar'garine
mar'garite
mar'gin
mar'ginal
margina'lia
mar'grave
mar'gravine
mar'guerite
Ma'rian
mar'igold
marinade'
mar'inate
marine'
mar'iner
Mariol'ater
Mariol'atry
marionette'
mar'ish
Ma'rist
mar'ital
mar'itime
mar'joram
mark
marked
mark'er
mar'ket
mar'ketable
mar'ket-day
mar'ket-garden
mar'ket-gardener
mar'keting
mar'ket-man
mar'ket-place
mar'ket-woman
mark'ing
marks'man
marks'manship
marl
marla'ceous
marled
mar'line
mar'line-spike
mar'ling
marl'-pit
marl'y
mar'malade
marmora'ceous
marmo'real
marmo'rean
mar'moset
mar'mot
Mar'onite
maroon'
maroon'er
mar'plot
marque
marquee'
mar'quess
mar'queterie
mar'quetry
mar'quis
mar'quisate
marred
mar'riage
mar'riageable
mar'ried
mar'rier
mar'ring
mar'row
mar'row-bone
mar'rowfat
mar'rowy
mar'ry
mar'rying
Mars
Marsa'la
Marseillaise'
marsh
mar'shal
mar'shalcy
mar'shalled
mar'shaled
mar'shaller
mar'shaler

{ mar'shalling
{ mar'shaling
mar'shalsea
marsh'iness
marsh'-mallow
marsh' marigold
marsh'y
marsu'pial
marsu'pium
mart
martel'lo-tow'er
mar'ten
mar'tial
Mar'tian
mar'tin
martinet'
mar'tingale
Marti'ni
Mar'tinmas
mart'let
mar'tyr
mar'tyrdom
mar'tyred
mar'tyring
martyrolog'ical
martyrol'ogist
martyrol'ogy
mar'vel
{ mar'velled
{ mar'veled
{ mar'velling
{ mar'veling
{ mar'vellous
{ mar'velous
{ mar'vellously
{ mar'velously
mar'zipan
mas'cle
mas'cot
mas'culine
mash
mashed
mash'er
mash'ing
mash'y
mask
masked
mask'er
mask'ing
mas'lin
ma'son
mason'ic
ma'sonry
Maso'rah
Masoret'ic
Mas'orite
masquerade'
masquera'ded
masquera'der
masquera'ding
Mass, mass
mas'sacre
mas'sacred
mas'sacrer
mas'sacring

massage
mass'-book
mas'sé
masse'ter
masseur'
masseuse'
mass'iness
mass'ive
mass'ively
mass'iveness
mass'-meeting
mass'y
mast
mast'ed
mas'ter
mas'ter-builder
mas'tered
mas'terful
mas'tering
mas'ter-key
mas'terless
mas'terly
mas'terpiece
mas'tership
mas'ter-stroke
mas'terwork
mas'tery
mast'-head
mas'tic
mas'ticable
mas'ticate
mas'ticated
mas'ticating
mastica'tion
mas'ticator
mas'ticatory
mas'tiff
mas'todon
mas'toid
mat
mat'ador
match
match'able
matched
match'er
match'ing
match'less
match'lock
match'-maker
match'-making
mate
ma'té
ma'ted
ma'telote
ma'ter
mate'rial
mate'rialism
mate'rialist
materialis'tic
material'ity
mate'rialize
mate'rialized
mate'rializing
mate'rially
mate'ria med'ica
matériel'
mater'nal

mater'nity
math
mathemat'ic
{ *mathemat'ical*
{ *mathemat'ically*
mathemati'cian
mathemat'ics
mathe'sis
mat'in
mat'inal
mat'inée
ma'ting
mat'ins
mat'rass
ma'trice
mat'ricidal
mat'ricide
matric'ulate
matric'ulated
matric'ulating
matricula'tion
matrimo'nial
matrimo'nially
mat'rimony
ma'trix
ma'tron
ma'tronage
ma'tronal
ma'tronly
matross'
mat'ted
mat'ter
mat'ting
mat'tock
mat'tress
mat'urate
mat'urated
matura'tion
matu'rative
mature'
matured'
mature'ly
mature'ness
matures'cence
matu'ring
matu'rity
matuti'nal
maud
maud'lin
mau'gre
maul
mauled
maul'ing
maul'stick
maund
maund'er
maun'dered
maun'dering
Maun'dy Thurs-day
Mau'ser
mausole'um
mauve
ma'vis
mavourneen
maw
mawk'ish

maw'worm
maxil'la
max'illar
maxil'lary
maxil'liform
max'im
max'imum
May
may
may'*be*
May'-day
May'flower
may'hap
may'hem
may'ing
mayonnaise'
may'or
may'oral
may'oralty
may'oress
May'pole
maz'ard
mazarine'
maze
ma'zily
ma'ziness
mazur'ka
ma'zy
me
mead
mead'ow
mead'ow-grass
mead'ow-sweet
mead'owy
mea'gre
mea'grely
mea'greness
meal
meal'ie
meal'iness
meal'man
meal'-time
meal'y
meal'y-mouthed
mean
mean'der
mean'dered
mean'dering
mean'est
mean'ing
mean'ingless
mean'ly
mean'ness
means
meant
mean'time
mean'while
mease
mea'sled
mea'sles
mea'sly
meas'urable
meas'urably
meas'ure
meas'ured
meas'ureless
meas'urement
meas'urer
meas'uring

meat
mechan'ic
{ *mechan'ical*
{ *mechan'ically*
mechani'cian
mechan'ics
mech'anism
mech'anist
mechanog'ra-
phist
mechanog'raphy
Mech'lin
mecom'eter
meco'nium
med'al
medal'lic
medal'lion
med'allist
med'allurgy
med'dle
med'dled
med'dler
med'dlesome
med'dling
me'dia
mediae'val
mediae'valism
me'dial
me'dian
me'diant
medias'tine
mediasti'num
me'diate
me'diated
me'diately
me'diating
media'tion
me'diatize
me'diatized
me'diator
mediato'rial
media'trix
med'icable
med'ical
med'ically
med'icament
med'icate
med'icated
med'icating
medica'tion
med'icative
medic'inal
medic'inally
med'icine
med'ico-chirur'-
gical
med'ico-le'gal
medie'val
medie'valism
me'diocre
medioc'rity
med'itate
med'itated
med'itating
medita'tion
med'itative
Mediterra'nean

me'dium
med'lar
med'ley
Médoc'
medul'la
med'ullary
medul'line
medu'sa
meed
meek
meek'en
meek'ly
meek'ness
meer'schaum
meet
meet'en
meet'ing
meet'ing-house
meet'ly
meg'acosm
meg'alith
megalith'ic
megalon'yx
megalosau'rus
meg'ascope
meg'aphone
megathe'rium
me'grim
meio'sis
melancho'lia
melanchol'ic
mel'ancholy
Melane'sian
mel'anism
mel'anite
melas'ma
meldom'eter
mêlée'
mel'ilot
me'liorate
meliora'tion
mellif'erous
mellif'ic
mellifica'tion
mellif'luence
mellif'luent
mellif'luous
mel'lite
mellit'ic
mel'lone
mel'low
mel'lowed
mel'lowing
mel'lowness
melo'deon
melo'dious
melo'diously
melo'diousness
mel'odist
mel'odize
melodra'ma
melodramat'ic
melodramat'ical
melodram'atist

mel'ody
mel'on
melt
melt'ed
melt'er
melt'ing
melt'ingly
mem'ber
mem'bered
*mem'ber*ship
membrana'ceous
mem'brane
membranif'erous
membra'niform
membranol'ogy
mem'branous
memen'to
mem'oir
memorabil'ia
memorabil'ity
mem'orable
mem'orably
memoran'da
memoran'dum
memo'rial
memo'rialist
memo'rialize
memo'rialized
memo'rializing
memor'iter
mem'orize
mem'orized
mem'orizing
mem'ory
Mem'phian
men
men'ace
men'aced
men'acer
men'acing
men'acingly
ménage'
menag'erie
mend
mend'able
menda'cious
menda'ciously
menda'ciousness
mendac'ity
mend'ed
mend'er
men'dicancy
men'dicant
mendic'ity
mend'ing
me'nial
menin'geal
menin'ges
meningi'tis
menis'cal
menis'coid
menis'cus
Men'nonite
men'ses
men'strual
men'struate
menstrua'tion
men'struous
men'struum
mensurabil'ity
men'surable
men'sural
mensura'tion
men'tal
men'tality
men'thol
men'tion
men'tionable
men'tioned
men'tioning
men'tor
mento'rial
men'u
Mephistophe'lian
mephit'ic
mephit'ical
mephi'tis
meph'itism
mer'cantile
Mer'cédès
mer'cenarily
mer'cenary
mer'cer
mer'cerize
mer'cerized
mer'cery
mer'chandise
mer'chant
mer'chantable
mer'chantman
mer'ciful
mer'cifully
mer'ciless
mer'cilessly
mercu'rial
mercu'rialist
mercu'rialize
mercu'rify
mer'cury
mer'cy
mer'cy-seat
mere
*mere'*ly
meretri'cious
merge
merged
mer'ging
merid'ian
merid'ional
meringue'
meri'no
mer'it
mer'ited
mer'iting
merito'rious
merle
mer'lin
mer'ling
mer'lon
mer'maid
mer'man
merop'idan
Merovin'gian
mer'rier
mer'riest
mer'rily
mer'riment
mer'ry
mer'ry-andrew
mer'rymaking
mer'rythought
mesdames'
mesdemoiselles'
meseems'
mesenter'ic
mes'entery
mesh
meshed
mesh'ing
mesh'y
mesmer'ic
mes'merism
mes'merist
mesmeriza'tion
mes'merize
mes'merized
mes'merizer
mes'merizing
mesne
mesoco'lon
mes'olabe
mes'osperm
mesotho'rax
mesotho'rium
mes'otype
mess
mes'sage
messed
mes'senger
Messi'ad
Messi'ah
Messi'ahship
Messian'ic
mes'sieurs
mes'sing
mess'mate
mes'suage
mestee'
mesti'zo
met
metab'asis
metab'ola
metabo'lian
metabol'ic
metacar'pal
metacar'pus

metach'ronism
met'acism
me'tage
metagram'matism
metal'
metalep'sis
metalep'tic
metal'lic
metallif'erous
metal'liform
met'alline
met'aline
met'allist
met'alist
metalliza'tion
metaliza'tion
met'allize
met'alize
met'allized
met'alized
met'allizing
met'alizing
metallog'raphy
met'alloid
metalloid'al
metallur'gic
metallur'gical
met'allurgist
met'allurgy
met'al-man
metamer'ic
metamor'phic
metamor'phism
metamor'phist
metamor'phose
metamor'phosed
metamor'phosis
met'aphor
metaphor'ic
metaphor'ical
metaphor'ically
met'aphorist
met'aphrase
met'aphrast
metaphras'tic
metaphys'ic
metaphys'ical
metaphysi'cian
metaphys'ics
met'aplasm
metapto'sis
metarrhe'a
metas'tasis
metastat'ic
metatar'sus
metath'esis
metathet'ical
metatho'rax
me'tayer
metazo'on
mete
me'ted
metempsycho'sis
metempto'sis
me'teor
meteor'ic

me'teorite
meteor'ograph
meteorograph'ic
meteorog'raphy
me'teoroid
me'teorolite
meteorolog'ic
meteorolog'ical
meteorol'ogist
meteorol'ogy
meteorom'eter
meteoros'copy
me'ter
metheg'lin
meth'ene
meth'ide
methinks'
meth'od
method'ic
method'ical
method'ically
Meth'odism
Meth'odist
methodis'tic
methodis'tical
meth'odize
meth'odized
meth'odizer
meth'odizing
*me*thought'
meth'yl
meth'ylate
meth'ylated
meth'ylene
methyl'ic
me'tier
me'ting
meton'ic
metonym'ic
meton'ymy
met'ope
metopos'copy
met'ra
me'tre, me'ter
met'ric
met'rical
met'rochrome
met'rograph
metrol'ogy
met'ronome
metronom'ic
metron'omy
metronym'ic
metrop'olis
metropol'itan
met'tle
met'tled
met'tlesome
mew
mewed
mew'ing
mewl
mewled
mewl'er

mewl'ing
mews
Mex'ican
mez'zanine
mez'zo
mez'zotint
mezzotin'to
mi'asm
mias'ma
mias'mal
miasmat'ic
miasmat'ical
mias'matist
mi'ca
mica'ceous
mice
Mich'aelmas
mick'le
micracous'tic
mi'crobe
microceph'alous
mi'crocosm
microcos'mic
microcos'mical
micrograph'ophone
microg'raphy
microl'ogy
microm'eter
micromet'ric
micronom'eter
mi'cro-or'ganism
mi'crophone
microphon'ics
microph'onous
mi'croscope
microscop'ic
microscop'ical
micros'copist
micros'copy
microzo'on
micturi'tion
mid
mid'day
mid'den
mid'dle
mid'dle-aged
mid'dle-class
mid'dleman
mid'dle*most*
mid'dling
mid'dy
midge
midg'et
Mid'ianite
mid'land
mid'*most*
mid'night
mid'rib
mid'riff
mid'ship
mid'shipman
midst

mid'stream
mid'summer
mid'way
mid'-wicket
mid'wife
mid'wifery
mid'winter
mien
miff
might
might'ier
might'iest
might'ily
might'iness
mightst
might'y
mignonette'
migraine'
mi'grate
mi'grated
mi'grating
migra'tion
mi'gratory
mika'do
Milanese'
milch
mild
mild'er
mild'est
mil'dew
mil'dewed
mil'dewing
mild'ly
mild'ness
mile
mile'age
Mile'sian
mile'-stone
mil'foil
mil'iary
mil'itant
mil'itarism
mil'itary
mil'itate
mil'itated
mil'itating
mili'tia
milk
milked
milk'er
milk'ier
milk'iest
milk'ing
milk'iness
milk'maid
milk'man
milk'-pail
milk'-pan
milk'sop
milk'-tooth
milk'-warm
milk'-white
milk'wort
milk'y

Milky Way
mill
mill'-cog
mill'-dam
milled
millena'rian
millena'rianism
mil'lenary
millen'nial
millen'nialist
millen'nium
mil'lepede
mil'lepore
mill'er
mill'erite
mill'er's-thumb
milles'imal
mil'let
mill'-head
mil'liard
mil'liary
mill'igram
milli'gramme
milli'litre
mill'iliter
mill'imetre
mill'imeter
mil'liner
mil'linery
mill'ing
mil'lion
millionaire'
mill'ionary
mil'lionth
mill'-pond
mill'-race
mill'stone
mill'-wheel
mill'wright
mil'reis
milt
Milton'ic
milt'wort
mil'vine
mil'vus
mime
mim'eograph
mimet'ic
mimet'ically
mim'ic
mim'ical
mim'icked
mim'icker
mim'icking
mim'icry
mimog'rapher
mimo'sa
mina'cious
minac'ity
min'aret
min'atory
mince
minced
mince'-meat
mince'-pie
min'cing

min'cingly
mind
mind'ed
mind'er
mind'ful
mind'ing
mind'less
mine
mined
mi'ner
min'eral
min'eralist
mineraliza'tion
min'eralize
min'eralized
min'eralizer
min'eralizing
mineralog'ic
mineralog'ical
mineral'ogist
mineral'ogy
min'eral wa'ters
Miner'va
min'gle
min'gled
min'gler
min'gling
min'iate
min'iature
min'iaturist
Min'ié
min'ify
min'ikin
min'im
min'imize
min'imized
min'imizing
min'imum
mi'ning
min'ion
min'ister
min'istered
ministe'rial
ministe'rialist
ministe'rially
min'istering
min'istrant
ministra'tion
min'istress
min'istry
min'ium
min'iver
mink
min'nesinger
min'now
mi'nor
minor'ity
Min'otaur
min'ster
min'strel
min'strelsy
mint
mint'age
mint'ed
mint'er
mint'ing
min'uend
minuet'

mi'nus
min'ute
minute'
min'uted
min'ute-book
min'ute-gun
min'ute-hand
minute'ly
minute'ness
minu'tiae
min'uting
minx
mi'ny
Mi'ocene
mir'acle
mirac'ulous
mirac'ulously
mirage'
mire
mired
mirif'ic
mi'riness
mir'ror
mir'rored
mirth
mirth'ful
mirth'fully
mirth'fulness
mirth'less
mir'y
mir'za
misadven'ture
misadven'turous
misadvised'
misalli'ance
misallied'
mis'anthrope
misanthrop'ic
misan'thropist
misan'thropy
misapplica'tion
misapplied'
misapply'
misapply'ing
misapprehend'
misapprehend'ed
misapprehend'-ing
misapprehen'-sion
misappro'priate
misappro'priated
misappro'priating
misappropria'-tion
mis*become'*
mis*be*com'ing
misbegot'ten
misbehave'
misbehaved'
misbeha'ving
misbeha'viour
misbelief'
misbelieve'
misbelieved'
misbeliev'er
misbeliev'ing
miscal'culate
miscal'culated
miscal'culating
miscalcula'tion
miscall'
miscalled'
miscall'ing
miscar'riage
miscar'ried
miscar'ry
miscar'rying
miscast'
miscellana'rian
miscella'nea
miscella'neous
miscella'neously
miscel'lanist
miscel'lany
mischance'
mischarge'
mis'chief
mis'chief-maker
mis'chievous
mis'chievously
mischoose'
mis'cible
mis'citation
miscite'
miscomputa'tion
miscompute'
misconceive'
misconceived'
misconceiv'ing
misconcep'tion
misconduct
misconjec'ture
misconstruc'tion
miscon'strue
miscon'strued
miscon'struing
miscount'
mis'creant
miscue'
misdate'
misdat'ed
misdat'ing
misdeal'
misdeed'
misdeem'
misdemean'
misdemean'ant
misdemean'our
misdirect'
misdirect'ed
misdirect'ing
misdirec'tion
misdo'
misdo'er
misdo'ing
mise
misemploy'
misemployed'
misemploy'ing
misemploy'ment
misen'ter
misen'try
mi'ser
mis'erable
mis'erably
misere're
miser'icord
mi'serly
mis'ery
misfea'sance
misfire'
misfit'
misform'
misformed'
misfor'tune
misframed'
misgave'
mis*give'*
mis*giv'en*
mis*giv'*ing
misgot'ten
mis*gov'ern*
mis*gov'erned*
mis*gov'erning*
mis*gov'ernment*
misguid'ance
misguide'
misguid'ed
misguid'ing
mishap'
mishear'
mishear'ing
mish'-mash
Mish'nah
mish'nic
misimprove'
{ mis*inform'*
{ mis*informed'*
mis*informa'tion*
misinter'pret
misinterpreta'tion
misinter'preted
misinter'preter
misinter'preting
misjoin'
misjoin'der
misjoined'
misjoin'ing
misjudge'
misjudged'
misjudg'ing
misjudg'ment
mislaid'
mislay'
mislay'ing
mis'le
mislead'
mislead'er
mislead'ing
misled'
misman'age
misman'aged
misman'age-ment
misman'ager
misman'aging

mismark'
mismarked'
mismark'ing
mismatch'
mismeas'ure
mismeas'ured
mismeas'uring
misname'
misnamed'
misnam'ing
misno'mer
misnum'ber
misog'amist
misog'amy
misog'ynist
misog'yny
mis'pickel
misplace'
misplaced'
misplace'ment
misplac'ing
misplead'
misplead'ed
misplead'ing
mispoint'
mispoint'ed
mispoint'ing
misprint'
misprint'ed
misprint'ing
mispri'sion
misprize'
misprized'
mispriz'ing
mispronounce'
mispronounced'
mispronounc'ing
mispronuncia'-tion
mis*propor'tion*
mis*propor'tioned*
mis*propor'tion*ing
misquota'tion
misquote'
misquot'ed
misquot'ing
misread'
misread'
misread'ing
misrecite'
misreck'on
misreck'oned
misreck'oning
misrelate'
misrela'tion
mis*remem'ber*
mis*remem'ber*-[ed
misreport'
misreport'ed
misreport'ing
mis*represent'*
mis*represent'ed*
mis*representa'tion*
mis*represent'*ing
misrule'
miss

mis'sal
missed
mis'sel
mis'sel-thrush
mis-send'
mis-sent'
mis-serve'
mis-served'
mis-serv'ing
miss-fire'
mis-shape'
mis-shaped'
mis-sha'pen
mis'sile
miss'ing
mis'sion
mis'sionary
mis'sioner
mis'sis
mis'sive
mis-spell'
mis-spelled'
mis-spell'ing
mis-spelt'
mis-spend'
mis-spend'ing
mis-spent'
mis-state'
mis-sta'ted
mis-state'ment
mis-sta'ting
mist
mista'kable
mistake'
mista'ken
mista'king
mistaught'
misteach'
misteach'ing
mis'ter
misterm'
mis*think'*
misthought
mistime'
mistimed'
mistim'ing
mist'iness
mis'tletoe
mist'-like
mistook'
mis'tral
mistranslate'
mistransla'ted
mistransla'ting
mistransla'tion
mis'tress
mistrust'
mistrust'ed
mistrust'ful
mistrust'ing
mistune'
mistuned'
mistun'ing
mist'y
mis*under*stand'
mis*under*stand'ing
mis*under*stood'
misu'sage
misuse', *v.*
misuse', *n.*

misused'
misu'ser
misu'sing
miswrite'
miswrit'ing
miswrit'ten
miswrote'
miswrought'
misyoke'
misyoked'
mite
mi'ter
mit'igable
mit'igant
mit'igate
mit'igated
mit'igating
mitiga'tion
mit'igative
mit'igator
mitrailleuse'
mi'tral
mi'tre
mi'tred
mi'triform
mi'tring
mitt
mit'ten
mit'timus
mi'ty
mix
mix'able
mixed
mix'edly
mix'en
mix'er
mix'ing
mixtilin'eal
mixtilin'ear
mix'tion
mix'ture
miz'en, miz'zen
miz'enmast
miz'zle
miz'zled
miz'zling
miz'zly
mnemon'ic
mnemon'ical
mnemon'ics
mnem'otechny
moan
moaned
moan'ful
moan'ing
moat
moat'ed
mob
mob'-cap
mobbed
mob'bing
mob'bish
mo'bile
mobil'ity

mobiliza'tion
mo'bilize
mo'bilized
mo'bilizing
mob'-law
moboc'racy
moc'casin
mo'cha
mock
mocked
mock'er
mock'ery
mock'-heroic
mock'ing
mock'ing-bird
mock'-orange
mock'-turtle
mo'co
mo'dal
modal'ity
mode
mod'el
mod'elled-eled
mod'eller-eler
mod'elling-eling
mod'erate, *n.*, *a.*
mod'erate, *v.*
mod'erated
mod'erately
mod'erating
modera'tion
mod'eratism
modera'to
mod'erator
mod'eratrix
mod'ern
mod'ernism
mod'ernist
moder'nity
moderniza'tion
mod'ernize
mod'ernized
mod'ernizer
mod'ernizing
mod'ernness
mod'est
mod'estly
mod'esty
mod'icum
modifiabil'ity
mod'ifiable
modifica'tion
mod'ified
mod'ifier
mod'ify
mod'ifying
modil'lion
mo'dish
mo'dishly
mo'dist
modiste'
mod'ulate
mod'ulated
mod'ulating
modula'tion
mod'ulator

mod'ule
mod'ulus
mo'dus
mod'wall
Moesogoth'ic
mofus'sil
Mogul'
mo'hair
Moham'medan
Moham'medan-ism
Moham'medan-ize
Moham'medan-ized
Mo'hawk
Mohi'can
Mo'hock
mo'hur
moi'dore
moi'ety
moil
moiled
moil'ing
moi'neau
moire
moiré'
moist
mois'ten
mois'tened
mois'tening
moist'ness
mois'ture
mo'lar
mo'lary
molas'ses
mold
mole
molec'ular
molecular'ity
mol'ecule
mole'-eyed
mole'-hill
mole'-hole
mole'skin
molest'
molesta'tion
molest'ed
molest'er
molest'ing
Mol'inism
Mol'inist
mol'lah
mol'lient
mol'lifiable
mollifica'tion
mol'lified
mol'lifier
mol'lify
mol'lifying
Mollus'ca
mollus'can
mollus'cous
mol'lusk

Mo'loch
molosse'
molos'sus
molt
mol'ten
mo'ly
molyb'dena
molyb'denous
molybde'num
mome
mo'ment
mo'mentarily
mo'mentary
mo'mently
momen'tous
momen'tum
Mo'mus
mon'achal
mon'achism
mon'ad
Monadel'phia
monadelph'ian
monadelph'ous
monad'ic
monad'ical
monan'drian
monan'drous
mon'arch
monar'chic
monar'chical
mon'archist
mon'archize
mon'archy
monaste'rial
mon'astery
monas'tic
monas'tical
monas'tically
monas'ticism
monas'ticon
Mon'day
mon'etary
mon'etize
mon'ey
mon'ey-broker
mon'eyed
mon'eyer
mon'eyless
mon'ger
Mon'gol
Mongo'lian
mon'goose
mon'grel
monil'iform

mon'ism
mon'ist
moni'tion
mon'itive
mon'itor
monito'rial
mon'itory
mon'itress
monk
monk'ery
mon'key
monk'hood
monk'ish
monk's'-hood
monocar'dian
monocar'pous
monoceph'alous
monoc'eros
mon'ochord
monochromat'ic
mon'ochrome
monochron'ic
mon'ocle
monocli'nous
Monocotyle'don
monoc'racy
mon'ocrat
monoc'ular
mon'ocule
monoc'ulous
Monodac'tylous
mon'odelph
mon'odist
mon'odon
mon'odrama
monodramat'ic
mon'ody
monog'amist
monog'amous
monog'amy
monogen'esis
monogenet'ic
monog'enism
monog'enist
monogenist'ic
mon'ogram
mon'ograph
monog'rapher
monograph'ic
monog'raphist
monog'raphy
monog'yny
monogyn'ian
mon'olith

monolith'ic
monol'ogy
mon'ologue
monom'achy
monoma'nia
monoma'niac
monometal'lic
monomet'allism
monomet'allist
monom'eter
monomet'ric
mono'mial
monop'athy
monoper'sonal
monopet'alous
monoph'onous
mon'ophthong
monophthon'gal
monophyl'lous
mon'oplane
monop'olism
monop'olist
monop'olize
monop'olized
monop'olizer
monop'olizing
monop'oly
monop'teral
mon'optote
mon'orail
{ mon'orime
{ mon'orhyme
monosep'alous
monosper'mous
monospher'ical
mon'ostich
monostroph'ic
monosyllab'ic
mon'osyllable
mon'otheism
mon'otheist
monotheis'tic
mon'otone
monot'onous
monot'ony
mon'otreme
mon'otype
monotyp'ic
monox'ide
monseigneur'
monsieur'

monsoon'
mon'ster
mon'strance
*monstros'*ity
mon'strous
*mon'strous*ly
montan'ic
Mon'tanism
Mon'tanist
mon'tant
mon'te
mon'tem
month
month'ly
mon'ument
{ monumen'tal
{ monumen'tally
moo
mood
mooed
moo'ing
mood'ily
mood'iness
mood'y
moon
moon'beam
moon'-calf
mooned
moon'-eyed
moon'ish
moon'less
moon'light
moon'lighter
moon'lighting
moon'lit
moon'-raker
moon'-raking
moon'shee
moon'shine
moon'shiny
moon'stone
moon'struck
moon'wort
moon'y
moor
moor'age
moor'-cock
moored
moor'-fowl
moor'-game
moor'-grass
moor'-hen
moor'ing
moor'ish
moor'land
moor'-stone
moor'y
moose
moose'wood
moot
moot'able
moot'-case
moot'ed
moot'er
moot'ing
mop

mope
moped
mo'ping
mo'pish
mo'pishness
mopped
mop'pet
mop'ping
mop'sy
moraine'
mor'al
morale'
mor'alist
moral'ity
moraliza'tion
mor'alize
mor'alized
mor'alizer
mor'alizing
mor'ally
mor'als
morass'
morato'rium
Mora'vian
Mora'vianism
mor'bid
morbid'ity
mor'bidly
mor'bidness
morbif'ic
morbil'lous
morbose'
mor'bus
morceau'
morda'cious
mordac'ity
mor'dant
more
moreen'
morel'
morel'lo
moreo'ver
Moresque'
morganat'ic
mor'gay
morgue
mor'ibund
moril'lon
mo'rion
Moris'co
Mor'mon
Mor'monism
Mor'monite
morn
morn'ing
morn'ing-star
moroc'co
morone'
morose'
morose'ly
morose'ness
Mor'pheus
mor'phia
mor'phine
morpholog'ic
{ morpholog'ical
{ morpholog'ically
morphol'ogy
mor'ris
mor'ris-dance
mor'ris-pike
mor'row
morse
mor'sel
mort
mor'tal
mortal'ity
mor'tally
mor'tar
{ *mort'gage*
{ *mort'gaged*
mortgagee'
mort'gager
mort'gaging
mort'gagor
mortif'erous
mortifica'tion
mor'tified
mor'tifier
mor'tify
mor'tifying
mor'tise
mor'tised
mor'tising
mort'main
mor'tuary
mo'rus
Mosa'ic, mosa'ic
moschatel'
Moselle'
Mos'lem
mosque
mosqui'to
moss
moss'clad
moss'iness
moss'-trooper
moss'y
most
most'ly
mot
mote
moth
moth'-eaten
moth'er
moth'erhood
moth'ering
moth'er-in-law
moth'erless
moth'erly
moth'er-of-pearl
moth'er-wit
moth'ery
moth'y
mo'tif
motif'ic
motil'ity
mo'tion
mo'tioned
mo'tioner
mo'tioning
mo'tionless
mo'tive
motiv'ity
mot'ley
mot'mot
mo'tograph
motom'eter
mo'tor
mo'tor-bus'
mo'tor-car
mo'tor-cy'cle
moto'rial
mo'torist
mo'tory
mot'tle
mot'tled
mot'to
mouf'flon
mould
mould'able
mould'ed
mould'er
mould'ered
mould'ering
mould'iness
mould'ing
mould'warp
mould'y
moult'
moult'ed
moult'ing
mound
mount
mount'able
moun'tain
moun'tain ash
mountaineer'
moun'tainous
mount'ebank
mount'ed
mount'er
mount'ing
mourn
mourned
mourn'er
mourn'ful
mourn'fully
mourn'fulness
mourn'ing
mourn'ing-ring
mouse
moused
mouse'-ear
mous'er
mouse'-hole
mouse'tail
mouse'trap
mous'ing

moustache'
mous'y
mouth
mouthed
mouth'er
mouth'ful
mouth'ing
mouth'piece
{ mov'able
{ move'able
mov'ables
move
moved
move'less
move'ment
mov'er
mov'ing
mov'ingly
{ mow (of hay)
{ mow (to grimace)
mow (to cut)
mowed
mow'er
mow'ing
mown
Mr.
Mrs.
much
mu'cid
mu'ciform
mu'cilage
mucilag'inous
mucip'arous
muck
muck'-heap
muck'worm
muck'y
mu'coid
mucos'ity
mu'cous
mu'cronate
mu'culent
mu'cus
mud
mud'dily
mud'diness
mud'dle
mud'dled
mud'dler
mud'dling
mud'dy
muez'zin
muff
muf'fin
muffineer'
muf'fle
muf'fled
muf'fler
muf'fling
muf'ti
mug
mug'get
Muggleto'nian
mug'gy
mug'wump
mulat'to
mul'berry
mulch
mulched

mulct
mulct'ed
mulct'ing
mulc'tuary
mule
muleteer'
mulieb'rity
mu'lish
mu'lishness
mull
mul'lah
mulled
mul'ler
mul'let
mulligataw'ny
mul'ling
mul'lion
multan'gular
multiartic'ulate
multicap'sular
multiden'tate
multifa'rious
multifa'riously
mul'tifid
multiflo'rous
mul'tifold
mul'tiform
multiform'ity
multilat'eral
multilin'eal
multil'oquence
multil'oquent
multino'mial
multip'arous
multipar'tite
mul'tiped
mul'tiplane
mul'tiple
mul'tiplex
mul'tipliable
multiplicand'
mul'tiplicate
multiplica'tion
mul'tiplicative
mul'tiplicator
multiplic'ity
mul'tiplied
mul'tiplier
mul'tiply
mul'tiplying
multi'potent

multipres'ence
multira'diate
multis'onous
multispi'ral
mul'titude
multitu'dinary
multitu'dinous
mul'tivalve
multival'vular
Multo'ca
multoc'ular
mum
mum'ble
mum'bled
mum'bler
mum'bling
mum'bo-jum'bo
mummed
mum'mer
mum'mery
mummifica'tion
mum'mified
mum'miform
mum'mify
mum'ming
mum'my
mump
mump'er
mump'ing
mump'ish
mumps
munch
munched
munch'er
munch'ing
mun'dane
mun'dic
mundifica'tion
mundif'icative
mun'go
munic'ipal
municipal'ity
munif'icence
munif'icent
mu'niment
muni'tion
munjeet'
mun'nion
mu'ral
mur'der
mur'dered
mur'derer
mur'deress
mur'derous
mur'derously
mur'dress
mu'riate
mu'riated
muriat'ic
mu'ricate
mu'ricated

mu'riform
mu'rine
murk
murk'ily
murk'y
mur'mur
mur'mured
mur'murer
mur'muring
mur'murous
mur'phy
mur'rain
{ mur'rhine
{ mur'rine
mur'za
mus'cadel
mus'cadine
mus'cardine
mus'cat
mus'catel
mus'cle
mus'cled
mus'coid
muscol'ogy
mus'cose
muscos'ity
muscova'do
Mus'covite
mus'cular
muscular'ity
mus'culous
muse
mused
muse'ful
mu'ser
muse'um
mush
mush'room
mu'sic
mu'sical
mu'sically
mu'sic-hall
musi'cian
mu'sic-master
mu'sic-stool
mu'sing
musk
mus'ket
musketeer'
musketoon'
mus'ket-proof
mus'ketry
musk'iness
musk'-rat
musk'y
mus'lin
mus'lin-de-laine
muslinet'
mus'quash
mus'role
muss
mus'sel

Mus'sulman
must
mustache'
mustach'io
mustach'ioed
mus'tang
mus'tard
mustee'
mus'teline
mus'ter
mus'tered
mus'tering
mus'ter-roll
mus'tily
mus'tiness
mus'ty
mutabil'ity
mu'table
mu'tably
mu'tage
mu'tate
mu'tated
muta'tion
mute
mute'ly
mute'ness
mu'tilate
mu'tilated
mu'tilating
mutila'tion
mu'tilator
mutineer'
mu'tinied
mu'tinous
mu'tinously
mu'tiny
mu'tinying
mu'tism
mut'ter
mut'tered
mut'terer
mut'tering
mut'ton
mu'tual
mutual'ity
mu'tually
mu'tule
muz'zle
muz'zled
muz'zle-loader
muz'zling
my
my'all-wood
mycolog'ic
mycol'ogist
mycol'ogy
mynheer'
myograph'ic
myog'raphist
myog'raphy
myolog'ic
myol'ogist
myolog'ical

myol'ogy
my'ope
myo'pia
myop'ic
my'opsy
my'opy
my'osin
myo'sis
myosit'ic
myot'omy
myr'iad
myr'iagram
{ myr'ialitre
{ myr'ialiter
{ myr'iametre
{ myr'iameter
myr'iapod
myr'iarch
myr'icin
myriora'ma
myr'ioscope
myr'midon
myrob'alan
myrrh
myr'rhine
myr'tiform
myr'tle
myself'
mys'tagogue
myste'riarch
myste'rious
myste'riously
mys'tery
mys'tic
mys'tical
mys'tically
mys'ticism
mystifica'tion
mys'tificator
mys'tified
mys'tify
mys'tifying
myth
myth'ic
myth'ical
myth'ically
mythog'rapher
mythog'raphy
mythol'oger
mytholog'ic
{ mytholog'ical
{ mytholog'ical- [ly
mythol'ogist
mythol'ogize
mythol'ogizing
myth'ologue
mythol'ogy (or)
myth'oplasm
my'thus

N

nab
nabbed
nab'bing
na'bob
nac'arat
na'cre
nacré'
na'creous
na'crite
na'dir
nag
nagged
nag'ging
Nai'ad
naïf
nail
nail'-brush
nailed
nail'er
nail'ery
nail'ing
nail'-scissors
nain'sook
naïve, naive
naïve'ly
naïveté'
na'ked
na'kedly
na'kedness
na'mable
namby-pam'by
name
named
name'less
name'ly
na'mer
name'sake
na'ming
nankeen'
Nantes
nap
nape
na'pery
naph'tha
naphthal'ic
naph'thaline
Napier'ian
Na'pier's bones
na'piform
nap'kin
Napo'leon
Napoleon'ic
nap'piness
nap'ping, nap'py
Narcis'sus
narco'sis
narcot'ic
narcot'ical

nar'cotine
nar'cotism
nar'cotize
nar'cotized
nar'cotizing
nard
nard'ine
na'res
nar'ghile
narrate'
narra'ted
narra'ting
narra'tion
nar'rative
narra'tor
nar'row
nar'rowed
nar'rower
nar'row-gauge
nar'rowing
nar'rowly
nar'row-mind'ed
nar'row-mind'ed-ness
nar'rowness
nar'thex
nar'whal
na'sal
nasal'ity
nasaliza'tion
na'salize
na'salized
na'salizing
na'sally
nas'cent
na'sicornous
na'siform
nasol'ogy
nas'tier
nas'tiest
nas'tily
nas'tiness
nastur'tium
nas'ty
na'tal
natali'tial
na'tant
nata'tion
natato'rial
na'tatory
nath'less
na'tion
na'tional
na'tionalism
national'ity
nationaliza'tion
na'tionalize
na'tionalized
na'tionalizing

na'tionally
na'tionhood
na'tive
nativ'ity
nat'rolite
na'tron
nat'ter
nat'tily
nat'ty
nat'ural
nat'uralism
nat'uralist
naturalis'tic
naturaliza'tion
nat'uralize
nat'uralized
nat'uralizing
nat'urally
nat'uralness
na'ture
naught
naugh'tier
naugh'tiest
naugh'tily
naugh'tiness
naugh'ty
nauma'chia
nau'machy
naus'copy
nau'sea
nau'seant
nau'seate
nau'seated
nau'seating
nausea'tion
nau'seous
nautch
nautch'-girl
nau'tical
nau'tilite
nau'tilus
na'val
na'varch
na'varchy
nave
na'vel
navette'
navic'ular
navigabil'ity
nav'igable
nav'igate
nav'igated
nav'igating
naviga'tion
nav'igator
nav'vy, na'vy
nawab'
nay

Nazarene'
Naz'arite
Naz'aritism
naze
nazir'
neap
neaped
Neapol'itan
neap'tide
near
*near*ed
near'er
near'est
near'ing
near'ly
near'ness
near'sighted
neat
neat'-cattle
neat'er
neat'est
neat'herd
neat'ly
neat'ness
neb
neb'ula
neb'ular
neb'ule
nebulos'ity
neb'ulous
necessa'rian
nec'essarily
nec'essariness
nec'essary
necessita'rian
neces'sitate
neces'sitated
neces'sitating
neces'sitous
neces'sity
neck
neck'cloth
neck'erchief
neck'lace
neck'tie
necrol'atry
necrolog'ic
necrolog'ical
necrol'ogist
necrol'ogy
nec'romancer
nec'romancy
necroman'tic
nec'ronite
necrop'olis
necroscop'ic
necro'sis
necrot'omy
nec'tar
necta'real
necta'rean
necta'reous
nectarif'erous
nec'tarine
necta'rium
nec'tarize
nec'tarous
nec'tary
né *or* née
need

need'ed
need'er
need'ful
need'ier
need'iest
need'ily
need'iness
need'ing
nee'dle
nee'dle-book
nee'dleful
nee'dle-gun
nee'dle-shaped
need'less
need'lessly
need'lessness
nee'dlewoman
nee'dlework
needs
need'y
ne'er
nefan'dous
nefa'rious
nega'tion
neg'ative
neg'atived
neg'atively
neglect', *neglect'ed*
neglect'er
*neglect'*ful
*neglect'*ing
negligé'
neg'ligence
neg'ligent
neg'ligently
neg'ligible
negotiabil'ity
nego'tiable
nego'tiate
nego'tiated
nego'tiating
negotia'tion
nego'tiator
nego'tiatory
ne'gress
ne'gro
ne'groid
ne'groloid
ne'gus
neigh
neigh'bour-bor
neigh'boured
neigh'bourhood
neigh'bouring
neigh'bourliness
neigh'bourly
neighed, neigh'-[ing
nei'ther
Neme'an
Nem'esis
nen'uphar
neog'amist
neog'raphy
Ne'ocene
neolith'ic
neolo'gian
neolog'ical
neol'ogism
neol'ogist
neol'ogize

neol'ogy
Neono'mian
ne'ophyte
Neoplaton'ic
Neoplat'onism
Neoplat'onist
neoter'ic
Neozo'ic
nepen'the
neph'eline
neph'ew
neph'oscope
nephral'gia
nephral'gy
neph'rite
nephrit'ic
nephri'tis
nephrol'ogy
nephrot'omy
nep'otal
nep'otism
nep'otist
Nep'tune
Neptu'nian
Nep'tunist
Ne'reid
ne'roli
nerva'tion
nerve, nerved
nerve'less
nerv'ine
nerv'ing
nerv'ous
nerv'ously
ner'vure
nes'cience
nes'cient
ness
nest
nest'ed
nest'-egg
nest'ing
nes'tle
nes'tled
nes'tling
Nes'tor
Nesto'rian
Nesto'rianism
net
neth'er
neth'er*most*
net'ted
net'ting
net'tle
net'tled
net'tler
net'tle-rash
net'tle-wort
net'tling
net'work
neu'ral
neural'gia
neural'gic
neural'gy
neurasthe'nia
neu'rine
neuri'tis
neurog'raphy
neurol'ogist
neurol'ogy

neurop'ter
Neurop'tera
neurop'teran
neuro'sis
neurot'ic
neurot'omy
neu'ter
neu'tral
neutral'ity
neutraliza'tion
neu'tralize
neu'tralized
neu'tralizer
neu'tralizing
neu'trally
nev'er
nev'ermore
nevertheless'
new
new'-born
new'-comer
new'el
new'er
new'est
newfan'gled
new-fash'ioned
new'ish
new'laid
new'ly
new'-made
new'ness
news
news'-agent
news'boy
news'man
news'monger
news'paper
news'room
news'vendor
news'*writer*
news'y
newt
Newto'nian
New'-*year*
next
nex'us
nib
nibbed
nib'ble
nib'bled
nib'bler
nib'bling
nice
nice'ly
Ni'cene
nice'ness
ni'cer
ni'cest
ni'cety
niche
niched
nick
nicked
nick'el
nick'ing
nick'-nack
nick'name
nick'named
nick'naming
Nicola'itan

nico'tian
nico'tianin
nic'otine
nic'tate
nic'tated
nic'tating
nicta'tion
nictita'tion
nide
nid'get
nid'ificate
nidifica'tion
nid'ulant
nid'ulate
nidula'tion
ni'dus
niece
niel'lo
nig'gard
nig'gardliness
nig'gardly
nig'ger
nig'gle
nig'gler
nig'gling
nigh
nigh'ness
night
night'-blooming
night'cap
night'dress
night'fall
night'-fire
night'gown
night'-hawk
night'ingale
night'jar
night'-light
night'ly
night'man
night'mare
night'-piece
night'-porter
night'shade
night'shirt
night'-stool
night'-time
night'-train
night'-walker
night'-walking
night'-watch
night'-watcher
nigres'cent
nigrifica'tion
nig'rin
nig'rine
ni'hilism
ni'hilist
nihilis'tic
nihil'ity
nil, nill
Nilom'eter
Ni'loscope
Nilot'ic
nimbif'erous
nim'ble
nim'bleness
nim'bler
nim'blest
nim'bly

nim'bus
nim'iny-piminy
nin'compoop
nine
nine'fold
nine'pence
nine'pins
nine'score
nineteen'
nineteenth'
nine'tieth
nine'ty
nin'ny
nin'nyhammer
ninth
ninth'ly
nip
nipped
nip'per
nip'perkin
nip'pers
nip'ping
nip'ple
nip'py
Nirva'na
Ni'san
ni'si pri'us
nit
ni'trate, *n.*
ni'trate, *v.*
ni'tre
ni'tric
nitrifica'tion
ni'trified
ni'trify
ni'trite
ni'trogen
nitrog'enous
nitrog'enize
nitro-glyc'erine
nitrom'eter
nitromuriat'ic
ni'trose
ni'trous
ni'trous ox'ide
nit'ty
niv'eous
nivette'
nix
nix'ie
Nizam'
no
Noa'chian
No'ah's ark
nob
nob'ble
nobil'ity
no'ble
no'bleman
no'bleness
noblesse'
no'bly
no'body
no'cent
noctambula'tion
noctam'bulism
noctam'bulist
noctilu'cous
noctiv'agant
noctivaga'tion

noc'tograph
noc'tuary
noc'tule
noc'turn
noctur'nal
noc'turne
noc'uous
nod
no'dal
nod'ded
nod'der
nod'ding
nod'dle
nod'dy
node
nodose'
nodos'ity
no'dous
nod'ular
nodula'tion
nod'ule
nod'uled
nod'ulose
No'el
noet'ic
nog
nog'gin
nog'ging
no'how
noise
noised
noise'less
noise'lessly
noise'lessness
noisette'
nois'ily
nois'iness
nois'ing
noi'some
noi'someness
nois'y
no'lens vo'lens
nom'ad
nomad'ic
nom'adism
nom'adize
nom'adized
nom'adizing
no'mancy
nom'arch
nom'bril
nom de guerre'
nom de plume'
nome
no'menclator
no'menclature
no'mial
nom'ic
nom'inal
nom'inalism
nom'inalist
nominalist'ic
nom'inally
nom'inate
nom'inated
nom'inating
nomina'tion
nominati'val
nom'inative
nom'inator
nominee'
nomog'enist
nomog'eny
nomolog'ical
nomol'ogy
non-accept'ance
non'age
nonagena'rian
nonages'imal
non'agon
non-appear'ance
non-arri'val
non-attend'ance
nonce
non'chalance
non'chalant
non'chalantly
non-com'batant
non-commis'-sioned
non-commis'-sioned of'ficer
non-commit'tal
non-conduct'or
Nonconform'ist
Nonconform'ity
non-content'
non-*deliv'ery*
non'descript
none
non-effect'ive
non-effi'cient
non-elect'
nonen'tity
nones
non-essen'tial
none'such
non-exist'ence
nonil'lion
nonju'ring
Nonju'ror
non-nat'ural
non-observ'ance
non-obe'dience
nonpareil'
nonpay'ment
non-*perform'ance*
non'plus
non'plussed
non'plussing
non-*produc'tion*
non-res'idence
non-res'ident
non-resist'ance
non'sense
nonsen'sical
nonsen'sically
non'-stop
non'such
non'suit
non'suited
non'suiting
non-us'er
noo'dle
nook
noolog'ical
nool'ogist
nool'ogy
noon
noon'day
noon'tide
noose
noosed
noos'ing
no'pal
nor
no'ria
norm
nor'ma
nor'mal
nor'malize
nor'mally
Nor'man
norn
Nor'roy
Norse
Norse'man
north
north-east'
north-east'er
north-east'erly
north-east'ern
north'erly
north'ern
north'erner
north'ern*most*
North'man
Northum'brian
north'ward
north'wardly
north'wards
north-west'
north-west'er
north-west'erly
north-west'ern
Norwe'gian
nose
nose'bag
nose'gay
nosog'raphy
nosolog'ical
nosol'ogist
nosol'ogy
noson'omy
nostal'gia
nostal'gic
nos'tril
nos'trum
not
no'ta be'ne
notabil'ia
notabil'ity
no'table
no'tably
notal'gia
nota'rial
no'tary
no'tate
nota'tion
notch
notched
notch'ing
note
note'-book
no'ted
note'-paper
note'worthy
noth'ing
*noth'ing*ness
no'tice

no'ticeable
no'ticeably
no'tice-board
no'ticed
no'ticing
notifica'tion
no'tified
no'tify
no'tifying
no'ting
no'tion
no'tional
notori'ety
noto'rious
noto'riously
notwithstand'ing
nougat'
nought
nou'menal
nou'menon
noun
nour'ish
nour'ishable
nour'ished
nour'isher
nour'ishing
nour'ishment
nous
Nova'tian
Nova'tianism
nova'tion
nov'el
novelette'
nov'elist
nov'elty
Novem'ber
nov'enary
noven'nial
nover'cal
nov'ice
novi'ciate
novilu'nar
novi'tiate
now
now'adays
no'way
now'el
no'where
no'wise
nox'ious
nox'iously
nox'iousness
noyau'
noz'zle
nuance'
Nu'bian
nubif'erous

nu'bile
nucif'erous
nu'ciform
nu'cleal
nu'clear
nu'cleated
nu'clei
nu'cleiform
nu'cleus
nuda'tion
nude
nude'ly
nude'ness
nudge
nudged
nudg'ing
nu'dity
nugac'ity
nu'gatory
nug'get
nui'sance
null
nul'lah
nullifica'tion
nullifid'ian
nul'lified
nul'lifier
nul'lify
nul'lifying
nul'lity
numb
numbed [numb)
numb'er (more
num'ber, num'-
num'bering [bered
num'berless
num'bers
num'bles
numb'ly
numb'ness
nu'merable
nu'meral
nu'merary
nu'merate
nu'merated
nu'merating
numera'tion
nu'merative
nu'merator
numer'ic
numer'ical
numer'ically
nu'merous
nu'merously
numismat'ics
numis'matist
numismatol'ogy

num'mular
num'mulary
num'skull
nun
nun'cheon
nun'cio
nuncu'pative
nun'dinal
nun'nery
nup'tial
nup'tials
nurse
nursed
nurse'-maid
nurs'ery
nurs'eryman
nurs'ing
nurs'ling
nur'ture
nur'tured
nur'turing
nut
nu'tant
nuta'tion
nut'-brown
nut'cracker
nut'-gall
nut'hatch
nut'-hook
nut'meg
nut'-oil
nu'trient
nu'triment
nutrimen'tal
nutri'tion
nutri'tious
nu'tritive
nu'tritively
nu'tritiveness
nut'-screw
nut'shell
nut'ted
nut'ter
nut'ting
nux
nux vom'ica
nuz'zle
nuz'zled
nuz'zling
nyan'za
nyctalo'pia
nyc'talopy
nyl'ghau
nymph
nym'pha
nym'phal
nymphe'an

O

O
oaf
oaf'ish
oak
oak'-apple
oak'en
oak'-tree
oak'um
oar
oar'age
oared
oars'man
oa'sis
oast
oat
oat'cake
oat'en
oath
oat'meal
obbliga'to
obcor'date
ob'duracy
ob'durate
ob'durately
ob'durateness
o'beah
obe'dience
obe'dient
obe'diently
obei'sance
obei'sant
ob'elisk
ob'elus
obese'
obes'ity
obey'
obeyed'
obey'er
obey'ing
obfus'cate
obfus'cated
obfus'cating
obfusca'tion
o'bi
o'bit
ob'iter
obit'ual
obit'uary
object, object'ed
*object'*ing
objec'tion
objec'tionable
objec'tive
*objec'tive*ly
*objec'tiv*ism
*objec'tiv*ist
*objectiv'*ity
ob'jectless
object'or
objura'tion
ob'jurgate
ob'jurgated
ob'jurgating
objurga'tion
objur'gatory
ob'late
obla'tion
ob'ligate, *adj.*
ob'ligate, *v.*
ob'ligated
ob'ligating
obliga'tion
ob'ligatorily
ob'ligatory
oblige'
obliged'
obligee'
obli'ger
obli'ging
obli'gingly
ob'ligor
oblique'
oblique'ly
obliq'uity
oblit'erate
oblit'erated
oblit'erating
oblitera'tion
obliv'ion
obliv'ious
obliv'iously
ob'long
ob'longish
ob'loquy
obmutes'ence
obnox'ious
o'boe
o'boist
ob'ol
ob'ole
ob'olus
obo'vate
obrep'tion
obrepti'tious
obscene'
obscene'ly
obscene'ness
obscen'ity
obscur'ant
obscur'antism
obscur'antist
obscura'tion
obscure'
obscured'
obscure'ly
obscure'ness
obscur'ing
obscu'rity
obsecra'tion
ob'sequies
obse'quious
obse'quiously
obse'quiousness
observ'able
observ'ably
observ'ance
observ'ant
observa'tion
observa'tional
obser'vative
observ'atory
observe'
observed'
observ'er
observ'ing
observ'ingly
obsess'ion
obsid'ian
obsid'ional
obsoles'cence
obsoles'cent
ob'solete
ob'stacle
obstet'ric
obstetri'cian
ob'stinacy
ob'stinate
ob'stinately
obstipa'tion
obstrep'erous
obstrep'erously
obstric'tion
obstruct'
obstruct'ed
obstruct'er
obstruct'ing
obstruc'tion
obstruc'tionist
obstruc'tive
ob'struent
obtain'
obtain'able
obtained'
obtain'er
obtain'ing
obtain'ment
obtest'
obtesta'tion
obtest'ed
obtest'ing
obtrude'
obtru'ded
obtru'der

obtru'ding
obtru'sion
obtru'sive
obtru'sively
obtru'siveness
obtund'
obtund'ed
ob'turator
obtuse'
obtuse'-angled
obtuse'-angular
obtuse'ly
obtuse'ness
obtu'sion
obverse
obverse'ly
obvert'
obvert'ed
obvert'ing
ob'viate
ob'viated
ob'viating
ob'vious
ob'viously
ob'volute
o'ca
ocari'na
occa'sion
occa'sional
occa'sionalism
occa'sionally
occa'sioned
occa'sioning
occa'sive
oc'cident
occiden'tal
occip'ital
oc'ciput
occlude'
occlu'sion
occult'
occulta'tion
occult'ing
occult'ism
occult'ly
occult'ness
oc'cupancy
oc'cupant
occupa'tion
oc'cupied
oc'cupier
oc'cupy
oc'cupying
occur'
occurred'
occur'rence
occur'rent
occur'ring
o'cean
Ocea'nian
ocean'ic
o'ceanward
o'cellate
o'cellated
o'celot
ochra'ceous
o'chre, o'cher
o'chreous
o'chry

oc'tachord
oc'tad
oc'tagon
octag'onal
octahe'dral
octahe'dron
octan'dria
octan'drous
octan'gular
oc'tant
oc'tarch
oc'tarchy
oc'tateuch
octa'val
oc'tave
octa'vo
octen'nial
octet'
octil'lion
Octo'ber
octodec'imo
octoden'tate
octogena'rian
octog'enary
oc'tonary
octonoc'ular
octopet'alous
oct'opod
oc'topus
octoroon'
octosper'mous
oc'tostyle
octosyllab'ic
octosyl'lable
octroi' *or*
oc'tuple
oc'ular
oc'ularly
oc'ulate
oc'ulated
oc'uliform
oc'ulist
od
o'dal
o'dalisque
odd
Odd'fellows
odd'ity
odd'ly
odd'ment
odd'ness
odds
ode
ode'on
od'ic
od'ically
O'din
o'dious
o'diously
o'dium
o'dize
o'dized
o'dizing
odom'eter
odomet'rical
odom'etry
odontal'gia
odontal'gic

odontal'gy
odon'to
odontolog'ical
odontol'ogy
o'dorant
odorif'erous
o'dorous
o'dorously
o'dour, o'dor
o'dourless
o'dyl
odyl'ic
o'dylism
Od'yssey
oecumen'ic
oecumen'ical
oenom'eter
o'er
oesoph'agus
of
off
off'al
off'-chance
offence'
offence'less
offend'
offend'ed
offend'er
offend'ing
offen'sive
offen'sively
offen'siveness
of'fer
of'fered
of'ferer
of'fering
of'fertory
off'*hand*
of'fice
of'fice-bearer
of'fice-copy
of'ficer
of'ficered
of'ficering
offi'cial
offi'cialism
offi'cially
offi'ciate
offi'ciated
offi'ciating
offi'ciator
offic'inal
offi'cious
offi'ciously
offi'ciousness
off'ing
off'scouring
off'scum
offset
offset'ting
off'shoot
off'-side
off'spring
off'ward
oft
oft'en
oft'ener
oft'entimes
oft'times

ogee'
og'ham, og'am
ogi'val
o'give
o'gle
o'gled
o'gler
o'gling
o'gre
o'gress
Ogyg'ian
oh
ohm
oho'
oil
oil'cake
oil'cloth
oiled
oil'er
oil'ery
oil'iness
oil'ing
oil'man
oil'-painting
oil'-shop
oil'skin
oil'stone
oil'-tree
oil'y
oint
oint'ment
Ojib'way
oka'pi
o'konite
ok'ra
old
old age
old'en
old'er
old'est
old-fash'ioned
old'ish
old'ness
old'-style
old'wife
oleag'inous
olean'der
oleas'ter
o'leate
ole'fiant
ole'ic
oleif'erous
o'lein
o'leo
o'leograph
oleomar'garine
oleom'eter
o'leoresin
o'leous
olera'ceous
olfac'tion
olfac'tory
olib'anum
ol'igarch
oligarch'ic
oligarch'ical
ol'igarchy
o'lio

ol'itory
oliva'ceous
ol'ive
ol'ive-branch
ol'iver
ol'ivine
ol'la
olla podri'da
Olym'piad
Olym'pian
Olym'pic
om'bre
ombrom'eter
o'mega
om'elet, om'elette
o'men
omen'tum
o'mer
om'inous
om'inously
om'inousness
omis'sible
omis'sion
omis'sive
omit'
omit'ted
omit'ting
om'nibus
omnifa'rious
omnif'erous
omnif'ic
om'niform
omniform'ity
omnig'enous
omnipar'ity
omnip'otence
omnip'otent
omnipres'ence
omnipres'ent
omnis'cience
omnis'cient
om'nium
omniv'ora
omniv'orous
omophag'ic
omphal'ic
om'phalos
omphalot'omy
on
on'ager
once
oncot'omy
one
one-eyed
one'-horse
oneirocrit'ic
oneirol'ogy
onei'romancy
oneiros'copy
one'ness
on'erary
on'erous
oneself'
one'-sided
on'ion
on'looker
on'ly

on'omancy
onomas'tic
onomas'ticon
onomatol'ogy
onomatoma'nia
onomatopoe'ia
on'rush
on'set
on'slaught
ontolog'ical
ontol'ogism
ontol'ogist
ontol'ogy
o'nus
*on'*ward
on'ycha
onych'ia
on'ychomancy
on'yx
o'olite
oolit'ic
oolog'ical
ool'ogist
ool'ogy
Oo'pak
ooze
oozed
oo'zing
oo'zy
opac'ity
opa'cous
o'pah
o'pal
opalesce'
opalesced'
opales'cence
opales'cent
o'paline
o'palize
o'palized
opaque'
ope
o'pen
open-air'
o'pened
o'pener
o'pen-handed
o'pen-hearted
o'pening
o'penly
o'pen-mouthed
o'penness
o'pen-work
op'era
op'era bouffe
op'era-cloak
op'era-glass
operam'eter
op'erant
op'erate
op'erated
operat'ic
operat'ically
op'erating
opera'tion
op'erative
op'erator
oper'cular
oper'culate

oper'culated
oper'culum
operet'ta
op'erose
oph'icleide
ophid'ian
ophiol'ogist
ophiol'ogy
oph'iomancy
o'phite
Ophiu'chus
ophthal'mia
ophthal'mic
ophthal'moscope
o'piate
opine'
opined'
opin'ing
opin'ion
opin'ionated
opin'ionative
opisom'eter
opis'thograph
o'pium
o'pium-eater
opodel'doc
opop'anax
opos'sum
op'pidan
oppo'nency
oppo'nent
opportune'
opportune'ly
opportune'ness
opportu'nism
opportu'nist
opportu'nity
oppo'sable
oppose'
opposed'
oppo'ser
oppo'sing
op'posite
opposi'tion
opposi'tionist
oppos'itive
oppress'
oppressed'
oppress'ing
oppres'sion
oppress'ive
oppress'ively
oppres'siveness
oppress'or
oppro'brious
oppro'briously
oppro'brium
oppugn'
oppug'nancy
oppug'nant
oppugned'
oppugn'er
oppugn'ing
opsiom'eter
op'tative
op'tic
op'tical
opti'cian
op'tics
op'tigraph
op'timacy
op'timate
optima'tes
op'time
op'timism
op'timist
optimis'tic
op'timize
op'tion
op'tional
optom'eter
op'ulence
op'ulent
op'us
opus'cule
opus'culum
or
or'acle
orac'ular
orac'ularly
orac'ulous
orac'ulum
o'ral
o'rally
or'ange
orangeade'
Or'angeism
Or'angeman
or'angery
orang'-outang'
ora'tion
or'ator
orato'rial
orator'ical
orator'ically
orato'rio
or'atory
orb
orbed
or'bic
or'bical
orbic'ular
orbic'ulate
orb'ing
or'bit
or'bital
orb'y
orc, ork
Orca'dian
or'chard
or'charding
or'chardist
or'chestra
orches'tral
orchestra'tion
orches'tric
or'chid
orchida'ceous
orchid'eous
or'chil
or'chis
or'cine
ordain'
ordained
ordain'er
ordain'ing
or'deal
or'der
or'dered
or'derer
or'dering
or'derliness
or'derly
ordinaire'
or'dinal
or'dinance
or'dinant
or'dinarily
or'dinary
or'dinate
ordina'tion
ord'nance
or'donnance
or'dure
ore
or'gan
organette'
organ'ic
organ'ical
organ'ically
or'ganism
or'ganist
or'ganizable
organiza'tion
or'ganize, or'gan-
or'ganizer [*ized*
or'ganizing
organog'raphist
organog'raphy
organol'ogy
or'ganum
or'ganzine
or'gasm
or'gies
orguinette'
or'gy, or'gie
o'riel
o'rient
orien'tal
orien'talism
orien'talist
orien'talize
orien'tate
orienta'tion
or'ifice
or'iflamme
orig'anum
Or'igenism
Or'igenist
or'igin
orig'inal
original'ity
orig'inally
orig'inate
orig'inated
orig'inating
origina'tion
orig'inative
orig'inator
oril'lion
o'riole
Ori'on
orismol'ogy
or'ison
orle

or'lop
or'molu
or'nament
ornamen'tal
ornamenta'tion
or'namented
or'namenting
ornate'
ornith'olite
ornithol'ogist
ornithol'ogy
orog'eny
orog'raphy
orol'ogy
o'rotund
or'phan
or'phanage
or'phaned
Orphe'an
Or'phic
or'phrey
or'piment
or'pine, or'pin
or'rery
or'ris
or'thodox, or'thodoxy
orthodrom'ic
orthod'romy
orthoep'ic
orthoep'ical
or'thoepist
or'thoepy
orthog'rapher
orthograph'ic
orthograph'ical
orthog'raphist
orthog'raphy
orthol'ogy
orthomet'ric
orthom'etry
orthopae'dic
orthop'ter
Orthop'tera
orthop'teran
orthop'terous
or'tive
or'tolan
orts
oryctog'raphy
oryctol'ogy
os'cheocele
os'cillate
os'cillated
os'cillating
oscilla'tion
os'cillatory
os'citancy
os'citant
oscita'tion
os'culant
os'culate
os'culated
os'culating
oscula'tion
os'culatory
os'cule
o'sier
o'siered
Osi'ris

Osman'li
os'mazome
os'mium
osmom'eter
os'mose
osmot'ic
Osmun'da
os'prey
os'selet
os'seous
Ossian'ic
os'sicle
ossif'erous
ossif'ic
ossifica'tion
os'sified
os'sifrage
os'sify
os'sifying
ossiv'orous
os'suary
ostensibil'ity
osten'sible
osten'sibly
osten'sive
ostenta'tion
ostenta'tious
ostenta'tiously
os'teocele
os'teocope
osteog'raphy
osteol'oger
osteol'ogist
osteol'ogy
osteop'athy
os'teophone
osteot'omy
os'tiary
os'tler
os'tracism
os'tracize
os'tracized
os'tracizing
os'trich
Os'trogoth
otacous'tic
otal'gia
otal'gic
otal'gy
oth'er
oth'erwise
otherworld'liness
o'tiose
otog'raphy
otol'ogy
otop'athy
otot'omy
ot'tar, ot'ter
ot'to
ot'toman, Ot'toman
oubliette'
ouch
ought
ounce
our
ouranog'raphy
ourol'ogy
ouros'copy
ours

ourselves'
oust
oust'ed
oust'er
oust'ing
out
out*bal'ance*
outbid'
outblown'
outbound'
out'break
out'burst
out'cast
out'*come*
out'crop
out'cry
outdo'
outdone'
outdoor'
out'er, out'er*most*
outface'
outfaced'
out'fall
out'fit
out'fitter
outflank'
out*gen'eral*
out*go'*
out'going
out'goings
outgrow'
outgrown'
out-Her'od
out'house
out'ing
out'lander
outland'ish
outlast'
out'law
out'lawed
out'lawing
out'lawry
out'lay
out'let
out'lier
out'line
out'lined
outlive'
out'look
out'lying
out'*most*
out*num'ber-ed*
out*num'ber*ing
out-of-date'
out-of-doors'
out'-patient
out'post
out'pour
out'pouring
out'put
out'rage
out'raged
outra'geous
outra'geously
out'raging
outre'
outreach'
outride'
out'rider
out'rigger

out'right
outrun'
outsail'
outsell'
out'set
outshine'
out'side
outsi'der
out'skirt
out'spoken
outspread'
outstand'ing
outstretch'
outstretched'
outstretch'ing
outstrip'
out-talk'
outvote'
out'-voter
outvo'ted
outwalk'
out'ward
out'ward-bound
out'wardly
out'wards
outwear'
outweigh'
outweighed'
outwit'
outwit'ted
outwit'ting
outwork
ou'zel
o'va
o'val
ovalbu'men
oval'bumin
ova'rian
ova'rious
o'vary
o'vate
o'vate-oblong
ova'tion
ov'en
o'ver
*over*act'
*over*act'ed
*o'ver*all
*o'ver*alls
*over*arch'
*over*awe'
*over*awed'
*over*aw'ing
overbal'ance
overbal'anced
overbal'ancing
*over*bear'
*over*bear'ing
*o'ver*board
*over*bur'den
*over*came'
*o'ver*cast
*over*charge
*over*cloud'
*o'ver*coat
overcome'
*over*com'ing

*over*crowd'
*over*crowd'ed
*over*crowd'ing
*over*do'
*over*do'ing
*over*done'
*over*dose
*o'ver*draft
*over*draw'
*over*drawn'
*over*due'
over-es'timate *v.*
o'ver-es'timate *n.*
*over*flow
*over*flowed'
*over*flow'ing
*over*grow'
*over*grown'
*o'ver*growth
*over*hang
*over*haul'
*over*hauled'
*over*haul'ing
*over*head'
*over*hear'
*over*heard'
*over*heat'
*over*hung'
*over*joyed'
*over*laid'
*o'ver*land
*over*lap'
*over*lay
*over*lay'ing
*over*leap'
*over*lie'
*over*load
*over*look'
*over*looked'
*over*look'ing
*o'ver*mantel
*over*mas'ter
*over*match'
*over*much'
*over*night'
*over*paid'
*over*pass'
*over*pay'
*o'ver*plus
*over*poise'
*over*pow'er
*over*pow'ered
*over*pow'ering
*over*pow'eringly
over-ran'
*over*rate'
*over*ra'ted
*over*ra'ting
*over*reach'
*over*reached'
*over*reach'ing
over-right'eous
*over*rule'
*over*ruled'
*over*ru'ler
*over*ru'ling
*over*run'
*over*run'ning
*over*see'
*o'ver*seer

*o'ver*set
*over*shade'
*over*shad'ow
*o'ver*shoe
*over*shoot'
*over*shot'
*o'ver*sight
*over*sleep'
*over*slept'
*over*spent'
*over*spread'
*over*step'
*over*stepped'
*over*stock'
*over*strain'
*over*strew'
*over*strung'
o'vert
*over*take'
*over*ta'ken
*over*task'
*over*tax'
*over*taxed'
*over*threw'
*over*throw'
*over*throw'ing
*over*thrown'
*o'ver*time
o'vertly
*over*took'
*over*top'
overtrade'
o'verture
*over*turn'
*over*turned'
*over*ween'
*over*ween'ing
*over*weigh'
*o'ver*weight
*over*whelm'
*over*whelmed'
*over*whelm'ing
*o'ver*wise
*o'ver*work
*o'ver*wrought
ovic'ular
Ovid'ian
o'viduct
ovif'erous
o'viform
ovig'erous
o'vine
ovip'arous
ovipos'it
ovipos'itor
o'visac
o'void
ovoi'dal
o'volo
ovol'ogy
ovo-vivip'arous
o'vular
o'vule
o'vum
owe
owed
ow'elty
Ow'enite
owes
ow'ing

owl
owl'er
owl'et
owl'ing
owl'ish
owl'-like
own
owned
own'er
own'erless
own'ership
own'ing
ox
ox'alate
oxal'ic
ox'en
ox'eye
ox'-eyed
ox'-fly
oxidabil'ity
ox'idable
ox'idate
ox'idated
ox'idating
oxida'tion
ox'idator

ox'ide
oxidiz'able
ox'idize
ox'idized
ox'idizement
ox'idizing
ox'lip
Oxo'nian
ox'-tail
ox'-tongue
oxyac'id
ox'ygen
ox'ygenate
ox'ygenated
ox'ygenating
oxygena'tion
oxyg'enator
ox'ygenizable
ox'ygenize
ox'ygenized
ox'ygenizement
ox'ygenizing
oxyg'enous
ox'ygon
oxyg'onal

oxyhy'drogen
ox'ymel
oxymu'riate
oxymuriat'ic
ox'yopy
oxyph'ony
ox'ytone
oy'er
oyes', oyez'
oys'ter
oys'ter-bed
oys'ter-catcher
oys'ter-knife
oys'ter-shell
oys'ter-woman
ozona'tion
o'zone
ozonif'erous
ozonifica'tion
o'zonize
o'zonized
o'zonizing
ozonom'eter
ozonomet'ric
ozonom'etry

P

pa
pab'ular
pabula'tion
pab'ulous
pab'ulum
pac'a
pace
paced
pa'cer
pacha', pasha'
pacha'lic, pasha'lic
pachydac'tylous
pach'yderm
pachyder'mal
pachyder'mata
pachyder'matous
pacif'ic
pacifica'tion
pacif'icator
pacif'icatory
pac'ified
pac'ifier
pac'ify
pac'ifying
pac'ing
pack
pack'age
packed
pack'er
pack'et
pack'et-boat
pack'et-ship
pack'horse
pack'ing
pack'ing-case
pack'ing-needle
pack'man
pack'thread
pack'wax
pa'co
pa'cos
pact
pac'tion
pac'tional
Pacto'lian
pad
pad'ded
pad'ding
pad'dle
pad'dle-box
pad'dled
pad'dler
pad'dle-wheel
pad'dling
pad'dock
pad'dy
pa'dishah
pad'lock
pad'locked
pa'dre
padro'ne
pad'uasoy
pae'an, pae'on
paedobap'tism
paedobap'tist
paedol'ogy
pa'gan
pa'ganish
pa'ganism
pa'ganize
pa'ganized
page
pag'eant
pag'eantry
paged
pag'inal
pagina'tion
pa'ging
pago'da
pagu'rian
pah
paid
paidol'ogy
pail
pail'ful
pain
pained
pain'ful
pain'fully
pain'ing
pain'less
pain'lessly
pain'lessness
pains
pains'taker
pains'taking
paint
paint'-box
paint'-brush
paint'ed
paint'er
paint'ing
pair
paired
pair'-horse
pair'ing
pair'ing-off
pair'ing-time
paja'mas
pal
pal'ace
pal'adin
{ pal'aeograph / pal'eograph
{ palaeog'rapher / paleog'rapher
{ palaeograph'ic / paleograph'ic
{ palaeog'raphist / paleog'raphist
{ palaeog'raphy / paleog'raphy
{ palaeolith'ic / paleolith'ic
{ palaeolog'ical / paleolog'ical
{ palaeol'ogist / paleol'ogist
{ palaeol'ogy / paleol'ogy
{ palaeontol'ogy / paleontol'ogy
palaeothe'rium
{ palaeozo'ic / paleozo'ic
palae'stra
palae'stric
{ palankeen' / palanquin'
pal'atable
pal'atal
pal'ate
pala'tial
palat'inate
pal'atine
pala'ver
pala'vered
pala'vering
pale
palea'ceous
paled
pale'-eyed
pale'-face
pale'-faced
pale'ness
Palestin'ian
pales'tra
pales'tric
pal'etot
pal'ette
pal'frey
Pa'li
palil'logy
pal'impsest
pal'indrome
pa'ling
palingene'sia
palingen'esis

pal'inode
palisade'
palisad'ed
palisa'ding
palisa'do
pa'lish
pall
Palla'dian
palla'dium
pal'let
pal'lial
palliasse'
pal'liate
pal'liated
pal'liating
pallia'tion
pal'liative
pal'liatory
pal'lid
pal'lidness
pall'ing
pal'lium
pall-mall'
pal'lor
palm
pal'mar
pal'mary
pal'mate, *n.*
pal'mate, *adj.*
pal'mated
palmed
palm'er
palmet'to
palm'ier
palm'iest
pal'min
palm'ing
pal'miped
palm'ist
pal'mister
pal'mistry
palm'-leaf
palm'-oil
palm'-tree
palm'y
palp
palpabil'ity
pal'pable
pal'pably
palpa'tion
pal'pebral
pal'pebrous
pal'piform
palpig'erous
pal'pitate
pal'pitated
pal'pitating
palpita'tion
pals'grave
pal'sied
pal'sy
pal'sying
pal'ter
pal'tered
pal'terer
pal'tering
pal'trier
pal'triest
pal'trily
pal'triness
pal'try
palu'dal
palu'dament
palu'dinous
pa'ly
pam
pam'pas
pam'pas-grass
pam'per
pam'pered
pam'perer
pam'pering
pam'phlet
pamphleteer'
pamphleteer'ing
pam'pre
pan
panace'a
panace'an
pana'da
panama'
pan'cake
pancra'tium
pan'creas
pancreat'ic
Pande'an
pan'dect
pan'demic
pandemo'nium
pan'der
pan'dered
pan'dering
pandicula'tion
Pando'ra
pando'ra
pandore'
pan'dour
pan'dy
pane
paned
panegyr'ic
pan'egyrist
pan'egyrize
pan'el
pan'el(l)ed
pan'el(l)ing
pang
pangen'esis
Pan-German
pango'lin
Pan-Hellen'ic
Pan-Hel'lenism
Pan-Hel'lenist
pan'ic
pan'icle
pan'ic-stricken
pan'ic-struck
Panislam'ic
paniv'orous
panjan'drum
pan'nage
pan'nel
pan'nier
pan'nikin
pan'oplied
pan'oply
panop'ticon
panora'ma
panoram'ic
pan'-pipe
Panslav'ic
Panslav'ism
Panslav'ist
pansoph'ical
pan'sophy
panstereora'ma
pan'sy
pant
pan'tagraph
pantalettes'
pantalets'
pantaloon'
pantech'nicon
pant'ed
pant'er
pan'theism
pan'theist
pantheist'ic
pantheol'ogy
Panthe'on
pan'ther
pan'tile
pant'ing
pan'tler
pan'tofle
pan'tograph
pantograph'ic
pantog'raphy
pantolog'ic
pantol'ogist
pantol'ogy
pantom'eter
pantom'etry
pan'tomime
pantomim'ic
pan'tomimist
pantomor'phic
pan'ton
pantoph'agist
pantoph'agy
pan'try
pants
pap
papa'
pa'pacy
pa'pal
pa'parchy
papav'erous
papaw'
pa'per

pa'per-cutter
pa'pered
pa'pering
pa'per-maker
pa'per-weight
pa'pery
Pa'phian
pa'pier-mâ'ché
papiliona'ceous
papil'la
pap'illary
pap'illate
pap'illose
pa'pist
papis'tic
papis'tical
pa'pistry
papoose'
pappes'cent
pap'pous
pap'py
Pap'uan
pap'ula
pap'ular
pap'ulous
papyra'ceous
papyr'ograph
papyrog'raphy
papy'rus
par
par'able
parab'ola
parabol'ic
parabol'iform
parab'olist
parab'oloid
Paracel'sian
Paracel'sist
parach'ronism
par'achute
par'achutist
par'aclete
paracros'tic
parade'
parad'ed
par'adigm
para'ding
paradis'aical
par'adisal
par'adise
par'adox
paradox'ical
par'affin
paragen'esis
parago'ge
paragog'ic
par'agon
par'agram
paragram'matist
par'agraph
paragraph'ic
par'akeet
paral'dehyde
paralip'sis
paralipom'ena
parallac'tic
par'allax
par'allel
par'alleled
parallele'piped
parallelepip'edon
par'allelism
parallel'ogram
paral'ogism
paral'ogize
paralysa'tion
par'alyse-lyze
par'alysed
par'alysing
paral'ysis
paralyt'ic
paramat'ta
param'eter
par'amount
par'amour
par'anymph
par'apegm
par'apet
par'apeted
par'aph
paraphernа'lia
par'aphrase
par'aphrased
par'aphrasing
par'aphrast
paraphras'tic
paraple'gia
par'aplegy
par'asang
par'ascene
parasce'nium
parasele'ne
par'asite
parasit'ic
parasit'ical
par'asitism
parasol'
parasolette'
parasyllab'ic
parath'esis
paravail'
par'boil
par'boiled
par'boiling
par'buckle
par'cel
par'cel(l)ed
par'cel(l)ing
par'cenary
par'cener
parch
parched
parch'ing
parch'ment
pard
par'don
par'donable
par'doned
par'doner
par'doning
pare
pared
paregor'ic
parem'bole
paren'chyma
parenchym'atous
parenet'ic
pa'rent
pa'rentage
paren'tal
paren'thesis
parenthet'ic
parenthet'ical
paren'ticide
pa'rentless
pa'rer
par'gasite
par'get
par'geter
par'geting
parhe'lic
parhe'lion
pa'riah
pari'al
Pa'rian
pari'etal
pari'etary
pa'ring
par'ish
parish'ioner
Paris'ian
parisol'ogy
parisyllab'ic
par'ity
park
par'lance
par'ley
par'leyed
par'leying
par'liament
parliamenta'rian
parliamen'tary
par'lour
par'lous
par'lousness
Parmesan'
Parnas'sian
paro'chial
parod'ic
par'odied
par'odist
par'ody
par'odying
par'ol
parole'
par'onym
paron'ymous
paron'ymy
par'oquet
parot'id
paroti'tis
par'oxysm
paroxys'mal
parquet'
par'quetry

parr
par'rakeet
parrici'dal
par'ricide
par'ried
par'rot
par'ry
par'rying
parse
parsed
Parsee'
Par'seeism
pars'er
parsimo'nious
parsimo'niously
parsimo'nious-ness
par'simony
pars'ing
pars'ley
pars'nip
par'son
par'sonage
part
partake'
parta'ken
parta'ker
parta'king
part'ed
part'er
parterre'
parthen'ic
Par'thenon
Parthen'ope
par'tial
par'tialism
par'tialist
partial'ity
par'tially
part'ible
partic'ipant
partic'ipate
partic'ipated
partic'ipating
participa'tion
partic'ipative
partic'ipator
particip'ial
par'ticiple
par'ticle
partic'ular
partic'ularism
partic'ularist
particular'ity
partic'ularize
partic'ularized
partic'ularizing
*partic'ular*ly
part'ing
par'tisan
par'tisanship
par'tite
parti'tion
parti'tioned
parti'tioning
par'titive

part'let
part'ly
part'ner
part'nership
partook'
par'tridge
parts
partu'rient
parturi'tion
par'ty
par'ty-col'oured
par'ty-spirit
parure'
par'venu
pas
pas'chal
pash
pasha'
pasigraph'ic
pasig'raphy
pasque'-flower
pas'quin
pasquinade'
pass
pass'able
pass'ably
passade'
pas'sage
pas'sant
pass'-book
passed
passé(e)
pas'senger
pass'er
pass'er-by'
pas'serine
passibil'ity
pass'ible
pas'sim
pass'ing
pass'ing-bell
pas'sion
pas'sional
pas'sionate
pas'sionately
pas'sion-flower
pas'sionist
pas'sionless
Pas'sion-play
Pas'sion Week
pas'sive
pas'sively
pas'siveness
passiv'ity
Pass'*over*
pass'port
pass'*word*
past
paste
paste'board
pa'sted
pas'tel
pas'tern
Pasteur'ism
Pasteur'ize
pastic'cio
pas'til
pastille'
pas'time
pa'sting

pas'tor
pas'toral
pastora'le
pas'torate
pa'stry
pa'stry-cook
pas'turable
pas'turage
pas'ture
pas'tured
pas'turing
pas'ty
pat
Patago'nian
patch
patched
patch'er
patch'ing
patchou'li
patch'work
patch'y
pate
pâté'
patel'la
patel'liform
pat'en
pat'ent
pat'entable
pat'ented
patentee'
pat'enting
paterfamil'ias
pater'nal
pater'nity
pat'ernos'ter
path
Pathan'
pathet'ic
pathet'ically
path'less
pathog'eny
pathognomon'ic
pathog'nomy
patholog'ic
patholog'ical
patholog'ically
pathol'ogist
pathol'ogy
pa'thos
path'way
pa'tience
pa'tient
pa'tiently
pat'ina
pat'ly
patois'
pa'triarch
patriar'chal
pa'triarchate
patriar'chic
pa'triarchy
patri'cian
pat'ricidal

pat'ricide
patrimo'nial
pat'rimony
pat'riot
patriot'ic
patriot'ically
pat'riotism
Patripas'sian
patris'tic
patrol'
patrolled'
patrol'ling
pa'tron
pat'ronage
pat'ronal
pa'troness
pat'ronize
pat'ronized
pat'ronizer
pat'ronizing
patronym'ic
patroon'
pat'ten
pat'ter
pat'tered
pat'tering
pat'tern
pat'ty
pat'ty-pan
pat'ulous
pau'city
Paul'ine
Paul'ist
paunch
pau'per
pau'perism
pauperiza'tion
pau'perize
pau'perized
pau'perizing
pause
paused
paus'er
paus'ing
pave
pavé'
paved
pave'ment
pa'ver
pavil'ion
pa'ving
pa'viour, pa'vior
pa'vo
pav'onine
paw
pawed
paw'ing
pawl
pawn
pawn'broker
pawned
pawnee'
pawn'er
pawn'shop
pawn'-ticket
pax
pax'wax
pay

pay'able
pay'-day
payee'
pay'er
pay'ing
pay'master
pay'ment
pay'nim
pea
peace
peace'able
peace'ably
peace'ful
peace'fully
peace'maker
peace'-offering
peace'-officer
peach
pea'-chick
peach'-tree
peach'y
pea'cock
pea'fowl
pea'hen
pea'-jacket
peak
peaked
peak'ish
peal
pealed
peal'ing
pean
pea'nut
pear
pearl
pearl'-ash
pearled
pearl'-stitch
pearl'y
pear'main
pear'-shaped
pear'-tree
peas'ant
peas'antry
peas'cod, pease'-[cod
pease
pease'-pudding
pea'-soup
pea'shooter
peat
peat'-moss
peat'y
peb'ble
peb'bled
peb'bly
peb'ble-stone
pecan'
peccabil'ity
pec'cable
peccadil'lo
pec'cancy
pec'cant
pec'cary
pecca'vi
peck
pecked
peck'er
peck'ing
pec'ten
pec'tinal

pec'tinate
pec'tinated
pectina'tion
pec'tine
pec'tolite
pec'toral
pec'ulate
pec'ulated
pec'ulating
pecula'tion
pec'ulator
{ *pecu'liar*
{ *peculiar'ity*
pecu'liarize
*pecu'liar*ly
pecu'niarily
pecu'niary
ped'agogic
ped'agogism
ped'agogue
ped'al
peda'lian
pedal'ity
ped'ant
pedan'tic
ped'antry
ped'ate
ped'dle
ped'dled
ped'dling
ped'estal
pedes'trial
pedes'trian
pedes'trianism
pedes'trianize
ped'icel
ped'icellate-late
ped'icelled-led
ped'icle
pedic'ular
pedicula'tion
pedic'ulous
ped'icure
pedig'erous
ped'igree
ped'iment
ped'imented
ped'ipalp
ped'lar
ped'lary
pedobap'tism
pedobap'tist
ped'omancy
pedom'eter
pedomet'ric
pedun'cle
pedun'cular
pedun'culate
peek
peel

peeled
peel'er
peel'ing
peen
peep
peeped
peep'er
peep'-hole
peep'ing
peer
peer'age
peer'ess
peer'ing
peer'less
peer'lessness
pee'vish
pee'vishly
pee'vishness
pee'wit, pe'wit
peg
Peg'asus
pegged
peg'ger
peg'ging
pe'gomancy
peg'-top
peiram'eter
peiras'tic
pek'an
pek'oe
pel'age
Pela'gian
Pela'gianism
Pelargo'nium
pel'erine
pelf
pel'ican
Pe'lion
pelisse'
pell
pel'lage
pella'gra
pel'let
pel'licle
pellic'ular
pel'litory
pell-mell'
pellu'cid
pellucid'ity
Peloponne'sian
pelt
pel'tate
pel'tated
pelt'ed
pelt'ing
pelt'ry
pel'vic
pel'vis
pem'mican
pen
pe'nal
pen'alty
pen'ance
Pena'tes
pence
penchant'
pen'cil
pen'cilled-led
pen'cilling-ling

pen'-cutter
pend'ant
pend'ence
pend'ency
pend'ent
penden'tive
pen'dicle
pend'ing
pendrag'on
pendulos'ity
pen'dulous
pen'dulum
penetrabil'ity
pen'etrable
penetra'lia
pen'etrant
pen'etrate
pen'etrated
pen'etrating
penetra'tion
pen'etrative
pen'guin
pen'holder
pen'icil
penicil'late
penin'sula
penin'sular
penin'sulate
penin'sulated
pen'itence
pen'itency
pen'itent
peniten'tial
peniten'tiary
pen'itently
pen'knife
pen'man
pen'manship
pen'nant
pen'nate
penned
pen'niform
pennig'erous
pen'niless
pen'non
pen'ny
penny-a-li'ner
pennyroy'al
pen'nyweight
pen'nywise
pen'nyworth
penol'ogy
pen'sile
pen'sion
pen'sionary
pen'sioned
pen'sioner
pen'sioning
pen'sive
pen'sively
pen'siveness
pent
pen'tachord
pen'tacle
pentac'rinite
pentacros'tic

pentadac'tyl
pen'tagon
pentag'onal
pen'tagram
pen'tagraph
pentagyn'ia
pentahe'dral
pentahe'dron
pentam'eter
pentan'dria
pentan'gular
pentapet'alous
pentaphyl'lous
pen'tarchy
pentasper'mous
pen'tastich
pen'tastyle
Pen'tateuch
pentaton'ic
Pen'tecost
pen'tecostal
pent'house
penult'
penul'tima
penul'timate
penum'bra
penum'bral
penu'rious
penu'riously
penu'riousness
pen'ury
pe'on
pe'onage
pe'ony
peo'ple
peo'pled
*peo'pl*ing
pep
pep'per
pep'percorn
pep'pered
pep'pergrass
pep'pering
pep'permint
pep'pery
pep'sin
pep'tic
pep'toid
pep'tone
per
peradven'ture
peram'bulate
peram'bulated
peram'bulating
perambula'tion
peram'bulator
per an'num
perceiv'able
perceive'
perceived'
perceiv'er
perceiv'ing
per cent'

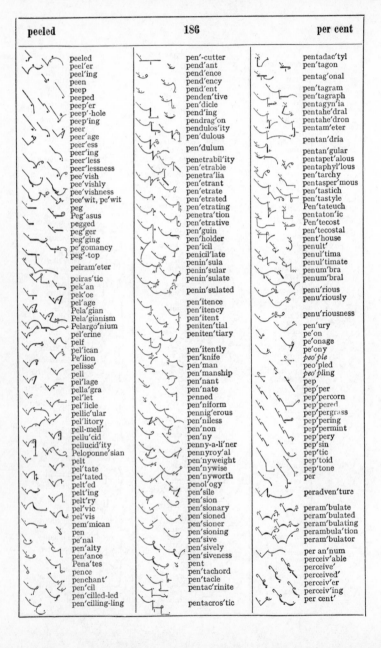

percent'age
per cen'tum
per'cept
perceptibil'ity
percep'tible
percep'tibly
percep'tion
percep'tive
perceptiv'ity
perch
perched
perchance'
perch'er
perch'ing
perchlo'rate
perchlo'ric
perchlo'ride
percip'ience
percip'iency
percip'ient
per'coid
per'colate
per'colated
per'colating
percola'tion
per'colator
percuss'
percussed'
percuss'ing
percus'sion
percus'sion-cap
percuss'ive
percu'tient
perdi'tion
perdu'
per'egrinate
peregrina'tion
per'egrinator
per'egrine
per'emptorily
per'emptoriness
per'emptory
peren'nial
per'fect
per'fected
per'fecter
perfectibil'ity
perfect'ible
per'fecting
perfec'tion
perfec'tionism
perfec'tionist
perfect'ive
per'fectly
per'fectness
perfer'vid
perfi'cient
perfid'ious
perfid'iously
perfid'iousness
per'fidy
perfo'liate
perfo'liated
per'forate
per'forated
per'forating
perfora'tion
per'forative
per'forator
perforce'
perform'
*perform'*able
perform'ance
performed'
perform'er
*perform'*ing
perfume'
perfumed'
perfu'mer
perfu'mery
perfunc'torily
perfunc'toriness
perfunc'tory
perfuse'
perfu'sive
pergame'neous
perhaps'
pe'ri
per'ianth
pericar'diac
pericar'dial
pericar'dian
pericar'dic
pericardi'tis
pericar'dium
per'icarp
pericar'pial
per'iclase
peric'ope
pericra'nium
per'iderm
per'idrome
per'igee
perihe'lion
perihexahe'dral
per'il
per'illed-led
per'illing-ling
per'ilous
per'ilously
per'ilousness
perim'eter
pe'riod
period'ic
period'ical
period'ically
periodic'ity
perios'teum
peripatet'ic
periph'eral
peripher'ic
periph'ery
per'iphrase
periph'rasis
periphras'tic
peripneumo'nia
peripneumon'ic
peripneu'mony
perip'teral
perip'terous
perip'tery
per'iscope
periscop'ic
per'ish
per'ishable
per'ished
per'isperm
perispher'ic
perissol'ogy
peristal'tic
peristreph'ic
per'istyle
perisys'tole
perit'omous
peritonae'um
peritoni'tis
perityphli'tis
per'iwig
per'iwinkle
per'jure
per'jured
per'jurer
per'juring
per'jury
perk
perked
per'kin
perk'y
per'manence
per'manency
per'manent
per'manently
perman'ganate
permeabil'ity
per'meable
per'meate
per'meated
per'meating
permea'tion
permis'sible
permissibil'ity
permis'sion
permis'sive
permis'sively
permis'sory
permit
permit'ted
permit'ter
permit'ting
permu'table
permuta'tion
per'nancy
perni'cious
perni'ciously
perni'ciousness
pernocta'tion
per'one
perone'al
perora'tion
perox'ide
perpend'
perpendic'ular
perpendicular'ity
perpendic'ularly

per'petrate
per'petrated
per'petrating
perpetra'tion
per'petrator
perpet'ual
perpet'ually
perpet'uate
perpet'uated
perpet'uating
perpetua'tion
perpetu'ity
perphos'phate
perplex'
perplexed'
perplex'ing
perplex'ity
per'quisite
perquisi'tion
per'ron
perroquet'
per'ry
perscruta'tion
per'se
per'secute
per'secuted
per'secuting
persecu'tion
per'secutor
persecu'trix
persever'ance
persevere'
persevered'
persever'ing
persever'ingly
Per'sian
Per'sic
persiflage'
persist'
persist'ed
persist'ence
persist'ency
persist'ent
persist'ing
persist'ingly
persist'ive
per'son
per'sonable
per'sonage
per'sonal
personal'ity
per'sonally
per'sonalty
per'sonate
per'sonated
per'sonating
persona'tion
per'sonator
personifica'tion
person'ified
person'ify
person'ifying
personnel'
perspec'tive
perspec'tograph
perspectog'raphy
perspica'cious

perspicac'ity
perspicu'ity
perspic'uous
perspirabil'ity
perspir'able
perspira'tion
perspir'atory
perspire'
perspired'
perspir'ing
persua'dable
persuade'
persua'ded
persua'ding
persua'sible
persua'sion
persua'sive
persua'sively
persua'siveness
persua'sory
persul'phate
persulta'tion
pert
pertain'
pertained'
pertain'ing
pertina'cious
pertina'ciously
pertinac'ity
per'tinence
per'tinency
per'tinent
per'tinently
pert'ly
pert'ness
perturb'
perturb'ance
perturba'tion
perturb'ate
perturbed'
perturb'ing
peruke'
peru'sal
peruse'
perused'
peru'ser
peru'sing
Peru'vian
pervade'
perva'ded
perva'ding
perva'sion
perva'sive
perverse'
perverse'ly
perverse'ness
perver'sion
perver'sity
perver'sive
pervert
pervert'ed
pervert'er
pervert'ible
pervert'ing
per'vious
per'viousness

pesade'
pes'sary
pes'simism
pes'simist
pessimis'tic
pest
Pestaloz'zian
pes'ter
pes'tered
pes'terer
pes'tering
pest'-house
pestif'erous
pes'tilence
pes'tilent
pestilen'tial
pes'tle
pet
pet'al
pet'alled-led
petalif'erous
petal'iform
pet'aline
pet'alite
pet'alless
pet'aloid
pet'alous
petard'
pet'asus
pete'chiae
Peter's pence
Pe'ter-wort
pet'iolar
pet'iolate
pet'iole
petiol'ule
petit'
petite'
peti'tion
peti'tionary
peti'tioned
peti'tioner
peti'tioning
petit maî'tre
petre'an
pet'rel
petres'cence
petres'cent
petrifac'tion
petrifac'tive
petrif'ic
petrifica'tion
pet'rified
pet'rify
pet'rifying
Pe'trine
pet'rol
petro'leum
pet'rolin
{ petrolog'ical
{ petrolog'ically
petrol'ogist
petrol'ogy
pet'ronel
petrosi'lex
petrosili'cious

pet'rous
pet'ted
pet'tichaps
pet'ticoat
pet'tier
pet'tiest
pet'tifogger
pet'tifoggery
pet'tifogging
pet'tily
pet'tiness
pet'ting
pet'tish
pet'tishly
pet'tishness
pet'titoes
pet'to
pet'ty
pet'ulance
pet'ulancy
pet'ulant
pet'ulantly
Petu'nia
petunt'se
pew
pewed
pe'wit / pee'wit
pew'-opener
pew'ter
pew'terer
pew'tery
pfen'nig
phac'oid
phaenog'amous
pha'eton
phagede'na
phageden'ic
phal'ange
phalan'geal
phalan'ger
phalan'gian
phalanste'rian
phal'anstery
phal'anx
phal'lic
phal'lical
phal'lus
phanerog'amous
phan'tascope
phan'tasm
phantas'ma
phantasmago'ria
phantasmagor'ic
phantas'mal
phantas'mascope
phan'tasy
phan'tom
Pharaon'ic
pharisa'ic
pharisa'ical
phar'isaism

pharise'an
Phar'isee
phar'iseeism
pharmaceu'tic
pharmaceu'tical
pharmaceu'tist
phar'macist
phar'macolite
pharmacol'ogist
pharmacol'ogy
pharmacopoe'ia
phar'macy
pha'ro
Pha'ros
pharyn'gal
pharyn'geal
pharyngi'tis
pharyngot'omy
phar'ynx
phase
pha'sis
pheas'ant
pheas'antry
phee'sy
phenac'etin
phen'gite
phen'icin
phe'nix
phenoga'mian
phenog'amous
phe'nol
phenol'ogist
phenol'ogy
phenom'ena
phenom'enal
phenom'enon
phe'on
phi'al
Philadel'phian
philan'der
philan'derer
philan'dering
philanthrop'ic
philan'thropist
philan'thropy
philatel'ic
philat'elist
philat'ely
philharmon'ic
Phil'hellene
Philhellen'ic
Philhel'lenism
Philhelle'nist
phil'ibeg
Philip'pian
philip'pic
Phil'ippine
Phil'istine

Phil'istinism
philol'oger
philolog'ic
philolog'ical
philol'ogist
philol'ogy
phil'omath
philomath'ic
philom'athy
phil'omel
Philome'la
philope'na
philopolem'ical
philoprogen'itiveness
philos'opher
philosoph'ic
philosoph'ical
philosoph'ically
philos'ophism
philos'ophist
philos'ophize
philos'ophized
philos'ophizing
philos'ophy
philotech'nic
phil'tre, phil'ter
phiz
phlebi'tis
phlebol'ogy
phlebot'omist
phlebot'omy
phlegm
phlegmat'ic
phleg'mon
phleme
phlogis'tic
phlogis'ton
phlox
pho'ca
pho'cine
Phoe'bus
Phoeni'cian
phoe'nix
phone
phonet'ic
phonet'ically
phonet'ics
phonetiza'tion
pho'nic
pho'nical
pho'nics
pho'nograph
phonog'rapher
phonograph'ic
phonog'raphy
pho'nolite
phonol'ogist
phonol'ogy
phonom'eter
pho'notype
phonotyp'ic

pho'notypist
pho'notypy
phos'gene
phos'phate
phos'phene
phos'phide
phos'phite
phos'pholite
phos'phor
phos'phorate
phos'phorated
phos'phorating
phosphoresce'
phosphores'cence
phosphores'cent
phosphor'ic
{ phos'phorous
{ phos'phorus
phos'phuret(t)ed
pho'to
photogen'ic
photog'eny
pho'tograph
photog'rapher
photograph'ic
photog'raphy
photogravure'
photolithog'raphy
photolog'ic
photol'ogy
photom'eter
photomet'ric
photom'etry
photopho'bia
photop'sia
pho'topsy
pho'tosphere
pho'totype
phototypog'raphy
photozincog'raphy
phrase
phrased
phra'seogram
phraseol'ogist
phraseol'ogy
phra'sing
phrenet'ic
phren'ic
phreni'tis
phrenolog'ical
phrenol'ogist
phrenol'ogy
phren'sy
Phryg'ian
phthis'ic
phthis'ical
phthis'icky
phthisiol'ogy
phthi'sis
phylac'tery
phy'larch
phy'larchy
phyllo'dium
phyl'lopod
phylloxe'ra
physian'thropy

phys'ic
phys'ical
phys'ically
physi'cian
phys'icist
phys'icked
phys'icking
physico-log'ical
physico-theol'ogy
phys'ics
physiognom'ic
physiogn'omist
physiogn'omy
physiog'ony
physiog'raphy
physiolog'ic
{ physiolog'ical
{ physiolog'ically
physiol'ogist
physiol'ogy
physique'
phytiv'orous
phytog'eny
phytog'raphy
phytolog'ical
phytol'ogist
phytol'ogy
phyton'omy
phytoph'agous
phytot'omy
Phytozo'a
phytozo'on
pi
piac'ular
pi'a ma'ter
pi'anist
pia'no
pian'o
pianofor'te
pias'tre, pias'ter
piaz'za
pi'broch
pi'ca
picador'
pic'amar
Pic'ard
picaroon'
picayune'
pic'cadilly
pic'calilli
pic'caninny
pic'colo
pick
pick'aback
pick'axe
picked
pick'er
pick'erel
pick'et
pick'eted
pick'eting
pick'ing
pick'le
pick'led
pick'ling
pick'lock

pick'-me-up
pick'pocket
pick'thank
Pickwick'ian
pic'nic
pic'nicking
picotee'
pic'ric
pic'rolite
pic'romel
picros'mine
picrotox'in
Pict
Pict'ish
pic'tograph
picto'rial
pic'ture
pic'ture-book
pic'tured
pic'ture-frame
pic'ture-gallery
picturesque'
picturesque'ness
pic'turing
pic'ul
pid'dle
pid'dled
pid'dler
pid'dling
pid'gin
pie
pie'bald
piece
pieced
piece'meal
piece'ner
piec'ing
pied
pier
pier'age
pierce
pierce'able
pierced
pier'cer
pier'cing
pier'-glass
Pie'rian
pi'errot
pier'-table
Pi'etism, pi'etism
Pi'etist, pi'etist
Pietist'ic
pi'ety
piezom'eter
pig
pig'eon
pig'eon-breasted
pig'eongram
pig'eon-hearted
pig'eon-hole
pig'eon-house

pig'eonry
pig'eon-toed
pig'gery
pig'gin
pig'gish
pig'headed
pig'-iron
pig'-lead
pigme'an
pig'ment
pigmen'tal
pig'mentary
pigmenta'tion
pig'my
pignora'tion
pig'-nut
pig'skin
pig'sty
pig'tail
pike
piked
pike'man
pike'staff
pilas'ter
pilas'tered
pilau'
pilch
pil'chard
pile
pi'leate
pi'leated
piled
pile'-driver
pi'ler
piles
pil'fer
pil'fered
pil'ferer
pil'fering
pilgar'lick
pil'grim
pil'grimage
pilig'erous
pi'ling
pill
pil'lage
pil'laged
pil'lager
pil'laging
pil'lar
pil'lar-box
pil'lared
pil'larist
pill'-box
pil'lion
pil'loried
pil'lory
pil'low
pil'low-case
pil'lowed
pil'lowing
pil'low-slip
pil'lowy
pi'lose
pilos'ity
pi'lot
pi'lotage
pi'loted
pi'lot-fish
pi'loting
pi'lous
Pil'sener
pil'ular
pi'lum
pim'elite
Pimen'ta
pimen'to
pimp
pimped
pim'pernel
pimp'ing
pim'ple
pim'pled
pim'ply
pin
pin'afore
pinas'ter
pin'-case
pince'-nez
pin'cers
pinch
pinch'beck
pinched
pinch'er
pinch'ing
pin'cushion
Pindar'ic
Pin'darism
Pin'darist
pine
pin'eal
pine'apple
pined
pi'nery
pine'-tree
pi'ney
pin'fold
ping
ping'-pong
pin'hole
pi'nic
pi'ning
pin'ion
pin'ioned
pin'ioning
pin'ite
pink
pinked
pink'er
pink'ing
pin'-money
pin'nace
pin'nacle
pin'nate
pin'nated
pinned
pin'ner
pin'ning
pin'niped
pin'nock
pin'nule
pin'point
pin'-prick
pint
pin'tail
pin'tle
pi'ny
pioneer'
pioneered'
pioneer'ing
pi'ous
pi'ously
pip
pipe
pipe'-case
pipe'-clay
piped
pipe'-fish
pipe'-laying
pi'per
pip'erine
pipette'
pi'ping
pipistrel'
pip'it
pip'kin
pip'pin
pi'quancy
pi'quant
pique
piqu'e
piqued
piqu'ing
pi'racy
pi'rate
pi'rated
pirat'ical
pi'rating
pirn
pirogue'
pirouette'
pis'cary
piscato'rial
pis'catory
Pis'ces
piscicul'ture
piscicul'turist
pis'ciform
pisci'na
pis'cinal
pis'cine
pisciv'orous
pisé'
pish
pis'iform
pis'mire
pis'olite
pista'chio
pistareen'
pis'til
pistilla'ceous
pis'tillate
pistillif'erous
pis'tol
pistole'
pis'tolet
pis'ton
pit
pit'-a-pat
pitch
pitch'-black
pitch'-blende
pitch'-dark
pitched
pitch'er
pitch'er-plant
pitch'fork

pitch'ing
pitch'-pine
pitch'-pipe
pitch'y
pit'eous
pit'eously
pit'fall
pith
pith'ily
pith'iness
pith'less
pit'-hole
pith'y
pit'iable
pit'ied
pit'ier
pit'iful
pit'ifully
pit'iless
pit'ilessness
pit'man
Pitman'ic
Pit'manite
pit'-saw
pit'tacal
pit'tance
pit'ted
pit'ting
pitu'itary
pit'uite
pitu'itous
pit'y
pit'ying
pit'yingly
pityri'asis
pit'yroid
più
piv'ot
piv'otal
pix
pix'ing
pix'y
placabil'ity
pla'cable
pla'cableness
plac'ard
plac'arded
plac'arding
pla'cate
pla'cated
pla'cating
place
place'bo
placed
place'man
placen'ta
placen'tal
placenta'tion
pla'cer
pla'cet
plac'id
placid'ity
plac'idly
pla'cing
plac'itory
plack'et
plac'oid
placoi'dean
plafond'

pla'gal
pla'giarism
pla'giarist
pla'giarize
pla'giarized
pla'giarizing
pla'giary
plagihe'dral
plague
plagued
pla'guer
pla'guily
pla'guing
pla'guy
plaice
plaid
plaid'ing
plain
plain'-dealing
plain'er
plain'est
plain'ly
plain'ness
plain'-speaking
plain'-spoken
plaint
plain'tiff
plain'tive
plain'tively
plain'tiveness
plait
plait'ed
plait'er
plait'ing
plan
pla'nary
planch
plan'chet
planchette'
plane
planed
pla'ner
plan'et
planeta'rium
plan'etary
plan'etoid
plane'-tree
plan'etule
plan'gent
planim'eter
planimet'ric
planim'etry
pla'ning
pla'ning-mill
planipet'alous
plan'ish
plan'ished
plan'isphere
plank
planked
plank'ing
plank'y
planned
plan'ner
plan'ning

plano-con'cave
plano-con'ical
plant
plant'able
plan'tain
plan'tar
planta'tion
plant'ed
plant'er
plant'icle
plan'tigrade
plant'ing
plant'let
plant'ule
plaque
plash
plashed
plash'ing
plash'y
plasm
plas'ma
plasmat'ic
plas'ter
plas'tered
plas'terer
plas'tering
plas'tery
plas'tic
plas'ticine
plastic'ity
plastog'raphy
plas'tron
plat
plat'band
plate
plateau'
pla'ted
plate'ful
plate'-glass
plat'en
pla'ter
plate'-warmer
plat'form
plat'ina
pla'ting
platinif'erous
plat'inize
plat'inized
plat'inizing
plat'inode
plat'inoid
plat'inotype
plat'inous
plat'inum
plat'itude
platom'eter
Platon'ic
Pla'tonism
Pla'tonist
Pla'tonize
Pla'tonized
Pla'tonizing
platoon'

plat'ted
plat'ter
plat'ting
plat'ypus
plau'dit
plau'ditory
plausibil'ity
plau'sible
plau'sibly
plau'sive
play
play'bill
played
play'er
play'fellow
play'ful
play'fully
play'fulness
play'goer
play'ground
play'house
play'ing
play'mate
play'thing
play'time
play'wright
play'-*writer*
plea
plead
plead'able
plead'ed
plead'er
plead'ing
plead'ingly
pleas'ant
pleas'antest
pleas'antly
pleas'antness
pleas'antry
please
pleased
pleas'er
pleas'ing
*pleas'ur*able
pleas'ure
pleas'ure-boat
*pleas'ur*ing
pleat
plea'ted
plebe'ian
plebe'ianism
pleb'iscite
plebs
plec'trum
pled
pledge
pledged
pledgee'
pledg'er
pledg'et
pledg'ing
Plei'ad
Plei'ades
Plei'ocene
Pleiosau'rus
Pleis'tocene
ple'narily
ple'narty
ple'nary

plenilu'nar
plenip'otence
plenip'otent
plenipoten'tiary
ple'nist
plen'itude
plen'teous
plen'teously
plen'tiful
plen'tifully
plen'tifulness
plen'ty
ple'num
ple'onasm
pleonas'tic
plesiomor'phism
ple'siosaur
Plesiosau'rus
pleth'ora
plethor'ic
pleu'ra
pleu'risy
pleurit'ic
pleuro-pneu-[mon'ia
plex'iform
plexim'eter
plex'ure
plex'us
pliabil'ity
pli'able
pli'ancy
pli'ant
pli'ca
pli'cate
pli'cated
plica'tion
plic'ature
plied
pli'er
pli'form
plight
plight'ed
plight'er
plight'ing
plinth
Pli'ocene
Pliosau'rus
plod
plod'ded
plod'der
plod'ding
plonge
plot
plot'ted
plot'ter
plot'ting
plough
plough'able
plough'boy
ploughed
plough'er
plough'ing
plough'man
plough'share
plough'-tail
plov'er
pluck

plucked
pluck'er
pluck'ier
pluck'iest
pluck'ily
pluck'iness
pluck'ing
pluck'y
plug
plugged
plug'ging
plum
plu'mage
plumassier'
plumb
plumbag'inous
plumba'go
plum'bean
plum'beous
plumb'er
plumb'ery
plum'bic
plumbif'erous
plumb'ing
plumb'-line
plum'-cake
plume
plumed
plume'let
plu'mery
plumig'erous
plu'miliform
plum'ing
plu'miped
plu'mist
plum'met
plum'ming
plu'mous
plump
plump'er
plump'ness
plum'-pudding
plum'-tree
plu'mule
plu'my
plun'der
plun'dered
plun'derer
plun'dering
plunge
plunged
plun'ger
plun'ging
pluper'fect
plu'ral
plu'ralism
plu'ralist
plural'ity
plu'ralize
plu'ralized
plu'ralizing
plurilit'eral

plus
plush
plu'tarchy
plutoc'racy
plu'tocrat
Pluto'nian
Pluton'ic
Plu'tonism
Plu'tonist
plu'vial
pluviom'eter
plu'vious
ply
ply'ing
pneumat'ic
pneumat'ics
pneumatol'ogy
pneumatom'eter
pneumo'nia
pneumon'ic
pneumoni'tis
pnyx
po'a
poach
poach'ard
poached
poach'er
poach'ing
poach'y
pock
pock'et
pock'et-book
pock'et-compass
pock'eted
pock'et-handker-chief
pock'eting
pock'et-knife
pock'et-money
pock'-mark
pock'y
po'co
poc'uliform
pod
pod'agra
pod'agral
podag'ric
pod'ded
podestà'
podg'y
po'dium
podophyl'lin
pod'osperm
poecilit'ic
poe'cilopod
po'em
po'esy
po'et
poetas'ter
po'etess
poet'ic
poet'ical
poet'ics
po'et-lau'reate
po'etry

pog'gy
poign'ancy
poign'ant
poign'antly
poikilit'ic
poinset'tia
point
point'blank
point'ed
point'el
point'ing
point'er
point'less
points'man
poise
poised
pois'ing
poi'son
poi'soned
poi'soner
poi'soning
poi'sonous
poi'trel
poke
poked
po'ker
poke'weed
po'king
po'ky
polac'ca
pola'cre
po'lar
polarim'eter
polarim'etry
polar'iscope
polar'ity
polariza'tion
po'larize
po'larized
po'larizer
po'larizing
pol'der
pole
pole'ax,-axe
pole'cat
poled
pol'emarch
polem'ic
polem'ical
polem'ics
polem'oscope
pole'-star
police'
policed'
police'man
pol'icied
pol'icy
po'ling
pol'ish
Po'lish (of Po-land)
pol'ishable
pol'ished
pol'isher
pol'ishing
polite'
polite'ly

polite'ness
politesse'
pol'itic
polit'ical
polit'ically
politi'cian
pol'itics
pol'ity
pol'ka
poll
Poll (Polly)
pol'lard
poll'-book
polled
pol'len
poll'er
pollicita'tion
poll'ing
pollinif'erous
pol'linose
pol'liwig
pol'liwog
poll'-tax
pollute'
pollu'ted
pollu'ter
pollu'ting
pollu'tion
Pol'lux
po'lo
polonaise'
polo'ny
polt
poltroon'
poltroon'ery
polyacous'tic
Polyadel'phia
Polyan'dria
polyan'dry
polyan'thus
pol'yarchy
polyb'asite
polycar'pous
pol'ychord
pol'ychroite
polychromat'ic
pol'ychromy
polycotyle'don
polyc'racy
polydac'tyl
polydip'sia
Polyga'mia
polyg'amist
polyg'amous
polyg'amy
polygas'tric
polyg'enous
pol'yglot
pol'ygon
polyg'onal
polyg'onous
polyg'ony

Polyg'onum
pol'ygram
pol'ygraph
polygraph'ic
polygraph'ical
polyg'raphy
pol'ygyn
Polygyn'ia
polyg'yny
polyhe'dral
polyhe'dric
polyhe'dron
polyhe'drous
Polyhym'nia
polymath'ic
polym'athy
polymor'phism
polymor'phous
pol'yneme
Polyne'sian
polyno'mial
polyon'ymous
polyon'ymy
polyop'tron
polyora'ma
pol'yp, pol'ype
pol'ypary
polyp'ean
polypet'alous
polyph'agous
polyphar'macy
Polyphe'mus
pol'yphone
polyphon'ic
pol'yphonist
polyph'ony
polyphyl'lous
Pol'ypi
pol'ypidom
polypif'erous
pol'ypod
pol'ypody
pol'ypous
polyprismat'ic
pol'ypus
pol'yscope
polysep'alous
pol'ysperm
polysper'mous
pol'ystyle
polysyllab'ic
polysyl'lable
polytech'nic
pol'ytheism
pol'ytheist
polytheis'tic
polytheis'tical

polyzo'ic
polyzo'na
polyzo'nal
polyzo'on
pom'ace
poma'ceous
pomade'
poman'der
poma'tum
pome
pomegran'ate
pom'elo
pomif'erous
pom'mel
pom'mel(l)ed
pom'mel(l)ing
pomolog'ical
pomol'ogist
pomol'ogy
Pomo'na
pomp
pom'padour
Pompe'ian
pom'pion
pom'-pom
pompos'ity
pom'pous
pom'pously
pon'cho
pond
pon'der
ponderabil'ity
pon'derable
pon'derance
pon'dered
pon'derer
pon'dering
ponderos'ity
pon'derous
pond'weed
po'nent
pongee'
pon'go
pon'iard
pon'tac
pon'tage
pontee'
Pon'tic
pon'tiff
pontif'ic
pontif'ical
pontif'icate, *n.*
pontif'icate, *v.*
pon'tine
pontonier'
pontoon'
po'ny
pood
poo'dle
pooh
pooh-pooh'
pooh-poohed'
pool
pool'er
pool'ing
poop
pooped

poop'ing
poor
poor'-box
poor'er
poor'est
poor'house
poor'-john
poor'-law
poor'ly
poor'ness
poor'-rate
pop
pope
pope'dom
pope'-joan
pope'ling
po'pery
pope's'-eye
pop'-gun
pop'injay
po'pish
pop'lar
pop'lin
poplit'ic
popped
pop'pet
pop'ping
pop'py
pop'ulace
pop'ular
popular'ity
populariza'tion
pop'ularize
pop'ularized
pop'ularizer
pop'ularizing
pop'ularly
pop'ulate
pop'ulated
pop'ulating
popula'tion
pop'ulin
pop'ulist
pop'ulous
pop'ulousness
por'cate
por'cated
porce'lain
porch
por'cine
por'cupine
pore
pored
po'riform
po'ring
po'rism
porismat'ic
po'rite
pork
pork'-butcher

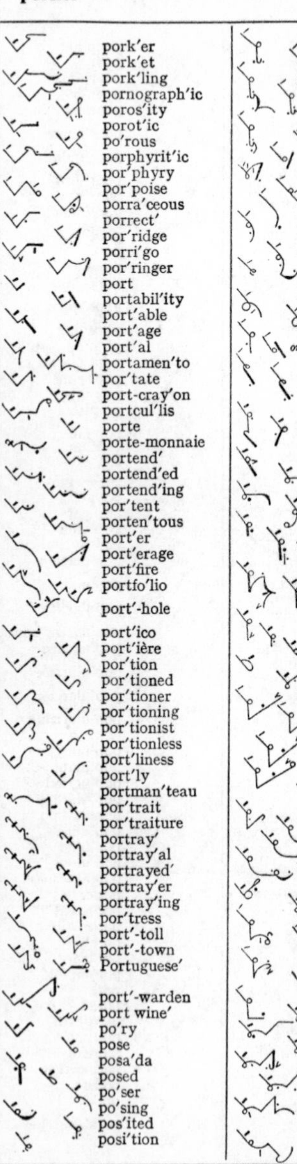

pork'er
pork'et
pork'ling
pornograph'ic
poros'ity
porot'ic
po'rous
porphyrit'ic
por'phyry
por'poise
porra'ceous
porrect'
por'ridge
porri'go
por'ringer
port
portabil'ity
port'able
port'age
port'al
portamen'to
por'tate
port-cray'on
portcul'lis
porte
porte-monnaie
portend'
portend'ed
portend'ing
por'tent
porten'tous
port'er
port'erage
port'fire
portfo'lio
port'-hole
port'ico
port'ière
por'tion
por'tioned
por'tioner
por'tioning
por'tionist
por'tionless
port'liness
port'ly
portman'teau
por'trait
por'traiture
portray'
portray'al
portrayed'
portray'er
portray'ing
por'tress
port'-toll
port'-town
Portuguese'
port'-warden
port wine'
po'ry
pose
posa'da
posed
po'ser
po'sing
pos'ited
posi'tion

pos'itive
pos'itively
pos'itivism
pos'itiveness
pos'itivist
pos'net
posolog'ical
posol'ogy
pospol'ite
pos'se
possess'
possessed'
possess'ing
posses'sion
possess'ive
possess'or
possess'ory
pos'set
possibil'ity
pos'sible
pos'sibly
post
post'able
post'age
post'al
post'boy
post'-captain
post'card
post'-chaise
post'date
post'dated
post'dating
post-dilu'vial
post-dilu'vian
pos'tea
post'ed
post'-entry
post'er
poste restante'
poste'rior
posterior'ity
poste'riorly
poste'riors
poster'ity
pos'tern
postfix'
postfixed'
postfix'ing
post'-free'
post-haste'
post'-horse
post'humous
pos'til
postil'ion
postil'lion
post'ing
postique'
post'man
post'mark
post'master
postmerid'ian
post merid'iem
post-mor'tem
post'-note
postnup'tial

post-ob'it
post'-office
post'-paid
postpone'
postponed'
postpone'ment
postpon'ing
postposi'tion
postpos'itive
postpran'dial
postsce'nium
post'script
post'-town
pos'tulant
pos'tulate, *n.*
pos'tulate, *v.*
pos'tulated
pos'tulating
postula'tion
pos'tulatory
pos'ture
pos'ture-mas'ter
post'-war'rant
po'sy
pot
po'table
potage'
potamog'raphy
potamol'ogy
pot'ash
potas'sa
potas'sium
pota'tion
pota'to
po'tatory
pot'-boiler
pot'-boy
potch
poteen'
po'tency
po'tent
po'tentate
poten'tial
potential'ity
poten'tially
po'tently
potheen'
poth'er
pot'-herb
poth'ered
poth'ering
pot'hook
pot'-house
pot'-hunter
po'tion
pot'latch
pot'-luck
pot'-man
potpourri'
pot'sherd
pot'-shop
pot'-shot
pot'tage

pot'ted
pot'ter
pot'tered
pot'tering
pot'tery
pot'ting
pot'tle
pot'walloper
pot'walloping
pouch
pouched
pouch'ing
pouchong'
poudrette'
poul'dron
poulp
poul'terer
poul'tice
poul'ticed
poul'ticing
poul'try
poul'try-*yard*
pounce
pounce'-box
pounced
poun'cet-box
pounc'ing
pound
pound'age
pound'ed
pound'er
pound'ing
pour
poured
pour'er
pour'ing
poussette'
pout
pout'ed
pout'er
pout'ers
pout'ing
pout'ingly
pov'erty
pow'der
pow'ders
pow'dered
pow'der-horn
pow'dering
pow'der-mill
pow'der-monkey
pow'dery
pow'er
pow'erful
pow'erfully
pow'erless
pow'wow
pox
poy
praam, pram
*practic*abil'ity
prac'ticable
prac'ticably
prac'tical
practical'ity

prac'tically
prac'tice
prac'tise
prac'tised
prac'tiser
prac'tising
practi'tioner
prae'cipe
praecor'dia
praemuni're
praeno'men
praetex'ta
prae'tor
praetor'ian
praeto'rium
pragmat'ic
pragmat'ical
prag'matism
prag'matist
prai'rie
prai'rie-dog
prai'rie-hen
prai'rie-wolf
praise
praised
prais'er
praise'worthiness
praise'worthy
prais'ing
prance
pranced
pranc'ing
pran'dial
prank
pranked
prank'ing
prank'ish
prase
pras'inous
prate
pra'ted
pra'ter
prat'ic
pra'ting
pratique
prat'tle
prat'tled
prat'tler
prat'tling
prav'ity
prawn
prax'is
pray
prayed
prayer (prays)
pray'er (one who
prayer'-book
prayer'ful
prayer'fully
prayer'fulness
prayer'less
prayer'lessness
prayer'-meeting
pray'ing

preach
preached
preach'er
preach'ing
preach'ment
pre'acquaint'
pre-acquaint'ance
pre-acquaint'ed
pre-adam'ic
pre-ad'amite
preadmon'ish
preadmon'ished
preadmoni'tion
pream'ble
preantepenul'timate
prearrange'
preassur'ance
preau'dience
preb'end
preb'endal
preb'endary
preca'rious
preca'riously
prec'ative
prec'atory
precau'tion
precau'tionary
precau'tioned
precau'tious
precede'
prece'ded
prece'dence
prece'dency
prece'dent, *a.*
prec'edent, *n.*
prec'edented
prec'edently
prece'ding
precen'tor
precen'torship
pre'cept
precep'tive
precep'tor
precepto'rial
precep'tory
precep'tress
preces'sion
pre'cinct
precios'ity
pre'cious
pre'ciously
pre'ciousness
pre'cipe
prec'ipice
precip'ient
precip'itance
precip'itancy
precip'itant
precip'itate, *n.,a.*
precip'itate, *v.*

precip'itated
precip'itating
precipita'tion
precip'itator
precip'itous
pré'cis
precip'itously
precise'
precise'ly
precise'ness
{ precis'ian
{ precis'ion
preci'sionist
preci'sive
preclude'
preclud'ed
preclu'ding
preclu'sion
preclu'sive
preco'cious
preco'ciousness
precoc'ity
precog'itate
precog'itated
precog'itating
precogita'tion
precogni'tion
preconceive'
preconceived'
preconceiv'ing
preconcep'tion
preconcert
preconcert'ed
preconcert'ing
precontract
precord'ial
precurs'ive
precurs'or
precurs'ory
preda'cious
pred'atorily
pred'atory
predeces'sor
predestina'rian
predes'tinate. *n.,a.*
predes'tinate, *v.*
predes'tinated
predes'tinating
predestina'tion
predes'tinator
predes'tine
predes'tined
predes'tining
predeter'minate
predetermina'-
tion
predeterm'ine
predeterm'ined
predeterm'ining
pre'dial
predicabil'ity
pred'icable

predic'ament
pred'icant
predicate, *n.*
pred'icate, *v.*
pred'icated
pred'icating
predica'tion
predic'ative
pred'icatory
predict'
predict'ed
predict'ing
predic'tion
predict'ive
predict'or
predilect'
predilec'tion
predispo nent
predispose'
predisposed'
predispos'ing
predisposi'tion
predom'inance
predom'inancy
predom'inant
predom'inate
predom'inated
predom'inating
predomina'tion
predoom'
predoomed'
pre-elect'
pre-elect'ed
pre-elec'tion
pre-em'inence
pre-em'inent
pre-empt'
pre-emp'tion
preen
preened
pre-engage'
pre-engage'ment
preen'ing
{ pre-*estab'lish*
{ pre-*estab'lished*
pre-*estab'lishing*
pre-exam'ine
pre-exam'ined
pre-exam'ining
pre-exist'
pre-exist'ed
pre-exist'ence
pre-exist'ent
pre-exist'ing
pref'ace
pref'aced
pref'acer
pref'acing
prefato'rial

pref'atory
pre'fect
pre'fecture
prefer'
pref'erable
pref'erably
pref'erence
preferen'tial
or
preferen'tially
or
prefer'ment
preferred'
prefer'rer
prefer'ring
prefigura'tion
prefig'urative
prefig'ure
prefig'ured
prefig'uring
prefix'
prefixed'
prefix'ing
preflora'tion
preg'nancy
preg'nant
prehen'sible
prehen'sile
prehen'sion
prehen'sory
prehistor'ic
prejudge'
prejudged'
prejudg'ing
prejudg'ment
prejudica'tion
{ *prej'udice*
{ *prej'udiced*
{ *prejudi'cial*
{ *prejudi'cially*
prej'udicing
prel'acy
prel'ate
prelat'ic
prelat'ical
prel'atism
prel'atist
prelec'tion
prelec'tor
preliba'tion
prelim'inarily
prelim'inary
prel'ude
prelud'er
prelu'ding
prelu'sive
prelu'sively
prelu'sory
premature'
premature'ly
prematur'ity
premed'itate

premed'itated
premed'itating
premedita'tion
prem'ier
première'
prem'iership
premillen'nial
prem'ise, prem'iss
premise'
premised'
prem'ises
pre'mium
premon'ish
premon'ished
premon'ishing
premoni'tion
premon'itor
premon'itory
Premon'strant
premorse'
premuni'tion
preno'men
prenom'inal
pren'tice
preoc'cupancy
preoccupa'tion
preoc'cupied
preoc'cupy
preoc'cupying
pre-ordain'
pre-ordained'
pre-ordain'ing
pre-ordina'tion
prepaid'
prep'arable
prepara'tion
prepar'ative
prepar'atory
prepare'
prepared'
prepar'edly
prepar'edness
prepar'er
prepar'ing
prepay'
prepay'ing
prepay'ment
prepense'
prepol'lence
prepol'lency
prepol'lent
prepon'derance
prepon'derancy
prepon'derant
prepon'derate
prepon'derated
prepon'derating
prepondera'tion
preposi'tion
preposi'tional
prepos'itive
prepos'itor
prepossess'
prepossessed'
prepossess'ing
prepossess'ion
pre-possess'or
prepos'terous
prepos'terously
pre'puce
Pre-Raph'aelite
Pre-Raph'aelitism
prereq'uisite
prerog'ative
pres'age, *n.*
presage', *v.*
presaged'
presa'ging
pres'byope
presbyo'pia
pres'byter
Presbyte'rian
Presbyte'rianism
pres'bytery
pre'science
pre'scient
prescribe'
prescribed'
prescri'ber
prescri'bing
pre'script
prescriptibil'ity
prescript'ible
prescrip'tion
prescript'ive
pres'ence
pres'ence-chamber
present
present'able
presenta'tion
present'ative
present'ed
presentee'
present'er
present'iment
present'ing
pres'ently
present'ment
preserv'able
preserva'tion
preserv'ative
preserv'atory
preserve'
preserved'
preserv'er
preserv'ing
preside'
presi'ded
pres'idency
pres'ident
presiden'tial
pres'identship
presid'er
presidi'al
presid'iary
presid'ing
presignifica'tion
presig'nified
presig'nify
presig'nifying
press
pressed
press'er
press'-gang
press'ing
press'ingly
press'man
pres'sure
press'-work
prestidigita'tion
prestidig'itator
prestige'
prest'imony
prestis'simo
pres'to
presu'mable
presu'mably
presume'
presumed'
presum'er
presu'ming
presump'tion
presump'tive
presump'tuous
presump'tuously
presump'tuousness
presuppo'sal
presuppose'
presupposed'
presuppo'sing
presupposi'tion
pretence'-tense'
pretend'
pretend'ed
pretend'er
pretend'ing
preten'sion
preten'tious
preterhu'man
preterimper'fect
pret'erite
preteri'tion
pretermis'sion
pretermit'
pretermit'ted
pretermit'ting
preternat'ural
preterper'fect
preterpluper'fect
pre'text, *n.*

pretext', *v.*
pre'tor
preto'rial
preto'rian
preto'rium
pret'tier
pret'tiest
pret'tily
pret'tiness
pret'ty
pret'zel
prevail'
prevailed'
prevail'ing
prev'alence
prev'alency
prev'alent
prevar'icate
prevar'icated
prevar'icating
prevarica'tion
prevar'icator
preve'nient
prevent'
prevent'able
prevent'ative
prevent'ed
prevent'er
prevent'ing
preven'tion
preven'tional
prevent'ive
pre'vious
pre'viously
previ'sion
prey
preyed
prey'er
pri'apism
price
price'-current
priced
price'less
pric'ing
prick
pricked
prick'er
prick'ing
prick'le
prick'le-back
prick'liness
prick'ly
prick'ly pear
pride
prid'ed
pri'ding
pried
prie-dieu
pri'er
priest
priest'craft
priest'ess
priest'hood
priest'like
priest'liness

priest'ly
priest'-ridden
prig
prig'gery
prig'gish
prig'gism
prill
prim
pri'macy
pri'ma
pri'ma don'na
pri'mage
pri'mal
pri'marily
pri'mary
pri'mate
prima'tial
primat'ical
prime
primed
prime'ly
prime'ness
pri'mer
prim'er
prime'val-ae'val
primige'nial
pri'mine
pri'ming
primi'tiae
primi'tial
prim'itive
prim'ness
primogen'itive
primogen'itor
primogen'iture
primord'ial
prim'rose
prim'ula
pri'mum mo'bile
prince
prince'dom
prince'ly
prince's feath'er
prin'ce's-metal
prin'cess
prin'cipal
principal'ity
prin'cipally
princip'ia
princip'iant
prin'ciple
prin'cipled
prink
prinked
prink'ing
print
print'ed
print'er
print'ing
print'ing-office
pri'or
pri'orate
pri'oress
prior'ity
pri'ory

prise
prism
prismat'ic
prismat'ical
pris'moid
prismoid'al
pris'on
pris'on-base
pris'oner
pris'oner's base
pris'on-van
pris'tine
prith'ee
pri'vacy
pri'vate
privateer'
privateer'ing
privateers'man
pri'vately
priva'tion
priv'ative
priv'et
priv'ilege
priv'ileged
priv'ileging
priv'ily
priv'ity
priv'y
prize
prized
prize'-fight
prize'-fighter
prize'-fighting
prize'man
prize'-money
priz'ing
pro
pro'a
prob'abilism
prob'abilist
probabil'ity
prob'able
prob'ably
pro'bang
pro'bate, *n.*
pro'bate, *v.*
proba'tion
proba'tional
proba'tionary
proba'tioner
pro'bative
pro'batory
probe
probed
pro'bing
prob'ity
prob'lem
problemat'ic
problemat'ical
probos'cis
proce'dure
proceed'
proceed'ed
proceed'ing
pro'ceeds
procella'rian
pro'cess
proces'sion

proces'sional
proces'sionist
pro'chronism
proclaim'
proclaimed'
proclaim'er
proclaim'ing
proclama'tion
procliv'ity
procon'sul
procon'sular
procon'sulary
procon'sulate
procon'sulship
procras'tinate
procras'tinated
procras'tinating
procrastina'tion
procras'tinator
procras'tinatory
pro'creant
pro'create
pro'created
pro'creating
procrea'tion
pro'creative
pro'creator
procrust'ean
proc'tor
procto'rial
procum'bent
procur'able
procura'tion
proc'urator
procure'
procured'
procure'ment
procur'er
procur'ess
procur'ing
Pro'cyon
prod
prod'ded
prod'ding
prod'igal
prodigal'ity
prod'igally
prodig'ious
prodig'iously
prod'igy
prodrom'ata
prod'romus
prod'uce, *n.*
produce', *v.*
produced'
produ'cer
produ'cible
produ'cing
prod'uct
produc'tile

produc'tion
produc'tive
*produc'tive*ly
*produc'tive*ness
pro'em
proe'mial
profana'tion
profane'
profaned'
profane'ly
profane'ness
profa'ner
profa'ning
profan'ity
profess'
professed'
profess'edly
profess'ing
profes'sion
profes'sional
profes'sionalism
profes'sionally
profess'or
professo'rial
professo'riate
profess'orship
prof'fer
prof'fered
prof'ferer
prof'fering
{ *profi'ciency*
{ *profi'cient*
{ *profi'ciently*
pro'file
pro'filist
prof'it
prof'itable
prof'itably
prof'ited
prof'iting
prof'itless
prof'ligacy
prof'ligate
profound'
profound'est
profound'ly
profun'dity
profuse'
profuse'ly
profuse'ness
profu'sion
prog
progen'itive
progen'itor
progen'iture
prog'eny
prognath'ic
prog'nathous
progno'sis
prognos'tic
prognos'ticable
prognos'ticate
prognos'ticated
prognos'ticating

prognostica'tion
prognos'ticator
prognos'ticatory
{ pro'gram
{ pro'gramme
pro'gress, *n.*
progress', *v.*
progressed
progress'ing
progres'sion
progres'sional
progres'sionist
progress'ive
progress'ively
progress'ivism
prohib'it
prohib'ited
prohib'iter
prohib'iting
prohibi'tion
prohibi'tionary
prohibi'tionist
prohib'itive
prohib'itively
prohib'itory
{ *project*
{ *project'ed*
project'ile
*project'*ing
projec'tion
project'or
projec'ture
projet
prolap'se
prolap'sus
pro'late
prola'tion
prolegom'ena
prolegom'enary
prolegom'enon
prolep'sis
prolep'tic
proletaire'
proleta'rian
proleta'rianism
proleta'riat
pro'letary
pro'licide
prolif'erous
prolif'ic
prolifica'tion
pro'lix
prolix'ity
proloc'utor
pro'logue
prolong'
prolonga'tion
prolonge'
prolonged'
prolong'er
prolong'ing
prolu'sion
promenade'
promena'ded
promena'der

promena'ding
Prome'thean
prom'inence
prom'inency
prom'inent
prom'inently
promis'cuous
promis'cuously
prom'ise
prom'ised
promisee'
prom'iser
prom'ising
prom'issorily
prom'issory
prom'ontory
promote'
promo'ted
promo'ter
promo'ting
promo'tion
promo'tive
prompt
prompt'-book
prompt'ed
prompt'er
prompt'ing
prompt'itude
prompt'ly
prompt'uary
prom'ulgate
prom'ulgated
prom'ulgating
promulga'tion
prom'ulgator
promulge'
promulged'
promulg'er
promulg'ing
pro'nate
prona'tion
prona'tor
prone
prone'ness
prong
pronged
pronom'inal
pro'noun
pronounce'
pronounce'able
pronounced'
pronounce'ment
pronounc'er
pronounc'ing
pronunciamen'to
pronuncia'tion
pronunc'iatory
proof
proof'-reader
proof'-sheet

prop
propagan'da
propagan'dism
propagan'dist
prop'agate
prop'agated
prop'agating
propaga'tion
prop'agator
propel'
propelled'
propel'ler
propel'ling
propend'ent
propense'
propen'sion
propen'sity
prop'er
prop'erly
prop'erty
proph'ecy
proph'esied
proph'esier
proph'esy
proph'esying
proph'et
proph'etess
prophet'ic
prophet'ical
prophylac'tic
propin'quity
propi'tiable
propi'tiate
propi'tiated
propi'tiating
propitia'tion
propi'tiator
propi'tiatory
propi'tious
propi'tiously
pro'plasm
prop'olis
propone'
propo'nent
propor'tion
propor'tionable
propor'tional
propor'tionally
propor'tionate
propor'tionately
propor'tioned
propor'tioning
propor'tionment
propo'sal
propose'
proposed'
propos'er
propos'ing
proposi'tion
proposi'tional
propound'

propound'ed
propound'er
propound'ing
propped
prop'ping
proprae'tor
propri'etary
propri'etor
propri'ety
pro-proc'tor
propt
propul'sion
propul'sive
propylae'um
prop'ylon
pro ra'ta
prore
pro-rec'tor
prorec'torate
proroga'tion
prorogue'
prorogued'
prorogu'ing
prosa'ic
prosa'ical
pro'saism
pro'saist
prosce'nium
proscribe'
proscribed'
proscri'ber
proscri'bing
proscrip'tion
proscrip'tive
prose
prosec'tor
pros'ecute
pros'ecuted
pros'ecuting
prosecu'tion
pros'ecutor
pros'ecutrix
prosed
pros'elyte
pros'elyted
pros'elyting
pros'elytism
pros'elytize
pros'elytized
pros'elytizing
pro'ser
pro'sily
pro'siness
pro'sing
pro-sla'very
prosodi'acal
proso'dial
proso'dian
pros'odist
pros'ody
prosopopoe'ia
prospect
prospec'tion
prospec'tive
prospec'tively

prospec'tor
prospec'tus
pros'per
pros'pered
pros'pering
prosper'ity
pros'perous
pros'perously
pros'tate
prostat'ic
pros'thesis
prosthet'ic
pros'titute
pros'tituted
pros'tituting
prostitu'tion
pros'titutor
pros'trate, *a.*
pros'trate, *v.*
prostra'ted
prostra'ting
prostra'tion
pro'style
pro'sy
prosyl'logism
protag'onist
prot'asis
protat'ic
pro'tean
protect'
protect'ed
protect'ing
protec'tion
protec'tionist
protect'ive
protect'or
protect'oral
protect'orate
protecto'rial
protect'ress
protect'rix
pro'tégé
pro'teid
pro'tein
pro tem'pore
pro'test, *n.*
protest', *v.*
Prot'estant
Prot'estantism
protesta'tion
protest'ed
protest'er
protest'ing
protest'ingly
Pro'teus
proth'esis
prothono'tary
protho'rax
pro'tocol
pro'togine
protomar'tyr
pro'toplasm
protoplas'mic
pro'toplast
protoplas'tic
pro'tosalt
pro'totype
protox'ide
protox'idize
protox'idized
protox'idizing
Protozo'a
protozo'ic
protozo'on
protract'
protract'ed
protract'ing
protract'ile
protrac'tion
protract'ive
protract'or
protrude'
protru'ded
protru'ding
protru'sile
protru'sion
protru'sive
protu'berance
protu'berant
protu'berate
protu'berated
protu'berating
proud
proud'er
proud'est
proud'ly
proud'ness
prov'able
prov'ably
prove
proved
provedore'
prov'en
Proven'çal
prov'ender
prov'er
prov'erb
prover'bial
prover'bialism
prover'bialist
prover'bially
provide'
provi'ded
prov'idence
prov'ident
providen'tial
providen'tially
prov'idently
provi'der
provi'ding
prov'ince
provin'cial
provin'cialism
provin'cialist
provincial'ity
prov'ing
provi'sion
provi'sional
provi'sionally
provi'sionary
provi'sioned
provi'sioning
provi'so
provi'sory
provoca'tion
provoc'ative
provo'kable
provoke'
provoked'
provo'ker
provo'king
provo'kingly
prov'ost
prow
prow'ess
prowl
prowled
prowl'er
prowl'ing
prox'imal
prox'imate
prox'imately
proxim'ity
prox'imo
prox'y
prude
pru'dence
pru'dent
pruden'tial
pru'dently
pru'dery
pru'dish
pru'dishly
pru'dishness
prune
pruned
prunel'la
prunel'lo
pru'ner
prunif'erous
pru'ning
pru'ning-hook
pru'rience
pru'riency
pru'rient
prurig'inous
pruri'go
Prus'sian
prus'siate
prus'sic
pry
pry'ing
pry'ingly
prytane'um
pryt'anis
pryt'any
psalm
psalm'-book
psalm'ist
psalmod'ic
psalm'odist
psalm'ody
psalt'er
psalt'ery
pseu'do
pseu'dograph
pseudog'raphy
pseudol'ogist
pseudol'ogy
pseudomor'-phous

pseu'donym
pseudon'ymous
pseu'doscope
pshaw
psilan'thropist
psitta'ceous
pso'ra
psori'asis
psor'ic
psy'chic
psych'ical
psycholog'ic
{ psycholog'ical
{ psycholog'ically
psychol'ogist
psychol'ogy
psy'chomancy
psycho'sis
psychrom'eter
psychrom'etry
ptar'migan
pteriplegis'tic
pterodac'tyl
pter'opod
ptis'an
Ptolema'ic
pto'maïne
pty'alin
pty'alism
ptys'magogue
pu'beral
pu'berty
pu'bes
pubesc'ence
pubesc'ent
pu'bic
pub'lic
pub'lican
publica'tion
public-house'
pub'licist
public'ity
*pub'lic*ly
pub'lic-spirited
{ *pub'lish*
{ *pub'lished*
pub'lisher
*pub'lish*ing
puccoon'
puce
puck
puck'er
puck'ered
puck'ering
puck'ery
pud'der
pud'dering
pud'ding
pud'ding-stone
pud'dingy
pud'dle
pud'dled
pud'dler
pud'dling
pud'dly
pu'dency

pudic'ity
pu'erile
pueril'ity
puer'peral
puer'perous
puff
puff'-ball
puffed
puff'er
puff'ery
puff'in
puff'iness
puff'ing
puff'y
pug
pug'-dog
pug'g(a)ree
pug'ging
pu'gil
pu'gilism
pu'gilist
pugilist'ic
pugna'cious
pugnac'ity
pug'nosed
puis'ne
pu'issance
pu'issant
puke
puked
pu'king
pul'chritude
pule
puled
pu'ler
pu'ling
pul'k(h)a
pull
pull'-back
pulled
pull'er
pull'et
pull'ey
pull'ing
Pull'man-car
pul'lulate
pul'monary
pulmon'ic
pulp
pulped
pulp'iness
pulp'ing
pul'pit
pulp'ous
pulp'y
pul'que
puls'ate
puls'ated
puls'atile
puls'ating
pulsa'tion
puls'ative
puls'atory
pulse
pulsed
pulse'-glass
pulse'less
pulsif'ic

pulsim'eter
puls'ing
pulsom'eter
pulta'ceous
pulv'erable
pulvera'ceous
pulv'erine
pulveriza'tion
pulv'erize
pulv'erized
pulv'erizer
pulv'erizing
pulv'erous
pulver'ulent
pulv'inated
pul'vis
pu'ma
pum'ice
pump
pumped
pump'er
pump'ernickel
pump'-handle
pump'ing
pum'pion
pump'kin
pun
punch
punched
punch'eon
punch'er
punchinel'lo
punch'ing
punc'tate
punc'tated
punc'tiform
punctil'io
punctil'ious
punct'ual
punctual'ity
punct'ually
punct'uate
punct'uated
punct'uating
punctua'tion
punct'uator
punct'ure
punct'ured
punct'uring
pun'dit
pung
pun'gence
pun'gency
pun'gent
Pu'nic
pu'nier
pu'niest
pu'niness
pun'ish
pun'ishable
pun'ished
pun'isher
pun'ishing
pun'ishment
pu'nitive
pu'nitory

punk
pun'ka
punned
pun'ner
pun'net
pun'ning
pun'ster
punt
punt'er
punt'ing
punt'ist
pu'ny
pup
pu'pa
pu'pil
pu'pilage
pu'pil(l)ary
pupip'arous
pupiv'orous
pupped
pup'pet
pup'pet-show
pup'ping
pup'py
pup'pyism
pura'na
puran'ic
pur'blind
pur'chasable
pur'chase
pur'chased
pur'chase-money
pur'chaser
pur'chasing
pure
pure'ly
pure'ness
pur'er
pur'est
pur'fle
purga'tion
pur'gative
purgato'rial
pur'gatory
purge
purged
pur'ger
pur'ging
purifica'tion
pu'rificative
pu'rificator
pu'rificatory
pu'rified
pu'rifier
pu'riform
pu'rify
pu'rifying
Pu'rim
pur'ism
pur'ist
Pu'ritan
Puritan'ic
Puritan'ical

Pu'ritanism
pu'rity
purl
purled
pur'lieu
pur'lin
pur'ling
purloin'
purloined'
purloin'er
purloin'ing
purpar'ty
pur'ple
pur'pled
pur'pling
pur'plish
purport', *v.*
pur'port, *n.*
purport'ed
purport'ing
pur'pose
pur'posed
pur'poseful
pur'poseless
pur'posely
pur'poser
pur'posing
purpres'ture
pur'pure
purpu'real
pur'purin
purr
purred
pur'ree
pur'ring
purse
pursed
purse'ful
purse'-net
purse'-pride
purse'-proud
purs'er
purs'ing
purs'lane
pursu'able
pursu'al
pursu'ance
pursu'ant
pursue'
pursued'
pursu'er
pursu'ing
pursuit'
pur'suivant
purs'y
pur'tenance
pu'rulence
pu'rulency
pu'rulent
purvey'
purvey'ance
purveyed'
purvey'ing
purvey'or
pur'view
pus
Pu'seyism
Pu'seyist

Pu'seyite
push
pushed
push'er
push'ful
push'ing
push'-pin
pusillanim'ity
pusillan'imous
puss
pus'sy
pus'tular
pus'tulate, *a.*
pus'tulate, *v.*
pus'tulated
pustula'tion
pus'tule
pus'tulous
put
puta'men
pu'tative
putchuk'
pu'teal
pu'tid
put'log
put'-off
putrefac'tion
putrefac'tive
pu'trefied
pu'trefy
pu'trefying
putres'cence
putres'cent
putres'cible
pu'trid
putrid'ity
put'ter
put'tied
put'ting
put'ty
put'tying
put-up'
puz'zle
puz'zled
puz'zle-headed
puz'zler
puz'zling
puzzola'no
pyae'mia
pyc'nite
pyc'nodont
pyc'nostyle
pye
py'garg
pygmae'an / pygme'an
pyg'my
pyja'mas
pyl'agore
pylor'ic
pylo'rus
pyr'acanth
pyral'lolite
pyr'amid

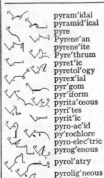

pyram'idal
pyramid'ical
pyre
Pyrene'an
pyrene'ite
Pyre'thrum
pyret'ic
pyretol'ogy
pyrex'ial
pyr'gom
pyr'iform
pyrita'ceous
pyri'tes
pyrit'ic
pyro-ac'id
py'rochlore
pyro-elec'tric
pyrog'enous
pyrol'atry
pyrolig'neous
pyrolith'ic
pyrol'ogist
pyrol'ogy
pyrolu'site
py'romancy
pyroman'tic
pyrom'eter
pyromet'ric
pyrom'etry
pyromor'phite
pyromorph'ous
py'rope
{ pyroph'orous
{ pyroph'orus
pyr'oscope
pyro'sis
pyros'malite
pyrotech'nic
pyrotech'nics
pyrotech'nist
py'rotechny
py'roxene
pyroxyl'ic
Pyr'rhic
pyr'rhite
pyr'rholite
pyr'rhonism
pyr'rhonist
pyr'rhotine
Pythagore'an
Pythag'orism
Pyth'ian
py'thon
py'thoness
python'ic
py'thonism
pyx
pyxid'ium
pyx'is

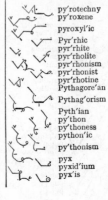

Q

qua
quab
quack
quacked
quack'ery
quack'ing
quack'ish
quack'salver
quad
quad'ra
Quadrages'ima
quad'rangle
quadran'gular
quad'rans
quad'rant
quad'rat
quad'rate, *a.*
quad'rate, *n.*
quadrat'ic
quadra'trix
quad'rature
quadren'nial
quad'rible
quadricap'sular
quad'ricorn
quadridec'imal
quadriden'tate
quad'rifid
quad'rifoil
quad'riform
quadri'ga
quadrigena'rious
quadrilat'eral
quadrilit'eral
quadrille'
quadril'lion
quadrilo'bate
quad'rilobed
quadriloc'ular
quadrino'mial
quadrinom'ical
quadripar'tite
quadriphyl'lous
quad'rireme
quadrisyllab'ic
quadrisyl'lable
quad'rivalve
quadrivalv'ular
quadriv'ial
quadroon'
Quadru'mana
quad'rumane
quadru'manous
quad'rune
quad'ruped
quad'ruple
quad'rupled
quadru'plicate, *a.*
quadru'plicate, *v.*
quadru'plicated
quadru'plicating
quadruplica'tion
quad'rupling
quaest'or
quaff
quaffed
quaff'er
quaff'ing
quag
quag'ga
quag'gy
quag'mire
quail
quailed
quail'ing
quaint
quaint'ly
quaint'ness
quake
quaked
qua'ker
qua'keress
qua'kerish
Qua'kerism
qua'king
qual'ifiable
qualifica'tion
qual'ificative
qual'ificator
qual'ified
qual'ifier
qual'ify
qual'ifying
qual'itative
qual'ity
qualm
qualm'ish
qualm'ishly
quan'dary
quantifica'tion
quan'titative
quan'tity
quan'tum
quar'antine
quar'rel
quar'relled-led
quar'reller-ler
quar'relling-ling
quar'relsome
quar'ried
quar'rier
quar'ry
quar'rying
quart
quar'tan
quarta'tion
quar'ter
quar'terage
quar'ter-day
quar'ter-deck
quar'tered
quar'terfoil
quar'tering
quar'terly
quar'termaster
quar'tern
quarteroon'
quar'ters
quar'ter-sessions
quar'terstaff
quartet'-ette'
quar'tile
quar'tine
quar'to
quar'tole
quartz
quartzif'erous
quartz'ose
quartz'y
quash
quashed
quash'ee
quash'ing
qua'si
quassa'tion
quas'sia
quas'sin
quater'nary
quater'nion
quater'nity
quatorze'
quat'rain
quat'refoil
qua'ver
qua'vered
qua'verer

qua'vering
quay
quay'age
queach'y
quean
quea'siness
quea'sy
queen
queen'ing
queen'like
queen'ly
queen'-post
queen's met'al
queer
queer'ish
queer'ly
quelch
quell
quelled
quell'er
quell'ing
quench
quench'able
quenched
quench'er
quench'ing
quench'less
quer'citron
que'ried
querimo'nious
que'rist
quern
quer'ulous
quer'ulously
quer'ulousness
que'ry
que'rying
quest
ques'tion
ques'tionable
*ques'tionable*ness
ques'tionably
ques'tionary
ques'tioned
ques'tioner
ques'tioning
ques'tionist
ques'tionless
quest'man
quest'or
queue
queued
quib'ble
quib'bled
quib'bler
quib'bling
quick
quick'en
quick'ened
quick'ener
quick'ening
quick'er
quick'-grass
quick'lime
quick'ly
quick'ness
quick'sand
quick'set
quick'-sighted
quick'silver
quick'step
quick'-witted
quid
quid'dity
quid'dle
quid'dled
quid'dler
quid'dling
quid'nunc
quid pro quo
quiesce'
quiesced'
quies'cence
quies'cency
quies'cent
quies'cing
qui'et
qui'eted
qui'eter
qui'etest
qui'eting
qui'etism
qui'etist
quietist'ic
qui'etly
qui'etness
qui'etude
quie'tus
quill
quill'-driver
quilled
quill'let
quill'ing
quill'wort
quilt
quilt'ed
quilt'er
quilt'ing
qui'nary
qui'nate
quince
quince'-tree
quincun'cial
quin'cunx
quindec'agon
quin'ine
Quinquages'ima
quinquan'gular
quinquefo'liate
quinquelit'eral
quinquen'nial
quinquepar'tite
quin'quereme
quinquesyl'lable
quin'quevalve
quin'quifid
quinqui'na
quin'sy
quint
quin'tain
quin'tal
quin'tan
quintess'ence
quintessen'tial
quintet'-ette'
quintil'lion
quin'tuple
quintu'plicate
quin'zaine
quip
qui'pu, quip'pu
quire
Quiri'nal
quirk
quirked
quirk'ish
quirt
quit
quitch
quit'claim
quite
quit'-rent
quits
quit'table
quit'tance
quit'ted
quit'ter
quit'ting
quiv'er
quiv'ered
quiv'erful
quiv'ering
quiv'eringly
qui vive
Quixot'ic
quixot'ically
quix'otism
quix'otry
quiz
quizzed
quiz'zer
quiz'zical
quiz'zing
quiz'zing-glass
quod'libet
quoin
quoit
quon'dam
quo'rum
quo'ta
quo'table
quota'tion
quote
quo'ted
quo'ter
quoth
quotid'ian
quo'tient
quo'ting
quo'tum

R

rab
rab'bet
rab'beted
rab'beting
rab'bi
rab'bin
{ Rabbin'ic
{ rabbin'ic
rabbin'ical
rab'binism
rab'binist
rab'bit
rab'ble
rab'blement
rabdol'ogy
rab'i
rab'id
rab'idly
rab'idness
ra'bies
ra'ca
raccoon'
race
race'-course
raced
race'-horse
raceme'
ra'cer
rachil'la
ra'chis
ra'cial
ra'cier
ra'ciest
ra'cily
ra'ciness
ra'cing
rack
racked
rack'er
rack'et
rack'eted
rack'eting
rack'ety
rack'ing
rack'-rent
rack'-renter
raconteur'
{ racoon'
{ raccoon'
rac'quet
ra'cy
rad'dle
ra'dial
ra'diance
ra'diancy
ra'diant
ra'diantly
ra'diary

Radia'ta
ra'diate
ra'diated
ra'diating
radia'tion
ra'diator
rad'ical
rad'icalism
radical'ity
rad'ically
rad'icant
rad'icate, *a.*
rad'icate, *v.*
rad'icated
rad'icating
radica'tion
rad'icle
radic'ular
ra'dii
radiom'eter
rad'ish
ra'dius
ra'dix
raf'fia
raf'fish
raf'fle
raf'fled
raf'fler
raf'fling
raft
raft'er
raft'ered
raft'ing
rafts'man
rag
rag'amuffin
rage
raged
ra'ger
rag'-fair
rag'ged
rag'gedness
rag'ging
ra'ging
rag'lan
rag'man
ragout'
rag'-shop
rag'stone
rag'wort
raid
rail
railed
rail'er
rail'ing
rail'lery
rail'road
rail'way

rai'ment
rain
rain'bow
rain'drop
rained
rain'fall
rain'-gauge
rain'ier
rain'iest
rain'iness
rain'ing
rain'less
rain'-proof
rain'-water
rain'y
rais'able
raise
raised
rais'er
rai'sin
rais'ing
{ ra'ja
{ ra'jah
Rajpoot'
rake
raked
rakee'
rake'-hell
ra'ker
ra'king
ra'kish
ra'kishness
râle
ral'lied
ral'lier
ral'ly
ral'lying
ram
Ramadan'
ram'ble
ram'bled
ram'bler
ram'bling
ram'ekin
ra'meous
ramifica'tion
ram'ified
ram'iform
ram'ify
ram'ifying
rammed
ram'mer
ram'ming
ram'mish
ram'my
ra'mous
ramp
rampa'cious

rampage'
rampaged'
rampa'ging
ram'pancy
ram'pant
ram'part
ramped
ramp'ing
ram'pion
ra'mus
ram'rod
ram'shackle
ram'sons
ram'ulous
ran
rances'cent
ranch
ranch'man
ran'cho
ran'cid
rancid'ity
ran'cidness
ran'cour-or
ran'corous
ran'corously
rand
randan'
ran'dom
ra'nee
rang
range
ranged
ran'ger
ran'ging
ra'nine
rank
ranked
rank'er
rank'ing
ran'kle
ran'kled
ran'kling
rank'ly
rank'ness
ran'sack
ran'sacked
ran'sacker
ran'sacking
ran'som
ran'somed
ran'somer
ran'soming
ran'somless
rant
rant'ed
rant'er
Rant'erism
rant'ing
rant'y
Ranun'culus
rap
rapa'cious
rapa'ciously
rapa'ciousness
rapac'ity
rape
Raph'aelism
Raph'aelite
Raph'aelitism
ra'phe
raph'ides
raph'igraph
raph'ilite
rap'id
rapid'ity
rap'idly
ra'pier
rap'ine
rapparee'
rapped
rappee'
rap'per
rap'ping
rapport'
rapprochement
rapscal'lion
rapt
rap'tor
rapto'rial
rapto'rious
rap'ture
rap'turous
ra'ra a'vis
rare
rarefac'tion
rar'efiable
rar'efied
rar'efy
rar'efying
rare'ly
rare'ness
rar'er
rar'ity
ras'cal
rascal'ity
rascal'lion
ras'cally
rase
rash
rash'er
rash'ly
rash'ness
raso'rial
rasp
rasp'atory
rasp'berry
rasped
rasp'er
rasp'ing
ra'sure
rat
ratafi'a
ratan'
rat'any
ratch
ratch'et
ratch'il
rate
rateabil'ity
rate'able
rate'ably
rate'-book
ra'ted
rate'payer
rate'payers
ra'ter
rath'er
ratifica'tion
rat'ified
rat'ifier
rat'ify
rat'ifying
ra'ting
ra'tio
ratioc'inate
ratiocina'tion
ratioc'inative
ra'tion
ra'tional
rationa'le
ra'tionalism
ra'tionalist
rationalist'ic
rational'ity
ra'tionalize
ra'tionally
rat'lin
ratoon'
rats'bane
rat'-tail
rattan'
rat'ted
ratteen'
rat'ten
rat'ter
rat'ting
rat'tle
rat'tled
rat'tler
rat'tlesnake
rat'tling
rau'city
rau'cous
rav'age
rav'aged
rav'ager
rav'aging
rave
raved
rav'el
rave'lin
rav'elled / rav'eled
rav'elling / rav'eling
ra'ven
rav'en
rav'ened
rav'ener
rav'ening
rav'enous
rav'enously
ra'ver
rav'in
ravine'
ra'ving
rav'ish
rav'ished
rav'isher
rav'ishing
rav'ishment
raw
raw'-boned
raw'-head
raw'ish
raw'ness
ray
ra'yah
rayed
ray'less

raze
razed
razee'
ra'zing
ra'zor
ra'zor-bill
reabsorb'
reabsorp'tion
reach
reach'able
reached
reach'er
reach'ing
react'
reac'tion
reac'tionary
react'ive
read
read, *p. tense*
read'able
readdress'
readdressed'
readdress'ing
read'er
read'ier
read'iest
read'ily
read'iness
read'ing
read'ing-book
read'ing-room
readjust'
readjust'ed
readjust'ing
readjust'ment
readmis'sion
readmit'
read'y
read'y-made
reaffirm'
reaffor'est
rea'gent
re'al
real'gar
re'alism
re'alist
realist'ic
real'ity
re'alizable
realiza'tion
re'alize
re'alized
re'alizing
re'ally
realm
re'alty
ream
rean'imate
rean'imated
rean'imating
reanima'tion
reannex'
reannexa'tion
reap
reaped
reap'er
reap'ing
reap'ing-hook
reappear'
reappear'ance

reappoint'
reappoint'ing
re*appoint'ment*
reappor'tion
rear
rear-ad'miral
reared
rear'er
rear'ing
rear'-*guard*
rear'mouse
re-arrange'
re-arranged'
re-arrang'ing
re-arrange'ment
rear'ward
reascend'
rea'son
rea'sonable
rea'sonableness
rea'sonably
rea'soned
rea'soner
rea'soning
reassem'ble
reassert'
re-assess'
reassign'
reassign'ing
re*assign'ment*
reassume'
reassu'rance
reassure'
reast'y
re'bate, *n.*
rebate', *v.*
reba'ted
rebate'ment
reba'ting
re'beck
reb'el
rebel'
rebelled'
rebel'ling
rebell'ion
rebell'ious
rebound'
re-bound'
rebound'ed
rebound'ing
rebuff'
rebuffed'
rebuff'ing
re*build'*
re*build'ing*
rebuilt'
rebuke'
rebuked'
rebu'ker
rebu'king
re'bus
rebut'
rebut'tal
rebut'ted
rebut'ter
rebut'ting
recal'citrant
recal'citrate
recal'citrated
recal'citrating

recalcitra'tion
recalesce'
recales'cence
rec*all'*
rec*alled'*
rec*all'*ing
recant'
recanta'tion
recant'ed
recant'er
recant'ing
recapit'ulate
recapit'ulated
recapit'ulating
recapitula'tion
recapit'ulatory
recap'tion
recap'ture
recast'
recede'
rece'ded
rece'ding
receipt'
receipt'-book
receipt'ed
receipt'ing
receiv'able
receive'
received'
receiv'er
receiv'ership
receiv'ing
re'cency
recen'sion
re'cent
re'cently
re'centness
recep'tacle
receptac'ular
receptibil'ity
recep'tible
recep'tion
recep'tive
receptiv'ity
recep'trix
recess'
recessed'
reces'sion
reces'sional
Rech'abite
recharge'
réchauffé
recheat'
recherché
rechoose'
recid'ivist
rec'ipe
recip'iency
recip'ient
recip'rocal
reciprocal'ity
recip'rocally
recip'rocate
recip'rocated
recip'rocating
reciproca'tion
reciproc'ity
reci'sion
reci'tal
recita'tion

recitative'
recitati'vo
recite'
reci'ted
reci'ter
reci'ting
reck
recked
reck'ing
reck'less
reck'lessly
reck'lessness
reck'on
reck'oned
reck'oner
reck'oning
reclaim'
reclaim'able
reclaim'ant
reclaimed'
reclaim'ing
reclama'tion
réclame
rec'linate
reclina'tion
recline'
reclined'
recli'ner
recli'ning
reclose'
recluse'
reclu'sion
reclu'sive
recoal'
recogni'tion
rec'ognizable
recog'nizance
rec'ognize
rec'ognized
rec'ognizer
rec'ognizing
rec'ognizor
recoil'
recoiled'
recoil'er
recoil'ing
recoil'ment
recoin'
recoin'age
recollect'
re-collect'
recollect'ed
recollect'ing
re-collect'ing
recollec'tion
re-collec'tion
recollect'ive
recombina'tion
recombine'
recommence'
recommenced'
recommenc'ing
recommend'
recommend'able
recommenda'tion
recommend'a'ory
recommend'ed
recommend'er
recommend'ing
recommit'
recommit'ted
recommit'ting
recommit'ment
recommit'tal
rec'ompense
rec'ompensed
rec'ompensing
recompose'
recomposed'
recompos'ing
recomposi'tion
rec'oncilable
rec'oncilably
rec'oncile
rec'onciled
rec'oncilement
rec'onciler
reconcilia'tion
reconcil'iatory
rec'onciling
rec'ondite
reconduct'
recon'naissance
reconnoi'tre
reconnoi'tred
reconnoi'tring
recon'quer
reconsid'er
reconsidera'tion
reconsid'ered
reconsid'ering
reconstruct'
reconstruct'ed
reconstruct'ing
reconstruc'tion
reconvert'
reconvey'
reconvey'ance
recop'y
record
recorded'
record'er
record'ing
recount'
recount'ed
recount'ing
recoup'
recouped'
recoup'ing
recoup'ment
recourse'
recov'er
re-cov'er
recov'erable
recov'ered
recov'erer
recov'ering
recov'ery
rec'reancy
rec'reant
rec'reate
re-create'
rec'reated
rec'reating
re-creat'ing
recrea'tion
re-crea'tion
rec'reative
rec'rement
recremen'tal
recrementi'tial
recrementi'tious
recrim'inate
recrimina'tion
recrim'inative
recrudes'cence
recruit'
recruit'ed
recruit'er
recruit'ing
rec'tal
rect'angle
rect'angled
rectan'gular
rectangular'ity
rec'tifiable
rectifica'tion
rec'tified
rec'tifier
rec'tify
rec'tifying
rectilin'eal
rectilin'ear
rec'titude
rec'tor
rec'toral
rec'torate
recto'rial
rec'tory
rec'tum
recum'bence
recum'bency
recum'bent
recu'perate
recu'perated
recu'perating
recupera'tion
recu'perative
recu'perator
recur'
recurred'
recur'rence
recur'rent
recur'ring
recurv'ate
recurv'ous
rec'usancy
rec'usant
recusa'tion
red
rédacteur'
redac'tion
redac'tor
redan'
red'breast
red'cap
red'coat
red'cross
red'den
redden'dum
red'dened
red'dening
red'dish
red'dle
redeem'
redeem'able
redeemed'
redeem'er
redeem'ing
redemp'tible

redemp'tion
redemp'tionary
redemp'tioner
redemp'tive
Redemp'torist
redemp'tory
red'-eye
red'-gum
red'-handed
red'head
redhibi'tion
redhib'itory
red'-hot
red'ingote
redin'tegrate
redin'tegrated
redin'tegrating
redintegra'tion
redispose'
redistrib'ute
redistribu'tion
red'-letter
red'ness
red'olence
red'olency
red'olent
redoub'le
redoubt'
redoubt'able
redoubt'ed
redound'
redound'ed
redound'ing
redraw'
redress'
redress'able
redressed'
redress'ing
redress'ive
red'root
red'shank
red'-*short*
red'skin
red'start
red'-streak
red'-tape
red-ta'pish
red-ta'pism
red'top
reduce'
reduced'
redu'cent
redu'cible
redu'cing
reduct'
reduc'tion
reduc'tive
redun'dance
redun'dancy
redun'dant
redu'plicate
redu'plicated
redu'plicating
reduplica'tion
redu'plicative
red'wing
re-ech'o
re-ech'oed
re-ech'oing
reed

reed'en
reed'ing
reed'less
reed'y
reef
reefed
reef'er
reef'ing
reef'y
reek
reeked
reek'ing
reek'y
reel
re-elect'
re-elect'ed
re-elect'ing
re-elec'tion
reeled
re-el'igible
reel'ing
re-embark'
re-embarked'
re-embark'ing
reem'ing
re-enact'
re-enact'ment
re-enforce'
re-enforced'
re-enforce'ment
re-engage'
re-en'ter
re-en'tered
re-en'tering
re-en'trance
re-en'try
reer'mouse
re-*estab'lish*
re-*estab'lished*
re-*estab'lish-ment*
reeve
reeved
reev'ing
re-examina'tion
re-exam'ine
re-exam'ined
re-exam'ining
re-export
refash'ion
refash'ioned
refash'ioning
refec'tion
refec'tive
refec'tory
refer'
ref'erable
referee'
ref'erence
referen'dary
referen'dum
referen'tial
referred'
refer'rer
refer'rible
refer'ring
refine'
refined'
refi'nedly
refine'ment
refi'ner

refi'nery
refi'ning
refit'
refit'ted
refit'ting
reflect'
reflect'ed
reflect'ible
reflect'ing
reflec'tion
reflect'ive
reflect'or
re'flex, *n.* and *a.*
reflex', *v.*
reflexed'
reflexibil'ity
reflex'ible
reflex'ive
reflores'cence
ref'luence
ref'luent
re'flux
reform'
re-form'
reform'able
reforma'tion
re-forma'tion
reform'ative
reform'atory
reformed'
reform'er
*reform'*ing
reform'ist
refract'
refract'ed
refract'ing
refrac'tion
refract'ive
refrac'torily
refrac'toriness
refrac'tory
re-frac'ture
ref'ragable
refrain'
refrained'
refrain'ing
refrangibil'ity
refran'gible
refresh'
refreshed'
refresh'er
refresh'ing
refresh'ment
refrig'erant
refrig'erate
refrig'erated
refrig'erating
refrigera'tion
refrig'erative
refrig'erator
refrig'eratory
reft
ref'uge
refugee'
reful'gence
reful'gency
reful'gent
refund'
refund'ed
refund'ing

refund'ment
refu'sable
refu'sal
refuse
refused'
refu'ser
refu'sing
refu'table
refuta'tion
refu'tatory
refute'
refut'ed
refut'ing
regain'
regained'
regain'ing
re'gal
regale'
regaled'
regale'ment
rega'lia
rega'ling
regal'ity
re'gally
regard'
regard'ant
regard'ed
regard'ful
regard'ing
regard'less
regat'ta
Re'gel
re'gency
regen'eracy
regenerate, *n., a.*
regen'erate, *v.*
regen'erated
regen'erating
regenera'tion
regen'erative
regen'erator
regen'eratory
re'gent
regermina'tion
reg'icidal
reg'icide
régime'
reg'imen
reg'iment
regimen'tal
regimen'tals
regi'na
re'gion
reg'ister
reg'istered
reg'istering
reg'istrar
reg'istrarship
registra'tion
reg'istry
re'gius
reg'let
reg'nal
reg'nancy
reg'nant
regorge'
regorged'
regrant'
regrate'
regra'ted

regra'ter
regra'ting
re'gress, *n.*
regress', *v.*
regres'sion
regress'ive
regret'
regret'ful
regret'ted
regret'ting
reg'ular
regular'ity
reg'ularly
reg'ulate
reg'ulated
reg'ulating
regula'tion
reg'ulative
reg'ulator
reg'uli
reg'ulus
regur'gitate
regurgita'tion
rehabil'itate
rehabil'itated
rehabilita'tion
rehang'
re'hash
rehear'
reheard'
rehear'ing
rehears'al
rehearse'
rehearsed'
rehears'er
rehears'ing
reheat'
Reichs'rath
Reichs'tag
rei'gle
reign
reigned
reign'ing
reimburse'
reimbursed'
reimburse'ment
reimburs'ing
reimprint'
rein
reincarna'tion
rein'deer
reined
reinforce'
reinforced'
reinforce'ment
reinforc'ing
rein'ing
rein'less
reins
reinsert'
re*inspec'tion*
reinstall'
reinstate'
reinstat'ed
reinstate'ment
reinstat'ing
re*insur'ance*
reinsure'
reintroduce'
re*introduc'tion*

reinvest'
re*invest'ment*
reis'sue
reis'sued
reis'suing
reit'erate
reit'erated
reit'erating
reitera'tion
reit'erative
reject'
reject'able
reject'ed
reject'er
reject'ing
rejec'tion
reject'ive
reject'ment
rejoice'
rejoiced'
rejoi'cing
rejoin'
rejoin'der
rejoined'
rejoin'ing
reju'venate
reju'venated
reju'venating
rejuvenes'cence
rejuvenes'cent
rekin'dle
rekin'dled
rekin'dling
relaid'
relais'
reland'
relapse'
relapsed'
relaps'er
relaps'ing
relate'
rela'ted
rela'ting
rela'tion
rela'tional
rela'tionship
rel'ative
rel'atively
rela'tor
relax'
relax'ant
relax'ation
relax'ative
relaxed'
relax'ing
relay'
re-lay'
releas'able
release'
released'
release'ment
releas'er
releas'ing
rel'egate
rel'egated
rel'egating
relega'tion
relent'
relent'ed
relent'ing

relent'less
relent'lessly
relet'
rel'evance
rel'evancy
rel'evant
reliabil'ity
reli'able
reli'ance
reli'ant
rel'ic
rel'ict
relied'
relief'
reli'er
reliev'able
relieve'
relieved'
reliev'ing
relie'vo
relight'
relig'ion
relig'ionism
relig'ionist
religios'ity
relig'ious
relig'iously
{ *relin'quish*
{ *relin'quished*
*relin'quish*ing
relin'quishment
rel'iquary
relique'
rel'ish
rel'ishable
rel'ished
rel'ishing
relive'
reloan'
relu'cent
reluc'tance
reluc'tancy
reluc'tant
reluc'tantly
relume'
relumed'
relu'mine
relu'mined
relu'ming
rely'
rely'ing
remade'
remain'
remain'der
remained'
remain'ing
remains'
remake'
remand'
remand'ed
remand'ing
remand'ment
rem'anent
rem'anet
remark'
re-mark'
{ *remark'able*
{ *remark'ably*
remarked'
*remark'*ing

remar'riage
remar'ried
remar'ry
remar'rying
reme'diable
reme'dial
rem'edied
rem'ediless
rem'edy
rem'edying
{ *remem'ber*
{ *remem'bered*
*remem'*bering
*remem'*brance
*remem'*brancer
rem'iform
rem'igrate
remind'
remind'ed
remind'er
remind'ful
remind'ing
reminis'cence
reminis'cent
rem'iped
remise', *n.*
remise', *v.*
remised'
remis'ing
remiss'
remissibil'ity
remiss'ible
remis'sion
remiss'ive
remiss'ly
remiss'ness
remiss'ory
remit'
remit'tal
remit'tance
remit'ted
remit'tent
remit'ter
remit'ting
rem'nant
remod'el
remod'elled
remod'elling
remon'etize
remon'strance
remon'strant
remon'strate
*remon'stra*ted
*remon'strat*ing
*remon'strat*or
rem'ora
remorse'
remorse'ful
remorse'less
remote'
remote'ly
remote'ness
remo'ter
remo'test
remould'
remount'
removabil'ity
remov'able
remov'al
remove'

removed'
remov'ing
Rem'phan
remunerabil'ity
remu'nerable
remu'nerate
remu'nerated
remu'nerating
remunera'tion
remu'nerative
remu'neratory
Renaissance'
re'nal
rename'
ren'ard
renas'cence
renas'cent
rencon'tre
rencoun'ter
rend
rend'er
ren'dered
ren'dering
ren'dezvous
rend'ible
rend'ing
rendi'tion
ren'egade
renew'
renew'able
renew'al
renewed'
renew'er
renew'ing
ren'iform
reni'tency
reni'tent
ren'net
renounce'
renounced'
renounce'ment
renoun'cer
renoun'cing
ren'ovate
ren'ovated
ren'ovating
renova'tion
ren'ovator
renown'
renowned'
rent
rent'able
rent'al
rente (Fr.)
rent'ed
rent'er
rent'ing
rent'-roll
re*num'ber-ed*
renuncia'tion
reoc'cupy
reop'en
reop'ened
reop'ening
reordain'
re*organiza'tion*
{ reo*r'ganize*
{ reo*r'ganized*
rep
repack'

repaid'
repair'
repair'able
repaired'
repair'er
repair'ing
repand'
rep'arable
repara'tion
repar'ative
repartee'
repass'
repassed'
repass'ing
repast'
repay'
repay'able
repay'ing
repay'ment
repeal'
repealabil'ity
repeal'able
repealed'
repeal'er
repeal'ing
repeat'
repeat'ed
repeat'edly
repeat'er
repeat'ing
repel'
repel'lance
repel'lant
repelled'
repel'lence
repel'lency
repel'lent
repel'ler
repel'ling
repent'
repent'ance
repent'ant
repent'ed
repent'ing
repeo'ple
repercuss'
repercussed'
repercuss'ing
repercus'sion
repercuss'ive
répertoire'
rep'ertory
rep'etend
repeti'tion
repeti'tious
repine'
repined'
repi'ner
repi'ning
replace
replaced'
replace'ment
repla'cing
replant'
replen'ish
replen'ished
replen'ishing
replen'ishment
replete'
reple'ted
replete'ness
reple'ting
reple'tion
replev'iable
replev'ied
replev'in
replev'y
replev'ying
rep'lica
rep'licant
rep'licate, *n.*, *a.*
rep'licate, *v.*
rep'licated
rep'licating
replica'tion
replied'
repli'er
reply'
reply'ing
report'
report'ed
report'er
report'ing
reporto'rial
repos'al
repose'
reposed'
repos'ing
repos'it
repos'ited
repos'iting
repos'itory
repossess'
reposses'sion
repoussé'
reprehend'
reprehend'ed
reprehend'ing
reprehen'sible
reprehen'sion
reprehen'sive
reprehen'sory
represent'
represent'able
representa'tion
represent'ative
represent'ed
represent'ing
repress'
repressed'
represser'
repress'ing
repres'sion
repress'ive
reprieve'
reprieved'
repriev'ing
reprimand
reprimand'ed
reprimand'ing
reprint
reprint'ed
reprint'ing
repri'sal
reprise'
reproach'
reproach'able
reproached'
reproach'ful
reproach'fully
reproach'ing
rep'robate, *a.*
rep'robate, *n.*, *v.*
rep'robated
rep'robating
reproba'tion
rep'robative
reproduce'
reproduced'
re***produc'tion***
re***produc'tive***
reproof'
reprov'able
reprov'al
reprove'
reproved'
reprov'er
reprov'ing
reprov'ingly
repta'tion
rep'tatory
rep'tile
Reptil'ia
reptil'ian
repub'lic
repub'lican
repub'licanism
repub'licanize (or)
repub'licanized
repub'licanizing
re***publica'tion***
{ re***pub'lish***
{ re***pub'lished***
re***pub'lish***ing
repu'diable
repu'diate
repu'diated
repu'diating
repudia'tion
repu'diator
repug'nance
repug'nancy (or)
repug'nant
repulse' (or)
repulsed'
repuls'er
repuls'ing
repul'sion
repul'sive
repul'sively
repul'siveness
repur'chase
rep'utable
rep'utably
reputa'tion
repute'
repu'ted
repu'ting
request'
request'ed
request'ing (or)
req'uiem
requir'able
require'
required'
require'ment
requir'ing
req'uisite
requisi'tion
requisi'tioned

requisi'tioning
requis'itive
requi'tal
requite'
requi'ted
requi'ting
rere'dos
re-resolve'
rere'ward
resale'
rescind'
rescind'able
rescind'ed
rescind'ing
rescind'ment
rescis'sion
rescis'sory
rescribe'
re'script
rescrip'tive
rescrip'tively
res'cuable
res'cue
res'cued
res'cuer
res'cuing
research'
reseat'
reseize'
resell'
resem'blance
resem'ble
resem'bled
resem'bling
resent'
resent'ed
resent'er
resent'ful
resent'ing
resent'ment
reserva'tion
reserve'
reserved'
reserv'edly
reserv'er
reserv'ing
reserv'ist
res'ervoir
reset'
reset'ting
reset'tle
reset'tlement
reship'
reship'ment
reside'
resi'ded
res'idence
res'idency
res'ident
residen'tial
residen'tiary
resi'der
resi'ding
resid'ual
resid'uary
res'idue
resid'uum
resign'
resigna'tion
resigned'

resign'edly
resignee'
resign'er
resign'ing
resil'ience
resil'iency
resil'ient
res'in
resinif'erous
res'inous
resist'
resist'ance
resist'ant
resist'ed
resist'er
resistibil'ity
resist'ible
resist'ing
resist'ive
resist'less
res'oluble
res'olute
res'olutely
resolu'tion
resolvabil'ity
resolv'able
resolve'
resolved'
resolv'ent
resolv'er
resolv'ing
res'onance
res'onant
res'onator
resorb'
resorbed'
resorb'ent
resorb'ing
resorp'tion
resort'
resort'ed
resort'ing
resound'
resound'ed
resound'ing
resource'
resource'less
respect'
*respect*abil'ity
*respect'*able
*respect'*ably
respect'ant
respect'ed
respect'er
*respect'*ful
*respect'*fully
*respect'*fulness
*respect'*ing
respect'ive
*respect'ive*ly
respell'
respirabil'ity
respir'able
respira'tion
respira'tional
res'pirator
respir'atory
respire'
respired'
respir'ing

res'pite
res'pited
res'piting
resplen'dence
resplen'dency
resplen'dent
respond'
respond'ed
respond'ence
respond'ent
respond'ing
response'
responsibil'ities
responsibil'ity
respon'sible
respon'sion
respon'sive
respon'sively
respon'siveness
rest
res'tant
restaurant
restau'rateur
rest'ed
rest'ful
rest'fully
rest'fulness
rest'ing
restitu'tion
rest'ive
rest'ively
rest'iveness
rest'less
rest'lessly
rest'lessness
restor'able
restora'tion
restora'tionist
restor'ative
restore'
restored'
restor'er
restor'ing
restrain'
restrain'able
restrained'
restrain'edly
restrain'er
restrain'ing
restraint'
restrict'
restrict'ed
restrict'ing
restric'tion
restrict'ive
restrict'ively
rest'y
result'
result'ance
result'ant
result'ed
result'ing
resum'able
resume'
résumé'
resumed'
resum'ing
resump'tion
resump'tive
resu'pinate

resur'gence
resur'gent
resurrec'tion
resurrec'tionist
resurvey'
resus'citant
resus'citate
resus'citated
resus'citating
resuscita'tion
resus'citative
resus'citator
reswear'
resworn'
ret
reta'ble
re'tail, *n., a.*
retail', *v.*
retailed'
retail'er
retail'ing
retain'
retain'able
retained'
retain'er
retain'ing
retake'
retal'iate
retal'iated
retal'iating
retalia'tion
retal'iative
retal'iatory
retard'
retarda'tion
retard'ative
retard'ed
retard'ing
retch
retched
retch'ing
reten'tion
reten'tive
reten'tively
reten'tiveness
re'tiary
ret'icence
ret'icency
ret'icent
ret'icle
retic'ular
retic'ulate, *a.*
retic'ulate
retic'ulated
reticula'tion
ret'icule
re'tiform
ret'ina
ret'inal
retinas'phalt
ret'inite
ret'inoid
ret'inue
reti'ral
retire'
retired'
retire'ment
retir'er
retir'ing
retort'

retort'ed
retort'er
retort'ing
retor'tion
retouch'
retouched'
retouch'ing
retour'
retrace'
retrace'able
retraced'
retra'cing
retract'
retract'ability
retract'able
retract'ed
retract'ible
retract'ile
retract'ing
retrac'tion
retract'ive
retract'or
retread'
retreat'
retreat'ed
retreat'er
retreat'ing
retrench'
retrenched'
retrench'ing
retrench'ment
retrib'ute
retrib'uted
retrib'uting
retribu'tion
retrib'utive
retrib'utory
retriev'able
retriev'al
retrieve'
retrieved'
retriev'er
retriev'ing
retroac'tion
retroact'ive
ret'rocede
ret'roceded
retroce'dent
retroced'ing
retroces'sion
retroduc'tion
ret'roflex
ret'roflexed
retrograda'tion
ret'rograde
ret'rograded
ret'rograding
retrogres'sion
retrogres'sive
retropul'sive
retrorse'ly
ret'rospect
retrospec'tion
retrospec'tive
*retrospec'tive*ly
retrover'sion
ret'rovert
ret'roverted
ret'roverting
return'

return'able
returned'
return'ing
retuse'
reu'nion
reunite'
reuni'ted
revac'cinate
revaccina'tion
reveal'
reveal'able
revealed'
reveal'er
reveal'ing
reveil'le
rev'el
revela'tion
rev'elled / rev'eled
rev'eller / rev'eler
revel'lent
rev'elling / rev'eling
rev'elry
reven'dicate
revendica'tion
revenge'
revenged'
revenge'ful
reven'ger
reven'ging
rev'enue
rever'berant
rever'berate
rever'berated
rever'berating
reverbera'tion
rever'beratory
revere'
revered'
rev'erence
rev'erenced
rev'erencing
rev'erend
rev'erent
reveren'tial
reveren'tially
rev'erently
rever'er
rev'erie
revers', *sing.*
revers', *pl.*
revers'al
reverse'
reversed'
reverse'ly
revers'ible
revers'ing
rever'sion
rever'sionary
rever'sioner
revert'
revert'ant
revert'ed
revert'er
revert'ible
revert'ing
revert'ive
rev'ery

revest'
review'
review'able
review'al
reviewed'
review'er
review'ing
revile'
reviled'
revi'ler
revi'ling
revi'sal
revise'
revised'
revi'ser
revi'sing
revis'ion
revis'ional
revis'ionary
revis'it
revi'val
revi'valism
revi'valist
revive'
revived'
revi'ver
revivifica'tion
reviv'ified
reviv'ify
reviv'ifying
revi'ving
revivis'cence
revivis'cent
revi'vor
revocabil'ity
rev'ocable
revoca'tion
rev'ocatory
revoke'
revoked'
revo'king
revolt'
revolt'ed
revolt'er
revolt'ing
rev'oluble
rev'olute
revolu'tion
revolu'tionary
revolu'tionist
revolu'tionize
revolu'tionized
revolu'tionizing
revolve'
revolved'
revolve'ment
revolv'ency
revolv'er
revolv'ing
revul'sion
revul'sive
reward'
reward'able
reward'ed
reward'er
reward'ing
rewrite'
rewrit'ten
rex
rey'nard

rhabar'barate
rhabdol'ogy
rhab'domancy
Rhadaman'thine
Rhadaman'tine
{ Rhae'tian
{ Rhe'tian
rhapsod'ic
rhapsod'ical
rhap'sodist
rhap'sodize
rhap'sodized
rhap'sodizing
rhap'sody
Rhen'ish
rheom'eter
rheom'etry
rhe'ostat
Rhe'tian, Rhae'- [tian
rhet'oric
rhetor'ical
rhetor'ically
rhetori'cian
rheum
rheumat'ic
rheum'atism
rheum'ic
rheum'y
rhi'no
rhinoce'rial
rhinoc'eros
rhinoplas'tic
rhi'noplasty
rhi'noscope
rhinos'copy
rhizo'ma
rhi'zome
rhizoph'agous
Rho'dian
rho'dium
Rhododen'dron
rhodomontade'
rhomb
rhom'bic
rhom'boid
rhom'boidal
rhom'bus
rhu'barb
rhumb
rhyme
rhymed
rhym'er
rhyme'less
rhyme'ster
rhym'ic
rhym'ing
rhym'ist
rhythm
rhyth'mic
rhyth'mical
rhyth'mus
ri'al
Rial'to
rib
rib'ald
rib'aldry
{ rib'and
{ rib'band
ribbed
rib'bing

rib'bon
rib'boned
rib'boning
Rib'bonism
Ri'bes
rib'ston
rice
rice'-bird
rice'-paper
rice'-water
rich
rich'er
rich'es
rich'ly
rich'ness
rick
rick'ets
rick'ety
rick'ing
rick'shaw
ric'ochet
ricochet'ted
ricochet'ting
rid
rid'dance
ride'able
rid'den
rid'der
rid'ding
rid'dle
rid'dled
rid'dler
rid'dling
ride
rideau'
ri'der
ri'derless
ridge
ridged
ridge'way
ridg'ing
rid'icule
rid'iculed
rid'iculer
rid'iculing
ridic'ulous
ridic'ulously
ridic'ulousness
ri'ding
ri'ding-hood
ri'ding-master
ridot'to
rife
riff'raff
ri'fle
ri'fle corps
ri'fled
ri'fleman
ri'fler
ri'fle-shot
ri'fling
rift
rift'ed
rift'ing
rift'less
rif'ty
rig
rigadoon'
Ri'gel
rigged

rig'ger
rig'ging
right
right'-about
right'-angle
right'-angled
right'ed
right'eous
right'eously
right'eousness
right'er
right'ful
right'fully
right'fulness
right'*hand*
right'-handed
right'ing
right'ly
right'-minded
right'-minded-ness
right'ness
rig'id
rigid'ity
rig'idly
rig'idness
rig'marole
rig'or
rig'orist
rig'orous
rig'orously
rig'our
Rig-ve'da
rile
riled
rilie'vo
ril'ing
rill
rilled
rill'et
rill'ing
rim
rime
rimed
ri'mer
rime'ster
ri'ming
rimmed
rim'ming
rimose'
rimos'ity
ri'mous
rim'ple
rim'pled
rim'pling
ri'my
rind
rin'derpest
rin'dle
ring
ring'-bolt
ring'-bone
ring'-dove
ringed
rin'gent
ring'er
ring'-fence
ring'ing
ring'leader
ring'let
ring'-shaped

ring'tail
ring'-tailed
ring'worm
rink
rink'er
rink'ing
rinse
rinsed
rins'ing
ri'ot
ri'oted
ri'oter
ri'oting
ri'otous
ri'otously
ri'otousness
rip
ripa'rian
ripe
ripe'ly
ri'pen
ri'pened
ripe'ness
ri'pening
ri'per
ripie'no
ripped
rip'per
rip'ping
rip'ple
rip'pled
rip'pling
rip'-rap
rise
ris'en
ri'ser
risibil'ity
ris'ible
ris'ibly
ri'sing
risk
risked
risk'er
risk'ing
risk'y
ris'sole
rite
ritornel'lo
rit'ual
rit'ualism
Rit'ualist
ritualist'ic
rit'ually
ri'val
ri'valled-led
ri'valling-ling
ri'valry
ri'valship
rive
rived
riv'en
riv'er
riv'er-horse
riv'et
riv'eted
riv'eting
rivière'
ri'ving
ri'vose
riv'ulet

rix'-dollar
roach
road
road'-hog
road'side
road'-stead
road'ster
road'way
roam
roamed
roam'er
roam'ing
roan
roar
roared
roar'er
roar'ing
roast
roast'ed
roast'er
roast'ing
rob
robbed
rob'ber
rob'bery
rob'bin
rob'bing
robe
robed
Rob'ertine
rob'in
rob'inet
ro'bing
rob'in-red'breast
ro'borant
ro'burite
robust'
robust'ious
robust'ly
robust'ness
roc
roc'ambole
roccel'lic
roch'et
rock
rock'-bound
rock'-crystal
rocked
rock'er
rock'ery
rock'et
rock'iness
rock'ing
rock'ing-*chair*
rock'ing-horse
rock'ing-stone
rock'-oil
rock'-rose
rock'-salt
rock'work
rock'y
roco'co
rod
rode
ro'dent
Roden'tia
rodomontade'
roe
roe'buck
roga'tion

rogue
rogu'ery
rogu'ish
rogu'ishly
rogu'ishness
roil
roiled
roil'ing
roil'y
roist'erer
rôle, roll
roll'-*call*
rolled
roll'er
roll'er-skate
rol'lick
rol'licked
rol'licking
roll'ing
roll'ing-pin
roll'ing-stock
ro'ly-po'ly
Roma'ic
romal'
ro'man, Ro'man
romance'
romanced'
roman'cer
roman'cing
roman'cist
Romanesque'
Roman'ic
Ro'manish
Ro'manism
Ro'manist
Ro'manize
Ro'manized
Ro'manizing
{ Romansch'
{ Romansh'
roman'tic
roman'tically
roman'ticism
roman'ticist
Rom'any
Ro'mic
Ro'mish
Ro'mist
romp
romped
romp'ing
romp'ish
ron'deau
ron'del
Rönt'gen rays
rood
roof
roofed
roof'ing
roof'less
roof-tree
roof'y
rook
rooked
rook'ery
room
room'ful
room'iness
room'y
roost

roost'ed
roost'er
roost'ing
root
root'ed
root'-house
root'ing
root'let
root'-stock
root'y
ropal'ic
rope
roped
rope'-maker
rope'-making
ro'per
ro'pery
rope'walk
rope'-yarn
ro'piness
ro'py
roqu'elaure
ro'ral
rorif'erous
ror'qual
Rosa'ceae
rosa'ceous
ro'sary
rose
ro'seal
ro'seate
rose'bud
rose'-colour
rose'-coloured
rose'mary
rose'ola
roset', rosette'
rose'-water
rose'wood
Rosicru'cian
ros'ied
ro'sier
ro'siest
ros'in
ros'iny
ross
ros'tel
ros'tellate
ros'ter
ros'tral
ros'trate
ros'trated
ros'trum
ros'ulate
ro'sy
rot
ro'ta
ro'tary
ro'tate
rotate'
rota'ted
rota'ting
rota'tion
ro'tative
rota'tor
ro'tatory
rote
roth'er-nail
ro'tifer
Rotif'era

rot'ted
rot'ten
rot'tenness
rot'ting
rotund'
rotun'da
rotun'dity
rotund'ness
rou'ble
rou'cou
rou'é
rouge
rouged
Rouge Drag'on
rouge-et-noir'
rough
rough'-cast
rough'-draft
rough'-draw
rough'en
rough'ened
rough'ening
rough'er
rough'-hew
rough'-hewed
rough'-hewing
rough'-hewn
rough'ing
rough'ish
rough'ly
rough'ness
rough'-rider
rough'shod
roug'ing
roulade'
rouleau'
roulette'
roulet'ted
rounce
roun'cival
round
round'about
round'ed
round'el
round'elay
round'er
round'*hand*
Round'head
round'house
round'ing
round'ish
round'let
round'ly
round'ness
round-rob'in
round'-shoul-[dered
roup
rouse
roused
rous'er
rous'ing
rout
route
rout'ed
routine'
rout'ing
rove
roved
ro'ver
ro'ving

row (a rank)
row (a tumult)
row'able
row'an-tree
row'-boat
row'dy
row'dyish
row'dyism
rowed
row'el
row'elled, -led
row'elling-ling
row'en
row'er
row'ing
row'land
row'lock
roy'al
roy'alism
roy'alist
roy'ally
roy'alty
roys'terer
rub
rubbed
rub'ber
rub'bing
rub'bish
rub'bishy
rub'ble
rub'bly
rubefa'cient
ru'bellite
rube'ola
rubes'cence
rubes'cent
ru'bican
ru'bicel
Ru'bicon
ru'bicund
rubicun'dity
ru'bied
rubif'ic
ru'biform
ru'bify
rubig'inous
ru'bric
ru'brical
ru'bricate
ru'bricist
rub'stone
ru'by
ruche
ruch'ing
ruck
ruc'tion
rudd
rud'der
rud'dier
rud'diest
rud'diness
rud'dle
rud'dock
rud'dy
rude
rude'ly
rude'ness
ruden'ture
ru'der
ru'dest
ru'diment
rudimen'tal
rudimen'tary
Rudolph'ine
rue
rued
rue'ful
rue'fully
rue'fulness
rue'ing
rufes'cent
ruff
ruffed
ruf'fian
ruf'fianism
ruf'fianly
ruff'ing
ruf'fle
ruf'fled
ruf'fling
ru'fous
rug
ru'gate
rug'ged
rug'gedly
rug'gedness
ru'gous
ru'in
ru'inate
ruina'tion
ru'ined
ru'ining
ru'inous
rule
ruled
ru'ler
ru'ling
rum
rum'ble
rum'bled
rum'bling
ru'men
ru'minal
ru'minant
ru'minate
ru'minated
ru'minating
rumina'tion
ru'minator
rum'mage
rum'maged
rum'maging
rum'mer
ru'mour
ru'mor
ru'moured
ru'mored
ru'mourer
ru'morer
ru'mouring
ru'moring
rump
rum'ple
rum'pled
rum'pling
rum'pus
run
run'agate
run'away
run'cinate
run'dle
rund'let
rune
rung
ru'nic
run'let
run'nel
run'ner
run'net
run'ning
runt
rupee'
rup'tion
rup'ture
rup'tured
rup'turing
ru'ral
ru'ralist
ru'ralize
ru'rally
ruse
rush
rushed
rush'er
rush'ing
rush'light
rush'y
rusk
russ
rus'set
rus'seting
rus'sety
Rus'sian
Rus'sianism
rust
rust'ed
rus'tic
rus'ticate
rus'ticated
rus'ticating
rustica'tion
rustic'ity
rust'iness
rust'ing
rus'tle
rus'tled
rus'tling
rust'y
rut
ruth
ruthe'nium
ruth'less
ruth'lessly
ruth'lessness
ru'tile
rye
ry'otti

S

sabadil'la
Sabae'an, Sabe'an
Sab'aoth
Sabbata'rian
Sabbata'rianism
Sab'bath
Sabbat'ic
Sabbat'ical
Sab'batism
Sabe'an
Sa'beism
Sabel'lian
Sabel'lianism
Sa'bian
Sa'bianism
Sab'ine
sa'ble
sabot'
sa'bre
sab'retache
sac
saccade'
sac'cate
sacchar'ic
sacchar'ify
saccharim'eter
sac'charine
sac'charoid
sac'cule
sacerdo'tal
sacerdo'talism
sa'chem
sachet'
sack
sack'age
sack'but
sack'cloth
sacked
sack'er
sack'ful
sack'ing
sacque
sac'rament
sacramen'tal
sacramenta'rian
sacra'rium
sa'cred
sa'credly
sa'credness
sac'rifice
sac'rificed
sac'rificer
sacrifi'cial
sac'rificing
sac'rilege
sacrile'gious
sacrile'gist

sac'ristan
sac'risty
sac'rosanct
sa'crum
sad
sad'den
sad'der
sad'dest
sad'dle
sad'dle-bag
sad'dled
sad'dler
sad'dlery
sad'dle-shaped
sad'dle-tree
sad'dling
Sadduce'an
Sad'ducee
Sad'duceeism
sad'-iron
sad'ly
sad'ness
safe
safe-con'duct
safe'*guard*
safe'-keeping
safe'ly
saf'er
saf'est
safe'ty
safe'ty-lamp
safe'ty-valve
saf'flower
saf'fron
saf'frony
sag
sa'ga
saga'cious
saga'ciously
sagac'ity
sag'amore
sage
sage'ly
sag'gar, sag'ger
sagit'ta
sagit'tal
Sagitta'rius
sag'ittary
sag'ittate
sa'go
sagoin'
sa'gy
sa'hib
sa'ic
saice
said
sail

sail'able
sail'cloth
sailed
sail'er
sail'ing
sail'-loft
sail'maker
sail'or
sail'-yard
sain'foin
saint
saint'ed
saint'like
saint'liness
saint'ly
Saint-Simo'nian
Saint-Si'monist
Saint-Si'monite
Saint Vi'tus's [dance
saith
sake
sak'é
sa'ker
sal
salaam'
sala'cious
sal'ad
salaman'der
salaman'drine
sal'aried
sal'ary
sale
sale'able
sale'ableness
sal'ep
salera'tus
sale'-room
sales'man
sales'woman
Sal'ic
sal'icin, sal'icine
sali'cylate
salicyl'ic
sa'lient
salif'erous
sal'ifiable
salifica'tion
sal'ified
sal'ify
sal'ifying
salina'tion
sa'line
sali'va
sali'val
sal'ivant
sal'ivary
sal'ivate

sal'ivated
sal'ivating
saliva'tion
sal'lenders
sal'let
sal'lied
sal'low
sal'lowness
sal'ly
sal'lying
sally-lunn'
sal'ly-port
salmagun'di
salm'on
salm'onet
salm'onoid
salm'on-trout
salon'
saloon'
saloop'
sal'picon
sal'pinx
sal'sify
salsil'la
salt
sal'tant
sal'tate
salta'tion
saltato'rial
saltato'rious
sal'tatory
salt'cellar
salt'ed
salt'er
salt'ern
sal'tier
salt'ing
sal'tire
salt'ish
salt'ness
saltpe'tre
salt'y
salu'brious
salu'brity
sal'utarily
sal'utariness
sal'utary
saluta'tion
salu'tatory
salute'
salu'ted
salu'ter
salutif'erous
salu'ting
salvabil'ity
sal'vable
sal'vage
salva'tion
Salva'tionist
sal've
salve, *v.t.*, and *n.*
salve, *v.t.*
salver
salv'ing
sal'vo
sal volat'ile
sal'vor

sam'ara
Samar'itan
Sam'bo
same
same'ness
Sa'mian
sa'miel
sam'ite
sam'let
Samothra'cian
samovar'
samp
sam'pan
sam'phire
sam'ple
sam'pler
sanabil'ity
san'ative
sanato'rium
san'atory
sanctifica'tion
sanc'tified
sanc'tifier
sanc'tify
sanc'tifying
sanctil'oquent
sanctimo'nious
sanctimo'nious-ness
sanc'timony
sanc'tion
sanc'tioned
sanc'tioning
sanc'titude
sanc'tity
sanc'tuary
sanc'tum
sanc'tus
sand
san'dal
san'dalled, -led
san'dal-wood
san'darac
sand'-bag
sand'ed
Sandema'nian
sand'-eel
san'derling
san'ders
san'dever
sand'hill
sand'iness
sand'ing
san'diver
sand'-paper
sand'piper
sand'stone
sand'wich
sand'y
sane
sane'ness
sang
sangaree'
sang-froid'
san'giac
Sangrail'-greal'
sanguif'erous

sanguifica'tion
san'guinarily
san'guinary
san'guine
san'guinely
sanguin'eous
sanguiniv'orous
sanguisu'gous
San'hedrim
San'hedrin
san'icle
sa'nies
sa'nious
sanita'rian
san'itary
sanita'tion
san'ity
san'jak
sank
san'pan
sans
sansculotte'
San'skrit
sans souci'
san'talin
san'tonine
sap
sap'ajou
sap'an-wood
sap'id
sapid'ity
sa'pience
sa'pient
sapinda'ceous
sap'less
sap'ling
sapodil'la
sapona'ceous
saponac'ity
sapon'ifiable
saponifica'tion
sapon'ified
sapon'ify
sapon'ifying
sap'onine
sap'onule
sa'por, sa'pour
saporif'ic
saporos'ity
sapped
sap'per
Sap'phic
sap'phire
sap'phirine
sap'piness
sap'ping
sap'py
saproph'agan
sap'-wood
sar'aband
Sar'acen
Saracen'ic
sar'casm
sarcas'tic
sarcas'tically

sarce'net
sar'cocarp
sar'cocele
sar'cocol
sar'code
sar'colite
sarcol'ogy
sarco'ma
sarco'matous
sarcoph'agi
{ sarcoph'agous
{ sarcoph'agus
sarcoph'agy
sar'cous
sard
sar'dine
sardine'
Sardin'ian
sar'dius
sardon'ic
sar'donyx
sark
sark'ing
sar'lak
Sarma'tian
Sarmat'ic
sar'ment
sa'ros
sar'plar
sar'rasin
sarsaparil'la
sar'sen
sarse'net
sarto'rial
sarto'rius
sash
sashed
sash'-frame
sash'-line
sas'safras
Sas'senach
sas'soline
sas'tra
sat
Sa'tan
satan'ic
satan'ical
satch'el
sate
sa'ted
sateen'
sat'ellite
sa'tiable
sa'tiate
sa'tiated
sa'tiating
satia'tion
sati'ety
sat'in
satinet(te)'
sa'ting
sat'in-wood
sat'iny
sat'ire
satir'ic
satir'ical
satir'ically

sat'irist
sat'irize
sat'irized
sat'irizing
satisfac'tion
*satisfac'tori*ly
satisfac'tory
sat'isfiable
sat'isfied
sat'isfier
sat'isfy
sat'isfying
sa'trap
sa'trapy
Sat'suma
sat'urable
sat'urant
sat'urate, *adj.*
sat'urate, *v.*
sat'urated
sat'urating
satura'tion
Sat'urday
Sat'urn
Saturna'lia
Saturna'lian
Satur'nian
sat'urnine
sat'urnist
sat'yr
sauce
sauce'-boat
sauce'box
sauced
sauce'pan
sau'cer
sau'cier
sau'ciest
sau'cily
sau'ciness
sauc'ing
saucisson'
sau'cy
sauer'kraut
Saumur
saun'ter
saun'tered
saun'terer
saun'tering
Sau'ria
sau'rian
sau'roid
sau'sage
sausage-roll'
sauté
Sauterne'
sa'vable, save'-able
sav'age
sav'agely
sav'ageness
sav'agery
savan'nah
savant'
save
save'-all
saved
sav'eloy
sa'ver

sav'in, sav'ine
sa'ving
sa'vingly
sa'vings-bank
sa'viour
sa'vour, sa'vor
sa'voured
sa'vourily
sa'vouriness
sa'vouring
sa'vourless
sa'voury
savoy'
Savoy'ard
saw
saw'dust
sawed
saw'fish
saw'ing
saw'mill
sawn
saw'ney
saw'-pit
saw'yer
sax'atile
sax'horn
saxic'avous
sax'ifrage
Sax'on
Sax'onism
Sax'onist
say
say'est
say'ing
says
scab
scab'bard
scabbed
scab'bier
scab'biest
scab'biness
scab'bing
scab'by
sca'bies
sca'bious
sca'brous
scad
scaf'fold
scaf'folder
scaf'folding
scagl'ia
scaglio'la
sca'la
scal'able
scalade'
scald
scald'ed
scald'er
scald'-head
scal'dic
scald'ing
scale
scaled
scalene'
sca'ler
sca'liness

scal'ing
scall
scal'lawag
scalled
scall'ion
scal'lop
scal'loped
scal'loping
scal'lywag
scalp
scalped
scal'pel
scalp'er
scalp'ing
scalp'ing-knife
scal'y
scam'ble
scam'bled
scam'bling
scam'mony
scamp
scam'per
scam'pered
scam'pering
scan
scan'dal
scan'dalize
scan'dalized
scan'dalizing
scan'dal-monger
scan'dalous
scan'dalously
scan'dent
Scandina'vian
scanned
scan'ning
scan'sion
Scanso'res
scanso'rial
scant
scant'ier
scant'iest
scant'ily
scant'iness
scant'ing
scan'tle
scant'ling
scant'ly
scant'ness
scant'y
scape
scape'goat
scape'grace
scape'ment
scaph'ite
scap'olite
scap'ple
scap'ula
scap'ular
scap'ulary
scar
scar'ab
scar'abee
scar'amouch
scarce
scarce'ly
scarce'ness

scar'city
scare
scare'crow
scared
scarf
scarfed
scarf'ing
scarf'skin
scarifica'tion
scar'ificator
scar'ified
scar'ify
scar'ifying
sca'ring
sca'rious
scarlati'na
scarlati'nous
scar'let
scarp
scarped
scarred
scar'ring
scathe
scathed
scathe'less
sca'thing
scat'ter
scat'ter-brained
scat'tered
scat'terer
scat'tering
scaup
scav'enge
scav'enger
scav'enging
scenar'io
scene
scene'-painter
sce'nery
scene'-shifter
sce'nic
sce'nical
scenograph'ic
scenog'raphy
scent
scent'ed
scent'ing
scent'less
scep'tic, skep'tic
scep'tical
scep'ticism
scep'tre
scep'tred
scep'treless
sched'ule
sched'uled
sche'ma
sche'matism
sche'matist
scheme
schemed
sche'mer
sche'ming
sche'mist
scher'zo

schism
schismat'ic
schismat'ical
schist
schist'ose
schist'ous
{ schnapps
{ schnaps
schol'ar
schol'arlike
schol'arly
schol'arship
scholas'tic
scholas'tically
scholas'ticism
scho'liast
scho'lium
school
school'-board
school'-book
*school'*boy
school'-days
schooled
*school'*fellow
*school'*girl
*school'*house
*school'*ing
*school'*man
*school'*master
*school'*mate
*school'*mistress
*school'*room
school'-teacher
school'-teaching
schoon'er
schorl
schorla'ceous
schottische'
sci'agraph
sciagraph'ic
sciag'raphy
sciat'ic
sciat'ica
sciat'ical
sci'ence
scien'tial
scientif'ic
scientif'ical
scientif'ically
sci'entist
sci'licet
scil'litin-tine
scim'itar
scin'coid
scincoid'ian
scintil'la
scin'tillant
scin'tillate
scin'tillated
scin'tillating
scintilla'tion
sci'olism
sci'olist
sci'on
sciop'tic

scirrhos'ity
scir'rhus
scis'sel
scis'sile
scis'sion
scis'sors
scis'sure
scitamin'eous
Sclavo'nian
Sclavon'ic
scler'ogen
sclero'sis
sclerot'ic
scobs
scoff
scoffed
scoff'er
scoff'ing
scold
scold'ed
scold'er
scold'ing
scol'ecite
scol'lop
Scolopen'dra
scom'beroid
sconce
scone
scoop
scooped
scoop'er
scoop'ing
scoop'net
scope
sco'piform
scorbu'tic
scorch
scorched
scorch'er
scorch'ing
scorch'ingly
score
scored
scor'er
sco'ria
scoria'ceous
scorifica'tion
sco'rified
sco'riform
sco'rify
sco'rifying
scor'ing
sco'rious
scorn
scorned
scorn'er
scorn'ful
scorn'fully
scorn'ing
Scor'pio
scor'pion
scor'tatory
scor'za
Scot

Scotch, scotch
scotched
scotch'ing
Scotch'man
sco'ter
scot'-free'
sco'tia
Scot'icè
Sco'tist
sco'tograph
scoto'mia
Scots
Scots'man
Scot'ticism
Scot'tish
scoun'drel
scoun'drelism
scoun'drelly
scour
scoured
scour'er
scourge
scourged
scour'ger
scour'ging
scour'ing
scout
scout'ed
scout'ing
scov'el
scow
scowl
scowled
scowl'ing
scrab'ble
scrab'bled
scrab'bling
scrag
scrag'ged
scrag'gily
scrag'giness
scrag'gy
scram'ble
scram'bled
scram'bler
scramb'ling
scranch
scrap
scrap'-book
scrape
scraped
scra'per
scra'ping
scratch
scratched
scratch'ing
scrawl
scrawled
scrawl'er
scrawl'ing
scrawn'y
scray
scream
screamed
scream'er
scream'ing
scree
screech
screeched

screech'ing
screech'-owl
screed
screen
screened
screen'ing
screes
screw
screw'-driver
screwed
screw'ing
screw'-jack
screw'-pine
scrib'ble
scrib'bled
scrib'bler
scrib'bling
scribe
scribed
scri'bing
scrim'mage
scrimp
scrimped
scrim'shaw
scrip
scrip'-holder
script
scripto'rial
scripto'rium
Scrip'tural
Scrip'turalist
Scrip'turally
Scrip'ture
Scrip'ture-reader
Scrip'turist
scriv'ener
scriv'enery
scrobic'ulate
scrof'ula
scrof'ulous
scroll
scrolled
scroll'work
scro'tum
scrub
scrubbed
scrub'ber
scrub'bier
scrub'biest
scrub'bing
scrub'by
scruff
scrum'mage
scru'ple
scru'pled
scru'pling
scrupulos'ity
scru'pulous
scru'pulously
scru'pulousness
scruta'tor
scru'tatory
scrutineer'
scru'tinize
scru'tinized
scru'tinizer

scru'tinizing
scru'tiny
scrutoire'
scud
scud'ded
scud'ding
scu'di
scu'do
scuf'fle
scuf'fled
scuf'fler
scuf'fling
sculk
sculked
sculk'er
scull
sculled
scull'er
scull'ery
scull'ing
scull'ion
scul'pin
sculp'tor
sculp'tural
sculp'ture
sculp'tured
sculpturesque'
sculp'turing
scum
scum'ble
scumb'ling
scummed
scum'mer
scum'mings
scup'per
scurf
scurf'ier
scurf'iest
scurf'iness
scurf'y
scur'rile
scurril'ity
scur'rilous
scur'rilously
scur'ried
scur'ry
scur'rying
scur'vily
scur'viness
scur'vy
scut
scu'tage
scu'tate
scutch
scutched
scutch'eon
scutch'ing
scute
scu'tel
scu'tellate
scu'tellated
scutel'lum
scutif'erous
scu'tiform
scut'tle
scut'tled
scut'tling

scu'tum
scym'itar
scythe
scythed
Scyth'ian
sea
sea'board
sea'-born
sea'-borne
sea'-breach
sea'-breeze
sea'-captain
sea'-chart
sea'coast
sea'-cow
sea'-dog
sea'-elephant
sea'farer
sea'faring
sea'-fight
sea'-gauge
sea'-girt
sea'-green
sea'-gull
sea'-horse
sea'-kale
sea'-king
seal
sealed
sea'-leopard
seal'er
sea'-level
seal'ing
seal'ing-wax
sea'-lion
seal'skin
seam
sea'man
sea'manship
sea'-mark
seamed
seam'er
sea'-mew
seam'ing
seam'less
sea'-mouse
seam'ster
seam'stress
seam'y
séance'
sea'-pie
sea'plane
sea'port
sear
search
search'able
searched
search'er
search'ing
seared
sear'ing
sea'-room
sea'-rover
sea'scape
sea'-serpent
sea'-shell
sea'shore
sea'sick
sea'-sickness
sea'side

sea'-snail
sea'son
sea'sonable
sea'soned
sea'soner
sea'soning
sea'son-ticket
seat
seat'ed
sea'-term
seat'ing
sea'-urchin
sea'-wall
sea'ward
sea'-water
sea'-weed
sea'worthiness
sea'worthy
seba'ceous
sebac'ic
se'bate
sebun'dy
se'cant
secede'
sece'ded
sece'der
sece'ding
secern'
secerned'
secern'ing
seces'sion
seces'sionist
seclude'
seclu'ded
seclu'ding
seclu'sion
seclu'sive
sec'ond
sec'ondarily
sec'ondary
sec'ond-best
sec'onded
sec'onder
sec'ond-*hand*
sec'onding
sec'ondly
sec'ond-rate
sec'onds
sec'ond sight
se'crecy
se'cret
secretaire'
secreta'rial
secreta'riat
sec'retary
sec'retary-bird
sec'retaryship
secrete'
secre'ted
secre'ting
secre'tion
secre'tive
secre'tiveness
se'cretly
se'cretness
secre'tory
sect
secta'rian
secta'rianism

secta'rianize
sect'arist
sect'ary
sec'tile
sec'tion
sec'tional
sec'tor
sec'ular
sec'ularism
sec'ularist
secular'ity
seculariza'tion
sec'ularize
sec'ularized
sec'ularizing
sec'ularly
sec'und
sec'undine
secur'able
secure'
secured'
secure'ly
secur'er
secu'riform
secur'ing
secu'rity
sedan'
sedate'
sedate'ly
sedate'ness
sed'ative
se'dent
sed'entarily
sed'entariness
sed'entary
sede'runt
sedge
sedg'y
sed'iment
sedimen'tary
sedi'tion
sedi'tionary
sedi'tious
seduce'
seduced'
seduce'ment
sedu'cer
sedu'cible
sedu'cing
seduc'tion
seduc'tive
seduc'tively
sedu'lity
sed'ulous
sed'ulously
see
seed
seed'-bud
seed'ed
seed'ier
seed'iest
seed'iness
seed'less
seed'ling
seeds'man
seed'-time
seed'-vessel

seed'y
see'ing
seek
seek'er
seek'ing
seem
seemed
seem'er
seem'ing
seem'ingly
seem'lier
seem'liest
seem'liness
seem'ly
seen [sees)
se'er (one who
seer (a prophet)
sees
see'-saw
see'-sawed
see'-sawing
seethe
seethed
seeth'er
seeth'ing
seg'gar
seg'ment
seg'mental
segmenta'tion
seg'regate
seg'regated
seg'regating
segrega'tion
Seid'litz
seigneu'rial
seign'ior
sei'gniorage
sei'gniory
seine
sein'er
sein'ing
seis'in
seis'mic
seis'mograph
seismom'eter
seiz'able
seize
seized
seiz'er
sei'zin
seiz'ing
sei'zure
se'lah
sel'dom
select'
select'ed
select'ing
selec'tion
select'ive
select'man
select'ness
select'or
sel'enate
sele'niate
selen'ic
sel'enide
selenif'erous
sel'enite
selenit'ic
sele'nium

selenog'rapher
selenograph'ic
selenog'raphy
self
self-con'fident
self-con'scious
self-control'
self-defence'
self-deni'al
self-esteem'
self-ev'ident
self-help'
self-*in'terest*
self-*in'terested*
self'ish
*self'ish*ly
self'ishness
self-love'
self-made'
self-possessed'
self-posses'sion
self-reli'ance
self-reli'ant
self-rely'ing
self-right'eous
self-right'eous- [ness
self'same
self-will'
self-willed'
sell
sell'er
sell'ing
sel'vage / sel'vedge
sel'vaged / sel'vedged
sel'vagee
selves'
sem'aphore
semaphor'ic
sematol'ogy
sem'blance
semée
semeiog'raphy
semeiolog'ical
semeiol'ogy
semeiot'ic
semes'ter
semes'tral
semes'trial
semi-an'nual
sem'ibreve
sem'icircle
semicir'cular
semico'lon
semicu'bical
semi-detached'
semi-diam'eter
semilu'nar
sem'inal
sem'inarist
sem'inary
sem'inate
semina'tion
seminif'erous
seminif'ic
sem'iped
sem'iquaver

Semit'ic
sem'itone
semivow'el
semoli'na
sempervi'rent
sempiter'nal
sem'pre
semp'ster
semp'stress
se'nary
sen'ate
sen'ate-house
sen'ator
senato'rial
senato'rian
sen'atorship
send
send'er
send'ing
sen'ega
senes'cence
sen'eschal
sen'green
se'nile
senil'ity
se'nior
senior'ity
sen'na
sen'night
sen'nit
senoc'ular
señor'
seño'ra
señori'ta
sen'sate, *adj.*
sen'sate, *v.*
sen'sated
sensa'tion
sensa'tional
sensa'tionalism
sensa'tionalist
sensa'tionary
sense
sense'less
sense'lessly
sense'lessness
{ *sensibil'ity*
sen'sible
sen'sibly
sensif'erous
sensif'ic
sens'ism
sen'sitive
sen'sitively
sen'sitiveness
sen'sitize
sen'sitized
sen'sitizing
senso'rial
senso'rium
sen'sory
sen'sual
sen'sualism
sen'sualist
sensual'ity
sen'sualize
sen'sualized
sen'sualizing
sen'sually
sen'suous
sent
sen'tence
sen'tenced
sen'tencing
senten'tial
senten'tious
senten'tiously
senten'tiousness
sen'tiency
sen'tient
sen'timent
sentimen'tal
sentimen'talism
sentimen'talist
sentimental'ity
sentimen'talize
sentimen'talized
sentimen'talizing
sentimen'tally
sen'tinel
sen'try
sen'try-box
sep'al
sep'aloid
separabil'ity
sep'arable
sep'arate, *adj.*
sep'arate, *v.*
sep'arated
sep'arately
sep'arateness
sep'arating
separa'tion
sep'aratism
sep'aratist
sep'arative
sep'arator
sep'aratory
se'pia
se'poy
sept
septan'gular
septa'ria
sep'tate
Septem'ber
Septem'brist
septem'vir
sep'tenary
septen'nial
septen'trional
septet', septette'
sept'foil
sep'tic
septicae'mia
sep'tical
sep'ticidal
septic'ity
septifa'rious
septif'erous
septilat'eral
septin'sular
septuagena'rian
septuage'nary
Septuages'ima
Sep'tuagint
sep'tum
sep'tuple
sepul'chral
sep'ulchre
sep'ulture
sequa'cious
sequac'ity
se'quel
se'quence
se'quent
sequen'tial
seques'ter
seques'tered
seques'tering
seques'trate
seques'trated
seques'trating
sequestra'tion
seq'uestrator
se'quin
sera'glio
sera'i
seralbu'men
ser'aph
seraph'ic
ser'aphim
ser'aphine
seras'kier
Serbo'nian
sere
serenade'
serena'ded
serena'der
serena'ding
serena'ta
serendip'ity
serene'
serene'ly
serene'ness
seren'ity
serf
serf'dom
serge
ser'geancy [-jeancy
ser'geant-jeant
or
ser'geant-ma'jor
se'rial
se'rially
se'riate
seria'tim
seri'ceous
se'ries
or
ser'in
serio-com'ic
se'rious
se'riously
se'riousness
ser'jeant
ser'mon
ser'monize
ser'monized
ser'monizer
ser'monizing
seron'

seroon'
seros'ity
ser'otine
se'rous
ser'pent
serpen'tiform
ser'pentine
ser'pentry
serpi'go
ser'rate
ser'rated
ser'rature
ser'ried
ser'rulate
serrula'tion
se'rum
serv'ant
serve
served
serv'er
Ser'vian
serv'ice
serv'iceable
serv'iceableness
serviette'
serv'ile
serv'iiely
servil'ity
serv'ing
serv'ing-man
serv'itor
serv'itude
ses'ame
ses'amoid
ses'amum
sesquial'tera
sesquicar'bonate
sesquidu'plicate
sesquip'edal
ses'quitone
sess
ses'sile
ses'sion
ses'sional
sess'pool
ses'terce
sestet', sestette'
set
se'ta
seta'ceous
setif'erous
se'tiform
set'-off
se'ton
se'tous
sett
settee'
set'ter
set'ting
set'tle
set'tled
set'tlement
set'tler
set'tling
set'tlor
set'-to
set'wall
sev'en
sev'enfold
sev'ennight
seventeen
seventeenth
sev'enth
sev'enthly
sev'entieth
sev'enty
sev'er
sev'eral
sev'erally
sev'eralty
sev'erance
severe'
sev'ered
severe'ly
sever'er
sever'est
sev'ering
sever'ity
sew
sew'age
sewed
sew'er (who sews)
sew'er (a drain)
sew'erage
sew'ing
sew'ing-machine
sewn
sex
sexagena'rian
sexag'enary
Sexages'ima
sexan'gular
sexen'nial
sex'less
sext
sex'tain
sex'tant
sextet'
sex'tile
sextil'lion
sex'ton
sex'toness
sex'tuple
sex'ual
sex'ualist
sexual'ity
sex'ually
sforza'to
sfuma'to
shab
shab'bier
shab'biest
shab'bily
shab'biness
shab'by
shab'rack
shack
shack'le
shack'led
shack'les
shack'ling
shad
shad'dock
shade
sha'ded
shades
sha'dier
sha'diest
sha'dily
sha'diness
sha'ding
shad'ow
shad'owed
shad'owing
shad'owy
sha'dy
shaft
shaft'ed
shaft'ing
shag
shag'giness
shag'gy
shagreen'
shah
shake
sha'ken
sha'ker
Sha'kerism
sha'kier
sha'kiest
sha'kiness
sha'king
shak'o
Shakspe'rian
sha'ky
shale
shall
shalloon'
shal'lop
shallot', shalot'
shal'low
shal'lower
shal'lowness
shalt
sha'ly
sham
sha'man
Sha'manism
sham'ble
sham'bled
sham'bling
shame
shamed
shame'faced
shame'ful
shame'fully
shame'less
shame'lessness
sha'ming
shammed
sham'mer
sham'ming
sham'my
shampoo'
shampooed'
shampoo'er
shampoo'ing
sham'rock
shan'dygaff
shank
shanked
shank'er
shank'ing

shan't
shan'ty
shape
shaped
shape'less
shape'liness
shape'ly
sha'ping
shard
share
shared
share'holder
shar'er
sha'ring
shark
sharked
shark'er
shark'ing
sharp
sharped
sharp'-edged
sharp'en
sharp'ened
sharp'ening
sharp'er
sharp'est
sharp'ing
sharp'ly
sharp'ness
sharp'-set
sharp'shooter
sharp-sight'ed
sharp-wit'ted
shas'ter
shat'ter
shat'tered
shatt'ering
shat'ters
shat'tery
shave
shaved
shave'ling
sha'ven
sha'ver
shav'ing
shav'ing-brush
shawl
shawm
she
sheaf
shear
sheared
shear'er
shear'ing
shear'man
shears
shear'-steel
shear'water
sheat'-fish
sheath
sheathe
sheathed
sheath'er
sheath'ing
sheath'y
sheave
shebeen'
Shechi'nah

shed
shed'der
shed'ding
sheen
sheen'y
sheep
sheep'-cot
sheep'-dog
sheep'fold
sheep'-hook
sheep'ish
sheep'ishly
sheep'ishness
sheep'-pen
sheep'-run
sheep's'-eye
sheep'skin
sheep'-stealer
sheep'-stealing
sheer
sheered
sheer'-hulk
sheer'ing
sheers
sheer'water
sheet
sheet'-anchor
sheet'ing
sheets
sheik, sheikh
shek'el
Sheki'nah
shel'drake
shel'duck
shelf
shelf'y
shell
shellac', shell'-lac
shelled
shell'-fish
shell'ing
shell'work
shell'y
shel'ter
shel'tered
shel'tering
shel'terless
shel'tie, shel'ty
shelve
shelved
shelves
shelv'ing
shelv'y
Shem'ite
Shemit'ic
She'ol
shep'herd
shep'herdess
sher'bet
sherd
shereef', -rif'
sher'iff
sher'ry
shew
shi'ah

shib'boleth
shie
shield
shield'ed
shield'ing
shield'less
shift
shift'ed
shift'er
shift'ier
shift'iest
shift'ing
shift'less
shift'y
Shi'ite
{ shille'la(g)h
{ shilla'lah
shil'ling
shil'ly-shally
Shi'loh
shi'ly
shim'mer
shim'mered
shim'mering
shin
shin'dy
shine
shined
shi'ner
shi'ness
shin'gle
shin'gled
shin'gles
shin'gling
shin'gly
shi'nier
shi'niest
shi'ning
Shinto
shi'ny
ship
ship'board
ship'-builder
or
ship'-*building*
ship'-carpenter
ship'-chandler
ship'master
ship'mate
ship'ment
ship'-money
ship'-*own*er
shipped
ship'per
ship'ping
ship'shape
ship'wreck
ship'wrecked
ship'wright
ship'yard
shire
shire'-town
shirk
shirked
shirk'ing
shirt

shirt'ed
shirt'ing
shirt'less
shit'tah
shive
shiv'er
shiv'ered
shiv'ering
shiv'ery
shoad
shoal
shoal'iness
shoal'y
shoar
shoat
shock
shocked
shock'-headed
shock'ing
shod
shod'dy
shoe
shoe'black
shoe'ing
shoe'-leather
shoe'less
shoe'maker
shoe'making
sho'er
shoe'-string
shone
shook
shoon
shoot
shoot'er
shoot'ing
shoot'ing-star
shop
shop'keeper
shop'lifter
shop'man
shop'ping
shop'walker
shop'-woman
shore
shored
shore'less
shor'ing
shorl
shorn
short
*short'*coming
short'en
short'ened
short'ener
short'ening
short'er
*short'*est
short'hand
short-han'ded
*short'*horn
*short'*horned
short'-lived
*short'*ly
*short'*ness
shorts
short-sight'ed
short-sight'ed-ness
shot
shote

shot'free
shot'ten
should
shoul'der
shoul'der-belt
shoul'der-blade
shoul'dered
shoul'dering
shoul'der-knot
shout
shout'ed
shout'er
shout'ing
shove
shoved
shov'el
shov'elful
shov'elled / shov'eled
shov'eller / shov'eler
shov'elling / shov'eling
shov'ing
show
show'-bill
show'bread
show'-case
showed
show'er
show'er
show'er-bath
show'ered
show'ering
show'erless
show'ery
show'ily
show'iness
show'ing
show'man
shown
show'room
show'y
shrank
shrap'nel
shred
shred'ded
shred'ding
shrew
shrewd
shrewd'ly
shrewd'ness
shrew'ish
shrew'-mole
shrew'-mouse
shriek
shrieked
shriek'ing
shriev'alty
shrift
shrike
shrill
shrill'ness
shril'ly
shrimp
shrimp'ing
shrine
shrink

shrink'age
shrink'er
shrink'ing
shrive
shrived
shriv'el
shriv'elled
shriv'elling
shriv'en
shri'ving
shroff
shroff'age
shroud
shroud'ed
shroud'ing
Shrove'tide
Shrove Tues'day
shrub
shrub'bery
shrub'biness
shrub'by
shrug
shrugged
shrug'ging
shrunk
shrunk'en
shud'der
shud'dered
shud'dering
shuf'fle
shuf'fled
shuf'fler
shuf'fling
shu'mac
shun
shunned
shun'ning
shunt
shunt'ed
shunt'er
shunt'ing
shut
shut'ter
shut'ting
shut'tle
shut'tlecock
shwan'pan
shy
shy'er
shy'est
shy'ing
shy'ly
shy'ness
si
sial'agogue
Siamese'
Sibe'rian
sib'ilance
sib'ilancy
sib'ilant
sibila'tion
sib'yl
sib'ylline
sic, sic'ca
sic'cative
sic'city
sice
Sicil'ian
sick

sick'-bed
sick'en
sick'ened
sick'ening
sick'ish
sick'le
sick'led
sick'lewort
sick'lied
sick'liness
sick'-list
sick'ly
sick'ness
sick'-room
side
side'board
si'ded
side'ling
side'long
si'deral
side'real
sid'erite
siderog'raphy
sid'eroscope
side'-saddle
side'-table
side'walk
side'wise
si'di
si'ding
si'dle
si'dled
si'dling
siege
sieg'ing
si'enite
sien'na
sier'ra
sies'ta
sieve
sift
sift'ed
sift'er
sift'ing
sigh
sighed
sigh'er
sigh'ing
sight
sighted
sight'ing
sight'less
sight'lessness
sight'liness
sight'ly
sight'-seeing
sight'-seer
sig'il
sigilla'ria
sig'moid
sigmoid'al
sign
sig'nal
sig'nalize
sig'nalized
sig'nalizing
{ sig'nalled
{ sig'naled
{ sig'naller
{ sig'naler
{ sig'nalling
{ sig'naling
sig'nally
sig'nalman
sig'natory
sig'nature
sign'-board
signed
sign'er
sig'net
signif'icance
signif'icancy
signif'icant
signif'icantly
significa'tion
signif'icative
sig'nificator
signif'icatory
{ *sig'nified*
{ *sig'nify*
*sig'nify*ing
sign'ing
si'gnior
sign'-manual
si'gnor
signo'ra
signori'na
si'gnory
sign'-painter
sign'-post
Sikh
si'lence
si'lenced
si'lencer
si'lencing
si'lent
si'lently
sile'sia
Sile'sian
si'lex
silhouette'
sil'ica
sil'icate
sil'icated
sili'ceous
silicif'erous
silic'ified
silic'ify
silic'ifying
sili'cium
sil'icle
sil'icon
silic'ulose
sil'iqua
sil'iquiform
sil'iquose
silk
silk'en
silk'iness
silk'worm
silk'y
sill
sil'labub, syl'la- [bub
Sil'lery
sil'lier
sil'liest
sil'lily
sil'liness
sillom'eter
sil'lon
sil'ly
si'lo
silt
silt'ed
silt'ing
Silu'rian
silu'ridan
sil'va
sil'van
sil'ver
sil'vered
sil'verer
sil'ver-grey
sil'vering
sil'verling
sil'versmith
sil'ver-stick
sil'ver-tree
sil'very
simar'
simaru'ba
sim'ia
sim'ian
sim'ilar
similar'ity
sim'ilarly
sim'ile
simil'itude
sim'ilor
sim'ious
sim'itar
sim'mer
sim'mered
sim'mering
simo'niac
simoni'acal
Simo'nian
sim'ony
simoom'
simoon'
si'mous
sim'per
sim'pered
sim'perer
sim'pering
sim'ple
sim'ple-minded
simple-mind'edness
sim'pleness
sim'pler
sim'plest
sim'pleton
simplic'ity
simplifica'tion
sim'plified
sim'plify
sim'plifying
sim'ply
simula'crum

sim'ulate
sim'ulated
sim'ulating
simula'tion
simulta'neous
simulta'neously
sin
Sinait'ic
Sina'pis
sin'apism
since
sincere'
sincere'ly
sincer'ity
sincip'ital
sin'ciput
sin'don
sine
si'necural
si'necure
si'necurism
si'necurist
si'ne di'e
si'ne quâ non'
sin'ew
sin'ewed
sin'ewy
sinfo'nia
sin'ful
sin'fully
sin'fulness
sing
singe
singed
singe'ing
sing'er
sing'er
Singhalese'
sing'ing
sing'ing-book
sing'ing-master
sing'ing-*school*
sin'gle
sin'gled
sin'gle-handed
sin'gle-hearted
sin'gle-minded
single-mind'ed-ness
sin'gleness
sin'gle-stick
sin'gling
sin'gly
sing'song
sin'gular
singular'ity
sin'gularly
sin'ical
sin'ister
sin'istral
sin'istrous
sink
sink'er
sink'-hole
sink'ing
sink'ing-fund
sin'less
sin'lessness
sinned

sin'ner
sin'net
sin'ning
sin'-offering
sin'ter
Sin'too
sin'uate
sin'uated
sin'uating
sinua'tion
sin'uose
sinuos'ity
sin'uous
si'nus
sip
si'phon
siphon'ic
siphon'ifer
siphonif'erous
si'phuncle
siphun'cular
sipped
sip'ping
sir
sir'car *or* sir'kar
sir'dar
sire
si'ren
sirene'
siri'asis
Sir'ius
sir'loin
siroc'co
sir'rah
sir'up
sir'upy
sis'kin
sis'ter
sis'terhood
sis'ter-in-law
sis'terly
Sis'tine
sis'trum
Sisyph'ean
sit
site
sith
sithe
sitol'ogy
sit'ter
sit'ting
sit'ting-room
sit'uate
sit'uated
situa'tion
sitz'-bath
Si'vaism
Sivan'
six
six'fold
six'pence
six'penny
six'score
sixteen
sixteenth
sixth
sixth'ly
six'tieth
six'ty
si'zable

si'zar
size
size'able
sized
siz'el
si'zer
si'zing
si'zy
sjam'bok
skald
skate
skat'ed
ska'ter
ska'ting
skedad'dle
skeet
skeg
skein
skel'eton
skep'tic
sker'ry
sketch
sketch'-book
sketched
sketch'er
sketch'ily
sketch'ing
sketch'y
skew
skew'-back
skew'-bridge
skewed
skew'er
ski
skid
skid'ded
skid'ding
skiff
ski'-ing
skil'ful
skil'fully
skil'fulness
skill
skilled
skil'let
skil'ling
skil'ly
skim
skimmed
skim'mer
skim'-milk
skim'ming
skim'mington
skin
skin'-deep
skin'flint
skin'ful
skink
skinned
skin'ner
skin'nier
skin'niest
skin'ning
skin'niness
skin'ny
skip

skipped
skip'per
skip'ping
skir'mish
skir'mished
skir'misher
skir'mishing
skir'ret
skirt
skirt'ed
skirt'ing
skirt'ing-board
skit
skit'tish
skit'tishly
skit'tle-alley
skit'tles
ski'ver
skow
skulk
skulked
skulk'er
skulk'ing
skull
skull'cap
skunk
skur'ry
sky
sky'-blue
sky'ey
sky'-high
sky'ish
sky'lark
sky'larking
sky'light
sky'-rocket
sky'-sail
sky'-scraper
slab
slab'ber
slab'bered
slab'berer
slab'bering
slab'biness
slab'by
slack
slacked
slack'en
slack'ened
slack'ening
slack'ing
slack'ly
slack'ness
slag
slag'gy
slaie
slain
slake
slaked
slake'less
sla'king
slam
slammed
slam'ming
slan'der
slan'dered
slan'derer
slan'dering
slan'derous
slan'derously
slang
slanged
slang'ing
slang'y
slant
slant'ed
slant'ing
slant'ingly
slant'wise
slap
slap'-dash
slapped
slap'ping
slash
slashed
slash'er
slash'ing
slat
slatch
slate
sla'ted
slate'-pencil
sla'ter
sla'ting
slat'tern
slat'ternliness
slat'ternly
sla'ty
slaugh'ter
slaugh'terer
slaugh'ter-house
slaugh'tering
slaugh'terous
Slav
slave
slaved
slave'-driver
slave'holder
slave'holding
slave'-*owner*
sla'ver
slav'er
slav'ered
slav'erer
slav'ering
sla'very
slave'-ship
slave'-*trade*
sla'ving
sla'vish
sla'vishly
sla'vishness
Slavon'ic
slay
slay'er
slay'ing
sleave
slea'zy, slee'zy
sled
sled'ded
sled'ding
sledge
sledge'-hammer
sleek
sleeked
sleek'ing
sleek'ly
sleek'ness
sleep
sleep'er
sleep'ier
sleep'iest
sleep'ily
sleep'iness
sleep'ing
sleep'less
sleep'lessness
sleep'-walker
sleep'-walking
sleep'y
sleet
sleet'iness
sleet'y
sleeve
sleeve'-link
sleigh
sleigh'-bell
sleigh'ing
sleight
slen'der
slen'derly
slen'derness
slept
sleuth
sleuth'-hound
slew
sley
slice
sliced
sli'cer
sli'cing
slick
slid
slid'der
slide
sli'der
sli'ding
sli'ding-scale
slight
slight'ed
slight'er
slight'est
slight'ing
slight'ingly
slight'ly
slight'ness
sli'ly
slim
slime
slimed
sli'miness
sli'ming
slim'ness
sli'my
sling
sling'er
sling'ing
slink
slink'ing

slip
slip'-knot
slipped
slip'per
slip'periness
slip'pery
slip'ping
slip'shod
slip'-slop
slit
slit'ter
slit'ting
slit'ting-mill
sliv'er
sloam
sloat
slob'ber
slob'bered
slob'berer
slob'bering
sloe
slog
slo'gan
slogged
slog'ger
slog'ging
sloid, sloyd
sloop
slop
slop'-basin
slope
sloped
slo'ping
slop'-pail
slopped
slop'piness
slop'ping
slop'py
slop'-shop
slosh
slosh'y
slot
sloth
sloth'ful
sloth'fully
sloth'fulness
slot'ted
slot'ting
slouch
slouched
slouch'hat
slouch'ing
slough (a bog)
slough (a cast [skin)
sloughed
slough'ing
slough'y
slough'y
slov'en
slov'enliness
slov'enly
slow
slow'ly
slow'ness
slow'-worm
slub
slub'ber
slub'bered
slub'bering
sludge
slue
slued
slug
slug'gard
slug'gish
slug'gishly
slug'gishness
sluice
slui'cy
slu'ing
slum
slum'ber
slum'bered
slum'berer
slum'bering
slum'berous
slum'ming
slump
slung
slunk
slur
slurred
slur'ring
slush
slush'y
slut
slut'tish
slut'tishly
sly
sly'-boots
sly'ly
sly'ness
smack
smacked
smack'ing
small
small'age
small'-arms
small'er
small'ness
small'pox
smalt
smalt'ine
smarag'dine
smarag'dite
smart
smart'ed
smart'en
smart'ened
smart'ening
smart'er
smart'est
smart'ing
smart'ly
smart'-money
smart'ness
smash
smashed
smash'er
smash'ing
smat'ter
smat'tered
smat'terer
smat'tering
smear
smeared
smear'ing
smear'y
smec'tite
smell
smelled
smell'er
smell'ing
smell'ing-bottle
smell'ing-salts
smell'-less
smelt
smelt'ed
smelt'er
smelt'ery
smelt'ing
smew
smick'er
smil'acin
smile
smiled
smi'ler
smi'ling
smi'lingly
smirch
smirched
smirch'ing
smirk
smirk'ing
smit
smite
smi'ter
smith
smith'ery
smith'ing
smith'y
smi'ting
smitt
smit'ten
smock
smock'-frock
smoke
smoked
smoke'less
smo'ker
smo'kier
smo'kiest
smo'kily
smo'kiness
smo'king
smo'ky
smooth
smoothed
smooth'er
smooth'-faced
smooth'ing
smooth'ly
smooth'ness
smorzan'do
smorza'to
smote
smoth'er
smoth'ered
smoth'ering
smoul'der

smoul'dered
smoul'dering
smoul'dry
smudge
smudged
smudg'ing
smug
smug'gle
smug'gled
smug'gler
smug'gling
smut
smutch
smutched
smutch'ing
smut'ted
smut'tily
smut'tiness
smut'ting
smut'ty
snack
snaf'fle
snaf'fled
snaf'fling
snag
snag'gy
snail
snail'-like
snail'-shell
snake
snake'-root
snake'-stone
snake'-wood
sna'kish
sna'ky
snap
snap'dragon
snap'-shot
snapped
snap'per
snap'ping
snap'pish
snap'pishly
snapt
snare
snared
snar'er
snar'ing
snarl
snarled
snarl'er
snarl'ing
snar'y
snatch
snatched
snatch'er
snatch'ing
snatch'ingly
snath
sneak
sneaked
sneak'er
sneak'ier
sneak'iest
sneak'ing
sneak'ingly
sneak'-up
sneak'y
sneer

sneered
sneer'er
sneer'ing
sneer'ingly
sneeze
sneezed
sneez'ing
snick
snick'er
snick'ered
snick'ering
sniff
sniffed
sniff'ing
snif'fle
snig'ger
snig'gered
snig'gering
snig'gle
snig'gled
snig'gling
snip
snipe
snipped
snip'ping
snip'-snap
sniv'el
sniv'el(l)ed
sniv'el(l)er
sniv'el(l)ing
snob
snob'bery
snob'bish
snob'bishly
snood
snooze
snore
snored
snor'er
snor'ing
snort
snort'ed
snort'er
snort'ing
snot
snot'ter
snout
snow
snow'ball
snow'bird
snow'blind
snow'-drift
snow'-drop
snowed
snow'flake
snow'ing
snow'-shoe
snow'slip
snow'-storm
snow'-white
snow'y
snub
snubbed
snub'bing
snuff
snuff'-box
snuffed
snuff'ers
snuff'ing
snuf'fle

snuf'fled
snuf'fles
snuf'fling
snuff'-taker
snuff'y
snug
snugged
snug'gery
snug'ging
snug'gle
snug'gled
snug'gling
snug'ly
so
soak
soak'age
soaked
soak'er
soak'ing
soap
soap'-bubble
soaped
soap'ier
soap'iest
soap'ing
soap'-stone
soap'-suds
soap'wort
soap'y
soar
soared
soar'ing
sob
sobbed
sob'bing
so'ber
so'bered
so'bering
so'berly
so'berness
sobri'ety
so'briquet
soc
soc'age
so'-called
sociabil'ity
so'ciable
so'ciably
so'cial
so'cialism
so'cialist
socialist'ic
social'ity
so'cialize
so'cialized
so'cializing
so'cially
soci'ety
Socin'ian
Socin'ianism
sociolog'ic
sociolog'ical
sociol'ogist
sociol'ogy
sock
sock'et
so'cle

soc'man
Soc'otrine
Socrat'ic
Socrat'ical
Socrat'ically
Soc'ratism
sod
so'da
so'dalite
sodal'ity
so'da-water
sod'ded
sod'den
sod'ding
sod'dy
so'dium
sod'omy
soev'er
so'fa
sof'fit
sof'ism
soft
sof'ten
sof'tened
sof'tener
sof'tening
soft'ly
soft'ness
sog'gy
soho
soi-disant'
soil
soiled
soil'ing
soirée'
soj'ourn
soj'ourned
soj'ourner
soj'ourning
soke
Sol
so'la
sol'ace
sol'aced
sol'acement
sol'acing
solana'ceous
solan'der
so'lan-goose
sol'anine
sola'no
so'lar
sola'rium
solariza'tion
so'larize
so'larized
so'larizing
sola'tium
sold
sol'dan
sol'der
sol'dered
sol'derer
sol'dering
sol'dier
sol'diering
sol'dierly
sol'diery
sole
sol'ecism
sol'ecist
solecis'tic
sol'ecize
soled
sole'ly
sol'emn
sol'emness
solem'nity
solemniza'tion
sol'emnize
sol'emnized
sol'emnizer
sol'emnizing
sol'emnly
so'len
so'lenite
so'lenoid
sol'-fa
sol'-faing
solfana'ria
solfata'ra
solic'it
solic'itant
solicita'tion
solic'ited
solic'iting
solic'itor
solic'itor- *gen'eral*
solic'itous
solic'itously
solic'itude
sol'id
solidar'ity
solidifica'tion
solid'ified
solid'ify
solid'ifying
sol'idism
sol'idist
solid'ity
sol'idly
solidun'gulous
solifid'ian
solifid'ianism
solil'oquize
solil'oquized
solil'oquizing
solil'oquy
sol'iped
sol'ipede
solip'edous
solitaire'
solita'rian
sol'itarily
sol'itariness
sol'itary
sol'itude
soliv'agant
solmiza'tion
so'lo
so'loist
Sol'omon's-seal
sol'stice
solsti'tial
solubil'ity
sol'uble
so'lus
solute'
solu'tion
solvabil'ity
solv'able
solve
solved
solv'ency
solv'end
solv'ent
solv'er
solv'ing
somatol'ogy
somatot'omy
som'bre, somber
som'breness
som'brous
some
some'body
some'*how*
some'one
som'ersault
som'erset
some'thing
some'time
some'times
some'what
some'where
so'mite
somnambula'-tion
somnam'bulator
somnam'bulism
somnam'bulist
somnif'erous
somnif'ic
somnil'oquence
somnil'oquism
somnil'oquist
somnip'athy
som'nolence
som'nolency
som'nolent
son
so'nance
so'nant
sona'ta
sonati'na
song
song'ster
song'stress
sonif'erous
son'-in-law
son'net
sonneteer'
son'neting

Son'nite
sonom'eter
sonorif'ic
sono'rous
sono'rously
son'ship
Soo'der
Soo'dra
soo'fee
soo'feeism
soon
soo'nee
soon'er
soot
soot'ed
sooth
soothe
soothed
sooth'er
sooth'ing
sooth'ingly
sooth'say
sooth'sayer
sooth'saying
soot'ier
soot'iest
soot'iness
soot'y
sop
soph
so'phi
soph'ism
soph'ist
sophis'tic
sophis'tical
sophis'ticate
sophis'ticated
sophis'ticating
sophistica'tion
sophis'ticator
soph'istry
soph'omore
sophomor'ic
soporif'erous
soporif'ic
so'porous
sopped
sop'ping
sopra'nist
sopra'no
sorb
Sor'bonist
Sorbonne'
sor'cerer
sor'ceress
sor'cerous
sor'cery
sor'des
sor'did
sor'didly
sor'didness
sor'dine
sore
sore'ly
sore'ness
sor'er
sor'est

sor'go
sori'tes
sorn
sorned
sorn'er
sorn'ing
soro'sis
sor'rel
sor'rier
sor'riest
sor'rily
sor'row
sor'rowed
sor'rowful
sor'rowfully
sor'rowing
sor'ry
sort
sort'able
sort'ed
sort'er
sor'tie
sor'tilege
sortile'gious
sort'ing
so'-so
sospi'ro
sostenu'to
sot
soteriol'ogy
so'thic
sot'tish
sot'tishness
sot'to vo'ce
sou
soubrette'
souchong'
soufflé'
souf'fle
sough
sought
soul
soul'ful
soul'fully
soul'fulness
soul'less
soul'lessly
soul'lessness
soul'-stirring
sound
sound'board
sound'ed
sound'er
sound'est
sound'ing
sound'ing-board
sound'ings
sound'less
sound'ly
sound'ness
soup
soupçon'
sour
source
soured
sour'ing
sour'ish
sour'krout-crout
sour'ly

sour'ness
sous
souse
soused
sous'ing
soutane'
sou'terrain
south
Southcott'ian
South'down
south-east'
south-east'er
south-east'erly
south-east'ern
south'erly
south'ern
south'erner
south'ing
south'*most*
south'ron
south'ward
south-west'
south-west'er
south-west'erly
south-west'ern
souvenir'
sov'ereign
sov'ereignty
sow (pig)
sow (to scatter)
sowar'
sow'bread
sowed
sow'ens
sow'er
sow'ing
sown
soy
spa
space
spaced
spac'ing
spa'cious
spa'ciously
spa'ciousness
spad'dle
spade
spade'ful
spadi'ceous
spadille'
spa'dix
spado'ne
spa'hi
spake
spall
spalt
span
span'drel
span'gle
span'gled
span'gler
span'gling
Span'iard
span'iel
Span'ish
spank

spanked
spank'er
spank'ing
spanned
span'ner
span'ning
spar
spare
spared
spare'ness
spa'rer
spare'rib
sparge
spa'ring
spa'ringly
spark
spark'le
spark'led
spark'ler
spark'ling
spark'lingly
spar'ling
spa'roid
sparred
spar'ring
spar'row
spar'row-hawk
spar'ry
sparse
sparse'ly
sparse'ness
Spar'tan
spasm
spasmod'ic
spasmod'ical
spasmod'ically
spasmol'ogy
spas'tic
spastic'ity
spat
spatha'ceous
spathe
spath'ic
spath'iform
spat'ter
spat'terdashes
spat'tered
spat'tering
spat'ula
spat'ulate
spav'in
spav'ined
spawn
spawned
spawn'er
spawn'ing
spay
spayed
spay'ing
speak
speak'able
speak'er
speak'ing
speak'ing-trumpet
speak'ing-tube
spear
speared
spear'ing
spear'mint
spear'wort
spe'cial
spe'cialist
special'ity
spe'cialize
spe'cialized
spe'cially
spe'cialty
spe'cie
spe'cies
specif'ic
specif'ical
specif'ically
specifica'tion
specif'icness
spec'ified
spec'ify
spec'ifying
spec'imen
spe'cious
spe'ciously
speck
specked
speck'ing
speck'le
speck'led
speck'ling
spec'tacle
spec'tacled
spec'tacles
spectac'ular
specta'tor
spectato'rial
specta'tress
specta'trix
spec'tral
spec'tre
spec'troscope
spec'trum
spec'ular
spec'ulate
spec'ulated
spec'ulating
specula'tion
spec'ulative
spec'ulator
spec'ulatory
spec'ulum
sped
speech
speech'ified
speech'ify
speech'ifying
speech'less
speed
speed'ily
speed'ing
speed'well
speed'y
speiss
spell
spell'-bound
spelled
spell'er
spell'ing
spell'ing-book
spelt
spel'ter
spen'cer
spend
spend'er
spend'ing
spend'thrift
Spense'rian
spent
sperm
spermace'ti
spermat'ic
spermatozo'a
spew
spewed
spew'er
spew'ing
sphac'elate
sphacela'tion
sphac'elus
sphag'nous
sphene
sphe'noid
sphenoid'al
sphere
sphered
spher'ic
spher'ical
spher'ically
spheric'ity
spher'icle
spher'ics
sphe'ring
sphe'roid
spheroi'dal
spherom'eter
spher'ule
spher'ulite
spher'y
sphinc'ter
sphinx
sphrag'ide
sphragis'tics
sphyg'mic
sphygmom'eter
spi'cate
spi'cated
spicca'to
spice
spiced
spi'cer
spi'cery
spi'cier
spi'ciest
spi'ciness
spi'cing
spick'nel
spic'ular
spic'ulate
spic'ule
spic'uliform
spiculig'enous
spi'cy
spi'der
spig'ot

spike
spiked
spike'let
spike'nard
spi'king
spi'ky
spile
spil'ikin
spill
spilled
spill'er
spill'ing
spilt
spin
spina'ceous
spin'ach
spi'nal
spin'dle
spin'dle-tree
spin'dling
spine
spined
spin'el
spines'cent
spin'et
spinif'erous
spin'naker
spin'ner
spin'neret
spin'nery
spin'ney
spin'ning
spin'ning-jen'ny
spin'ning-wheel
spinos'ity
spi'nous
Spino'zism
Spino'zist
spin'ster
spin'ule
spin'ulous
spi'ny
spir'acle
spi'ral
spi'rally
spi'rant
spira'tion
spire
spir'it
spir'ited
*spir'it*ing
spir'itist
*spir'it*less
spirito'so
spir'itous
*spir'it*ual
*spir'it*ualism
*spir'it*ualist
*spirit*ualis'tic
*spirit*ual'ity
*spirit*ualiza'tion
*spir'it*ualize
*spir'it*ualized
*spir'it*ualizer
*spir'it*ualizing
*spir'it*ually
*spir'it*ualty
spirituelle'

spir'ituous
spirt
spirt'ed
spirt'ing
spir'y
spis'sated
spis'situde
spit
spitch'cock
spite
spi'ted
spite'ful
spite'fully
spite'fulness
spit'fire
spi'ting
spit'ted
spit'ter
spit'ting
spit'tle
spittoon'
splanchnol'ogy
splash
splash'-board
splashed
splash'er
splash'ing
splash'y
splay
splayed
splay'-foot
splay'-footed
spleen
spleen'ish
spleen'y
splen'dent
splen'did
splen'didly
splen'dour,-or
splenet'ic
splenet'ical
splen'ic
spleniza'tion
sple'nocele
splenol'ogy
splice
spliced
spli'cing
splint
splin'ter
splin'tered
splin'tering
splin'tery
split
split'ter
splotch
splotch'y
splut'ter
splut'tered
splut'tering
spod'omancy
spod'umene
spoil
spoiled
spoil'er
spoil'ing
spoilt
spoke

spo'ken
spoke'-shave
spokes'man
spo'liate
spo'liated
spo'liating
spolia'tion
spo'liative
spo'liator
sponda'ic
sponda'ical
spon'dee
spon'dyl-dyle
sponge
sponged
spon'ger
spon'giform
spon'giness
spon'ging
spon'ging-house
spon'giole
spon'giolite
spon'gious
spon'gy
spon'sal
spon'sion
spon'sor
sponso'rial
spontane'ity
sponta'neous
sponta'neously
spontoon'
spook
spool
spoon
spoon'bill
spoon'drift
spoon'ful
spoon'-meat
spoon'y
spoor
sporad'ic
spore
spor'ran
sport
sport'ed
sport'ful
sport'fully
sport'fulness
sport'ing
sport'ive
sport'iveness
sports'man
spor'ule
sporulif'erous
spot
spot'less
spot'lessness
spot'ted
spot'ter
spot'tiness
spot'ting
spot'ty
spou'sal
spouse
spouse'less
spout
spout'ed
spout'er

spout'ing
sprack
sprag
sprain
sprained
sprain'ing
sprang
sprat
sprawl
sprawled
sprawl'er
sprawl'ing
spray
spray'er
spread
spread'er
spread'ing
spree
sprent
sprig
sprigged
sprig'ging
sprig'gy
spright'liness
spright'ly
spring
spring'bok
springe
spring'er
spring'-halt
spring'iness
spring'ing
spring'-tide
spring'-time
spring'y
sprin'kle
sprin'kled
sprin'kler
sprin'kling
sprint
sprit
sprite
sprit'sail
sprod
sprout
sprout'ed
sprout'ing
spruce
spruced
spruce'ly
spruce'ness
spru'cing
sprung
sprunt
spry
spud
spue
spume
spumed
spumes'cence
spumif'erous
spu'miness
spu'ming
spu'mous
spun
spunge
spunk
spur
spur'gall

spurge
spu'rious
spu'riously
spu'riousness
spur'ling
spurn
spurned
spurn'er
spurn'ing
spurred
spur'rer
spur'rier
spur'ring
spur'royal
spur'ry
spurt
spurt'ed
spurt'ing
sput'ter
sput'tered
sput'terer
sput'tering
spu'tum
spy
spy'-glass
spy'ing
squab
squab'bish
squab'ble
squab'bled
squab'bler
squab'bling
squab'by
squad
squad'ron
squal'id
squalid'ity
squal'idness
squall
squalled
squall'er
squall'ing
squall'y
squa'loid
squal'or
squa'ma
squama'ceous
squa'miform
squamig'erous
squa'mipen
squa'moid
squa'mous
squan'der
squan'dered
squan'derer
squan'dering
square
squared
square'ly
square'ness
squar'er
square'-rigged
squar'ing
squar'ish
squar'rous
squash
squashed

squash'er
squash'ing
squash'y
squat
squat'ted
squat'ter
squat'ting
squaw
squawk
squawked
squawk'er
squawk'ing
squeak
squeaked
squeak'er
squeak'ing
squeak'y
squeal
squealed
squeal'ing
squeam'ish
squeam'ishly
squeam'ishness
squee'gee
squeez'able
squeeze
squeezed
squeez'er
squeez'ing
squelch
squib
squib'bing
squid
squill
squint
squint'ed
squint'er
squint'-eyed
squint'ing
squire
squire'archy
squireen'
squire'ship
squirm
squirmed
squirm'ing
squir'rel
squirt
squirt'ed
squirt'ing
stab
Sta'bat Ma'ter
stabbed
stab'ber
stab'bing
stabil'ity
sta'bilizator
sta'ble
sta'bled
sta'ble-keeper
sta'bleness
sta'bling
stab'lish
sta'bly
stacca'to

stack
stacked
stack'er
stack'ing
stac'te
stad'dle
sta'dia
sta'dium
stadt'holder
stadt'holderate
staff
stag
stage
stage'-coach
stage'-player
sta'ger
stage'-struck
sta'gey
stag'ger
stag'gered
stag'gering
stag'hound
sta'ging
stag'irite
stag'nancy
stag'nant
stag'nate
stag'nated
stag'nating
stagna'tion
staid
stain
stained
stain'er
stain'ing
stain'less
stain'lessness
stair
stair'case
stair'-rod
stair'way
staith(e)
stake
staked
stake'holder
sta'king
stalac'tic
stalac'tiform
stal'actite
stalactit'ic
stal'agmite
stalagmit'ic
stal'der
stale
stale'mate
stale'ness
stalk
stalked
stalk'er
stalk'ing
stalk'less
stalk'y
stall
stall'age
stalled
stall'-fed
stall'-feed
stall'-feeding
stall'ing
stal'lion
stal'wart
sta'men
stam'ina
stam'inal
stam'inate, *adj.*
stam'inate, *v.*
stamin'eous
staminif'erous
stam'mer
stam'mered
stam'merer
stam'mering
stamp
stamped
stampede'
stamp'er
stamp'ing
stanch
stanched
stanch'ing
stan'chion
stanch'less
stand
stand'ard
stand'ard-bearer
standardiza'tion
stand'ardize
stand'ardized
stand'ardizing
stand'er
stand'ing
stand'ish
stand'point
stand'still
stang
stan'hope
stank
stan'nary
stan'nate
stan'nic
stannif'erous
stann'yel
stan'za
stanza'ic
sta'pes
staph'yline
staphylo'ma
sta'ple
sta'pled
sta'pler
star
star'board
starch
Star'-Chamber
starched
starch'er
starch'ing
starch'y
stare
stared
star'er
star'fish
star'-flower
star'-gazer
star'-gazing
star'ing
stark
star'less
star'light
star'like
star'ling
star'lit
star'ost
star'osty
starred
star'riness
star'ring
star'ry
star'-spangled
start
start'ed
start'er
start'ful
start'ing
start'ing-point
start'ing-post
start'le
start'led
start'ling
starva'tion
starve
starved
starve'ling
starv'ing
star'wort
state
state'craft
sta'ted
sta'tedly
state'hood
state'lier
state'liest
state'liness
state'ly
state'ment
sta'ter
state'room
States' *Gen'eral*
states'man
states'manlike
states'manship
stat'ic
stat'ical
stat'ics
sta'ting
sta'tion
sta'tional
sta'tionary
sta'tioned
sta'tioner
sta'tionery
sta'tioning
sta'tist
statis'tic
statis'tical
statis'tically
statisti'cian
statis'tics
sta'tive
stat'uary
stat'ue
stat'ued
statuesque'
statuette'
stat'ure

sta'tus
stat'utable
stat'ute
stat'ute-book
stat'utory
staunch
stau'rolite
stau'rotypous
stave
staved
sta'ving
stay
stayed
stay'er
stay'ing
stay'lace
stay'maker
stays
stay'sail
stead
stead'fast, sted'-[fast
stead'fastly
stead'fastness
stead'ied
stead'ier
stead'iest
stead'ily
stead'iness
stead'y
stead'ying
steak
steal
steal'er
steal'ing
stealth
stealth'ily
stealth'iness
stealth'y
steam
steam'boat
steamed
steam'-engine
steam'er
steam'-gauge
steam'-gun
steam'-hammer
steam'ing
steam'-pipe
steam'-ship
steam'-tug
steam'y
ste'arate
stear'ic
ste'arin
ste'atite
steatit'ic
steatom'atous
steed
steel
steeled
steel'er
steel'iness
steel'ing
steel'-plated
steel'y
steel'yard
steen'ing
steep

steeped
steep'ing
stee'ple
stee'plechase
steep'ness
steep'y
steer
steer'age
steered
steer'er
steer'ing
steers'man
steeve
steeved
steev'ing
steg'anopod
stegnot'ic
stein
ste'la
stel'echite
ste'lene
stel'lar
stel'lary
stel'late
stel'lated
stellif'erous
stel'liform
stel'lion
stel'lular
stelog'raphy
stem
stem'less
stemmed
stem'ming
stem'ple
stench
sten'cil
sten'cilled / sten'ciled
sten'cilling / sten'ciling
stenog'rapher
stenograph'ic
stenograph'ical
stenog'raphist
stenog'raphy
sten'otype
sten'otypy
sten'tor
stento'rian
step
step'brother
step'*child*
step'-dame
step'-daughter
step'father
stephano'tis
step'mother
steppe
stepped
step'per
step'ping
step'ping-stone
step'sister
step'son
stept
stercora'ceous

ster'corary
sterco'rianism
stere
ster'eo
stereograph'ic
stereog'raphy
stereom'eter
stereomet'ric
stereom'etry
stereop'ticon
ster'eoscope
stereoscop'ic
stereos'copist
stereot'omy
ster'eotype
ster'eotyped
ster'eotyper
stereotyp'ic
ster'eotyping
stereotypog'raphy
ster'ile
steril'ity
ster'ilize
ster'ling
stern
ster'nal
stern'-board
stern'-chase
stern'er
stern'est
stern'ly
stern'*most*
stern'ness
sternocos'tal
stern'-post
stern'-sheets
ster'num
sternuta'tion
sternu'tative
sternu'tatory
ster'torous
stet
stethom'eter
steth'oscope
stethoscop'ic
ste'vedore
stew
stew'ard
stew'ardess
stew'ardship
stewed
stew'ing
sthen'ic
st'b'ial
stib'iated
stib'ious
stib'ium
stich
stich'ic
stich'omancy
stichom'etry
stick
stick'er
stick'iness
stick'ing
stick'le
stick'leback

stick'led
stick'ler
stick'ling
stick'y
stiff
stiff'en
stiff'ened
stiff'ening
stiff'er
stiff'ly
stiff'-neck
stiff'-necked
stiff'ness
sti'fle
sti'fled
sti'fling
stig'ma
Stigma'ria
stig'mata
stigmat'ic
stigmat'ical
stig'matize
stig'matized
stig'matizing
sti'lar
stil'bite
stile
stilet'to
still
stil'lage
still'-born
stilled
still'er
still'ing
still'life
still'ness
still'-room
stil'ly
stilt
stilt'ed
stilt'ing
Stil'ton
stilt'y
stim'ulant
stim'ulate
stim'ulated
stim'ulating
stimula'tion
stim'ulative
stim'ulator
stim'ulus
sting
sting'er
stin'gier
stin'giest
stin'gily
stin'giness
sting'ing
sting'less
stin'go
stin'gy
sting'y
stink
stink'ard
stink'er
stink'ing
stint
stint'ed
stint'er

stint'ing
stipe
sti'pend
stipend'iary
stip'ple
stip'pled
stip'pling
stipula'ceous
stip'ular
stip'ulary
stip'ulate, *adj.*
stip'ulate, *v.*
stip'ulated
stip'ulating
stip'ulation
stip'ulator
stip'ule
stip'uled
stir
stirk
stirred
stir'rer
stir'ring
stir'rup
stitch
stitched
stitch'er
stitch'ing
stith'y
stive
stived
sti'ver
stiv'ing
stoat
stock
stockade'
stock'-broker
stock'-dove
stocked
stock'-fish
stock'holder
stockinet'
stock'ing
stock-in-*trade*
stock'ish
stock'-jobber
stock'-jobbing
stock'-list
stocks
stock'still
stock'-taking
stock'y
stock'-yard
sto'ic
sto'ical
stoicheiom'etry
sto'icism
stoke
stoked
stoke'-hole
sto'ker
sto'king
stole
stoled
sto'len
stol'id
stolid'ity
sto'lon
stom'ach

stom'achal
stom'ached
stom'acher
stomach'ic
stomach'ical
stom'achless
stom'ach-pump
sto'mapod
stone
stone'-blind
stone'-*cold*
stone'crop
stone'-cutter
stoned
stone'-fruit
stone'-mason
sto'ner
stone's'-throw
stone'-still
stone'ware
sto'niness
sto'ning
sto'ny
sto'ny-heart'ed
stood
stook
stool
stoom
stoop
stooped
stoop'er
stoop'ing
stoop'ingly
stop
stop'-cock
stop'gap
stop'page
stopped
stop'per
stop'ping
stop'ple
stop'-watch
stor'age
sto'rax
store
stored
store'house
store'keeper
store'room
store'ship
sto'rey, sto'ry
sto'ried
sto'ring
stork
stork's'-bill
storm
stormed
storm'ier
storm'iest
storm'iness
storm'ing
storm'y
Stor'thing
sto'ry
sto'ry-book
sto'ry-teller

sto'ry-telling
stoup
stour
stout
stout'er
stout'ly
stout'ness
sto'vaine
stove
stow
stow'age
stow'away
stowed
stow'ing
stra'bism
strabis'mus
strad'dle
strad'dled
strad'dling
Stradiva'rius
strag'gle
strag'gled
strag'gler
strag'gling
straight
straight'en
straight'ened
straight'ener
straight'ening
straightfor'ward
straightfor'ward-ness
straight'ly
straight'ness
straight'way
straik
strain
strained
strain'er
strain'ing
strait
strait'en
strait'ened
strait'-jacket
strait'-laced
strait'ly
strait'ness
strait'-waistcoat
strake
stramin'eous
stramo'nium
stram'ony
strand
strand'ed
strand'ing
strange
strange'ly
strange'ness
stran'ger
stran'gle
stran'gled
stran'gles
stran'gling
stran'gulated
strangula'tion
stran'gury
strap

straphang'er
strappa'do
strapped
strap'per
strap'ping
strass
stra'ta
strat'agem
stratarith'metry
strateget'ical
strateg'ic
strateg'ical
strat'egist
strat'egy
strath
strath'spey
stratifica'tion
strat'ified
strat'iform
strat'ify
strat'ifying
stratoc'racy
stratog'raphy
stra'tum
stra'tus
straw
straw'berry
straw'-colour
straw'y
stray
strayed
stray'er
stray'ing
streak
streaked
streak'ing
streak'y
stream
streamed
stream'er
stream'ing
stream'let
stream'y
street
strel'itz
strength
strength'en
strength'ened
strength'ener
strength'ening
strength'less
stren'uous
stren'uously
stren'uousness
stress
stretch
stretched
stretch'er
stretch'ing
strew
strewed
strew'ing
stri'a

stri'ae
stri'ate
stri'ated
stria'tion
strick'en
strick'le
strict
strict'er
strict'est
strict'ly
strict'ness
stric'ture
stric'tured
strid'den
stride
stri'dent
stri'ding
strid'ulous
strife
strig'il
stri'gose
stri'gous
strike
stri'ker
stri'king
stri'kingly
string
string'-board
string'-course
stringed
strin'gency
string'ent
string'er
string'-halt
string'iness
string'ing
string'y
strip
stripe
striped
stri'ping
strip'ling
stripped
strip'per
strip'ping
stript
strive
striv'en
stri'ver
striv'ing
strob'ile
strode
stroke
stroked
stro'ker
strokes'man
stro'king
stroll
strolled
stroll'er
stroll'ing
stromat'ic
strom'bite
strom'bus
strong
stron'ger
stron'gest
strong'hold
strong'ish
strong'ly

strong'minded
strong-mind'ed-ness
strong'room
stron'tia
stron'tian
stron'tianite
stron'tium
strop
stro'phe
stroph'ic
stroph'iolate
stroph'iolated
strove
strow
strowed
strow'ing
strown
struck
struc'tural
struc'ture
strug'gle
strug'gled
strug'gling
strum
stru'ma
strummed
strum'ming
stru'mous
strum'pet
strung
strut
stru'thious
strut'ted
strut'ter
strut'ting
strych'nia
strych'nin,-nine
stub
stubbed
stub'bed
stub'bing
stub'ble
stub'bly
stub'born
stub'bornly
stub'bornness
stub'by
stuc'co
stuc'coed
stuc'coer
stuc'coing
stuck
stuck'-up
stud
stud'ded
stud'ding
stu'dent
stud'ied
stu'dio
stu'dious
stu'diously
stud'y
stud'ying
stu'fa
stuff
stuffed
stuff'er
stuff'ier
stuff'iest
stuff'iness
stuff'ing
stuff'ing-box
stuff'y
stultifica'tion
stul'tified
stul'tifier
stul'tify
stul'tifying
stum
stum'ble
stum'bled
stum'bler
stum'bling
stum'bling-block
stummed
stum'ming
stump
stumped
stump'iness
stump'ing
stump'-orator
stump'-oratory
stump'y
stun
stung
stunk
stunned
stun'ner
stun'ning
stunt
stunt'ed
stunt'ing
stupe
stupefa'cient
stupefac'tion
stupefac'tive
stu'pefied
stu'pefier
stu'pefy
stu'pefying
stupen'dous
stupen'dously
stu'pid
stupid'ity
stu'pidly
stu'por
stu'pose
stu'prate
stupra'tion
stur'dier
stur'diest
stur'dily
stur'diness
stur'dy
stur'geon
sturio'nian
stut'ter
stut'tered
stut'terer
stut'tering
sty
Styg'ian
stylagalma'ic
sty'lar
style
styled
sty'let
sty'liform
sty'ling
sty'lish
sty'lishly
sty'list
sty'lite
sty'lobate
sty'lograph
stylograph'ic
stylog'raphy
sty'loid
sty'lus
styp'tic
styptic'ity
Styx
suabil'ity
su'able
sua'sion
sua'sive
suave
suave'ly
suav'ity
sub
subac'etate
subac'id
sub-a'gency
sub-a'gent
subal'pine
sub'altern
subalter'nate
suba'queous
subas'tral
subaudi'tion
sub'base
subbra'chial
subbra'chian
subcla'vian
sub-commit'tee
sub-con'tract
subcon'trary
subcor'date
subcos'tal
subcuta'neous
sub'deacon
sub'dean
subdivide'
subdivi'ded
subdivi'ding
subdivis'ible
subdivi'sion
subdom'inant
subdu'able
subdu'al
subduce'
subduced'
subdu'cing
subduct'
subduct'ed
subduct'ing
subduc'tion
subdue'
subdued'
subdu'er
subdu'ing
sub'duple

sub'-editor
su'berate
suber'ic
su'berin-ine
suberose'
su'berose
su'berous
sub'genus
subi'odide
su'bito
subja'cent
{ *subject,*
{ *subject'ed, p.t.*
subject'ing
subjec'tion
subjec'tive
*subjec'tive*ly
subjec'tivism
subjectiv'ity
sub'ject-matter
subjoin'
subjoined'
subjoin'ing
sub ju'dice
sub'jugate
sub'jugated
sub'jugating
subjuga'tion
sub'jugator
subjunc'tion
subjunc'tive
sublapsa'rian
sublapsa'rianism
sublap'sary
sublate'
subla'tion
sublease'
sublet'
subleva'tion
sub-libra'rian
sub'limate, *n., a.*
sub'limate, *v.*
sub'limated
sub'limating
sublima'tion
sublime'
sublimed'
sublime'ly
subli'ming
sublim'ity
sublu'nar
sub'lunary
sub'marine
submax'illary
subme'diant
submerge'
submerged'

submer'gence
submer'ging
submerse'
submersed'
submers'ing
submer'sion
submis'sion
submiss'ive
submiss'ively
submiss'iveness
submit'
submit'ted
submit'ting
submul'tiple
subnas'cent
subor'dinacy [*a.*
subor'dinate, *n.*,
subor'dinate, *v.*
subor'dinated
subor'dinating
subordina'tion
suborn'
suborna'tion
suborned'
suborn'er
suborn'ing
subo'vate
subpoe'na
subpoe'naed
subpoe'naing
sub'*principal*
subrep'tion
subroga'tion
sub ro'sa
sub'salt
{ *subscribe'*
{ *subscribed'*
subscri'ber
*subscrib'*ing
sub'script
subscrip'tion
sub'section
sub'sequence
sub'sequent
sub'sequently
subserve'
subserved'
subserv'ience
subserv'iency
subserv'ient
subside'
subsi'ded
subsi'dence
subsid'iarily
subsid'iary
subsi'ding
sub'sidize
sub'sidized
sub'sidizing
sub'sidy
subsist'
subsist'ed
subsist'ence

subsist'ent
subsist'ing
sub'soil
sub'species
sub'stance
substan'tial
substantial'ity
substan'tially
substan'tials
substan'tiate
substan'tiated
substan'tiating
substantia'tion
sub'stantive
sub'stantively
sub'stitute
sub'stituted
sub'stituting
substitu'tion
substitu'tional
substitu'tionary
sub'stitutive
sub'strate
substra'tum
substruc'ture
sub'style
subsul'phate
subsul'tory
sub'tangent
subtend'
subtend'ed
subtend'ing
subtense'
subter'fluent
sub'terfuge
subterra'nean
subterra'neous
sub'tile
subtil'ity
subtiliza'tion
sub'tilize
sub'tilized
sub'tilizing
sub'tilty
sub'tle
sub'tlety
sub'tly
subton'ic
subtract'
subtract'ed
subtract'er
subtract'ing
subtrac'tion
subtract'ive
sub'trahend
su'bulate
su'bulated
sub'urb
subur'ban
sub'urbs
subven'tion

subver'sion
subver'sive
subvert'
subvert'ed
subvert'er
subvert'ible
subvert'ing

sub'way
succeda'neous
succeda'neum
succeed'
succeed'ed
succeed'ing
succen'tor
success'
success'ful
success'fully
succes'sion
succes'sional
succes'sionist
succes'sive
succes'sively
success'or
succif'erous
suc'cinate
suc'cinated
succinct'
succinct'ly
succinct'ness
succin'ic
suc'cinite
suc'cinous
suc'cour-cor
suc'coured-cored
suc'courer-corer
suc'couring-cor- [ing
suc'culence
suc'culency
suc'culent
succumb'
succumbed'
succumb'ing
succus'sion
succus'sive
such
suck
sucked
suck'er
suck'ing
suck'le
suck'led
suck'ling
suc'tion
sucto'rial
sucto'rian
Sudanese'
suda'tion
su'datory
sud'den
sud'denly
sud'denness
sudorif'erous
sudorif'ic
sudorip'arous
Su'dra
suds
sue
sued
suède

su'er
su'et
su'ety
suf'fer
suf'ferable
suf'ferance
suf'fered
suf'ferer
suf'fering
suffice'
sufficed'
suffi'ciency
suffi'cient
suffi'ciently
suffi'cing
suffix
suffixed'
suffix'ing
suffla'tion
suf'focate
suf'focated
suf'focating
suffoca'tion
suf'focative
suf'fragan
suf'fragette
suf'frage
suf'fragism
suf'fragist
suffuse'
suffused'
suffu'sing
suffu'sion
su'fi
sug
sug'ar
sug'ar-cane
sug'ared
sug'ariness
sug'aring

sug'ar-loaf
sug'ar-plum
sug'ary
suggest'
suggest'ed
suggest'er
suggest'ing
sugges'tion
suggest'ive
suggest'ively
su'icidal
su'icide
su'icidism
su'ing
suit
suitabil'ity
suit'able
suit'ableness
suit'ably
suite
suit'ed
suit'ing
suit'or
sul'cate
sul'cated
sulk
sulk'ily
sulk'iness
sulks

sulk'y
sul'len
sul'lenly
sul'lenness
sul'lied
sul'ly
sul'lying
sul'phate
sulphat'ic
sul'phide
sul'phite
sul'phonal
sul'phosalt
sul'phosel
sul'phur
sul'phurate, *n.*, *a.*
sul'phurate, *v.*
sul'phurated
sul'phurating
sulphura'tion
sulphu'reous
sul'phuret
sul'phuretted
sulphu'ric
sul'phuring
sul'phurous
sul'phury
sul'tan
sulta'na
sul'taness
sul'tanry
sul'trily
sul'triness
sul'try
sum
su'mac, su'mach
Suma'tran
sum'marily
sum'marize
sum'marized
sum'marizing
sum'mary
summa'tion
summed
sum'mer
sum'mered
sum'mer-house
sum'mering
sum'mersault
sum'merset
sum'ming
sum'mit
sum'mon
sum'moned
sum'moner
sum'moning
sum'mons
sum'mum
bo'num
sump
sump'ter
sump'tuary
sump'tuous
sump'tuously
sump'tuousness
sun
sun'beam
sun'burnt
Sun'day
sun'der

sun'dial
sun'down
sun'-dried
sun'dries
sun'dry
sun'fish
sun'flower
sung
sunk
sunk'en
sun'light
sun'like
sun'lit
Sun'na
sun'nier
sun'niest
sun'niness
sun'ning
Sun'nite
sun'ny
sun'rise
sun'rising
sun'set
sun'shade
sun'shine
sun'shiny
sun'stroke
sup
su'per
su'perable
superabound'
superabun'dance
superabun'dant
superadd'
superaddi'tion
superangel'ic
superan'nuate
superan'nuated
superan'nuating
superannua'tion
superb'
superb'ly
supercar'go
supercil'ious
supercil'iously
supercil'iousness
superdom'inant
superem'inence
superem'inent
superer'ogate
supereroga'tion
supererog'atory
superex'cellence
superex'cellent
superfi'cial
superfi'cialist
superficial'ity
superfi'cially
superfi'cies
su'perfine
superflu'ity
super'fluous
superhu'man
superimpose'
superimposed'
superimpos'ing
superincum'bent
superinduce'
superinduced'
superinduc'ing
superintend'
superintend'ed
superintend'ence
superintend'ency
superintend'ent
superintend'ing
supe'rior
superior'ity
super'lative
super'latively
superlu'nar
superlu'nary
supermun'dane
super'nal
superna'tant
supernat'ural
supernat'uralism
supernat'uralist
supernat'urally
supernu'merary
superphos'phate
superpose'
superposed'
superposi'tion
superroy'al
su'persalt
supersat'urate
supersatura'tion
superscribe'
superscribed'
superscri'bing
superscrip'tion
supersede'
superse'deas
superse'ded
superse'ding
superse'dure
supersen'sual
superses'sion
supersti'tion
supersti'tious
supersti'tiously
superstra'tum
superstruc'ture
supersul'phate
superton'ic
supervene'
supervened'
superve'nient
superve'ning
superven'tion
supervi'sal
supervise'
supervised'
supervi'sing
supervi'sion
supervi'sor
supervi'sory
su'pinate
supina'tion
supine
supine'ly
supine'ness
supped
sup'per
sup'perless
sup'ping
supplant'
supplanta'tion
supplant'ed
supplant'er
supplant'ing
sup'ple
sup'pled
sup'plement
supplemen'tal
supplemen'tary
sup'pleness
sup'pliant
sup'plicant
sup'plicate
sup'plicated
sup'plicating
supplica'tion
sup'plicator
sup'plicatory
supplied'
suppli'er
supplies'
supply'
supply'ing
support'
support'able
support'ed
support'er
support'ing
suppo'sable
suppose'
supposed'
suppo'sing
supposi'tion
supposi'tional
suppositi'tious
suppos'itive
suppos'itory
suppress'
suppressed'
suppress'ing
suppres'sion
suppress'ive
suppress'or
sup'purate
sup'purated
sup'purating
suppura'tion

sup'purative
supra-ax'illary
supracil'iary
supralapsa'rian
supramun'dane
supra-or'bital
suprem'acy
supreme'
supreme'ly
su'ra
su'rah
su'ral
sur'base
sur'basement
surbed'
surcharge'
surcharged'
surcharg'ing
sur'cingle
sur'coat
surd
sure
sure'-footed
*sure'*ly
*sure'*ness
*sur'*est
*sure'*ty
*sure'*tyship
surf
sur'face
sur'feit
sur'feited
sur'feiting
surge
surged
sur'geon
sur'geoncy
sur'gery
sur'gical
sur'ging
sur'gy
su'ricate
sur'liness
sur'ly
surmise'
surmised'
surmi'sing
surmount'
surmount'able
surmount'ed
surmount'er
surmount'ing
surmul'let
sur'name
sur'named
sur'naming
surpass'
surpass'able
surpassed'
surpass'ing
sur'plice
sur'plus
sur'plusage
surpri'sal
surprise'
surprised'

surpri'sing
surrebut'
surrebut'ted
surrebut'ter
surrebut'ting
surrejoin'
surrejoin'der
surren'der
surren'dered
surrenderee'
surren'derer
surren'dering
surrepti'tious
surrepti'tiously
sur'rogate
surround'
surround'ed
surround'ing
sursol'id
surtout'
sur'turbrand
surveil'lance
survey
survey'al
surveyed'
survey'ing
survey'or
survey'orship
survi'val
survive'
survived'
survi'ving
survi'vor
survi'vorship
susceptibil'ity
suscep'tible
suscep'tibly
suscep'tive
sus'pect, *n.*
suspect', v.
suspect'able
suspect'ed
suspect'er
*suspect'*ing
suspend'
suspend'ed
suspend'er
suspend'ing
suspense'
suspensibil'ity
suspen'sible
suspen'sion
suspen'sory
suspi'cion
suspi'cious
suspi'ciously
suspira'tion
suspire'
suspired'
suspir'ing
sustain'
sustain'able
sustained'
sustain'er

sustain'ing
sustain'ment
sus'tenance
sustenta'tion
sut'ler
suttee'
suttee'ism
sut'tle
su'ture
su'zerain
su'zerainty
swab
swabbed
swab'ber
swab'bing
swad'dle
swad'dled
swad'dling
swag
swage
swagged
swag'ger
swag'gered
swag'gerer
swag'gering
swag'ging
swain
swale
swaled
swal'ing
swal'low
swal'lowed
swal'lower
swal'lowing
swal'lowtail
swal'low-tailed
swal'lowwort
swam
swamp
swamped
swamp'ing
swamp'y
swan
swan'pan
swans'down
swap
swapped
swap'ping
sward
sware
swarm
swarmed
swarm'ing
swarth
swarth'ily
swarth'iness
swarth'y
swash
swash'-buckler
swash'ing
swath
swathe
swathed
swa'thing
sway
swayed
sway'ing
sweal
swealed
sweal'ing

swear
swear'er
swear'ing
sweat
sweat'ed
sweat'er
sweat'iness
sweat'ing
sweat'y
Swede
Swedenbor'gian
Swedenbor'gian-ism
Swe'dish
sweep
sweep'er
sweep'ing
sweep'ings
sweep'stakes
sweep'y
sweet
sweet'bread
sweet'brier
sweet'en
sweet'ened
sweet'ener
sweet'ening
sweet'er
sweet'est
sweet'heart
sweet'ing
sweet'ish
sweet'ly
sweet'meat
sweet'ness
sweet'pea
sweet'-scented
sweet'-smelling
sweet'-will'iam
swell
swelled
swell'ing
swel'ter
swel'tered
swel'tering
swel'try
swept
swerve
swerved
swerv'ing
swift
swift'er
swift'est
swift'ly
swift'ness
swig
swill
swilled
swill'er
swill'ing
swim
swim'mer
swim'ming
swim'mingly
swin'dle
swin'dled
swin'dler
swin'dling
swine

swine'herd
swing
swinge
swinged
swinge'ing
swin'gel
swing'er
swing'ing
swin'gle
swin'gled
swin'gling
swi'nish
swipe
swirl
swirl'ed
swirl'ing
Swiss
switch
switch'back
switch'board
switched
switch'ing
switch'man
Swit'zer
swiv'el
swoll'en
swoon
swooned
swoon'ing
swoop
swooped
swoop'ing
swop
swopped
swop'ping
sword
sword'-belt
sword'-blade
sword'-cane
sword'ed
sword'fish
sword'-shaped
swords'man
swore
sworn
swum
swung
Syb'arite
Sybarit'ic
syc'amine
syc'amore
syce
sycee'
syc'ophancy
syc'ophant
sycophan'tic
syc'ophantize
sy'enite
syenit'ic
syl'labary
syllab'ic
syllab'ically
syllabica'tion
syl'lable
syl'labub
syl'labus
syllep'sis
syl'logism
syllogis'tic
syllogiza'tion

syl'logize
syl'logized
syl'logizer
syl'logizing
sylph
sylph'id
syl'va
syl'van
syl'vanite
syl'vate
sym'bol
symbol'ic
symbol'ical
symbol'ically
sym'bolism
sym'bolist
symboliza'tion
sym'bolize
sym'bolized
sym'bolizing
symbolog'ical
symbol'ogy
sym'metric
symmet'rical
symmet'rically
sym'metrize
sym'metry
sympathet'ic
sympathet'ical
sympathet'ically
sym'pathize
sym'pathized
sym'pathizer
sym'pathizing
sym'pathy
symphon'ic
sympho'nious
sym'phonist
sym'phony
sym'physis
sympiesom'eter
sym'ploce
sympo'siac
sympo'siarch
sympo'siast
sympo'sium
symp'tom
symptomat'ic
symptomatol'ogy
sympto'sis
synae'resis
synagog'ical
syn'agogue
synale'pha
syn'archy
synarthro'sis
syncar'pous
syn'chronal
syn'chronism
syn'chronize
syn'chronized
syn'chronizing
syn'chronous
syncli'nal
syn'cline

syn'copal
syn'copate
syn'copated
syn'copating
syncopa'tion
syn'cope
syn'copist
syncret'ic
syn'cretism
syn'cretist
syndac'tylous
syndesmo'sis
syn'dic
syn'dicate
syn'drome
synec'doche
syne'chia
syn'epy
syner'esis
synerget'ic
syn'ergist
syn'ergy
Syngene'sia
syn'graph
synize'sis
synneuro'sis
syn'od
syn'odal
synod'ic
synod'ical
syn'odist
syn'onym
synonym'ic
synon'ymist
synon'ymize
synon'ymous
synon'ymously
synon'ymy
synop'sis
synop'tic
synop'tical
synop'tically
syno'via
syno'vial
syntac'tic
syntac'tical
syn'tax
syntax'is
syntect'ic
syntere'sis
synteret'ic
synther'mal
syn'thesis
synthet'ic
synthet'ical
synthet'ically
syn'tomy
synton'ic
syph'ilis
syphilit'ic
sy'phon
sy'ren
Syr'iac
Syr'iacism
Syr'ian
Syr'ianism
Syr'iasm
syrin'ga
syr'inge
syr'inged
syr'inging
syringot'omy
syr'inx
syrt
syr'tic
syr'up
syr'upy
systal'tic
sys'tem
systemat'ic
systemat'ical
systemat'ically
sys'tematism
sys'tematist
sys'tematize
sys'tematized
sys'tematizer
sys'tematizing
system'ic
systemiza'tion
sys'temize
sys'temized
sys'temizer
sys'tem-maker
sys'tole
systol'ic
sys'tyle
syz'ygy

T

tab
tab'ard
tab'aret
tabasheer'
tab'bied
tab'binet
tab'by
tab'bying
tab'ernacle
tab'ernacled
tab'ernacling
ta'bes
tabet'ic
tab'idly
tab'idness
tabif'ic
tab'itude
tab'lature
ta'ble
tableau'
tableau' vivant
ta'ble-cloth
ta'bled
ta'ble d'hôte
ta'ble-land
ta'blespoon
ta'blespoonful
tab'let
ta'ble-talk
ta'bling
taboo'
tabooed'
taboo'ing
ta'bor
ta'bored
tab'oret
tab'ouret
tab'ret
tab'ular
tab'ula ra'sa
tab'ularize
tab'ulate
tab'ulated
tab'ulating
tabula'tion
tab'ulator
tac'amahac
tache (med.term)
tache (sugar pan)
tachom'eter
tachygraph'ic
tachyg'raphy
tac'it
tac'itly
tac'iturn
taciturn'ity
tack
tacked
tack'er
tack'ing
tack'le
tack'led
tack'ling
tacks'man
tact
tact'ful
tact'fully
tac'tic
tac'tical
tacti'cian
tac'tics
tac'tile
tactil'ity
tac'tion
tact'ual
tad'pole
tael
tae'nia
taff'erel
taf'feta
taff'rail
taf'fy
tafi'a
tag
tagged
tag'ging
tagl'ia
Tagliaco'tian
tag'rag
tail
tail'age
tailed
tail'ing
tail'less
tai'lor
tai'loress
tai'loring
tail'-piece
tail'zie
taint
taint'ed
taint'ing
taint'less
tain'ture
take
take'-in
ta'ken
take'-off
ta'ker
ta'king
ta'kingly
ta'kingness
tal'apoin
tal'bot
talc
tal'cite
talck'y
talc'ose
talc'ous
tale
tale'bearer
tale'bearing
tal'ent
tal'ented
ta'les
ta'lesman
tal'iped
tal'isman
talisman'ic
talk
talk'ative
talked
talk'ee-talk'ee
talk'er
talk'ing
tall
tal'lage
tall'er
tall'est
tal'lied
tall'ness
tal'low
tal'low-chandler
tal'lowy
tal'ly
tally-ho'
tal'lying
tal'lyman
Tal'mud
Talmud'ic
Tal'mudist
tal'on
tal'oned
talook', taluk'
talook'ah
talook'dar
taluk'dar
ta'lus
tamabil'ity
ta'mable
tame'able
ta'mableness
tame'ableness
tam'arack
tam'arin
tam'arind
tam'arisk
tam'bour
tambourine'
tame
tameabil'ity
tame'able
tame'ableness
tamed

tame'less
tame'ly
tame'ness
ta'mer
ta'ming
Tam'many
Tam-o'-Shant'er
tamp
tamped
tam'per
tam'pered
tam'perer
tam'pering
tamp'ing
tam'pion
tam'poe
tam'-tam
tan
tan'ager
tan'dem
tang
tan'gency
tan'gent
tangen'tial
tangerine'
tangibil'ity
tan'gible
tan'gle
tan'gled
tan'gling
tan'gly
tan'ist
tan'istry
tank
tank'ard
tan'nage
tan'nate
tanned
tan'ner
tan'nery
tan'nic
tan'nier
tan'nin
tan'ning
tan'sy
tan'talite
tan'taliza'tion
tan'talize
tan'talized
tan'talizer
tan'talizing
tan'talum
tan'tamount
tan'tivy
tan'trum
tan'-yard
tap
tape
ta'per
ta'pered
ta'pering
tap'estry
tap'eti
tape'worm
tap'-house
tapio'ca
ta'pir
ta'pis
tapped
tap'per

tap'pet
tap'ping
tap'-room
tap'-root
tap'ster
tar
tarantel'la
tar'antism
taran'tula
tarax'acum
tarboosh'
tar'digrade
tar'dily
tar'diness
tar'dy
tare
tar'entism
taren'tola
tar'get
targeteer'
Tar'gum
Tar'gumist
tar'iff
{ tar'iff-*reform'*
{ Tar'iff *Reform'*
tar'in
tar'latan
tarn'
tar'nish
tar'nished
tar'nishing
tarpau'lin
Tarpe'ian
tar'ragon
tar'ras
tarred
tar'ried
tar'rier
tar'ring
tar'rock
tar'ry, *adj.*
tar'ry, *v.*
tar'rying
tar'sal
tarse
tar'sus
tart
tar'tan
Tar'tar, tar'tar
Tarta'rean
tar'tar-emet'ic
tarta'reous
tartar'ic
tartariza'tion
tar'tarize
tar'tarized
tar'tarizing
{ tar'tarous
{ Tar'tarus
tart'ish
tart'ly
tart'ness
tar'trate
Tartuffe'
tar'-water
task
tasked
task'er
task'ing
task'master

task'-work
Tasma'nian
tas'sel
{ tas'selled
{ tas'seled
{ tas'selling
{ tas'seling
{ ta'stable
{ taste'able
taste
ta'sted
taste'ful
taste'fully
taste'less
taste'lessness
ta'ster
ta'stily
ta'sting
ta'sty
tat
ta'-ta'
tat'ter
tatterdema'lion
tat'tered
tat'ting
tat'tle
tat'tled
tat'tler
tat'tling
tattoo'
tattooed'
tattoo'ing
taught
taunt
taunt'ed
taunt'er
taunt'ing
taunt'ingly
tau'riform
tau'rine
tau'rocol
Tau'rus
taut
tau'tochrone
{ tautolog'ical
{ tautolog'ically
tautol'ogist
tautol'ogize
tautol'ogized
tautol'ogizing
tautol'ogy
tautophon'ical
tautoph'ony
tav'ern
tav'ern-keeper
taw
taw'drily
taw'driness
taw'dry
tawed
taw'er
taw'ery
taw'ing
taw'niness
taw'ny
tax
taxabil'ity
tax'able
taxa'tion
taxed

tax'er
tax'-gatherer
tax'i
tax'iarch
tax'icab
taxider'mic
tax'idermist
tax'idermy
taxim'eter
tax'ing
taxon'omy
tax'payer
taz'za
tea
tea'-caddy
teach
teach'able
teach'ableness
teach'er
tea'-chest
teach'ing
tea'cup
tea'cupful
tea'-dealer
tea'-garden
teague
teak
tea'kettle
teal
team
team'ster
tea'pot
tear (a drop)
tear (to rend)
tear'er
tear'ful
tear'fully
tear'fulness
tear'ing
tease
teased
tea'sel, tea'zle
teas'er
tea'-service
teas'ing
tea'spoon
tea'spoonful
teat
tea'-table
tea'-urn
tea'zle
tea'zled
tea'zler
tea'zling
Tebet'
Tebeth'
tech'ily
tech'iness
tech'nical
technical'ity
tech'nically
tech'nics
technique'
technolog'ic
technolog'ical
technol'ogist
technol'ogy
tech'y
tecton'ic
ted

ted'ded
ted'der
ted'ding
Te De'um
te'dious
te'diously
te'dium
tee
teem
teemed
teem'ing
teem'less
teens
teeth
teethe
teeth'ing
teeto'tal
teeto'tal(l)er
teeto'talism
teeto'tum
teg
teg'men
tegmen'tum
teg'ular
teg'ument
tegumen'tal
tegumen'tary
tehee'
teil
tei'noscope
telamo'nes
tela'rian
telau'tograph
teleg'ony
tel'egram
tel'egraph
tel'egraphed
telegraph'ic
tel'egraphing
teleg'raphist
teleg'raphy
teleolog'ical
teleol'ogy
Teleosau'rus
telepath'ic
telep'athist
telep'athy
tel'ephone
telephon'ic
tel'escope
telescop'ic
tel'esis
telesmat'ic
tel'estich
tel'ewriter
tel'ic
tell
tell'er
tell'ing
tell'-tale
tellu'ral
tel'lurate
tel'luretted
tellu'rian
tellu'ric
tel'lurite
tellu'rium
tel'lurous
temera'rious
temer'ity

tem'per
tem'perament
temperamen'tal
temperamen'tally
tem'perance
tem'perate
tem'perately
tem'perative
tem'perature
tem'pered
tem'pering
tem'pest
tempes'tuous
tempes'tuously
tempes'tuousness
tem'plar
tem'ple
tem'plet
tem'po
tem'poral
temporal'ity
tem'porally
tem'porarily
tem'porary
temporiza'tion
tem'porize
tem'porized
tem'porizer
tem'porizing
tempt
temptabil'ity
tempt'able
tempta'tion
tempt'ed
tempt'er
tempt'ing
tempt'ress
ten
tenabil'ity
ten'able
ten'ace
tena'cious
tena'ciously
tenac'ity
tenac'ulum
tenaille'
ten'ancy
ten'ant
ten'antable
ten'anted
ten'anting
ten'antless
ten'antry
tench
tend
tend'ed
ten'dency
ten'der
ten'dered
ten'derer
ten'der-hearted
ten'dering
ten'derly
ten'derness
tend'ing
ten'dinous
ten'don
ten'dril
ten'ebrous
ten'ement

tenemen'tal
tenemen'tary
tenes'mus
ten'et
ten'fold
te'nioid
ten'nis
ten'nis-court
ten'nis-lawn
ten'on
ten'or
tenot'omy
ten'pence
ten'penny
ten'-pins
tense
tense'ly
tense'ness
tensibil'ity
ten'sible
ten'sile
ten'sion
ten'sity
ten'sive
ten'sor
tent
ten'tacle
tentac'ular
tentac'ulum
ten'tative
ten'tatively
tent'ed
ten'ter
ten'ter-hook
tenth
tenth'ly
tent'ing
tento'rium
tenuifo'lious
tenu'ity
ten'uous
ten'uously
ten'uousness
ten'ure
tepefac'tion
tep'efied
tep'efy
tep'efying
tep'id
tepid'ity
ter'aph
ter'aphim
teratol'ogy
terce
ter'cel
tercen'tenary
ter'ebinth
terebin'thine
Tere'do
terete'
tergem'inal
tergem'inate
tergif'erous
ter'giversate
tergiversa'tion
ter'gum
term
ter'magancy
ter'magant
termed

term'er
Ter'mes
ter'minable
ter'minal
ter'minate, *a.*
ter'minate, *v.*
ter'minated
ter'minating
termina'tion
termina'tional
ter'minative
ter'minator
ter'minatory
ter'miner
term'ing
ter'minism
ter'minist
{ terminolog'ical
{ terminolog'ically
terminol'ogy
ter'minus
ter'mite
term'less
tern
ter'nary
ter'nate
Terpsichore'an
ter'ra
ter'race
ter'raced
ter'racing
ter'ra-cot'ta
ter'ra firma
ter'ra incog'nita
ter'rapin
terra'queous
terrene'
ter'reous
terre'plein
terres'trial
ter'rible
ter'ribly
ter'rier
terrif'ic
ter'rified
ter'rify
ter'rifying
terrig'enous
territo'rial
territo'rialism
territo'rially
ter'ritory
ter'ror
ter'rorism
ter'rorist
ter'rorize
terse
terse'ly
terse'ness
ter'tial
ter'tian
ter'tiary
ter'za-ri'ma
terzet'to
tes'sellar
tes'sellate
tes'sellated
tes'sellating
tessella'tion
tes'seral

tes'sular
test
tes'ta
test'able
testa'cea
testa'cean
testacel'la
testaceol'ogy
testa'ceous
tes'tacy
tes'tament
testamen'tary
tes'tate, *n.* & *a.*
tes'tate, *v.*
testa'tor
testa'trix
test'ed
test'er
tes'ticle
testifica'tion
tes'tified
tes'tifier
tes'tify
tes'tifying
tes'tily
testimo'nial
tes'timony
tes'tiness
test'ing
testoon'
test'-paper
testu'dinal
testu'dinate
testu'do
tes'ty
tetan'ic
tet'anus
tetch'ily
tetch'iness
tetch'y
tête
tête'-à-tête'
teth'er
teth'ered
teth'ering
tetrabran'chiate
tet'rachord
tet'radrachm
tet'ragon
tetrag'onal
tetrahe'dral
tetrahe'dron
tetram'eter
tet'rapla
tet'rapod
tet'rarch
tet'rarchate
tet'rarchy
tet'rastich
tet'rastyle
tetrasyl'lable
tet'ter
Teu'ton
Teuton'ic
tew'el, tu'el
te'whit
Tex'an
text
text'book
text'-*hand*

tex'tile
texto'rial
tex'tual
tex'tualist
textual'ity
tex'tually
tex'tuary
tex'ture
thal'amus
tha'ler
Thali'a
thal'lium
{ Tham'muz
{ Tam'muz
than
thane
{ *thank*
{ *thanked*
{ *thank'ful*
{ *thank'fully*
*thank'*fulness
*thank'*ing
*thank'*less
*thank'*lessness
thank'-offering
thanks
*thanks' giv*ing
*thank'*worthy
that
thatch
thatched
thatch'er
thatch'ing
thau'matrope
thaumatur'gic
thaumatur'gist
thau'maturgy
thaw
thawed
thaw'ing
thaw'y
the
thean'thropism
the'archy
the'atine
the'atre, the'ater
theat'ric
theat'rical
theat'rically
The'ban
the'ca
the'codont
the'cophore
thee
theft
the'iform
the'ine
their
*their*s
the'ism
the'ist
theist'ic
theist'ical
them
theme
Them'is
themselves'
then
thence
thenceforth'
thencefor'ward
theobro'ma
theobro'mine
{ theoc'racy
{ theoc'rasy
theocrat'ic
theocrat'ical
theod'icy
theod'olite
theog'ony
theolo'gian
{ theolog'ical
{ theolog'ically
theol'ogist
the'ologue
theol'ogy
theom'achy
the'omancy
theop'athy
theoph'any
theophilosoph'ic
theopneus'tic
theopneu'sty
theor'bo
the'orem
theoret'ic
theoret'ical
theoret'ically
the'orist
the'orize
the'orized
the'orizer
the'orizing
the'ory
theosoph'ic
theos'ophist
theos'ophy
therapeu'tic
therapeu'tical
there
*there'*about
*there*af'ter
*there*at'
*there*by'
*there*for'
there'fore
*there*from'
*there*in'
*there*of'
*there*on'
*there*out'
*there*to'
*there*upon'
*there*with'
*there*withal'
the'riac
theri'acal
theriot'omy
ther'mal
ther'mic
Thermidor'
thermo-
dynam'ics
thermo-elec'-
tricity
thermol'ogy
thermom'eter
thermomet'ric
thermomet'rical
ther'moscope
ther'mostat
thermot'ics
ther'motypy
thesau'rus
these
the'sis
Thes'pian
Thessalo'nian
thet'ic
thet'ical
the'tis
theur'gist
the'urgy
thews
they
Thibe'tan
thick
thick'en
thick'ened
thick'ening
thick'er
thick'est
thick'et
thick'head
thick'-headed
thick'ish
thick'ly
thick'ness
thick'-set
thief
thieve
thieved
thiev'ery
thieves
thiev'ing
thiev'ish
thigh
thigh'-bone
thill
thill'er
thills
thim'ble
thim'bleful
thim'blerig
thim'blerigger
thim'blerigging
thin
thine
thing
think
*think'*able
think'er
*think'*ing
thin'ly
thinned
thin'ner
thin'ness
thin'nest
thin'ning
thin'nish
thin'-skinned
third
*third'*ing
*third'*ly
*third*s
thirl'age
thirst
thirst'ed
thirst'er
thirst'ier

thirst'iest
thirst'ily
thirst'iness
thirst'ing
thirst'y
thirteen
thirteenth
thir'tieth
thir'ty
this
this'tle
this'tly
thith'er
thith'erward
thole
thole'-pin
thol'obate
Thomae'an
Tho'mism
Tho'mist
Tho'mite
Thompso'nian
Thompso'nian-[ism
thong
Thor
thorac'ic
tho'rax
tho'ria
tho'rite
tho'rium
thorn
thorn'-apple
thorn'-bush
thorn'-hedge
thorn'y
thor'ough
thor'oughbass
thor'oughbred
thor'oughfare
thor'oughgoing
thor'oughly
thor'oughness
thor'ough-paced
thor'oughwort
thorp
those
Thoth
thou
though
thought
thought'ful
thought'fully
thought'fulness
thought'less
thought'lessly
thought'lessness
thou'sand
thou'sandfold
thou'sandth
Thra'cian
thral'dom
thrall
thrap'ple
thrash
thrashed
thrash'er
thrash'ing
thrason'ical
thrave
thread
thread'bare
thread'ed
thread'en
thread'ing
thread'-shaped
thread'worm
thread'y
threap
threat
threat'en
threat'ened
threat'ener
threat'ening
three
three'-cornered
three'-decker
three'fold
three'-legged
three'pence
three'penny
three'score
threne
thren'ody
thresh
thresh'er
thresh'old
threw
thrice
thrid
thrift
thrift'ily
thrift'iness
thrift'less
thrift'lessness
thrift'y
thrill
thrilled
thrill'ing
thrive
thrived
thriv'en
thri'ving
throat
throat'iness
throat'wort
throat'y
throb
throbbed
throb'bing
throe
throm'bus
throne
throned
throng
thronged
throng'ing
thro'ning
thros'tle
thros'tling
throt'tle
throt'tled
throttle-valve
throt'tling
through
throughout'
throve
throw
throw'er
throw'ing
thrown
throw'ster
thrum
thrummed
thrum'ming
thrush
thrust
thrust'er
thrust'ing
thrust'ings
thud
thud'ded
thud'ding
thug
thug'gee
thug'gery
thug'gism
Thu'le
thumb
thumbed
thumb'ing
thumb'screw
thumb'-stall
thum'mim
thump
thumped
thump'er
thump'ing
thun'der
thun'derbolt
thun'derclap
thun'dered
thun'derer
thun'dering
thun'der-shower
thun'der-storm
thun'derstruck
thun'dery
thu'rible
thurif'erous
thurifica'tion
thurl
Thurs'day
thus
thwack
thwacked
thwack'ing
thwaite
thwart
thwart'ed
thwart'ing
thy
thy'ine
thy'ite
thyme
thy'mus
thym'y
thy'roid
thyrse
thyr'soid
thyr'sus
thyself'
tia'ra
Tibe'tan
tib'ia
tib'ial
tic
tic'-douloureux
tick
ticked
tick'en

tick'et
tick'eted
tick'eting
tick'ing
tick'le
tick'led
tick'ler
tick'ling
tick'lish
tick'seed
tick'-tack
tid
ti'dal
tid'bit
tide
ti'ded
tide'-gauge
tide'less
tide'mill
tide'waiter
tide'way
ti'dier
ti'diest
ti'dily
ti'diness
ti'ding
ti'dings
ti'dy
tie
tied
tier
ti'er
tierce
tier'cel
tierce'let
tiff
tif'fany
tif'fin
tig
tige
ti'ger
ti'ger-cat
ti'gerish
ti'ger-lily
tight
tight'en
tight'ened
tight'ening
tight'er
tight'est
tight'ly
tight'ness
tights
ti'gress
ti'grine
tike
til'bury
tile
tile'-earth
tiled
til'er
til'ing
till, *n.* and *v.*
till, prep.
till'able
till'age
tilled
till'er
till'ering
till'ing

til'mus
tilt
tilt'ed
tilt'er
tilth'
tilt'-hammer
tilt'ing
tim'bal, tym'bal
tim'ber
tim'bered
tim'bering
tim'bre
tim'brel
time
timed
time'-honoured
time'-keeper
time'less
time'liness
time'ly
time'piece
time'-server
time'-serving
time'-table
time'-worn
tim'id
timid'ity
tim'idly
ti'ming
ti'mist
timoc'racy
timoneer'
tim'orous
tim'orously
Timo'thean
tin
tin'cal
tinct
tincto'rial
tinc'ture
tinc'tured
tinc'turing
tin'der
tin'der-box
tine
tin'ea
tin'foil
ting
tinge
tinged
tinge'ing
ting'ing
tin'gle
tin'gled
tin'gling
tink
tinked
tink'er
tink'ered
tink'ering
tink'ing
tin'kle
tin'kled
tin'kling
tin'man
tinned
tin'ner
tin'ning
tin'ny
tin'-plate

tin'sel
tin'selled / tin'seled
tin'selling / tin'seling
tin'smith
tint
tint'ed
tint'ing
tintinnab'ulary
ti'ny
tip
tip'-cat
tipped
tip'per
tip'pet
tip'ping
tip'ple
tip'pled
tip'pler
tip'pling
tip'sily
tip'staff
tip'sy
tip'toe
tip'-top
tip'ulary
tirade'
tire
tired
tire'less
tire'lessness
tire'some
tire'someness
tir'ing
Tiro'nian
'tis
Tish'ri
tis'ical
Tis'ri
tis'sue
tis'sued
tis'suing
tit
Ti'tan
Tita'nian
titan'ic
titanif'erous
ti'tanite
tita'nium
tit'-bit
tith'able
tithe
tithed
ti'ther
ti'thing
ti'thing-man
tit'illate
tit'illated
tit'illating
titilla'tion
tit'ivate
tit'lark
ti'tle
ti'tled
ti'tle-page
ti'tling
tit'mouse
tit'rate

tit'rated
tit'rating
tit'ter
tit'tered
tit'tering
tit'tle
tit'tle-tattle
tit'ular
tit'ulary
tiv'y
tme'sis
to
toad
toad'-eater
toad'ied
toad'stone
toad'stool
toad'y
toad'ying
toad'yism
toast
toast'ed
toast'er
toast'ing
toast'ing-fork
toast'-master
toast'-rack
tobac'co
tobac'conist
tobog'gan
tobog'ganing
toc'sin
tod
to-day'
tod'dle
tod'dled
tod'dling
tod'dy
to-do'
to'dy
toe
tof'fee, tof'fy
toft
to'ga
togeth'er
tog'gery
tog'gle
toil
toiled
toil'er
toi'let
toil'ing
toilinet(te)'
toil'less
toil'some
toil'-worn
toise
Tokay'
to'ken
to'la
told
toled
Tole'do
tol'erable
tol'erably
tol'erance
tol'erant
tol'erate
tol'erated
tol'erating
tolera'tion
toll
toll'-booth
toll'-bridge
tolled
toll'er
toll'-gate
toll'-gatherer
toll'-house
toll'ing
toll'man
tol'zey
tolt
tolu'
tom'ahawk
toma'to
tomb
tom'bac
tombed
tom'boy
tomb'stone
tom'-cat
tom'-cod
tome
tomen'tous
tom'-fool
tomfool'ery
tomin'
tom-nod'dy
to-mor'row
tom'pion
tom'-tit'
tom'-tom
ton
ton (*Fr.*)
to'nal
tonal'ity
tone
toned
tone'less
ton'ga
tongs
tongue
tongued
tongue'-shaped
tongue'-tied
tongu'ing
ton'ic
ton'ically
tonic'ity
to-night'
to'ning
ton'ka
ton'nage
ton'sil
ton'sillar
ton'silar
tonsillit'ic
tonsilli'tis
tonso'rial
ton'sure
ton'sured
tontine'
to'ny
too
took
tool
tooled
tool'ing
toon, tun
toon'-wood
toot
toot'ed
toot'er
toot'ing
tooth
tooth'ache
tooth'-brush
toothed
tooth'ing
tooth'less
tooth'leted
tooth'pick
tooth'some
tooth'wort
top
top'arch
top'archy
to'paz
top'-boots
top'-coat
tope
toped
to'per
to'ping
topgal'lant
toph
topha'ceous
top'-heavy
To'phet
to'phus
top'ic
top'ical
top'knot
top'man
top'mast
top'*most*
topog'rapher
topograph'ic
topog'raphy
topped
top'per
top'ping
top'ple
top'pled
top'pling
top'sail
topsy-tur'vy
topt
toque
toquet'
tor
torch
torch'-bearer
torch'-light
tore
toreu'tic
torment
torment'ed
torment'er
tor'mentil
torment'ing
torment'or
torment'ress
torn
torna'do
to'rous
torpe'do
tor'pid
torpid'ity

tor'pified
tor'pify
tor'pifying
tor'pitude
tor'por
tor'quated
torque
torqued
torrefac'tion
tor'refied
tor'refy
tor'refying
tor'rent
torren'tial
Torricel'lian
tor'rid
torse
tor'sel
tor'sion
tor'so
tort
torteau'
tor'tile
tor'tious
tor'tive
tor'toise
tor'toise-shell
tortuos'ity
tor'tuous
tor'ture
tor'tured
tor'turer
tor'turing
tor'ulous
to'rus
To'ry
To'ryism
toss
tossed
toss'ing
tost
tot
to'tal
total'ity
to'talize
to'tally
to'tem
to'temism
toth'er
tot'ter
tot'tered
tot'tering
tot'tery
toucan'
touch
touched
touch'er
touch'-hole
touch'iness
touch'ing
touch'-me-not
touch'stone
touch'wood
touch'y
tough
tough'en
tough'ened
tough'ening
tough'er
tough'est

tough'ish
tough'ly
tough'ness
toupee'
toupet'
tour
tourbil'lion
tour'ing
tour'ist
tour'maline
tour'nament
tour'ney
tour'niquet
tournure'
touse
toused
tous'ing
tou'sle, tou'zle
tou'sled / tou'zled
tou'sling / tou'zling
tout
tout'ed
tout'er
tout'ing
tow
tow'age
to'ward
to'wardly
to'wardness
to'wards
towed
tow'el
tow'elling / tow'eling
tow'er
tow'ered
tow'ering
tow'ery
tow'ing
to-wit'
tow'-line
town
town-clerk'
town'-crier
town'-hall'
town'-house
towns'-folk
town'ship
towns'man
towns'people
town'-talk'
tow'ser
tow'y
tox'ic
tox'ical
toxicol'ogist
toxicol'ogy
toxoph'ilite
toy
toyed
toy'ful
toy'ing
toy'ish
toy'-shop
trabea'tion
trace
trace'able
traced

tra'cer
tra'cery
tra'ces
trache'a
trache'ae
tra'cheal
trache'ocele
tracheot'omy
tra'chyte
tra'cing
tra'cing-paper
track
tracked
track'ing
track'less
tract
tractabil'ity
tract'able
tract'ably
Tracta'rian
Tracta'rianism
trac'tate
trac'tile
tractil'ity
trac'tion
tract'ive
trac'tor
trac'tory
tract'rix
trade
tra'ded
trade'-mark
trade'-price
tra'der
trade'-sale
*trades'*folk
*trades'*man
trades-u'nion
trade-u'nion
trade'-wind
*tra'd*ing
tradi'tion
tradi'tional
tradi'tionally
tradi'tionary
tradi'tionist
trad'itor
traduce'
traduced'
tradu'cent
tradu'cer
tradu'cing
traduc'tion
traduc'tive
traf'fic
traf'ficked
traf'ficker
traf'ficking
trag'acanth
trag'alism
trage'dian
trag'edy
trag'ic
trag'ical
trag'ically
tragi-com'edy
tragi-com'ic
tragi-com'ical
trail
trailed

trail'ing
train
train'able
train'-band
train'-bearer
trained
train'er
train'ing
train'-oil
traipse
trait
trai'tor
trai'torous
trai'torously
trai'tress
traject
trajec'tion
traject'ory
tram
tram'-car
tram'mel
{ tram'melled
{ tram'meled
{ tram'melling
{ tram'meling
tramon'tane
tramp
tramped
tramp'ing
tram'ple
tram'pled
tram'pler
tram'pling
tram'-road
tram'way
trance
tran'quil
tranquil'lity
tranquilliza'tion
tran'quillize
tran'quillized
tran'quillizer
tran'quillizing
tran'quilly
transact'
transact'ed
transact'ing
transac'tion
transac'tor
transal'pine
transatlan'tic
transcend'
transcend'ed
transcend'ence
transcend'ency
transcend'ent
transcenden'tal
transcenden'talism
transcenden'talist
transcenden'tally
transcen'dently
transcend'ing
transcribe'
transcribed'
transcri'ber
transcri'bing
tran'script
transcrip'tion
transcrip'tive
tran'sept

transfer
trans'ferable
transferee'
transfer'ence
trans'feror
transferred'
transfer'rer
transfer'ring
transfigura'tion
transfig'ure
transfig'ured
transfig'uring
transfix'
transfixed'
transfix'ing
transfix'ion
trans'fluent
transform'
transform'able
transforma'tion
transform'ative
transformed'
transform'er
transform'ing
transfuse'
transfused'
transfu'sible
transfus'ing
transfu'sion
transfu'sive
transgress'
transgressed'
transgress'ing
transgres'sion
transgres'sional
transgress'ive
transgress'or
tranship'
tranship'ment
tran'sient
tran'siently
tran'sientness
transil'ience
transil'iency
transil'ient
trans'it
transi'tion
transi'tional
trans'itive
trans'itorily
trans'itoriness
trans'itory
transla'table
translate'
transla'ted
transla'ting
transla'tion
transla'tive
transla'tor
transla'tory
transla'tress
translit'erate
transloca'tion
translu'cence
translu'cency
translu'cent
translu'cid

trans'migrate
trans'migrated
trans'migrating
transmigra'tion
trans'migrator
transmi'gratory
transmissibil'ity
transmis'sible
transmis'sion
transmis'sive
transmit'
transmit'tal
transmit'tance
transmit'ted
transmit'ter
transmit'tible
transmit'ting
transmutabil'ity
transmu'table
transmuta'tion
transmuta'tionist
transmute'
transmu'ted
transmu'ter
transmu'ting
tran'som
transpa'rence
transpa'rency
transpa'rent
transpierce'
transpierced'
transpierc'ing
transpir'able
transpira'tion
transpir'atory
transpire'
transpired'
transpir'ing
transplant'
transplanta'tion
transplant'ed
transplant'er
transplant'ing
transplen'dent
transport
transportabil'ity
transport'able
transporta'tion
transport'ed
transport'er
transport'ing
transpo'sal
transpose'
transposed'
transpo'sing
transposi'tion
transposi'tional
transpos'itive
transship'
transship'ment
transshipped'
transship'ping
transubstan'tiate
transubstan'tiated
transubstan'tiating
transubstantia'tion
transuda'tion
transu'datory
transude'
transu'ded

transu'ding
transvec'tion
transver'sal
transverse'
transverse'ly
transvola'tion
trap
trapan'
trapanned'
trapan'ning
trap'-door
trapeze'
trape'zian
trape'ziform
trape'zium
trapezohe'dron
trap'ezoid
trapezoid'al
trap'pean
trapped
trap'per
trap'ping
trap'pings
Trap'pist
trap'pous
trash
trash'y
trass
traumat'ic
trav'ail
trav'ailing
trav'el
trav'elled
trav'eled
trav'eller
trav'eler
trav'elling
trav'eling
trav'ersable
trav'erse
trav'ersed
trav'erser
trav'erse-table
trav'ersing
trav'ertine
trav'ertin
trav'estied
trav'esty
trav'estying
trav'is
trawl
trawled
trawl'er
trawl'ing
trawl'-net
tray
treach'erous
treach'ery
trea'cle
tread
tread'er
tread'ing
tread'le
tread'mill
trea'son
trea'sonable
treas'ure
treas'ured
treas'urer
trea'sure-trove
treas'uring
treas'ury
treat
treat'able
treat'ed
treat'er
treat'ing
trea'tise
treat'ment
trea'ty
treb'le
treb'le clef
treb'led
treb'ling
treb'ly
treb'uchet
tree
tree'-frog
tree'nail
tref'le
tre'foil
treil'lage
trek
trel'lis
trel'lised
trel'lising
treman'do
trem'ble
trem'bled
trem'bler
trem'bling
Tremel'la
tremen'dous
tremen'dously
trem'olite
trem'olo
trem'or
trem'ulous
trem'ulousness
trench
trench'ant
trenched
trench'er
trench'erman
trench'ing
trend
trend'ed
trend'ing
tren'tal
trepan'
trepang'
trepanned'
trepan'ner
trepan'ning
trephine'
trepida'tion
tres'pass
tres'passed
tres'passer
tres'passing
tress
tressed
tress'ure
tress'ured
tress'y
tres'tle
tres'tle-tree
tret
trev'et
trey
tri'able
tri'ad
tri'al
tri'alogue
trian'drian
trian'drous
tri'angle
tri'angled
trian'gular
triangular'ity
trian'gularly
trian'gulate
trian'gulated
trian'gulating
triangula'tion
tri'archy
Tri'as, tri'as
Trias'sic
tri'bal
tribe
trib'let
tribom'eter
tri'brach
tribula'tion
tribu'nal
trib'unary
trib'unate
trib'une
trib'utarily
trib'utary
trib'ute
tricap'sular
trice
tricen'nial
tricen'tenary
trichi'na
trichino'sis
tri'chord
trichot'omous
trichot'omy
tri'chroism
trick
tricked
trick'ery
trick'ing
trick'ish
trick'ishness
trick'le
trick'led
trick'ling
trick'ster
trick'-track
trick'y
tric'linate
triclin'iary
triclin'ic
tricoc'cous
tri'colour
tri'coloured
tricor'poral
tricus'pid
tricus'pidate
tri'cycle
tridac'tylous
tri'dent
triden'tate
tridentif'erous
Triden'tine
tridiapa'son
tried

trien'nial
trien'nially
tri'er
tri'erarch
trifa'rious
tri'fid
trifis'tulary
tri'fle
tri'fled
tri'fler
tri'fling
tri'flingly
triflo'ral
triflo'rous
trifo'liate
trifo'liated
trifo'liolate
Trifo'lium
tri'foly
trifo'rium
tri'form
triform'ity
tri'furcated
trig
trig'amous
trig'amy
trigged
trig'ger
trig'ging
tri'glyph
tri'gon
trig'onal
trigonomet'ric
trigonom'etry
tri'gram
trigrammat'ic
tri'graph
Trigyn'ia
trihe'dral
trihe'dron
trilat'eral
trilin'gual
trilit'eral
tri'lithon
trill
trilled
trill'ing
tril'lion
trilo'bate
tri'lobed
tri'lobite
triloc'ular
tril'ogy
trim
trimes'ter
trimes'tral
trimes'trial
trim'eter
trimet'ric
trim'ly
trimmed
trim'mer
trim'ming
trim'ness
tri'nal
trine
trinerv'ate
trinerved'
trin'gle
Trinita'rian
Trinita'rianism
trin'ity
trin'ket
trin'ketry
trinoc'tial
trino'mial
tri'o
trioc'tile
tri'olet
tri'onal
tri'or
trip
tripar'tite
triparti'tion
tripe
trip'edal
tripen'nate
triper'sonal
triper'sonalist
tripersonal'ity
tripet'alous
trip'-hammer
tri'phone
triph'thong
triphthon'gal
triph'yline
triphyl'lous
trip'le
trip'led
trip'let
trip'licate, *n.*, *a.*
trip'licate, *v.*
triplica'tion
triplic'ity
trip'ling
trip'lite
tri'pod
tripo'dian
trip'ody
trip'oli
tri'pos
tripped
trip'per
trip'ping
trip'pingly
trip'sis
trip'tote
trip'tych
tri'reme
trirhomboid'al
trisect'
trisect'ed
trisect'ing
trisec'tion
trisep'alous
trisper'mous
trist
trisul'cate
trisyllab'ic
trisyl'lable
trite
trite'ly
trite'ness
tri'theism
tri'theist
tritheist'ic
Tri'ton
tri'tone
trit'urable
trit'urate
trit'urated
trit'urating
tritura'tion
tri'umph
trium'phal
trium'phant
trium'phantly
tri'umphed
trium'pher
tri'umphing
trium'vir
trium'viral
trium'virate
tri'une
triun'ity
tri'valve
trivalv'ular
triv'et
triv'ial
trivial'ity
triv'ium
triweek'ly
tro'car
trocha'ic
trochan'ter
tro'chee
tro'chil
troch'ilus
tro'chings
troch'lea
tro'choid
trod
trodd'en
trog'lodyte
Tro'jan
troll
trolled
trol'ley
troll'ing
trol'lop
trom'bone
tromp, trompe
trompille'
tro'na
troop
trooped
troop'er
troop'ing
troop'-ship
trope
troph'ic
tro'phied
tro'phy
trop'ic
trop'ical
tro'pist
tropolog'ical
tropol'ogy
trot
troth
trot'ted
trot'ter
trot'ting
trou'badour
troub'le
troub'led
troub'ler
troub'lesome
troub'ling
troub'lous

trough
trounce
trounced
troun'cing
troupe
trou'sers
trousseau'
trout
trouvère
tro'ver
trow
trow'el
{ trow'elled
{ trow'eled
troy
troy' weight
tru'ancy
tru'ant
truce
truck
truck'age
trucked
truck'er
truck'ing
truck'le
truck'le-bed
truck'led
truck'ler
truck'ling
truck'man
tru'culence
tru'culency
tru'culent
trudge
trudged
trudg'ing
true
tru'er
tru'est
truf'fle
trug
tru'ism
trull
tru'ly
trump
trumped
trump'ery
trump'et
trump'eted
trump'eter
trump'et-tongued
trump'ing
trun'cal
trun'cate, *adj.*
trun'cate, *v.*
trun'cated
trun'cating
trunca'tion
trun'cheon
trun'dle
trun'dle-bed
trun'dled
trun'dling
trunk
trunk'-hose
trun'nel
trun'nion
trun'nioned
truss
trussed

truss'el
truss'ing
trust
trust'deed
trust'ed
trustee'
trustee'ship
trust'er
trust'ful
trust'fully
trust'ier
trust'iest
trust'ily
trust'iness
trust'ing
trust'ingly
trust'worthiness
trust'worthy
trust'y
truth
truth'ful
truth'fully
*truth'*fulness
truth'less
truths
trutta'ceous
try
try'ing
try'sail
tryst
tryst'ing
Tsar
Tsarit'sa
tset'se
tub
tu'ba
tu'bal
tub'bing
tub'by
tube
tubed
tu'ber
tu'bercle
tu'bercled
tuber'cular
tuber'culate
tuber'culin
tuberculo'sis
tuber'culous
tuberif'erous
tu'berose
tuberos'ity
tu'berous
tu'bicorn
tu'biform
tu'bing
tu'bipore
tu'bular
tubulate, *adj.*
tu'bulate, *v.*
tu'bule
tu'bulicole
tu'buliform
tu'bulous
tuck
tucked
tuck'er
tuck'et
tuck'ing
Tu'dor

Tues'day
tu'fa
tufa'ceous
tuff
tuft
tuft'ed
tuft'-hunter
tuft'-hunting
tuft'ing
tuft'y
tug
tug'boat
tugged
tug'ger
tug'ging
tui'tion
tui'tionary
tu'lip
tu'lipist
tulipoma'nia
tu'lip-tree
tulle
tum'ble
tum'bled
tum'ble-down
tum'bler
tum'blerful
tum'bling
tum'brel
tum'bril
tumefac'tion
tu'mefied
tu'mefy
tu'mefying
tu'mid
tumid'ity
tu'mour
tu'mular
tu'muli
tu'mult
tumul'tuary
tumul'tuous
tumul'tuously
tumul'tuousness
tu'mulus
tun
tu'nable
tune
tuned
tune'ful
tune'fully
tune'less
tu'ner
tung'state
tung'sten
tung'stic
Tun'gus
tu'nic
tu'nicary
tu'nicate
tu'nicated
tu'nicle
tu'ning
tu'ning-fork
Tunis'ian
Tunk'er
tun'nage
tun'nel
{ tun'nelled
{ tun'neled

tun'nelling
tun'neling
tun'ny
tup
tu'pelo
Tura'nian
tur'ban
tur'bary
tur'bid
turbid'ity
tur'bidly
tur'bidness
turbinate, *adj.*
tur'binate, *v.*
tur'binated
tur'bine
tur'bit
tur'bot
tur'bulence
tur'bulency
tur'bulent
Turc'ism
Turk'ism
Tur'coman
tureen'
turf
turfed
turf'iness
turf'ing
turf'y
tur'gent
turges'cence
turges'cency
turges'cent
tur'gid
turgid'ity
Turk
tur'key
tur'key-buzzard
tur'key-cock
Turk'ish
Turk'ism
Turk's'-cap
tur'malin
tur'meric
tur'moil
tur'moiled
tur'moiling
turn
turn'coat
turned
turn'er
turn'ery
turn'ing
turn'ing-point
tur'nip
turn'key
turn'out
turn'over
turn'pike
turn'plate
turn'sole
turn'spit
turn'stile
turn'stone
turn'table
tur'pentine
tur'peth
tur'pitude
turquoise'

tur'ret
tur'reted
tur'ret-ship
tur'rilite
tur'tle
tur'tle-dove
turves
Tus'can
tush
tusk
tusked
tusk'er
tusk'y
tus'sle
tus'sled
tus'sock
tus'sock-grass
tus'socky
tut
tu'telage
tu'telar
tu'telary
tu'tenag
tu'tor
tu'torage
tu'tored
tu'toress
tuto'rial
tu'toring
tu'tors
tut'san
tut'ti
tut'ty
tu-whit'
tu-whoo'
tuyère'
twad'dle
twad'dled
twad'dler
twad'dling
twain
twaite
twang
twanged
twang'ing
twan'gle
twank
twan'kay
twank'ing
'twas
twat'tle
twat'tling
tway'blade
tweak
tweaked
tweak'ing
tweed
twee'dle
twee'dled
twee'dling
tweel
twee'ny-maid
tweer
twee'zers
twelfth
twelfth'-night
twelve
twelve'month
twelve'pence
twelve'penny

twen'tieth
twen'ty
twen'tyfold
twi'bill, twy'bill
twice
twice'-told
twid'dle
twid'dled
twid'dling
twig
twig'gy
twi'light
twill
twilled
twill'ing
twin
twine
twined
twinge
twinged
twinge'ing
twin'ing
twin'kle
twin'kled
twin'kling
twin'ling
twinned
twin'ning
twirl
twirled
twirl'ing
twist
twist'ed
twist'er
twist'ing
twit
twitch
twitched
twitch'er
twitch'ing
twit'ted
twit'ter
twit'tered
twit'tering
twit'ting
'twixt
two
two'-decker
two'-edged
*two'*fold
two'-handed
two'-legged
two'-lobed
two'pence
two'penny
twos
Tychon'ic
tycoon'
tye
ty'ing
ty'ler
tym'bal
tym'pan
tympan'ic
tympanit'ic
tympani'tis
tym'panum
tym'pany
ty'pal
type

type'writer
type'writing
type'written
Typho'ean
ty'phoid
Ty'phon
typhoon'
{ ty'phous
{ ty'phus
typ'ic
typ'ical
typ'ically
typifica'tion
typ'ified

typ'ify
typ'ifying
ty'pist
ty'po-
typog'rapher
typograph'ic
typograph'ical
typog'raphy
typ'olite
typol'ogy
tyran'nic
tyran'nical
tyran'nically
tyran'nicide

tyr'annize
tyr'annized
tyr'annizing
tyr'annous
tyr'anny
ty'rant
tyre
Tyr'ian
ty'ro
Tyrolese'
Tyrtae'an
Tzar
Tzari'na

U

ubi'ety
u'biquist
ubiquita'rian
ubiq'uitary
ubiq'uitous
ubiq'uity
u'dal
ud'der
udom'eter
ug'lier
ug'liest
ug'lily
ug'liness
ug'ly
uh'lan, u'lan
uit'lander
ukase'
ul'cer
ul'cerate
ul'cerated
ul'cerating
ulcera'tion
ul'cerous
Ulema'
ulig'inous
ul'lage
ulma'ceous
ul'mic
ul'min, ul'mine
ul'na
ul'ster
ulte'rior
ulte'riorly
ul'tima
ul'tima ra'tio
ul'timate
ul'timated
ul'timately
ul'timating
ultima'tum
ul'timo
ul'tra
ul'traism
ul'traist
ultramarine'
ultramon'tane
ultramon'tanism
ultramon'tanist
ultramun'dane
ul'ulate
um'bel
um'bellar
um'bellate
um'bellated
umbellif'erous
um'ber
um'bered

umbil'ic
umbil'ical
umbil'icate
umbili'cus
um'bo
um'bonate
um'bonated
um'bra
umbrac'uliform
um'brage
umbra'geous
umbrel'la
umbrif'erous
um'pirage
um'pire
unabashed'
unaba'ted
una'ble
unabridged'
unaccent'ed
unaccept'able
unaccom'modating
unaccom'panied
unaccount'able
unaccount'ably
unaccus'tomed
un*acknowl'edged*
unacquaint'ed
unadorned'
unadul'terated
unadvi'sable
unadvi'sedly
unaffect'ed
unaffect'edly
unaid'ed
unallied'
unalloyed'
unal'terable
unal'terably
unal'tered
unambi'tious
una'miable
unanim'ity
unan'imous
unan'imously
unan'swerable
unan'swerably
unan'swered
unappre'ciated
unapprised'
unapproach'able
unappro'priated
unarmed'
unascertained'
unasked'

unaspi'ring
unassail'able
unassailed'
unassist'ed
unassort'ed
unassu'ming
unattached'
unattain'able
unattempt'ed
unattend'ed
unattract'ive
u'nau
unauthen'tic
unau'thorized
unavail'able
unavail'ing
unavoid'able
unavoid'ably
unaware'
unawares'
unbal'anced
unbar'
unbear'able
unbear'ably
unbecom'ing
unbefit'ting
unbegot'ten
unbelief'
unbeliev'er
unbeliev'ing
unbeloved'
unbend'
unbend'ing
unbent'
unbi'as
unbi'ased
unbid'den
unbind'
unbit'
unbleached'
unblem'ished
unblest'
unblush'ing
unbolt'
unborn'
unbor'rowed
unbos'om
unbought
unbound'ed
unbound'edly
unbri'dle
unbrok'en
unbroth'erly
unbuck'le
unbur'den
unbur'ied
unbut'ton
un*called'*

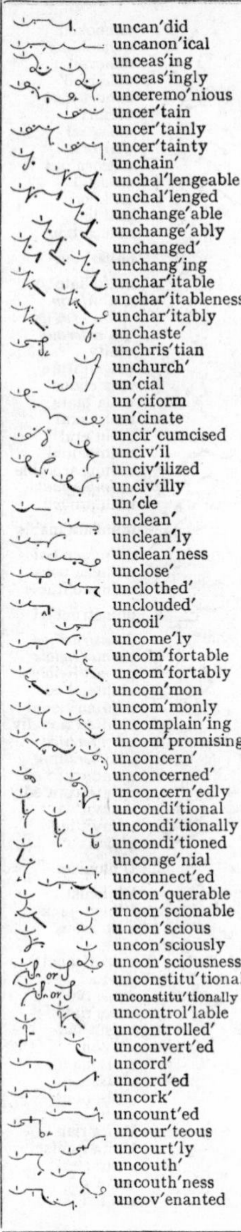

uncan′did
uncanon′ical
unceas′ing
unceas′ingly
unceremo′nious
uncer′tain
uncer′tainly
uncer′tainty
unchain′
unchal′lengeable
unchal′lenged
unchange′able
unchange′ably
unchanged′
unchang′ing
unchar′itable
unchar′itableness
unchar′itably
unchaste′
unchris′tian
unchurch′
un′cial
un′ciform
un′cinate
uncir′cumcised
unciv′il
unciv′ilized
unciv′illy
un′cle
unclean′
unclean′ly
unclean′ness
unclose′
unclothed′
unclouded′
uncoil′
uncome′ly
uncom′fortable
uncom′fortably
uncom′mon
uncom′monly
uncomplain′ing
uncom′promising
unconcern′
unconcerned′
unconcern′edly
uncondi′tional
uncondi′tionally
uncondi′tioned
uncongé′nial
unconnect′ed
uncon′querable
uncon′scionable
uncon′scious
uncon′sciously
uncon′sciousness
unconstitu′tional
unconstitu′tionally
uncontrol′lable
uncontrolled′
unconvert′ed
uncord′
uncord′ed
uncork′
uncount′ed
uncour′teous
uncourt′ly
uncouth′
uncouth′ness
uncov′enanted

uncov′er
uncreat′ed
unc′tion
unc′tuous
uncul′tivated
uncur′rent
uncut′
unda′ted
undaunt′ed
undaunt′edly
undec′agon
undeceive′
undeci′ded
undefend′ed
undefiled′
undefined′
undeliv′ered
undeni′able
undeni′ably
un*denomina′tional*
un′der
un′der-agent
*under*bid′
*un′der*bred
*un′der*brush
un′der-clerk
*un′der*clothing
*un′der*current
*un′der*done
*under*dose′
*un′der*drain
under-es′timate, *v*
under-es′timate, *n*
under-es′timated
under-es′timating
*under*foot′
*under*go′
*under*go′ing
*under*gone′
*under*grad′uate
*un′der*ground
*un′der*growth
un′derhand
*un′der*handed
*under*hung′
*under*lay′
*un′der*lease
*under*let′
*under*lie′
*under*line
*under*lined′
*un′der*ling
*under*ly′ing
*under*mine′
un′dermost
*under*neath′
*under*pin′
*under*pin′ning
*under*rate′
*under*run′
*under*score′
under-sec′retary
*under*sell′
*un′der*shot
*un′der*sized
*un′der*soil
*under*stand′
*under*stand′ing
*under*stood′

*un′der*strapper
*un′der*study
*under*take′
*under*tak′en
*un′der*taker
*under*ta′king
*under*took′
*under*val′ue
*un′der*wear
*under*went′
*un′der*wood
*under*work′
*under*write′
un′derwriter
undeserved′
undeserv′ing
undesigned′
undesign′ing
undesir′able
undetect′ed
unde′viating
undid′
undigest′ed
undig′nified
undimin′ished
undimmed′
undis′ciplined
undisguised′
undismayed′
undisturbed′
undivi′ded
undo′
undo′er
undo′ing
un′done
undoubt′ed
undoubt′edly
undress′
undue′
un′dulant
un′dulate
un′dulated
un′dulating
undula′tion
un′dulatory
undu′ly
undu′tiful
undy′ing
unearned′
unearth′
unearthed′
unearth′ing
unearth′ly
uneas′ily
uneas′iness
uneas′y
uned′ucated
unembar′rassed
unemployed′
unencum′bered
unend′ing
unendur′able
unendur′ably
unengaged′
unenlight′ened
unen′viable
unen′viably
une′quable
un*e′qual*
un*e′qualled*

une'*qually*
unequiv'ocal
unequiv'ocally
uner'ring
uner'ringly
unessen'tial
une'ven
une'venly
une'venness
unevent'ful
unexam'pled
unexcep'tionable
unexcep'tionably
unexhaust'ed
un*expect'ed*
un*expect'ed*ly
unexplained'
unexplored'
unexpressed'
un*extin'guish*able
un*extin'guished*
unfad'ed
unfad'ing
unfail'ing
unfail'ingly
unfair'
unfair'ly
unfair'ness
unfaith'ful
unfaith'fulness
un*famil'iar*
un*famil'iar*ly
unfash'ionable
unfash'ionably
unfash'ioned
unfast'en
unfast'ened
unfast'ening
unfath'omable
unfa'vourable
unfa'vourably
unfeel'ing
unfeel'ingly
unfeigned'
unfeign'edly
unfelt'
unfem'inine
unfet'tered
unfil'ial
unfin'ished
unfit'
unfit'ly
unfit'ness
unfit'ted
unfit'ting
unfix'
unfixed'
unfix'ing
unflag'ging
unflat'tering
unfledged'
unflinch'ing
unfold'
unfold'ed
unfold'ing
unforeseen'
unfore*told'*
unfor*giv'en*
unfor*giv'*ing
unformed'
unfor'tunate
unfor'tunately
unfound'ed
unfrequent'ed
unfre'quently
unfriend'ly
unfruit'ful
unfruit'fulness
unfulfilled'
unfurl'
unfurled'
unfurl'ing
unfur'nished
ungain'ly
ungen'erous
ungen'erously
unge'nial
ungen'tle
un*gen'tleman*ly
ungod'liness
ungod'ly
un*gov'ern*able
un*gov'ern*ably
ungrace'ful
ungrace'fully
ungrace'fulness
ungra'cious
ungra'ciously
ungrammat'ical
ungrate'ful
ungrate'fully
unground'ed
ungrudg'ing
un'gual
unguard'ed
unguard'edly
un'guent
un'guentary
unguen'tous
unguic'ulate
unguic'ulated
un'gulate
un'gulated
unhal'lowed
unhand'
unhand'some
unhand'somely
unhan'dy
unhap'pily
unhap'piness
unhap'py
unharmed'
unhar'ness
unhar'nessed
unhar'nessing
unhealth'iness
unhealth'y
unheard'
unheed'ed
unheed'ing
unhes'itating
unhes'itatingly
unhinge'
unhinged'
unhing'ing
unhitch'
unho'liness
unho'ly
unhon'oured
unhook'
unhooked'
unhook'ing
unhorse'
unhorsed'
unhors'ing
unhurt'
uniax'ial
u'nicorn
unicorn'ous
unide'al
unifa'cial
unif'ic
unifica'tion
uniflo'rous
unifo'liate
u'niform
uniform'ity
u'niformly
u'nify
unigen'iture
unig'enous
unila'biate
unilat'eral
unilit'eral
unimpaired'
unimpeach'able
un*impor'tant*
unimproved'
uninflam'mable
un*influen'tial*
uningen'uous
uninhab'itable
uninstruct'ed
un*instruct'ive*
un*intel'ligible*
un*intel'ligibly*
unintend'ed
uninten'tional
uninten'tionally
un*in'terested*
un*in'terest*ing
uninterrupt'ed
uninterrupt'edly
uninvit'ed
uninvit'ing
u'nion
U'nionism
U'nionist
U'nion Jack
unip'arous
u'niped
uniper'sonal
unique'
unise'rial
unise'riate
unisex'ual
u'nison
u'nisonance
u'nisonant
u'nisonous
u'nit
Unita'rian
Unita'rianism
u'nitary
unite'
uni'ted

uni'tedly
uni'ter
uni'ting
uni'tion
u'nity
u'nivalve
u'nivalved
univalv'ular
univer'sal
*Univer'sal*ism
*Univer'sal*ist
universal'ity
univer'salize
univer'salized
univer'sally
u'niverse
univer'sity
univ'ocal
unjust'
unjust'ifiable
unjust'ifiably
unjust'ly
unkempt'
unken'nel
unken'nelled
unken'nelling
unkind'
unkind'ly
unkind'ness
un'knowable
unknit'
unknow'ingly
unknown'
unlace'
unlaced'
unlac'ing
unlade'
unlatch'
unlatched'
unlatch'ing
unlaw'ful
unlaw'fully
unlaw'fulness
unlearn'
unlearned'
unlearn'ed
unleav'ened
unless'
unlet'tered
unli'censed
unlike'
unlike'ly
unlike'ness
unlim'ited
unlink'
unliq'uidated
unload'
unload'ed
unload'ing
unlock'
unlocked'
unlock'ing
unloose'
unloved'
unlove'liness
unlove'ly
unluck'ily
unluck'y
unmade'

unmaid'enly
unmake'
unmak'ing
unman'
unman'ageable
unman'ly
unmanned'
unman'nered
unman'nerly
unmar'ried
unmask'
unmasked'
unmask'ing
unmatched'
unmean'ing
unmen'tionable
unmer'ciful
unmer'cifully
unmer'ited
unmil'itary
unmind'ful
unmin'gled
unmista'kable
unmit'igated
unmixed'
unmoor'
unmoth'erly
unmoved'
unmur'muring
unmu'sical
unmuz'zle
unmuz'zled
unnamed'
unnat'ural
unnat'urally
unnec'essarily
unnec'essary
unneigh'bourly
unnerve'
unnerved'
unnerv'ing
unno'ted
unno'ticed
unnum'bered
un*objec'tionable*
unoblig'ing
unobserv'able
unobserv'ant
unobserv'ing
unobtru'sive
unoc'cupied
unoffend'ing
unoffi'cial
unoffi'cious
uno'pened
un*or'ganized*
unostenta'tious
unostenta'tiously
unpack'
unpacked'
unpack'ing
unpaid
unpal'atable
unpar'alleled
unpar'donable
unpar'donably
un*parliament'ary*

unpatriot'ic
unpaved'
unperceiv'able
unperceived'
unphilosoph'ical
unpin'
unpinned'
unpin'ning
unpit'ied
unpit'ying
unpleas'ant
unpleas'antly
unpleas'antness
unpleas'ing
unpoet'ical
unpol'ished
unpollut'ed
unpop'ular
unpopular'ity
unprac'tical
un*prac'tised*
unprec'edented
un*prej'udiced*
unpremed'itated
unprepared'
unprepossess'ing
unpretend'ing
unprin'cipled
unprint'ed
un*produc'tive*
unprofes'sional
unprof'itable
unprof'itably
unprom'ising
unpronounce'able
unpropi'tious
unpros'perous
unpros'perously
unprotect'ed
unprovi'ded
unprovoked'
un*pub'lished*
unpun'ished
unqual'ified
unquench'able
{ un*ques'tionable*
{ un*ques'tionably*
unques'tioned
unques'tioning
unqui'et
unqui'etly
unrav'el
{ unrav'elled
{ unrav'eled
{ unrav'elling
{ unrav'eling
unread'
unread'able
unread'y
unre'al
unreal'ity
unre'alizable
or
unre'alized
unrea'sonable

unrea'sonableness
unrea'sonably
unredeemed'
unregen'eracy
unregen'erate
unreg'istered
unrelent'ing
unreli'able
un*remem'bered*
unremit'ting
unremun'erative
unrepent'ing
un*represent'ed*
unrequi'ted
unreserve'
unreserved'
unreserv'edly
unresist'ing
unrest'
unrest'ing
unrestrained'-nt'
unrestrict'ed
unreward'ed
unrid'dle
unrig'
unright'eous
unright'eously
unright'eousness
unripe'
unri'val(l)ed
unrobe'
unroll'
unrolled'
unroll'ing
unroman'tic
unroof'
unroofed'
unroof'ing
unruf'fled
unru'liness
unru'ly
unsad'dle
unsad'dled
unsad'dling
unsafe'
unsafe'ly
unsaid'
unsale'able
unsanc'tified
un*satisfac'tori*ly
un*satisfac'tory*
unsat'isfying
unsa'vory
unsay'
unsay'ing
unscathed'
unschol'arly
un*schooled'*
unscientif'ic
unscrew'
unscrewed'
unscrew'ing
unscrip'tural
or
unscru'pulous
unscru'pulously
unscru'pulous- [ness
unseal'
unsealed'
unseal'ing
unseam'
unsearch'able
unsea'sonable
unsea'sonably
unseat'
unseat'ed
unseat'ing
unsea'worthy
unsec'onded
unsecta'rian
unsee'ing
unseem'ly
unseen'
un*self'ish*
un*self'ish*ly
un*self'ishness*
unser'viceable
unset'tle
unset'tled
unset'tling
unsex'
unshack'le
unshak'en
unsheathe'
unsheathed'
unsheath'ing
unship'
unshipped'
unship'ping
unshod'
unshrink'ing
unshrinkingly
unsight'liness
unsight'ly
unskil'ful
unskil'fulness
unskilled'
unsmoked'
unso'ciable
unso'cial
unsoiled'
unsold'
unsolic'ited
unsophis'ticated
unsort'ed
unsought'
unsound'
unsound'ly
unsound'ness
unspa'ring
unspa'ringly
unspeak'able
unspeak'ably
unspent'
unspot'ted
unsta'ble
unstaid'
unstained'
unstead'ily
unstead'iness
unstead'y
unstint'ed
unstop'
unstopped'
unstring'
unstrung'
unstud'ied
un*substan'tial*
unsuccess'ful
unsuccess'fully
unsuit'able
unsuit'ably
unsuit'ed
unsul'lied
unsum'moned
unsung'
unsupport'ed
unsurpassed'
unsuscep'tible
un*suspect'ed*
un*suspect'*ing
unsuspi'cious (or)
unsuspi'ciously (or)
unsustained'
unswathe'
unswathed'
unswath'ing
unswayed'
unsweet'ened
unswerv'ing
un*sympathet'ic*
unsystemat'ic
untaint'ed
untam'able-eable
untast'ed
untaught'
unten'able
un*thank'ful*
un*thank'fully*
un*thank'*fulness
un*think'*able
un*think'*ing
un*think'*ingly
unthought'ful
unthrift'y
unti'dy
untie', untied'
until'
untime'ly
untir'ing
un'to
un*told'*
unto'ward
untract'able
untrained'
untram'melled
untram'meled
untrav'elled
untrav'eled
un*tried'*
untrod'
untrod'den
untrue'
untru'ly
untruth'
untu'tored
untwine'
untwined'
untwin'ing
untwist'
untwist'ed
untwist'ing
unty'ing

unused'
unu'*sual*
unu'*sually*
unut'terable
unval'ued
unva'ried
unvar'nished
unva'rying
unveil'
unveiled'
unveil'ing
unver'ified
unwa'rily
unwa'riness
unwar'like
unwar'rantable
unwar'rantably
unwar'ranted
unwa'ry
unwav'ering
unwea'ried
unwea'riedly
unwea'ry
unweave'
unweav'ing
unwel'*come*
unwell'
unwept'
unwhole'some
unwhole'someness
unwield'iness
unwield'y
unwill'ing
unwill'ingly
unwill'ingness
unwind'
unwind'ing
unwise'
unwise'ly
unwit'tingly
unwit'ty
unwom'anly
unwont'ed
unwont'edness
unworld'ly
unworn'
unwor'thily
unwor'thiness
unwor'thy
unwound'
unwov'en
unwrit'ten
unwrought
unyield'ing
unyoke'
unyoked'
unyok'ing
up
u'pas
upbraid'
upbraid'ed
upbraid'er
upbraid'ing
upcast'
upheav'al
upheave'
upheaved'
upheav'ing
upheld'
up'hill
uphold'
uphold'er
uphold'ing
uphol'ster
uphol'sterer
uphol'stery
up'land
uplift'
uplift'ed
uplift'ing
upon'
up'per
up'per*most*
upraise'
upraised'
uprais'ing
uprear'
upreared'
uprear'ing
up'right
up'rightly
up'rightness
upris'en
upris'ing
up'roar
uproar'ious
uproot'
uproot'ed
uproot'ing
uprose'
upset'
upset'ting
up'shot
up'side
up'spring
upstairs'
up'start
up'-stroke
up'-train
upturn'
upturned'
upturn'ing
up'ward
up'wards
Ura'lian
u'ranite
ura'nium
uranog'raphy
uranol'ogy
uranos'copy
U'ranus
u'rate
ur'ban
urbane'
urban'ity
ur'chin
Ur'du
u'rea
ure'ter
ure'thra
urge
urged
ur'gency (or)
ur'gent
ur'gently
ur'ger
ur'ging
u'ric
u'rim
u'rinal
u'rinary
u'rinate
u'rinative
u'rine
u'rinous
urn
uros'copy
Ur'sa Major
Ur'sa Minor
ur'siform
ur'sine
Ur'suline
u'rus
us
u'sable
u'sage
u'sance
use
used
use'ful
use'fully
use'fulness
use'less
use'lessly
use'lessness
u'ser
ush'er
ush'ered
ush'ering
u'sing
us'quebaugh
ust'ion
ustula'tion
u'sual, u'sually
u'sufruct
usufruct'uary
u'surer
us'urious
usu'riously
usurp'
usurpa'tion
usurped'
usurp'er
usurp'ing
u'sury
uten'sil
u'terine
u'terus
utilita'rian
utilita'rianism (or)
util'ity
utiliza'tion
u'tilize
u'tilized
u'tilizing
ut'*most*

Uto'pia
Uto'pian
Uto'pianism
u'tricle
utric'ular
ut'ter

ut'terable
ut'terance
ut'tered
ut'terer
ut'tering
ut'terly
ut'ter*most*

u'vea
u'veous
u'vula
u'vular
uxo'rial
uxo'rious
uxo'riousness

V

va'cancy
va'cant
vacate'
vaca'ted
vaca'ting
vaca'tion
vac'cinate
vac'cinated
vac'cinating
vaccina'tion
vac'cinator
vac'cine
vac'cinist
vac'illancy
vac'illant
vac'illate
vac'illated
vac'illating
vacilla'tion
vac'uist
vacu'ity
vac'uous
vac'uum
va'de-me'cum
vag'abond
vag'abondage
vag'abondism
vag'abondize
vaga'ry
vagi'na
vagi'nal
vag'inant
vag'inate
vag'inated
va'grancy
va'grant
vague
vague'ly
vague'ness
vail
vain
vain'er
vain'est
vainglo'rious
vainglo'riously
vainglo'ry
vain'ly
vair
vair'y
vai'vode
vakeel'
val'ance
vale
valedic'tion
valedic'tory
va'lence
Valençiennes
val'entine

vale'rian
val'et (or)
valetudina'rian
valetu'dinary
Valhal'la
val'iant
val'iantly
val'id
valid'ity
val'idly
val'inch
valise'
Valkyr'ie
val'ley
val'lum
valo'nia
val'orous
val'orously
val'our
valse
val'uable
valua'tion
val'uator
val'ue
val'ued
val'ueless
val'uer
val'uing
val'vate
valve
valved
valv'let
valv'ular
valv'ule
vam'brace
vamp
vamped
vamp'er
vamp'ing
vam'pire
vam'plet
van
vana'dium
Van'dal
vandal'ic
van'dalism
vandyke'
vane
vang
van'*guard*
vanil'la
van'ish
van'ished
van'ishing
van'ity
van'quish
van'quishable
van'quished

van'quisher
van'quishing
van'tage
van'tage-ground
vap'id
vapid'ity
vap'idly
va'porable
vaporif'ic
va'porizable
vaporiza'tion
va'porize
va'porized
va'porizing
va'porous
va'pour, va'por
va'pour-bath
va'poured
va'pourer
va'pouring
va'pourish
va'pours
va'poury, va'pory
variabil'ity
va'riable
va'riableness
va'riably
va'riance
va'riant
varia'tion
var'ices
var'icocele
var'icose
va'ried
va'riegate
va'riegated
va'riegating
variega'tion
vari'ety
va'riform
va'riformed
vari'ola
vari'olar
variola'tion
variol'ic
va'riolite
va'rioloid
vari'olous
vario'rum
va'rious
va'riously
va'rix
var'let
var'nish
var'nished
var'nisher
var'nishing
va'ry

va'rying
vas'cular
vascular'ity
vasculif'erous
vase
vas'eline
vas'iform
vas'sal
vas'salage
vast
vast'er
vast'est
vast'ly
vast'ness
vast'y
vat
Vat'ican
Vat'icanism
vat'icide
vatic'inal
vatic'inate
vatic'inated
vatic'inating
vaticina'tion
vaude'ville
Vaudois'
vault
vault'ed
vault'er
vault'ing
vaunt
vaunt'ed
vaunt'er
vaunt'ing
vaunt'ingly
vauque'linite
veal
vec'tor
Ve'da
vedette'
veer
veered
veer'ing
veg'etable
veg'etal
vegeta'rian
vegeta'rianism
veg'etate
veg'etated
veg'etating
vegeta'tion
veg'etative
ve'hemence
ve'hemency
ve'hement
ve'hemently
ve'hicle
vehic'ular
vehm'gericht
veh'mic
veil
veiled
veil'ing
vein
veined
vein'ing
vein'less
vein'ous
vein'y
veld, veldt

vel'licate
vel'licated
vellica'tion
vel'lum
veloc'ipede
veloc'ity
ve'lum
vel'vet
vel'veted
velveteen'
vel'veting
vel'vety
ve'nal
venal'ity
venat'ic
vena'tion
vend
vend'ed
vendee'
vend'er
vendet'ta
vendibil'ity
vend'ible
vend'ing
vendi'tion
vend'or=vend'er
{ vend'or (legal term)
vendue'
veneer'
veneered'
veneer'ing
ven'erable
ven'erate
ven'erated
ven'erating
venera'tion
ven'erator
vene'real
ven'ery
venesec'tion
Vene'tian
ven'geance
venge'ful
venge'fully
ve'nial
venial'ity
veni're
ven'ison
ven'om
ven'omed
ven'omous
ven'omously
ve'nous
vent
vent'age
vent'ed
ven'ter
vent'-hole
ven'tiduct
ven'tilate
ven'tilated
ven'tilating
ventila'tion
ven'tilator
vent'ing
ven'tose
vent'-peg
vent'-pin
ven'tral

ven'tricle
ven'tricose
ventrilocu'tion
ventrilo'quial
ventril'oquism
ventril'oquist
ventril'oquize
ventril'oquized
ventril'oquizing
ventril'oquy
ven'ture
ven'tured
ven'turer
ven'turesome
ven'turin
ven'turing
ven'turous
ven'turously
ven'ue
ven'ulose
Ve'nus
vera'cious
vera'ciously
verac'ity
veran'da
vera'tria
vera'trine
verb
ver'bal
ver'balism
ver'balist
verbal'ity
ver'balize
ver'balized
ver'balizing
ver'bally
verba'tim
Verbe'na
ver'biage
verbose'
verbose'ly
verbos'ity
ver'dancy
ver'dant
ver'dantly
verd-antique'
ver'derer
ver'dict
ver'digris
ver'diter
ver'dure
ver'dured
ver'durous
verge
verged
ver'ger
ver'ging
verid'ical
ver'iest
ver'ifiable
verifica'tion
ver'ified
ver'ify
ver'ifying
ver'ily
verisim'ilar
verisimil'itude
ver'itable
ver'ity
ver'juice

ver'meil
vermeol'ogist
vermeol'ogy
vermicel'li
vermi'ceous
ver'micide
vermic'ular
vermic'ulate, *a.*
vermic'ulate, *v.*
vermic'ulated
vermicula'tion
ver'micule
vermic'ulous
ver'miform
ver'mifuge
vermil'ion
ver'min
ver'minate
vermina'tion
ver'minous
vermiv'orous
ver'muth
vernac'ular
ver'nal
verna'tion
ver'nicose
ver'nier
vero'nal
Veronese'
veron'ica
verr'ucose
ver'sant
ver'satile
versatil'ity
verse
versed
ver'sicle
ver'sicolour
ver'sicolor
ver'sicoloured
ver'sicolored
versifica'tion
ver'sified
ver'sifier
ver'sify
ver'sifying
ver'sion
verst
ver'sus
versute'
vert
ver'tebra
ver'tebrae
ver'tebral
vertebra'ta
ver'tebrate, *n.*, *a.*
ver'tebrate, *v.*
ver'tebrated
ver'tex
ver'tical
ver'tically
ver'ticil
vertic'illate
vertig'inous
ver'tigo
ver'vain
verve
ver'y
vesi'ca
ves'ical

ves'icant
ves'icate
ves'icated
ves'icating
vesica'tion
ves'icatory
ves'icle
vesic'ular
vesic'ulate
vesic'ulous
ves'per
ves'peral
ves'pertine
ves'piary
ves'sel
vest
Ves'ta
ves'tal
vest'ed
vestia'rian
ves'tiary
vestib'ular
ves'tibule
ves'tige
vest'ing
vest'ment
ves'try
ves'tryman
vest'ure
vest'ured
vesu'vian
vetch
vet'eran
veterina'rian
vet'erinary
ve'to
ve'toed
ve'toer
ve'toing
ve'toist
vettu'ra
vetturi'no
vex
vexa'tion
vexa'tious
vexa'tiously
vexed
vex'er
vex'il
vex'illar
vex'illary
vexilla'tion
vex'ing
vi'a
viabil'ity
vi'able
vi'aduct
vi'al
viam'eter
vi'and
viat'ic
viat'icum
via'tor
vi'brant
vi'brate
vi'brated
vi'bratile
vi'brating
vibra'tion
vi'brative

vi'bratory
vibur'num
vic'ar
vic'arage
vic'aress
vica'rial
vica'riate
vica'rious
vica'riously
vice
vi'ce
vice-ad'miral
vice-*chair'*man
vice-cham'ber-lain
vice-chan'cellor
vice-con'sul
vicege'rency
vicege'rent
vic'enary
vicen'nial
vice-pres'ident
vice-*prin'cipal*
vice-re'gal
vice'roy
viceroy'alty
vi'ce ver'sa
vic'inage
vic'inal
vicin'ity
vic'ious
vic'iously
vic'iousness
vicis'situde
vic'tim
vic'timize
vic'timized
vic'timizing
vic'tor
Victo'ria
victo'ria
victorine'
victo'rious
victo'riously
vic'tory
vict'ual
vict'ualled
vict'ualler
vict'ualling
vict'uals
vicu'na
vi'de
videl'icet
vidette'
vie
vied
Viennese
view
viewed
view'er
view'ing
view'less
vig'il
vig'ilance
vig'ilant
vig'ilantly
vignette'
vig'or, vig'our
vig'orous
vig'orously

Vi'king
vile
vile'ly
vile'ness
vi'ler
vi'lest
vilifica'tion
vil'ified
vil'ifier
vil'ify
vil'ifying
vil'la
vil'lage
vil'lager
vil'lain
vil'lainous
vil'lainously
vil'lainy
villat'ic
vil'leinage
vil'li
vil'lous
vim
vim'inal
vimin'eous
vina'ceous
vinaigrette'
vincibil'ity
vin'cible
vin'culum
vin'dicable
vin'dicate
vin'dicated
vin'dicating
vindica'tion
vin'dicative
vin'dicator
vin'dicatory
vindic'tive
vindic'tively
vindic'tiveness
vine
vine'-clad
vin'egar
vi'nery
vine'yard
vi'nous
vin'tage
vin'tager
vint'ner
vi'ny
vi'ol
vi'ola
vi'olable
viola'ceous
vi'olate
vi'olated
vi'olating
viola'tion
vi'olator
vi'olence
vi'olent
vi'olently
violes'cent
vi'olet
violin'
violin'ist
vi'olist
violoncel'list
violoncel'lo

violo'ne
vi'per
vi'perine
vi'perous
vira'go
vires'cent
vir'gate
Virgil'ian
vir'gin
vir'ginal
virgin'ity
vir'go
vir'gulate
virid'ity
vir'ile
viril'ity
virtu'
vir'tual
vir'tually
vir'tue
virtuo'so
vir'tuous
vir'tuously
vir'tuousness
vir'ulence
vir'ulent
vir'ulently
vi'rus
vis
vi'sa
vi'saed
vis'age
vis-à-vis'
vis'cera
vis'ceral
vis'cid
viscid'ity
viscos'ity
vis'count
vis'countess
vis'cous, vis'cus
visé'
Vish'nu
visibil'ity
vis'ible
vis'ibly
Vis'igoth
Visigoth'ic
vi'sion
vi'sionariness
vi'sionary
vis'it
vis'itable
vis'itant
visita'tion
visite'
vis'ited
vis'iter
vis'iting
vis'itor
visito'rial
vis'or, viz'or
{ vis'ored
{ viz'ored
vis'ta
vis'ual
visual'ity
vis'ualize
vi'tal
vi'talism

vital'ity
vitaliza'tion
vi'talize
vi'talized
vi'talizing
vi'tally
vi'tals
vi'tiate
vi'tiated
vi'tiating
vitia'tion
vit'iculture
vit'reous
vitres'cence
vitres'cent
vitres'cible
vitrifac'tion
vit'rifiable
vitrifica'tion
vit'rified
vit'riform
vit'rify
vit'rifying
vit'riol
vit'riolate
vit'riolated
vit'riolating
vitriola'tion
vitriol'ic
vit'riolizable
vitrioliza'tion
vit'riolize
vit'riolized
vit'riolizing
vit'uline
vitu'perate
vitu'perated
vitu'perating
vitupera'tion
vitu'perative
vitu'perator
viva'ce
viva'cious
viva'ciously
vivac'ity
viva'rium
viv'ary
vi'va vo'ce
vives
viv'ianite
viv'id
viv'idly
viv'idness
vivifica'tion
viv'ified
viv'ify
viv'ifying
vivip'arous
vivisec'tion
vivisec'tor
vix'en
vix'enish
viz'ard
vizier'
vizier'ate
viz'or
viz'ored
vo'cable
vocab'ulary
vocab'ulist

vo'cal
vocal'ic
vo'calism
vo'calist
vocal'ity
vocaliza'tion
vo'calize
vo'calized
vo'calizing
vo'cally
voca'tion
voc'ative
vocif'erate
vocif'erated
vocif'erating
vocifera'tion
vocif'erous
vocif'erously
vogue
voice
voiced
voice'less
voic'ing
void
void'able
void'ance
void'ed
void'er
void'ing
void'ness
vo'lant
Volapük'
vol'atile
volatil'ity
vol'atilizable
volatiliza'tion
vol'atilize
vol'atilized
vol'atilizing
volcan'ic
volcanic'ity
vol'canist
volcan'ity
vol'canize
volca'no
vole
volée'
volita'tion
voli'tion
vol'itive
volks'raad
vol'ley
vol'leyed
vol'leying
vol'plane
volt
volta'ic
vol'taism
voltam'eter
vol'taplast
vol'tatype
voltigeur'
volubil'ity
vol'uble
vol'ubly
vol'ume
vol'umed
volumet'ric
volu'minous
vol'untarily
vol'untary
vol'untaryism
volunteer'
volunteered'
volunteer'ing
volupt'uary
volupt'uous
volupt'uously
volupt'uousness
volute'
volu'ted
volu'tion
vo'mer
vo'merine
vom'ica
vom'it
vom'ited
vom'iting
vom'itive
vom'ito
vom'itory
vomituri'tion
vora'cious
vora'ciously
vorac'ity
vor'tex
vor'tical
vor'tically
vor'ticel
vo'taress
vo'tary
vote
vo'ted
vo'ter
vo'ting
vo'tive
vo'tively
vouch
vouched
vouchee'
vouch'er
vouch'ing
vouch'or
vouchsafe'
vouchsafed'
vouchsafe'ment
vouchsaf'ing
voussoir'
vow
vowed
vow'el
vow'el(l)ed
vow'er
vow'ing
vox pop'uli
voy'age
voy'aged
voy'ager
voyageur'
voy'aging
voy'al
vraisemblance'
Vulca'nian
Vulcan'ic
Vul'canist
vul'canite
vulcaniza'tion
vul'canize
vul'canized
vul'canizing
vul'gar
vul'garism
vulgar'ity
vul'garize
vul'garized
vul'garizing
vul'garly
Vul'gate
vulnerabil'ity
vul'nerable
vul'nerary
vul'pine
vul'ture
vul'turine
vy'ing

W

wab'ble
wab'bled
wab'bling
wack'e
wad
wad'ded
wad'ding
wad'dle
wad'dled
wad'dler
wad'dling
wade
wa'ded
wa'der
wa'ding
wa'fer
wa'fered
wa'fering
waf'fle
waft
waft'age
waft'ed
waft'er
waft'ing
wag
wage
waged
wa'ger
wa'gered
wa'gerer
wa'gering
wa'ges
wagged
wag'gery
wag'ging
wag'gish
wag'gishly
wag'gle
wag'gled
wag'gling
wa'ging
wag'(g)on
wag'(g)onage
wag'(g)oner
wagonette'
wag'tail
Waha'bi
waif
wail
wailed
wail'er
wail'ing
wain
wain'scot
wain'scot(t)ed
wain'scot(t)ing
waist
waist'band
waist'coat
wait
wait'ed
wait'er
wait'ing
wait'ing-maid
wait'ress
waits
waive
waived
waiv'er
waiv'ing
wake
waked
wake'ful
wake'fully
wake'fulness
wa'ken
wa'kened
wa'kener
wa'kening
wa'ker
wa'king
Walden'ses
wale
waled
Walhal'la
walk
walked
walk'er
walk'ing
walk'ing-stick
wall
Wal(l)a'chian
walled
wall'er
wal'let
wall'-eye
wall'-eyed
wall'flower
wall'-fruit
wall'ing
wall'-knot
wal'lop
wal'loped
wal'loping
wal'low
wal'lowed
wal'lower
wal'lowing
wall'-paper
wal'nut
wal'rus
waltz
waltzed
waltz'ing
wam'ble
wampee'
wam'pum
wan
wand
wan'der
wan'dered
wan'derer
wan'dering
wane
waned
wa'ning
wanghee'
wan'ly
wanned
wan'ness
wan'ning
want
want'ed
want'ing
wan'ton
wan'toned
wan'toning
wan'tonly
wan'tonness
want'wit
wap'entake
wap'iti
war
war'ble
war'bled
war'bler
war'bling
war'-cry
ward
war'-dance
ward'ed
ward'en
ward'enry
ward'er
ward'ing
ward'-mote
ward'robe
ward'room
ward'ship
ware
ware'house
ware'housed
ware'houseman
ware'housing
wares
war'fare
war'horse
wa'rily
wa'riness
war'like

war'lock
warm
warmed
warm'er
warm'est
warm'-hearted
warm'-hearted-[ness
warm'ing
warm'ing-pan
warm'ly
warmth
warn
warned
warn'er
warn'ing
war'-office
warp
war'-paint
war'-path
warped
warp'ing
war'rant
war'rantable
war'ranted
warrantee'
war'ranter
war'ranting
war'rantor
war'ranty
warred
war'ren
war'rener
war'ring
war'rior
war'-song
wart
wart'wort
wart'y
war'-whoop
war'worn
wa'ry
was
wase
wash
wash'-ball
wash'-board
wash'-bowl
washed
wash'er
wash'erwoman
wash'house
wash'ing
wash'-leather
wash'-stand
wash'-tub
wash'y
wasp
wasp'ish
wasp'ishly
was'sail
was'sailer
wast
waste
waste'book
wast'ed
waste'ful
waste'fully
waste'-gate
waste'ness
waste'pipe
wa'ster
wa'sting
wast'rel
watch
watch'-case
watch'-dog
watched
watch'er
watch'ful
watch'fully
watch'fulness
watch'-glass
watch'-*guard*
watch'-house
watch'ing
watch'maker
watch'man
watch'-night
watch'-tower
watch'*word*
wa'ter
wa'terage
wa'ter-butt
wa'ter-cart
wa'ter-closet
wa'tercourse
wa'tercress
wa'tered
wa'terfall
wa'ter-fowl
wa'teriness
wa'tering
wa'tering-place
wa'terish
wa'ter-lily
wa'ter-logged
wa'terman
wa'ter-mark
wa'termelon
wa'ter-mill
wa'ter-plane
wa'ter-pot
wa'terproof
wa'ter-ram
wa'ter-rat
wa'ter-rate
wa'ter-rot
wa'ter-rotted
wa'ter-rotting
wa'tershed
wa'ter-soak
wa'terspout
wa'tertight
wa'terway
wa'ter-work
wa'terwort
wa'tery
Wat'teau
wat'tle
wat'tled
wat'tling
waul, wawl
wave
waved
wave'less
wave'let
wave'-like
wave'-offering
wa'ver
wa'vered
wa'verer
wa'vering
wave'son
wa'viness
wa'ving
wa'vy
wawl
wax
waxed
wax'en
wax'-end
wax'iness
wax'ing
wax'wing
wax'work
wax'y
way
way'-bill
way'bread
way'farer
way'faring
waylaid'
waylay'
way'layer
way'laying
way'-mark
way'side
way'ward
way'wardly
way'wardness
way'wode
way'worn
wayz'goose
we
weak
weak'en
weak'ened
weak'ener
weak'ening
weak'er
weak'est
weak'-eyed
weak'ling
weak'ly
weak'ness
weal
weald
weald'en
wealth
wealth'ier
wealth'iest
wealth'y
wean
weaned
wean'ing
wean'ling
weap'on
weap'oned
wear
wear'able
wear'er

wear'ied
wear'ier
wear'iest
wear'ily
wear'iness
wear'ing
wear'isome
wear'isomeness
wear'y
wear'ying
wea'sand
wea'sel
weath'er
weath'er-beaten
weath'er-board
weath'er-bound
weath'ercock
weath'ered
weath'er-gage
weath'er-glass
weath'ering
weath'erly
weath'erwise
weave
weav'er
weav'ing
wea'zen
web
webbed
web'bing
web'by
web'-foot
web'footed
wed
wed'ded
wed'ding
wedge
wedged
wedge'-shaped
wedg'ing
Wedg'wood ware
wed'lock
Wednes'day
wee
weed
weed'ed
weed'er
weed'ery
weed'ing
weed'ing-hook
weed'less
weed'y
week
week'-day
week'ly
weel
ween
weened
ween'ing
weep
weep'er
weep'ing
weep'ing wil'low
weev'er
weev'il
weft
weige'lia

weigh
weigh'able
weigh'age
weigh'-bridge
weighed
weigh'er
weigh'-house
weigh'ing
weight
weight'ed
weight'ier
weight'iest
weight'ily
weight'iness
weight'ing
weight'less
weight'y
weir
weird
welch'er
wel'*come*
wel'comed
wel'comer
wel'coming
weld
weld'ed
weld'ing
wel'fare
wel'kin
well
well'aday
well'-being
well'-bred
well'-doer
well'-doing
well'-done
well'-dressed
welled
wel'ling
Wellingto'nia
Wellingto'nian
well'-known
well'-met
well'nigh
well'-spring
well'-wisher
Welsh
welsh'er
Welsh'man
welt
welt'ed
wel'ter
wel'tered
wel'tering
welt'ing
wen
wench
wend
wend'ed
wend'ing
wen'ny
went
wept
were
were'wolf
Werne'rian
wert
Wes'leyan
Wes'leyanism

west
west'erly
west'ern
west'ing
west'ward
wet
weth'er
wet'ness
wet'-nurse
wet'ted
wet'ter
wet'test
wet'ting
wet'tish
wey
whack
whacked
whack'er
whack'ing
whale
whale'-boat
whale'bone
whale'man
wha'ler
wha'ling
whap
wharf
wharf'age
wharf'ing
wharf'inger
what
whatev'er
what'-not
*what*soev'er
wheal
wheat
wheat'ear
wheat'en
whee'dle
whee'dled
whee'dler
whee'dling
wheel
wheel'barrow
wheel'-carriage
wheeled
wheel'er
wheel'-horse
wheel'-house
wheel'ing
wheel'wright
wheeze
wheezed
wheezing'
wheez'y
whelk
whelm
whelmed
whelm'ing
whelp
whelped
whelp'ing
when
whence
whencesoev'er
whenev'er
whensoev'er
where

where'about
where'abouts
whereas'
whereat'
whereby'
where'fore
where*in'*
whereinsoev'er
wherein'to
whereof'
whereon'
wheresoev'er
where*to'*
whereun'to
whereupon'
wherev'er
wherewith'
wherewithal'
wher'ry
whet
wheth'er
whet'slate
whet'stone
whet'ted
whet'ter
whet'ting
whew
whew'ellite
whey
whey'ey
whey'ish
which
*which*ev'er
*which*soev'er
whiff
whiffed
whiff'ing
whif'fle
whif'fled
whif'fler
whif'fletree
whif'fling
Whig
Whig'garchy
Whig'gery
Whig'gish
Whig'gism
while
whiled
whil'ing
whi'lom
whilst
whim
whim'brel
whim'per
whim'pered
whim'pering
whim'sey
whim'sical
whimsical'ity
whim'sically
whim'wham
whin'
whinchat
whine
whined
whi'ner
whi'ning
whi'ningly
whin'nied
whin'ny
whin'nying
whin'stone
whip
whip'-cord
whip'-hand
whipped
whip'per
whip'per-in
whip'per-snap'-[per
whip'pet
whip'ping
whip'ping-post
whip'pletree
whip'poorwill
whip'powill
whip'-staff
whip'-stick
whip'-stock
whipt
whir, whirr
whirl
whirl'about
whirled
whirl'igig
whirl'ing
whirl'pool
whirl'wind
whirred
whir'ring
whisk
whisked
whisk'er
whisk'ered
whis'key, whis'ky
whisk'ing
whis'per
whis'pered
whis'perer
whis'pering
whist
whis'tle
whis'tled
whis'tler
whis'tling
whit
white
white'bait
whit'ed
whi'ten
whi'tened
whi'tener
white'ness
whi'tening
whites
white'smith
white'throat
white'wash
white'washed
white'washer
white'washing
white'weed
white'wood
whith'er
whithersoev'er
whi'ting
whi'tish
whit'leather
whit'low
Whit'sun
Whit'-Sunday
Whit'suntide
whit'tle
whit'tled
whit'tling
whi'ty-brown
whiz
whizzed
whiz'zing
who
whoa
*who*ev'er
whole
whole'ness
whole'sale
whole'some
whole'someness
whol'ly
whom
whomsoev'er
whoop
whooped
whoop'ing
whoop'ing cough
whop
whopped
whop'per
whop'ping
whore
whore'dom
whore'monger
whor'ish
whorl
whorled
whort
whor'tleberry
whose
*whose*soev'er
*who'*so
*who*soev'er
why
wick
wick'ed
wick'edly
wick'edness
wick'er
wick'ered
wick'er-work
wick'et
Wic'liffite
wide
wide'awake
wide'ly
wi'den
wi'dened
wide'ness
wi'dening
wi'der
wide'spread
wi'dest
widge'on
wid'ow
wid'owed
wid'ower

wid'owhood
width
wield
wield'ed
wield'er
wield'ing
wield'y
wife
wife'hood
wife'less
wife'like
wife'ly
wig
wigged
wig'ging
wight
wig'wag
wig'wam
wild
wild'cat
wild'er
wil'der
wil'dered
wil'dering
wil'derness
wild'est
wild'-fire
wild'ly
wild'ness
wile
wil'ful
wil'fully
wil'fulness
wi'lier
wi'liest
wi'lily
wi'liness
will
willed
wil'ling
wil'lingly
wil'lingness
will-o'-the-wisp
wil'low
wil'lowed
wil'lowy
will'-with-a-wisp
wil'ly
wil'iy-nil'ly
wil'some
wilt
wilt'ed
wilt'ing
wi'ly
wim'ble
wim'ple
wim'pled
wim'pling
win
wince
winced
winc'er
winch
winch'ing
winc'ing
wind (moving air)
wind (to turn round)

wind'age
wind'-bound
wind'ed
wind'er
wind'fall
wind'-gall
wind'ier
wind'iest
wind'iness
wind'ing
wind'ing-sheet
wind'lass
win'dle
wind'mill
win'dow
win'dow-glass
win'dow-sash
win'dow-seat
wind'pipe
wind'row
wind'ward
wind'y
wine
wine'-bibber
wine'-cellar
wine'-glass
wing
winged
wing'ed
wing'ing
wing'less
wing'y
wink
winked
wink'er
wink'ing
win'kle
win'ner
win'ning
win'ning-post
win'now
win'nowed
win'nower
win'nowing
win'some
win'ter
win'tered
win'tergreen
win'tering
win'terly
win'try
wi'ny
winze
wipe
wiped
wi'per
wi'ping
wire
wire'draw
wire'drawer
wire'drawing
wire'-gauze
wire'less
wire'-pulling
wire'worm
wir'iness
wir'y
wis'dom
wise

wise'acre
wise'ly
wi'ser
wi'sest
wish
wished
wish'er
wish'ful
wish'fully
wish'ing
wish'y-washy
wisp
wist
Wista'ria
wist'ful
wist'fully
wis'tonwish
wit
witch
witch'craft
witch'-elm
witch'ery
witch'ing
wit'enagemote
with
withal'
withdraw'
withdraw'al
withdraw'er
withdraw'ing
withdraw'ing-room
withdrawn'
withdrew'
withe
withed
with'er
with'ered
with'ering
with'ers
withheld'
withhold'
withhold'en
withhold'er
withhold'ing
within'
without'
withstand'
withstand'ing
withstood'
with'y
wit'less
wit'ling
wit'ness
wit'nessed
wit'nessing
wit'ted
wit'ticism
wit'tier
wit'tiest
wit'tily
wit'tiness
wit'tingly
wit'ty
wit'wal
wive
wived
wi'vern
wives
wi'ving

wiz'ard
wiz'ardry
wiz'en
wiz'ened
woad
Wo'den
woe
woe'begone
woe'ful, wo'ful
woe'fully, wo'ful-
woe'some [ly
woke
wold
wolf
wolf'-fish
wolf'ish
wolf'ram
wolf's'-bane
wolverine'
wom'an
wom'an-ha'ter
wom'anhood
wom'anish
wom'ankind
wom'anliness
wom'anly
womb
wom'bat
wom'en
won
won'der
won'dered
won'derful
won'derfully
won'derfulness
won'dering
won'deringly
won'derment
won'drous
won'drously
won't
wont
wont'ed
wont'edness
woo
wood
wood'-ashes
wood'bine
wood'chat
wood'-chuck
wood'cock
wood'cut
wood'-cutter
wood'ed
wood'en
wood'house
wood'iness
wood'ing
wood'land
wood'less
wood'-louse
wood'man
wood'-note
wood'-nymph
wood'pecker
wood'-pigeon
wood'roof
woods'man
wood'ward
wood'work
wood'-worker
wood'y
wooed
woo'er
woof
woof'y
woo'ing
woo'ingly
wool
wool'comber
woold
woold'er
woold'ing
wool'fell
wool'-gathering
wool'len
wool'liness
wool'ly
wool'pack
wool'sack
wootz
word
word'-book
word'ed
*word'*ily
*word'*iness
*word'*ing
word'y
wore
work
work'able
work'aday
work'bag
work'-box
work'-day
worked
work'er
work'house
work'ing
work'ing-day
work'ing-man
work'man
work'manlike
work'manly
work'manship
work'shop
work'shy
work'woman
world
world'liness
world'ling
world'ly
world'ly-minded
world'-wide
worm
worm'-eaten
wormed
wor'mil
worm'ing
worm'like
worm'wood
worm'y
worn
wor'nil
worn'-out
wor'ried
wor'rier
wor'ry
wor'rying
worse
wor'ship
wor'shipful
wor'shipfully
wor'shipped
wor'shipper
wor'shipping
worst
worst'ed
worst'ing
wort
worth
wor'thier
wor'thiest
wor'thily
wor'thiness
worth'less
worth'lessness
wor'thy
wot
would
would'-be
wound (a hurt)
wound (did
wound'ed [wind)
wound'ing
wound'wort
woura'li
wove
wo'ven
wrack
wraith
wran'gle
wran'gled
wran'gler
wran'gling
wrap
wrap'page
wrapped
wrap'per
wrap'ping
wrasse
wrath
wrath'ful
wrath'fully
wreak
wreaked
wreak'ing
wreath
wreathe
wreathed
wreath'ing
wreath'y
wreck
wreck'age
wrecked
wreck'er
wreck'ing
wren
wrench

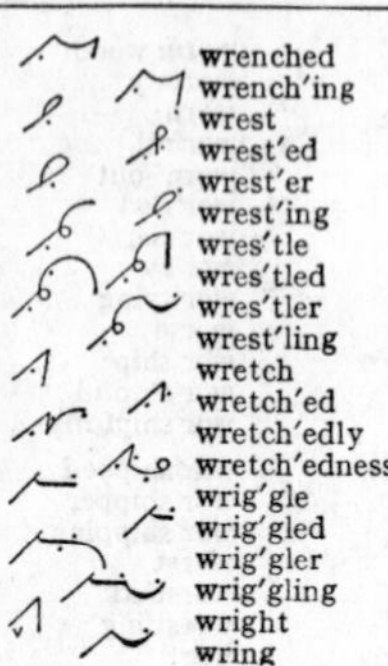

wrenched
wrench'ing
wrest
wrest'ed
wrest'er
wrest'ing
wres'tle
wres'tled
wres'tler
wrest'ling
wretch
wretch'ed
wretch'edly
wretch'edness
wrig'gle
wrig'gled
wrig'gler
wrig'gling
wright
wring

wring'-bolt
wring'er
wring'ing
wrin'kle
wrin'kled
wrin'kling
wrin'kly
wrist
wrist'band
wrist'let
writ
write
wri'ter
*wri'ter*ship
writhe
writhed
wri'thing
wri'ting
wri'ting-book
wri'ting-desk

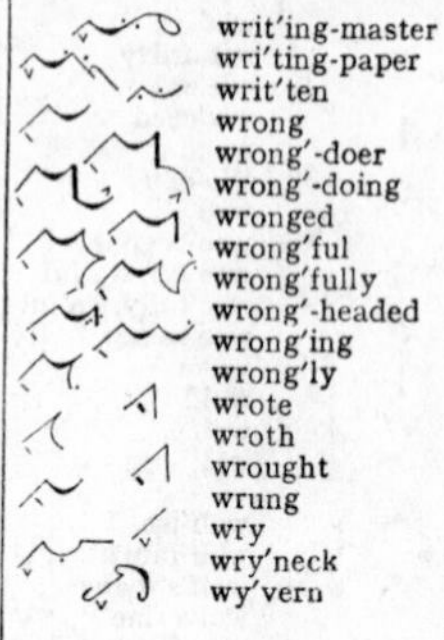

writ'ing-master
wri'ting-paper
writ'ten
wrong
wrong'-doer
wrong'-doing
wronged
wrong'ful
wrong'fully
wrong'-headed
wrong'ing
wrong'ly
wrote
wroth
wrought
wrung
wry
wry'neck
wy'vern

X

Xan'thian
xan'thic
xan'thin-thine
xan'thogen
Xan'thous
xe'bec
xe'nium
xenog'amy
xenogen'esis
xenoma'nia

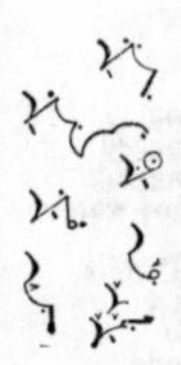

xeroph'agy
xerophthal'my
xero'sis
xe'rotes
Xiph'ias
xiph'oid
xy'lite
xy'lograph

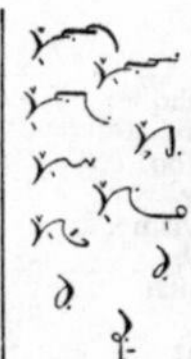

xylog'rapher
xylograph'ic
xylog'raphy
xyloi'dine-din
xy'lonite
xyloph'agous
xy'lophone
xyst
xys'ter
xys'tus

Y

yacht
yacht'er
yacht'ing
ya'ger
Yahoo'
yak
yam
Yan'kee
Yan'keeism
yap
yap'on
yap'ping
yard
yard'-arm
*yard'*stick
yarn
yar'row
yash'mak
yat'aghan
yaup
yaw
yawed
yaw'ing
yawl
yawn
yawned
yawn'ing
ycleped', yclept'
ye
yea
yean
yeaned
yean'ing
year
year'-book
*year'*ling
*year'*ly
yearn
yearned
yearn'ing

yeast
yeast'y
yelk
yell
yelled
yell'ing
yel'low
yel'lower
yel'lowest
yel'low fe'ver
yel'lowish
yelp
yelped
yelp'ing
yen'ite
yeo'man
yeo'manry
yerk
yerked
yerk'ing
yes
yes'ter
yes'terday
yes'ternight
yet
yew
yew'en
yew'tree
Yid'dish
yield
yield'ed
yielder
yield'ing
yield'ingly
yield'ingness
ylang'-ylang
yo'del

yo'del(l)ing
yoke
yoked
yoke'-fellow
yo'kel
yo'king
yolk
yon
yon'der
yore
you
young
*young'*er
young'est
*young'*ish
*young'*ling
*young'*ster
youn'ker
your
*your*self'
*your*selves'
youth
youth'ful
youth'fulness
youths
yt'tria
yt'trious
yt'trium
yuc'ca
yufts
yu'lan
Yule
Yule'-tide
yun'gan
Yunx
yure
Yur'ga

Z

zac'cho
zaf'fre
Zam'bo
za'ny
za'nyism
zare'ba
zar'nich
zax
za'yat
Ze'a
zeal
zeal'ot
zeal'otism
zeal'otry
zeal'ous
zeal'ously
ze'bra
ze'bu
zech'in
zech'stein
zed
zed'oary
zeit'geist
zemindar'
zemin'dary
zena'na
Zend
Zend-Aves'ta
zen'dik
zen'ith
ze'olite
zeolit'ic
zeph'yr
Zeph'yrus
ze'ro
zest
zest'ful
ze'ta
zetet'ic
zeug'ma
zeux'ite
zib'et
zie'ga
zif
zigan'ka

zig'zag
zig'zagged
zig'zagging
zim'ent-water
zinc
zincif'erous
zinck'y
zin'co
zin'code
zinc'ograph
zincog'rapher
zincograph'ic
zincog'raphy
zinc'ous
zin'giber
Zi'on
Zi'onism
zir'con
zirco'nia
zirco'nium
zith'er
zith'ern
zo'cle
zo'diac
zodi'acal
zo'etrope
zo'har
Zo'ilism
Zo'laism
zoll'verein
zo'nal
zone
zoned
zo'nular
zo'nule
zoo
zoog'eny
zoog'rapher
zoog'raphy
zool'atry
zo'olite
zoolit'ic
zool'oger

zoolog'ic
zoolog'ical
zool'ogist
zool'ogy
zoomor'phism
zoon'omy
zooph'agan
zooph'agous
zoophor'ic
zooph'orus
zo'ophyte
zoophyt'ic
zoophytol'ogy
zo'osperm
zoot'omist
zoot'omy
Zoroas'trian
Zoroas'trianism
zos'ter
Zouave'
zounds
zu'folo
Zu'lu
zumolog'ical
zumol'ogist
zumol'ogy
zumom'eter
zygodac'tyl
zygodac'tylous
zygomat'ic
zyme
zymolog'ic
zymolog'ical
zymol'ogist
zymol'ogy
zymom'eter
zymot'ic
zy'thum

Proper Names

A

Aar
Aar'on
Abbe'ville
Ab'botsford
Ab'diel
Ab'dul-Hamid'
Abed'nego
A'bel
Ab'elard
Abera'von
Ab'ercorn
Ab'ercrombie
Aberdare'
Aberdeen'
Aberdeen'shire
Aberdour'
Abergaven'ny
Ab'ernethy
Aberyst'with
Abie'zer
Ab'igail
Abim'elech
Ab'ingdon
Ab'inger
Ab'ney
Aboukir', Abukir'
A'braham
A'bram
Abruz'zo
Ab'salom
Abyssin'ia
Aca'dia
Acapul'co
Ac'cra, Ac'ra
Ac'crington
Achai'a
Ach'eron
Ach'ill, Ach'il
Achil'les
Achit'ophel
Ach'met
A'cis
Ack'ermann
Ack'worth
Ac'land
A'cre
Actæ'on
Ac'ton
A'da
Adair'
Ad'am
Ad'derbury
Ad'dingham
Ad'dington
Ad'dison
Ad'ela
Ad'elaide
Adeli'na
Adel'phi
A'delung
A'den
Adiron'dacks
Ad'ler
Adol'phus
Ado'nis
A'drian
Adria'na
Adriano'ple
Adriat'ic
Adul'lam
Æge'an
Æne'as
Æs'chylus
Æscula'pius
Æ'sop, E'sop
Afghanistan'
Af'rica
Africa'nus
Agamem'non
Ag'atha
Agincourt
Ag'lionby
Ag'nes
Ag'new
A'gra
A'gram
Agric'ola
Agrip'pa
Agrippi'na
A'hab
Ahasue'rus
A'haz
Ahazi'ah
Ahith'ophel
Ah'med
Ai'kin
Ains'worth
Air'drie
Aire'dale
Aix
Aix-la-Chapelle'
Aix-les-Bains'
Ajmir'
Ak'enside
Ak'ron
Alaba'ma
Alad'din
Al'aric
Alas'ka
Al'ban
Alba'ni
Alba'nia
Al'bans, St.
Al'bany
Al'bemarle
Al'bert
Alber'ta
Al'bigenses
Al'bion
Al'cester
Alces'tis
Alcibi'ades
Al'cides
Ald'borough
Ald'bourne
Aldeb'aran
Alde'burgh
Al'den
Al'derbury
Al'dermanbury
Al'derney
Al'dersgate
Al'dershot
Al'derson
Al'derston
Ald'gate
Al'dington
Al'dridge
Ald'wych
Alençon
Alep'po
Alessan'dria
Alexan'der
Alexan'dria
Alexandri'na
Alex'is
Alfie'ri
Alfon'so
Al'ford
Al'fred
Al'freton
Algeci'ras
Alge'ria
Al'gernon

Algiers'
Algo'a
Al'ice
Alic'ia
Al'ison
Allahabad'
Al'lan
All'church
All'cott
Al'leghany
Al'legheny (city)
Al'len
Al'lendale
Al'lerton
Al'lingham
Al'lington
Al'loa
Al'lonby
Al'mack's
Alm'ondbury
Aln'wick
Alon'zo
Alphe'us
Alphon'so
Alping'ton
Alps
Alsace'
Alsa'tia
Al'sop
Al'ston
Al'tenburg
Althæ'a
Al'thorp
Al'ton
Alto'na
Altoo'na
Al'trincham, Al'tringham
Al'va
Alve'ley
Al'verstoke
Al'verstone
Al'verthorpe
Amade'us
Am'adis
Amaryl'lis
Amazo'nia
Am'berg
Am'berley
Am'bleside
Am'brose
Ame'lia
Amer'ica
Am'ersham
Ames'bury
Am'herst
Amiens'
Am'lwch
Am'mon
A'mos
Ampt'hill
Am'sterdam
A'my
Anac'reon
A'nak
An'andale
Anani'as
Andalu'sia

An'daman
An'derson
An'derston
An'des
Andor'ra
An'dover
An'drew
An'drews, St.
Androm'ache
Androm'eda
Androni'cus
An'dros
Aner'ley
Angel'ica
Angel'ico
Angeli'na
An'gelo
An'glesey
Ango'la
Anguil'la
An'gus
Anjou
Ann *or* Anne
Annam'
An'nan
An'nandale
Annap'olis
Annes'ley
An'nibal
An'selm
An'son
An'sted
An'stey
An'struther
An'thony,-tony
Antig'onus
Anti'gua
Antilles
An'tioch
Antip'ater
Antip'atris
Antoinette'
Anto'nio
Anto'nius
An'tony
An'trim
Ant'werp
Aos'ta
Apach'e
Apel'les
Ap'ennines
Aphrodi'te
Apol'lo
Apollo'nius
Apol'lyon
Ap'pleby
Ap'pledore
Ap'plegate
Ap'pleton
Aps'ley
Aq'uila
Aqui'nas
Arabel'la
Ara'bia
Ar'agon
A'ram

Ar'arat
Ara'tus
Arbroath'
Ar'buthnot / Arbuth'not
Arca'dia
Archela'us
Arch'ibald
Archime'des
Arco'le
Arcot'
Arctu'rus
Ar'dagh
Ardee'
Ar'den
Ardennes'
Ard'glass
Ard'ing
Ard'leigh
Ardnamur'chan
Ardros'san
Ard'wick
Areop'agus
Arequi'pa
Arethu'sa
Ar'gentine
Ar'gos
Argyll'
Ariad'ne
A'riel
Arimathæ'a
Arios'to
Aristar'chus
Aristi'des
Aristoph'anes
Ar'istotle
Arizo'na
Ar'kansas
Ark'low
Ark'wright
Armaged'don
Armagh'
Arme'nia
Armin'ius
Arm'ley
Arm'strong
Arnaud'
Arne
Arn'heim
Ar'nold
Ar'not
Ar'ran
Ar'reton
Ar'rowsmith
Artaxerx'es
Ar'temis
Artemis'ia
Ar'thur
Arthu'rian
Ar'undel
As'aph
As'cham
Ashan'ti, Ashantee

Ash'bourne
Ash'burnham
Ash'burton
Ash'by-de-la-Zouch
Ash'cott
Ash'er
Ash'ford
Ash'ley
Ash'over
Ash'ton
Ash'ton-*under*-Lyne
Ash'well
A'sia
As'kew
Asmode'us
Aspa'sia
As'quith
Assam'
Assi'si
Assump'tion
Assyr'ia
Ast'bury
Ast'ley
As'ton
Astrakhan'
Astu'rius

Asun'cion
Athana'sius
Ath'elstan
Athe'ne
Ath'ens
Ath'erstone
Ath'erton
Athlone'
Ath'ol
Athy'
At'kins
At'kinson
Atlan'ta
At'terbury
At'tercliffe
At'tica
At'tila
At'tleborough
At'wood
Au'brey
Au'burn
Auck'land
Au'denshaw
Aud'ley
Au'drey
Augs'burg
Augus'ta
Augus'tine

Augus'tine, St.
Augus'tus
Aumale'
Aure'lia
Aure'lius
Aus'tell, St.
Aus'terlitz
Aus'tin
Australa'sia
Austra'lia
Aus'tria
Autol'ycus
A'va
Ave'bury
Ave'ning
Aver'nus
Av'ignon
Av'ington
A'von
Ax'bridge
Ax'minster
Ayles'bury
Ayles'ford
Ayl'sham
Ayr
Ayr'shire
A'zof *or* A'zov
Azores'

B

Ba'al
Ba'alim
Bab'bage
Ba'bel
Bab-el-Man'deb
Bab'ington
Bab'ylon
Bac'chus
Bach
Ba'cup
Badajos'
Bad'cock
Ba'den
Ba'den-Pow'ell
Bad'ham
Bad'minton
Baed'eker
Baf'fin Bay
Bagdad', Bagh'dad
Bage'hot, Bag'ot
Bag'shaw
Bag'shot
Bag'ster
Baha'ma
Bail'don
Bai'ley
Bain'bridge
Baines
Bain'ton

Bai'reuth, Bay'reuth
Bake'well
Baku'
Ba'la
Ba'laam
Bal'beck
Bal'combe
Bal'dock
Bald'win
Bâle
Balfe
Bal'four
Bal'guy
Bal'ham
Ba'liol
Balkan'
Bal'lantyne
Ballarat'
Ballina'
Ballinasloe'
Ballymo'ney
Ballyshan'non
Balmor'al
Bal'tic
Bal'timore
Baluchistan'
Balzac'
Bam'berg

Bam'ford
Bamp'ton
Ban'bury
Ban'croft
Ban'don
Banff
Bangalore'
Bangkok'
Ban'gor
Ban'ham
Banks
Ban'nerman
Ban'nister
Ban'nockburn
Ban'quo
Ban'tam
Ban'try
Ban'well
Barab'bas
Barba'dos
Bar'bara
Barbaros'sa
Bar'bary
Bar'bauld
Barcelo'na
Bar'clay
Bar'dolph
Bar'ford
Bar'ham

Bar'low
Bar'mouth
Bar'nabas
Bar'naby
Bar'nard Castle
Barn'by
Barnes
Bar'net
Bar'ningham
Barns'bury
Barns'ley
Barn'staple
Barn'well
Baro'da
Bar'rett
Bar'rington
Bar'row-in-Fur'-ness
Bar'ry
Barthol'omew
Bartimæ'us
Bart'lett
Bar'ton
Ba'ruch
Bas'church
Bas'ford
Ba'sel
Bas'il
Ba'singhall
Ba'singstoke
Bas'kerville
Bassa'nio
Basse'-Terre'
Bas'sett
Bas'singbourne
Bas'sora
Bast'wick
Basu'toland
Bata'via
Bat'combe
Bate'man
Bates
Bath
Batheast'on
Bathford'
Bath'gate
Bath'sheba
Bath'urst
Bathwick'
Bat'ley
Bat'tenberg
Bat'tersea
Bava'ria
Baw'try
Bax'ter
Bay'ard
Bayeux'
Bay'ley
Bayonne'
Bea'consfield
Beale
Bea'minster
Bea'mish
Be'atrice
Beat'tie

Beau'champ
Beau'fort [Hants
Beau'lieu (in
Beauma'ris
Beau'mont
Beb'ington
Bec'cles
Bechua'naland
Beck'et
Beck'ett
Beck'ford
Beck'ingham
Beck'ington
Beck'ley
Beck'with
Be'dale
Bed'dington
Bed'does
Bede
Bed'ford
Bed'lington
Bed'minster
Bed'win
Bed'worth
Bee'cher
Bee'chey
Beel'zebub
Beer'sheba
Bees, St.
Bees'ton
Bee'thoven
Beh'men
Beh'ring
Beirut', Beyrout'
Belfast'
Bel'ford
Bel'gium
Belgrade'
Bel'grave
Be'lial
Belin'da
Belisa'rius
Belize'
Bel'la
Bel'lamy
Bel'larmine
Bel'lerby
Beller'ophon
Bel'lingham
Bel'more
Beloochistan'
Bel'per
Belshaz'zar
Bel'ton
Bel'voir
Belzo'ni
Bem'bridge
Bena'res
Ben'digo
Ben'edick
Ben'enden
Ben'gal
Bengue'lla

Ben Lo'mond
Ben Nev'is
Benin'
Ben'jamin
Ben'nett
Ben'nington
Ben'son
Ben'tham
Ben'tinck
Bent'ley
Ben'ton
Béranger'
Berar'
Ber'bera
Berbice'
Bere Al'ston
Bereni'ce
Bere Re'gis
Ber'esford
Beresi'na
Ber'gen
Berke'ley
Berkhamp'sted
Berks
Berk'shire
Ber'lin
Ber'mondsey
Bermu'das
Ber'nard
Berne
Bern'hardt
Ber'ridge
Ber'tha
Ber'tillon
Ber'tram
Ber'vie
Ber'wick
Bes'ant, Besant'
Bes'ley
Bess
Bes'sie
Beth'any
Beth'el
Bethes'da
Beth'lehem
Beth'nal Green
Beth'une
Bet'sey
Beu'lah
Bev'an
Bev'eridge
Bev'erley
Bewd'ley
Bex'hill
Bex'ley
Bey'rout
Be'za
Bhutan'
Biarritz'
Bices'ter
Bick'ersteth
Bick'ley
Bid'denden

Bid'dulph
Bid'dy
Bid'eford
Bid'stone
Bier'ley
Big'gleswade
Big'low
Bihar'
Bilba'o
Billeric'ay
Bil'linge
Bil'lingham
Bil'lingsgate
Bil'lingshurst
Bil'ston
Bin'field
Bing'ham
Bing'hamton
Bing'ley
Bin'ney
Bi'on
Birk'beck
Birk'enhead
Bir'kett
Bir'mah
Bir'mingham
Bir'rell
Bir'stall
Bis'cay
Bish'op's Cas'tle
Bish'opsgate
Bish'op's Stort'-ford
Bish'opthorpe
Bish'opton
Bis'ley
Bis'marck
Bit'ton
Black'burn
Black'friars
Black'heath
Black'ley
Black'lock
Black'more
Black'pool
Black'stone
Blackwall'
Black'wood
Blag'don
Blai'na
Blaine
Blair
Blairgow'rie
Blake
Blake'ney
Blan'chard
Blanche
Bland'ford
Blan'tyre
Blar'ney
Blay'don

Blen'heim
Blen'kinsopp
Bletch'ingley
Bloem'fontein
Blom'field
Bloom'field
Blooms'bury
Blount
Blu'cher
Blyth
Boadice'a
Boaner'ges
Bo'az
Boccac'cio
Bod'enham
Bod'min
Boe'thius
Bog'nor
Bogota'
Bogue
Bohe'mia
Boileau'
Bokha'ra
Bol'ingbroke
Bol'ivar
Boliv'ia
Bolo'gna
Bol'ton
Bo'ma
Bombay'
Bo'naparte
Bonar Law'
Bon'iface
Bonn
Bon'nycastle
Bon'sall
Bon'vilstone
Bootan'
Boo'tle
Bordeaux'
Bordes'ley
Bore'ham
Bor'gia
Bor'neo
Bornu'
Bor'oughbridge
Bor'oughgreen
Bor'stal
Bosanquet
Bos'castle
Bos'cawen
Bos'nia
Bos'phorus
Bossuet'
Bos'ton
Bos'well
Bos'worth
Botes'dale
Bo'tha
Both'well
Bot'ley
Bou'cher
Bough'ton
Boulanger'

Boulogne'
Bour'bon
Bour'chier
Bourn
Bourne'mouth
Bou'verie
Bo'vey Tra'cey
Bow
Bow'den
Bowes
Bow'ling
Bowness'
Box'ford
Boyd
Boyle
Brack'ley
Brad'bourne
Brad'field
Brad'ford
Brad'laugh
Brad'ley
Brad'ninch
Brad'shaw
Brad'well
Bra'dy
Braemar'
Brah'ma
Braid'wood
Brails'ford
Brain'tree
Braith'waite
Bram'field
Bram'ley
Bramp'ton
Bran'denburg
Bran'don
Bras'sey
Braun'ston
Brazil'
Breage
Brech'in
Breck'nock
Brec'on
Brem'en
Brem'ner
Brent'ford
Brent'wood
Bres'lau
Brest
Bre'ton
Brett
Bri'an
Bria'reus
Bridge'port
Bridg'et
Bridge'town
Bridg'north
Bridg'water
Brid'lington
Brid'port
Bri'erley
Brigg
Brig'ham
Brig'house
Bright'lingsea
Brigh'ton
Brig'stock

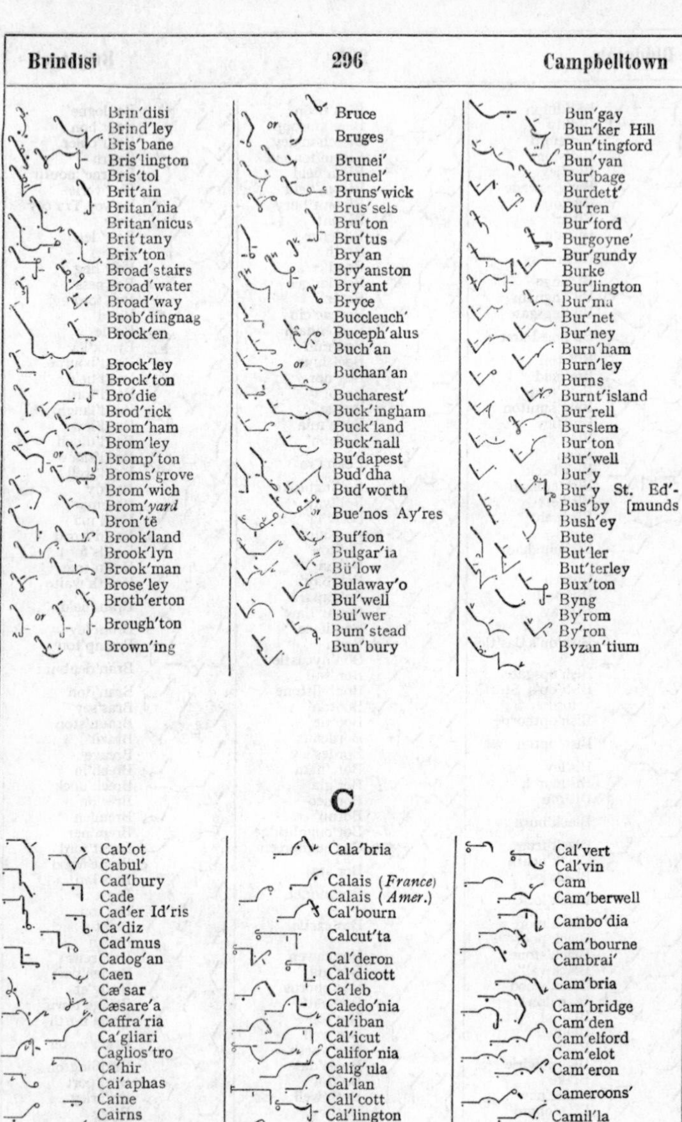

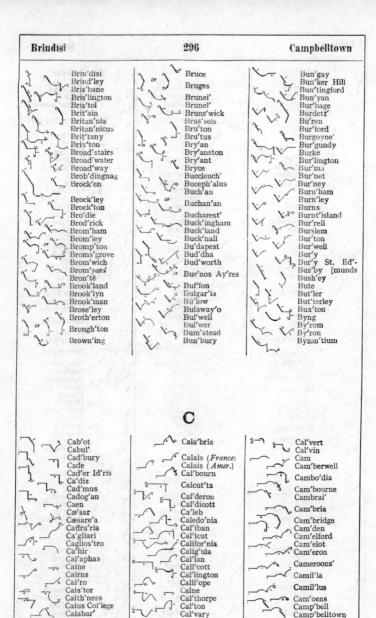

Brin'disi
Brind'ley
Bris'bane
Bris'lington
Bris'tol
Brit'ain
Britan'nia
Britan'nicus
Brit'tany
Brix'ton
Broad'stairs
Broad'water
Broad'way
Brob'dingnag
Brock'en
Brock'ley
Brock'ton
Bro'die
Brod'rick
Brom'ham
Brom'ley
Bromp'ton
Broms'grove
Brom'wich
Brom'*yard*
Bron'tē
Brook'land
Brook'lyn
Brook'man
Brose'ley
Broth'erton
Brough'ton
Brown'ing

Bruce
Bruges
Brunei'
Brunel'
Bruns'wick
Brus'sels
Bru'ton
Bru'tus
Bry'an
Bry'anston
Bry'ant
Bryce
Buccleuch'
Buceph'alus
Buch'an
Buchan'an
Bucharest'
Buck'ingham
Buck'land
Buck'nall
Bu'dapest
Bud'dha
Bud'worth
Bue'nos Ay'res
Buf'fon
Bulgar'ia
Bü'low
Bulaway'o
Bul'well
Bul'wer
Bum'stead
Bun'bury

Bun'gay
Bun'ker Hill
Bun'tingford
Bun'yan
Bur'bage
Burdett'
Bu'ren
Bur'ford
Burgoyne'
Bur'gundy
Burke
Bur'lington
Bur'ma
Bur'net
Bur'ney
Burn'ham
Burn'ley
Burns
Burnt'island
Bur'rell
Burslem
Bur'ton
Bur'well
Bur'y
Bur'y St. Ed'munds
Bus'by
Bush'ey
Bute
But'ler
But'terley
Bux'ton
Byng
By'rom
By'ron
Byzan'tium

C

Cab'ot
Cabul'
Cad'bury
Cade
Cad'er Id'ris
Ca'diz
Cad'mus
Cadog'an
Caen
Cæ'sar
Cæsare'a
Caffra'ria
Ca'gliari
Caglios'tro
Ca'hir
Cai'aphas
Caine
Cairns
Cai'ro
Cais'tor
Caith'ness
Caius Col'lege
Calabar'

Cala'bria
Calais (*France*)
Calais (*Amer.*)
Cal'bourn
Calcut'ta
Cal'deron
Cal'dicott
Ca'leb
Caledo'nia
Cal'iban
Cal'icut
Califor'nia
Calig'ula
Cal'lan
Call'cott
Cal'lington
Calli'ope
Calne
Cal'thorpe
Cal'ton
Cal'vary

Cal'vert
Cal'vin
Cam
Cam'berwell
Cambo'dia
Cam'bourne
Cambrai'
Cam'bria
Cam'bridge
Cam'den
Cam'elford
Cam'elot
Cam'eron
Cameroons'
Camil'la
Camil'lus
Cam'oens
Camp'bell
Camp'belltown

Camp'den
Campea'chy
Campe'che
Cam'perdown
Ca'naan
Can'ada
Can'berra
Candahar'
Can'dia
Can'dy
Cane'a
Can'ford
Cannes
Can'ning
Can'nington
Can'nock
Can'onbury
Canos'sa
Cano'va
Can'terbury
Can'ton
Canton'
Cantyre'
Canute'
Caper'naum
Cape Town
Cap'per
Ca'pri
Cap'ulet
Caracal'la
Cara'cas
Carac'tacus
Car'diff
Car'digan
Ca'rey
Carew'
Car'ibbee
Carin'thia
Car'isbrooke
Car'leon
Carlisle'
Car'low
Carls'bad
Carl'ton
Carlyle'
Carmar'then
Car'mel
Carnar'von
Carnat'ic
Carneg'ie
Carn'forth
Caroli'na
Car'oline
Carpa'thian
Carra'ra
Car'rick
Carrickfer'gus
Car'rington
Car'roll
Car'ron
Carruth'ers
Carshal'ton
Car'son

Car'thage
Carthage'na
Car'ton
Cart'wright
Cash'el
Cashmere'
Cas'pian Sea
Cas'quets
Cassan'dra
Cas'sel
Castile'
Castlebar
Cas'tleford
Castlerea'
Cas'tleton
Castries'
Cat'aline
Catalo'nia
Cat'ford
Cath'arine
Cathay'
Cath'erine
Ca'to
Ca'ton
Cat'tegat
Cat'terick
Catul'lus
Cau'casus
Caus'ton
Cav'an
Cav'endish
Cavour'
Caw'dor
Cawnpore'
Caw'thorne
Cax'ton
Cayenne'
Cay'ley
Cay'thorpe
Cec'il
Cecil'ia
Cel'ebes
Ce'lia
Cel'sus
Cen'ci
Cenis'
Cer'berus
Ce'res
Cervan'tes
Cetewa'yo
Cetin'je, Cet- [ti'nge
Ceylon'
Chad'wick
Chalde'a
Chal'font
Chal'lis
Chal'mers
Chalons'
Cham'berlain
Cham'bers
Chan'dos
Chan'ning
Chan'trey
Chap'lin
Chap'man
Chard

Char'field
Char'ing Cross
Charl'bury
Charlemagne'
Charles
Charles'ton
Charles'town
Charleville'
Char'lotte
Char'lottetown
Charl'ton
Char'minster
Char'mouth
Cha'ron
Char'terhouse
Charyb'dis
Chateaubriand'
Chat'ham
Chat'teris
Chat'terton
Chau'cer
Chautau'qua
Chea'dle
Cheapside'
Ched'dar
Cheet'ham
Chelms'ford
Chel'sea
Chel'tenham
Chep'stow
Cherbourg'
Cher'iton
Cher'rington
Cher'son
Chert'sey
Ches'ham
Chesh'ire
Ches'hunt
Ches'ter
Ches'terfield
Ches'terton
Chet'wynd
Chev'iot
Chey'ne
Chica'go
Chich'ester
Chilcomp'ton
Chil'ders
Chil'e, Chil'i
Chil'ham
Chill'cott
Chil'lingworth
Chimbora'zo
Ching'ford
Chip'penham
Chip'perfield
Chip'ping Norton
Chip'stead
Chis'holm
Chis'lehurst
Chis'wick
Chitral'
Chlo'e
Cholm'ondeley
Chopin'
Chorassan'

Chor'ley
Chor'leywood
Chorl'ton
Christ
Christ'church
Christia'na
Christia'nia
Chris'tie
Christi'na
Chris'topher
Chrys'ostom
Chubb
Church'ill
Chuz'zlewit
Cic'ero
Cimabu'e
Cincinna'ti
Cincinna'tus
Cinderel'la
Cin'derford
Circas'sia
Cir'ce
Ci'rencester
Clackman'nan
Clac'ton-on-Sea
Clan'ricarde
Clap'ham
Clap'perton
Clap'ton
Cla'ra
Clare
Clare'mont
Clar'ence
Clar'endon
Claris'sa
Clark
Clark'son
Clat'worthy
Claude'
Clau'dio
Clau'dius
Clav'erhouse
Cla'vering
Clav'erton
Clay'ton
Clea'ton
Cleck'heaton
Clemenceau'
Clem'ent
Clementi'na
Clem'entson
Cleopa'tra
Clerk'enwell
Cler'mont
Cleve'don
Cleve'land
Cleves
Clif'ford
Clif'ton
Clin'ton
Cli'o

Clith'ero
Clive
Clogher
Clonmel'
Clo'vis
Cloyne
Clut'terbuck
Clyde
Coal'brookdale
Coat'bridge
Cobb
Cob'bett
Cob'den
Cob'lenz
Co'burg
Coch'in Chi'na
Coch'rane
Cock'burn
Cock'erham
Cock'ermouth
Cock'erton
Cod'rington
Cœur de Lion'
Cog'geshall
Co'gnac
Coh'en
Coke
Col'chester
Cold'stream
Cole'ford
Cole'man
Colen'so
Coleraine'
Cole'ridge
Coles'hill
Col'lard
Col'lett
Col'lier
Col'lingbrook
Col'lingham
Col'lingwood
Col'lins
Col'linson
Col'man
Colne
Cologne'
Colom'bia
Colom'bo
Colon'na
Colora'do
Colquhoun'
Col'ston
Col'ton
Colum'bia
Colum'bus
Col'ville
Col'vin
Co'mo
Comp'ton
Comte
Concor'dia
Conde'
Confu'cius
Con'gleton
Con'go
Con'greve

Con'naught
Connect'icut
Con'nell
Con'nor
Con'rad
Con'stable
Con'stance
Con'stantine
Constantino'ple
Con'way
Cooke
Cook'ham
Cooks'town
Coop'er
Coorg, Kurg
Co'os
Cope'land
Copenha'gen
Coper'nicus
Cop'ley
Cop'perfield
Cop'pleston
Copt'hall
Corday'
Corde'lia
Cordil'leras
Cor'dova
Core'a, Kore'a
Corel'li
Corfe
Corfu'
Cor'inth
Coriola'nus
Cork
Corna'ro
Corneille'
Corne'lia
Corne'lius
Corn'hill
Corn'wall
Cornwal'lis
Coroman'del
Correg'gio
Cor'sham
Cor'sica
Corun'na
Cos'ham
Cos'sington
Cos'ta Ri'ca
Cot'ham
Cots'wold
Cot'tenham
Cot'tesmore
Cott'rell
Cour'land
Courte'nay / Court'ney
Coutts
Cov'ent Gar'den
Cov'entry
Cov'erdale
Cov'erley
Cov'ington
Cow'bridge

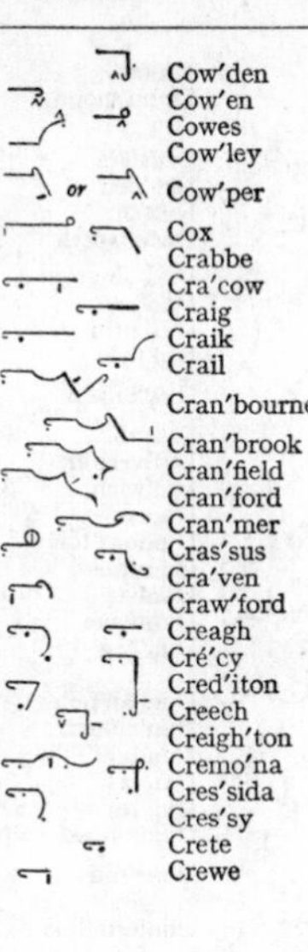

Cow’den
Cow’en
Cowes
Cow’ley
Cow’per
Cox
Crabbe
Cra’cow
Craig
Craik
Crail
Cran’bourne
Cran’brook
Cran’field
Cran’ford
Cran’mer
Cras’sus
Cra’ven
Craw’ford
Creagh
Cré’cy
Cred’iton
Creech
Creigh’ton
Cremo’na
Cres’sida
Cres’sy
Crete
Crewe

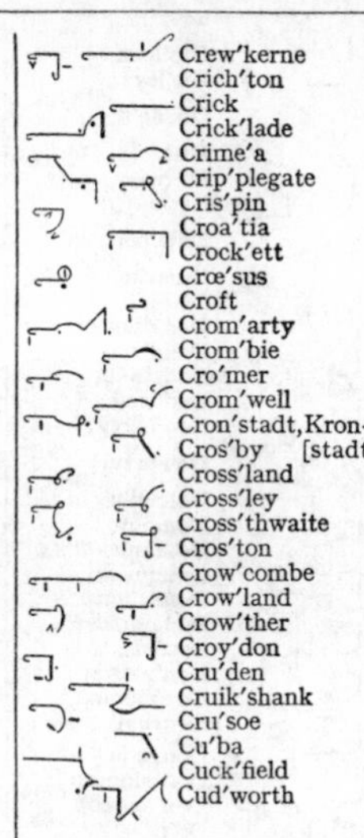

Crew’kerne
Crich’ton
Crick
Crick’lade
Crime’a
Crip’plegate
Cris’pin
Croa’tia
Crock’ett
Crœ’sus
Croft
Crom’arty
Crom’bie
Cro’mer
Crom’well
Cron’stadt, Kron-[stadt
Cros’by
Cross’land
Cross’ley
Cross’thwaite
Cros’ton
Crow’combe
Crow’land
Crow’ther
Croy’don
Cru’den
Cruik’shank
Cru’soe
Cu’ba
Cuck’field
Cud’worth

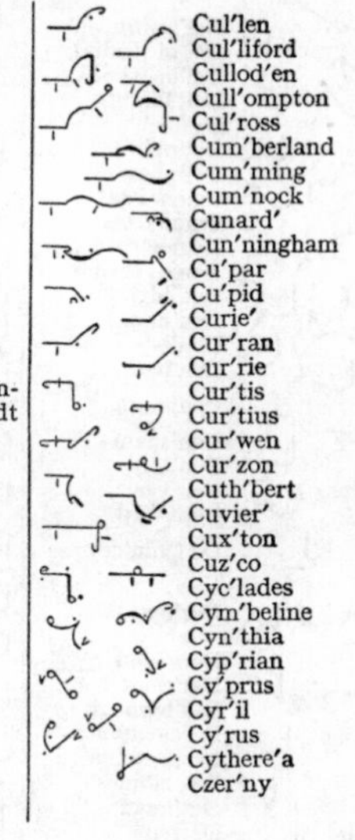

Cul’len
Cul’liford
Cullod’en
Cull’ompton
Cul’ross
Cum’berland
Cum’ming
Cum’nock
Cunard’
Cun’ningham
Cu’par
Cu’pid
Curie’
Cur’ran
Cur’rie
Cur’tis
Cur’tius
Cur’wen
Cur’zon
Cuth’bert
Cuvier’
Cux’ton
Cuz’co
Cyc’lades
Cym’beline
Cyn’thia
Cyp’rian
Cy’prus
Cyr’il
Cy’rus
Cythere’a
Czer’ny

D

Dac’ca
Dag’enham
Da’gon
Daho’my
Daim’ler
Dako’ta
Dalhou’sie
Dalkeith’
Dal’las
Dalma’tia
Dalrym’ple
Dal’ston
Dal’ton
Daly
Dal’ziel
Dam’aris
Damas’cus
Dam’ien
Damiet’ta
Dam’ocles
Da’mon
Dam’pier
Dan
Dan’bury
Dan’by
Dan’iel

Dan’te
Dan’ton
Dan’ube
Dan’vers
Dan’zig
Daph’ne
D’Arblay’
Dar’by
Dardanelles’
Dar’field
Da’rien
Dari’us
Darjee’ling
Dar’laston
Dar’lington
Darm’stadt
Dar’racq
Dart’ford
Dart’mouth
Dar’ton
Dar’wen
Dar’win
Dauphine’
Dau’phiny
Dav’enham
Dav’enport

Dav’entry
Da’vey
Da’vid
Da’vid’s, St.
Da’vidson
Da’vies, Da’vis
Da’vison
Dav’itt
Da’vos
Da’vy
Daw’ley
Daw’lish
Daw’son
Day’ton
Dea’kin
Deans
Deb’enham
Deb’orah
Dec’ca
Dec’can
Deck’er
Ded’dington
Ded’ham
Dee
Defoe’
Delago’a
De la Rue’

Del'aware
Del'hi (India)
Del'hi (U.S.A.)
Deli'lah
Delisle'
Del'phi
Del'phos
Demera'ra
Deme'trius
Democ'ritus
Demos'thenes
Den'bigh
Den'ham
Den'is
Den'man
Den'mark
Den'sham
Den'ton
Den'ver
Dept'ford
De Quin'cey
Der'by
Dere'ham
Der'went
Des'borough
Descartes'
Desdemo'na
Des Moines
Det'mold
Detroit'
Det'tingen
Dev'ereux
De Vin'ne
Devi'zes
Dev'on
Dev'onport
Dew'ar
Dews'bury
Dian'a
Dib'din
Dick
Dick'ens
Dick'inson
Dick'see
Diderot'
Di'do
Didot'
Dids'bury
Dieppe
Dig'by
Dijon'
Dilke
Dil'lon
Di'nah
Din'gle
Ding'wall
Din'ton
Diocle'tian
Diodo'rus Sic'u-[lus
Diog'enes
Dionys'ius

Dip'lock
Dis'ley
Disrae'li
Diss
Di'ves
Dix'on
Dnie'per
Dnies'ter
Dodd
Dod'dington
Dodd'ridge
Dods'well
Dod'well
Dog'berry
Do'herty
Dolgel'ly
Dombey
Dom'inic
Domini'ca
Domit'ian
Donaghadee'
Don'ald
Don'aldson
Don'caster
Donegal'
Dongo'la
Don'nington
Don'oghue
Do'ra
Dor'cas
Dor'chester
Doré'
Dor'king
Dor'noch
Dor'othy
Dor'rington
Dor'rit
D'Orsay'
Dor'set
Dort
Douay'
Doug'las
Dove'dale
Do'ver
Dow'ling
Down'end
Down'ham
Downpat'rick
Down'shire
Down'ton
Doyle
Drake
Dray'ton
Dres'den
Dreyfus'
Drif'field
Drogh'eda
Droit'wich
Dro'more
Dron'field
Dront'heim

Drood
Drum'mond
Dru'ry
Drusil'la
Dry'den
Dub'lin
Duck'worth
Dud'dington
Dud'ley
Duf'ferin
Duf'field
Duk'infield
Duluth'
Dul'verton
Dul'wich
Dumas'
Dumbar'ton
Dumfries'
Dunbar'
Dunblane
Dun'can
Duncan'non
Dun'church
Dundalk'
Dundas'
Dundee'
Dundon'ald
Dune'din
Dunferm'line
Dungan'non
Dungar'van
Dungeness'
Dunkirk'
Dun'lop
Dunman'way
Dunmore'
Dun'mow
Dunn
Dunra'ven
Dun'stable
Dun'stan
Dun'ster
Dur'ban
Dü'rer
Dur'ham
Dur'rant
Durs'ley
Dur'ward
Dut'ton
Dvor'ak
Dwight
Dwi'na
Dym'oke
Dy'mond
Dy'sart
Dy'son

E

Ea'ling
Eames
Earl's Court
Earn'shaw
Ears'don
Eas'ington
Eas'ingwold
East'bourne
East' Ham
East In'dies
East'ington
Eas'ton
Ea'ton
Ebene'zer
E'bro
Ec'cles
Ec'clesfield
Ec'cleshall
Ecclesias'tes
Ecclesias'ticus
Ec'cleston
Ec'uador
Ed'dystone
Ed'gar
Edg'baston
Edge'combe
Edge'hill
Edge'worth
Edge'worthtown
Ed'inburgh
Ed'ison
E'dith
Ed'mondson
Ed'monton
Ed'mund
E'dom
Ed'ward
Ed'win
Eg'bert
Ege'ria
Eg'erton
Eg'ham
Eg'linton
Eg'remont
E'gypt
Eir'e
Elaine'
El'ba
Elbe
El'don
El Dora'do
El'eanor
Elea'zar

Elephan'ta
El'gar
El'gin
E'li
E'lia
Eli'as
El'ibank
Elie'zer
Eli'hu
Eli'jah
El'iot
Eli'sha
Eli'za
Eliz'abeth
El'land
El'len
El'lenborough
Elles'mere
El'liott
El'lis
El'lison
Elm'sley
El'phinstone
Elsinore'
El'tham
El'ton
E'ly
El'zevir
Eman'uel
Em'ary
Em'bleton
Em'den
Em'erson
Em'ery
Em'ily
Em'ma
Emman'uel
Ems'worth
En'dor
Endym'ion
En'field
Engadine'
Enghien'
Eng'land
E'nid
En'nis
Enniscor'thy
Enniskil'len
E'noch
En'sor
Eph'esus
E'phraim
Epicte'tus
Epicu'rus
Ep'ping
Ep'som
Ep'worth
Eras'mus

Er'ato
Er'furt
Er'ic
E'rie
Er'in
Er'ith
Er'nest
Er'skine
Erze'rum
E'sau
Escula'pius
Es'dras
Esh'er
Esk
Es'mond
Es'senden
Es'sex
Es'ther
Estremadu'ra
Eth'el
Eth'elbald
Eth'elbert
Eth'elred
Eth'elwald
Eth'elwulf
Ethio'pia
Et'na
Eto'lia
E'ton
Eu'clid
Eugene'
Eugénie'
Eu'nice
Euphra'tes
Eurip'ides
Eu'rope
Euryd'ice
Euse'bius
Eus'tace
Eus'ton
Eutro'pius
Eux'ine
E'va
Ev'an
Evan'geline
Ev'ans
Ev'ansville
Eve
Ev'elyn, *Eng.*
Ev'elyn, *Scotch*
Ev'erard
Ev'erest
Ev'erett
Ev'ersley

Ev'erton
Eve'sham
Ew'art
Ew'ell
Ew'ing

Ex'bourne
Ex'bury
Ex'eter
Ex'minster
Ex'mouth

Ex'ton
Ey'lau
Eyre
Eze'kiel
Ez'ra

F

Fa'bian
Fabric'ius
Fair'bairn
Fair'fax
Fair'field
Fair'ford
Fa'kenham
Fal'coner
Fal'kirk
Falk'land
Fallieres'
Fal'mouth
Fal'staff
Fan'ny
Far'aday
Fare'ham
Far'ingdon
Far'leigh
Farn'borough
Farn'don
Farn'ham
Farn'worth
Far'oe Is'lands
Far'quhar
Far'ragut
Far'rar
Far'ringdon
Fa'scist
Fasho'da
Faust
Faus'tus
Fav'ersham
Faw'cett
Fawkes (Guy)
Fayette'
Feath'erstone
Felic'ia
Fe'lix
Fel'lenberg
Felt'ham
Fel'ton
Fen'church
Fénelon'
Fen'ning
Fen'ton

Fen'wick
Fer'dinand
Fer'gus
Fer'guson
Ferman'agh
Fermoy'
Fernan'dez
Ferra'ra
Fer'riby
Fer'ro
Fer'ry
Fer'rybridge
Festin'iog
Fes'tus
Feth'ard
Fev'ersham
Fez
Fez'zan
Field'ing
Fie'sole
Figaro'
Fig'gins
Fi'ji
Fildes'
Fill'more
Fil'ton
Finch'ley
Find'lay
Fin'don
Fin'gal
Finisterre'
Fin'land
Fin'lay
Fins'bury
Fish'er
Fish'guard
Fitzclar'ence
Fitzger'ald
Fitzher'bert
Fitzmau'rice
Fitzos'born
Fitzpat'rick
Fitz'roy
Fitzwil'liam
Flamborough

Flan'ders
Flax'man
Flax'ton
Fleet'wood
Flem'ing
Fletch'er
Flint
Flix'ton
Flod'den
Flo'quet
Flo'ra
Flor'ence
Flor'ida
Flush'ing
Foles'hill
Fol'jambe
Folke'stone
Folk'ingham
Fol'let
Fontainebleau'
Fon'tenoy
Forbes
Ford
Ford'ham
Ford'ingbridge
For'dyce
For'far
Formo'sa
For'res
For'ster
Forsyth'
For'tescue
Forth
Fortrose'
Fortuna'tus
Fort Wayne
Fos'ter
Foth'ergill
Foth'eringay
Foulis
Fow'ler
Fox'hill
Fram'ingham
Fram'lingham
Framp'ton
France
Fran'ces
Fran'cis
Franco'nia

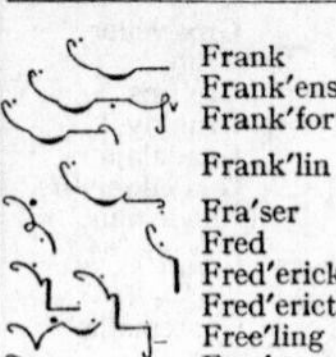

Frank
Frank'enstein
Frank'fort
Frank'lin
Fra'ser
Fred
Fred'erick
Fred'ericton
Free'ling
Free'man
Free'town

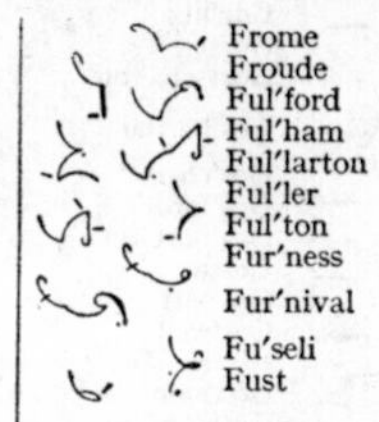

Fre'mantle
Frere
Freycinet'
Fri'bourg
Friend'ly Isles
Fries'land
Frod'sham
Froe'bel
Frog'more
Froissart'

Frome
Froude
Ful'ford
Ful'ham
Ful'larton
Ful'ler
Ful'ton
Fur'ness
Fur'nival
Fu'seli
Fust

G

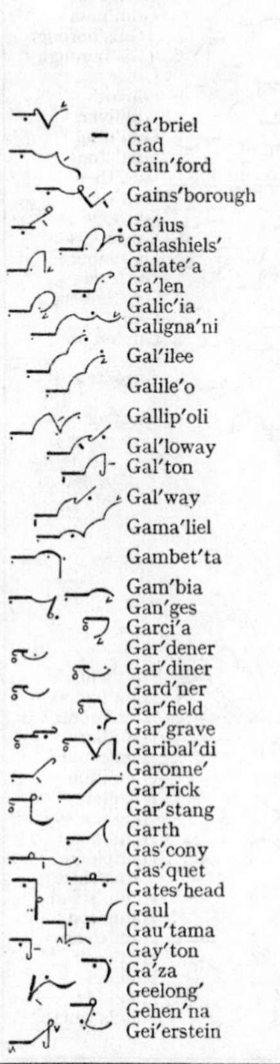

Ga'briel
Gad
Gain'ford
Gains'borough
Ga'ius
Galashiels'
Galate'a
Ga'len
Galic'ia
Galigna'ni
Gal'ilee
Galile'o
Gallip'oli
Gal'loway
Gal'ton
Gal'way
Gama'liel
Gambet'ta
Gam'bia
Gan'ges
Garci'a
Gar'dener
Gar'diner
Gard'ner
Gar'field
Gar'grave
Garibal'di
Garonne'
Gar'rick
Gar'stang
Garth
Gas'cony
Gas'quet
Gates'head
Gaul
Gau'tama
Gay'ton
Ga'za
Geelong'
Gehen'na
Gei'erstein

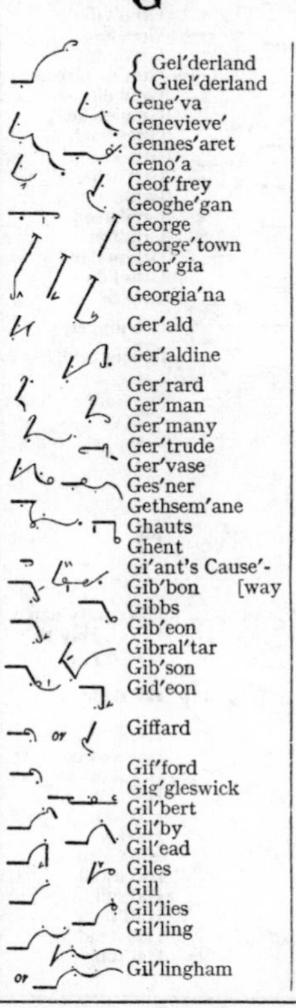

Gel'derland / Guel'derland
Gene'va
Genevieve'
Gennes'aret
Geno'a
Geof'frey
Geoghe'gan
George
George'town
Geor'gia
Georgia'na
Ger'ald
Ger'aldine
Ger'rard
Ger'man
Ger'many
Ger'trude
Ger'vase
Ges'ner
Gethsem'ane
Ghauts
Ghent
Gi'ant's Cause'way
Gib'bon
Gibbs
Gib'eon
Gibral'tar
Gib'son
Gid'eon
Giffard
Gif'ford
Gig'gleswick
Gil'bert
Gil'by
Gil'ead
Giles
Gill
Gil'lies
Gil'ling
Gil'lingham

Gil'pin
Giot'to
Glad'stone
Glam'is
Glamor'gan
Glan'ville
Glas'gow
Glas'tonbury
Glencoe'
Glenelg'
Glent'ham
Glos'sop
Glouces'ter
Glouces'tershire
Glo'ver
Go'a
God'alming
God'dard
God'frey
Godi'va
God'manchester
Godol'phin
God'win
Goe'the
Gol'car
Golcon'da
Gold Coast
Gol'die
Gol'gotha
Goli'ath
Gomor'rah
Gon'dar
Good Hope, Cape of
Good'enough
Good'rich
Good'year
Gor'bals
Gor'don
Goree'
Gorgonzo'la

Gör'litz
Gorst
Gortschakoff'
Gos'berton
Gos'chen
Gos'ford
Gos'port
Gosse
Gos'sett
Gos'well
Go'tha
Go'tham
Goth'ard, St.
Goth'land
Got'tenburg
Göt'tingen
Gough
Gould
Gounod'
Gow'er
Grac'chus
Grace'church
Graf'ton
Gra'ham
Gra'hamstown
Grain'ger
Gram'pian
Grana'da
Gran'by
Grand'ison
Grand Rap'ids
Grange'mouth
Grant'ham
Gran'ville

Gras'mere
Grat'tan
Graves
Graves'end
Gray's Inn
Gray'son
Great Brit'ain
Great'ham
Greaves
Greece
Green'land
Green'law
Green'ock
Green'wich
Green'wood
Greg'ory
Greig
Grena'da
Greno'ble
Gren'ville
Gres'ford
Gresh'am
Gret'na Green
Grev'ille
Grey'stoke
Gries'bach
Grif'fin
Grif'fith
Grims'by
Grin'stead
Grin'ton
Gri'qualand
Grisel'da
Grisons'
Gro'ningen
Groom'bridge

Gros'venor
Grote
Gro'tius
Grun'dy
Guadalaja'ra
Guadalquiv'ir
Guadeloupe'
Guam
Guatema'la
Guel'derland
Guelph
Guerns'ey
Guia'na
Guild'ford
Guin'ea
Guin'evere
Guin'ness
{Guis'borough
{Gis'borough
Guise
Guizot'
Gul'liver
Gun'ning
Gun'ston
Gün'ther
Gun'ton
Gur'ney
Gusta'vus
Gu'tenberg
Guth'rie
Gut'tenberg
Guy
Guy'on
Guzerat'
Gwa'lior

H

Haar'lem
Habak'kuk
Häck'el
Hack'et, Hack'ett
Hack'ney
Had'den
Had'denham
Had'dington
Had'leigh
Ha'drian
Haeck'el
Ha'fiz
Ha'gar
Hagg'ai
Hague
Hah'nemann
Hail'sham

Hai'nau,-y'nau
Hai'ti, Hay'ti
Hak'luyt
Hal'dane
Hales
Hales'owen
Hal'ifax
Hal'lam
Hal'lett
Hal'ley
Hal'liford
Hal'liwell
Hal'sall
Hals'bury
Hal'stead
Hal'ton

Halt'whistle
Ham'bleton
Ham'brook
Ham'burg
Ham'erton
Ham'ilton
Ham'let
Ham'mersmith
Ham'mond
Hamp'den
Hamp'shire
Hamp'stead
Hamp'ton
Ham'stead
Han'cock
Han'del
Hand'ley
Hands'worth

Han'ley
Han'nah
Han'nan
Han'nibal
Han'over
Han'sard
Hants
Han'way
Han'well
Han'worth
Haps'burg
Har'borne
Har'court
Hard'castle
Hardicanute'
Har'ding
Hard'inge
Hard'wick
Har'dy
Hares'field
Hare'wood
Har'lech
Har'lem
Har'ley
Har'lington
Har'lowe
Har'man
Har'old
Har'penden
Har'riet
Har'rington
Har'ris
Har'risburg
Har'rison
Har'rogate
Har'row
Har'rowby
Har'ry
Hart'field
Hart'ford
Hart'ington
Hart'land
Hart'lebury
Hart'lepool
Hart'ley
Hartz
Har'vard
Har'vey
Har'well
Har'wich
Har'wood
Has'lingden
Has'tings
Hat'field
Hat'ton
Haugh'ton
Havan'a
Hav'ant
Hav'elock
Hav'erfordwest
Hav'erhill
Ha'vre
Hawai'i
Hawar'den
Hawes

Haw'ick
Hawkes'bury
Hawkes'worth
Haw'kins
Haw'ley
Haw'thorne
Hay'dn
Hay'don
Hayes
Hay'ley
Hay'man
Hay'ti
Hay'ward
Hay'wood
Haz'litt
Head'ingly
Head'ington
Hea'ly
Heath'cote
Heath'field
Hea'ton
Heav'itree
Heb'denbridge
He'be
He'ber
Heb'rides
He'bron
Hec'ate
Heck'ington
Hec'la
Hec'tor
Hec'uba
Hed'ingham
He'don
He'gel
Hei'delberg
Heigh'am
Hei'ne
Hel'en
Hel'ena
Hele'na, St.
Hel'ens, St.
Hel'iers, St.
Hel'igoland
Héloise'
Helps
Hel'ston
Hel'ton
Helve'tia
Hem'ans
Hem'el Hemp'stead
Hem'merde
Hem'mings
Hems'well
Hems'worth
Hen'bury
Hen'derson
Hen'don
Hene'age
Hen'field
Hen'gist
Hen'ley
Henriet'ta
Hen'ry
Hen'singham

Hep'tonstall
Heracli'tus
Herat'
Her'bert
Hercula'neum
Her'cules
Her'eford
Her'komer
Her'mes
Herne
Her'od
Herod'otus
Her'rick
Herrn'hutt
Her'schell,-schel
Hert'ford
Hert'fordshire
Her'vey
Herzegovi'na
He'siod
Hes'se Cas'sel
Hes'se Darm'-stadt
Hes'ter
Hev'ersham
Hew'orth
Hex'ham
Heytes'bury
Hey'wood
Hezeki'ah
Hiawa'tha
Hiber'nia
Hicks
Hicks'-Beach
Hig'gins
High'bury
High'gate
High'lands
High'worth
Hil'ary
Hil'da
Hil'desheim
Hil'lier
Hil'lington
Hills'borough
Hil'perton
Hil'ton
Hima'laya
Him'maleh
Hinck'ley
Hind'ley
Hin'du
Hindustan'
Hin'ton
Hippar'chus
Hippoc'rates
His'cock
Hispa'nia
Hitch'cock
Hitch'in
Hoad'ly
Ho'bart

Hobbes
Hob'house
Hobo'ken
Hodge
Hodg'es
Hod'son
Hoey
Ho'fer
Hoff'mann
Ho'garth
Hogg
Hohenlin'den
Hohenzol'lern
Hol'beach
Hol'beck
Hol'bein
Hol'born
Hol'brook
Hol'croft
Holds'worth
Hol'inshed
Hol'land
Hol'linwood
Hol'loway
Holl'ywood
Hol'man
Holmes
Hol'stein
Holt
Hol'yhead
Hol'yoake
Hol'yoke
Hol'y Land
Hol'ywell
Hom'burg
Ho'mer
Hom'erton
Hondu'ras
Hong Kong'
Hon'iton
Honolu'lu

Hook'er
Hoop'er
Hop'kins
Hor'ace
Hora'tio
Hora'tius
Hor'field
Horn'castle
Hor'ner
Horn'sey
Hor'sa
Horse'fall
Hor'sham
Hors'ley
Horten'sius
Hor'ton
Hor'wich
Hose'a
Hoth'am
Hot'spur
Hough
Hough'ton
Houns'low
Hous'ton
Hove
How'ard
How'den
Howe
How'ell
How'itt
Hox'ton
Hoy'land
Huas'car
Hub'bard
Hu'bert
Hud'dersfield
Hu'dibras
Hud'son

Huer'ta
Hugh
Hughes
Hu'gli
Hu'go
Hul'lah
Hulme
Hul'ton
Hum'ber
Hum'boldt
Hume
Hum'mel
Hum'phrey
Hum'phreys
Hun
Hun'fleet
Hun'gary
Hun'gerford
Hun'slet
Hun'stanton
Hunt'ingdon
Hunt'ingford
Hunt'ington
Hunt'ley
Hurd
Hu'ron
Hurst
Hu'sey
Hus'kisson
Huss
Hutch'ings
Hutch'inson
Hut'ton
Hux'ley
Huy'gens
Hyde
Hyderabad'
Hy'geia
Hy'men
Hypa'tia
Hythe

I

Ia'go
I'an
Ib'sen
Ice'land
Ich'abod
I'colmkill
I'da
I'daho
Id'desleigh
Igna'tius
Il'chester
Il'ford
Il'fracombe
Il'keston

Ilk'ley
Illinois'
Illyr'ia
Il'minster
Imman'uel
In'cledon
In'dia
India'na
Indianap'olis
In'dus
In'gelow
In'gersoll
Ing'ham
In'gleborough
In'gleton

In'glis
In'goldsby
In'gram
Ink'erman
In'man
Inns'bruck
Inns'pruck
Invera'ry
Invercar'gill
Inverness'
Io'na
Io'nian Isles
I'owa
Ips'wich

Iqui'que
Irawa'di
Ire'land
Ire'ne
Ire'ton
Irkutsk'
Iroquois'
Ir'vine
Ir'ving
Ir'win
I'saac
I'saacson
Is'abel
Isabel'la
Isai'ah
Iscar'iot
Ish'mael
Ish'maelites
I'sis
I'sla
Isle of Wight'
Isle'worth
Is'lington
Isoc'rates
Ispahan'
Is'rael
Is'sachar
Is'tria
It'aly
Itch'en
Itha'ca
Ithu'riel
I'vanhoe
Ives, St.
Iv'iza
I'vory Coast
Ixi'on

J

Ja'besh
Ja'bez
Jack'son
Ja'cob
Jae'ger
Ja'el
Jaf'fa
Ja'go, St.
Jamai'ca
James
Jame'son
James'town
Janei'ro, Rio de
Jan'et
Ja'nus
Japan'
Ja'pheth
Jaques
Jar'dine
Jar'row
Jar'vis
Ja'son
Jas'per
Jas'sy
Ja'va
Jay
Jebb
Jed'burgh
Jed'do
Jeff
Jef'ferson
Jef'feries / Jef'fries
Jef'frey
Jehoi'achin
Jehoi'akim
Jeho'vah
Je'hu
Jek'yll
Jel'licoe
Jemi'ma
Je'na
Jen'kins
Jen'kinson
Jen'ner
Jen'net
Jen'nings
Jen'ny
Jeremi'ah
Jer'emy
Jer'icho
Jerome
Jer'rold
Jer'ry
Jer'sey
Jeru'salem
Jer'vaulx
Jer'vis
Jes'se
Jes'sica
Jes'sie
Jes'sop
Je'sus
Jeune
Jew'ry
Jez'ebel
Jim
Jo'achim
Joan
Joan'na
Job
Joe
Jo'el
Johan'nesburg
John
John'son
John'stone
Johore'
Jo'nah
Jo'nas
Jon'athan
Jones
Jor'dan
Jor'tin
Jos'celyn
Jo'seph
Jo'sephine
Jose'phus
Josh'ua
Josi'ah
Josi'as
Jou'bert (Dutch)
Joubert' (French)
Jove
Joyce
Ju'an
Ju'ba
Ju'dah
Ju'das
Judd
Jude
Jude'a
Ju'dith
Ju'dy
Jugur'tha
Ju'lia
Ju'lian
Julia'na
Ju'liet
Ju'lius
Jung'frau
Ju'nius
Ju'no
Ju'piter
Ju'ra
Jus'tin
Justin'ian
Jus'tus
Jut'land
Ju'venal

K

Ka'bul
Kal'mucks
Kamchat'ka
Kampa'la
Kandahar'
Kan'sas
Kant
Karls'ruhe
Kars
Kars'lake
Kashmir'
Kate
Kath'arine
Kean
Kear'ley
Keat'ing
Keats
Ke'ble
Kedle'ston
Keel'ing
Keene
Keigh'ley
Keith
Keke'wich
Kel'loe
Kel'ly
Kel'sall
Kel'sey
Kel'son
Kelve'don
Kem'ble
Kemp
Kem'pis
Kemp'sey
Ken'dal
Ken'drick
Ken'elm
Ken'ilworth
Ken'nard
Ken'nedy
Ken'nerley
Ken'net
Ken'nington
Ken'rick
Ken'sal Green
Ken'sington
Ken'sit
Kent
Kent'ish Town
Kentuck'y
Ken'wyn
Ken'yon
Keogh
Kep'ler

Kerr or
Ker'ry
Ker'shaw
Kes'teven
Kes'wick
Ketch
Ket'tering
Khartoum' Khar- [tum'
Khi'va
Khorassan'
Kid'derminster
Kid'welly
Ki'ef, Ki'eff
Ki'kuyu
Kilbir'nie
Kilbride'
Kil'burn
Kil'da
Kildare'
Kild'wick
Kilken'ny
Killala'
Killaloe'
Killar'ney
Kil'lyleagh
Kilmain'ham
Kilmar'nock
Kilmore'
Kil'ner
Kilrush'
Kil'wyn
Kim'berley
Kimbolton
Kincar'dine
King'lake
Kings'bridge
King's Coun'ty
Kings'down
Kings'land
Kings'ley
King's Lynn
King's Norton'
Kings'ton
King'ston-on-Thames (or)
Kings'town

Kingswin'ford
Kings'wood
King'ton
King'Will'iam's [Town
Kinross'
Kinsale'
Kin'son
Kintyre'
Kip'ling
Kirk'by
Kirkcal'dy
Kirkcud'bright
Kirk'dale
Kirk'ham
Kirkhea'ton
Kirk'lington
Kirkpat'rick
Kirkwall'
Kir'riemuir
Kir'wan
Kitch'ener
Klon'dike
Klop'stock
Knares'borough
Knel'ler
Knight'on
Knights'bridge
Knollys
Knot'tingley
Knowles
Knox
Knut
Knuts'ford
Koch
Kohat'
Kon'go
Kön'igsberg
Kore'a
Ko'riacs
Koss'uth
Kra'cow
Krapot'kin
Kron'stadt
Krug'er
Ku'belik
Kuch'ing
Kumas'si
Kurdistan'
Ku'rile
Kyrle

L

Labouchere'
Labrador'
Labuan'
Lac'cadive
Lace'by
Lacedæ'mon
La Chaise'
La'cy
Ladrones'
Lady'smith
Lafayette'
Lafontaine'
La'gos
Lahore'
Laing
La'kenham
Lamartine'
Lam'berhurst
Lam'bert
Lam'beth
Lam'bourne
Lamb'ton
Lammermoor'
Lammermuir'
Lam'peter
Lan'ark
Lan'cashire
Lan'caster
Lan'celot
Lan'chester
Land'port
Land'seer
Land's End
Lane' End
Lang
Lang'dale
Lang'ford
Lang'ham
Lang'horne
Lang'ley
Lang'port
Lan'gridge
Lang'ton
Languedoc'
Lans'downe
Laodice'a
Laplace'
Lap'land
La Pla'ta
Lapu'ta
Lar'bert
Laris'sa

Lark'field
Lark'ins
Las'celles
Las'sa
Lataki'a
La'tham
La'thom
Lat'imer
Lattakoo'
Lau'ban
Laud
Lau'der
Laugh'ton
Launces'ton
Lau'ra
Lau'rier
Lausanne'
Lavalette'
Lava'ter
La'venham
Lav'ington
Lavin'ia
Lavoisier'
Lawes
Law'rence
Law'rie
Law'son
Law'ton
Lay'cock
Lay'ard
Laz'arus
Leach
Lead'enhall
Le'ah
Leake
Leam'ington
Lean'der
Lear
Leath'erhead
Leb'anon
Lebrun'
Leckhamp'ton
Leck'y
Leclerc'
Led'bury
Leeds
Leek
Lees
Lee'ward Is'lands
Lefe'vre
Legge
Leghorn'
Legrand'

Leib'nitz
Leices'ter
Leices'tershire
Leigh
Leigh'ton Buz'-
Lein'ster [zard
Leip'sic, Leip'zig
Leith
Lei'trim
Lel'and
Lem'nos
Len'nox, Len'ox
Len'ton
Le'o [(Eng.)
Leom'inster
Leom'inster
Leon [(U.S.A.)
Leon'ard
Leon'idas
Leono'ra
Le'opold
Lepan'to
Le Queux'
Ler'wick
Le Sage'
Les'lie
Les'seps
Les'sing
Le'the
Letit'ia
Levant'
Le'ven
Lev'eridge
Le'vi
Lew'enhoeck
Lew'es, Lew'is
Lew'isham
Lex'ington
Ley'burn
Ley'den
Ley'land
Ley'ton
Ley'tonstone
Lha'sa
Lib'anus
Libe'ria
Lib'ya
Lich'field
Lid'dell
Lid'don
Lidg'ett
Lie'big
Liége'
Lif'ford

Light'foot
Lil'lian
Lille
Lil'leshall
Lil'liput
Lil'ly
Li'ma
Lim'ber
Lim'burg
Lime'house
Limer'ick
Limps'field
Lin'coln
Lin'colnshire
Lind'field
Lind'sey
Lin'ley
Linlith'gow
Linnæ'us
Lin'thwaite
Lin'ton
Lin'wood
Li'onel
Lip'ari
Lip'pe
Lip'ton
Lis'bon
Lis'burn
Lis'keard
Lisle (or)
Lis'more
Lis'ter
Liszt
Lithua'nia
Lit'tlebury
Lit'tleham
Lit'tlejohn
Lit'tleport
Lit'tleton
Liv'erpool (or)
Liv'ersedge
Liv'ingstone
Livo'nia
Liv'y
Llan'daff (or) (And so with the eight following words)
Llando'very
Llanel'ly
Llanfyl'lin
Llangol'len
Llan'idloes
Llano'ver
Llanrwst'
Llewel'yn
Lloyd

Loan'go
Locha'ber
Lock'hart
Lock'wood
Lock'yer
Lo'di
Loffo'den
Lof'tus
Lo'gan
Loh'engrin
Loire
Lo'mas
Lo'max
Lom'bard
Lom'bardy
Lom'broso'
Lo'mond
Lon'don
Londonder'ry
Long'don
Long'fellow
Long'ford
Longi'nus
Long'ley
Long'man
Long'port
Long'ton
Lons'dale
Loo'choo
Lo'pez (or)
Lore'burn
Loren'zo
Loret'to
Lorne
Lorraine'
Los An'geles
Lostwith'iel
Lothar'io
Loth'bury
Lo'thian
Lot'ty
Lou'don
Lough'borough
Loughrea'
Lough'ton
Lou'is
Loui'sa
Lou'isburg
Louise'
Louisia'na
Lou'isville
Lourdes
Louth (or)
Louvre
Love'lace
Lov'ell
Low'ell

Lowes'toft
Lowndes
Lowth
Low'ther
Loyo'la (or)
Lub'bock
Lü'beck
Lu'can
Lu'cas
Luc'ca
Lucerne'
Lu'cia
Lu'cian
Lu'cifer
Lu'cius
Luck'now
Lucre'tia
Lucre'tius
Lu'cy
Lud'denden
Lud'ford
Lud'gate
Lud'low
Lud'wick
Lud'wig
Luke
Lul'lington
Lum'ley
Lun'dy
Lu'nenbourg
Lup'ton
Lush
Lush'ington
Lusita'nia
Lu'ther
Lu'ton
Lut'terworth
Lux'emburg
Lux'or
Lyc'idas
Lycur'gus
Lydd
Lyd'gate
Lyd'ia
Lyd'ney
Ly'ell
Lyg'on
Lyl'y
Lyme
Lyme Re'gis
Lym'ington
Lyn'combe
Lynd'hurst
Lyne'ham
Lynn
Ly'ons (or)
Lyt'tleton
Lyt'ton

M

Ma'bel
Macad'am
Macao'
Macar'thy
Macart'ney
Macas'sar
Macau'lay
Macbeth'
Mac'cabees
Mac'clesfield
Macdon'ald
Macduff'
Macedo'nia
Macgreg'or
Machiavel'li
Ma'chin
Mackay'
Macken'zie
Macknight'
Maclar'en
Maclean'
Macleod'
MacMah'on
Macmil'lan
Macnama'ra
Macpher'son
Macquar'ie
Macrea'dy
Macroom'
Madagas'car
Mad'an
Mad'dox
Madei'ra
Madeleine'
Made'ley
Mad'ison
Madras'
Madrid'
Mæce'nas
Maes'tricht
Mafeking'
Mag'dala
Mag'dalen
Mag'deburg
Magel'lan

Ma'gog
Mahan'
Mahom'et
Mahony
Mahrat'ta
Maida' Hill
Maid'enhead
Maid'stone
Maine
Main'waring
Mait'land
Major'ca
Maju'ba
Mal'abar
Malac'ca
Mal'achi
Mal'aga
Mal'aprop
Mala'ya
Mal'colm
Mal'den
Mal'dive
Mal'don
Mallin'son
Malmes'bury
Malone'
Malo'ny
Mal'pas
Mal'ta
Mal'thus
Mal'ton
Mal'vern
Malvi'na
Mana'gua
Manas'seh
Manas'ses
Man'chester
Man'dalay
Mandin'go
Mangotsfield'
Manil'la
Manitoba'
Man'ley
Man'nering
Mann'heim
Man'ning
Man'ningtree
Mans'field
Man'son
Man'ton
Man'tua

Marajo'
Marañon'
Mar'athon
Mar'burg
Marcel'lus
Marco'ni
Mar'den
Maren'go
Mares'field
Mar'garet
Mar'gate
Mar'gery
Mari'a
Mari'enburg
Mar'ion
Ma'rius
Marjori'banks
Mark
Mark'ham
Mark'land
Marl'borough
Mar'low
Mar'maduke
Mar'mion
Marmontel'
Mar'mora
Mar'ple
Marque'sas
Mars
Mars'den
Marseilles'
Mar'shall
Mar'shalsea
Mar'sham
Marsh'field
Mar'ston
Martaban'
Mar'tha
Mar'tin
Mar'tineau
Martinique'
Mar'tock
Mar'ton
Ma'ry
Ma'ryborough
Ma'ryland
Mar'ylebone

Ma'ryport
Mas'eru
Mash'am
Masho'naland
Massachu'setts
Masséna'
Mas'sey
Mas'singer
Mas'terman
Matabe'le
Math'er
Math'eson
Matil'da
Mat'lock
Matth'ew
Matthi'as
Maud
Maureta'nia
Mau'rice
Maurit'ius
Maw'gan
Maximil'lian
Max'well
Mayence'
May'field
May'hew
May'nard
May'nooth
May'o
Mazep'pa
Mazzi'ni
M'Car'thy
McCor'quodale
McCul'loch
McKay'
McKen'na
McKin'ley
McKin'non
Meagher
Meath
Mec'ca
Meck'lenburg
Mede'a
Med'ici
Medi'na
Mediterra'nean
Med'way
Mei'ningen
Melanch'thon
Mel'ba
Mel'bourne
Mel'combe
Mel'huish
Melic'ent
Melin'da
Melis'sa
Mel'moth
Melpom'ene
Mel'rose
Mel'tham
Mel'ton Mow'-bray

Mel'ville
Me'mel
Mem'phis
Men'ai
Men'delssohn
Menpes
Menton'
Mento'ne
Mentz
Men'zies
Mephistoph'eles
Merca'tor
Mer'edith
Merion'eth
Mer'lin
Mer'riman
Mer'ryweather
Mer'sey
Merthyr Tyd'fil
Mer'ton
Me'shech
Mes'mer
Mesopota'mia
Messi'na
Met'calfe
Methu'selah
Metz
Meux
Mex'borough
Mex'ico
Mey'er
Meyn'ell
Mi'cah
Micaw'ber
Mi'chael
Mich'ie
Mich'igan
Mick'lethwaite
Mi'das
Mid'delburg
Mid'dleham
Mid'dlesbrough
Mid'dlesex
Mid'dleton
Mid'dlewich
Mid'hurst
Mid'somer Norton'
Mil'an *or* Milan'
Mil'bourne
Mil'denhall
Mil'dred
Mile End
Miles
Mil'ford
Millais'
Mil'lard
Mills
Mil'ner
Miln'thorpe
Mil'ton
Mil'verton

Milwau'kee
Minchinhamp'-ton
Min'den
Mine'head
Miner'va
Minneap'olis
Minneso'ta
Minor'ca
Min'ories
Mi'nos
Min'to
Mirabeau'
Miran'da
Mir'field
Mir'iam
Mississipp'i
Missolong'hi
Missou'ri
Mitch'am
Mitch'ell
Mitch'elstown
Mit'ford
Mithrida'tes
Miz'pah
Mo'ab
Mobile'
Mo'cha
Mod'bury
Mod'der
Mode'na
Mof'fat
Mogador'
Moham'med
Mo'hawk
Moi'ra
Mold
Molda'via
Moles'worth
Molière'
Mol'ly
Mo'loch
Molt'ke
Mol'ton
Moluc'ca
Momba'sa
Mo'mus
Mon'aco
Mon'aghan
Monck
Moncrief'
Mond
Monde'go
Mongo'lia
Monk'house
Monk'land
Monk'ton
Mon'mouth
Monroe'
Monro'via
Mon'tagu
Montaigne'
Monta'na

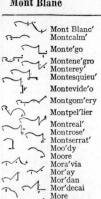

Mont Blanc'
Montcalm'
Monte'go
Montene'gro
Monterey'
Montesquieu'
Montevide'o
Montgom'ery
Montpel'lier
Montreal'
Montrose'
Montserrat'
Moo'dy
Moore
Mora'via
Mor'ay
Mor'dan
Mor'decai
More
More'a
Moreau'
More'cambe
Mores'by
More'ton
Mor'gan

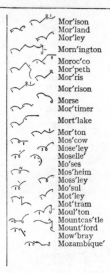

Mor'ison
Mor'land
Mor'ley
Morn'ington
Moroc'co
Mor'peth
Mor'ris
Mor'rison
Morse
Mor'timer
Mort'lake
Mor'ton
Mos'cow
Mose'ley
Moselle'
Mo'ses
Mos'heim
Moss'ley
Mo'sul
Mot'ley
Mot'tram
Moul'ton
Mountcas'tle
Mount'ford
Mow'bray
Mozambique'

Mozart'
Moz'ley
Mül'hausen
Mü'ller
Mullingar'
Mul'lins
Mum'ford
Munchau'sen
Mundel'la
Mu'nich
Munro'
Mun'ster
Murat'
Mur'cia
Mur'phy
Mur'ray
Muscat'
Mus'covy
Mus'grave
Mus'selburgh
Mus'well Hill
My'att
My'ers
My'ott
My'ra
Mysore'

N

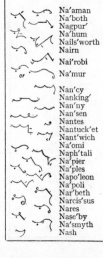

Na'aman
Na'both
Nagpur'
Na'hum
Nails'worth
Nairn
Nai'robi
Na'mur *or*
Nan'cy
Nanking'
Nan'ny
Nan'sen
Nantes
Nantuck'et
Nant'wich
Na'omi
Naph'tali
Na'pier
Na'ples
Napo'leon
Na'poli
Nar'beth
Narcis'sus
Nares
Nase'by
Na'smyth
Nash

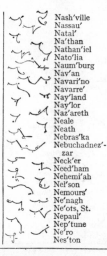

Nash'ville
Nassau'
Natal'
Na'than
Nathan'iel
Nato'lia
Naum'burg
Nav'an
Navari'no
Navarre'
Nay'land
Nay'lor
Naz'areth
Neale
Neath
Nebras'ka
Nebuchadnez'-zar
Neck'er
Need'ham
Nehemi'ah
Nel'son
Nemours'
Ne'nagh
Ne'ots, St.
Nepaul'
Nep'tune
Ne'ro
Nes'ton

Nes'tor
Neth'erlands
Neu'burg
Neuchâtel'
Neu'stadt
Neva'da
Nev'ille
Nev'in
Nev'is
New'ark
{ New'berry / New'bery }
New'borough
New'bridge
{ New'burgh / New'burg }
New'burn
New'bury
New'castle *or* Newcas'tle
Newcastle-on-Tyne *or*
New'castle-*under*-Lyme'
{ New'comb / New'come }
New'digate
New'enden
New'ent

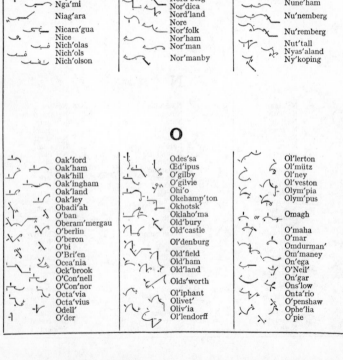

Newfound'land
New'gate
New Hamp'shire
Newha'ven
New'ington
New Jer'sey
New'land
New'man
New'market
New Mex'ico
Newnes
Newn'ham
New Or'leans
New'port
New'quay
New'ry
New South Wales
New'ton
New'town
Newtownards'
New York
New York City
New Zea'land
Ney
Nga'mi
Niag'ara
Nicara'gua
Nice
Nich'olas
Nich'ols
Nich'olson

Nick'leby
Nicobar'
Nicode'mus
Nicosi'a
Nie'buhr
Nie'per
Nie'ster
Ni'gel
Ni'ger
Nige'ria
Nile
Nil'sson
Nim'rod
Nine' Elms
Nin'eveh
Nin'field
Nin'ian, St.
Ni'obe
Nix'on
No'ah
Noakes
No'bel
No'el
Noot'ka Sound
No'ra
Nord'berg
Nor'dica
Nord'land
Nore
Nor'folk
Nor'ham
Nor'man
Nor'manby

Nor'mandy
Nor'manton
Nor'ris
Northal'lerton
North'am
Northamp'ton
North Caroli'na
North'cote
North Dako'ta
North'field
North'fleet
North'leach
Nor'throp
Northum'berland
North'wood
Nor'ton
Nor'way
Nor'wich
Nor'wood
Not'tingham
Not'ting Hill
No'va Sco'tia
No'va Zem'bla
Novgorod'
Nu'bia
Nu'gent
Nu'ma
Nun'eaton
Nune'ham
Nu'nemberg
Nu'remberg
Nut'tall
Nyas'aland
Ny'koping

O

Oak'ford
Oak'ham
Oak'hill
Oak'ingham
Oak'land
Oak'ley
Obadi'ah
O'ban
Oberam'mergau
O'berlin
O'beron
O'bi
O'Bri'en
Ocea'nia
Ock'brook
O'Con'nell
O'Con'nor
Octa'via
Octa'vius
Odell'
O'der

Odes'sa
Œd'ipus
O'gilby
O'gilvie
Ohi'o
Okehamp'ton
Okhotsk'
Oklaho'ma
Old'bury
Old'castle
Ol'denburg
Old'field
Old'ham
Old'land
Olds'worth
Ol'iphant
Olivet'
Oliv'ia
Ol'lendorff

Ol'lerton
Ol'mütz
Ol'ney
Ol'veston
Olym'pia
Olym'pus
Omagh
O'maha
O'mar
Omdurman'
Om'maney
On'ega
O'Neil'
On'gar
Ons'low
Onta'rio
O'penshaw
Ophe'lia
O'pie

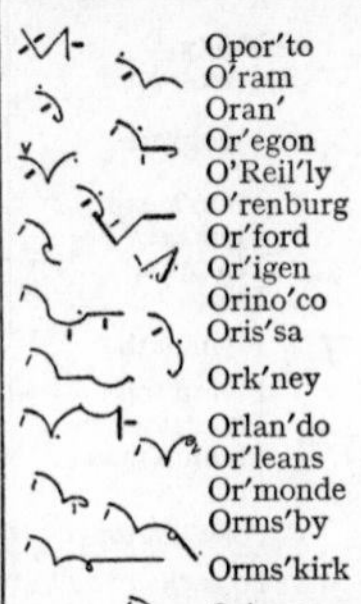

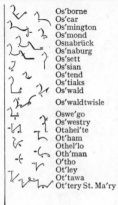

Opor'to
O'ram
Oran'
Or'egon
O'Reil'ly
O'renburg
Or'ford
Or'igen
Orino'co
Oris'sa
Ork'ney
Orlan'do
Or'leans
Or'monde
Orms'by
Orms'kirk
Or'mus
Or'pen
Or'pheus
Or'pington
Or'ton

Os'borne
Os'car
Os'mington
Os'mond
Osnabrück
Os'naburg
Os'sett
Os'sian
Os'tend
Os'tiaks
Os'wald
Os'waldtwisle
Oswe'go
Os'westry
Otahei'te
Ot'ham
Othel'lo
Oth'man
O'tho
Ot'ley
Ot'tawa
Ot'tery St. Ma'ry

Ot'way
Oudh, Oude
Oui'da
Oul'ton
Oun'dle
Ou'ral
Ouse
Ou'tram
O'verbury
O'verend
O'verton
Overys'sel
Ov'id
Ovie'do
O'vingham
O'wen
Ows'ley
Ow'ston
Ox'enden
Ox'ford
Ox'ley

P

Pacif'ic
Pad'dington
Pad'dy
Pa'derborn
Paderew'ski
Pad'iham
Pad'stow
Pad'ua
Pagani'ni
Pag'et
Paine
Paign'ton
Pains'wick
Pais'ley
Pak'enham
Palermo'
Pal'estine
Pa'ley
Pal'grave
Pal'issy
Pal'las
Pal'liser
Pall Mall
Pal'mer
Palm'erston
Palmy'ra
Pamir'
Pam'pas
Pampelu'na

Pamphyl'ia
Panama'
Pan'cras, St.
Pando'ra
Pang'bourne
Pank'hurst
Pap'ua
Paracel'sus
Paraguay'
Paramar'ibo
Paramat'ta
Parana'
Par'fitt
Par'is
Par'ker
Park'gate
Park'hurst
Par'kinson
Par'ma
Parnas'sus
Par'nell
Pa'ros
Par'ry
Par'sons
Par'sonstown
Pas'cal
Pass'more
Pasteur'
Patago'nia

Pat'ernoster Row
Pat'erson
Pat'more
Pat'mos
Pat'na
Pa'ton
Pat'rick
Pat'ten
Pat'terson
Pat'ti
Pat'tingham
Pat'tison
Paul
Pauli'na
Pauline'
Paul'ton
Paunce'fote
Pausa'nias
Pavi'a
Pawtuck'et
Pax'ton
Payne
Pea'body
Pearce
Pear'son
Pear'y
Pease
Peck'ham
Peck'sniff
Pe'dro
Pee'bles

Peel
Peg'asus
Peg'gy
Pegu'
Pe'ipus
Pekin'
Peking'
Pela'gius
Pelew' Islands
Pel'ham
Pell
Pem'berton
Pem'bridge
Pem'broke
Pem'bury
Penden'nis
Pen'dleton
Pene'lope
Penn
Pen'nant
Pen'nefather
Pen'nington
Pen'niston
Pennsylva'nia
Pen'rith
Pen'ryn
Pens'ford
Pent'land
Pen'tonville
Pen'wortham
Penzance'
Peo'ria
Pep'in
Pepys
Per'cival
Per'cy
Per'egrine
Per'gamos
Per'icles
Per'kins
Perks
Pernambu'co
Perranzab'uloe
Per'rin
Per'ry
Persep'olis
Per'sia
Perth
Peru'
Peru'gia
Peshaw'ar
Pestaloz'zi
Pesth
Pe'ter
Pe'terborough
Pe'terchurch
Pe'terhead
Pe'tersfield
Pe'tersham

Peth'erton
Pe'trarch
Pet'rograd
Pet'worth
Pev'ensey
Pev'eril
Pew'sey
Pha'raoh
Phe'be
Phelps
Pheni'cia, Phœni'cia
Phid'ias
Philadel'phia
Phile'mon
Phil'ip
Phil'ippine
Phil'ipstown
Philis'tia
Phil'lack
Phil'lips
Phil'lis
Phill'pott
Phin'ehas
Phin'eas
Phipps
Phryg'ia
Phyl'lis
Piccadil'ly
Pick'ering
Pick'ett
Pick'ford
Pick'wick
Pied'mont
Pierce
Pier'pont
Pietermar'itz-burg
Pig'ott
Pi'late
Pil'kington
Pil'lau
Pil'ton
Pin'dar
Piner'o
Pin'kerton
Pin'ner
Pin'nock
Pir'ie
Pi'sa
Pit'man
Pit'tington
Pitts'burg
Pi'us
Pizar'ro
Plais'tow
Plantag'enet
Plas'sey
Pla'ta
Pla'to
Platt
Plau'tus
Play'fair
Plev'na

Plin'y
Plumb'land
Plump'tre
Plum'stead
Plun'ket
Plu'tarch
Plu'to
Plym'outh
Plymp'ton
Plym'stock
Plynlim'mon
Po
Pock'lington
Po'cock
Poe
Poincaré'
Poitiers'
Po'land
Pole'-Ca'rew
Polk
Pol'lard
Pol'lock
Pollokshaws'
Pol'ly
Po'lo
Polo'nius
Polyb'ius
Polyne'sia
Pomera'nia
Pomo'na
Pompadour'
Pompe'ii
Pom'pey
Pondicher'ry
Pon'doland
Pon'sanooth
Pon'sonby
Pon'tefract *or* Pom'fret
Pon'tesbury
Pon'typool
Poole
Poo'na
Pop'lar
Por'lock
Por'son
Portadown'
Port'au-Prince'
Port'bury
Port'chester
Por'teus
Port Glas'gow
Por'tia
Port'ishead
Port'land
Portmad'oc
Port'man

Por'tobel'lo
Por'to Ri'co
Port Said'
Port'sea
Ports'mouth
Por'tugal
Po'sen
Pos'tlethwaite
Pot'iphar
Poto'mac
Poto'si
Pots'dam
Pot'terne
Pot'tersham
Pou'lett
Poul'ton
Pow'ell (or)
Pow'erscourt
Pow'ick
Pow'is, Powys (or)
Pow'nall
Poyn'ter
Poyn'ton
Praed

Prague
Pratt
Preiss'nitz
Pren'dergast
Pres'burg
Pres'cott
Prest'bury
Presteign'
Pres'ton
Pres'tonpans
Prest'wich
Preto'ria
Pri'am
Prid'eaux
Priest'ley
Prin'gle
Pri'or
Pris'cian
Priscil'la
Pritch'ard
Procrus'tes
Proc'tor
Prome'theus
Pros'pero
Pros'ser
Proth'eroe
Prout

Provence'
Prus'sia
Psy'che
Ptol'emy
Pud'sey
Pu'gin
Pules'ton
Pull'man
Pu'lo Pinang'
Pulte'ney
Punjab'
Pur'beck
Pur'brook
Pur'cell
Pur'fleet
Pur'nell
Pu'sey
Put'ney
Put'son
Put'tenham
Puy de Dôme'
Pygma'lion
Pym
Pyr'enees
Pytch'ley
Pythag'oras

Q

Quarles
Quatre Bras'
Quebec'
Queen'borough
Queen'hithe
Queen's' Coun'ty

Queens'ferry
Queens'land
Queens'town
Quen'don
Quen'tin
Quet'ta
Queux

Qui'loa
Quin
Quin'cy
Quintil'ian
Quin'tin
Qui'to
Quix'ote

R

Rabelais'
Ra'chel
Racine'
Rad'cliffe
Rad'ford
Rad'ipole
Rad'nor
Rad'stock
Raf'fles

Rag'lan
Ragu'sa
Raikes
Rain'ford
Rain'ham
Rain'hill (or)
Ra'leigh, -legh (or)
Ralph
Ram'eses

Ram'illies
Rams'bottom
Rams'den
Ram'sey
Rams'gate
Ran'dall
Ran'dolph

Rangoon'
Ran'som
Raph'ael
Ra'pin
Ras'selas
Rat'cliffe
Rath'bone
Rath'down
Rathdow'ney
Rath'gar
Rathmines'
Rat'isbon
Ra'venglass
Raven'na
Ra'venscroft
Ra'vensworth
Raw'cliffe
Raw'don
Raw'lings
Raw'linson
Raw'son
Raw'tenstall
Ray'mond
Ray'ner
Reade
Read'ing
Reay
Rebec'ca
Red'bridge
Red'burn
Red'car
Red'fern
Red'gauntlet
Red'grave
Red'hill
Red'land
Red'mond
Red'ruth
Red Sea
Reeves
Reg'gio
Regi'na
Reg'inald
Reid
Rei'gate
Rem'brandt
Rem'ington
Re'mus
Renan'
Ren'del
Rend'ham
René'
Ren'frew
Ren'nell
Ren'nie
Ren'shaw
Ren'wick
Rep'ton
Ret'ford
Reu'ben
Reuss

Reu'ter
Reyk'javik
Reyn'olds
Rheims
Rhine
Rho'da
Rhode'sia
Rhode' I'sland
Rhodes
Rhon'dda
Rhone
Rhys
Rib'chester
Ricar'do
Rich'ard
Rich'ardson
Richelieu'
Rich'mond
Rich'ter
Rick'etts
Rick'mansworth
Ridd'ell
Ridge'mount
Ridge'way
Ridge'well
Rid'ley
Rien'zi
Riev'aulx
Ri'ga
Ril'lington
Ring'wood
Ri'o Janei'ro
Rip'ley
Rip'on
Rit'chie
Rit'son
Rivie'ra
Riv'ington
Riz'zio
Rob'ert
Rob'ertson
Rob'espierre
Rob'in Hood
Rob'inson
Rob Roy
Rob'son
Roch'dale
Rochefort'
Rochefoucauld'
Rochelle', La
Roch'ester
Rock Fer'ry
Rock'hampton
Rock'ingham
Rod'erick
Rodg'er
Rod'ney
Rog'er
Rog'ers
Ro'land
Rollin'

Rome
Ro'meo
Rom'ford
Rom'illy
Rom'ney
Rom'sey
Rom'ulus
Ron'aldshay
Ro'nan, St.
Roose'velt
Ro'per
Ro'sa
Ros'alind
Ros'amond
Roseau'
Ros'cius
Roscoe'
Roscom'mon
Rose'bery
Rosel'la
Roset'ta
Rosh'erville
Ross
Rosset'ti
Rossi'ni
Rosyth'
Roth'erfield
Roth'erham
Roth'erhithe
Rothe'say
Roths'child
Roth'well
Rot'terdam
Rouen'
Rouma'nia
Roume'lia
Rousseau'
Rowe'na
Row'land
Row'ley
Row'ton
Rox'burgh
Rox'bury
Rox'well
Roys'ton
Roy'ton
Rua'bon
Ru'bens
Ru'binstein
Ru'dall
Rudge
Rudg'wick
Ru'dolph
Rud'yard
Ru'fus
Rug'by
Ruge'ley
Rum'ford
Rum'sey
Run'ciman
Run'corn

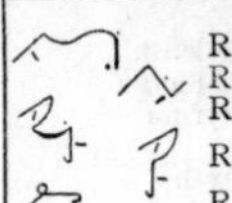

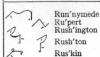

Run'nymede
Ru'pert
Rush'ington
Rush'ton
Rus'kin
Rus'sell
Rus'sia
Ruth
Ruth'erford
Ruth'erglen
Ru'thin
or
Ruth'ven
Rut'land
Ryde
Rye
Ry'mer
Rys'wick

S

Saar
Sabi'na
Sachev'erell
Sack'ville
Sad'dleworth
Saf'fron Wal'den
Sag'inaw
Saha'ra
or St. John
Sal'adin
Salaman'ca
Sal'amis
Sal'combe
Sa'lem
Saler'no
Sal'ford
Salis'bury
Salee'
Sal'lust
Sal'ly
Salm'on
Salo'me
Saloni'ca
Sal'taire
Salt'ash
Salt'er
Salt'ford
Salt' Lake Cit'y
Salvador'
Salz'burg
Samarkand'
Sama'ria
Samo'a
Sa'mos
Samp'son
Sam'son
Sam'uel
San Anto'nio
San'cho Pan'za
San'croft
Sandakan'
San'dall
San'deman
San'ders
San'derson
Sand'ford
Sand'gate
Sand'hurst
San'diford
San Domin'go
San'down
Sand'ringham
Sand'wich
Sandys
or
San Francis'co
San José'
San'key
San Re'mo
San Sal'vador
San'ta Cruz
San'ta Fé
Santia'go
Sant'ley
Sapphi'ra
Sapph'o
Saragos'sa
Sa'rah
Saraje'vo
Sarato'ga
Sara'wak
Sardanapa'lus
Sardin'ia
Sark
Sa'rum
Saskatch'ewan
Saul
Saun'ders
Saun'derson
Sauterne'
Savan'nah
Savonaro'la
Savoy'
Saw'bridgeworth
Saw'ston
Saw'try
Saxe-Al'tenburg
Saxe-Co'burg Go'tha
Saxe-Mei'ningen
Saxe-Wei'mar
Sax'mundham
Sax'ony
Sayce
Scal'iger
Scandina'via
Scar'borough
Schaffhau'sen
Schil'ler
Schles'wig
Schoef'fer
Schrevel'ius
Schu'bert
Schus'ter
Schwartz
Schwarz'burg
Schwerin'
Scil'la
Scil'ly Isles
Sci'o
Scip'io
Sclavo'nia
Scot'land
Scott
Scran'ton
Scrym'geour
Scul'coates
Scu'tari
Scyth'ia
Sea'combe
Sea'ford
Sea'forth
Sea'ham
Searle
Sea'ton
Seat'tle
Sebas'tian
Sebas'topol
Sedan'
Sed'berg
Sedge'field
Sedge'moor
Sedg'ley
Sedg'wick
See'ley
Sego'via
Seine
Sel'borne
Sel'by
Sel'den

Seli'na
Sel'kirk
Selous'
Sel'wyn
Semir'amis
Senaar'
Sen'eca
Senegal'
Senegam'bia
Seoul'
Serampore'
Seringapatam'
Serve'tus
Ser'via
Seth
Sev'enoaks
Sev'ern
Sev'ille
Sèvres
Seychelles'
Sey'mour
Sha'drach
Shad'well
Shaftes'bury
{ Shak'spere
Shake'speare
Shanghai'
Shan'non
Shap'wick
Shar'land
Sha'ron
Shaw
She'ba
Sheep'shanks
Sheerness'
Shef'field
Shef'ford
Shel'burne
Shel'don
Shel'ley
Shel'ton
Shem
Shen'stone
Shep'pard
Shep'pey
Shep'ton Mal'let
Sher'borne
Sher'idan
Sher'lock
Sher'man
Sher'win
Sher'wood
Shet'land
Shil'lingstone
Ship'ton
Shiraz'
Shir'ley
Shoe'buryness
Shore'ditch
Shore'ham
Shot'ley
Shrews'bury
Shrop'shire
Shuttle'worth
Shy'lock

Siam'
Sibe'ria
Sib'ford
Sic'ily
Sid'bury
Sid'cot
Sid'dons
Sid'mouth
Sid'ney
Si'don
Sie'mens
Sien'a
Sier'ra Leo'ne
Sig'ismund
Sikhs
Sile'sia
Silk'stone
Silva'nus
Sil'verton
Silves'ter
Sil'via
Sim'eon
Sim'kin
Sim'la
Simms
Si'mon
Simp'kin
Sim'plon
Simp'son
Si'nai
Sin'clair
Sin'clairtown
Sind'bad
Sind, Sindh
Singapore'
Sin'gleton
Sing Sing
Si'on
Sioux
Si'rach
Sis'era
Sismon'di
Sis'yphus
Sith'ney
Sit'tingbourne
Ska'raborg
Skeat
Skel'ton
Skibbereen'
Skid'daw
Skin'ner
Skip'ton
Skye
Slade
Slap'ton
Slea'ford
Sles'wick
Sli'go
Sloane
Slo'per
Slough
Small'bridge
Smal'ley
Smar'den
Smea'ton
Smeth'wick
Smith
Smith'ers
Smith'field

Smolensk'
Smol'lett
Smyr'na
Smyth
Snaith
Snel'ling
Snen'ton
Snod'grass
Snow'don
Snow'hill
Soci'nus
Soc'rates
Sod'bury
Sod'om
Sofa'la
Sofi'a
So'ham
So'ho
So'lent
Soleure'
Solihull'
Sol'omon
So'lon
Sol'way Firth
Soma'liland
Som'ers
Som'erset
Som'ersham
Som'erstown
Som'erton
Som'erville
Sophi'a
Soph'ocles
Sophro'nia
So'phy
Soth'eby
Soudan'
South'am
Southamp'ton
South'borough
South'bourne
South Caroli'na
South'cott
South Dako'ta
Southend'
Sou'they
South'gate
South Mol'ton
South'port
South'sea
South Shields
South'wark
South'well
South'wick
South'wold
Sow'erby
Spain
Spal'ding
Spar'ta
Speen
Speen'hamland

Spen'cer
Spen'nithorne
Spen'ser
Spi'cer
Spils'by
Spino'za
Spi'on Kop
Spit'alfields
Spit'head
Spitzberg'en
Spoon'er
Spring'field
Spur'geon
Sta'cey
Staf'fa
Staf'ford
Staines
Stain'land
Stal'bridge
Sta'lybridge
Stamboul'
Stam'ford
Stand'ish
Stand'lake
Stan'field
Stan'ford
Stan'hope
Stan'ley
Stan'ningley
Stan'ton
Stan'well
Sta'plefield
Sta'pleford
Sta'pleton
Star'key
Staun'ton
Stave'ley
Steb'bing
Sted'man
Stel'la
Sten'nett
Ste'phen
Ste'phens
Ste'phens, St.
Ste'phenson
Step'ney
Sterne
Ste'vens
Ste'venson
Ste'venton
Stew'art
Stew'arton
Steyn
Stil'lington
Stil'ton
Stir'ling
Stock'bridge
Stock'holm

Stock'land
Stock'port
Stocks'field
Stock'ton
Stock'well
Stock'with
Stod'dart
Sto'gumber
Stoke
Stoke New'ing-ton
Stokes'ley
Stone
Stone'bridge
Stone'ham
Stone'haven
Stone'henge
Stone'house
Stony'hurst
Stor'noway
Stort'ford
Stoth'ert
Stour
Stour'bridge
Stour'port
Stour'ton
Stow'ell
Stow'market
Strabane'
Stra'bo
Strachan
Stra'chey
Strad'brooke
Straf'ford
Stral'sund
Strang'ford
Stranraer'
Stran'ton
Stras'burg
Strat'ford
Strathco'na
Strat'ton
Strauss
Streat'ham
Stre'litz
Stret'ford
Stret'ton
Strick'land
String'er
Strom'boli
Stromness'
Strood
Stroud
Strutt
Stu'art
Stub'bing
Stubbs

Stud'ley
Stur'minster
Stutt'gart
Styr'ia
Styx
Sua'bia
Sua'kin
Su'cre
Sudan'
Sud'bury
Sude'ley
Sue
Sueto'nius
Su'ez
Suf'folk
Sul'livan
Sul'ly
Suma'tra
Sum'ner
Sun'derland
Surat'
Sur'biton
Surinam'
Sur'rey
Su'san
Susan'na
Sus'sex
Sut'cliffe
Suth'erland
Sut'ton Cold'field
Suva
Swaff'ham
Swain'son
Swam'merdam
Swan'age
Swan'bourne
Swan'sea
Swa'ziland
Swe'den
Swe'denborg
Swin'burne
Swin'don
Swine'fleet
Swin'ey
Swin'ford
Swin'stead
Swin'ton
Swith'in, St.
Swith'un, St.
Swit'zerland
Syd'enham
Syd'ney
Sykes
Syl'la
Syl'via
Sy'monds
Sy'mons
Sy'ra
Syr'acuse
Syr'ia

T

Taba'go
Tabas'co
Tab'itha
Ta'bor
Tac'itus
Tad'caster
Tad'more
Taft
Ta'gus
Tahi'ti
Tain
Tait
Talave'ra
Tal'bot
Talleyrand'
Ta'mar
Tamerlane'
Tam'worth
Tam'many
Tanganyi'ka
Tangier'
Tang'ye
Tanjore'
Tan'talus
Tap'lin
Ta'ranto
Tar'land
Tarle'ton
Tarn
Tar'porley
Tar'quin
Tar'rant
Tar'sus
Tar'tary
Tar'vin
Tasma'nia
Tas'so
Tate
Tat'tenhall
Tat'tersall
Tauch'nitz
Taun'ton
Tav'erner
Tav'istock
Ta'vy
Tay
Tay'ler
Tay'lor
Ted
Tees
Teheran'
Teign'mouth
Tel-el-Kebir'
Telem'achus
Tel'ford
Tell
Tem'pe
Tem'pleton
Ten'bury
Ten'by
Teneriffe'
Ten'nent
Tennessee'
Ten'niel
Ten'nyson
Ten'terden
Ter'ence
Terpsich'ore
Terr'a del Fue'go
Ter'ry
Tertul'lian
Tet'bury
Tewkes'bury
Tex'as
Tex'el
Thack'eray
Tha'les
Thame
Thames
Than'et
Thatch'am
Thebes
Thel'wall
Themis'tocles
The'obald
Theoc'ritus
Theodo'ra
The'odore
Theod'oret
Theodo'sia
Theodo'sius
Theoph'ilus
There'sa
Thermop'ylæ
Thes'saly
Thet'ford
Thibet', Tibet'
Thiers'
Thirsk
Thom'as
Thom'asine
Thomp'son
Thom'son
Thor
Thorn'aby
Thorn'bury
Thorne
Thor'ney
Thorn'hill
Thorn'ley
Thorn'ton
Thorpe
Thrap'stone
Thucyd'ides
Thur'low
Thur'so
Thwaites
Ti'ber
Tibe'rias
Tibe'rius
Tibet', Thibet'
Tibul'lus
Tice'hurst
Tich'borne
Tich'field
Tick'ell
Tid'denham
Tid'dington
Tides'well
Tien' Tsin
Ti'gris
Til'bury
Til'ley
Tillicoul'try
Til'lingham
Til'lotson
Timbuc'too
Timbuk'tu
Timo'leon
Ti'mon
Tim'othy
Tims'bury
Tin'dal
Tintag'el
Tippera'ry
Tippoo Sah'ib
Tip'ton
Tita'nia
Ti'tian
Ti'tus
Tiv'erton
Tiv'oli
Toba'go
Tobi'as
To'bit
Tobolsk'
To'by
Todd
Tod'morden

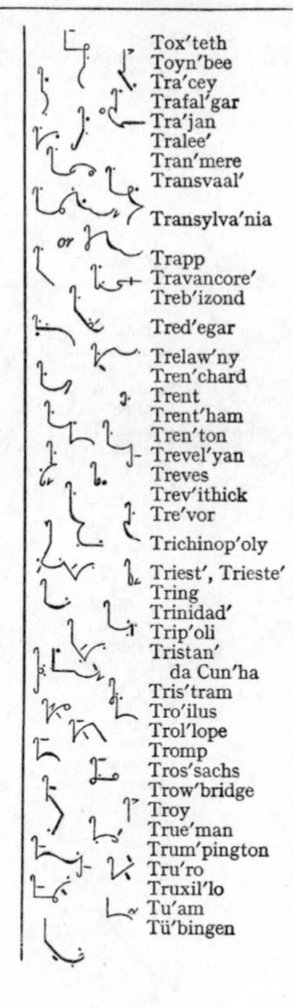

To'go
Tokay'
To'kyo
Tole'do
Tolle'mache
Tol'stoi
Tom
Tom'kins
Tom'linson
Tomp'kins
Ton'bridge
Ton'ga
Tongata'bu
Tonquin'
To'ny
Tooke
Toot'ing
Top'lady
Tops'ham
Top'sy
Torbay'
Tor'nea
Toron'to
Torquay'
Tor'rington
Torto'la
Tortu'ga
Tort'worth
Tot'nes
Tot'tenham
Tot'tington
Toulon'
Toulouse'
{ Tournay'
{ Tournai'
Tours
Towces'ter
Town'er
Town'ley
Towns'end

Tox'teth
Toyn'bee
Tra'cey
Trafal'gar
Tra'jan
Tralee'
Tran'mere
Transvaal'
Transylva'nia
Trapp
Travancore'
Treb'izond
Tred'egar
Trelaw'ny
Tren'chard
Trent
Trent'ham
Tren'ton
Trevel'yan
Treves
Trev'ithick
Tre'vor
Trichinop'oly
Triest', Trieste'
Tring
Trinidad'
Trip'oli
Tristan' da Cun'ha
Tris'tram
Tro'ilus
Trol'lope
Tromp
Tros'sachs
Trow'bridge
Troy
True'man
Trum'pington
Tru'ro
Truxil'lo
Tu'am
Tü'bingen

Tuck'er
Tud'denham
Tu'dor
Tuil'leries
Tullamore'
Tul'loch
Tul'ly
Tun'bridge Wells
Tu'nis
Tun'stall
Tup'per
Tu'rin
Turkestan'
Tur'key
Turn'bull
Tur'ner
Tur'pin
Tur'vey
Tur'ville
Tus'cany
Tussaud'
Tux'ford
Tweed
Tweed'mouth
Twer'ton
Twick'enham
Twi'ning
Twy'ford
Ty'burn
Tyldes'ley
Ty'ler
{ Tyn'dale
{ Tyn'dall
Tyne
Tyne'mouth
Tyr'ol
Tyrone'
Tyr'rel
Tyr'whitt
Ty'ssen
Tyt'ler

U

Ugan'da
Uist
Uji'ji
U'kraine
Ulles'thorpe
Ulls'water
Ulm
Ul'ster
Ul'verstone
Ulys'ses
U'na
Un'derwood

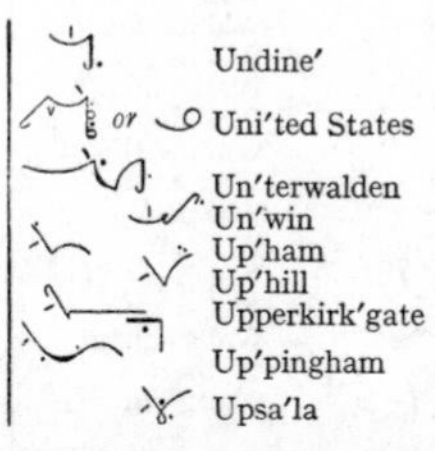

Undine'
Uni'ted States
Un'terwalden
Un'win
Up'ham
Up'hill
Upperkirk'gate
Up'pingham
Upsa'la

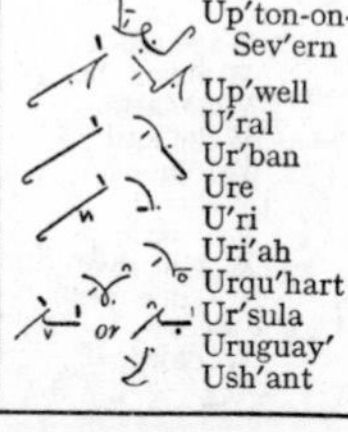

Up'ton-on-Sev'ern
Up'well
U'ral
Ur'ban
Ure
U'ri
Uri'ah
Urqu'hart
Ur'sula
Uruguay'
Ush'ant

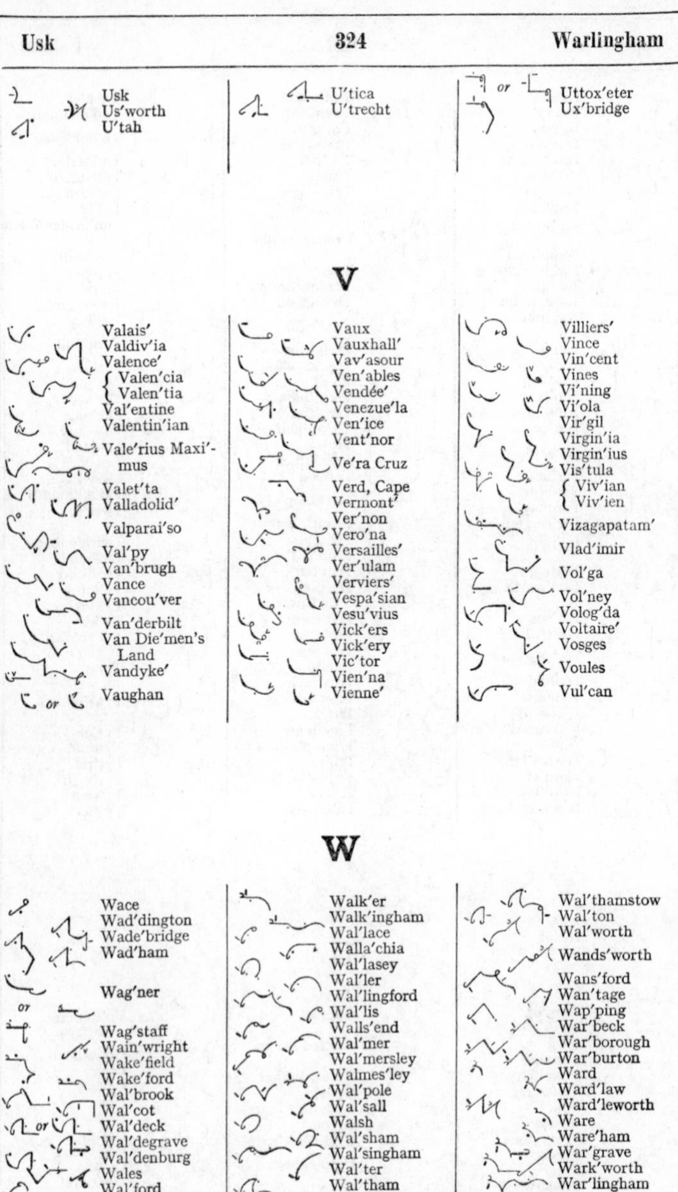

Usk
Us'worth
U'tah
U'tica
U'trecht
Uttox'eter
Ux'bridge

V

Valais'
Valdiv'ia
Valence'
Valen'cia
Valen'tia
Val'entine
Valentin'ian
Vale'rius Maxi'-mus
Valet'ta
Valladolid'
Valparai'so
Val'py
Van'brugh
Vance
Vancou'ver
Van'derbilt
Van Die'men's Land
Vandyke'
Vaughan
Vaux
Vauxhall'
Vav'asour
Ven'ables
Vendée'
Venezue'la
Ven'ice
Vent'nor
Ve'ra Cruz
Verd, Cape
Vermont'
Ver'non
Vero'na
Versailles'
Ver'ulam
Verviers'
Vespa'sian
Vesu'vius
Vick'ers
Vick'ery
Vic'tor
Vien'na
Vienne'
Villiers'
Vince
Vin'cent
Vines
Vi'ning
Vi'ola
Vir'gil
Virgin'ia
Virgin'ius
Vis'tula
Viv'ian
Viv'ien
Vizagapatam'
Vlad'imir
Vol'ga
Vol'ney
Volog'da
Voltaire'
Vosges
Voules
Vul'can

W

Wace
Wad'dington
Wade'bridge
Wad'ham
Wag'ner
Wag'staff
Wain'wright
Wake'field
Wake'ford
Wal'brook
Wal'cot
Wal'deck
Wal'degrave
Wal'denburg
Wales
Wal'ford
Walk'er
Walk'ingham
Wal'lace
Walla'chia
Wal'lasey
Wal'ler
Wal'lingford
Wal'lis
Walls'end
Wal'mer
Wal'mersley
Walmes'ley
Wal'pole
Wal'sall
Walsh
Wal'sham
Wal'singham
Wal'ter
Wal'tham
Wal'thamstow
Wal'ton
Wal'worth
Wands'worth
Wans'ford
Wan'tage
Wap'ping
War'beck
War'borough
War'burton
Ward
Ward'law
Ward'leworth
Ware
Ware'ham
War'grave
Wark'worth
War'lingham

War'minster
Warm'ley
War'ner
Warn'ford
War'ren
War'rington
War'saw
War'ton
War'wick
Wash'burne
Wash'ington
Wat
Wa'terbury
Wa'terford
Wa'terhouse
Waterloo'
Wa'terworth
Wat'ford
Wat'kins
Wat'son
Watt
Watteau'
Wat'ton
Watts
Wau'chope
Waugh
Wa'verley
Wear'mouth
Wea'verhead
Wea'vertree
Webb
Web'ber
We'ber
Web'ster
Wedg'wood
Wed'more
Wednes'bury
Wee'don
Weeks
Wei'-hai-wei
Wei'mar
Wel'bury
Welch
Wel'don
Wel'ford
Wel'ler
Welles'ley
Well'ingborough
Wel'lington
Wells
Welsh'pool
Wem
Wemyss
Wen'dover
Wen'lock
Went'worth
Wer'ner
Wert'heim
Wer'ther
Wes'ley

West'acott
West'bourne
West'bury
West'cott
West'field
West'gate
West In'dies
West'lake
West'land
West'ley
West'macott
West'meath
West'minster
West'morland
Wes'ton
Wes'ton-su'per-Mare
Westpha'lia
West'port
West Virgin'ia
Weth'erell
Wex'ford
Wey'man
Wey'mouth
Whal'ley
Whal'ton
Wharn'cliffe
Whar'ton
Whate'ly
Wheel'er
Whis'ton
Whit'aker
Whit'bread
Whit'by
Whit'church
White'chapel
White'hall
Whiteha'ven
White'head
White'house
Whit'field
Whit'horn
Whit'ley
Whit'man
Whit'minster
Whit'more
Whit'ney
Whit'taker
Whit'tier
Whit'tingham
Whit'tington
Whit'tlesea
Whit'wick
Wick
Wick'ham
Wick'low
Wic'liffe
Wid'combe
Wid'nes
Wiesba'den
Wig'an
Wight
Wight'man
Wig'ram
Wig'toft

Wigton' / Wig'town
Wil'berforce
Wil'cox
Wil'ford
Wil'frid
Wilhelmi'na
Wilkes
Wilkes'-Barre
Wil'kie
Wil'kins
Wil'kinson
Will
Wil'lenhall
Willes'den
Will'iam
Will'iams
Will'iamsburg
Will'iamson
Wil'lingdon
Wil'lingham
Wil'lington
Wil'lis
Will'oughby
Wills'bridge
Wil'ly
Wil'mington
Wil'mot
Wilms'low
Wil'na
Wil'son
Wil'ton
Wilt'shire
Wim'bledon
Wim'borne
Wincan'ton
Win'chelsea
Win'chester
Winch'more
Winck'worth
Win'dermere
Wind'ham
Wind'sor
Win'ford
Win'gate
Wing'field
Wing'ham
Win'grove
Win'ifred
Win'kle
Wink'ton
Win'laton
Winn'ipeg
Wins'low
Win'ster
Win'ston
Win'terbourne
Win'terton
Win'wick

Wirks'worth
Wis'bech
Wiscon'sin
Wise'man
With'am
With'ers
Wit'ney
Wit'tenberg
Wi'tu
Wo'burn
Wode'house
Wo'king
Wo'kingham
Wol'ga
Wol'laston
Wolse'ley
Wol'sey
Wol'singham
Wol'stanton
Wolverhamp'ton
or
Wol'verton
Wol'viston
Womb'well
or
Wood'bridge
Wood'bury
Wood'church
Wood'fall
Wood'ford
Wood'side
Wood'stock
Wood'ward
Woolhamp'ton
Wool'ley
Wool'los
Wool'ston
Wool'wich
Woot'ton
Woot'ton Bas'sett
Worces'ter
Worces'tershire
Words'ley
Words'worth
Working'ton
Work'sop
Wor'lington
Wor'lingworth
Wor'num
Wors'borough
Wors'ley
Wor'then
Wor'thing
Wor'thington
Wot'ton-*un'der-*Edge
Wrag'by
Wray
Wren
Wren'bury
Wren'tham
Wrex'ham
Wring'ton
Wroth'am
Wur'temberg
Wurz'burg
Wy'att
Wych'erley
Wyc'lif
Wyc'ombe
Wye
Wymond'ham
Wynd'ham
Wynn
Wyo'ming

X

Xan'adu
Xan'thus
Xantip'pe
Xav'ier
Xe'nia
Xen'ocles
Xenoc'rates
Xen'ophon
Xe'res
Xerx'es
Xul'la
Xu'ry

Y

Yale
Yar'borough
Yard'ley
Yar'mouth
Yar'row
Yates
or
Yat'ton
Yax'ley
Yeats
Yel'lowstone
Yem'en
Yenise'i
Yeo'vil
Yer'burgh
Yokoha'ma
Yon'kers
Yor'ick
York
Yosem'ite
Yost
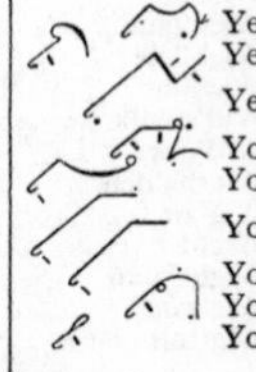
Yough'al
Youl'grave
Young
Young'husband
Youngs'town
Yox'all
Yox'ford
Yucatan'
Yu'kon
Y'verdon
Yvetot'

Z

Zach
Zacche'us
Zachari'ah
Zach'ary
Zad'kiel
Za'dok
Zambe'si
Zamen'hof
Zang'will
Zan'te

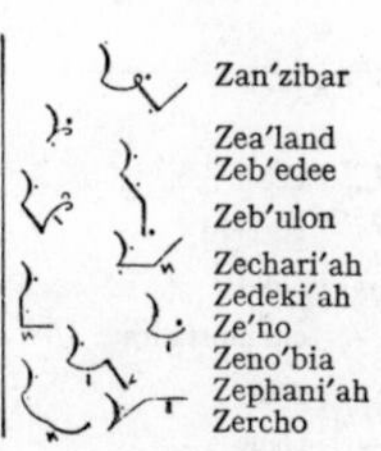

Zan'zibar
Zea'land
Zeb'edee
Zeb'ulon
Zechari'ah
Zedeki'ah
Ze'no
Zeno'bia
Zephani'ah
Zercho

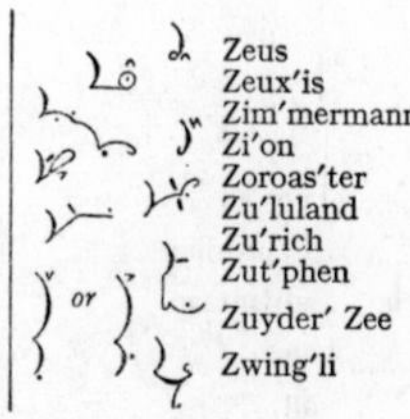

Zeus
Zeux'is
Zim'mermann
Zi'on
Zoroas'ter
Zu'luland
Zu'rich
Zut'phen
Zuyder' Zee
Zwing'li

Full List of Grammalogues

A

a *or* an
accord-ing
advantage
ah!
all
and
any
are
as
aught
awe
aye

B

balance
be
because
been
behalf
belief-ve-d
beyond
build-ing
but

C

call
called
can
cannot
care
cared
chair
chaired
cheer
cheered
child
circumstance
cold
come
could

D

dear
deliver-ed-y
deliverance
difference-t
difficult
do
doctor, Dr.
during

E

eh?
equal-ly
equalled

F

first
for
from

G

general-ly
generalization
gentleman
gentlemen
give-n
go
gold
great
guard

H

had
hand
has
have
he
him
himself
his
hour
how
however

I

importance-ant
impossible
improve-d-ment
in
influence
influenced
information
inscribe-d
inscription
instruction
instructive
is
it
itself

J

justification

L

language
large
largely
larger
liberty
Lord

M

me
member
mere
more
most
Mr.
much
myself

N

near
next
nor
northern
number-ed

O

O! oh!
of
on
opinion
opportunity
ought
our
ourselves
over

owe
owing
own

P

particular
people
pleasure
principal-ly
principle
put

Q

quite

R

rather
remark-ed
remember-ed

S

satisfaction
school
schooled
selfish-ness
sent
several
shall, shalt
short
should
significance
significant
signification
signify-ied
southern
speak
special-ly
spirit
subject-ed
subjection
subjective
sure
surprise
surprised

T

tell
thank-ed
that
the
their
them
themselves
there
therefore
thing
think
third
this
those
though
thus
thyself
till
to
to be
told
too
toward
towards
trade
tried
truth
two

U

under
usual-ly

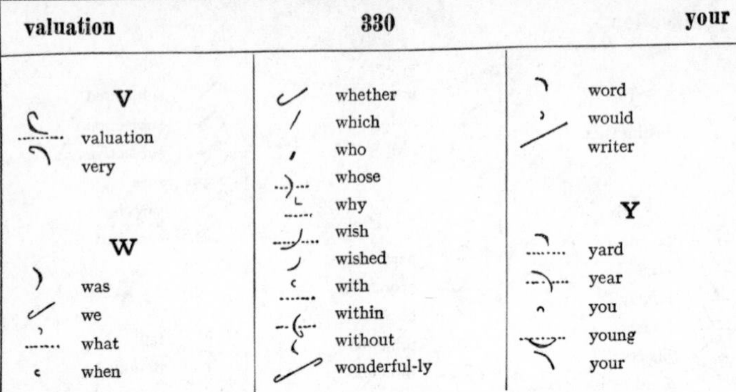

V

valuation
very

W

was
we
what
when
whether
which
who
whose
why
wish
wished
with
within
without
wonderful-ly
word
would
writer

Y

yard
year
you
young
your

Contractions

A

abandonment
acknowledge
administrator
administratrix
advertise-d-ment
altogether
amalgamate
amalgamation
anything
appointment
arbitrary
arbitrate
arbitration
arbitrator
architect-ure-al
assignment
attainment

B

bankruptcy

C

capable
certificate
character
characteristic
circumstantial
commercial-ly
contentment
contingency
cross-examination
cross-examined

D

danger
dangerous
defective
deficient-ly-cy
demonstrate
denomination-al
description
destruction
destructive
destructively
difficulty
discharge-d
distinguish-ed

E

efficient-ly-cy
electric
electrical
electricity
emergency
England
English
Englishman
enlarge
enlarger
enlightenment
entertainment
enthusiastic-iasm
especial-ly
esquire
establish-ed-ment
everything

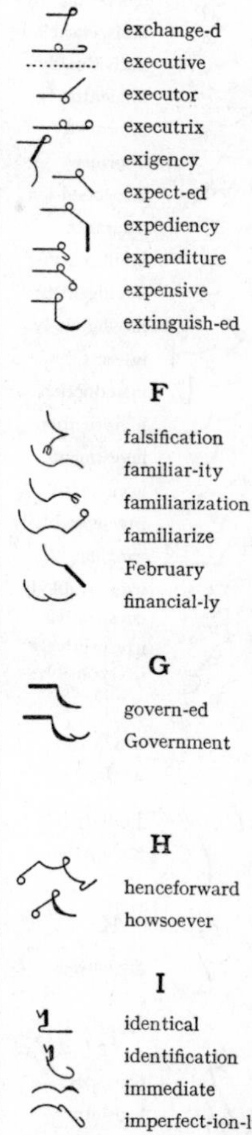

exchange-d
executive
executor
executrix
exigency
expect-ed
expediency
expenditure
expensive
extinguish-ed

F

falsification
familiar-ity
familiarization
familiarize
February
financial-ly

G

govern-ed
Government

H

henceforward
howsoever

I

identical
identification
immediate
imperfect-ion-ly

imperturbable
incandescence
incandescent
inconsiderate
inconvenience-t-ly
incorporated
independent-ly-ce
indispensable-ly
individual-ly
influential-ly
inform-ed
informer
inspect-ed-ion
insurance
intelligence
intelligent-ly
intelligible-ly
interest
introduction
investigation
investment
ironmonger
irrecoverable-ly
irregular
irremovable-ly
irrespective
irrespectively
irresponsible-ility

J

January
jurisdiction

K

knowledge

L

legislative
legislature

M

magnetic-ism
manufacture-d
manufacturer
manuscript
mathematical-ly
mathematician
mathematics
maximum
mechanical-ly
messenger
metropolitan
minimum
ministry
misfortune
monstrous
mortgage-d

N

neglect-ed
negligence
never
nevertheless
nothing
notwithstanding
November

O

object-ed
objection
objectionable
objective
obstruction
obstructive
oneself
organization
organize-d
organizer

P

parliamentary
passenger
peculiar-ity
perform-ed
performance
performer
perpendicular
perspective
practicable
practice
practise-d
prejudice-d-ial-ly
preliminary
probable-ly-ility
production
productive
proficient-ly-cy
project-ed
proportion-ed
proportionate-ly
prospect
prospective
prospectus
public
publication
publish-ed
publisher

Q

questionable-ly

R

ratepayers
recoverable
reform-ed
reformer
regular
relinquish-ed
remarkable-ly

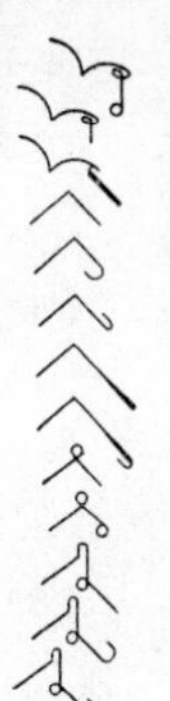

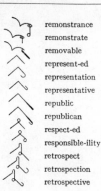

remonstrance
remonstrate
removable
represent-ed
representation
representative
republic
republican
respect-ed
responsible-ility
retrospect
retrospection
retrospective

S

satisfactory
sensible-ly-ility
something
stranger

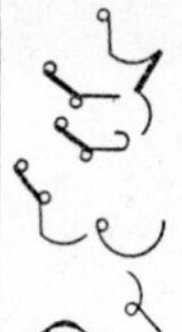

stringency
subscribe-d
subscription
substantial-ly
sufficient-ly-cy
suspect-ed
sympathetic

T

telegram
telegraphic
thankful-ly
thenceforward
together

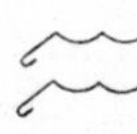

U

unanimity
unanimous-ly

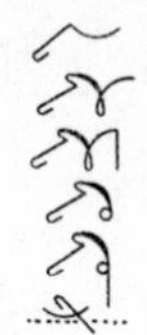

uniform-ity-ly
universal-ly
universality
universe
university
unprincipled

W

whatever
whenever
whensoever
whereinsoever
wheresoever
whithersoever

Y

yesterday

Phrase Logograms

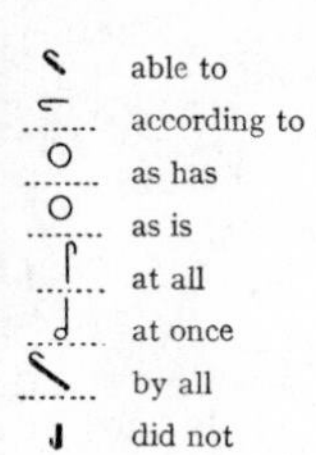

able to
according to
as has
as is
at all
at once
by all
did not

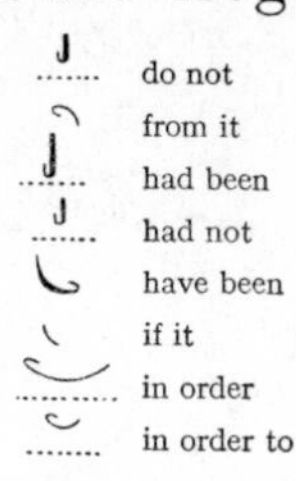

do not
from it
had been
had not
have been
if it
in order
in order to

in our
is as
is his
may not
out of
they are
till it
which have

APPENDIX

In addition to some further ordinary words not previously given in this Dictionary it has been thought desirable to include in this Appendix certain new words which have come into use during recent years.

A

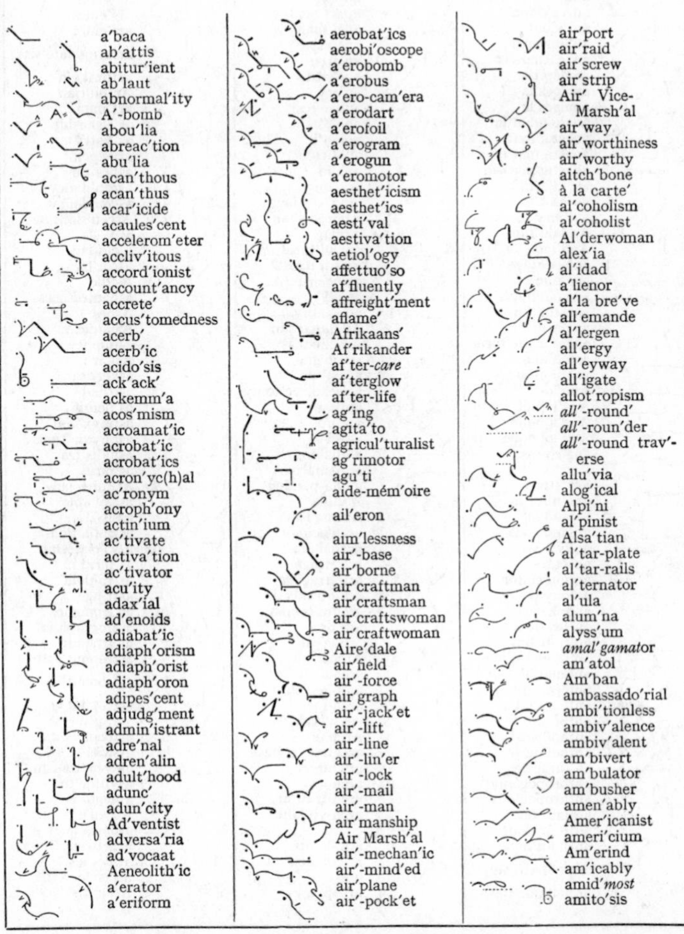

a'baca
ab'attis
abitur'ient
ab'laut
abnormal'ity
A'-bomb
abou'lia
abreac'tion
abu'lia
acan'thous
acan'thus
acar'icide
acaules'cent
accelerom'eter
accliv'itous
accord'ionist
account'ancy
accrete'
accus'tomedness
acerb'
acerb'ic
acido'sis
ack'ack'
ackemm'a
acos'mism
acroamat'ic
acrobat'ic
acrobat'ics
acron'yc(h)al
ac'ronym
acroph'ony
actin'ium
ac'tivate
activa'tion
ac'tivator
acu'ity
adax'ial
ad'enoids
adiabat'ic
adiaph'orism
adiaph'orist
adiaph'oron
adipes'cent
adjudg'ment
admin'istrant
adre'nal
adren'alin
adult'hood
adunc'
adun'city
Ad'ventist
adversa'ria
ad'vocaat
Aeneolith'ic
a'erator
a'eriform

aerobat'ics
aerobi'oscope
a'erobomb
a'erobus
a'ero-cam'era
a'erodart
a'erofoil
a'erogram
a'erogun
a'eromotor
aesthet'icism
aesthet'ics
aesti'val
aestiva'tion
aetiol'ogy
affettuo'so
af'fluently
affreight'ment
aflame'
Afrikaans'
Af'rikander
af'ter-*care*
af'terglow
af'ter-life
ag'ing
agita'to
agricul'turalist
ag'rimotor
agu'ti
aide-mém'oire
ail'eron
aim'lessness
air'-base
air'borne
air'craftman
air'craftsman
air'craftswoman
air'craftwoman
Aire'dale
air'field
air'-force
air'graph
air'-jack'et
air'-lift
air'-line
air'-lin'er
air'-lock
air'-mail
air'-man
air'manship
Air Marsh'al
air'-mechan'ic
air'-mind'ed
air'plane
air'-pock'et

air'port
air'raid
air'screw
air'strip
Air' Vice-Marsh'al
air'way
air'worthiness
air'worthy
aitch'bone
à la carte'
al'coholism
al'coholist
Al'derwoman
alex'ia
al'idad
a'lienor
al'la bre've
all'emande
all'ergen
all'ergy
all'eyway
all'igate
allot'ropism
all'-round'
all'-roun'der
all'-round trav'-erse
allu'via
alog'ical
Alpi'ni
al'pinist
Alsa'tian
al'tar-plate
al'tar-rails
al'ternator
al'ula
alum'na
alyss'um
*amal'gamat*or
am'atol
Am'ban
ambassado'rial
ambi'tionless
ambiv'alence
ambiv'alent
am'bivert
am'bulator
am'busher
amen'ably
Amer'icanist
ameri'cium
Am'erind
am'icably
amid'*most*
amito'sis

am'monal
ammon'iated
amoe'bic
amok'
amo'ral
amoral'ity
amorce'
amp'
amper'age
am'poule
am'putator
am'track
amus'edly
amyg'dalin
am'yloid
an'abranch
anacathars'is
analep'tic
analges'ia
analges'ic
analphabet'ic
anastig'mat
anastigmat'ic
anastig'matism
an(n)at'ta
an(n)at'to
an'bury
Andalu'sian
And'ine
an'ecdotage
ane'mic
anem'ograph
anesthet'ic
an'eurin
angin'a pec'toris
angio'ma
an'gle-iron
Ang'lo-
Ang'lophil
Ang'lophile
Ang'lophobe
ang'riness
ang'strom
ang'uiform
Anguil'la
anguin'eous
ankylo'sis
ann'ates
annun'ciator
an'onym
anoph'eles
an'swerless
an'te-bellum
an'te merid'iem
antenat'al
antepen'dium
antepran'dial
anthe'sis
anthol'ogist
anthol'ogize
an'thracene
anthropog'eny
anthropog'ony
antiadi'tis
anti-air'craft
antibiot'ic
antic'ipatively
anticlimac'tic

antihist'amine
antijuda'ic
antimalar'ial
antiph'onary
Antirrhin'um
anti-Semit'ic
antitet'anin
antithet'ics
anti-vac'cina-
tionist
anti-vivisec'tion
*an'y*time
*an'y*way
apart'heid
ape'-man'
apep'sy
ap'erçu
apé'ritif
ap'ery
aphae'resis
aph'esis
aphet'ic
aph'icide
aph'id
aph'ony
aphrodis'iac
Aphrodis'ian
a'pian
apicul'tural
apicul'turist
ap'ocentre
ap'od
apog'amy
Apollinar'ian
Apollinar'is
apolo'gia
aposi'tia
appendicec'tomy
appose'
ap'pro
aptot'ic
a'qualung
aquamarine'
a'qua-planing
A'quila
Arama'ism
aran'eology
arapai'ma
arb'itrage
arb'itrageur
*arbitra'tion*al
*arbitra'tion*ist
arb'or
arbor'eal
Archae'an
archais'tic
arch'-en'emy
arch-foe'
Arch'ibald
Arch'ie
archiepis'copate
ar'chitected
arch'let
arch-trait'or
arch-vill'ain
arc'-lamp
ar'cubalist
are
areop'agy

ar'gle-bar'gle
ar'gufier
ar'gufy
ar'gie-bar'gie
ar'gy-bar'gy
Ar'imasp
Arimas'pian
ario'so
aristol'ogy
Armagedd'on
arrange'able
ar'senate
ars'enic
art'efact
arteriosclero'sis
arthral'gia
Arthu'rian
art'ifact
ar'tisanship
ar'tistry
arus'pex
asbes'tic
ascen'dancy
ascen'dency
Ascen'siontide
asce'sis
ascid'ian
ascor'bic
As'dic
ashamed'ness
Ashes
Asian'ic
asinin'ity
Askar'i
askel'etal
aso'cial
as'pergill
asphyx'iant
asphyxia'tion
aspidis'tra
as'pirin
Asquith'ian
assay'able
assib'ilate
assibila'tion
asso'ciateship
as'terid
astrakhan'
astringe'
as'trodome
astrograph'ic
as'tronaut
astronaut'ical
astronaut'ics
astrophotog'-
raphy
astrophys'ics
a-swirl'
asynch'ronism
asyntac'tic
ateleio'sis
Athen'e
atherm'ic
atheto'sis
athlet'ics
ati'choo
Atlan'tis

atmosphe'rics
ato'cia
atomiza'tion
at'omizer
aton'al
Ats'
atta'ché-case
attui'tion
auberge'
aub'ergine
aubr(i)e't(i)a
auctor'ial
aud'ile
au'dio-
au'diophil(e)
au'ditize
au'ditress
au'rify
aur'ous
Auss'ie
Austra'lianism
aut'archy
aut'arky
authigen'ic
authoritar'ian
authorita'rianism
au'tism
aut'o
autobiog'raphist
aut'obus
autocop'yist
autocrit'ical
aut'ocycle
autodiagno'sis
autodidac'tic
autoerot'ic
autogen'esis
autog'eny
Autogir'o
autogravure'
autogyr'o
aut'oharp
autol'atry
autol'ogy
aut'omate
automa'tion
automat'ograph
automot'ive
auton'omism
autonomist'ic
aut'onym
autopian'o
auto-port'rait
auto-sugges'tion
aut'ovac
aut'o-wheel
auxanom'eter
auxom'eter
av'iarist
av'iate
a'viculture
av'idly
aviette'
av'ion
avoca'do
Av'ro
aware'ness
awear'y
awheel'
Ax'minster
Ayles'bury
azan'
Azil'ian
azote'a

B

bab'y-farm
bab'y-ribb'on
bab'y-sitt'er
bach'elor-girl'
bacill'icide
back'-ben'cher
back'-chat
back'-cloth
back'-down
back'fisch
back'-front
back'-log
back'mark'er
back'*num'ber*
back'-ped'al
back'scratch'er
back'scratch'ing
back-spa'cer
backwarda'tion
bacte'ricide
bacte'riform
bacteriol'ogist
bacteriolyt'ic
bac'terize
bad'dish
Bail'ey bridge
Bak'elite
Balaclav'a
balalaik'a
balbo'a
bald'-faced
bald'-headed
bald'ish
ballerin'a
balletomane'
balletoma'nia
ball'onet
ball'ot-pa'per
ball'y
ballyhoo'
bal'sa
band'itry
band'master
band'-saw
band'-wag'on
band'-wheel
Ban'ian
ban'jolin
banjule'le
banks'man
ban'thine
Bantu'
bap'tistry
barathe'a
barb'itone
barbiturate'
barbitur'ic
bardol'atry
bar'er
bar'est
bargee'
barg'ing
Barm'ecidal
barocyclonom'eter
bar'onetize
Baroque'
bar'rage
barrette'
bar'ristress
bar'row-boy
Bar'sac
bar'ysphere
bascol'ogy
bas'cule
bash
bashed
bash'ing
bas'ically
bas'inet
bask'er
bas'ket-ball
bass'o-profun'do
Basu'to
Bath'-*chair*
bathet'ic
bathom'eter
bathygraph'ical
bathym'eter
bathy'metry
bath'yscaphe
bath'yscope
bath'ysphere
bat'tle-cruis'er
bat'tleworthy
batt'y
baux'ite

bay'-rum
bazoo'ka
beach'comb'er
beach'-res'cue
beach'ward
beachwards
bead'ed
bead'ledom
bean'o
beaumon'tage
beauti'cian
beautifica'tion
beaux'ite
be'bop
bedaze'
bed'cover
bed'der
bed'fast
bed'-key
bed'-pan
bed'-rock
bed'-sit'ter
bed'-sit'ting-room
bed'spread
beech'y
beeftea'
beef'y
beer'-pump
before'-men'-tioned
begor'ra
beguine'
behav'iourism
behav'iourist
behove'
beige
bei'gnet
bel
belat'edness
belay'ing-pin
bel'ga
belit'tler
bell'-boy
bell'-buoy
bel'lite
bell'-punch
bell'push
belong'ings
bemus'edly
bemuse'ment
benatu'ra
Benedic'ite
Benedic'tiness
ben'efact
bénéficiaire'
Ben'elux
benig'nancy
béni'tier
ben'thos
ben'thoscope
bent'wood
benzyp'rine
ber'ber
berceuse'
ber'et
Berlin'

Bermu'dian
ber'ryless
ber'serk
Berth'a
bertillonage'
besiclom'eter
besmirch'
besmirched'
besmirch'ing
bête-noire
Beth'din
between'ness
between'time
between'whiles
bev'atron
bev'eler
bev'eller
bian'nual
bibcock'
bibe'lot
bibliop'egy
biblioph'ilist
biblioph'ily
bibliop'oly
bica'meral
bicon'vex
bicor'porate
bicyclette'
bien'nial
bifa'cial
biff
bifo'cal
bifo'cals
big'amize
big'amous
big'enous
big'ger
big'gest
bijou'terie
bike
biki'ni
bila'bial
biling'ualism
bill'-brok'er
bil'likin
bill'y
biman'ual
bi-month'ly
bi'nac
bing'o
binitar'ian
binitar'ianism
biochem'ical
biochem'ist
biochem'istry
biogeog'raphy
biophys'ics
bi'oscope
bipartisan'
bi-quar'terly
birch'-rod'
bird'call
birth'-control'
birth'-rate

bisen'sory
bi-week'ly
black'-flag
Black'-fri'ar
black'-jack
black'-list
Black Mari'a
black mar'ket
black'out
black'shirt
blade'less
blan'co
blastogen'esis
blath'er
blaz'er
blear'y
blephari'tis
bleth'er
blight'er
Blight'y
blind'-all'ey
blind'spot
blind'-worm
blink'ered
blink'ing
blip
blith'er
blith'ering
blitz
blitzed
blitz'krieg
blob
bloc
blondinette'
blood'-bath
blood'-group
blood'stock
blood'-transfu'sion
blos'somry
blotch'y
blow'lamp
blow'y
blue'-chip
blue'-eyed
blue'ing
blue'jacket
blue'-pen'cil
blue'print
Blues
bluette'
blu'ing
blus'tery
boat'-deck
boat'er
boat'-house
bob'ble
bob'by-dazzler
bob'bysock
bob'bysoxer
bob'sled
bob'sleigh
bob'wig
Bodo'ni
boff'in
bog'gle
bog'myrtle
Bo'gomilism

Bohair'ic
Bohem'ianism
boli'var
bolivia'no
boll'-weev'il
Bo'loism
bolom'eter
bolon'ey
Bol'shevik
Bol'shevism
Bol'shevist
bolt'-up'right
bomb'er
bond'stone
bone'head
bone'less
bone'-meal
bon'zoline
boo'by-prize
boo'by-trap
boo'gie-woo'gie
book'able
book'plate
boom'let
boom'slang
boon'gary
boost
boos'ter
boot'legger
boot'licker
boracif'erous
bor'der-line
bor'né
Bor'nean
born'ite
borsel'la
bort
Borz'oi
Bos'nian
bo'sun
bot'tle-green
bot'tle-neck
bot'tle-wash'er
bot'ulism
Boule
boul'ter
bou'rrée
bouse
boutique'
bov'rilize
box-calf'
box'-car
box'-office
box-resp'irator
box'-room
box'y
bra
bra'ces
brack'et
bract'eal
bract'eate
brad'ded
Brad'shaw
bradycar'dia
bradyphra'sia
bradyseism'
brae
brain'-*child*
brain'ily
brain'y
brain'-storm
brain'-wash
brain'wave
brak'ing
bramantesque'
branc'hia
branc'hiate
branch'ling
bran'dified
bran'dy-snap
bran'-tub
brass'erie
brass'-hat
brass'ière
bratt'ice
braze'less
break'-away
break even
break'-neck
breast'-stroke
breech'es-buoy
Bren
bretelle'
Bret'on
brick'-field
brick'-tea'
bridge'able
bridge'-head
bri'dle-path
brig'andry
Brig'hamite
bright'er
brill'iantine
brim'my
brink'manship
briquette'
bri'sance
bri'sant
brisk'er
brisk'est
bris'ling
Bris'tol
Brit'isher
broad'caster
Broad'land
broad'-mind'ed
broad'-mind'ed-ness
brochette'
brok'en-heart'ed
bron'choscope
Brontosaur'us
broth'erliwise
brum'ous
brune
brush'let
brutalita'rian
bub'ble-car
bub'ble-gum
buck'et-shop
buck'-rab'bit
buck'-shot
budg'erigar'
buff'ish
buf'flehead
budg'eting
bug'house
bu'glet
*build'*able
build'-up
bulb'il
Bul'gar
Bulga'rian
bul'ger
bul'imy
bull'doze
bull'dozer
bull'y-beef
bum'ming
Bun'desrat(h)
Bun'destag
bung'aloid
buoy'age
Burb'erry
bur'eaucrat
bureau'cratize
burg'le
Bur'goyne
burl'ing
Burm'an
bur'mite
bursic'ulate
bursi'form
bus
bush'-ba'by
bush'master
bus'iness-man'
bus'ker
butt'er-bean
butt'er-fingers
butt'er mus'lin
butyrom'eter
butt'on-ball
butt'on-wood
buzz
buzz'-bomb
by-elec'toral
by'pass
by'play

C

cabb'y
caboo'dle
ca'can'ny
cachaem'ia
cac'hinnate
cacogen'ics
cad'dish
Caesa'rean
Caesa'rean
caesa'reanist
caesa'rianist
café au lait
cafete'ria
cage'ling
cage'work
cake'let
cake'walk
cal'aber
calcic'olous
calcif'erous
cal'culiform
calefac'tor
calf'-love
caliol'ogy
*call'*able
call'-girl
cal'(l)iper
calm'ingly
cal'orie
cal'ycate
calyp'so
cam'aloté
cam'alote
camaraderie
cam'aron
cam'eloid
Cam'embert
camerlin'go
cam'i-knick'ers
cam'ion
cam'ouflage
cam'pan
camp'-bed
campim'eter
camp'-stool
cam'pus

can'apé
can'can
canc'roid
candes'cent
can'gan
canit'ies
canned
can'nery
can'ning
canoe'able
canoe'ing
canood'le
canoph'ilist
Canta'te
can'tor
capac'itance
capac'itor
cap'italism
capitalis'tic
Cappado'cian
cappucci'no
capric'cio
cap'tained
car'bide
carbo-hy'drate
carbona'do
car'bonite
car'bonizer
Carborun'dum
car'burate
carcin'ogen
carcinogen'esis
carcinogen'ic
carcinomato'sis
car'digan
car'dinally
card'-in'dex
car'diogram
car'diograph
career'ist
*care'*free
carn'ivore
car'rack
car'riole
car'ry-over
cartol'ogy
car'tomancy
cartoon'ing
cartoph'ilist
cartoph'ily
case'-book
case'-law
cash'able

cash'register
cassolette'
cast'-off
castra'to
cas'ualism
cas'ually
cas'uals
catagen'esis
cat'aloguable
cat'aloguer
catamoun'tain
cat'aractal
cat'-burg'lar
catch'-phrase
caten'ist
Cath'erine-wheel
cathex'is
cathod'ograph
cat'nap
cat's'*eye*
catt'ish
cat'tle-grid
catt'y
cauk
cavalier'ish
cav'endish
cavernic'olous
Celanese'
Cel'ebret
celes'ta
celeste'
cell'ophane
cem'balo
cemen'tite
cen'suses
cen'tibar
centill'ion
cen'timo
cen'trally
cen'trosphere
cen'trum
cephalal'gia
cephali'tis
ceram'ics
ceratosaur'us
cerebri'tis
ceroplas'tics
cert'ifiable
certif'icated
cer'vix
Cesar'ewitch
Ceylonese'
cha'-cha'
chaconne'
chaf'fing
Chagi'gah

chain'let
chair'oplane
Chalcolith'ic
chall'is
cham'bray
chamotte'
champlevé
chance'ful
chance'less
chan'cellory
chan'cy
change'-*o'ver*
chant'y
chap'pie
*char'acter*ful
*charactero*l'ogy
char'-la'dy
Char'leston
char'mante
char'melaine
char'meuse
chastis'able
chaton'
chat'tily
chau'ffer
chauf'feuse
Chazzan'
ché'chia
check'-up
Ched'ar
chedd'ite
cheek'y
cheep
cheer'io
cheese'-paring
chees'er
cheese'-straw
cheese'wood
chees'ing
cheiro-
Chell'ean
chemig'raphy
chem'itype
chemopsychi'a-
try
chem'urgy
cher'alite
chev'iot
chev'ronel
chib'ol
chid'ed
chig'oe
Chihua'hua
Chil'ean
chin'-deep
Chin'dit
Chinese' lan'tern
chin'-wag
chirop'odous
chirop'ody
chiroprac'tic
chiroprac'tor
chirop'tera
chirop'terous
chirp'y

chi'tal
chi'tin
chi'tosan
chit'tagong
chlor'idize
chlor'inate
chlo'rinize
cho'ate
choir'-screen
chok'iness
chop'-chop'
chop'py
cho'reograph
choreog'rapher
choreog'raphy
cho'riamb
chor'tle
chou
Chow
chris'mon
Christ'mas(s)y
chro'matoid
chro'mogram
chromoplas'tic
chrom'osome
chro'motype
chro'mo-typog'-
raphy
chrysobe'ryl
cic'ad
cid'aris
cin'e
cine-cam'era
cinemat'ic
cinematog'-
rapher
cinematograph'ic
cinematog'raphy
cinemat'oscope
cine-microg'-
raphy
cir'ca
circulariza'tion
circumam'bulate
circumben'dibus
cir'cus(s)y
cir'ri
cise'leur
cise'lure
cispon'tine
cis'sy
cith'er
cith'ern
cit'rin
cit'rus
cit'tern
citrom'eter
civ'vies
clair-de-lune'
clam'atory
clang'er
clans'woman
Clare'
clare-obscure'
Clarisse'
clark'ia
classifi'able
class'ism

class'-war'
class'y
claustrophob'ia
clav'ecin
clavicem'balo
claw'-ham'mer
clay'eyness
clear'able
clear'-cole'
clear'way
cleav'ers
cler'gywoman
clerk'ess
cleroden'dron
clev'erish
climatothe'rapy
clinic'ian
cli'quy
clock'wise
clo'nus
clos'et-play
close'-up
clos'ish
cloud'-burst
clo'verleaf
cluck'er
clumped
Clydes'dale
coach'work
coad'unate
coal'-bed
coal'-face
coal'-gas
coal'-hole
coal'ite
coal'-tar
coal'-trimmer
coars'en
coast'al
coatie'
coax'ial
cob'bly
coca'inist
coccinel'la
cock-a-hoop'
cock'amaroo
cocotte'
co'dices
co'ed'
co-ed'ucate
co-educa'tional
co-educa'tional-
ism
co-educa'tionist
coel'acanth
coe'liostat
coeliot'omy
coen'obite
coenobit'ical
cof'fee-mill
cof'finite
cog-nitum
coher'er
coiffeuse'
coif'fured

co-inhe'ritor
co-insure'
co'kery
co'ky
cold'-chisel
cold'-frame'
cold war
collae'mia
collage'
collaps'able
collectiviza'tion
collect'ivize
collin'ear
collog'raphy
col'lotypy
coll'ywobbles
colo'nialism
col'onizer
coloratu'ra
colorim'eter
col'our-cast
col'ourful
col'umnist
combe
combina'tions
comb'ings
come'-back
Com'inform
Com'intern
commercialese'
commère'
commissar'
commu'niqué
com'pensator
com'plimented
comprimar'ia
compul'sionist
comput'ative
com'radeship
Com'stockery
conca'vo-con'vex
conceivabil'ity
concep'tual
concep'tualize
concessionnaire'
con'chate
con'chiform
conchi'tis
con'chy
concres'cent
concu'bitancy
concu'bitant
condi'tionalism
condi'tionalist
condomin'ium
confer'ment
confer'rable
congen'erous
congen'ially
Congoese'
Congolese'
con'jee
conjunctivi'tis
con'ker
con'queress
conquist'ador
conscrip'tionist
conscrip'tive
conserv'ative-ness
consor'tium
con'sternate
con*strin'gency*
consubstan'tial-ist
con'tact
contadi'no
conte
Contemp'tibles
conter'minal
contin'uator
contin'uo
contin'uousness
contin'uum
con'tra-bass
con'tra-bassoon
contracep'tion
contracep'tive
contradistinc'-tive
con'trail
contrap'tion
contrapun'tal
contrast'ive
controllabil'ity
con'ular
conurba'tion
convec'tor
conven'tionalize
conversa'tional-ist
convex'o-convex
convey'or
cook'er
cool'ant
coomb
co-ord'inator
cop
copai'va
co'-pi'lot
cop'ra
cop'ulatory
cop'y-cat
cop'yholder
copy-*writ'er*
cor ang'lais
corg'i-y
corian'drol
corm
corn'eum
cor'ocore
Cor'pus Chris'ti
correc'titude
correl'ativism
corri'da
cor'roval
cors'etier
cors'etière
cors'let
Cort'isone
cor'yl
cos
coscoro'ba
cosh
cos'monaut
cosmop'olis
cos'mosphere
cosmothe'ism
cos'motron
cos'ter
cos'terdom
cost-plus
co'tinine
cott'er
cot'tolene
cot'ton wool'
cou'éism
coulomb'
coun'terblast
coun'ter-punch
coun'try-side
coup'élet
court'-bar'on
Courtelle'
court'ing
Cousteau'
couture'
couturier'
couturière'
cov'erage
cov'er-charge
cov'er-girl
cow'age
cowl'ing
crab'ber
crack'ajack
crack'erjack
crack'pot
crane'-fly
crash'-dive
crash'-land'ing
crass'ier
crawk
creak'y
cream'-laid
creativ'ity
creek'let
creep'age
crème
cremnophob'ia
cren'el
crêpe
crêpe de chine
crêpe'line
crep'uscle
cresco'graph
cret'inoid
crevette'
crick'le
crim'inaloid
crim'py
Croe'sus
croon
croon'er
croquette'
cross'-cut
cross-cut'
crossect'
cross'-over
cross'-patch
cross'-ref'erence
cross'-sec'tion

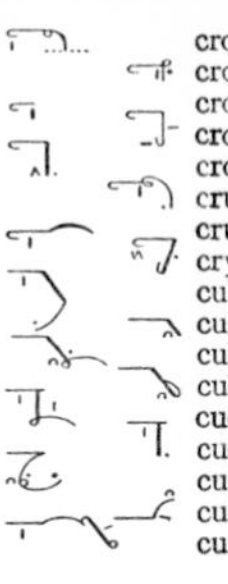

cross′*word*
croustade′
croûte
croûton′
crowd′ie
cru′cifer
crump
cry′ogen
cubb′ish
cubed
cub′ism
cub′ist
cud′dlesome
cud′dly
cu′licine
culottes′
cum′brous

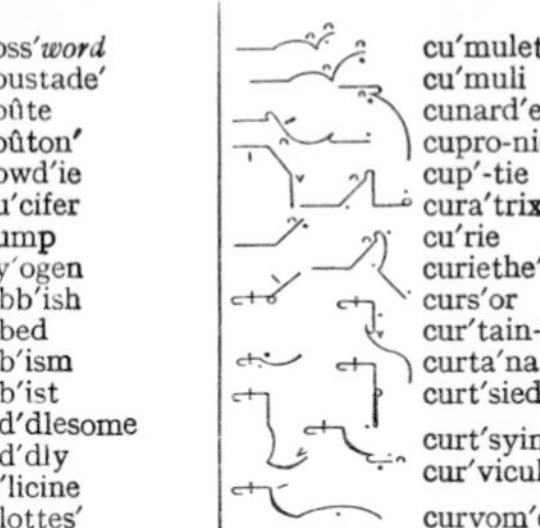

cu′mulet
cu′muli
cunard′er
cupro-nick′el
cup′-tie
cura′trix
cu′rie
curiethe′rapy
curs′or
cur′tain-fire
curta′na
curt′sied
curt′sying
cur′viculate
curvom′eter
cu′sec

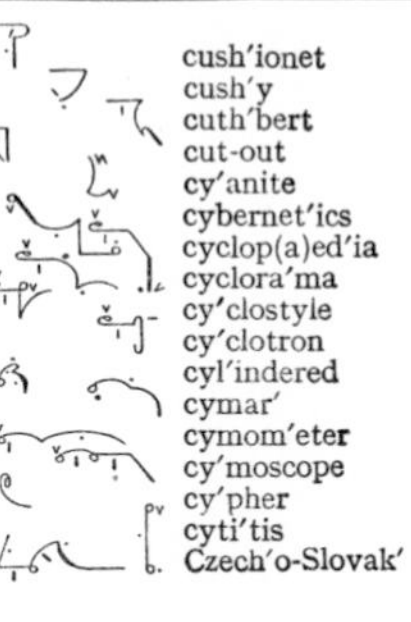

cush′ionet
cush′y
cuth′bert
cut-out
cy′anite
cybernet′ics
cyclop(a)ed′ia
cyclora′ma
cy′clostyle
cy′clotron
cyl′indered
cymar′
cymom′eter
cy′moscope
cy′pher
cyti′tis
Czech′o-Slovak′

D

dactyliog′raphy
dac′tylogram
dactylos′copy
dadd′y-long′-legs
Dail Ei′reann
Da′lai La′ma
dancette′
Dan′iel
dan′sant
dark′fall
dash′-board
date′-line
D′-Day
deactiva′tion
dead′-beat
dead′ freight
dead′-line
dead′ reck′oning
deaf′-aid
death′-mask
death-rat′tle
debag′
deb′itable
debunk′
debus′
decarteliza′tion
decel′erate
decelera′tion
decel′erator
decen′tralist
decentraliza′tion
dec′ibar
de′cibel
deck′-carg′o
declass′
declass′ify
decliv′itous
declutch′
decode′
decohe′rer

decoke′
décol′letage
decompress′
decontam′inate
decontrol′
decontrolled′
décor′
decuss′ately
deduct′able
deed′-poll
deep′-freeze
deep′ish
deer′skin
defeasibil′ity
defeat′ism
defeat′ist
defer′ment
defla′tionary
defla′tionist
deforma′tion
defrost′
degauss′
degres′sion
dehum′anize
dehyd′rate
de-ice′
deif′ic
dekk′o
delasse′ment
delate′
dela′tion
del cred′ere
delec′tify
delicatess′en
delict′
delic′tual
Deli′lah
delouse′
del′phine
Delphin′ium
del′ta-wing
démen′ti

demerar′a
democ′ratize
democ′ratized
démo′dé
demod′ed
demog′rapher
demoli′tionist
demote′
demo′tion
demus′tered
dena′ture
de′nier
de′nim
den′tine
depatria′tion
dependabil′ity
deportee′
depth′-charge
dep′utize
dera′cinate
derate′
derat′ing
dera′tion
Der′by
dere′gister
de rigueur′
dermatit′is
derv
desex′ualize
dessous′
detainee′
détente′
detrain′ment
de trop′
deuter′ium
deu′teron
deval′orize
deval′uate
de*valua′tion*
deval′ue
dever′bative
de′viable
devia′tionist
dev′il-box

dev'il-may-*care*
dev'ilment
diagnose'
dialec'tics
di'alled
diamant'é
diamet'rically
di'archy
di'athermy
dibb'er
di'chord
dichro'ic
dic'ta
dic'tograph
Die'sel
dietet'ics
dieti'cian
di'etist
dig'amist
dig'amy
digitor'ium
digs
dike'let
dilap'idate
dill'y-dally
dimorph'ic
dinar'
dingh'**y**
Din'ka
dink'y
dino'ceras
dinorn'is
din'osaur
din'othere
di'ode
diphylet'ic
dip'lon
di'pode
dipol'ar
di'pole
direc'tional
Direc'toire
dirn'dl
dirt'-track
disa'blement
disaffil'iate
disaffirma'tion
disassem'ble

disassocia'tion
disbud'
disburs'al
discern'ible
*discharge'*able
disc'-jock'ey
discog'raphy
disenti'tle
di'seur
di'seuse
disgrun'tled
disgrun'tlement
dishar'mony
dish'full
disincen'tive
disinfect'or
disli'kable
dismount'able
dispers'al
disrupt'
dissim'ilarly
disten'sile
distin'gué
distraint'
distrib'utism
distrib'utively
dis'tyle
disul'phide
disutil'ity
dith'er
div'agate
diverticulo'sis
divertic'ulum
divertimen'to
divertisse'ment
divi'sionism
divorce'able
divorcee'
dix'ie
dob'erman(n)
dock'er
dock'land
doc'torand
documenta'tion
dod'derer
dod'dery
dog'-coll'ar
dog'fight
dog'ging
doll'op

dol'men
doloro'so
dom'inance
doo'dle
doo'dlebug
dope
Dor'a
doss'-house
doub'le-bass'
doub'le-cross'
dough'-boy
dour
dow
down'grade
down'stream
down'wards
doyl'ey
drab'ly
Dracon'ian
dracon'iform
drag'ée
drain'less
dram'aturgy
dras'tically
drif'ter
dromophob'ia
drosom'eter
dry'-clean
dry'salt
dubb'in
Du'ce
duchesse'
duck'board
dud
duf'fle
dug'-out
dul'cin
dulcitone
Du'ma
dumb'-wait'er
duoden'al
dural'umin
duralumin'ium
du'rrie
dust'-jack'et
dy'namotor
dyne
dyspho'nia
dysur'ia

E

ear'let
ear'lierize
ear'-phone
earth'work
eas'tern***most***
east'wards
eau-de-nil
E'-boat
eb'onite
ebull'ience

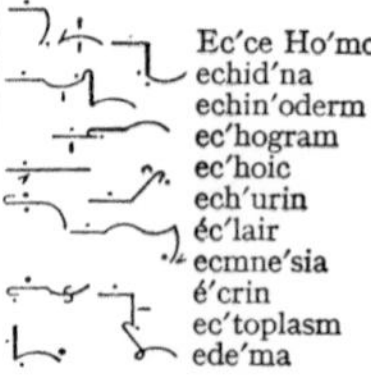

Ec'ce Ho'mo
echid'na
echin'oderm
ec'hogram
ec'hoic
ech'urin
éc'lair
ecmne'sia
é'crin
ec'toplasm
ede'ma

edem'atous
edg'ily
edg'y
edibil'ity
educand'
ed'ucatable
educa'tionalist
educa'tionally
Edward'ian
e'er
eff'ortfull

ef'fortlessness
egalitar'ian
egg'ery
eg'o
egocen'tric
egoman'ia
egoman'iac
eik'on
Einstein'ium
electrocu'tion
electromot'ive
elec'tron
electron'ic
electron'ics
electrostat'ics
electrotech'nics
electrothana'sia
electrothera-
peut'ics
electrothe'rapy
elev'enses
ellipsoi'dal
Élysée
Em'ber-Days
embouchure'
embrute'
embus'
ém'igré
emo'tionable
empa'radise
em'pathy
empen'nage
emphysem'a
emplace'ment
emplane'
empleoman'ia
employabil'ity
employ'able
empres'sé
emulsifica'tion
emul'sifier
emul'sify
encase'ment
encash'
encash'ment
encephalit'is
encir'clement
encrust'ed
encrust'ing
endocri'nal
en'docrine

endors'able
en'dorsee'
*Eng'lish*ism
*Eng'lish*woman
En'iac
enlace'
enlaced'
enlac'ing
en masse
en'osis
en pass'ant
enquired'
enquir'er
enquir'ing
enquir'y
en route
En'sa
en'teron
enthuse'
entrain'ment
en'trecôte
en'tredeux
enure'
enured
enure'sis
envi'sage
envi'saged
envi'saging
en'zyme
Eo'ka
e'olith
Eolith'ic
ép'ée
ep'iblast
epicen'tre
epicen'trum
epidi'ascope
epifoc'al
ep'igon
epinos'ic
episcopa'lia
epis'toler
epsil'on
equalitar'ian
equestrienne'
equil'ibrator
ergatoc'racy
erg'ograph
ergom'eter
erg'on
ergonom'ics
ergopho'bia
erig'eron
Er'os
erot'oman'ia
ersatz'
escapee'
escor'tage
escrow'
escud'o

espa'da
espadrille'
esperant'ist
espressiv'o
espress'o
essen'tialize
estam'inet
Esthon'ian
eth'ane
eth'icism
eth'os
eth'yl
etiquett'ical
é'tude'
eu'genist
euphon'ium
euphor'ia
euphor'ic
euph'ory
eurhyth'mics
Euro'mart
eur'yscope
eval'uate
evalua'ting
evalua'tion
even'tualize
evercir'culator
Ev'eryman
ev'illy
ex'calate
ex cathed'ra
exclo'sure
ex'eunt
exhibi'tionism
exhibi'tionist
ex'igible
existen'tial
existen'tialism
ex-lib'ris
Exo'nian
expan'sionist
expa'tiative
expend'able
expertise'
explicand'
explo'dent
ex-serv'ice
exten'dable
ex'travert
extrem'ism
ex'trovert
exuv'iate
eye'-bolt
eye'-op'ener
eye'-strain
*eye'*wash

F

Fa'bianism
fab'ulousness
fab'urden
fac'tional
fac'torize
fac'tual
fac'tum
fadd'ish
fade'-out
fag
fair'-haired
fairyol'ogy
fair'y-tale
Falang'e
fall'-out
famil'ial
faquir'
far'-flung
farm'stead
fas'cicule
fascine'
Fas'cism
fa'stener
fat'igable
feas'ibly
feath'er-weight
fea'tureless
feck'less
fell'ow-trav'eller
feme
fem'inism
fem'inist
fenestel'la
fer'al
ferro-conc'rete
fe'rrous
fe'rry-bridge
feuds
fi'breboard
fi'breglass
fib'riform
fib'rillose
fibro'sis
fibrosit'is
fictioneer'
fi'es'ta
fifth-col'umnist
figurine'
Fiji'an
fil'agree
fil'ibeg
Filipi'no
fi'lite
fill'ing-sta'tion
fin'alist
fin'alize
fin'alized
fing'er-print
fin'icky
fire'-bas'ket
fire'-control
fis'calism
fish'-plate
fiv'er
fives'
flag'-wagg'er
flak
flame'-projec'tor
flamm'enwerfer
flan
flap' jack
flap'ping
flash'-light
flash'-point
flat'-bott'omed
flav'in
flea'some
flèche
flee'ciness
fleet'er
flesh'monger
flex
flick'-knife
flicks
flight'-deck
flight'-lieuten'-ant
flip
float'-plane
flong
flood'-light
flood'lit
floor'-cloth
flos'culous
floun'cy
flow'sheet
'flu
fluid'ify
fluores'cence
fluores'cent
fly'-*ov'er*
fly'-past
fly'-*under*
fly'-weight
fo'ci
fond'er
food'-card
food'-stuff
fool'proof
foot'-can'dle
foot'-gear
foot'-hill
foo'tle
foot'ling
foot'-note
foot'-plate
foot'-slog
foot'-wear
fore'bear
fore'court
fore'*hand*
fore'hander
foresee'able
forestalled'
fore'stay
fore'*word*
forgett'ing
forgo'*ing*
form'alin
formato're
forsyth'ia
fortepia'no
forth'right
foss'ilate
fossila'tion
fos'ter-daught'er
fos'ter-mo'ther
fox'aline
fox'hole
fox'trot
frac'tionalist
frac'tionator
fraen'um
frame'up
Francoma'nia
Francopho'bia
frank'furter
fran'tically
frap'pé
Frau
Fräul'ein
fraz'zle
tree'-*hand*
free'-handed

free'hand'edness
free'lance
French'bean
French'woman
fre'num
fret'-saw
Freud'ian
fri'go
frill'ies
Fris'ian
Fritz
frizz'y
frog'man
frowz'iness
fruc'tuous
frum'piness
frum'pishly
fud'dy-duddy
Fueh'rer, Führer
fuel'ling
fug
fuga'to
full'-sized
full'y-fashioned
fumato'rium
func'tionalism
func'tioned
func'tioning
fundamen'talism
fundamen'talist
funk'-hole
funic'ulus
fur'cal
fuss'iness
fuss'-pot
fustanell'a
fu'tureless
fu'turism
futuris'tic
fyl'fot

G

gab'ardine
gad'about
gadg'et
gaffe
Gal'ilee
gall'ey-proof
gall'iot
gang'ster
gang'sterdom
gang'sterism
gas'-mask
gasp'er
gassed
gas'troscope
gâ'teau
gas't(e)ropod
gasterop'odous
gastrop'oda
gaudea'mus
Gau'leiter
ged'da
gee-whizz'
geig'er
Geig'er coun'ter
gel
gel'ignite
gen
gene
genet'icist
Geni'zah
gen'ocide
gen'otype
genteel'ism
geochronol'ogy
geophys'ical
geophys'icist
geophys'ics
geopol'itics
georgette'
geratol'ogy
ger'enuk
geriat'ric
geriatri'cian
geriat'rics
geri'atry
gerontoc'racy
gerontol'ogy
gerun'dive
gesta'po
get-at'-able
ghaf'fir
Ghana'ian
ghawa'zee
ghazee'yeh
ghoont
giantesque'
gibb'er
gig'olo
gigue
gilt'-edged
gim'bri
gimm'ick
gingivi'tis
gipp'o
glac'iere
glacieret'
glais'tig
glas'sichord
glass'-ware
gleep
glint
glissan'do
glob'al
glock'enspiel
glor'ia
glu'coside
gly'cerol
glyphog'raphy
G'-man
gnom'ish
goan'na
gob'bledegook
gob'bledygook
God'fearing
God'-forsaken
gold'-digger
gold'-leaf
goll'iwog
goll'y
gonorrhoe'a
good'-sized
goof
goof'y
goog'ly
gorg'onize
gorill'ine
gou'ache
Goud'a
gou'lash
gov'ernorate
goy
goy'a
gra'ben
Gr(a)e'cism
grallator'ial
gramophon'ic
gramoph'ony
grand'*child*
grandchil'dren
granolith'ic
grant-*in*-aid
grass'-wid'ow
gratic'ulate
grat'icule
grat'in
grav'el-voiced
grav'id
gravita'tional
greats
grey'ish
grey'wacke
grid
grimoire'
grits

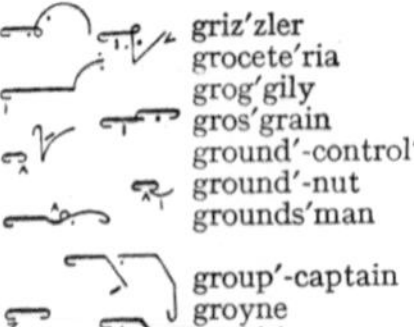

griz'zler
grocete'ria
grog'gily
gros'grain
ground'-control'
ground'-nut
grounds'man
group'-captain
groyne
grubb'y
gru'elling
Grun'dyism
gua'na
guana'co
*guard'*ant
guard'-ring
Guatema'lan
guern'sey
guest'-house
gui'chet
guid'on
guimpe
Guin'ean
guitar'ist
Gujara'ti
gum'boot'
gun'layer
gun'man
gush'ily
gymnade'nia
gymnot'us
gymp
gynaecoc'racy
gyniat'rics
gynoc'racy
gyp
gypsoph'ila
gyr'oplane
gyrosta'bilizer
gyr'ostat
gyrostat'ics
gyves

H

habutai'
hack'-saw
haematol'ogy
haemophil'ia
haem'ostat
haemostat'ic
hag'ioscope
hair'-*do*
hair'spring
hair'trigg'er
hair'-wave
Hai'tian
half-broth'er
half-nel'son
half-sis'ter
half'-sized
half'-tone
hal'ite
halito'sis
hallucino'sis
ham'burger
ham'-hand'ed
Hande'lian
*hand'*ler
*hand'*made
hand'-out
*hands'*breadth
*hand'*spun
hang'-over
hank'y-pank'y
han'sel
happ'i-coat
happ'y-*go*-luck'y
hara-ki'ri
hard'board
hard'-head'ed
hard'met'al
hard'spun
hare'wood
hari-ka'ri
harmon'ics
harmoniza'tion
Harro'vian
hart'(e)beest
hate'worthy
hat'trick
haught'ier
haul'ier
haute
have'lock
hay'wire
H'-bomb
head'-*on'*
head'phone
hear'ing-aid
heart'en
heart'ened
heart'ening
heav'enwards
heav'y-weight
Heb'ridean
heck'lephone
hec'ogenin
hec'tically
hectog'raphy
hef'ty
heir presump'-tive
hel'icopter
heliolith'ic
heliothe'rapy
hel'iotypy
hel'iport
hel'iscoop
Hell'ene
help'ing
hem'al
hemat'ic
hemianop'sia
hemino'pia
heminop'sia
hemip'tera
hem'-line
hemophil'ia
hem'ostat
hen'-harr'ier
hepatit'is
hep'-cat
Herbar'tian
here'abouts'
here*in*af'ter
here*to'*
hero'ics
he'roin
hes'ped
Hespe'ria
het'erodyne
hetero-sex'ual
heur'ism
hick'boo
hide'out
hi'fi
high'brow
highfalu'ting
high' freq'uency
hi'-jack
hi'-jacker
high'light
high'-treas'on
high'-up
hike
hi'ker
hind'sight
hip'ster
hir'able
hire'-pur'chase
hist'amine
hist'ogram
histor'iated
hitch'-hike
Hit'lerism
Hit'lerite
hoar'hound
hodom'eter
hodomet'rical
hodom'etry
hogg'in
hold'-up

holl'and
hombre
Hom'burg
Home'-*guard*
home'sickness
home'wards
home'work
homosex'ual
homosex'ualist
homosexual'ity
honk
honorif'ic
hon'ours
hood'lum
hoo'doo
hoo'ey
hook'-worm
hoop'-la
hoot'er
hore'hound
hor'mone
hors-d'oeuv're
Hor'us
hos'pitalize
hot'dog
hotel'ier

house'leek
hov'ercraft
hov'erplane
hug'-*me*-tight
huff
hul'a
hul'a-hoop
humanis'tic
human'ities
hu'manoid
hum'ble-pie
humding'er
hu'midor
humoresque'
hu'mous
humph
hun
hun'ger-strike
hurd'ler
hur'tling
hush'-boat
hush'-hush
hut'ment
huz'zy
hy'alite
hy'dro
hydrofluor'ic

hy'drofoil
hydrol'ogy
hyd'rophone
hydropon'ics
hydrothe'rapy
hyd'rovane
hy'dyne
hym'nary
hyp
hypermetrop'ia
hy'peron
hyperson'ic
hyph'enate
hyph'enated
hypnoanaesthe-s'ia
Hyp'nos
hypnos'is
hypnothe'rapy
hypoder'mis
hypoman'ia
hy'poscope
hypother'mia
hysterec'tomy

I

ib'id
ice'-break'er
iconom'eter
iden'ti-kit
id'ioplasm
Id'o
ig'loo
ilei'tis
illiq'uid
illu'sional
imbal'ance
imbecil'ic
immer'sal
immort'able
immu'nify
impair'ment
impa'la
impas'to
impas'toed
implementa'tion
importee'
impractical'ity
impressionis'tic
improv'isator
improv(v)isa-tor'e
inac'tivate

inadvis'able
inartic'ulacy
inartic'ulateness
incendiv'ity
incensed'
incens'ing
incin'erator
*in'*comer
incommunica'do
incon'dite
inconven'iently
independ'able
In'dianesque
Indianol'ogist
individ'ualist
individualis'tic
individ'uate
Indones'ian
induc'tance
indus'trialism
indus'trialist
industrializa'tion
indus'trialize
ined'ible
ined'ita
ined'ucable
ineducabil'ity

ineffec'tively
inesca'pable
inexac'titude
infan'tilism
infer'ably
infer'rably
infla'tionary
infla'tionism
infla'tionist
inflex'ional
inform'ative
inform'atory
in'fra
infra-red'
in'frastruc'ture
ingen'ium
in'gle-nook
ingrained'
ingrain'ing
inhal'ant
inhalato'rium
inhumane'
ini'tiand
ini'tial(l)ing

ini'tis
inju'ria
ink'er
ink'ily
in-law
inop'erable
inopex'ia
in'-pa'tient
in'put
insan'itary
inscript'
in'sert
insip'idness
insnare'
in'stancy
institu'tionalize
*instruc'tive*ly
*instruc'tive*ness
in'sulin
in'swept
*intelligent'*sia
interac'tion
interac'tive
intercep'tor
in'tercom
interdepart-men'tal

*in'terest*ingly
interferom'eter
interling'ual
interlocu'tion
internationale'
interned'
internee'
interpage'
In'terpol
interrela'tion
interrela'tionship
in'tersex
intersex'ual
in'ter*trade*
interzon'al
intra'da
intramus'cular
intran'sigence
intranspar'ent
intraven'ous
introjec'tion
in'trovert
intui'tional

in'vert
invi'able
invi'gilate
invigila'tion
invig'ilator
ion'ium
ioniza'tion
i'onize
ion'osphere
Ira'qi
Iroquois'
irrifran'gible
i'rrigant
ischiat'ic
isogon'ic
isola'tionism
isola'tionist
isomor'phic
is'otone
is'otope
is'otron
is'otype
Israel'i
ital'ics
it'emize
Izves'tia

J

jab
jaboran'di
jabot'
jacaran'da
jack'boot
Jack John'son
jack'pot
Jaff'a
jäg'er
jailed
Jamai'can
jamboree'
jam'my
jani'form
Jan'us
Japanes'ery
japon'ica
jardinière

jar'don
ja'to
Ja'van
jay'-wa'lker
jazz
jazz'er
jazz'ophone
jazz'y
jeep
Je'hu
jejune'
jemim'as
Jeremi'ah
jerque
jer'quer
Jew'ry
jigg'ery-pok'ery
jig'-saw
jin'gal(l)
jitt'er
jitt'erbug
jitt'ers
jitt'ery

jiu-jit'su
jive
jod'el
joint'less
jot'ter
journalese'
joy'-ride
joy'stick
judd'er
jug'ate
Ju'goslav
Jugoslav'ian
jug'ulate
ju'jit'su
juke'-box
jum'bo
ju'pati
juvenil'ia
juxtapose'

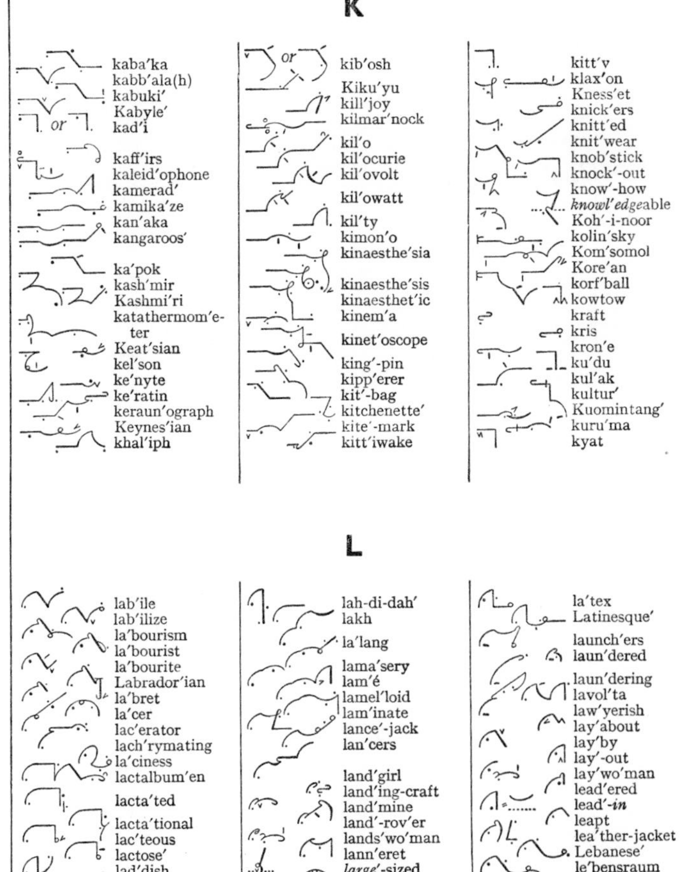

K

kaba'ka
kabb'ala(h)
kabuki'
Kabyle'
kad'i
kaff'irs
kaleid'ophone
kamerad'
kamika'ze
kan'aka
kangaroos'
ka'pok
kash'mir
Kashmi'ri
katathermom'e-ter
Keat'sian
kel'son
ke'nyte
ke'ratin
keraun'ograph
Keynes'ian
khal'iph

kib'osh
Kiku'yu
kill'joy
kilmar'nock
kil'o
kil'ocurie
kil'ovolt
kil'owatt
kil'ty
kimon'o
kinaesthe'sia
kinaesthe'sis
kinaesthet'ic
kinem'a
kinet'oscope
king'-pin
kipp'erer
kit'-bag
kitchenette'
kite'-mark
kitt'iwake

kitt'y
klax'on
Kness'et
knick'ers
knitt'ed
knit'wear
knob'stick
knock'-out
know'-how
*knowl'edge*able
Koh'-i-noor
kolin'sky
Kom'somol
Kore'an
korf'ball
kowtow
kraft
kris
kron'e
ku'du
kul'ak
kultur'
Kuomintang'
kuru'ma
kyat

L

lab'ile
lab'ilize
la'bourism
la'bourist
la'bourite
Labrador'ian
la'bret
la'cer
lac'erator
lach'rymating
la'ciness
lactalbum'en
lacta'ted
lacta'tional
lac'teous
lactose'
lad'dish
la-di-da'
lad'y-killer
lagrimo'so

lah-di-dah'
lakh
la'lang
lama'sery
lam'é
lamel'loid
lam'inate
lance'-jack
lan'cers
land'girl
land'ing-craft
land'mine
land'-rov'er
lands'wo'man
lann'eret
large'-sized
la'ser
last'ness
lateral'ity
la'test

la'tex
Latinesque'
launch'ers
laun'dered
laun'dering
lavol'ta
law'yerish
lay'about
lay'by
lay'-out
lay'wo'man
lead'ered
lead'-*in*
leapt
lea'ther-jacket
Lebanese'
le'bensraum
lecturette'
left'ism
left'ist

left′ward
left′wards
legginette′
legionnaire′
lem′on-cheese
lem′on-cheese-curd
len′ience
Len′inism
Len′inist
leprechaun′
lepros′ery
lep′ton
Les′bian
let′-up
leuchaem′ia
leucorrhoe′a
leucot′omy
leukaem′ia
lev
Lew′is gun
lew′isite
liaise′
liais′on off′icer
libid′inal
libid′o
lichenol′ogy
lid′o
life′buoy
life′line
life′manship
life-sav′er
life′-size
life′-sized

lig′er
light′houseman
li′lacky
lim′burger
li′miness
limnol′ogy
lim′ousine
lincrus′ta
linc′tus
lineal′ity
ling′erer
ling′ua franc′a
li′no
li′nocut
li′notyper
li′notypist
lip′-read
lip′stick
li′ra
li′re
lisle
lis′tener-*in*
lis′ten-*in*
lis′tening-*in*
litho′sis
lith′osphere
lit′tery
li′ver
liv′erish
load′-line
locale′
loca′ter

lockup′able
lo′ganberry
logis′tics
lon′geron
long′shore-man
long-term
look′er-*in*
look′-*in*
look′-*in*′
loop′y
lo′ran
loss′lead′er
loud′speak′er
lour
lour′ing
lou′ver
low′brow
lox
lud′o
Luft′waffe
lug′-*chair*
lum′ber-jacket
lu′men
lup′in(e)
lu′ringly
Lusita′nia
lus′trine
ly′cée
lych′-gate
ly′ricist
Lys′ol

M

Mac
maca′bre
McCar′thyism
Ma′cédoine
machine′-gun
machine′-tool
Macon′ochie
macra′mé
macra′mi
macrobiot′ics
mac′ron
madame′
madrigalesque′
maes′tro
Mae′West
Mag′dalen
mag′dalene
magnal′ium

magnet′o
mahara′nee
mail′able
maître d'hôtel′
maladjust′ment
mal′aise
mal′amute
mal′aprop
mal′apropism
malariol′ogy
mal′emute
mall′enders
malnutri′tion
malod′orous
mam′ba
mam′bo
mamill′a
Mancun′ian
man′*hand*le

man′ifolder
mann′equin or
manoeu′vrable
man′power
mara′ca
Ma′rathon
mar′blette
marca′to
marim′ba
marionet′tist
marks′woman
marm′ite
ma′rocain
mar′tenot
Marx′ian
Marx′ist
mascar′a
mas′cotry
ma′ser

mas'ochism
mas'ochist
masque
mastit'is
mas'turbate
masturba'tion
match'-board
match'wood
ma'tiness
mat'riarch
mat'ronhood
mat'tered
mat'ter-*of*-fact
ma'ty
mat'zo
Mau-Mau
maun'dy
Mauri'tian
max'imalist
max'imize
may'day
May'-fly
meat'less
Mecca'no
mechaniza'tion
mech'anize
med'itatively
mediumis'tic
megaloman'ia
meg'aton
megilp'
meis'tersinger
mela'no
mel'iorant
melis'ma
melismat'ic
meloma'nia
mel'ton
Men'delism
men'folk
men'hir
men'opause
Men'shevism
Men'shevist
*mer'e*st
mergan'ser
mésall'iance
mesolith'ic
Mess'rs.
metab'olism
metab'olon
metagal'axy
metapsych'ics
metapsychol'ogy
meteorette'
me'teorogram
meth'ane
metic'ulous
metic'ulously
metic'ulousness

met'opon
met'opryl
mho
miaow'
miaowed'
miaul'
Micaw'berish
mi'crobar
microbiol'ogy
microcop'ying
mic'rofilm
mi'crograph
mi'crogroove
mic'rolith
mic'rophone
microseismom'-eter
mi'crowave
mid'dlebrow
mign'on
mi'grant
mil'age
mil'ieu
mil'itantly
mil'itarist
militaris'tic
mill'board
millen'nialism
milliardaire'
mill'ibar
mill'ipede
Mil'vus
mince'meat
mine'-crat'er
mine field
mine'lay'er
mine'sweep'er
min'gy
min'icab
minifica'tion
min'imal
min'isub
minus'cule
min'ute-glass
minutis'simic
minx'ish
mirk
miscast'
misch'met'al
mis'erabilism
mis*han'd*ling
mis'sionist
mistak'enly
mistime'
mistri'al
mito'sis
mod'ena
modernis'tic
modis'tic
molest'ive
momen'tive
monau'ral

mondaine'
mon'dial
mon'golism
monochro'masy
monoclin'al
mon'omark
monotech'nic
monothema'tic
Monroe'ism
mon'tage
montbre'tia
Montessor'ian
monumen'talism
mo'ped
morator'ial
moren'do
Morse
mor'tar-board
morti'cian
motel'
motet'
mo'ther-craft
mot'ivate
motiva'tion
mo'torable
mot'orcade
mot'ordom
mot'orism
mot'orize
motorpho'bia
mot'orway
mousse
mo'vies
mozet'ta
mugg'ins
mug'wumpish
Mul'tigraph
Mul'tilith
multira'cial
muni'tioner
mus'covite
musicale'
musicolog'ical
musicol'ogist
musicol'ogy
musk'-deer
Mus'lim
mu'tant
muta'tional
muzz'y
myal'gia
mycel'ium
myelit'is
myrmecol'ogist
mys'tery-ship
mystique'
myxomato'sis

N

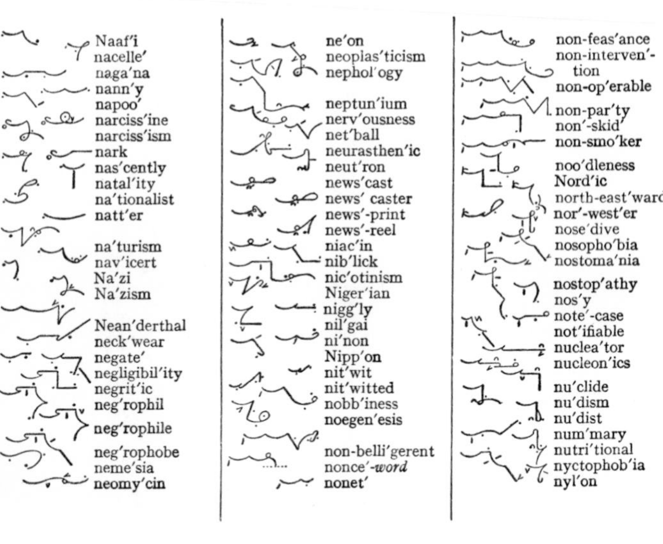

Naaf'i
nacelle'
naga'na
nann'y
napoo'
narciss'ine
narciss'ism
nark
nas'cently
natal'ity
na'tionalist
natt'er
na'turism
nav'icert
Na'zi
Na'zism
Nean'derthal
neck'wear
negate'
negligibil'ity
negrit'ic
neg'rophil
neg'rophile
neg'rophobe
neme'sia
neomy'cin

ne'on
neoplas'ticism
nephol'ogy
neptun'ium
nerv'ousness
net'ball
neurasthen'ic
neut'ron
news'cast
news' caster
news'-print
news'-reel
niac'in
nib'lick
nic'otinism
Niger'ian
nigg'ly
nil'gai
ni'non
Nipp'on
nit'wit
nit'witted
nobb'iness
noegen'esis
non-belli'gerent
nonce'-*word*
nonet'

non-feas'ance
non-interven'-
tion
non-op'erable
non-par'ty
non'-skid'
non-smo'ker
noo'dleness
Nord'ic
north-east'ward
nor'-west'er
nose'dive
nosopho'bia
nostoma'nia
nostop'athy
nos'y
note'-case
not'ifiable
nuclea'tor
nucleon'ics
nu'clide
nu'dism
nu'dist
num'mary
nutri'tional
nyctophob'ia
nyl'on

O

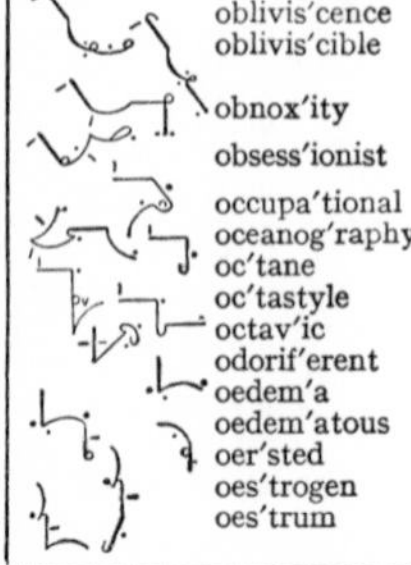

obelis'coid
oblivis'cence
oblivis'cible
obnox'ity
obsess'ionist
occupa'tional
oceanog'raphy
oc'tane
oc'tastyle
octav'ic
odorif'erent
oedem'a
oedem'atous
oer'sted
oes'trogen
oes'trum

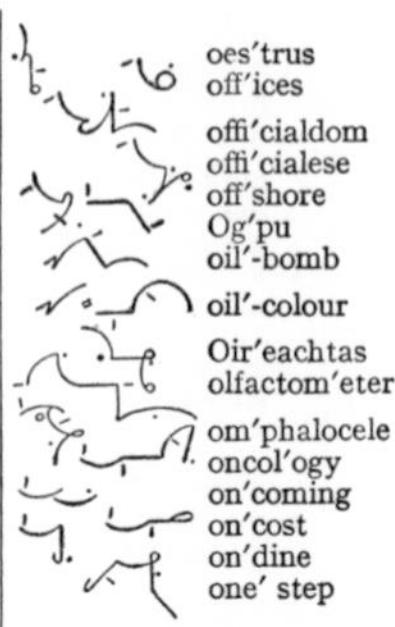

oes'trus
off'ices
offi'cialdom
offi'cialese
off'shore
Og'pu
oil'-bomb
oil'-colour
Oir'eachtas
olfactom'eter
om'phalocele
oncol'ogy
on'coming
on'cost
on'dine
one' step

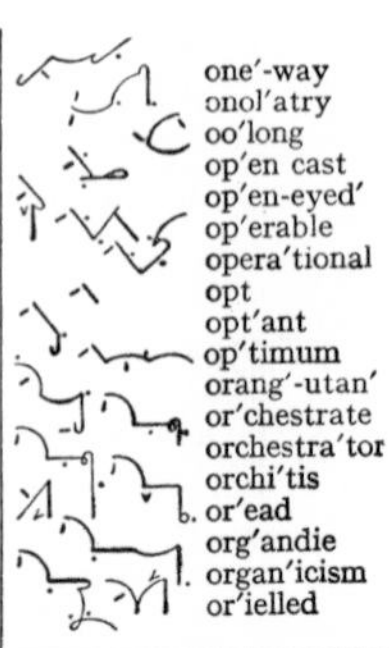

one'-way
onol'atry
oo'long
op'en cast
op'en-eyed'
op'erable
opera'tional
opt
opt'ant
op'timum
orang'-utan'
or'chestrate
orchestra'tor
orchi'tis
or'ead
org'andie
organ'icism
or'ielled

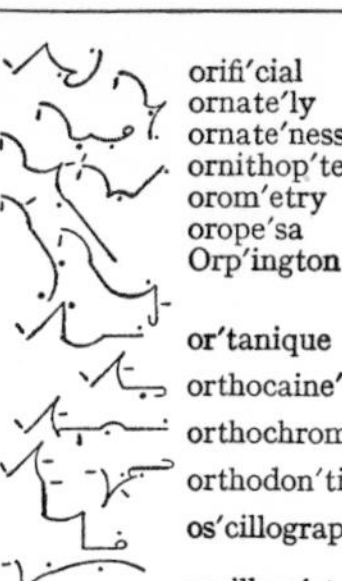

orifi'cial
ornate'ly
ornate'ness
ornithop'ter
orom'etry
orope'sa
Orp'ington
or'tanique
orthocaine'
orthochromat'ic
orthodon'tics
os'cillograph
oscillom'eter
osmos'is
osteoarthrit'is
os'teopath
osteop'athy

oti'tis
*our*self'
out'board
out'*buil'ding*
outclassed'
outdate'
outdat'ed
outmod'ed
outpoint'
outside'
out'size
out'skirts
out'sta'tion
out'-turn
ovenette'
*over*dress'
*o'ver*haul
*o'ver*heads
*over*insure'
*over*land'
*over*leaf'

*o'ver*lord
*o'ver*pass
*over*pay'ment
overproduc'tion
*over*proof'
*over*ride'
*over*rid'ing
*o'ver*sea
*over*seas'
*o'ver*shot
o'ver-staffed'
*o'ver*tone
o'vibos
own'er-driv'er
oxidiza'tion
oxim'eter
oxy-acet'ylene
oxymor'on
o'zonizer

P

pacif'icism
pa'cifism
pa'cifist
paediat'ric
paediat'rics
page'-boy
page'-proof
Pakista'ni
Palaeanthrop'ic
palais de danse
pall'y
panache'
pan'atrope
panchromat'ic
pan'da
pandore'
pan'ga
pan'icked
Panis'lamism
pan-sex'ualism
pan'thenol
pan'ties
pan'zer
pa'per-chase
pa'per-hanger
pa'per-mus'lin
pap'rika
pa'quined
parabel'lum
Paraguay'an or
paramil'itary

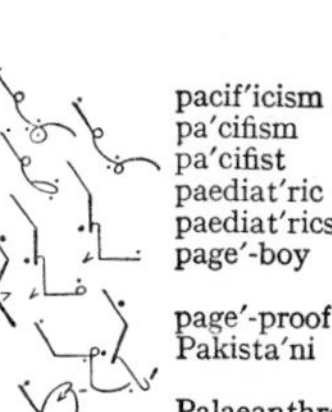

paranoi'a
par'anoid
paranoid'al
paraphre'nia
paraple'gic
parapsychol'ogy
pa'rasites
pa'ratrooper
pa'ratroops
paratyph'oid
pa'ravane
parimut'uel
park'in
paronomas'ia
parou'sia
pars'ec
Pars'eval
Parthenope'an
parti'tionist
part'-*own'er*
part'-song
part'-time
par'ty-line
pas'chaltide
pa'shalic
Pas'quin
passe-partout'
passim'eter
pass'key
pass'way
pastiche'
past'mas'ter
path'fin'der
pathogen'esis
pathogen'ic
pa'tio

patrilin'eal
pat'tress
pay'load
peak'y-faced
pear'lies
pea-soup'er
pêche Mel'ba
peck'ish
pedagog'ically
ped'icurist
pedi'tis
pedolog'ical
pedol'ogy
ped'oscope
ped'rail
peep'-toe
peeved
pej'orative
Pekinese'
Pekingese'
pela'gian
pela'gic
Pel'manism
pel'met
pelor'us
penaliza'tion
pe'nalize
pe'nalized
pe'nalizing
pen'-friend
penicill'in
pe'nis
penn'oned
penn'yfarth'ing
pen'sionable
pen'tode

pentste'mon
percep'tual
perfect'or
perigraph'ic
period'ogram
per'ishables
per'ishing
perm'alloy
per'mutate
pernick'etty
per'orate
per'orative
persev'erate
persevera'tion
persist'ently
persona'lia
pers'pex
perturb'ative
pese'ta
pe'so
pestol'ogy
pe'ter
pe'tered
peth'idine
petrogen'esis
pet'roglyph
petronel'la
phacoid'al
phalangi'tis
phare
phena'cetin
phenobar'bitone
phew
phillum'enist
phillum'eny
philog'ynist
philog'yny
Phil'omel
phob'ia
pho'bism
phoneti'cian
phonet'icist
phonet'icize
phon'etist
phon'ey
phon'ofilm
phon'ogram
phonolo'gic
pho'ny
phot'o-fin'ish
pho'togram
pho'ton
phot'ophone
photora'diogram
Phot'ostat
phra'try
Phur'nacite
physiothera-
peut'ic

physiothe'rapist
physiothe'rapy
piani'no
pianiss'imo
pi'aniste
Pianol'a
pian'o org'an
pick'elhaube
pick'-up
pic'togram
pic'ture-drome
piece'-goods
pie'cer
piece'-work
piece'-wor'ker
Pied'mont
pier'-head
pierrot'ic
pif'fle
pike'let
pil'ferage
pill'ionist
pill'iwinks
pill'wort
pil'ule
ping'er
pin'ball
pin'-head
pin'-stripe
pin'-ta'ble
pin'-up
pipe'dream
pipe'line
pip'-squeak
piquet'
pira'gua
pis'tillary
pistil'liform
pitch'blende
place'ment
plac'idness
plan'etkin
planetol'ogy
planog'raphy
plaquette'
plas'ticism
plas'ticizer
plate'layer
plat'inite
platitudinar'ian
platitud'inist
platitud'inize
platitud'inous
play'-pen
plena'rium
pli'antly
Plim'soll line
plim'solls
plumb'-bob
plumb'-rule
plumped
plump'est
plump'ish
pluranim'ity

pluren'nial
plus'-fours'
Plu'to
plutol'atry
plutocrat'ic
pluto-democ'racy
pluton'ium
pluton'omy
ply'wood
poch'ard
pochette'
po'dex
podg'iness
poilu'
poin'tillism
pois'on-gas
Polar'is
police'-court
police'woman
pol'icy-hold'er
pol'io
pol'iomyelit'is
polit'buro
poll'inate
pollina'tion
pol'linator
polon'ium
pol'tergeist
Polyg'ala
pol'ymer
pol'yonym
pol'ypoid
Pol'ythene
Pomeran'ian
pom'pon
ponce
pond-lil'y
pontoneer'
pon'y-tail
poplit'eal
popp'ycock
port'raitist
poseur'
posi'tional
pos'itron
postiche'
post-impres'sion-
ism
Post'master
Gen'eral
post'-war
pot'ful
pouf(f)e
pourboire'
pour'parler'
powd'er-house
powd'er-puff
pozzola'na
pozz'y
praetor'ial
pram
Prav'da

pre'cast
pred'ative
pred'ator
predecease'
predict'able
predic'tor
predom'inantly
pre'fab
prefab'ricate
prefab'ricated
preg'nable
premol'ar
premunir'e
pre-nat'al
presid'ium
pre'ssurize
pre'ttify
pre'view
pre'-war
prick'ling
primat'es
primip'arous
prince'let
proam'bient
proced'ural
process'
pro'cessed
proclit'ic
procryp'sis
prod'rome
productiv'ity
profitabil'ity
profiteer'ing
pro form'a
proges'terone

prolif'erate
pro'metal
promiscu'ity
prom'isor
prompt'ness
propagand'
propagan'dize
prop'agative
proparox'ytone
proper'din
prop'erty-man
prop'-net
propri'etress
pro'-rate
prospec'ted
prospec'ting
protag'onism
protec'tionism
Proteis'tic
prot'on
proton'ic
prov'ocator
providen'tialism
Pru'ssianism
Pru'ssianize
Pru'ssianized
psilan'thropism
psilos'is
psittacos'is
psych'e
psychiat'ric
psychi'atrist
psychi'atry
psycho-an'alyse
psycho-anal'ysis
psycho-an'alyst
psy'chogram

psych'ograph
psychog'raphy
psych'opath
psychop'athist
psychothera-peut'ics
psychother'apist
psychothe'rapy
psyphol'ogy
ptos'is
pub'licize
puck'a
pud'ent
puf'fet
puf'fily
pukk'a
pul'chritude
pull'-out
pull'over
Pul'motor
pump'-room
pumm'elled
pumm'elling
punch'-card
punch'-drunk
pup'ate
pup'petry
pur'chase-tax
purd'ah
pur'ée
pur'posive
purserette'
purse'-strings
Pu'ssyfoot
putsch
putt
pyl'on
pyorrhoe'a
Py'rex
pyrheliom'eter
pyrophot'ograph

Q

Q'-ship
quadragenar'ian
quadriling'ual
qua'druplet
quaint'er
quaint'est
qua'ntify

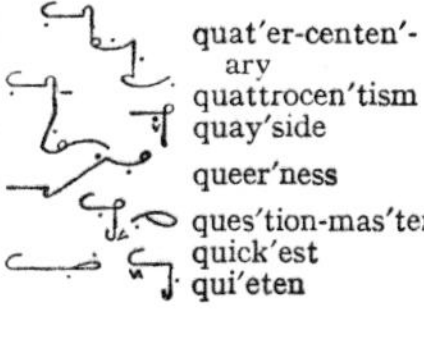

quat'er-centen'-ary
quattrocen'tism
quay'side
queer'ness
ques'tion-mas'ter
quick'est
qui'eten

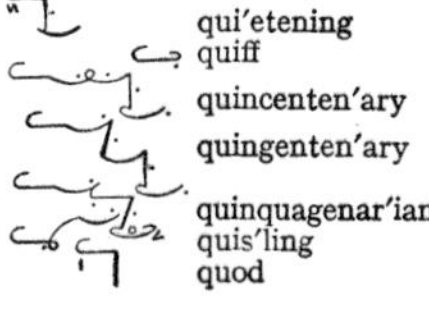

qui'etening
quiff
quincenten'ary
quingenten'ary
quinquagenar'ian
quis'ling
quod

R

Ra
raban'na
rabb'inate
rachit'is
ra'cialism
ra'cialist
raciol'ogy
racketeer'
rack'ets
rad
rad'ar
rad'ian
radif'erous
rad'io
rad'ioac'tive
radio-activ'ity
radiobiol'ogy
radiogenet'ics
rad'iogram
rad'iograph
radiog'raphy
radio-loca'tion
radiolo'gical
radiol'ogist
radiol'ogy
rad'iophone
rad'io*tel'egram*
rad'iotel'egraph
rad'iotel'ephone
rad'io-thera-peut'ics
rad'io-ther'apy
rad'ium
raff
rag'time
raid'ed
raid'er
raid'ing
rail'age
rail'head
rain'storm
rallentan'do
ram'ie
rampage'ous
ranch'ing
range'-fin'der
ranuncula'ceous
Raphaelesque'
rare'bit
rar'est
ras'ter
ratabil'ity
rat'able
ra'tably
ratine'
rationaliza'tion
ra'tioned
ra'tioning
rat'tat'
Ray'on
reac'tor
rearm'ament
recep'tionist
recip'rocator
recondi'tion
recon'stitute
reconstitu'tion
recrudes'cent
recruit'ment
redac'tor
re*deliv'er*
redeploy'
redeploy'ment
red'-shirt
refla'tion
*reform'*ism
refrac'tor
re'gional
reg'istrator
Reich
reimpose'
re'ject
rejuvena'tion
rejuv'enator
rejuv'enize
relativ'ity
rem
rem'igate
remiga'tory
remonstra'tion
*remon'stra*tive
remu'nerator
ren'tier
renun'ciative
renun'ciator
reorienta'tion
repat'riate
repatria'tion
repeat'able
repet'itive
replaceabil'ity
replace'able
replen'isher
rep'tant
reptil'iary
repulp
re-rubb'er
rescin'namine
resipis'cence
resit'
resource'ful
resource'fulness
responden'tia
respon'der
restart'
restart'er
rest'-house
result'ing
resurrect'
retir'ingly
retrogress'
retru'sible
reun'ionist
revaloriza'tion
reval'orize
re*valua'tion*
reval'ue
reval'ued
reval'uing
revanche'
reverb'erator
rev'erize
revet'ment
revict'ualment
revis'able
revis'ionism
revis'ionist
revue'
revu'ette
Rex'ine
rhat'any
rhe'ograph
rheol'ogy
rhes'us
rheu'matoid
rheumatol'ogy
rhine'stone
rhinol'ogist
rhinol'ogy
Rhode'sian
rhyme'let
rhythm'less
ric'inus

ric'ocheted
ricochet'ing
ri'dable
ridge'-pole
rid'ibund
right'ist
ring'hals
ring'-road
ring'ster
rins'er
rip'-roar'ing
ris'qué
riv'erside
riv'eter
road'-met'al
road'worthiness
road'worthy
rob'ot
robotesque'
ro'botism
ro'botize
rock'-bot'tom
rock'etry
rock'n'roll'
rode'o
roll'-on
romp'er

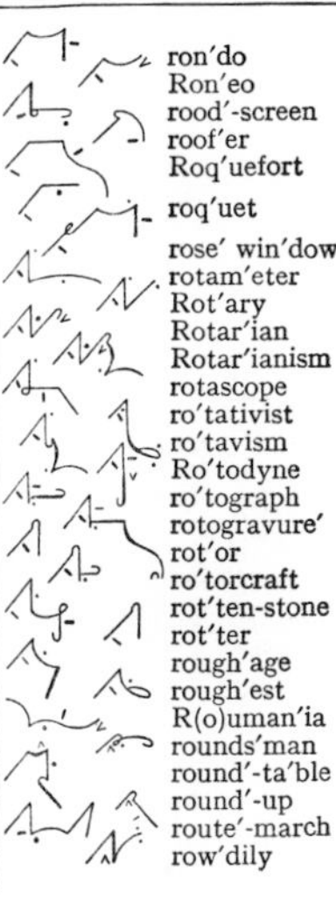
ron'do
Ron'eo
rood'-screen
roof'er
Roq'uefort
roq'uet
rose' win'dow
rotam'eter
Rot'ary
Rotar'ian
Rotar'ianism
rotascope
ro'tativist
ro'tavism
Ro'todyne
ro'tograph
rotogravure'
rot'or
ro'torcraft
rot'ten-stone
rot'ter
rough'age
rough'est
R(o)uman'ia
rounds'man
round'-ta'ble
round'-up
route'-march
row'dily

rowd'iness
roys'ter
ruba'to
rubb'erized
rubb'ery
ru'befy
rubel'la
Rubenesque'
ru'bify
rubri'cian
ruck'le
rudbeck'ia
ru'dish
Rug'by
rugg'er
rugose'
R(o)uman'ian
rumbus'tious
rumm'y
run'about
run'-down'
run'way
rurideca'nal
Rurita'nia
rust'less
rust'-proof
ruth'erford

S

Sab'aism
sad'dle-bar
sa'dism
safa'ri
safe'depos'it
safe'ty curtain
saff'ian
salabil'ity
sal'able
sal'ableness
sales'manship
sales'-tax
Sal'ian
sali'na
salin'ity
sal'vager
salvator'ian
sal'via
sam'ba
Sam Browne
Sam'oyed
sam'sonite
sand'bank
sand'-fly
sand'-glass
sand'-storm
sand'wich-man
sand'-yacht
San'forize
sanguiv'orous
sanse'rif

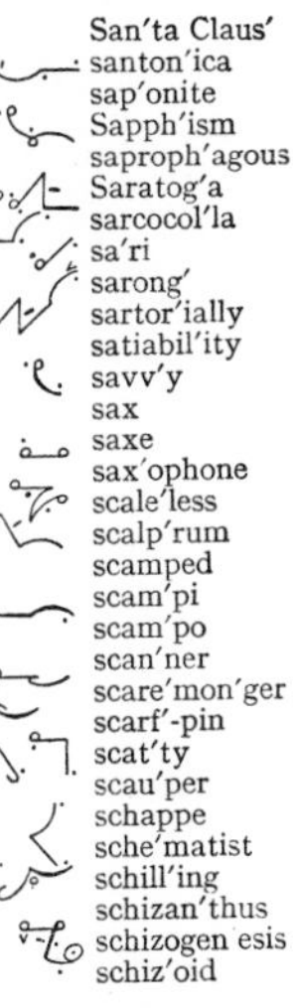
San'ta Claus'
santon'ica
sap'onite
Sapph'ism
saproph'agous
Saratog'a
sarcocol'la
sa'ri
sarong'
sartor'ially
satiabil'ity
savv'y
sax
saxe
sax'ophone
scale'less
scalp'rum
scamped
scam'pi
scam'po
scan'ner
scare'mon'ger
scarf'-pin
scat'ty
scau'per
schappe
sche'matist
schill'ing
schizan'thus
schizogen'esis
schiz'oid

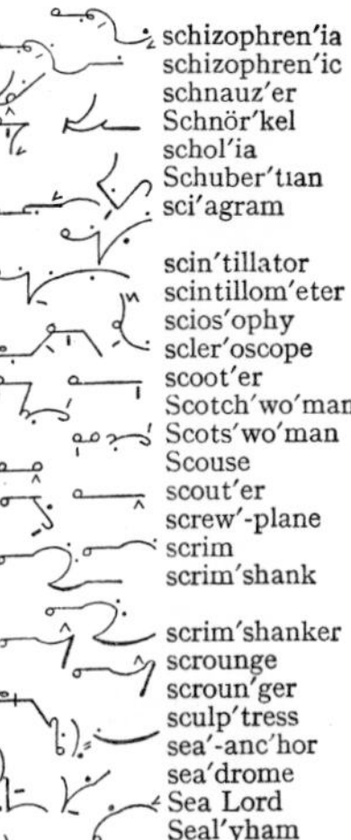
schizophren'ia
schizophren'ic
schnauz'er
Schnör'kel
schol'ia
Schuber'tian
sci'agram
scin'tillator
scintillom'eter
scios'ophy
scler'oscope
scoot'er
Scotch'wo'man
Scots'wo'man
Scouse
scout'er
screw'-plane
scrim
scrim'shank
scrim'shanker
scrounge
scroun'ger
sculp'tress
sea'-anc'hor
sea'drome
Sea Lord
Seal'yham
sea'manlike
sea'sonal

sea'squirt
sea'wards
se'bum
sec
sec'ateur
secc'o
sec'odont
sec'onal
sec'ondment
secon'do
sec'ond-rat'er
sec'onds-*hand*
secre'tin
se'cretive
se'cretiveness
sectionaliza'tion
sec'tionalize
sec'tionalized
sec'tionalizing
sec'tionize
se'dra
sed'ulousness
seer'craft
seer'*hand*
seg'mented
se'gno
seg'regable
segrega'tionist
seg'regator
seigno'ral
seise
seis'mogram
seismol'ogy
seis'moscope
selectiv'ity
self'-assur'ance
self-con'fidence
self-con'sequence
self-contained'
self-delu'sion
self-determina'-tion
self-explan'atory
self-expre'ssion
self'less
self'lessness
self-*respect'*
self-serv'ice
self-start'er
self-start'ing
Sel'lotape
seman'tic
seman'tics
semasiol'ogy
sem'en
semidocumen'-tary
sem'inar
Semit'ic
Sem'itism
sen
senes'cent
sep'arates
sep'sis
sep'ta
septcente'nary
sep'timal
ser'ialize

se'rif
serinette'
serol'ogy
serra'tion
serv'iced
serv'ice-man
Sesu'to
set'-back
se'tose
sev'enpence
sev'erable
sev'ery
sex'-appeal
sex'-kitten
sexol'ogy
sex'y
sforzan'do
shak'able
sham'ash
sham'ateur
shanghai'
shanghaied'
shan'tung
shar'able
sharp'ener
shav'able
Shav'ian
shav'ing-stick
shear'-hulk
shee'lah
shei'la
shellacked'
shellack'ing
shell'-crater
shell'-hole
shell'-proof
shell'-shock
shemoz'zle
She'raton
Sher'pa
shew'bread
shimm'y
Shin'toism
ship'-way
shire'-horse
shirt'y
shock'-troops
shoot'ing-brake
shoot'ing-stick
shop'-stew'ard
shore'wards
*short'*bread
*short'*cake
short'-circ'uit
*short'*fall
*short'*ish
short'-term
shot'gun
shov'er
show'-down
show'-girl
show'ground
show'manship
shroud'-line
si'al
sib'ilate
sib'lings
sick'-bay
sick'-berth

side'band
side'-car
side'-effect
side'-iss'ue
side'-light
side'-show
side'-slip
side'-step
side'-track
siffleur'
sight'-play'er
sight'-read'er
sight'-sing'er
si'gillate
sig'nary
sig'nature tune'
sig'net-ring
sign'-*writ'er*
sik'ra
sil'cot
silicos'is
silk'-screen
sil'ver gilt'
sil'verside
sil'verware
simplifi'er
simultane'ity
simultan'eous-ness
sin'ewless
singh
Sinn Fein'
sin'ogram
sinol'ogist
sin'ologue
sinol'ogy
sinophob'ia
sinusi'tis
Sioux
sis'al
siss'y
sitt'er-*in*
siz'zle
siz'zled
siz'zling
skee'ball
skel'etal
skep
skew'bald
skew'ing
ski'agram
ski'agraph
ski'er
skif'fle
skimp
skimped
skimp'ing
skit'tle
skivv'y
sky'line
sky'man
sky'troops
sky'way
slack'er
slack'est
sla'lom
slang'uage

slap'-happ'y
slap'jack
slap'stick
slat'ted
slaw
sleep'ing-sick'-ness
slid'able
slide'-rule
slimmed
slimm'ing
slink'er
slink'y
slip'road
slips
slit'-trench
Slov'ak
Slovene'
Sloven'ian
slow'coach
slow'er
slow'est
slow'-match
sloyd
smalm
smarm
smarm'y
smog
smoke'-bomb
smoke'-screen
smooth-tongued
snack'-bar
snark'y
sneak'ish
sneak'ishly
sneak'-thief
snib
snide
sniff'y
sni'per
snoek
snook
snook'er
snoop
snoop'er
snoozed
snooz'ing
snor'kel
snot
snott'y
snub'ber
snub'-nose
soak'away
soa've
Sobra'nje
sob'-sis'ter
sob'-stuff
socc'er
socializa'tion
so'ciogram
sociomet'ric
sociom'etry
sock'er
Socrate'an
So'fi
soft'wood
soigné
solid'ifiable
sol'idus
solu'tionist
Somal'
Soma'li
so'mascope
somat'ic
sombrer'o
somnam'bulance
somnam'bulant
sonan'tal
So'nar
son'ic
son'obuoy
sonor'ity
son'sy
son'tag
soon'est
sopp'y
sor'ghum
sorop'timist
SOS
Soudanese'
sound'-proof
sound'-track
sour'er
sour'est
Sou'saphone
soutache'
souteneur'
*sou'thern*ish
sou'thernmost
south'wards
Sov'iet
Sov'ietism
Sov'ietize
soy'a bean
space'-bar
space'man
space'-ship
space'-sta'tion
space'-suit
spade'-work
Spam
spar'sity
spar'terie
spate
spa'tial
spattee'
spear'head
spe'cialism
specializa'tion
spectrom'eter
spec'tropho-tom'eter
speedom'eter
speed'ster
speed'way
spell'ing-bee
spermatorrhoe'a
spermatozo'on
spid'er-man
spid'ery
spied
spif(f)'licate
spill'ikin
spin'dleage
spind'ly
spin'-drier
spin'drift
spirae'a
spir'itism
spiv
splendif'erous
splodge
splosh
spondul'icks
spon'sored
spoon'erism
spoon'-fed
spoon'-feed
sports'manlike
sports'wear
sports'wo'man
spot'-check
spot'light
spray'-gun
spring'-board
spring'-clean'ing
spring'like
sprint'er
spry'ly
spur'-wheel
sput'nik
sputt'eringly
spy'hole
squab'pie
squacc'o
squa'dron-lead'er
squails
squamif'erous
squam'ula
squam'ule
squan'derma'nia
square-built
squareleg
square'root
square-toed
square-toes
squash'iness
squaw'-man
squeal'er
squeezabil'ity
squidg'y
squiff'er
squiff'y
squig'gle
squinch
squir'archy
squire'dom
squirl
squirt'er
squit
stabiliza'tion
sta'bilizator
stab'ilizer
sta'ble-boy
sta'bler
stactom'eter
stad'holder
stage'-craft
stagg'erer

stag'horn
sta'ging-post
stag'-part'y
stair'wise
stakhan'ovite
stal'ag
stalagmom'eter
Stalinism
stam'ened
stam'inoid
stamped'ed
stan'dardizable
stand'-by
stand'-*in*
stand-off'ish
stand'-pipe
stand'-*to*
stan'iel
stan'nel
stan'notype
staph'yle
staphyli'tis
starch'ily
starch'iness
star'dom
star'-dust
star'ingly
star'let
star'osta
starr'y-eyed
star'-shaped
star'shell
star'-stone
start'ler
star'-turn
stas'is
stat'able
sta'tant
state'hood
state'less
states'wo'man
stat'ically
sta'tion-house
sta'tion-master
sta'tion-wag'on
sta'tism
stat'or
stat'oscope
stay'bolt
stay'-tape
steam'-chest
steam'-jack'et
steam'navv'y
steam'-pack'et
steam'-roll'er
steatopyg'ia
steatop'ygous
steel'-wool'
steel'work
steen'bok
steep'en
steep'er
steep'est
steep'ish
stee'ple-jack
steep'ly
steg'anogram
steg'anoped
stegno'sis
stegoph'ilist
Stein'berger
stein'bock
stel'larator
stell'ify
stemm'a
Sten
sten'ciller
stenoch'romy
sten'ograph
sten'otypist
sten'torphone
step'-dance
steph'anite
step'-ladd'er
step'ney
step'par'ent
step'-rock'et
ster'corate
ster'eobat
ste'reogram
ste'reograph
ste'reophonic
ste'reoph'ony
ste'reop'tics
ste'reos'copy
ste'reoson'ic
ste'reotypist
ste'reotypy
steriliza'tion
ste'rilizer
ster'nutator
stet'son
stib'ialism
stic'cado
stichar'ion
sticher'on
stichomyth'ia
stickabil'ity
stick'-*in*-the-mud
stick'-up
stiff'ener
stiff'est
stiff'ish
stigmatiza'tion
still'age
stilt'-wal'ker
stim'ulable
stim'y
stinged
stip'el
stip'pler
stirp'iculture
stir'ringly
stock'-breed'er
stock'hold'ing
stock'ist
stock'pile
stock'piling
stodge
stodg'y
stoke'hold
sto'ma
sto'mach-ache
stom'ata
stomatit'is
stom'atopod
stone'-dead
stone'-deaf
stone'-dress'er
stone'less
stone'-pit
stonewall'
stonewall'ing
stone'work
ston'ily
ston'y broke'
stooge
stool'-ball
stool'-pi'geon
stop'-press
stor'able
sto'rer
stor'iated
storiette'
stor'eyed
storm'bound
storm'-cen'tre
storm'-troops
storyette
stout'-heart'ed
stout'ish
sto'vaine
stow'er
strabot'omy
Strad
strafe
strafed
straf'ing
straight'away
straight'-edge
straight'er
straight'est
straight'-jet
strain'less
stran'glehold
stran'gler
Stratford'ian
stratig'raphy
stra'tocruis'er
strat'osphere
stratospher'ic
straw'berry-mark
straw'-board
stream'less
stream'line
stream'lined
stream'lining
street'-car
street'wa'lker
strepitos'o
streptococc'i
streptococ'cus
streptomy'cin
stressed
stress'ing
stret'to
strewn
strict'ish
strid'ulant
strife'less
strik'able
strike'-bound
strike'-break'er
string'-bean
string'less

strings
string'tie
strip'-mine
strip'-tease
strom'ata
strumi'tis
strutt'ingly
stud'-bolt
stud'entship
stud'-horse
stultil'oquence
stutt'eringly
style'less
styl'i
stylif'erous
styl'ishness
styl'ize
styl'o
stym'ie
sua'be
subacute'
subaquat'ic
subarc'tic
subar'id
subat'om
subax'illary
sub'bing
sub*e'qual*
sub'-head
sub-head'ing
subhu'man
sub-irriga'tion
*subjec'tive*ness
sub-lieuten'ant
sublin'ear
submersibil'ity
submers'ible
submon'tane
subnor'mal
subordina'tion-ism
subord'inative
sub'rogate
sub'sidist
subson'ic
substantiv'al
subsume'
subsump'tion
sub'title
subto'pia
subtro'pical
suburb'ia
succ'or
suc'rose
sudator'ium
suedette
sug'arless
sugges'tiveness
sul'fate
sul'fur
sull'age
sul'phonal
sul'phury
sul'tanate
summ'erish
summ'er-time
summ'ery
sum'ming-up
sump
sun'-bath
sun'-bathe
sun'-bathing
sun'-blind
sun'burn
sun'burned
sun'dae
Sun'dayfied
sun'dew
sun'-glasses
sun'-lamp
sun'less
sun'lighted
sunned
Sunn'i
sun'proof
sun'-ray
sun'spot
sun'stone
sun'struck
sun'-wor'ship
sup'erceles'tial
su'percharger
supercil'iary
su'per-du'per
superhet'
superhet'erodyne
superhigh'way
su'permarine
su'permarket
super-roy'al
supersen'sitive
supersen'sory
superson'ic
su'persound
su'pertax
sup'inator
suppos'edly
suppress'ible
sup'ra
supralapsar'ian-ism
supralun'ar
suprana'tional
surf'ace-car
surf'-board
surf'-boat
surfi'cial
surf'-riding
surre'alism
surre'alist
surrealist'ic
Sut'ra
svelte
swag'ger-cane
swag'ger-coat
Swahi'li
swan'herd
swank
swank'er
swank'iness
swank'y
swan'like
swan'neck
swan'nery
swan'-song
swan'-up'ping
swaraj'
swat
swat'ter
sway'er
swear'-*word*
sweat'er-girl
sweat'-shirt
sweep'ingly
sweet'ie
swerve'less
swerv'er
swift'let
swim'mable
swin'gletree
swip'er
swiz(z)
swiz'zle
sword'-dance
swords'manship
swot
syce
syc'ophantish
sycos'is
syll'abize
sylph'like
sym'centre
symmet'allism
sympathec'tomy
synchroniza'tion
syn'copator
syndicalis'tic
syn'ergism
synonym'ity
synthetiza'tion
syn'thetize
syn'thetized
syn'thetizing
syn'tony
syphilol'ogy
sys'tematy

T

tab'inet
ta'ble-mo'ney
ta'ble-spoon'ful
ta'ble-ware
tab'loid
tabu'
tack'y
tact'less
tact'lessness
tae'noid
taffetine'
tage'tes
Tahi'tian
tail'-dive
tail'-end
tail'or-made
tail'-spin
taj
take'-over
tal'ion
talk'ie
talk'ing-*to*
tall'owish
tall'ow-tree
tamein'
tamm'y
tam'pon
tan'aiste
tang'o
tan'gram
tank'er
tank'odrome
tantar'a
taoi'seach
tap'-bolt
tap'-dance
tape'-machine
tape'-measure
tape'-record'er
ta'radiddle
tard'o
tar'iff-wall
tarm'ac
tarmacad'am
tarn'ishable
ta'rradiddle
Tarragon'a
tars'ia
tarta'ric
tart'let
taseom'eter
tasim'eter
taste'fulness
taub'e
taurom'achy
tav'erner
tax'-free
tax'i-dancer
tax'ied
tax'i-plane
tax'y
tax'ying
tea'-cake
tea'-gown
team'-work
tear'-gas
tear'-jerk'er
tea'-rose
tear' shell
tear'-stained
teas'elled
teas'eller
teas'elling
tea'-tas'ter
techni'cian
Tech'nicolor
technoc'racy
Ted'dy boy
Ted'dy girl
teen'-age
teen'ager
telecam'era
tel'ecast
telecin'e
telecommunica'-tion
telecontrol'
tel'edu
tel'efilm
telegen'ic
telegraphese'
telekin'ema
telekines'is
tel'elens
tel'emark
telemechan'ics
telem'eter
tel'epheme
tel'ephoner
teleph'onist
teleph'ony
telepho'to
telepho'tograph
telephoto-graph'ic
telephotog'raphy
tel'eprinter
teleprompt'er
telerecord'ing
tel'eseme
tel'etype
tel'eview
tel'eviewer
tel'evise
tel'evised
tel'evision
tel'evisor
tel'pher
tel'pherage
tem'perish
tem'persome
tem'pi
tem'plate
tem'porariness
tempt'ingly
ten'ant-*in*-chief'
tenden'tious
tenden'tiousness
ten'derest
ten'derfoot
tenori'no
ten'pins
ten'tacled
tenu'to
tep'ee
tepee'
terce'let
ter'giversator
terminabil'ity
ter'mini
term'ly
terrain'
terric'olous
ter'rorized
ter'rorizing
Ter'ry
Ter'ylene
tess'erae
tessitur'a
testa'tion
test'-match
test'-tube
tetrath'lon
tet'ronal
Teu'tonize
Teu'tonized
thalas'sic

than'atism
thanatol'ogy
thanatopho'bia
thaw'er
thean'dric
the'ic
theli'tis
themat'ic
then'abouts
thenceaf'ter
theol'ogize
*there'*abouts
the'riomorph
therm
therm**i'on**
thermion'ic
thermion'ics
therm'ite
thermodu'ric
thermo-nuc'lear
thermoplas'tic
Ther'mos
thermostat'ic
Thessa'lian
thick'-skinned
*think'*ingly
third'-class
third'-rate
thir'tyish
tho'ron
thread'er
thread'like
thread'-mark
thread'-worm
three'-dimen'-
sional
three'-er
three'-lane
three'-ply
thremmatol'ogy
thresh'ing
thrill'er
thrip
throne'less
throp'ple
through'-put
through'way
throw'-back
throwee'
throw'-*in*
thrown'-silk
throw'-out
Thucydide'an
thumb'er
thumb'pot
thumb'-print
thun'der-cloud
thun'derous
Thurin'gian
thym'ol
thyroidi'tis
ti'ang
tia'rad
tia'raed
tick'eter
tick'et-*writ'er*
tidd'ler
tidd'ly-winks
ti'died
ti'dying
tight'ener
tight'ish
tight'ishly
ti'gon
til'de
til'ery
time'-lag
time'-sig'nature
time'-work
tin'dery
tin'ful
ti'nier
ti'niest
tin'-pan
tin'-pot
tint'er
tintom'eter
tin'ware
tip'-off
tip'toed
tip'toeing
ti'ringly
tir'o
ti'tler
Ti'toism
tob'y
tocca'ta
toc emma
*togeth'er*ness
togs
toile
tok'en
tol'booth
toll'-bar
toll'-*call*
tol'uene
tol'uol
tom'bola
tomen'tose
tomm'y
tomm'y-gun
tomm'y-rot
tone'-poem
tonn'eau
tonnelle'
tonsillec'tomy
tonsillot'omy
tooth'paste
toot'le
toot'sweet
topec'tomy
to'pee
top'-hat
top'-hole
top'i
top'iary
top'-lev'el
topon'ymy
tops
to'reador
torpe'doed
tor'turingly
tosh
totalitar'ian
totalita'rianism
tot'alizator
to'talizer
to'talled
to'talling
tote
touch'able
touch'-line
toured
tour'er
tour'ism
tous'y
tou'zle
tow'able
towns'woman
tow'-path
tow'sy
toxaem'ia
tox'in
toxoph'ily
track'-suit
*trades'*woman
trade u'nion
trade-un'ionism
trade-un'ionist
tradi'tionalism
traduce'ment
traf'ficator
tragedienne'
trag'icose
tra'gus
trainee'
train'-mile
transceiv'er
transdu'cer
transferabil'ity
transhum'ance
transir'e
transist'or
transi'tionary
transjor'dan
transla'tional
translatorese'
trans'migrant
transmigra'tion-
ism
transmitt'able
transmut'ative
transna'tional
transocean'ic
transpacif'ic
transuran'ic
transvest'
Transylva'nian
trapes
trattor'ia
traum'a
trav'elogue
trav'olator
treac'ly
tread'led
tread'ler
tread'ling
trea'sureship

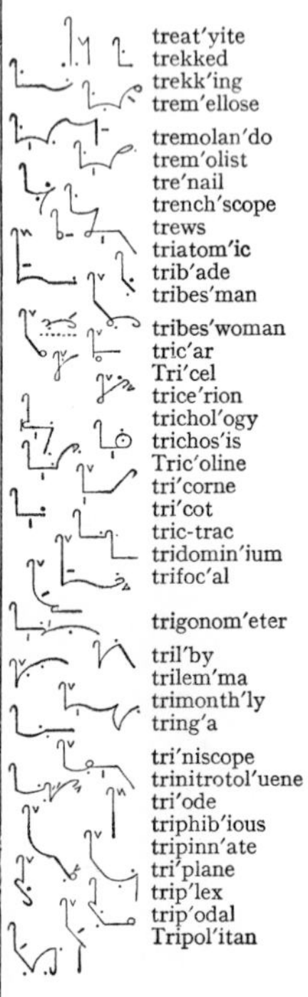

treat'yite
trekked
trekk'ing
trem'ellose
tremolan'do
trem'olist
tre'nail
trench'scope
trews
triatom'ic
trib'ade
tribes'man
tribes'woman
tric'ar
Tri'cel
trice'rion
trichol'ogy
trichos'is
Tric'oline
tri'corne
tri'cot
tric-trac
tridomin'ium
trifoc'al
trigonom'eter
tril'by
trilem'ma
trimonth'ly
tring'a
tri'niscope
trinitrotol'uene
tri'ode
triphib'ious
tripinn'ate
tri'plane
trip'lex
trip'odal
Tripol'itan

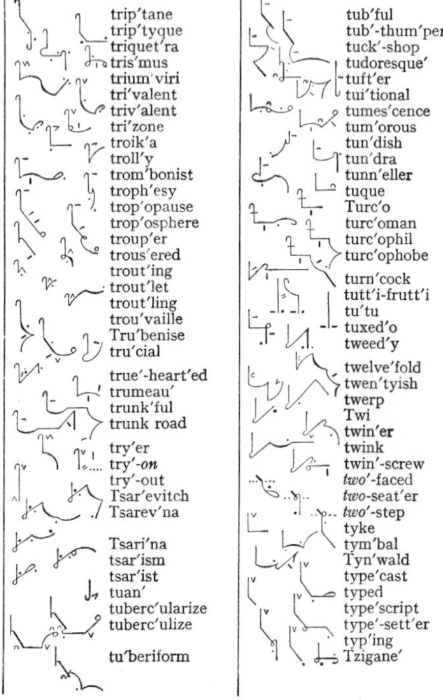

trip'tane
trip'tyque
triquet'ra
tris'mus
trium'viri
tri'valent
triv'alent
tri'zone
troik'a
troll'y
trom'bonist
troph'esy
trop'opause
trop'osphere
troup'er
trous'ered
trout'ing
trout'let
trout'ling
trou'vaille
Tru'benise
tru'cial
true'-heart'ed
trumeau'
trunk'ful
trunk road
try'er
try'-*on*
try'-out
Tsar'evitch
Tsarev'na
Tsari'na
tsar'ism
tsar'ist
tuan'
tuberc'ularize
tuberc'ulize
tu'beriform

tub'ful
tub'-thum'per
tuck'-shop
tudoresque'
tuft'er
tui'tional
tumes'cence
tum'orous
tun'dish
tun'dra
tunn'eller
tuque
Turc'o
turc'oman
turc'ophil
turc'ophobe
turn'cock
tutt'i-frutt'i
tu'tu
tuxed'o
tweed'y
twelve'fold
twen'tyish
twerp
Twi
twin'er
twink
twin'-screw
two'-faced
two-seat'er
two'-step
tyke
tym'bal
Tyn'wald
type'cast
typed
type'script
type'-sett'er
typ'ing
Tzigane'

U

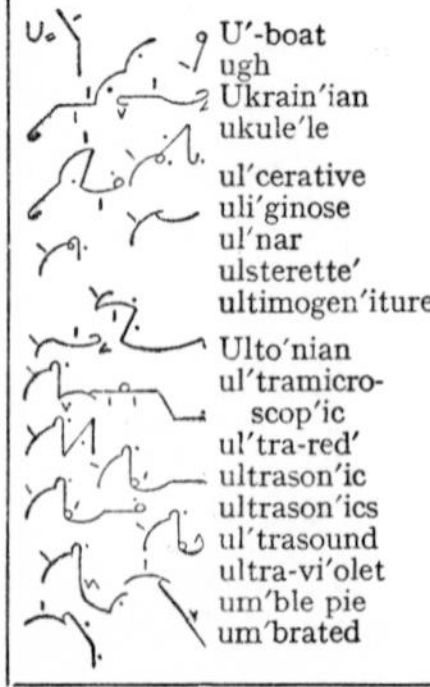

U'-boat
ugh
Ukrain'ian
ukule'le
ul'cerative
uli'ginose
ul'nar
ulsterette'
ultimogen'iture
Ulto'nian
ul'tramicro-scop'ic
ul'tra-red'
ultrason'ic
ultrason'ics
ul'trasound
ultra-vi'olet
um'ble pie
um'brated

umbrell'ad, -l'aed
Um'brian
um'laut
ump'teen
unafraid'
unambig'uous
unauthen'ticated
unbeknown'
un*believ'*able
unbesought'
uncan'ny
uncel'ebrated
unchar'ted
unchris'tianlike
uncomplimen'-tary
unconven'tional
unconvinced'

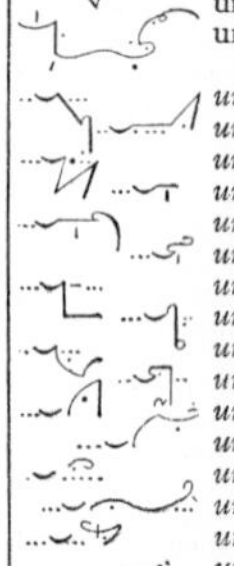

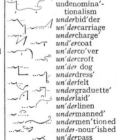

uncount'able
undenomina'-tionalism
*under*bid'der
*un'der*carriage
*under*charge'
*und'er*coat
*un'der*co'ver
*un'der*croft
un'der dog
*under*dress'
*un'der*felt
*under*graduette'
*under*laid'
*un'der*linen
*under*manned'
*under*men'tioned
under-nour'ished
*un'der*pass
*under*pay'

*under*pinned′
under-priv′ileged
under-produc′tion
*under*quote′
*un′der*self
*under*sell′
*un′der*side
*under*sign′
*un′der*signed′
*un′der*skirt
*un′der*song
*under*staffed′
*understand′*able
*under*state′
*under*state′ment
*under*stock
*un′der*tone
*un′der*water
*un′der*world
undeser′vedly
undeterred′
un′dies
undine′
un*discharged′*
undisclosed′
undisput′ed
un*disting′uished*
undraped′
un′dulator
uneconom′ic
uneconom′ical
uned′ifying
unemploy′able
Unes′co
unexcep′tional
unexplain′able
unexploit′ed
un*familiar′ity*
unfa′shioned
unferment′ed
unfert′ilized
unflav′oured
unforesee′able
unforewarned′
unforf′eited
unforgett′able
unfor*giv*′able
unfranked′
unget-at′-able
unham′pered
unhang′
unhelp′ful
unhope′ful
unhur′ried
unhygien′ic
unicam′eral
unicam′eralism
un′icycle
un′ified
un′ifying

uniling′ual
un*in′fluenced*
un*informed′*
uninspired′
unique′ly
unival′ent
unjus′tified
unlab′elled
unlab′oured
unladd′erable
unlament′ed
unlash′
unlashed
unleash′
unleashed′
unlocat′ed
unlov′able
unmarked′
unmeant′
unmerch′antable
unmod′ified
unmut′ilated
unnav′igable
unobtain′able
unobtrus′ively
unobtrus′iveness
unorth′odox
unpaged′
unperturbed′
unpredict′able
unpredictabil′ity
unpreten′tious
unpunc′tual
unpunctual′ity
unra′tioned
unrealis′tic
unreas′oning
unrec′ognizable
unrehearsed′
unrelat′ed
un*remark′able*
unrepen′tant
unresolved′
unreward′ing
unsan′itary
unsa′ted
unscram′ble
unscratched′
unscru′tinized
unseam′
unsecon′ded
unselfcon′scious
unshak′able
unsharp′ened
unshav′en
unsight′ed
unsigned′
unsmil′ing
unsol′vable

unspe′cified
unspi′ritual
unstamped′
unstarched′
unsta′ted
unstates′manlike
unstead′fast
unste′rilized
unstick′
unstim′ulated
unstitch′
unstitched′
unstressed′
unstuck′
unsuppressed′
unswa′llowed
unsymmet′rical
unsympathet′ically
untaxed′
unteach′able
untid′ily
untid′iness
untouch′able
untruth′ful
unvoiced′
unwear′ying
unwor′ded
unwor′kable
unwo′rried
unwove′
up′bringing
up′grade
up′keep
up′*most*
upp′ish
upp′ishly
upset′tingly
up′stage′
up′surge
up′swing
uraem′ia
uranom′etry
urb′anism
urb′anist
urb′anite
ur′ger
urina′tion
urn′-shaped
urol′ogy
urticar′ia
urt′icate
Uruguay′an (or)
usherette′
ut′ilizable
ut′ilizer

V

va'cillatingly
vac'ua
Vai'sya
val'ency
vale'ta
val'idate
valoriza'tion
val'orize
valu'ta
vamoos(e)'
vanette'
vap'orizer
var'iolate
var'iole
variom'eter
vars'ity
ve'gan
vegeta'tional
veil'less
vele'ta
veloc'itous
velom'eter
velours'
veloutine'
veneer'er
venereol'ogy
ven'ially
ven'tilative
Ve'ra
veran'dad
verifiabil'ity
verm'ian
ver'minicide
vernac'ularist
Ve'ronal
verruc'a
ver'sal
vertical'ity
Vert'oscope
vertu'
vet
vet'ted
vet'ting
vibra'to

vibrat'or
vice-pres'idency
vicere'gent
vice'reine
victimiza'tion
Victor'ianism
vid'eo
view'point
viginten'nial
vill'ainess
vill'ein
vil'lose
vin'egarish
vin'egary
vingt-et-un
vinicul'ture
vinol'ogy
vinom'eter
vin'yl
violabil'ity
violinist'ic
vip'erish
vi'ral
vire'ment
vir'ginhood
Virgin'ian
vir'gule
vi'ricide
virol'ogy
virt'ualism
virtual'ity
virtuos'ity
vis'cerate
viscom'etry
visc'ounty
vis'éed
vis'ile
visiogen'ic
visitator'ial
visualiza'tion
vis'ualized
vis'ualizing

Vit'a glass
vi'tagraph
vi'tamin
vit'amin
vi'tamine
vi'taminize
vitam'inous
vitell'in
vitell'us
vi'tiable
vi'tiator
vit'rine
vivipa'rity
voca'tional
vocif'erant
vocif'erator
vo'cule
vod'ka
voile
volan'te
vol'-au-vent
vol'et
vol'itant
vol'itate
Volks'wagen
vol'plane
vol'ta
vol'tage
voltam'eter
volte
volte-face
volu'meter
vom'er
vom'ica
voo'doo
vort'icism
vort'icist
Vul'can
Vul'canism
vulcanol'ogy
vul'picide
vul'turish
Vyn'ide

W

Waac
Waaf
Wad'dy
wa'di
Wafd
Wafd'ist
wage'-freeze
wagg'er
wagon-lit
waist'ed
waist'line
wait'ing-list
wait'ing-room
walk'ie-ta'lkie
walk'-out
walk'-over
wal'lah
wallaroo'
wall' game
wall'-less
wa'lloper
wa'nderingly
wan'derlust
wan'gle
wan'gled
wan'gler
wan'gling
wap'ens(c)haw
wa'ppens(c)haw
war'dress
war'-head
war'monger
war'ship
war'time
wash'able
wash'-out
wast'age
waste pap'er
watch'-spring
wa'ter-chute
wa'ter-divin'ing
wa'ter-finder
wa'ter-front
wa'ter-glass
Waterloo'
wa'tersid'er
wa'ter-tow'er
wa'ter-wag(g)'on
watt
watt'age
watt'meter
wave'-band
wave'-length
wav'eringly
wax'bill
wax' cloth
way'-leave
wea'ponless
wearabil'ity
wea'ther-board'-ing
wea'ther-chart
wea'ther-proof
wea'ther-side
Web'ley
weed'icide
weed'iness
weed'kill'er
week'-end
week-end'
week-en'der
Wehr'macht
weird'ness
Weis'mannism
Welch
wel'der
wel'farism
well-*bal'anced*
Well'ingtons
well-mann'ered
well-mean'ing
well' off
Well'sian
Welsh'ism
Wens'leydale
wes'ternism
wes'ternize
Westpha'lian
west'wards
whal'ery
whangee'
wharf'-ma'ster
wheat'meal
wheat'sheaf
wheel'-base
whim'perer
whim'sy
whir'ly-bird
whis'kery
whis'tle-stop
white'-coll'ar
white'-liv'ered
whit'er
whit'est
Whit'sun week
Whit' week
whole'-heart'ed
wholeheart'edly
whole-heart'ed-ness
whole'-meal
whoo'pee
wi'dish
wig'an
wil'debeest
wild'ish
wile'less
wil'lies
wil'low-ware
Wil'ton
Wilt'shire
win'cey
winceyette'
wind'bag
wind'cheater
wind'-cone
wind'-gauge
wind'-jammer
win'dow-dress'-ing
wind'-screen
wind'-sock
wind'-tunn'el
wine'press
wine'sap
wing'-comman'-der
wing'let
win'terish
wir'able
wired
wire'-haired
wire'lessed
wir'er
wir'ing
wise'-crack
wish'-bone
wish'tonwish
wit'an
witch'-*doc'tor*
witchol'ogy
wob'ble
wolf'-cub
wo'manishly
wo'manlike
won'derland
wonk'y
wood'craft
wood'-pulp
wood'ruff

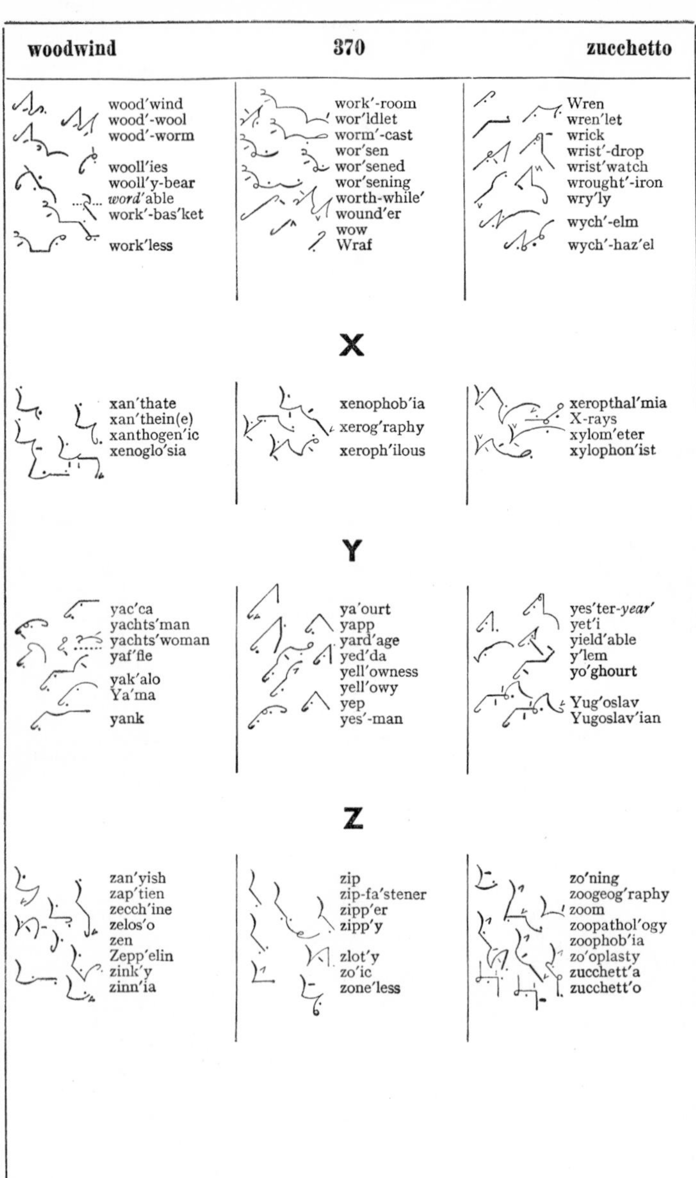
wood'wind
wood'-wool
wood'-worm
wooll'ies
wooll'y-bear
*word'*able
work'-bas'ket
work'less
work'-room
wor'ldlet
worm'-cast
wor'sen
wor'sened
wor'sening
worth-while'
wound'er
wow
Wraf
Wren
wren'let
wrick
wrist'-drop
wrist'watch
wrought'-iron
wry'ly
wych'-elm
wych'-haz'el
X
xan'thate
xan'thein(e)
xanthogen'ic
xenoglo'sia
xenophob'ia
xerog'raphy
xeroph'ilous
xeropthal'mia
X-rays
xylom'eter
xylophon'ist
Y
yac'ca
yachts'man
yachts'woman
yaf'fle
yak'alo
Ya'ma
yank
ya'ourt
yapp
yard'age
yed'da
yell'owness
yell'owy
yep
yes'-man
yes'ter-*year'*
yet'i
yield'able
y'lem
yo'ghourt
Yug'oslav
Yugoslav'ian
Z
zan'yish
zap'tien
zecch'ine
zelos'o
zen
Zepp'elin
zink'y
zinn'ia
zip
zip-fa'stener
zipp'er
zipp'y
zlot'y
zo'ic
zone'less
zo'ning
zoogeog'raphy
zoom
zoopathol'ogy
zoophob'ia
zo'oplasty
zucchett'a
zucchett'o